THROUGH DARKENING SPECTACLES

D1716311

Diamond Jenness, August 21, 1944.

THROUGH DARKENING SPECTACLES

Memoirs of Diamond Jenness

Diamond Jenness and Stuart E. Jenness

MERCURY SERIES
HISTORY PAPER 55
CANADIAN MUSEUM OF CIVILIZATION

© 2008 Canadian Museum of Civilization Corporation

Published by the
Canadian Museum of Civilization Corporation (CMCC)
100 Laurier Street
Gatineau, Quebec
K1A 0M8

© Mixed Sources
Product group from well-managed forests, controlled sources and recycled wood or fiber
www.fsc.org Cert no. SGS-COC-1854
© 1996 Forest Stewardship Council
FSC

Acting Manager, Publishing: Rosemary Nugent
Coordinator, Publishing: Rachel Locatelli
Technical Editor: Ian Dyck
Mercury Series Design: Hangar 13
Production Artist: Phredd Grafix
Printer: Delta Printing

Front cover photograph: Diamond Jenness, August 21, 1944. Photo by Y. Karsh, Neg. no. 9272, Yousuf Karsh Collection, Accession 1987-054, LAC.

Back cover photographs
Top: Diamond Jenness in winter attire at Collinson Point, northern Alaska, April 1914. Photo by G.H. Wilkins, CMC 50806.
Bottom: Diamond Jenness and son Stuart, July 1931.

Library and Archives Canada Cataloguing in Publication

Jenness, Diamond, 1886–1969

Through darkening spectacles : memoirs of Diamond Jenness / Diamond Jenness and Stuart E. Jenness.

(Mercury series)
(History paper ; 55)

This book contains an unpublished manuscript of recollections by Diamond Jenness with additional chapters written by Stuart E. Jenness. Cf. Abstract

Includes bibliographical references and index.
Includes abstract in French.
ISBN 978-0-660-19802-6
Cat. no.: NM23-4/55E

1. Jenness, Diamond, 1886–1969. 2. Jenness, Diamond, 1886–1969—Manuscripts. 3. Ethnologists—Canada—Biography. 4. Anthropologists—Canada—Biography. I. Jenness, Stuart E. (Stuart Edward), 1925– II. Canadian Museum of Civilization III. Title. IV. Title: Memoirs of Diamond Jenness. V. Series. VI. Series: History paper (Canadian Museum of Civilization) ; 55.

GN21.J36J36 2008   301.092   C2008-980013-3

Object of the Mercury Series

This series is designed to permit the rapid dissemination of information pertaining to the disciplines in which the Canadian Museum of Civilization Corporation is active. Considered an important reference by the scientific community, the Mercury Series comprises over 400 specialized publications on Canada's history and prehistory. Due to its specialized audience, the series consists largely of monographs published in the language of the author. In the interest of making information available quickly, normal production procedures have been abbreviated. As a result, grammatical and typographical errors may occur. Your indulgence is requested.

But de la collection Mercure

La collection Mercure vise à diffuser rapidement le résultat de travaux dans les disciplines qui relèvent des sphères d'activités du Musée canadien des civilisations. Considérée comme un apport important dans la communauté scientifique, la collection Mercure présente plus de 400 publications spécialisées portant sur l'héritage canadien préhistorique et historique. Comme la collection s'adresse à un public spécialisé, celle-ci est constituée essentiellement de monographies publiées dans la langue des auteurs. Pour assurer la prompte distribution des exemplaires imprimés, les étapes de l'édition ont été abrégées. En conséquence, certaines coquilles ou fautes de grammaire peuvent subsister : c'est pourquoi nous réclamons votre indulgence.

How to Obtain Mercury Series Titles

E-mail: publications@civilization.ca
Web: cyberboutique.civilization.ca
Telephone: 1 819 776-8387 or toll-free, in North America only, 1 800 555-5621
Mail: Mail Order Services
             Canadian Museum of Civilization
             100 Laurier Street
             Gatineau, Quebec K1A 0M8

Comment se procurer les titres parus dans la collection Mercure

Courriel :   publications@civilisations.ca
Web :   cyberboutique.civilisations.ca
Téléphone : 1 819 776-8387 ou sans frais, en Amérique du Nord seulement, 1 800 555-5621
Poste :   Service des commandes postales
             Musée canadien des civilisations
             100, rue Laurier
             Gatineau (Québec) K1A 0M8

Canada

To the Jenness family

ABSTRACT

Diamond Jenness (1886–1969), one of Canada's greatest scientists, served as Chief Anthropologist at the National Museum in Ottawa, Canada, from 1926 to 1948. During that period he strove passionately, but with mixed success, to improve the knowledge and welfare of Canada's Aboriginal peoples and to enhance the international reputation of the National Museum. His modesty prevented him from seeking fame for himself, but fame ultimately came to him as a result of his Native studies, scholarly publications, and brilliant scientific deductions.

Until now little has been known about this remarkable individual apart from his professional writings and activities. Having chosen to pursue his career as a government employee rather than as a university professor, he did not have the customary students to champion his teachings and spread his professional fame. Additionally, his personal life has remained private and largely unknown.

In the final three years of his life Diamond Jenness prepared a manuscript of recollections containing heretofore unpublished details of parts of his personal life. Now, more than thirty years later, I offer this quasi-biographical account of his life, comprising his original manuscript and a nearly equal number of additional chapters written by me. This book reveals details about his early years, his trials as Chief of Anthropology, his relationship with Marius Barbeau, his activities during both World Wars, his travels following retirement, and a variety of personal recollections of him. It also includes a revised and expanded list of his publications, a list of publications *about* him, and many photographs from his family's private collections. [S.E.J.]

RÉSUMÉ

Diamond Jenness (1886–1969), un des plus grands scientifiques du Canada, a été anthropologue en chef au Musée national du Canada, à Ottawa, de 1926 à 1948. Pendant cette période, il s'est efforcé passionnément, mais pas toujours avec succès, d'améliorer le savoir et le bien-être des peuples autochtones du Canada et d'accroître la réputation internationale du Musée national. Sa modestie l'empêchait de rechercher la gloire pour lui-même, mais ses études sur les Autochtones, ses publications spécialisées et ses brillantes déductions scientifiques l'ont finalement rendu célèbre.

Jusqu'ici, on ne connaissait pas grand-chose de cette personne remarquable en dehors de ses écrits et de ses activités professionnelles. Ayant choisi de poursuivre sa carrière en tant que fonctionnaire plutôt que d'occuper une chaire universitaire, il ne disposait pas des habituels étudiants pour se faire les champions de son enseignement et propager sa renommée professionnelle. En outre, sa vie personnelle est demeurée privée et en grande partie inconnue.

Au cours des dernières années de sa vie, Diamond Jenness a rédigé un manuscrit de souvenirs contenant des détails jusque-là inédits sur des parties de sa vie personnelle. Maintenant, plus de trente ans plus tard, j'offre ce récit quasi biographique de sa vie. Il comprend son manuscrit original et un nombre presque égal de chapitres supplémentaires de ma main. Ce livre révèle des détails sur ses premières années, ses épreuves en tant qu'anthropologue en chef, sa relation avec Marius Barbeau, ses activités au cours des deux guerres mondiales, ses voyages à la suite de sa retraite et divers souvenirs que j'ai de lui. Il présente également une liste revue et enrichie de ses publications, une liste de publications *sur* lui, et un bon nombre de photos provenant des collections privées de sa famille. [S.E.J.]

CONTENTS

Chapter 1: 1908: The Launching of an Innocent

**Chapter 2: 1912: The Ascent of Mount Madawana,
    Papua-New Guinea**

Chapter 3: 1913–16: The Canadian Arctic Expedition

Chapter 4: 1915–24: The Trials of a Polygamist

Chapter 5: 1916–22: The First World War and its Aftermath

Chapter 6: 1923–24: On a British Columbia Frontier

Chapter 7: 1924: Trekking the Yukon Telegraph Line

Chapter 8: 1925–26: A Friendship Lost

Chapter 9: 1926: Searching for Early Americans

LIST OF FIGURES AND MAPS

FOREWORD

The Canadian Museum of Civilization has employed many fine scholars in its 150-year history. Few, if any, have cast a longer shadow or contributed more to its collections, knowledge base and reputation than Diamond Jenness. An anthropologist in the days before archaeology and ethnology were quite as distinct as they are now, Jenness made major pioneering contributions to both disciplines. He was also an effective administrator, who led the Anthropology Division of the Geological Survey of Canada—as the Museum was then configured—through the lean and hungry years of the 1930s.

Jenness came to Canada from his native New Zealand on contract. In 1913 he was invited to participate as an anthropologist on the Canadian Arctic Expedition, sponsored by the Geological Survey of Canada. For just under two years—from the fall of 1914 to the summer of 1916—Jenness lived and worked with the Copper Inuit of the Central Canadian Arctic, a people who had been effectively contacted by the outside world only a few years earlier. After a period with the Canadian Forces in France (1917–1918) he returned to Canada and was hired full-time by the Museum. A flurry of publications followed, describing the Copper Inuit and their culture. Chief among them, and widely considered the single best description ever written of a Canadian Aboriginal society, was his monograph *The Life of the Copper Eskimo* (1922). He also brought to the Museum a large and invaluable collection of Copper Inuit tools and clothing.

Other achievements followed, of which only a few can be mentioned here. In 1925, while examining a donated archaeological collection from Baffin Island, Jenness noted that not all of the artifacts could be easily ascribed to relatively recent Inuit. On the basis of their form and apparent age, Jenness proposed the existence of an earlier, pre-Inuit culture, which he named Cape Dorset culture. Subsequent archaeological work has verified nearly all of his insights and conclusions about the age and importance of this extinct culture, now known simply as Dorset. The following year he led an archaeological expedition to the Bering Strait region of Alaska. Here he found evidence of early Inuit culture dating back nearly 2,000 years. Although he denied any particular abilities as an archaeologist, it was Diamond Jenness who first provided any real time depth to the prehistory of the North American Arctic. In 1932, he produced the classic *Indians of Canada*, long the authoritative source on the topic. In 1937 he was elected president of the prestigious Society for American Archaeology, and in 1939 was named president of the American Anthropological Association.

In 1926, Jenness was promoted to Chief of the Anthropology Division at the Geological Survey of Canada. I believe it would be fair to say that he was never a happy administrator. His promotion cost him a valued friendship—that of his colleague, the brilliant ethnologist and folklorist, Marius Barbeau. It also involved work he did not particularly enjoy. There were many within the Geological Survey who did not appreciate anthropology nor wish to spend money on it, and the government of the day was both tight-fisted and prudish. As Jenness wrote to a colleague, "The general feeling around the building seems to be that anthropology is half pornography, and what isn't spicy is so dull and uninteresting that no one will want to read it." The case in point involved Tom McIlwraith's description of the life and culture of the

Bella Coola First Nation of British Columbia (now known as the Nuxalk), which Jenness wanted to publish. The Minister responsible felt that this was inappropriate because the manuscript included a chapter on marital and sexual behaviour. In the words of the Minister, the Government of Canada could not publish anything which a nine-year-old girl could not read with perfect propriety. It was even proposed—as a compromise—that the offending chapter be published in Latin! (In the end, it was published elsewhere, and in English.)

In short, Jenness took up administration not because of vaunting ambitions, but because the task needed to be done. And in the end, perhaps his greatest achievement was in securing the continued existence of the Anthropology Division during the inter-war years. Budgets were cut and research programmes slashed, but a nucleus of scholarly activity survived, and the public continued to be served with top quality exhibitions and educational programs at the Victoria Memorial Museum Building in Ottawa. In his time at the Museum, Jenness was a defender and perhaps the greatest single practitioner of the modern, scholarly discipline of anthropology in Canada. And he is certainly among the founding fathers of the Canadian Museum of Civilization as it is today. But with the outbreak of war in 1939 he effectively disappeared, slipping away—almost gratefully one imagines—into military service. He spent the War in Intelligence, and although he did not retire until 1948 he never returned full-time to his administrative duties as Chief of Anthropology at the Museum. He died in1969.

I have long been a fan and admirer of Diamond Jenness. Much of my own archaeological research was inspired by Jenness and focused on the same geographic regions he pioneered. So it came as a happy surprise to learn that, late in life, he wrote these memoirs, and that with equally happy facility they were rescued from oblivion by his son, Stuart. Stuart Jenness has been a dedicated and talented chronicler of his father's career for some time. Perhaps his best-known previous contribution was the editing and annotation of his father's journal with the Canadian Arctic Expedition, published as *Arctic Odyssey: The Diary of Diamond Jenness* (1991). His role in bringing these memoirs to light—and in filling in the various gaps left by Diamond's natural modesty and reservation—completes the story of the Museum's, and perhaps Canada's, most accomplished anthropologist.

David Morrison
Director, Archaeology and History Division
Canadian Museum of Civilization
September 2007

PREFACE

Stuart E. Jenness

Almost forty years have passed since the death in 1969 of my New Zealand-born father, Diamond Jenness. He had served as Canada's second Chief Anthropologist between 1926 and 1948, always seeking to improve the understanding and quality of life of Canada's Aboriginal peoples, as had his predecessor, Dr. Edward Sapir, Canada's first Chief Anthropologist. Following his death, Jenness was remembered by such accolades as "Canada's most distinguished anthropologist," "The Father of Eskimo Archaeology," and the author of "one of the great works of world anthropology" (*The Indians of Canada*), and his accomplishments continue to linger in the minds of many of Canada's current anthropologists and others.

My father was an extremely modest man, so what is known about him is almost entirely from his professional activities—official letters, government publications, scientific articles, and unpublished reports. Little information has been available heretofore about his personal life. The longest biography of him is a 59-page account in a delightful book by Nansi Swayze, entitled *The Man Hunters*, published in 1960 for high school use in Canada. His biography in that book is followed by shorter biographies of his two colleagues at the National Museum of Canada, the ethnologist Marius Barbeau, and the archaeologist William Wintemberg. Swayze's account includes some information about my father that is found nowhere else, information that he mentioned to her when she interviewed him at his cottage in the summer of 1958. She was then studying anthropology under his friend, Professor Frederica de Laguna at Bryn Mawr College.

Research leading to a much more scholarly biography of my father has been under way for some two decades by Anthropology Professor Barnet Richling, formerly at Mount Saint Vincent University in Halifax but currently at the University of Winnipeg. Although he never met or talked with my father, he has tirelessly pursued in Canada, England, the United States, New Zealand, Australia, and perhaps elsewhere, archival evidence about my father and has already published nearly a dozen informative articles on one or other aspect of my father's life and activities. His detailed biography will be welcomed when it is ultimately published.

Meanwhile, there remains a need for more personal information about my father, the man whom History Professor J. Granatstein judged to have been one of Canada's greatest scientists, that quiet, intensely serious and loyal New Zealand-Canadian who gave so much during his lifetime for his adopted country. Therein lies the purpose of this book—to offer glimpses into my father's personal life and character so that historians and biographers may understand him better and thus arrive at more valid conclusions about his role, decisions, and actions during his professional years as Canada's leading anthropologist.

Here is how this book came to be. Sometime in the spring or summer of 1966, my father closed his portable typewriter for what he expected to be the last time. It had been his constant companion in the various countries he had visited during the eighteen years since his retirement, helping him produce an assortment of articles, books, and letters. He was 80 years old, had recently completed six years of stressful research and writing on what he regarded as his last important scholarly contribution (his five-volume study of Eskimo Administration)[1] in his life-long struggle to aid his Copper Eskimo friends in Canada's Arctic. He now expected to relax at his country home and reflect in peace and quiet upon the life thereafter and other such philosophical matters.

Alas, it was not to be. He soon found that he could not relax, for he was much too restless. Prevented on medical grounds—a weak heart—from driving his automobile, he could no longer escape from the near silence and isolation of the countryside by driving to town whenever the spirit moved him. Thus grounded and deprived of the mental stimulation he had obtained in the past from visiting his friends Bill Taylor, Richard Glover, Richard "Scotty" MacNeish, and one or two others at the National Museum, or from lunching with one or other of his sons, or from his archival research, he soon showed signs of a diminishing enjoyment of life. Although I never heard him complain of it, I am sure that his confinement in the small country bungalow and his increasing dependence on my mother prayed on his mind. He had always been positive and cheerful about life, and to see those traits slowly fading troubled me greatly.

One day, while we chatted quietly during one of my weekly visits, I suggested that he start writing about some of the unusual experiences he had had during his lifetime. I deliberately avoided using the word "autobiography" lest it deter him altogether. However, he showed no interest in my suggestion, dismissing it in fact with a wave of his hand and the comment, "No one would have any interest in reading about my life." I argued as best I could to the contrary, but to no avail. My suggestion simply did not appeal to him, so I said no more.

Sometime thereafter—I have no idea when or why—he must have recalled my suggestion. Quite unbeknownst to me, he retrieved his typewriter from his clothes closet where he had stored it and set to work. I did not know of this activity at the time, but my older brother Pete recently informed me that he had discussed it with our father once or twice. Father evidently completed his manuscript sometime in 1969, for early in November of that year, shortly before his death, he typed a letter to the assistant director of the University of Chicago Press, asking him if he would be interested in considering his latest manuscript for publication. Three years later, I found the letter inside the cover of his manuscript. It contained several inked corrections in father's handwriting, so I believe it is the rough draft of a letter he had intended to send. I do not think he sent it, however, for there was no answering letter from Chicago. A month later, father was gone.

I knew nothing of the existence of this final manuscript of his until three years after his death. While visiting my mother one day in 1972, I chanced to ask if she still had my father's Arctic diary. He had given a volume to me in the late 1950s after he published *Dawn in Arctic Alaska*, rather than discarding it as he had apparently intended to do. Then in 1962 he requested it back after the wife of famed explorer Vilhjalmur Stefansson wrote asking to borrow it. I had

---

[1]Rather begrudgingly described by one of my father's critics as "one of the major milestones of his career and a definitive work in northern studies" (Kulchynski, 1993, p. 27).

not seen it since. Having failed to examine it carefully at the time, I believed that volume to be his complete Arctic diary.

Mother responded that the diary was on the floor of his clothes closet. There among three pairs of shoes and a pair of brown boots, I found the familiar volume, which a brief perusal revealed covered only his first year in the Arctic. Beneath it lay three other volumes I had not previously seen. Two of them proved to be about his second and third years in the Arctic respectively, while he was in the Coronation Gulf region.

The fourth volume was in a two-holed binder, unlike the other three, which were bound. It contained a title page and table of contents, just as in a book, followed by a series of chapters telling about a number of events in his life in more-or-less chronological order. Mother quietly confirmed that these were indeed the memoirs I had asked my father to write some years previously, and then agreed to let me take the manuscript home to read. "Yes," I distinctly remember her saying, "You may read it, but then you must file it away carefully and never publish it, for it is really quite dreadful!" I was so elated to find the manuscript, I neglected to ask Mother why she thought its contents were so dreadful. Later that day, I returned home with the memoirs and the three Arctic-diary volumes in my possession, unaware that some years later I would become deeply involved in getting them all published.

When I first read my father's manuscript, I confess that I, too, was as disappointed as was my mother, although I was not nearly as negative in my judgement of it as she seemed to be. It was not its content that distressed me, for it contained charming new passages of writing like the ones in his *People of the Twilight*. What distressed me were the many significant activities in his life that he had not mentioned at all. At the time, I agreed entirely with Mother that the manuscript was not suitable for publication, and out of respect for her wishes, I put it in one of my file cabinets where it remained, largely forgotten, for the next thirty years! During those intervening years, I approached the same octogenarian age my father had been when he wrote his final manuscript.

Then one day in the summer of 2003, I remembered the manuscript and showed it to my son John, a college instructor in Vancouver at the time with several years of experience editing college textbooks for a well-known commercial publisher. He harboured many fond memories of visits with his grandfather and, in fact, carried his name (i.e., John Diamond Jenness). After reading several random passages, he turned to me and said, "Dad, this is delightful! You really ought to edit it and get it published." His obvious enthusiasm encouraged me to have another look at the manuscript some days later. My dear wife had passed away just a few weeks earlier, and I was desperately seeking something worthwhile to do to help me start along the long road to recovery from my grief. I was also aware then that in the intervening thirty-one years since I had taken possession of the manuscript, a considerable interest had arisen in my father's life and his contributions to the early developments of anthropology in Canada. Here then, with his virtually unknown final manuscript, was a real opportunity to provide a unique and valuable personal contribution about my father's life as seen through the eyes of one of his family. I promptly started to work on it.

Mother, over the years, had meticulously edited most of Father's manuscripts, and I found some of her comments pencilled in the margins of this one. She was an extremely talented and well-meaning individual, but judging from some of her marginal comments, she appears to have believed that an editor was supposed to be critical rather than constructively helpful. Perhaps hers was a form of "tough love," for she wanted my father's writing to be only the finest and was very proud of his literary achievements. I took note of her comments, which were scattered throughout this last manuscript of his, but did not agree with all of them. For example, her pencilled comments at the start of a chapter that I found separate from the manuscript, which described their trip around Europe in 1938, read, "This article interesting but not very important." Pencilled at the top of the same page in my father's handwriting is the single word "Reject." He had removed the chapter from his final draft, no doubt to avoid further argument. Fortunately, he did not throw it away, and when I located it and read it in 2003, I found it both informative and insightful and quickly restored it as Chapter 14. It includes information not found elsewhere about his efforts to establish trades with several European museums for early Canadian Indian artifacts. The Second World War commenced the next year, however, before any trading arrangements could be reached.

Almost two years of research followed while I sought to accumulate sufficient information to augment his manuscript with chapters about his Arctic work, his First World War activities, his difficult years as Chief Anthropologist, his change of career during the Second World War, and his post-retirement activities.

While I was carrying out my research on my father's activities, one topic cried out for discussion—the sensitive matter of my father's relationship with his fellow student and then museum associate, Marius Barbeau. The writing of Chapter 8, which deals with that topic, proved to be a major challenge. I am not aware that my father ever discussed the matter with anyone, although it would seem probable that he aired it quietly with my mother and perhaps one or two close friends during the late 1920s when I was too young to learn about it. Certainly he did not discuss it with me, nor was I aware during his lifetime of the severity and tragedy of their abruptly terminated friendship.

The most complete record of their conflict that I know about is in Barbeau's unpublished memoirs, which were typed from tape recordings of Barbeau made by the National Museum's folklore specialist, Carmen Roy, in 1957 and 1958, a decade after Barbeau's retirement. On these tapes, Barbeau discusses some topics in English, others in French. He generally spoke in French when he discussed his work in Quebec, but switched to English when he discussed his Indian work in British Columbia and elsewhere in Canada, and his activities at the National Museum. He spoke in English when he mentioned the details about his conflict with my father. Typescripts were created from both the English and the French segments of the taped recordings. The English segments were later translated into French, but the French segments were not translated into English. Thus, the English transcript of his memoirs is incomplete. That is of no concern here, however, for he did not talk about my father when he was taping in French. In this book, all passages quoted from Barbeau's memoirs are from the English transcript. Both English and French versions are carefully archived at the Canadian Museum of Civilization.

I do not expect that my father knew of the existence of Barbeau's memoirs, and, even had he known, I doubt if he would have sought them out. As far as I know, he himself left no personal account of the subject.

Many years later, following tape-recorded discussions with Barbeau in the 1960s, author Laurence Nowry prepared a detailed biography of Barbeau, in which he included a brief discussion of the Barbeau–Jenness association and the ultimate rift between them. The biography was published in 1995. In his account of the rift, Naury implies behavioural traits on my father's part that cast a dark shadow on my father's integrity. Had he understood anything of my father's background and strict English moral standards, I do not think that Nowry would have reached the same views on their relationship that he evidently did. In Chapter 8, I discuss the subject at greater length than did Nowry and arrive at a quite different conclusion.

I might be considered a trifle mad to undertake the editing and enlargement of my own father's recollections, the more so when he was an internationally known scientist, a pioneer in his field, and one known for his facility with the written word. And especially when I was not specifically trained in any of what I perceive to have been his three fields of specialization or loves—the *Classics* (his first love, the one that beckoned to him all his life like the sirens in his favourite book, Homer's *The Odyssey*); *Anthropology* (his acquired love, from which he ultimately received his major acclaim); and *Geography* (his life-long friend).

When I first examined my father's manuscript in 1972, it consisted of eleven more-or-less autobiographical essays. Each essay had little to do with the one preceding it or the one following it. I subsequently restored the chapter about his trip to Europe in 1938 (now No. 14) which my father had set aside, and split one of his chapters into two separate ones (now Nos. 6 and 7), thereby producing thirteen original chapters. To these thirteen chapters, I added nine that I had written, which detail many of my father's activities during the periods about which he did not write. I then inserted explanatory bridge passages (in italics) at the beginnings and/or ends of several chapters and added numerous footnotes containing reference citations or supplementary information, as well as two tables, three appendices, and references. At the request of my manuscript's first two reviewers, I placed Father's name under the title of the chapters he wrote and my name underneath each of the ones I wrote, in order to render the authorship of each chapter perfectly clear.

With regard to illustrations, my father originally included sixteen photographs and seven sketch maps with his manuscript. I retained twelve of his photographs and added forty-six others, most of which are previously unpublished pictures from the family collections. I retained one of his seven sketch maps, re-drew the other six, and drafted seven more.

Thus the book in your hands right now combines the labours of us both. Of my father's thirteen chapters, nine are original writings about unusual activities he experienced during his lifetime, and four are previously published articles. Of these latter four, one chapter (No. 12—"An Indian Medicine Man") differs from all the rest in that it focuses on the rigorous training a Coast Salish man underwent at a very early age in order to become a shaman, as told to my father in a series of meetings with that shaman in 1936.

The chapters I added deal with his Arctic experiences, his experiences in connection with the First and Second World Wars, a discussion of his controversial relationship with fellow ethnologist, Marius Barbeau, some of the problems he encountered in the twenty plus years he was Canada's Chief Anthropologist, and brief commentaries on the various places where he and my mother spent their winters after his retirement.

My final chapter covers an assortment of topics, including details about his museum office, his house in Ottawa, his cottage life on the Gatineau River north of Ottawa, his hobbies and sports activities, awards and honours received, and other aspects of his personal life. I included this chapter intentionally to reveal something of my father's warmth, compassion, generosity, modesty, patience, tolerance, industriousness, seriousness, constant search for knowledge, and occasional playfulness.

It also reveals something of his interest in people, especially but not exclusively the serious, well-educated ones. All were received kindly and warmly in his home. With serious friends, he enjoyed stimulating their investigative instincts with questions arising from the depth and breadth of his knowledge, the wealth of ideas he entertained, and by his quiet way of listening to what they had to say. I suspect that he also got satisfaction from encouraging them in their search for worthwhile goals. With the less scholarly, he listened with patience, tolerance, and politeness, sometimes even with mild amusement, and now and then offered an observation or two. His gentle and gentlemanly qualities endeared him to most people, young and old. Many women found his quiet manner and encyclopaedic knowledge fascinating, at times to mother's distress, but their conversations always remained on an intellectual level, never delving into the personal or sensual.

My father's manuscript carried the curious but meaningful title *Through Darkening Spectacles: Some Memories of a Taugenichts*. I suspect that he settled upon that title after some considerable reflection. I also suspect that his use of the German word "Taugenichts" (a good-for-nothing fellow) exemplified his gentle, whimsical, self-depreciating humour at that late stage in his life. Yet many readers may not understand either the implication of that word or its meaning, and two reviewers even remarked that it was quite unsuitable for the serious-minded, scholarly man he really was. I have therefore modified his title to *Through Darkening Spectacles: Memoirs of Diamond Jenness*, which happily also encompasses the biographical additions I have inserted and justifies the inclusion of my name alongside his on the title page.

The information I have added to Father's original chapters has given more emphasis to him as a family-oriented person than as a professional anthropologist. While he is best known for his accomplishments in the field of anthropology, the reader will soon discover that Father was a man with many interests, including such subjects as porcelain, art, music, church architecture and, of course, the Classics. Indeed, by 1939, his anthropological career lay largely behind him while he focused more and more on geographical topics.

My father included only five footnotes in his manuscript. These are found in Chapters 2, 4, 7, 12, and 19. To these I have added a great many more, by this means including secondary information that I considered to be both informative and interesting.

The following pages include many observations and vignettes on my father's family and life, about which little is currently available in print. To others I have left the task of discussing and analyzing his professional and administrative accomplishments, although I have dabbled slightly on the following pages in both subjects. The picture of Diamond Jenness that emerges from available publications is that of a quiet but dedicated scholar who tackled his scientific investigations methodically and without fanfare. He was highly regarded internationally because of his pioneer studies in Arctic archaeology and ethnology and through his book, *The Indians of Canada*, but much less so among the administration people he had to deal with within his own department (Deputy Minister Charles Camsell being a notable exception). How well I recall his frequent use of the well-known quotation, "A prophet is not without honour, save in his own country, and in his own house."[2] I think that may be how he saw himself—well respected abroad, but receiving little or no respect in his workplace or home—or then again, perhaps it was merely another example of his gentle wit.

As a government administrator, he sought to expand and develop Canada's knowledge of its Aboriginal peoples, to improve their way of life as much as he could, and to make the National Museum of Canada known far and wide. Seeking fame for himself was not one of his goals. The fame that did come to him resulted from the importance of his studies, publications, and intuitions, and not through his deliberate efforts to acquire it. To the end, he remained a private person, attracting little attention outside his office.

---

[2]The Gospel according to St. Matthew, Chapter 13, verse 57.

ACKNOWLEDGEMENTS

In my father's day, the Native or Aboriginal people who populated much of the southern part of what is now Canada were known as Indians, those living to the north of them beyond the tree-line in the Arctic as Eskimos. As an anthropologist, he attached no pejorative implications to the use of either term; they were simply the proper generic terms at the time for him to use. He has used them in that professional sense in all of his writings as well as in this last manuscript, and I have therefore retained his usage. The currently used words Inuit, Inuvialuit, Inupiat, and First Nations, all plural words, and their singular forms, came into common usage some years after Father's death.

I acknowledge with gratitude the assistance and encouragement of Dr. David A. Morrison, Director of the Archaeology and History Division, and Dr. Ian Dyck, Curator of Plains Archaeology, at the Canadian Museum of Civilization. Both read an early draft of the manuscript and made many valuable suggestions, virtually all of which resulted in improvements to the text. Dr. Morrison, who has published much on my father's work and prepared museum exhibits about my father, graciously agreed to write the Foreword that appears in this book, and provided frequent encouragement as manuscript preparations progressed. Dr. Dyck, who has also published on the history of the Museum, acted as technical editor, arranging to have my manuscript copy-edited, dealing calmly with the changes the copy-editor and I subsequently requested, and offering many suggestions that have led to significant improvements. He facilitated the manuscript's seemingly endless journey to publication with care, thoroughness, efficiency, and unlimited patience and I am greatly indebted to him for his very special assistance.

I very much appreciate the considerable assistance I received on many occasions over the past several years from the head archivist Geneviève Eustache, reference archivists Benoît Thériault and Patricia Forget, reference librarian Sylvia Mauro, audiovisual archives technician Jonathan Wise, and other members of the staff at the Canadian Museum of Civilization. They will readily recognize, I suspect, where my discussions with them have enabled me to add meaningful information in several parts of the manuscript and to greatly improve the final content of the book. Thank you all.

Dr. Derek Smith, adjunct professor of sociology and anthropology at Carleton University in Ottawa, read an early draft of my manuscript with special care and interest, for he had enjoyed numerous stimulating discussions with my father in the early 1960s when my father was writing his series of reports on Eskimo administration. Professor Smith made many thoughtful suggestions for the betterment of the manuscript, for which I am most grateful.

I offer special thanks to Victoria Barkoff for the copy-editing skills she employed in finding and correcting far more typographical errors in the manuscript than it should have held. I am further indebted to Rachel Locatelli, publishing coordinator, for her diligence, grace and professionalism in overseeing the design and production of the book.

On behalf of my late father and myself, I wish to thank the Directors of the Canadian Geographic Journal for permission to reproduce the essays on the ascent of Mount Madawana on Goodenough Island (Chapter 2), and to the British Columbia Provincial Museum for permission to reproduce the photograph and material on Old Pierre, the Indian medicine man (Chapter 12). The photographers of most of the pictures are identified in the captions and are here thanked. The remaining photographs (2, 3, 4, 18, 19, 22, 44, 47, 50, 53, 54, and 55) are from Jenness-family collections and their photographers are not known.

Throughout the preparation of this book I regularly received invaluable suggestions and encouragement from my son Dr. John Diamond Jenness and my daughter Mrs. Mary Gwendoline Montgomery. Unlike their grandfather Diamond and me, both of whom edited manuscripts as part of our respective government duties, they voluntarily spent many hours editing an early draft of this manuscript out of devotion to us both.

I have also benefited greatly from discussions with my two brothers, John (Pete) and Robert (Bob), the results of which have been incorporated within the following pages. They kindly supplied from their personal collections several of the photographs I have used. All in all, this book is in many ways the result of a family endeavour. However, I alone assume responsibility for any errors that may still lurk within its pages.

Lastly, I am eternally grateful to my late wife Jean and to both of my late parents for their constant care, love, and encouragement over the years. Without their special influences, this book would never have seen the light of day.

ABBREVIATIONS

AAAS	American Association for the Advancement of Science
CMC	Canadian Museum of Civilization, Gatineau, Quebec
CMN	Canadian Museum of Nature, Gatineau, Quebec
ERP	European Recovery Program
GSC	Geological Survey of Canada, Ottawa, Ontario
HBC	Hudson's Bay Company
LAC	Library and Archives Canada, Ottawa, Ontario
NMC	National Museum of Canada, Ottawa, Ontario
N.Z.	New Zealand
RCMP	Royal Canadian Mounted Police
RNWMP	Royal North-West Mounted Police (prior to 1920)

1908:
THE LAUNCHING OF
AN INNOCENT

1

Diamond Jenness

A slip of paper in my desk tells me that I first opened my eyes in Wellington, New Zealand,[1] in the year of grace A.D. 1886, but I myself do not recollect that momentous event. I do remember attending the Boy's High School (Wellington College)[2] and Victoria University College in that city,[3] and have always presumed that those two institutions must somehow have affected my destiny. I record them here merely to satisfy the curiosity of anyone who still believes that man is a rational being, living in a rational world in which causes precede effects and man turns the wheel of his own fate.

---

[1]In 1891, five years after my father's birth, my grandfather bought a large house named "Waihinga" in Lower Hutt and moved his family there. "Waihinga," is a Maori word meaning waterfall. The house and waterfall were on a hillside overlooking the Hutt River Valley, a few miles inland from Wellington.
[2]The Education Board in Wellington awarded him a two-year scholarship of fifteen pounds annually in January 1899 while he attended Wellington College (high school). A certificate signed by the secretary and announcing the award was in my possession at the time of writing (2006). In his senior year at the high school he was selected as "Head of the School" (Nemo, 1918, p. 36).
[3]Victoria University College of Wellington was founded in 1897 as the fourth and youngest college that comprised the University of New Zealand (Otago, Canterbury, and Auckland were the other three colleges), and was named in honour of the 60th Anniversary of Queen Victoria's reign. It opened in 1899 with less than 120 students, increasing to 254 by 1905. Until it was able to occupy its own building in 1904, college classes were held after 4 p.m. in the Girl's High School and in a few available rooms in other buildings nearby (Beaglehole, 1949, p. 27). The college became Victoria University of Wellington in the early 1960s with the dissolution of the University of New Zealand. The original campus where my father took classes is now part of the recently named Kelburn Campus of this university.

When my father attended the college it operated on two terms per year, offering the Bachelor's degree after three years. The final-year exams were set and subsequently marked in England and the degree was awarded a year later (Arthur Pomeroy, Professor of Classics, Victoria University, Wellington, personal communication, June 2004). My father commenced his college studies in February 1904, having just turned 18, and was therefore one of the college's earliest students and graduates. He received a Junior Scholarship of twenty pounds from the University of New Zealand, Wellington, tenable for three years, subject to his meeting certain conditions as set forth in the University of New Zealand Calendar. He completed his three years for a B.A. degree in 1907, and was awarded Senior Scholarships in Latin and Greek. He followed this with another year of study in Latin and Greek, and qualified for the M.A. degree with First Class Honours in April, 1908. He commenced his studies at Oxford in September of that year.

One of the college's four founding professors, John Rankine Brown, an Oxford-educated Scot from St. Andrews, professor of Latin and Greek, inspired a love for the classics in my father and was like "a

Figure 1 Diamond Jenness about 1890.
Photo by Wrigglesworth & Binns, Wellington, N.Z.

By the first decade of the twentieth century, Wellington's 200-strong community of sixty years earlier[4] had increased to nearly 50,000, and the tiny settlement in the almost circular harbour of Port Nicholson had become a southern-hemisphere megalopolis, capital of a Dominion of the British Empire. Its encircling hills, once covered with virgin forest, had been denuded by axe and fire, and houses were rapidly creeping up their steep slopes. Horse trams and horse buses circulated through the streets, and signs posted at convenient intervals exhorted citizens to "Wait here for Tram and Bus"—wherever, that is, their text had not been amended by the erasure of the *f* in *for* and the addition of a *p* to *Tram* and a *t* to *Bus*! As a foretaste of greater glories just over the horizon, an ingenious cable-tramway carried its passengers swiftly and easily up the hillside to an unfinished university building that overlooked the city, a building that glowed with an exciting new invention, electricity, while the high school I had attended continued to struggle along in the dim light of old-fashioned gas lamps.

From Wellington, a narrow-gauge railway carried its trains, with the help of two extra engines, up and over the slopes of the Rimutaka Mountains (where seasonable excursionists leaped off the front carriage in Kaitoki Gorge, crammed their mouths and fists with ripe wild blackberries, and scrambled aboard the second carriage as it drifted slowly by) into the Wairarapa Valley, and thence northward through the centre of the island to a still uncertain destination.

---

father to him" (Jenness, 1924c, p. 29). My father also greatly admired and was much influenced by Professor George W. von Zedlitz, who was also Oxford-educated and became the fledgling college's fifth professor late in 1901. He taught modern languages. My father attended his French classes. Von Zedlitz was born in Germany but raised in England. He lived less than a mile from my father's home in Lower Hutt, a Wellington suburb, and in the summer of 1906 invited my father to come to his home each Friday evening to read Homer's *Odyssey* with him in Greek (Jenness, 1963), a book and story my father treasured for the rest of his life.

[4]Wellington was founded in 1840 by the first group of English colonists to reach New Zealand. Matilda Minifie, Diamond Jenness' paternal grandmother, was one of those original colonists. She reached the Wellington area in March 1840 after 171 days at sea on the S.S. *Adelaide*, flagship of the London-based New Zealand Company. Then only fifteen years old, she and her four brothers, three of whom were older than she was, had been brought to New Zealand by her widowed mother Elizabeth Minifie (née Cox) from the London area. Matilda married Nathaniel Jenness in Wellington in August 1841 (Jenness and Jenness, 1998, p. 83–84).

Rumours were reaching the city of an even more revolutionary vehicle, the automobile, which might find its way before long across the South Pacific Ocean. In those dawning years of this twentieth century, I and other Wellingtonians of my generation fully understood that our city, if not the hub of the universe, stood in the very forefront of progress, and that our teachers were deliberately grooming us to become leaders in the changing world of Western civilization.

It is not easy for me today to look back at that primeval age and recall how mature I considered myself when I reached my twenty-first birthday. By that time, I had graduated from a university and travelled as widely as most of my countrymen—by bicycle over an arc of 100 miles from Wellington; by railway over twice that distance; by an ocean steamer that ferried between Wellington and Lyttleton, the port of Christchurch, in New Zealand's South Island, where I had spent four days at a remarkable Exhibition (or should I

Figure 2 Diamond Jenness' mother, Hannah Heayns, in 1870 at age 17, two years before her marriage to George Lewis Jenness.

Figure 3 "Waihinga," Diamond Jenness' home in Lower Hutt, N.Z., about 1931.

modernize and say Exposition?), which had been famous throughout the Dominion, even if it passed unnoticed by the rest of the world; and by paddle-steamer up the Wanganui River, renowned for its scenic beauty, but to our captain more memorable for its shallow water and shifting sandbars. In addition to being both scholar and traveller, I considered myself a latter-day Nimrod,[5] because in the hills behind my home I had shot a dozen rabbits in a single afternoon, and on the wilder hills of Wainui, nine miles away, tracked down and exterminated several wild pigs and wild goats that were destroying the scanty pastures of my cousin's sheep-station. It was with the calm detachment of Caesar when he crossed the Rubicon, therefore, that I weighed the prospect of crossing two oceans in order to round out my studies in England,[6] and to conduct a two- or three-year survey of Western Europe, the cradle of New Zealand civilization.

I

My first problem was to reach England. In that pre-aeroplane age the quickest and most interesting route carried the traveller [by steamship] from New Zealand to Australia, and from Australia via Ceylon and the Suez Canal through the Mediterranean and the Strait of Gibraltar to London, a voyage of about forty days, including brief stops at two or three coaling ports. One such port was Naples in southern Italy, a city rich in history and legends, as my classical studies had told me. A chance remark by my shipping agent now focussed my attention on this port.

"Every fortnight," he told me, "a vessel of our line calls at Naples and stays there about twelve hours. If a passenger wishes to remain longer and arranges his ticket beforehand, he can disembark there, stay two whole weeks, and continue his voyage on our next boat without extra charge."

---

[5] A mighty hunter, mentioned in the Bible, Genesis 10:8–9.

[6] Aided by a small graduating scholarship, he proceeded to Balliol College at Oxford University to continue his studies of the classics for the next three years (1908–1911). There he found that the school year was divided into three terms instead of the two terms he had been used to, and that he was expected to do the major part of his work during the long mid-term breaks and the summer vacations. For the Diploma in Anthropology, in addition to his regular courses, he attended lectures in human geography, comparative religion, psychology, the European Bronze Age, Egyptology, and osteology (Wallis, 1957, p. 787). My father's main Oxford teachers in anthropology were R.R. Marett of Exeter College (social anthropology), Professor Arthur Thomson (physical anthropology and Professor of Anatomy), and Henry Balfour (technology), Curator of the Pitt-Rivers Museum. Marett was the one who most influenced him. He also connected with Professor A.C. Haddon, Reader in Ethnology at Cambridge University and a founder of British anthropology. In addition to the lectures he attended, my father met weekly with his tutor, of which he had three during the three years he attended Oxford: A.W. Pickard-Cambridge, J.A. Smith, and A.D. Lindsay (B. Richling, pers. comm., 2004).

My father's time at Oxford was not fully consumed by his studies, however. In a letter dated Nov. 15, 1908, playfully addressed to "Sir William Buster [Whitehead], Bart.," a young nephew in New Zealand, he mentions that he went practice shooting twice a week, took military drill for an hour efore breakfast four mornings a week, went to Sunday concerts at various Oxford colleges, and occasionally strolled the neighbouring regions visiting ancient sights such as canal locks and churches. A postcard to his brother Fred, dated June 16, 1909, and written in extremely fine handwriting, reveals that so far during his summer term he was doing little shooting because of his limited funds, but had been swimming four times, one of which was unintentional, and had been boating almost every day, either rowing or punting, so was in fit condition.

Figure 4 The Jenness family, Lower Hutt, N.Z. about 1908. L. to r. (standing): Violet, Fred, Grace, Arthur, May; (seated): Amy, Diamond, Hannah, George Lewis, Will; (seated on floor): Leonard, Pearl.

The idea of roaming foot-loose for two weeks in Southern Italy caught my fancy. I booked my passage accordingly, and prior to my departure studied a book on Naples and its history, which a friend kindly placed at my disposal. Also I re-read, of course, Bulwer Lytton's *Last Days of Pompeii*.

The ocean liners to England via Suez did not service New Zealand directly, but made Sydney, Australia, their southern terminal. Passengers from Wellington connected with them through two smaller steamers, which crossed the 1,200 miles of the Tasman Sea in two and a half days. Sydney, although at that date four or five times larger than Wellington, possessed the same general character; the stranger felt that he was visiting not a genuine city, but an over-grown country town. No impatient automobiles demanded passage yet through its pedestrian-crowded streets, no sky-touching bridge spanned the gateway to its harbour, and no motorboats raced busily to and fro in that harbour's numerous inlets. Sparse woods, with here and there a few isolated houses, covered the sides of the inlets, and Manly Beach was no more than a cluster of cottages at one end of its now famous stretch of sand. Such at least is my recollection of Sydney in the winter of 1908.[7] Through the haze of years I recall a pleasant boat excursion ten or fifteen miles up the Lane River, and picture in my mind the quiet,

---

[7]My father left his home in New Zealand in July 1908, which in that southern part of the world would have been wintertime.

pastoral landscape along its banks. But very few other memories have survived the two days I spent in Sydney before embarking on my transoceanic liner.

The vessel called briefly at Melbourne, Adelaide, and Fremantle before heading out into the Indian Ocean. Nothing of note occurred until we reached Ceylon and docked in Colombo for the day and a half required for refuelling and for passengers to visit Buddha's shrine at Kandy, in the mountains. I did not join this Kandy excursion, but lingered in and around Colombo, for this was my first contact with any part of the Orient, and I was bewildered and fascinated by the new sights and sounds and odours—by the lush vegetation, the exotic temples, the hordes of dark-skinned people in strange dress, the pertinacious (and pernicious) salesmen, especially the vendors of imitation rubies and emeralds, the numberless mendicants of all ages, and the heart-rending evidences on every hand of over-population and grinding poverty.

Our passenger roll listed the names of three French priests who were returning to Europe after several years' service on a mission station at Yule Island, on the edge of one of the wildest and least explored regions of British New Guinea. Every day I walked the deck with one of them, a kindly-faced, middle-aged man who spoke no English and, consequently, was left very much on his own. However, he seemed not to mind the solitude, being an ardent connoisseur of cigars. At the hour when our vessel was due to leave Colombo, I saw him on deck haggling with a peddler over a large box of cigars for which the man was demanding an exorbitant price. Suddenly the steamer whistled to signal its departure, and loud shouts warned all non-passengers to disembark immediately. In well-simulated despair, the peddler thrust a cigar into the missionary's hand, urged him to test its quality quickly, and offered him the entire boxful at a bargain price. The good father lit the cigar, puffed on it contentedly for a minute and closed the deal. Just one hour later, when Ceylon was fading into the distance and the peddler probably singing a paean of victory in his home, his clerical victim angrily stalked to the rail of the ship and consigned the box and all its contents to the waters of oblivion.

Between Ceylon and the Red Sea, the Indian Ocean seemed twice as hot and humid as its eastern expanse between Ceylon and Australia. It sapped every remaining ounce of energy from the passengers, who spent twelve somnolent hours each day reclining in their deck chairs. Thousands of flying fish, taking to the air to escape the speedy bonito and other enemies, rippled the sea with gleaming flashes. I spent half my days leaning over the rail in vain efforts to calculate the average length of their flight. One flew onto our lower deck and, with the connivance of the chief steward, ended uncooked on a special platter in front of a tub-like gourmand who had alienated his fellow diners by his inordinately long, boarding-house reach. Diversions so fleeting, however, could not dispel the prevailing lassitude. My ship-companions submerged themselves in their deck chairs, and I, conforming to their regime, dozed away the languid hours. Imperceptibly, time ceased.

Then, toward noon one Sunday, a long whistle jerked my eyes open, and two seamen brushed by me dragging a long fire-hose. Other sailors were scurrying to the lifeboats. The ship was afire!

I, alone of all the passengers, seemed aware of it. The others remained dozing in their deck chairs. What should I do? Should I awaken them and run the risk of creating a panic? No, I must be calm. Clearly the fire was not of major proportions, at least not yet, for I could see no smoke. But what if it should grow, blaze out of control, and force us to take to the lifeboats? I could not hope to save my luggage, but should I not salvage one or two small valuables?

Outwardly calm and collected, I went down to my cabin, recovered my travellers cheques and one or two papers, and buttoned them safely in an inside pocket. Then I stepped out into the corridor again to return to the deck. Passing a sailor who was stowing away a small fire-hose, I remarked as casually as my nerves permitted,

"I imagine the fire is not very serious?" And he answered,

"Oh, no, it's not serious."

On deck the sailors had disappeared, the passengers were sleeping tranquilly, and all was quiet. With heart still pounding, I dropped into my deck chair and waited. Presently, the gong sounded for lunch, and everyone trooped sluggishly to the dining room. After the steward had served the soup, I said to my neighbour,

"You didn't hear the fire-alarm half an hour ago?" And he answered,

"You mean the fire-drill? I heard it. It sounds every Sunday around noon."

The Red Sea gave us a following wind, which brought no relief from the stifling heat, and Port Said, which we reached an hour before dark, was inferno itself. It was not safe to wander even down its main street, the captain warned us, and our vessel below deck was a fiery furnace. All through the night, noisy chains of workers, both men and women, ascended and descended the gang-planks, carrying on their shoulders baskets of coal which they emptied into the hold forty feet below, and the soot that arose as it fell buried the decks under two inches of black snow.

Release came the next morning. Fresh Mediterranean breezes blew the coal-dust from our noses and throats, and armies of playful dolphins leaping and bounding around the vessel escorted us halfway to Italy. The air was clear and invigorating, both sky and sea a deep blue. This was the voyage of the storybooks, I said to myself. And the hours passed quickly.

All too soon, we arrived at Naples and docked in full view of Mt. Vesuvius, whose violent eruptions in A.D. 79 had buried the ancient towns of Herculaneum and Pompeii under molten lava and ashes. Archaeologists had now undertaken to dig them out again, and the Naples Museum, filled to overflowing with the treasures scholars were unearthing, had become a Mecca for every student of ancient Greece and Rome. This region held those tourist resorts celebrated by a hundred romances, Naples itself, Salerno, Amalfi, and the Isle of Capri. Now, after weeks of travel, they lay within my view. The idle part of my voyage had ended. If I was to profit from this Neapolitan interlude, I would have to exert myself every hour of every day for the next two weeks. The Italian officials on the dock seemed eager to help me. They passed me through immigration and customs without opening a bag, and in a one-horse carriage which they pointed out to me I drove to my pre-notified *pension*.[8]

This *pension*, recommended by a friend in New Zealand, was located on the hillside in the oldest part of the city. I could speak barely a dozen words of Italian, but my hostess, who had been widowed the year before, knew a little English, and one of her two grown-up daughters spoke the language quite well. The family had been fairly prosperous until the father was stricken with a fatal illness, and it was holding together now partly by operating this very modest pension, and partly through the earnings of the oldest girl, who was employed in some business establishment. For the moment I was their only guest, but within a few days they

---

[8]A boarding house, providing both accommodation and meals.

expected a man and his wife from Turin, and at any hour of the day some unknown person might ring the bell and request lodging. They allotted me a spacious, high-ceilinged bedroom, showed me the cosy sitting room, which was provided with tourist literature and some illustrated Italian magazines, and at 7:30 p.m. served me an excellent dinner at one of the four small tables in the dining room.

Next morning, my first in Naples, I visited Herculaneum, where I suffered a sharp disappointment. All, or virtually all, the ruins lay underground, beneath houses that were still inhabited, and even with the aid of a guide it was impossible to distinguish one wall from another or to disentangle any coherent plan. Excavations had been slow and costly because the town had been engulfed by a river of molten lava, which had quickly congealed into solid rock. Temporarily, too, the work had been suspended through lack of funds, and all valuable specimens transferred to the Naples Museum. Fifty years later, after the Second World War, I visited Herculaneum again, and found the ancient town's skeleton open to the sky thirty or more feet below the level of the surrounding buildings. But in 1908, as my guide gloomily remarked, the place was interesting only to professional archaeologists. "Go on to Pompeii," he counselled me. "That city was buried not in lava but in ashes and pumice, which slowly changed into soft earth. Gangs of men are excavating there continuously, and you can walk through the old Roman streets and enter the Roman houses."

I hired a carriage to convey me to Pompeii, lunched at a small hotel just outside the gate of the old city, and spent the afternoon roaming through its streets. There were no other visitors, probably because the sun was scorching and the few tourists who had chosen this end-of-August period to vacation in Naples had sought shadier localities. Nor were there any professional guides, for which I was thankful, not because I could interpret correctly all that I was seeing, but because a chattering ignoramus irritates more travellers than he enlightens and never allows his victims to meditate in peace. I encountered a dozen workmen in groups of twos and threes, and one lone worker who offered to sell me two genuine Roman coins, but I saw no foreman or person in authority, although there must have been a superintendent somewhere in the vicinity. Not more than half the city had been excavated. Such remarkable dwellings as the "House of Mysteries" still lay concealed under solidified ashes. But for a classical student, as I was at that period, enough had been uncovered to hold one's interest for several days. There and then, I decided that I would visit a few places west of Naples first, then move into the hotel at the gate of Pompeii and from that base explore both Pompeii itself and the region to the south.

Over the next fortnight my wanderings included, naturally, an excursion to Pozzuoli, where a temple built in Roman days was submerged by the sea in the Middle Ages and its marble columns pitted with holes by that boring "ship's worm," the teredo. At the foot of nearby New Mountain (*Monte Nuovo*), which three centuries ago suddenly reared itself two hundred feet into the air, an acre of ground had been roped off because smoke or steam was issuing from two fumeroles. A cheerful Italian in the vicinity advised me not to stamp my feet too heavily, because the earth's crust on which I was standing was only eight feet thick, and beneath it glowed the flames of hell. Hot-footed, I moved away to what I trusted was safer ground, and proceeded along a very dusty road in the direction of Cumae, the home of Virgil's sibyl.

Vineyards sagging with bunches of ripe grapes now hemmed me in on both sides, the air was hot and stifling, and very soon I was parched with thirst. Lighting upon a small boy who was sitting at the roadside, I offered him ten *centesimi* (a penny) to bring me a bunch of good eating grapes. He brought me twelve bunches of twelve different varieties, and insisted that I sample all of them to discover my preference. Innocently I complied, and continued to sample them as I walked along, forgetting that Bacchus holds many a surprise in store for the thoughtless wayfarer. Then the jocular deity smote me of a sudden with disturbing queasiness, which drove me to shelter in a long tunnel that seemed to perforate a low hill. In that secluded spot I gradually dissociated myself from the grapes—or, as my Australian friends pronounce the word, "gripes". By that time, the sun had travelled a considerable distance and it was advisable to return to my *pension*.

I spent one entire morning in the Naples Museum, the first museum of classical archaeology I had ever entered, and it opened up a world I knew only from books. There for the first time I learned what sculpture could mean. Alone in one corner of an exhibition hall, in a circular chapel, stood a life-sized nude figure of a maiden so translucently pure and ethereal in its white marble that I caught my breath, and for some minutes could not withdraw my eyes from it. I do not remember the sculptor's name or date, but believe the figure was labelled *Psyche* and attributed to some Hellenistic artist of the third century B.C. Since then, I have wondered once or twice whether Wordsworth could possibly have carried this statue in his mind when he wrote

> Our birth is but a sleep and a forgetting:
> The Soul that rises with us, our life's Star,
> Hath had elsewhere its setting,
> And cometh from afar:
> Not in entire forgetfulness,
> And not in utter nakedness,
> But trailing clouds of glory do we come
> From God, who is our home.[9]

Needless to say, I was very young and impressionable in those days, and very ignorant and innocent. The years have now hardened not only my arteries but my mind, and so coarsened it that no wonderful vision of anything supremely good and beautiful will ever touch it again. But art must be something very real when it can transform a shapeless block of cold stone into an exquisite, breathing image that moves a man to his very core.

I lunched quickly after leaving the museum, then took the ferryboat to the Isle of Capri directly south of Naples across the bay. Three troubadours whose repertoire seemed limited to *Santa Lucia* made the round of the decks, and though none of them was an Enrico Caruso, their voices sounded very pleasant on the still sea. From the Capri dock, a boatman rowed me a mile along the coast to the Blue Grotto, whose pale-blue, phosphorescent waters are so eerily

---

[9]These lines are from an Ode by William Wordsworth (1770–1850) entitled *Intimations of Immortality from Recollections of Early Childhood.*

beautiful. Unlike the statue of *Psyche*, however, they left me cold and unmoved, possibly because I could not divest myself of the Christian tradition that our universe is divided into two worlds, an animate and an inanimate, and that while both can stir man's imagination, only the animate world engages his sympathies and his emotions. Many thinkers reject this dichotomy, and modern science strongly supports them, claiming that our universe is one, and that body and mind, matter and energy, are but two faces of the same coin. Nevertheless, man is a very conservative animal. The philosophical theories of his adult years limp far behind the ideas and habits that adhere to him in childhood, and it is the latter that continue to mould most of his thoughts and activities.

A surprise awaited me at the *pension*. Late August, my hostess told me, ushers in the summer carnival, and that evening thousands of young people wearing paper hats and masks could parade up and down the tree-lined park on the waterfront, blaring tin or cardboard trumpets in the faces of every one they met. Girls well brought up needed male escorts to protect them from boisterous youths, and to chaperone them at chance or pre-arranged encounters with favoured ones. My hostess' unattached daughters, lacking brothers, had begged their mother to let them conscript me. She had consented on condition that we return home by 10 p.m., and at the dinner table I was formally commissioned for that one evening only.

We reached the park, which was less than half a mile away, about 8:30 p.m. Already it was crowded, but the rowdier elements had not yet turned out in force and nearly all the masked promenaders were teen-aged school-children in bands of four or five, a few accompanied by their parents. The noisy, carefree multitude could have been harmless participants in a Sunday-school picnic. By 9:30 p.m. the festival's character was changing. The teenagers were thinning out, persons of eighteen years and older began to predominate, the crowd became less restrained and several incidents that began in play threatened to develop into serious quarrels. We then went home, the girls a little disappointed, I fear, at the dullness of an evening which their stolid, unimaginative escort had lacked the wit to enliven.

Two days later, I established myself at the hotel outside Roman Pompeii's gate and enjoyed a picnic lunch within the old city, leaning in restful solitude against the shady wall of a living-room whose aristocratic owner had been snatched away 1,829 years earlier to that bourne[10] from which no traveller returns. His ravisher, Mt. Vesuvius, confronted me, still pointing its graceful cone to the blue sky and wafting towards the empyrean a wisp of white smoke; and a faint breeze from the east began to fan my hot cheeks, just as it had fanned those of the light-hearted Pompeiians long ago, before the volcano blew off its top and vomited the black cloud of ashes that buried the doomed city in perpetual night. Might not such an explosion happen again, I mused; and was there any reason why I, and the hundreds of people in my neighbour-hood, should not share, perhaps that very day, the fate that overtook hundreds of Pompeiians many centuries ago?

Just as a boy feels almost irresistibly tempted to skate on thin ice, so I experienced a strong but irrational desire to look into the crater-jaw of this monstrous volcano and dare it to do its worst. I knew that a funicular railway from Naples carried tourists to very near its summit, but the American humorist Mark Twain had ridden up Vesuvius' face on a mule, and at this

---

[10]The River Styx.

period of my life I too preferred animal transport to locomotion in a lifeless machine. That evening, therefore, I broached the subject to my hotelkeeper, who undertook to enquire the next day about mules and guides and to make whatever arrangements seemed advisable. Meanwhile he suggested a minor excursion. At Castellammare, five miles away, he said, many springs from the mountain behind had been tapped and piped into a single building so that the public might profit, at little or no expense, from the various minerals which impregnated their waters. I could reach the place in one hour by carriage, and even if I was not interested in the region's geochemistry, I would certainly enjoy Castellammare's fine beach and the picturesque drive to and from the little town.

Now having sampled Neapolitan grapes but a few days before, I was in no haste to repeat the experiment with its mineral waters. However, I hired a carriage one afternoon and was driven to a long, galvanized-iron shed with a concrete floor and, down one side, a row of eighteen or twenty taps, from each of which hung a metal mug. Here, for the sum of ten *centesimi*, the same fee as to the boy in the vineyard, I received permission to sample, at my discretion of course, the water in any or all the taps in front of me. I sipped half a teaspoonful from Tap No. 1, very gingerly. It tasted strongly of sulphur, so strongly indeed that I forewent any further experimentation and accepted without trial or question the custodian's glowing description of the virtues in the other taps.

The coachman then came to my rescue. He conducted me away from the poisonous waters of this Stygian cavern and drove me a little off the homeward road to show me a hidden garden where the real waters of life had once reposed and later also dried up. It was enclosed within high walls, and its gate was shut and padlocked so that no one could see within, but by standing on the front seat of the carriage, I was able to peer over the wall. What I saw were four rows of from fifty to one hundred large amphorae or wine jars planted upright in the ground at equal intervals, each jar about three feet high and, so far as I could observe, empty. My coachman, if I understood him rightly, believed that they were Roman jars from which the wine had evaporated with the passage of years, and that the garden had been the cellar of some rich Pompeiian at the time of the eruption. But this seemed hardly credible. I suspected, rather, that they were modern jars of ancient shape, stored here for convenience by some wine merchant, though why he should have arranged them so geometrically I could not conjecture.

The Vesuvius guide presented himself at the door of the hotel one morning and arranged to meet me at 1:30 that afternoon, with two mules, in a tiny hamlet at the foot of the mountain. He brought with him a young boy, for what purpose I did not enquire, but after we began the ascent I noticed that my mule was advancing by fits and starts, and that every start coincided with a loud thump. Puzzled by this unbiological behaviour I looked back, and discovered that the boy was firmly grasping the mule's tail in his left hand and rhythmically beating a devil's tattoo on its rump with a cudgel. Then I remembered that Mark Twain had ascended the volcano with the same spasmodic motion until his rebellious animal kicked its tormentor down the mountainside. I was less fortunate, perhaps because I lacked his ability to appeal to a mule's higher nature, for my animal had lost all faith in humanity, had abandoned all hope of a better life, and with drooping head was enduring its bitter fate in silence.

We dismounted about five hundred feet from the summit and I climbed the rest of the way on foot, leaving the boy to take care of the mules. The trail wound among cinders and ashes, which at times felt distinctly warm under foot, and in two places my guide poked into the ground small scraps of paper which at once caught fire. We reached the rim of the crater without mishap, but could not see its bottom on account of a projecting spur, and we dared not walk around the rim because the demon below in the molten pot had already detected our presence and was bombarding us with flaming red fragments of crust, like showers of sparks from a cedar fire. Three times they almost reached where we were standing. On the third occasion, my guide turned about, shouted to me to follow him, and raced down the mountainside toward his mule. Nothing loath, I raced after him, mounted my animal, and gave it free rein to find its own way to safety for us both. It seemed to share our alarm, for it galloped down so precipitately that the boy could hardly keep up with it, despite the friendly assistance of its tail. Later I wondered whether fright had been its only spur, for I had seemed to hear the animal laughing at the boy's predicament, and subsequent experience with mules during the First World War convinced me that they often react like human beings, at times with even greater intelligence.

One other excursion I made before my fortnight expired, a trip round the Amalfi peninsula. Travelling by train to Salerno, where mediaeval Europe established its first medical university, I hired a two-horse carriage and drove leisurely along the rocky coast—with frequent stops to rest the horses, for the road was not paved—until we reached, late in the afternoon, the town of Amalfi and found lodging at the Hotel dei Cappucini, close to the old Norman-built cathedral. From the hotel's vine-shaded terrace, where the purple grapes hung in bunches over my head, I watched the fishermen draw up their small boats on the pebbly beach and spread out their nets, and at dusk, I dined there under a full moon while the sea glittered below me and only the occasional cry of a street urchin, and the soft patter of my waiter's feet, broke the stillness of the night. Silence, man's most precious heritage, has now almost escaped him. Three millenia ago the clang of an iron age fractured human peace and quiet, and today noisy machines of every size and shape unceasingly jar his nerves through his waking hours and shatter his nightly rest.

We drove on next day through Positano and across the peninsula to Sorrento, where I dismissed the carriage and caught a train to Pompeii. The liner from Australia called in at Naples the following morning, and by evening was carrying me through the western Mediterranean toward Gibraltar and England. Laden with high hopes mingled with an unreasoning sadness, the barque of my life was completing the last leg of its maiden voyage and bracing itself to enter regular service.

II

Twelve months later, along with hundreds of other youths, I was fortifying myself in England for the final examinations of my first year at Oxford University. The crucial tests came and went, leaving me breathless and apprehensive. Two days I waited. Then a short note reached my room, bidding me appear at ten o'clock the following morning in the great dining hall of the college to learn my fate.

Five minutes before the appointed hour, I joined four fellow students on the hall's long steps and filed in with them to a bench just inside its doorway. In the middle of the High Table at its far end, confronting us, sat the master of the college, flanked by two of its tutors, my own and one other.

A name was called, and the student beside me walked the length of the hall to the High Table, underwent judgement and was dismissed. I came third on the list. With loudly beating heart I mounted the low platform, seated myself in the lone chair directly across the table from the master and waited. My tutor recognized me with a faint smile and pushed a sheet of paper in front of the judge, who scanned it very gravely. He was a big man, a classical scholar famous for his profound knowledge of republican Rome, and he had spent many Christmas vacations in Cairo, where his familiarity with the details of Cicero's governorship in Asia Minor two thousand years before had qualified him to advise the British plenipotentiary in troubled Egypt how to deal with today's tangled problems in northeast Africa. Now he was the master of my college, and I too was studying Greek and Roman history. Simultaneously, however, I was dabbling in a new subject, anthropology, and the great scholar could spare little sympathy for a young upstart who wasted his time on a topic so useless. This morning I was sitting in front of him, awaiting his judgement.

He was frowning.

"Ah yes," he said at last. "This is the man who is trying to ride two horses at the same time," and, looking me sternly in the face, he added:

"Take care, young man, that you don't fall between them."

My tutor leaned forward and interceded.

"Mr. Jenness has been working very hard all year. As you see, his examiners have marked him a B. I hope that you will encourage him to return next year and pursue his studies more deeply."

The great man nodded his head, somewhat reluctantly, I thought, and wished me a pleasant vacation. With a grateful glance at my tutor I left the hall elated.

It was the beginning of June 1909. For the next three months, I was free to roam wherever my meagre finances would carry me. I remembered St-Jacut-de-la-Mer, and what a friend had told me about that obscure village on the north coast of French Brittany, just across the English Channel. There, he had said, I would find cheap but comfortable lodging in a high-walled convent, leisure and peace for all the study I was planning, pleasant bathing, and an intriguing countryside littered with relics of past centuries. What more could a man wish? At dawn the next morning, I strapped my suitcase to the carrier of my bicycle, hoisted a rucksack of books on to my back, crossed the Thames and headed for Southampton.

No motor-traffic clogged the highways of Europe in those days, and the roads, though macadamized,[11] had not been asphalted. Grades were more uneven than now: untroubled by the roar, the fumes and the dust of future automobiles, you pushed your bicycle up the steeper slopes and free-wheeled gaily down their farther sides, savouring the fresh clean air that brought the blood into your cheeks. No accident could befall you, nothing could mar your enjoyment

---

[11]British roads at the beginning of the Industrial Revolution were among the worst in Europe. Two great engineers played a major role in changing this: the Englishman, Thomas Telford (*Encyclopaedia Britannica*, 1956b, vol. 21, p. 914) and the Scotsman, John McAdam (*Encyclopaedia Britannica*, 1956a, vol. 14, p. 543). Early in the 1800s, the latter, after considerable experimentation, developed a system of road-making now known as "macadamizing." His roads had foot-thick sub-surfaces of small broken stones, which the wheels of the passing wagons ground together, with the stone dust filling the intervening spaces. Most of the minor roads in the country were built in this fashion. Years later the road surfaces were given coatings of bitumen or tar for added durability and comfort.

of the scenery unless you carelessly ran off the road or blew out one of your tires, and the latter mishap, which you could remedy yourself, seldom happened provided you avoided the flinty roads of Somersetshire, where I once suffered four punctures in a single morning. Nearly every English village contained an inn which at any hour of the day would set before you a hearty meal of bread, ham, and cheese, together with a pot of fresh tea, for the not extravagant sum of one shilling and sixpence, or thirty cents in United States currency. How pleasant it was, in those years before World War I, to wander young and carefree over the highways and byways of southern England when the days were long, the grass still green, and meadows gay with the late spring flowers.

I stopped for the night in Salisbury, wishing to attend an early morning service in its magnificent cathedral. The long narrow nave appeared empty when I slipped into a back pew the next morning, for there were only three other persons in the congregation, and they sat far forward near the chancel. Alone at the back, with my eyes half closed, I listened to the muted notes of the distant organ, drank in the fairyland colours of the stained-glass windows and felt myself immersed in the infinite. A mysterious light enveloped me, and the lofty ceiling seemed to float in the sky.

Salisbury's slender spire is the highest in England, and it has been pointing skyward for more than seven centuries. Its builders were men who spoke my own language. I had read their words, and their assessments of one another, in *The Canterbury Tales*. But at Stonehenge, only seven miles away, stood an even greater marvel, a tremendous circle of gigantic monolithic pillars, capped by lintels of nearly equal size and weight, which had resisted both man and weather for thirty-five centuries and probably longer.

After the morning service in Salisbury, I cycled out to Stonehenge to see its imposing structures and, standing beneath a lintel three times my height above the ground, asked myself—as thousands of others must have asked before me—"What race of man could have shaped these mighty stones and raised them to their present positions? What was the purpose of the monument? Was it a temple perhaps, roofless and wall-less, open on all sides to the life-giving sun? And what did the worshippers look like, what clothes did they wear, what language did they speak, those men, women and children who gathered inside their strange temple long ages ago?"

These thoughts haunted me all the way to Southampton. There the waters of the English Channel looked very troubled when I bought my ticket and walked up the gang-plank of the night ferry to St-Malo, and they communicated their uneasiness to me. Some distressing qualms troubled me during the night passage, but since they disappeared as soon as I planted my feet on the firm St-Malo dock, I felt no trepidation in wheeling my bicycle onto the much smaller ferryboat that crossed the mouth of St-Malo harbour to Dinard, on the opposite headland. But the channel waters resented this brazen attempt to escape without paying the customary scot, and at the harbour mouth they became so agitated that only with the greatest difficulty could I stand on my feet. Foolishly stubborn, I resisted payment until I staggered ashore on the Dinard Quay. There, nature prevailed, and made me disburse not only the full tariff, but a second fee, before she would allow me to mount my bicycle and, lightened in body and mind, start out on the road to St-Jacut-de-la-Mer, which my map told me was only eleven miles away.

A ride of two hours brought me to my destination. St-Jacut-de-la-Mer was a very small village[12] then inhabited mainly by women and children, for nearly all the men had sailed away

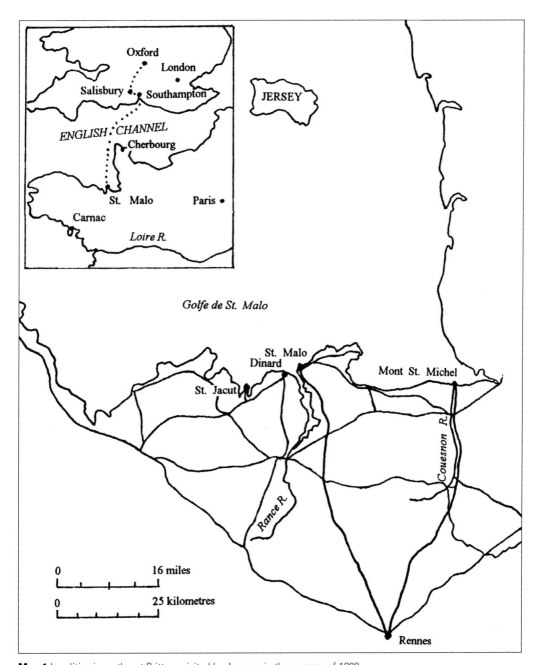

Map 1 Localities in northeast Brittany visited by Jenness in the summer of 1909.

[12]The village of St-Jacut-de-la-Mer has little significance today, for it is not even mentioned in *The Penguin Guide to France 1990* (Tucker, 1990), and is described in the more detailed *Blue Guide France* (Robertson, 1984, p. 265) only as a small resort located on a jagged reef at the north end of a promontory in the Baie de Lancieux.

in April to fish on the Newfoundland banks. There was no need to enquire the way to the convent, for it stood just 200 yards beyond the village on a rocky promontory—a rambling, three-storey building of perhaps seventy rooms inside a high wall broken by two gates, a wide carriage gate in front and a small postern gate that overlooked the sea. From the latter, a steep flight of stone steps led down to a rock-strewn beach, which the daily tide covered with several feet of water, rendering it too hazardous for bathing. Northeast of the convent, however, the pounding sea had created a small, half-moon cove of pure sand, and it was this beach which attracted vacationists from both France and England, some of whom returned year after year.

I have called my new home a convent, and such indeed it was during the greater part of the year. France had abolished closed nunneries about the start of the twentieth century, when it disestablished its Roman Catholic church, but at St-Jacut-de-la-Mer, the church, with the connivance of a devout peasantry, had circumvented the law by converting the local convent into a summer resort for three months of the year, then closing it during the other nine to all but nuns, who purified it of the iniquities brought in by the tourists and occupied it until the following summer. Just before the new season opened, they dispersed, to what place or places I do not know, but three or four remained behind and, with the help of the village women, attended to the needs of the vacationing laity.

It was the Soeur Gérante, the superintendent nun, who welcomed me when I rang the bell, registered me in her office and assigned me a "cell" on the second floor. Another nun then conducted me to my small, carpetless room, which actually contained everything I needed—a bed, a bureau, a small writing table, a straight-backed chair and, on the walls, two pegs on which to hang some of my clothes. I was their fourth guest, my conductress told me; three had arrived the day before, and more were expected at the weekend. At exactly twelve noon, the convent bell would ring for lunch, which would be served in the refectory on the ground floor. In the meantime, I could wander wherever I wished within their two-acre shrubbery, and of course (she added with a twinkle in her eye) I needed no permission to roam outside the convent wall.

Very soon I felt at home. New guests arrived almost daily, and after the second week, some began to depart again. In early July, I counted fifty, the majority of them French, but a dozen or more English.

About 7:30 each morning, a village youth trundled the local baker's bread in a hand-cart to the kitchen door, and Soeur Marthe, our ever-cheerful cook, removed her half of the tally stick from its hook to be notched with the number of loaves she purchased. (At the end of the summer I deposited one of her sticks, notched from tip to handle, in the Oxford museum.)[13] Early risers among us—I was one—accepted the noise as a signal to dress and, drifting into the refectory as the bell rang 8 a.m., we munched as much as we wished of the bread and sipped the hot chocolate which the good sister ladled into our bowls from her copper cauldron. Then we scattered until noon, flexibly adjusting each day's routine to the weather and the state of the tide, which every twelve hours rose as much as fifteen feet and covered most of the beaches. Apprehensive of the critical examinations in the year ahead, I tried to study each morning,

---

[13]The Pitt Rivers Museum, Oxford.

sometimes in my room, sometimes on a bench in a quiet corner of the shrubbery, and sometimes among the rocks below the postern gate.

In July, when the wild blackberries ripened on the road-side hedges, a few of us banded together to add that appetizing fruit to our breakfast. We rose about 5:30 a.m., cycled three or four miles to wherever the bushes seemed most heavily laden, filled our pails with the berries and carried them back to Soeur Marthe, who stewed them in a second cauldron and served them with our chocolate. Brittany's climate and soil seem especially designed for this fruit, for neither in England nor in New Zealand, to which country England carried the plant, have I seen more luscious berries. Twelve months later, when travelling in the Dordogne region of central France, I came upon berries which looked just as luscious as those of Brittany, but tasted as insipid as plain water, presumably owing to some nutritive deficiencies in the lime-stone soil. Today most of France's blackberry bushes have disappeared, and the few that survive conceal their leaves and berries under blankets of motor-car dust.

Our small summer colony provided a fair cross-section of English and French middle-class society in the first decade of the twentieth century. The fellow-guests whose acquaintance I most cultivated included an English manufacturer from the Midlands and two middle-aged English women, one the wife of a London lawyer and the other a university graduate who held some senior post in England's civil service. Then there was a French family from Paris, the father a prosperous merchant, his wife a vivacious lady in her prime-of-beauty period. More attracted and—let me confess—attractive to me than the mature parents were their two gadfly daughters, the elder about eighteen and the other some four years younger, for they corrected my schoolboy French with such hilarity that their mother often scolded them, and apologized to me for their disrespectful conduct toward a serious student who was also a foreigner. I did not apologize to either father or mother for my own egregious blunder when, quite innocently, I addressed their elder daughter by the familiar pronoun *tu*, "thou," instead of the respectful *vous*, "you"; but then no apology seemed called for, since the outraged indignation on the countenance of the startled girl withered not only me, but the flowers at my feet. Happily, she relented the next afternoon and, with the help of her sister, revived both myself and the flowers by pinning me against the convent wall for half an hour, and shrieking with laughter at my pitiful attempts to reproduce her pronunciation of those pernicious sounds French people insist on writing *r* and *u*.

One other guest often accompanied me to the bathing beach, a professor of philosophy in the University of Rennes, in central Brittany.[14] He it was who explained to me, with scholarly lucidity, why Protestantism has dominated northern Europe since the Reformation, but hardly dinted the countries bordering the Mediterranean Sea. Without a shadow of doubt, he declared, it was differences in the physical environment that caused the religious cleavage. Scandinavia and other northern countries lack colour: their skies are clouded, their seas dark and cold. Dark and gloomy, too, are their forests of fir and pine, which make their landscapes so stern and forbidding. The Mediterranean, on the other hand, is a region of light and colour as warm as the temperature; its sky and sea are blue, its atmosphere redolent of thyme and other

---

[14] Rennes has been the capital of Brittany since the tenth century. It was extensively damaged in 1944 during the Second World War.

fragrant herbs. Because man is an animal he must conform to his environment as other animals do, even if nature does not require him to change his colour with the seasons. Mediterranean peoples crave the warmth and brightness of the sun, and in winter, when their sun is too weak to warm their unheated homes, they sit on their doorsteps to enjoy its glow. Inevitably, therefore, they demand a sunny religion brightened by gorgeous vestments, colourful ceremonies and numerous feasts. But in northern Europe nature is harsh and unkind. From the cradle to the grave, she schools that region's inhabitants in a cold, unpoetic environment which makes them dour and unimaginative pragmatists. And their religion is cold and unimaginative also.

I suspect that this professor traced his lineage back to the prehistoric inhabitants of Brittany and southern England, for they too, if our archaeologists interpret correctly their monuments at Stonehenge and other places, were ardent sun-worshippers who regulated their lives by the movements of that orb and carefully noted its summer and winter solstices. Within a thirty-mile radius of St-Jacut-de-la-Mer, I examined several of the pillar-like *menhirs*[15] they had left behind, some still upright, others flat on the ground and half hidden by the vegetation. The largest, broken unfortunately into three pieces, measured over sixty feet long and must have weighed several tons. These stone pillars probably served various purposes. Some may have been simple grave-markers; others, perhaps, were structural parts of grave chambers originally covered with mounds of earth, but exposed and displaced by man in the course of the centuries; and still others may have been units in long alignments, such as those at Carnac[16] in Southern Brittany, which appear to have been associated with religious ceremonies.

There was much to see and do in the neighbourhood of St-Jacut. Cycling cost nothing, and its only competitors on the highways were other cyclists, some horse-drawn carts, and numerous pedestrians. The farmer who was mowing his hay beside the road gladly returned your greeting and, leaning on his scythe, discussed the harvest with you, or the state of the weather, or where you had fulfilled your military service. Every farm-house raised a few hens, in every country inn one pot of soup and another of coffee simmered all day on the stove, and you could lunch at any hour, as in England, not on ham, cheese and tea, but on rich soup, plain or savoury omelette, and coffee; and the charge rarely exceeded 1.50 francs, or roughly thirty-five cents U.S. Lodging too was cheap: you counted on paying five, or at the most six francs for a full dinner that included wine, a comfortable bed, and the regular continental breakfast of bread or roll and coffee. Most pleasant of all, no waiter or maidservant ever hovered around you waiting for a tip, although he or she would gratefully accept one if you offered it.

Country people everywhere welcomed tourists, especially if they understood French and struggled to speak that language, however painful the struggle might be to both speaker and listener. Before the first World War, indeed, tourists were a rare genus, except in Paris and a few other large cities, although Russia was then the only European country that demanded a

---

[15]Tall, upright, monumental stones.

[16]The village of Carnac, along the Atlantic coast, is world-famous for its large Stone-Age blocks of rock (megaliths) and dolmens (structures usually consisting of several large stone slabs set upright in the earth and capped by a large flat stone forming a roof). Rows of megaliths, a hundred yards wide and half a mile long, run alongside a road a mile from the village (Robertson, 1984, p. 293). The word *dolmen* is Celtic; the Welsh equivalent is *cromlech*. These stones are found in many parts of England and Ireland as well.

passport or a visa. At France's borders, customs' officials asked only two questions: "Have you any tobacco? Have you any matches?" For on those two articles their government maintained a strict monopoly.

One morning, five of my French friends invited me to join them in a picnic to a rocky islet in a neighbouring bay. A local fisherman would row us there, they said, and call for us again three hours later. We landed with two big hampers, one containing bread and wine, Omar Khayyam's favourite menu in the wilderness, the other filled with raw oysters, a luxury unknown to that Persian poet.[17] I too had never sampled them, and distinguished myself on this occasion only by my awkwardness in opening them and my inability to swallow more than six, however much I encouraged their passage with the good red wine. My companions succeeded where I failed; they voraciously emptied the whole basket. Then two of them, Paul and Héloïse, celebrated their victory by retiring to the shelter of a large rock and rending the calm air with the latest music-hall ditties. We others tried to flee, but were stopped by the water, and our nerves would certainly have broken under their caterwauling had not the wine, the oysters, and the warm sun combined to attack and silence them. The conquering allies then overpowered us also, and our entire party slumbered noisily until the fisherman returned in his boat and freighted us back to the mainland.

August arrived, and with it the annual week of pilgrimage to Mont-St-Michel, an ancient Benedictine fortress-abbey on a granite island off the mouth of the Couesnon River, some thirty miles east of St-Malo. The pilgrimage dates back to the eighth century A.D., when the cone-shaped crag, 160 feet high, carried on its precipitous northern face a lone chapel, erected by a missionary bishop at the command of the Archangel Michael. So many pilgrims from France, Ireland, England, and even Italy flocked to the new shrine that it was unable to accommodate them all, and its fame began to rival the much greater shrines of St. Peter in Rome and St. James of Compostella in northwestern Spain. In A.D. 966, a Duke of Normandy, ancestor of the William the Conqueror who seized the throne of England exactly one hundred years later, replaced the small chapel with a large abbey, which later generations destroyed, rebuilt, and further enlarged until it covered the greater part of the island.

The modern pilgrim reaches today's complex of buildings from the mainland over a mile-long causeway which ends at a gate in the encircling ramparts, whence a narrow street lined with ancient houses leads him uphill to the abbey proper and its part-Romanesque, part-Gothic church near the summit. From there he can watch the tide sweep over miles and miles of treacherous sand with the speed of a race-horse, cutting off all possibility of regaining the mainland except by the same causeway, now almost submerged by the water.[18]

In 1909, there was only one building outside the abbey gate, a humble restaurant that almost touched the rampart wall. When I dismounted there about 11 a.m. of a mid-week morning, ten or twelve country carts had parked beside it, and a few people were loitering at the open gateway, but there was no crowd. Without hesitation, I left my bicycle unguarded

---

[17]Oysters are plentiful along this northern Brittany coast, especially between St-Malo and Mont-St-Michel (Tucker, 1990, p. 275). Omar Khayyam authored *The Rubaiyat* in the twelfth century.

[18]By 2003, the accumulation of sand, slime, and sludge along this causeway was so nearly clogging its watery setting that the French authorities planned to rip up the road (built across it in 1879) and replace it with an electronic shuttle on stilts (Anonymous, 2003, p. A18).

Figure 5 Abbey of Mont-St-Michel, Brittany, France, a centuries-old symbol of man's undying hope in his ultimate destiny.
Photo by D. Jenness

among the carts, ascended the narrow street, and attached myself to a family that was examining an old thirteenth-century house, once the home of Bertrand du Guesclin, the renowned Breton warrior who liberated much of western France from the rule of England's Plantagenet kings. With my new acquaintances, I climbed the steps to the main abbey buildings, the cloister, the Merveille, the church, and the keep, in and through which small knots of people were drifting.

The abbey had been classified as a national monument, open to visitors between the appointed hours, and so great was the trust the government reposed in its public that nowhere on my round did I see any uniformed official, although there must have been several custodians on the island. Neither did I observe any sign of commercialism, apart from the restaurant at the gate. Yet there were at least one hundred visitors that morning, all French people, so far as I could judge, except myself. About half were peasants from the neighbouring countryside enjoying a rare holiday, and half seemed to be tourists from other parts of France who had come, three or four on bicycles, the rest by train to the railway station three miles away, thence on foot over the causeway.

After wandering through the abbey for perhaps an hour, I descended to the gateway, where a dozen people were standing in line outside the restaurant door. Another fifty or more were eating their lunches among the rocks below the ramparts, maintaining the while a careful watch on the hour and the tide. I found an unclaimed rock and ate my own bread and ham, then cycled back over the causeway to the mouth of the Couesnon River and joined a group of people waiting beside two rowboats which were to carry them upstream on the bore.[19]

---

[19]A high, abrupt tidal wave moving with great force in a narrow channel.

Half an hour later we saw the bore approaching. The sand-plain separating us from the island began to heave and quiver, dark patches spread over it, and a low wall of water suddenly disengaged itself and raced ominously in our direction. The boatmen shouted, the waiting passengers climbed hurriedly aboard, I lifted my bicycle over the side of the second boat and leaped in after it. Within two minutes the bore caught up with us. My boat pitched violently forward, its two rowers pulled with all their might to keep the bow facing upstream, and the banks of the river began to fly past us as fast as a man can run.

The bore carried us a full mile without slackening, and it continued to help us over most of the next three miles, where we disembarked at a small dock near the highway. It had been an exhilarating run, a fitting climax to a day of subdued but continuous excitement. There remained, of course, the thirty-five-mile bicycle ride back to St-Jacut-de-la-Mer, but in the quiet of the evening, that seemed almost relaxing.

III

More than forty years slipped by before I saw Mont-St-Michel again, and during that interval Brittany, and indeed the whole world, changed more profoundly than during the preceding four centuries. Man was striving to emancipate himself through the researches of his chemists and physicists, and he was no longer content to cling humbly to the surfaces of the lands and seas which had bounded the activities of his forefathers. He was flying through space with the speed of sound, and drilling through the depths of the ocean into the bowels of his mother earth. At the same time, he was secularizing his centuries-old religions, and transforming pious midsummer pilgrimages to holy shrines into frenetic tours to luridly advertised show-places, open at every season of the year to swell the coffers of a money-grubbing civilization.

In that changing world I too had changed, and had long since entered my second life-phase, for scientific man has reduced Shakespeare's seven ages to only two, an age of growth and an age of decay. In his age of growth, as I was during that summer of 1909 when I lived with the good nuns of St-Jacut-de-la-Mer, he is an optimist and a star-gazer, filled with energy and a zest for change without too much concern for its direction. But in his second age, when his physical and mental powers are waning, he fears innovation, clings to the familiar and the status quo, and looks back nostalgically to the world of his earlier years.

So in 1952, when my wife and I motored from southern to northern France by way of Brittany, the land through which we passed seemed altogether different from the one in which I had spent my student vacation, for I was seeing it through different eyes.

We crossed the Loire River and entered southern Brittany in mid-April, that glorious month when the fogs and chill of winter have ended, the sky is blue, the air transparent, and the fields green and gold from the flowering bushes of prickly gorse scattered among the fresh grass. We stayed two days in Carnac, the religious centre of the pre-historic megalith-builders, which in 1909 I had cycled one hundred miles out of my way to visit after the sea-bathing in St-Jacut-de-la-Mer had become a test of endurance and my college in England was calling me back to its lecture-halls. At that time, Carnac's inhabitants were dreaming in a Shangri-la untouched by the currents of unrest which were agitating so many regions of Eastern and Western Europe. Its women regularly donned each morning the picturesque black-and-white head-dress their mothers and grandmothers had worn in the Middle Ages, perhaps even in the age of stone, and strangers were so rare that no one in the sleepy little village paid any attention to them. But by 1952, the head-dresses had disappeared or were paraded only on special occasions, and Carnac had become a stopping-place for touring buses from half a dozen countries, as well as for the local bus which served this part of the coast. When we started to stroll among the long avenues of menhirs that led up to the great "altar-stone" a scant half-mile from our hotel, a pitiless guide insisted on reciting to us a bombastic epic about the supposed builders of the prehistoric monument, an epic composed by some commercial hack who had confused or combined the mediaeval Gestes de Roland with the Cornish legends about King Arthur and his Knights of the Round Table.

Saddened, unreasonably perhaps, by this travesty of history, we continued our circuit of the Breton Peninsula and reached at last the Mont-St-Michel. At the end of its causeway fourteen cars stood parked so close together that none could move without disarranging all the rest. And hard up against them two large buses were disgorging a gaggle of tourists who disregarded the open gate and narrow street that led straight up the mountain to meditation and prayer, but crowded into the postcard-and-trinket shops squeezed between the parking lot and the rampart, where they jostled one another in their eagerness to purchase a few mementos of their pilgrimage before the bus-drivers sounded their klaxons and whisked them away to another shrine. My wife and I, survivors of an outdated century, did not await the buses' signal, but wheeled our Volkswagen around and fled into the open country, where distance silenced the honking klaxons, and peaceful oxen grazing in quiet pastures invited us to re-enter a world of sanity.

The contemporaries of the architects who built Mont-St-Michel's great abbey fought to the death over the number of angels that could dance on the point of a needle, and today we mock their folly. But we who knight our "beatles" and extol our "goons,"[20] who appraise an abbey's lovely cloister and glorious view in terms of pieces of silver and tawdry banknotes of soiled paper, have we advanced one step beyond our mediaeval forefathers? Or is it not true that

"Knowledge grows but wisdom lingers; and the stone-age farmers laugh
When the electronic harvesters toss the wheat out with the chaff."

[My father commenced his studies at Oxford in the fall of 1908 and qualified after two years for the Diploma in Anthropology in the spring of 1910.[21] Three Certificates for Examination in Anthropology

---

[20]The Beatles were a wildly popular British musical quartet in the 1960s when my father wrote this chapter; "The Goon Show" was a popular British radio comedy program about the same time. It surprises me that he knew about either of these groups.

[21](Marett, 1920, p. 5). It was only the second year that the Diploma in Anthropology had been granted at Oxford. The French-Canadian, Marius Barbeau, and an American, Wilson Wallis, both Rhodes Scholars, also received their Diplomas in Anthropology that year. After my father underwent the requisite examination for the Diploma in Anthropology, one of his tutors (who had also been one of his examiners), Professor J.A. Smith of Balliol College, wrote on July 10, 1910: "I think you will find that Jenness will do credit to Balliol, as a field Anthropologist. We were very much struck by his work in the Diploma Examination. He actually beat the two B.Sc. men; and besides struck us as remarkably observant, and levelheaded, the two main qualities needed in an explorer;" (quoted in Nemo, 1918, p. 36).

in my possession at the time of writing (2006), signed between April 25 and early May 1910, indicate he studied Prehistoric Archaeology and Comparative Technology during one year and two terms with Henry Balfour, Physical Anthropology during three terms with Professor Arthur Thomson, and Social Anthropology during one year and two terms with R.R. Marett.

Unable to return to New Zealand during the summer breaks because of limited time and funds, he spent the summer of 1909 studying and bicycling about the countryside in northern France, as he has detailed in the foregoing chapter. The following summer, 1910, he accompanied his friend, Marius Barbeau, to Paris, where he met Professor Marcel Mauss, the eminent French anthropologist at the Sorbonne, under whom Barbeau had studied during school vacation breaks. After a few days in Paris, he journeyed south alone to the Dordogne region, where he spent several weeks investigating the prehistoric caves, where evidences of Cro-Magnon people had been found in the 1860s, including chipped flints, human bones, and cave drawings, and he collected archaeological

Figure 6 Candidates for the Diploma in Anthropology and their examiners, Oxford, 1910. L. to r. (standing): Candidates Wilson Wallis, Diamond Jenness, and Marius Barbeau; examiners, L. to r. (seated): Professor Arthur Thomson, R.R. Marett, and Henry Balfour.
Photo from Pitt Rivers Museum, Oxford University

artifacts around the little communities of Les Eyzies-de-Tayac, Laussel, Basse Laugerie and Haute Laugerie.[22] I suspect that he used a bicycle for transportation while staying at Les Eyzies-de-Tayac, renting one locally rather than bringing his own from Oxford. Upon his return to Oxford for his final year of study, he donated his resultant collection of 181 artifacts (chiefly scrapers and flakes) to the Pitt Rivers Museum. In 1952, he again visited the Les Eyzies region for a day or two, this time with his wife, Eilleen, while they were on their way north after a winter in southern Spain. It is reasonable to assume he showed her some of the sites where he had collected forty-one years earlier. On this occasion, however, he was more of an informed tourist than a researcher, and recorded his visit only by photographing local chateaus. In the spring of 1911, he completed his classics studies at Oxford and was granted a B.A. Literae Humaniores by the university.

Eager to obtain field experience in his newly acquired training of anthropology, he discussed with his teacher, R.R. Marett of Exeter College, the idea of spending a year studying the almost unknown native people in the eastern part of Papua-New Guinea, where his older sister May and her husband, Reverend Andrew Ballantyne, ran a missionary station. His idea was presented to the Committee of

---

[22]Les Eyzies-de-Tayac is about 41 km southeast of Perigueux, east of Bordeaux. Laussel lies 8 km east of Les Eyzies-de-Tayac; the two Laugerie's are some 2 to 3 km north of it, along the valley of the Vézère River. Staff at the Pitt Rivers Museum, Oxford, very kindly supplied me in June 2004 with photocopies of the pages on which my father's artifacts are listed in its accession books.

Anthropology at Oxford University, whose members were likely made aware of his limited financial resources and approved his project with the proviso that he should undertake an intensive study of one small area in that region rather than try to carry out a superficial survey of a larger region. He was then appointed Research Student, designated Oxford Scholar in Papua-New Guinea, and given funds for equipment, travel, and field expenses totalling £250, some of which came from the Committee, with the rest raised from nine Oxford colleges and three individual donors.[23] *It was the first time that the university supported such an anthropological endeavour.*[24] *One of the individual donors was Sir Arthur Evans (1851–1941), the Oxford archaeologist famous for his excavation of the palace at Knossos on the island of Crete early in the 1900s, and for other archaeological activities in Crete commencing in 1893, which collectively resulted in important discoveries concerning the early history of Greece and the eastern Mediterranean.]* [S.E.J]

---

[23]Marett, R.R., 1920, pp. 5–6.
[24]Edwards, E., 1994, p. 1.

1912:
THE ASCENT OF MOUNT MADAWANA, PAPUA-NEW GUINEA[1]

2

Diamond Jenness

[*My father sailed home to New Zealand in the summer of 1911, at the end of his third and final year at Oxford. He reached Wellington on October 25 and was royally received by his family, who had not seen him for three years. He stayed there only two weeks, then departed for Papua. He travelled first to Sydney, Australia, then after a few days continued on board the SS Matunga to Papua, with stops at Port Moresby and Samarai. From Samarai, a pearl trader took him by cutter to the small settlement of Bwaidoga on the southeast coast of Goodenough Island, which he reached on December 11. There he met his*

Figure 7 Diamond Jenness and his sisters at the Methodist mission at Bwaidoga, Goodenough Island, Papua-New Guinea, 1912. L. to r.: Grace Jenness Skinner, Diamond, May Jenness Ballantyne with son Alan, Reverend Andrew Ballantyne.

Photo by D. Jenness

---

[1]Much of this chapter is reproduced with the permission of the Directors of the Royal Canadian Geographical Society from the *Canadian Geographical Journal*, Vol. LXXIV, No. 3, March 1967, pp. 100–108. [*D.J.*]

sister, May, and his brother-in-law, Reverend Andrew Ballantyne, who operated the local Methodist mission station. My father lived with them and used the station as his base of operations for the next twelve months.

Goodenough Island is a volcanic island, part of the D'Entrecasteaux Islands (at that time called the D'Entrecasteaux Archipelago), just north of the eastern tip of Papua-New Guinea. Measuring some thirty by forty miles, it is said to be the highest island for its size in the world, its mountains rising some 8,000 feet above sea level. Its interior had never been explored when my father reached the island.

For the next twelve months, working alone and occasionally with his missionary brother-in-law, he carried out detailed anthropological studies on the habits, customs, arts, language, and religion of the natives in the surrounding region, who were thought to be a mixture of Melanesian and Papuan peoples. Although the region was readily accessible, its people had remained unstudied. Some were even known to practice cannibalism; my father, in fact, spent a few hours with a remote group whom he suspected sometimes followed that practice.

The region was experiencing a severe famine that year because of a long summer drought. Such droughts were not common there (the previous one having been in 1899–1901, and the next one not until 1946–1947), but all resulted in crop failures and famine, with devastating effects upon the native population. From their own meagre supplies, the people at the mission station struggled to support many of the nearly starving local natives, all the while hoping for the appearance of a trading boat that might be able to replenish their own greatly depleted food stock.

Although confined to working near the mission station much of the time because of his transportation and financial limitations, my father managed to visit nearly every village on the southern half of South Goodenough Island, and several on nearby North Ferguson Island when his brother-in-law had reason to go there. As time passed and my father's confidence and knowledge of the native language increased, he sometimes ventured even farther afield, using a local native as guide and companion.

Diseases abounded in the region. As a result, my father suffered frequently from ulcerous sores on his legs, which he described in a letter to his Oxford teacher, R.R. Marett, as "one of the natural plagues of this country."[2] He also mentioned that every scratch had to be treated immediately with an antiseptic; but even then, some of them had become infected. In another letter to his professor[3] he wrote of being laid up with "scrub itch" on his legs, which he attributed to wading through streams along the coast. Worst of all, however, were the malaria carrying mosquitoes. My father experienced his first two malarial attacks a month after his arrival. He apparently had several more attacks thereafter, and finally was forced to return to New Zealand to recuperate.[4]

With so little financial support or personnel, my father showed remarkable courage (some might rather call it naiveté) to undertake such a study in this unexplored region. He undertook it largely single-handed, though at times he was greatly aided by his experienced brother-in-law, who had mastered the language and custom, and fostered the trust of the native people. Had my father gotten ill, injured,

---

[2]Jenness to R.R. Marett, April 11, 1912, Committee for Anthropology Papers, File MS. UDC/C/2/4, Bodleian Library, Oxford University, Oxford, England.

[3]Jenness to R.R. Marett, January 20, 1912, Committee for Anthropology Papers, File MS. UDC/C/2/4, Bodleian Library, Oxford University, Oxford, England.

[4]Most of the details presented here have been obtained from Jenness and Ballantyne (1920).

or even been killed during one of his occasional journeys, there was little likelihood of search efforts being made to locate him. His situation was, therefore, quite different from that of Michael Rockefeller (son of wealthy New York State Governor Nelson Rockefeller), who in 1961 attempted an exploration and anthropological expedition into another remote part of New Guinea, disappeared, and became the object of many unsuccessful search parties.

In the following, account my father relates an unusual adventure he had during his year on Goodenough Island.] [S.E.J.]

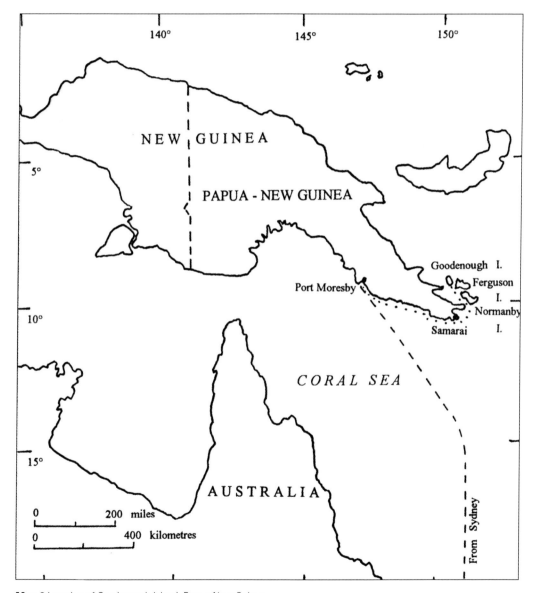

Map 2 Location of Goodenough Island, Papua-New Guinea.

In 1911, when I was completing my studies at Oxford University, my tutor[5] advised me to crown them, not with the leisurely European tour that had been so fashionable half a century before, but with an investigation of some of the unknown, or little known, aborigines of eastern New Guinea, that rugged tropical island which sits like a cap on Australia's head. And he backed up his advice by collecting the necessary funds for me from the university and its constituent colleges.

I then spent twelve months in the D'entrecasteaux Archipelago off the tip of eastern New Guinea, eleven of them on the northernmost island, Goodenough, at whose southeast corner the Methodist Church of Australia had recently planted a mission. Using this mission as my base, I reconnoitred both Goodenough Island and the adjacent coast of Fergusson Island, studying the language and customs of their inhabitants and, by way of relaxation, their butterfly population, some three hundred examples of which I sent to Oxford's Pitt-Rivers Museum, together with a few samples of its rich parasitical treasures—bat-fleas, etc.—for the Rothschild Museum in Tring, England, which specializes in that interesting branch of biological science. Curiosity drove me then to climb one of Goodenough's highest peaks, Mount Madawana, and it is that episode I am describing in this article, which I wrote immediately after I returned to sea-level, but laid aside and forgot for half a century.

Goodenough Island greatly changed during that half century. An exploration by the American biologist, Dr. L.J. Brass in or about 1950 failed to discover a single surviving clump of the thick-stemmed variety of bamboo which previously had flourished in many places, and on Mount Madawana had formed so dense a forest that my party was obliged to hack a trail through it.

More striking than any changes in the flora, however, has been the revolution in the aborigines themselves, who are now [1966] a civilized and literate people, fully aware of the vast and complicated world in which they occupy so tiny a niche. In 1912, when I lived among them, the majority had just replaced their shell knives with metal ones and fitted steel blades on the hand-adzes they used for chipping wood, but the only other sign of their contact with Europeans was the cotton loin-cloth which a few young men affected in place of the traditional banana leaf or stitched flax-leaves. The women, conservative like women everywhere, strictly maintained the customs of their grandmothers: they wore grass mini-skirts, two or three on top of one another, but none reaching more than half-way down the thighs. Both sexes carried on their daily chores in and around their hamlets of thatched huts as if no other land existed. They cultivated their plots of yams and taro and sweet potatoes, fished with baskets

---

[5] My father's tutor during his third year was A.D. Lindsay (B. Richling, personal communication). His main advisor was R.R. Marett of Exeter College, Oxford, and it was probably to him my father is referring here. In the early 1940s while training with the Canadian Army in England, my older brother John, at father's suggestion, visited Marett in Oxford. At some point in their conversation (as recalled to me by my brother in 2006), Marett remarked that although Jenness had been a good student of anthropology he greatly needed practical experience in his field, so Marett had encouraged him to undertake the specialized native studies in Papua–New Guinea. Ironically, in 1918 my father remarked that Marett "is a good philosophical anthropologist, but I don't imagine he would score very highly in field work!" (Jenness to Barbeau, letter dated February 15, 1918, Jenness correspondence, Box 206, Folder 27, Archives, CMC). Nevertheless, my father had the highest regard for his former teacher.

and nets on the coral reefs, cooked their food in rude clay pots, and hollowed from tree-trunks canoes so clumsy that they overturned and sank whenever a choppy sea broke off their outriggers. Every hamlet, whether it contained twenty huts or only two, was a kingdom unto itself. Ties of kinship generally preserved peace with near neighbours, but natives living only a league apart often hesitated to enter each other's hamlets lest an imprudent visit terminate abruptly in unfamiliar cooking-pots.

Cannibalism had been officially suppressed by the Australian magistrate who patrolled the archipelago once a year with a detachment of two or three native policemen, but rumours of fresh cases continued to circulate and it behooved every man, woman, and child to be circumspect. A fine old chief who entertained me in his hamlet confided to me that the roast pork we were eating was very tasty, but not half as tender as "long pig!"

The grammar of Goodenough's language was so simple that a stranger could learn the speech of any locality within a few weeks. But, as so often among illiterate peoples, every locality had developed a separate dialect, which diverged from other dialects in direct proportion to their remoteness, and natives who lived on the northern and western coasts of the island found it difficult to converse with those in the southeast around the mission station. There was no standard dialect, no "Malayan" trade jargon intelligible in every district. Every ten or fifteen miles, the traveller had to find a new interpreter.

Military operations from a fighter airbase in the north of the island during World War II uprooted many of the inhabitants and increased the linguistic confusion, which has left its mark in the discrepancies of the place-names on maps of the island. The hamlet names (or, more correctly, the names of the localities in which the hamlets lay, since the homes of shifting agriculturalists are very ephemeral) do not now coincide exactly with those in this chapter, but after more than fifty years that is not surprising.

The mountains of Goodenough Island, at the eastern end of New Guinea, culminate in three peaks, two of which, Tukekela and Mount Madawana, are about equal in height and loftier than the third. On their slopes, the natives told me, were many villages that no white man had visited, not even the local missionaries. Indeed at this time, 1912, the centre of the island was believed to be almost uninhabited, and I myself had lived nine months in the region studying the manners and customs of the natives without hearing of these villages in the mountains. I determined, therefore, to pay them a visit and, making my way up the coast to Belebele, the last missionary outpost in the north of the D'Entrecasteaux Archipelago, engaged two guides for the journey, Sali and Matakoi. The former's home lay in one of the hill villages close to the coast, but Matakoi came from farther back and could guide me over a large part of my route.

We started out in the early morning. One of the boys carried my blanket, wrapped in a sheet of oiled cloth, and my camera; the other a couple of aluminum pots and a little rice and tea. Toward noon we stopped to cook our lunch beside a small creek that flowed down from the hills near Dududu, and while we were resting were overtaken and passed by a band of Kwaiaudili natives who were returning to their home in the foothills. The first village we reached was Vewa, a small settlement on the brow of a hill overlooking the plain. The settlement had been built two years before by some Dududu people searching for new land on which to grow their crops. Nearby were their gardens, where a number of women were breaking up the soil, and beyond the women were the men, "ploughing" virgin land with long pointed stakes. They stood in line, with the stakes driven about six inches into the ground, and, at a signal from the end man, heaved and shouted simultaneously, turning a continuous furrow. Then they stepped back a pace and drove their stakes into the ground to heave a parallel furrow.

Steadily we made our way up one ridge and down another until we came to a second stream, where the Kwaiaudili travellers had halted for a few minutes to bathe in the cool water.

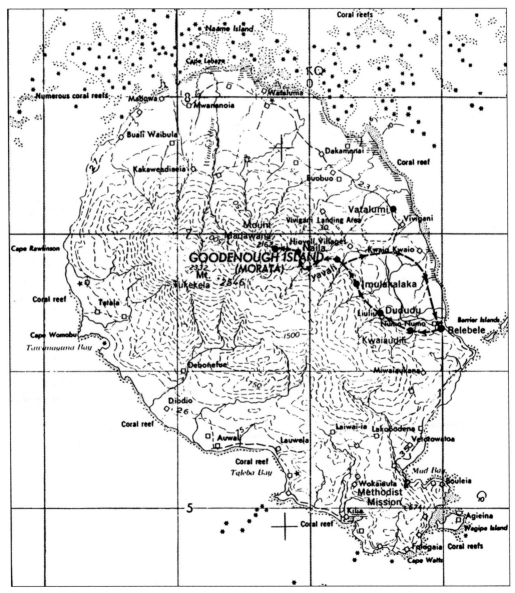

Map 3 Jenness' route to the summit of Mount Madawana in 1912, Goodenough Island, Papua-New Guinea.
Map from Jenness, 1967

As they were moving off in front of us, I looped my camera, a Reflex that weighed nearly ten pounds, over the shoulder of one of their young men, who accepted it without saying a word and carried it two miles to his village Mataboya. There he laid it on the ground, and was climbing up the log ladder into his hut when I called him back and gave him some tobacco, a payment that greatly surprised both him and his companions, who had regarded his burden as just the natural penalty of encountering a white man.

Since nearly all the inhabitants of Mataboya were working in their gardens some distance away, we did not linger, but pushed on to the larger village of Afufuya, where several natives had painted their faces black in mourning for a relative who had died two days before. From the description they gave me of his malady I suspected dysentery, but they themselves declared that a sorcerer of Dududu village had killed him by marking a cross on the path over which he was travelling and chanting a magic spell. I heard four weeks later that the two villages were at war with one another on this account. No real fighting had occurred, but each was avoiding the other's territory through fear of being attacked.

After talking for a while with the Afufuya natives, we continued on through the villages of Galalaunea, Mataisea and Kanio'o to Utalo, the home of some of Sali's relatives, who treated

Figure 8 Native family and animals relax below their hut, Goodenough Island, Papua-New Guinea, 1912. The fence in the upper left protects a vegetable garden.

Photo by D. Jenness

us to a bowlful of sweet potatoes that had been left over from the morning meal. Here, the women were busily weaving strong wicker baskets in preparation for the approaching yam harvest. While we were quietly talking in the shade of one of the houses, a party of strangers, men and women from the coast village of Vatalumi, suddenly appeared at a corner of the trail a few yards from the first hut and halted there, uncertain of the reception they would receive. My Utalo hosts shouted to them to come on, assuring them that all would be well, but I could see signs of trepidation on their faces as they filed quickly past us and vanished along the path.

After inviting our Utalo friends to visit us that evening and hold a sing-song, we moved before sunset to Sali's own home in Imulakalaka, a village about a hundred yards higher up. Most of its men were hunting kangaroos on the plain below and would not return until the next day. Sali introduced me to his aged father, who was too feeble to join any more in strenuous hunts. As we sat sheltered from the wind below the stone *tuwaka* or village platform, the old man pointed out to me a row of jaw-bones suspended from a horizontal pole near his hut, and declared with pride that they were trophies from the wild pigs he had killed in his younger days. I suspected, however, that most of them had belonged to tame pigs slaughtered for the village feasts.

The women and girls now began to drop in from the gardens, each carrying on her head a load of firewood, sweet potatoes, or bottles filled with water. One of them climbed a neighbouring tree to pluck fresh green leaves with which to line the inside of her clay cooking-pot. The vessel was black as ink on the outside, but the sweet potatoes she boiled in it and set before me would have tempted a gourmet.

When the full moon rose that evening the natives strewed some palm leaves under a coconut tree so that I could spread out my blanket, and they gathered near me to chant their songs. As they droned their weird and rather melancholy choruses, the moonlight shone fitfully through the trees on their dark bodies and grass-thatched huts, and a faint sound of cascading water reached the village from the stream below. Far off, I could see the dark line of the forest that separated the grass-clad coastal plain from the moonlit sea, while behind me towered the black mass of the mountain, of which I had now reached one of the foothills.

Next morning, after a farewell breakfast, we followed a narrow trail through these foothills to Ufuya, a hamlet of only two houses. Thence a descent into a ravine, succeeded by a steep climb up the opposite hillside, brought us after two long hours to Ilubobo, a large village on the brow of a ridge skirted by a raging torrent. Beyond the next ridge foamed another stream in whose bed we stopped to bathe before climbing a slippery grass slope to Iyavali, where we were immediately surrounded by a welcoming crowd that had watched our approach. One man collected a few sticks for us, a woman brought fire, and while my two boys cooked our rice they offered us cool green coconuts to quench our thirst. We in turn showed our good manners by leaving most of the rice for our hosts, very few of whom had seen this cereal before, and we enjoyed watching the gingerly manner in which the women scooped up a few grains with their fingers and tested them on their tongues. The excitement spread to a neighbouring village, Atamawaiawaia, whence a dozen or more natives, drawn by the loud chatter and the laughter, descended to inspect the unheralded strangers.

Thus far, my boy Matakoi had been our guide, but since he was unacquainted with the trails beyond Atamawaiawaia, I engaged a local native to take us the rest of our journey at the price of one stick of tobacco. The track ran back into the ranges along the slope of a grass-covered ridge strewn with enormous rocks. We came face to face with one of these rocks when we rounded a sudden corner. Its flat underside projected at an angle of about eighty degrees for some fifteen feet above our heads.

What astonished us, however, was not its mass, which was no novelty in this volcanic land, but the painted figures on its surface. They were too faint for us to decipher, but a few yards farther on we encountered a similar rock on which the figures seemed freshly drawn with black charcoal and edged with white dots. Our guide told us that the rock was known as "The Crow," that one figure represented a large lizard, another a frigate bird, and a third a bird called *ganawa*, but when I asked him their purpose he said that they carried no meaning, being merely the work of children. I then questioned a native and his wife who, with their young son, had climbed up from a garden below to enjoy a midday siesta in the rock's shadow, but they too were unable or unwilling to shed any light on the matter. After my return to the coast, however, I learned that the rock was the scene of magical rites designed to ensure a bountiful harvest.

About a mile from the painted rocks, our ridge turned sharply south to merge into the flank of Mount Tukekela, while Mount Madawana, the peak that I was hoping to ascend, rose opposite us across a steep ravine. We descended to the bottom of this ravine, startling a band of natives who were bathing in its stream. Their village, Naila, lay above us on top of an extremely steep slope, which they had laboriously terraced with logs and planted with sweet potatoes that they were already harvesting.

It was almost sunset when we entered their village, registered by my pocket barometer as lying 2,000 feet above sea level. I counted twenty houses in it, so that the population must have numbered about a hundred. The old chief received me cordially, and his son, one of the only three men who had left this mountain home to work on a white man's coconut plantation, brought out the fly of a large tent which he had received as part payment for his labour, set it up in the middle of the village, and made me a bed of palm leaves under it. While the women were preparing supper, my two boys boiled the remainder of our rice; but when the chief's wife brought us a great bowl filled with sweet potatoes we presented our rice-pot to her husband, who had eyed it with polite curiosity. Immediately a crowd of women gathered around him, all eager to sample the strange food that they had heard about but never seen.

I joined the men on the village platform after supper, but the women and children held themselves aloof, apparently too timid to approach a white man. They peered at me from out-of-the-way corners, or through the doors of their huts, always at a safe distance. Recalling a children's rigmarole that I had learned in one of the coast villages, I stooped down, tapped the ground with my fingers and chanted the refrain. The children drew nearer and nearer, and one or two with broad smiles began to imitate me. Then with a piece of string I made some of their own cat's cradle figures and held them out for their inspection. This turned the scale. Five minutes later a laughing crowd surrounded me, thronging so close that I felt like the robber baron when the rats invaded his castle. The natives could hardly believe that I was a white man, and kept asking my two boys who I was, how I came to speak their language and where I had learned their game.

I told them why I had come. Theirs was the highest village on the mountain's flank, they said. Their territory extended right to its summit, and they had planned to hunt kangaroos on its upper slopes the very next day. If I wished, I could join them.

Nothing could have suited me better. My new friends sat around me far into the night, talking and singing. Their low murmuring lulled me to sleep, and I knew no more till morning.

Before sunrise, the chief's wife brought me some breakfast and we began to climb the mountain, while my two boys, tired from the last day's tramp, remained behind in the village to rest. A winding trail along a ridge covered with burnt grass guided us the first thousand feet, but then we entered a dense forest where four men armed with large machete knives had to walk in front and hew out a path. The first man cleared a space just wide enough to squeeze his body through, and the other three enlarged it so that we who followed after met with almost no obstruction. They worked so expeditiously that hardly once were we obliged to halt and wait.

Above the zone of forest stretched a zone of bamboo through which also we were forced to hew a path, and above the bamboo came some 1,500 feet of grassy slopes and rocky precipices. We rested before attacking this last zone, which was by far the most difficult. We clambered between and over sharp crags that lined a precipice on one side or on both, and through long slippery grass where my boots slid back almost faster than I could raise them. Finally, about noon, we gained the summit 7,050 feet above sea level, a flat area, measuring less than a quarter of an acre, covered with large angular rocks.

The view from the summit was disappointing. Clouds of mist concealed the neighbouring mountains, the plains below, and the encircling sea. They lifted once to give me a glimpse of Wagifa and the mountains of Fergusson Island twenty miles away, but within a few seconds they closed in again, shutting out everything but the ground at our feet and the blazing sky overhead.

In the treetops of the forest, my companions had killed two *cuscus*,[6] and in the grassland below the summit, a small kangaroo. They now roasted these animals on top of a flat rock, kindling a fire with two sticks. While four men busied themselves with the cooking, the rest of us sought shelter from the burning sun, some in the shadow of the rocks, others under leafy branches raised over rock crevices. Two butterflies played around us. One I captured with my hat. It was bright green in colour, and striped, belonging to a species that I had not collected or noticed on the coast.

The descent was far easier than the ascent. Our rearguard fired the grass below the summit in the hope of securing another kangaroo, but the hope was vain. A few men gathered rushes for baskets, others cut some of the thickest bamboo stems for water-bottles. We reached the village again at sunset, and the chief's wife immediately set a bowl of food in front of me. Afterwards, men and women gathered for a sing-song, but all were weary and soon retired to their huts.

During both the ascent and the descent of the mountain, the natives had overwhelmed me with unexpected kindnesses. They had carried only one water bottle, and that they reserved for me alone. Whenever we stopped to rest two or three men stood over me to shield me from the fiery sun, and when we were climbing the rocks and crags one hand at least was always extended to help me up. Meanwhile, in the village below the women had vied with each other in presenting dishes of cooked food to my two boys, and when we left them the following morning, they heaped more food on us for the return journey. I had nothing to give them in return except one stick of tobacco, but I invited the old chief and his son to visit me on the

---

[6]A four-footed marsupial.

coast, when I could repay their hospitality in full measure. They promised to visit me when the new moon appeared, but they never came. Later I found out the reason: they were afraid that they might be killed and eaten in the hostile villages that lay between them and the coast.

We followed our old route past the painted rocks as far as Atamawaiawaia and Iyavali, then, instead of turning southward, descended at once to the village of Wakonai at the foot of the ranges. The chief of this village presented us with a few sweet potatoes as a token of his goodwill, and invited me to return and help him to hunt the wild pigs and kangaroos that were ravaging his gardens. My camera excited a great deal of curiosity in the village, not the mirror with its reflected image but the black bellows. One woman asked me whether it was some kind of tobacco.

From Wakonai our trail took us eastward over a broad grassy plain covered with loose scoria, but after three miles we turned off to another trail that led south through a forest claimed by the Belebele natives as their hunting reserve. This path, though narrow, was clear of undergrowth, and we hurried along it so as to reach the Belebele village before dark. We forded a fair-sized stream, and passed through a small open glade where the natives had suspended some wild pigs from cross-poles raised on forked stakes three feet above the ground, built fires underneath, and roasted them. The forest soon yielded to grassland again, and, traversing this, we entered Belebele village at sunset. Its inhabitants came out to welcome us as travellers returning from a perilous journey, for to them the mountains at their back were an unknown region inhabited by fierce cannibal tribes who consigned every stranger to the cooking-pot. Actually it was only a few years since Belebele itself had indulged in similar cannibalism, but now the village was "civilized," and its mission-hut, a bare half-mile away, offered us a welcome rest after our long tramp.

[*My father worked diligently during the dozen months he was in Papua, recording as much anthropological information as he could. However, after he experienced several attacks of malaria, his condition had deteriorated to such an extent by December that he was forced to return to New Zealand to recuperate. During his convalescence, he commenced the preparation of a general report on the natives he had been studying and sent it for revision to Reverend Ballantyne, whose knowledge of the natives and Goodenough Island and the surrounding islands he regarded as unsurpassed. The latter's unexpected demise from blackwater fever in 1915 shifted the responsibility of completing the report back to my father, who by then was otherwise occupied in the Canadian Arctic. Nevertheless, their joint efforts were published some years later in two reports, totalling almost 500 pages (Jenness and Ballantyne, 1920, 1928). My father also published a lengthy report separately on the Bwaidogan native grammar (Jenness 1926), and three popular articles about the Goodenough islanders (Jenness, 1919, 1923a, 1924a).*

While he was on Goodenough Island, he took a great many photographs and collected large numbers of native artifacts and butterflies, all of which he shipped along with some other natural history specimens to Oxford University late in 1912 or early in 1913.[7] *The ship carrying his material to Britain (the S.S. Turakina) had a serious fire during a stop in Rio de Janeiro, resulting in the loss of some of*

---

[7]Oxford University stipulated two conditions when providing their financial support for my father's work in Papua–New Guinea: he must publish the results of his fieldwork, and he must provide photographs and collections of material culture to the Pitt Rivers Museum (Edwards, 1994, and 2001, footnote 12, pp. 103–104). He met both conditions most satisfactorily.

the natural history items, but fortunately most of his collections reached their intended destination. The native artifacts, numbering 511 items,[8] and 470 glass negatives and 495 original prints[9] from his Papuan investigations, are lodged in the Pitt Rivers Museum at Oxford. The 300 or so butterfly specimens he collected on Goodenough Island are lodged in the Oxford University Natural History Museum in Oxford.[10]] [S.E.J.]

---

[8]The Pitt Rivers Museum holds 707 objects my father donated to it at different times: 511 are from Papua-New Guinea, 8 are Canadian Eskimo items collected between 1913 and 1916, and the rest are mainly from the Dordogne of central France.

[9]I donated my father's photograph album containing 419 prints from Papua to the Pitt Rivers Museum in 1988. He had carefully inserted and labelled in white ink all of the pictures in the album many years ago. He had also documented their subject matter on the backs of the 495 original prints he forwarded to the museum in 1913. Elizabeth Edwards at that museum assembled an exhibition of some of my father's Papuan photographs, which was shown at the Pitt Rivers Museum from November 1991 to May 1992. A year later, the photographs were shown at the Metropolitan Museum of Art, New York, from November 1992 to May 1993. According to Ms. Edwards, the 16 × 20 in. exhibit prints were given as a gift to the National Art Gallery and Museum of Papua-New Guinea in 1997 and are now in their collections after being exhibited in that country in 1998 for about three months.

[10]Dr. George C. McGavin, curator of Entomology at the Oxford University Museum of Natural History, confirmed in an e-mail message to me, dated May 7, 2004, that the butterflies were indeed in the possession of the museum, but suspected that the book in which they were originally recorded may have been one of the books destroyed during the aerial bombing of World War II. He added "The material would almost certainly have been added into the arranged foreign butterfly collection shortly after its arrival and the only way to locate the material now would be to look through the collections for it." Elizabeth Edwards of the Pitt Rivers Museum informed me in 2004 that she had seen the butterflies years ago and they were "rather beautiful."

1913–1916: THE CANADIAN ARCTIC EXPEDITION[1]

3

Stuart E. Jenness

Four months after returning to New Zealand from Papua-New Guinea to recuperate from malaria, my father sailed for Canada to join a three-year expedition into the Canadian Arctic. The experiences he had and the knowledge he gained during those three years played such an important role in his later professional life that they should be expressed at some length in his manuscript. Instead, he merely inserted the following statement:

> The author joined the scientific staff of a Canadian government expedition which, on June 17, 1913, under the command of Vilhjalmur Stefansson, sailed north from British Columbia to explore for three years the Arctic coast of Canada and the archipelago beyond it. He has related the story of those three years in two books: *The People of the Twilight* and *Dawn in Arctic Alaska*.[2] The scientific members of the expedition returned to southern Canada in the autumn of 1916, at the height of the First World War, and the author spent the ensuing winter at the government museum in Ottawa, cataloguing and arranging his specimens and notes; but as soon as spring broke he enlisted in Canada's overseas forces and served with a howitzer battery until the armistice.

After he returned from the war, he spent a lot of time writing about Canada's Eskimos, soon establishing himself as the expert on Canada's most northerly people. In addition to writing the two books he mentioned, which were for the general public, he was the main contributor to the series of scientific reports on the expedition's results published by the Canadian government. In all he authored eight of the series of sixty-four reports published between 1919 and 1946. He was unable to complete his ninth report, entitled "On contributions to the archaeology of western Arctic America," largely because of the demands on his time after his promotion in 1926 to Chief of the Division of Anthropology. That report was intended to describe his

---

[1]From its inception the expedition was planned as a three-year project and was known as the "Canadian Arctic Expedition of 1913–16." The Southern Party of scientists returned south in 1916 as scheduled, but Stefansson kept his Northern Party exploring in the Arctic until 1918 (Stefanssson, 1922). Early in 1919, shortly after Stefansson's return south, the Canadian government officially changed the name of the expedition to the "Canadian Arctic Expedition 1913–18," probably on his insistence (Jenness, 1991, footnote 1 to Prologue, p. 729).

[2]My father's Arctic diary (Jenness, 1913–1916; S.E. Jenness, 1991), published twenty-two years after his death, contains a much more detailed account of his Arctic experiences.

archaeological investigations on and near Barter Island, northern Alaska.[3] During the 1920s and 1930s my father also published many articles in scholarly journals as well as popular articles about the Eskimos in magazines and newspapers. Finally, between 1962 and 1968, he published a series of detailed studies on Eskimo administration in Alaska, Canada, Labrador, and Greenland[4] in which he managed to set forth much of the advice he had offered to the largely deaf ears of his federal government while in their employ. A number of the thoughts he expressed in these reports appeared in a more elementary form in an article in 1944.[5]

His eight Arctic Expedition reports and *The People of the Twilight* have been out of print for many years, and most of his articles about his Arctic experiences among the Eskimos are difficult to find. It seemed desirable, therefore, to include an overview of his Arctic experiences with this publication of his recollections.

In February 1913, while my father was recuperating at his family home in New Zealand, he received a cable inviting him to join a three-year scientific expedition to the Canadian Arctic. I have sometimes been asked why the Canadian government had looked so far afield for someone for its Arctic expedition. There is a simple answer.

Shortly after his return to New Zealand in December 1912, my father wrote to his Oxford teacher, R.R. Marett, about the relatively successful completion of his field studies in Papua. In his letter he also mentioned that he was currently unemployed and wondered if Marett knew of any anthropological work in Canada or elsewhere. Marett promptly wrote another of his former students, Marius Barbeau, who was working at the Victoria Memorial Museum in Ottawa. That letter, dated January 26, 1913,[6] reached Barbeau fortuitously a few days before the explorer Vilhjalmur Stefansson arrived in Ottawa seeking two anthropologists as well as financial assistance from the Canadian Government for the Arctic expedition he planned. Stefansson spoke to Dr. R.W. Brock, the Director of the Geological Survey of Canada, from whom he had received financial support and encouragement for his previous Arctic

---

[3]His Barter Island collection was ultimately studied in the early 1960s by an American archaeologist (Hall, 1987). See also S. Jenness (1990) for a more recent overview of the Barter Island investigations. American army personnel obliterated the sites my father had excavated when they built a landing strip and a Distant Early Warning radar station on the island in the 1950s.

[4]My father once told me that he had requested official permission to visit Eskimo communities in the northern U.S.S.R. in the early 1960s so that he could include a report on their administrative accomplishments in his series, but was turned down by the Canadian government because of the political tension then existing between the U.S.S.R. and the western powers. He said that he suspected his request was refused because the Russians had demanded to be allowed to send one of their scientists to the Canadian Arctic if he visited their Arctic. The Canadians and Americans had just installed a series of defensive radar stations (the DEW-line) across the Arctic as protection from possible incoming Russian intercontinental ballistic missiles or aircraft, and they did not want a Russian secret police officer (KGB) posing as a scientist to get anywhere near those stations.

[5]Jenness, 1944b. One can well imagine the embarrassment of the editor of the Queen's Quarterly to find that my father's name at the top of the first page of this article was listed as "Desmond" Jenness. My father would have merely shrugged the matter off with a smile.

[6]In his letter, Marett asked Barbeau "Can you find a more or less permanent job for D. Jenness, who has just finished with New Guinea. He's a splendid little chap, so competent and keen." (Marett to Barbeau, letter dated January 26, 1913, Barbeau Collection, Box 218, Folder 37, Archives, CMC).

expedition in 1908. Dr. Brock had created the Division of Anthropology at the museum in 1910, and it remained under his direction. He took Stefansson to the chief of that division, Dr. Edward Sapir, who in turn called in Barbeau. Stefansson explained his need for two anthropologists for his expedition and asked Barbeau if he would be interested. Barbeau was not, but recalled Marett's letter and recommended his friend Jenness who, he added, was at home in New Zealand and looking for work. Barbeau also mentioned another of his friends, the French anthropologist, Henri Beuchat.[7] Dr. Sapir cabled my father, and Barbeau wrote Beuchat.[8]

My father had hoped to continue his studies in Papua, but saw the work among the little-known, central Canadian-Arctic Eskimos as an opportunity that might greatly enhance his experience as well as his reputation. He accepted Dr. Sapir's cabled offer to join the Stefansson-led expedition.

For the next two months he worked furiously (a) to complete his Papuan report for Oxford, (b) to learn what he could about Stefansson and the expedition, (c) to determine and obtain the clothing, camera, rifle, and other items he would need, and (d) to recover fully from the malaria that had troubled him for many months. He then sailed for Canada, not to return for six years (three more than he expected).

The First Year: Northern Alaska

My father, in spite of having the farthest to travel to join the Canadian Arctic Expedition,[9] reached Victoria, British Columbia, before the arrival of the other members. While waiting for them, he spent his time poring over the books Dr. Sapir had sent him from Ottawa, as well as everything he could find about the North American Eskimos in British Columbia's Parliamentary Library. After much activity and confusion, the expedition members sailed north on June 17 on the overloaded, 29-year-old, reconditioned whaling ship *Karluk*. It reached Nome, Alaska, on July 9. Stefansson and his second-in-command, Dr. Rudolph M. Anderson, arrived the same day by coastal steamer from Seattle, having remained behind to obtain additional supplies. Stefansson promptly assessed the large amount of expedition supplies and equipment at Nome and purchased an additional schooner, the *Mary Sachs*, to ensure that all the men and supplies would get to Herschel Island.[10] Once there, the expedition would divide into a Northern (Exploration) Party and a Southern (Scientific) Party and thereafter operate independently. Stefansson's Northern Party was to explore the land and sea north of

---

[7]Barbeau, 1957–58, p. 15, Carmen Roy Collection, Box 622, Folder 1, Archives, CMC.

[8]Henri Beuchat had established a reputation by 1913 through his several publications on American ethnology and his work with the eminent anthropologist Marcel Mauss at Sorbonne University, Paris. In 1906 he had published, in collaboration with Mauss, *Essai sur les variations saisonnières des sociétés eskimos* (*L'Année Sociologique*, vol. 9, pp. 39–130), and in 1912 his own 773-page book, "Manuel d'archéologie américaine, Amérique Préhistorique, civilisations disparues." On the strength of Beuchat's publications and Barbeau's recommendation, Stefansson asked him to join the Arctic expedition as its chief ethnologist.

[9]He sailed from Auckland, New Zealand, on the S.S. *Makura* on April 11, reaching Victoria on April 30.

[10]Before leaving Victoria, Stefansson had arranged to purchase a second vessel, the schooner *Alaska*, of which he would take possession at Nome. The addition of the *Mary Sachs* thus augmented his fleet to three ships by the time he and his expedition left Nome.

Figure 9 Diamond Jenness (on left) and William McKinlay on the *Karluk* at the start of the Canadian Arctic Expedition, Esquimalt, B.C., 1913.

Photo C-086412, LAC

the mainland coast and carry out oceanographic studies in the Beaufort Sea. Dr. Anderson's scientific Southern Party was to study the mainland Arctic coast of Canada from Amundsen Gulf to Bathurst Inlet.

As Nome has no sheltered harbour, Stefansson had the *Karluk*, *Alaska*, and *Mary Sachs* moved up the coast a few miles to the shelter of Port Clarence. There, the expedition's men and ships remained for two weeks, waiting for additional supplies, for the completion of repairs to the *Alaska*, and for Stefansson to complete his business activities in Nome. Stefansson finally joined the others and ordered the *Karluk* and the *Mary Sachs* to start north on July 27, with the *Alaska* to follow when its repairs were completed. The two ethnologists, my father and Henri Beuchat, were on the *Karluk*. That ship soon

Figure 10 The scientific members of the Canadian Arctic Expedition at Nome, Alaska, July 1913. L. to r. (back row): Mamen, McConnell, Chipman, Wilkins (black hat), Malloch, Beuchat, O'Neill, Jenness, Cox, McKinlay; (front row): Dr. Mackay (with cane), Bartlett, Stefansson, Dr. Anderson, Murray, Johansen.

GSC 27790

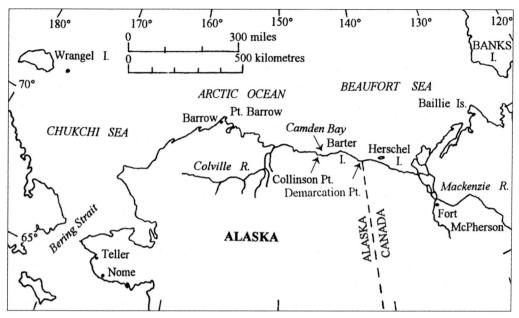

Map 4 Localities in Northern Alaska visited by Jenness in 1913–1914.

left the slower *Mary Sachs* far behind, and the two ships did not meet again. At Cape Smyth (now known as Barrow), the *Karluk* took on five Eskimos, sleds, *umiaks* (large skin boats), and dogs. It then rounded Point Barrow on August 9 without catching sight of the other two ships. Having trouble with ice, it edged its way cautiously eastward. The *Karluk's* captain was a competent Newfoundlander, Robert Bartlett, who, though well acquainted with eastern Arctic ice conditions, was unfamiliar with those of the western Arctic. To make matters worse, the summer of 1913 proved unusually severe for western Arctic navigation; not a single vessel reached Herschel Island and returned south that year. Three days east of Point Barrow, the *Karluk* became trapped in the ice,[11] and despite all efforts by its crew, failed to break free.

Two weeks later, Stefansson sent my father and Beuchat shoreward with six other men, sleds, dogs, and supplies. He hoped they would link up with the Southern Party (to which they rightfully belonged) and reach Herschel Island. They could then send news of their whereabouts south in compliance with contracts Stefansson had with an assortment of newspapers. This shore party soon ran into serious difficulties, however, and had to return to the *Karluk*.

---

[11]This entrapment resulted after Captain Bartlett, against the suggestions of Stefansson, followed a lead in the ice north from Cross Island to deeper water, the procedure he customarily employed in the Eastern Arctic to avoid entrapment. Bartlett's action resulted in considerable controversy and faultfinding over the years. The late historian, Dr. Gordon Smith, once told me that in the early 1960s he shared a government office with my father, and that they had many conversations about the expedition. During one such conversation my father revealed to him that on the afternoon of August 12, when Bartlett headed the *Karluk* seaward, Stefansson was not asleep, as has been suggested, but nervously pacing his cabin while Bartlett "put the ship into the ice." Stefansson's cabin was above my father's sleeping quarters. Stefansson could thus have ordered Bartlett to return to Cross Island, but was apparently unwilling or afraid to do so lest he draw the ire of the feisty sea captain.

Days passed. The *Karluk* remained immobilized in the ice. By September 19, Stefansson evidently concluded that it was caught in the ice for the rest of the winter, and announced that he would lead a small hunting party shoreward to obtain fresh caribou meat. Fortuitously, he decided to include my father in his hunting party.[12] On September 20, they left the ship and headed some twenty miles for shore, with two sleds and provisions for twelve days.

Two days later a severe storm broke up the ice between Stefansson's six-man hunting party and the *Karluk*. The ship was carried westward, never to be seen by them again. Thus stranded, they headed for the mouth of the Colville River, where Stefansson thought they might find an Eskimo family he had known in that area the previous year. He also hoped to acquire a supply of fish for his dogs to enable them to continue west to the Eskimo settlement at Cape Smyth. Sure enough, on October 5 they came upon the tent of his Eskimo friend, Aksiatak,[13] his wife, and three small children. Here Stefansson and his companions were all made welcome, remained for three days, and obtained from their host the supply of frozen fish they needed to reach Cape Smyth. That journey took them seven days, during which most of them suffered from frostbite and other ailments.[14] At Cape Smyth they obtained accommodation with Charles Brower, the local storekeeper,[15] from whom they learned that the *Karluk* had been sighted only once. It apparently was moving northwestward, but its present whereabouts was unknown.[16] They also learned that the Southern Party and the *Alaska* and *Mary Sachs* were three hundred miles to the east, ice-bound but safe at Camden Bay.

For the next fifteen days, Stefansson's party rested and recuperated from their injuries and afflictions, wrote letters and reports, had suitable fur garments sewn to replace the inadequate clothing they had brought from the ship, and arranged for supplies for their journey east to Camden Bay and the Southern Party. During this time, my father attended an Eskimo dance, was shown a number of string or cat's cradle figures—he had encountered a similar game played by the native people in Papua—and visited an Eskimo school.

Late in October, Stefansson decided that my father and an Eskimo interpreter should spend the winter with Aksiatak's family near the mouth of the Colville River, so that my father could acquire a basic knowledge of the local customs and language. Accordingly, my father,

---

[12]Beuchat was the older and more knowledgeable of the two ethnologists and the logical first choice for Stefansson to include in his hunting party, but his health had been somewhat less than perfect during the previous month. Additionally, this was a hunting party, and my father was the more competent of the two with a rifle.

[13]This is how my father spelled this man's name in the diary he kept in the Arctic (S.E. Jenness, 1991, pp. 13, 636), although years later he spelled it "Arksiatark" in his book, *Dawn in Arctic Alaska* (Jenness, 1957, p. 11).

[14]Between the time he left the *Karluk* and his arrival at Cape Smyth three weeks later, my father had several incapacitating attacks of ague, relapses from the malaria he had contracted in Papua the previous year, and was forced to ride on one of the sleds, well bundled in furs, until the attacks passed.

[15]Stefansson slept in the Brower house, while my father and his two white companions, George Wilkins, who some years later acquired world fame as the explorer Sir Hubert Wilkins (S.E. Jenness, 2004), and Burt McConnell, Stefansson's secretary, slept in Brower's store. The two young Eskimo guide/hunters brought from the *Karluk* slept somewhere in the village.

[16]For further information on the subsequent fate of the *Karluk* and the people who were on it, see Bartlett and Hale (1916), McKinlay (1975), and Niven (2000).

Wilkins, their young Eskimo hunter from the *Karluk*, Jimmy Asetsaq, and a newly hired young Eskimo from Point Hope, Anutisiak,[17] sledded east. They camped each night with native families who had gathered in the scattered, unoccupied cabins along the coast which they had passed during their westward journey. These natives were preparing to trap white foxes, then a major source of income for them.

The trip to Aksiatak's fishing lake took twelve days, during which both my father and Wilkins suffered severe facial frostbite. Stefansson had assured my father that he would catch up with them by the time they reached the fishing lake. He also instructed my father and Wilkins to lay in a supply of frozen fish for my father's dogs and also for Stefansson's dogs when he and his secretary McConnell arrived en route to join the Southern Party at Camden Bay. But Stefansson failed to put in an appearance until November 21. During the intervening three weeks, my father's group caught far less fish in their nets than they had anticipated, saw no caribou whatsoever, and killed only one fox and a few ptarmigan. By the time Stefansson and McConnell arrived, my father and his three companions were almost out of food, having used up all of their flour, sugar, and salt, with only a little remaining rice, oatmeal, and beans to feed themselves and their dogs.

Stefansson remained for three days. During that time, he acquired a supply of frozen fish from Aksiatak with which to feed his dogs on his journey eastward, and discussed his plans for my father's winter activities. Then he, McConnell, Wilkins, and Anutisiak headed east to rendezvous with the Southern Party.[18] My father remained behind with two young native assistants and what Stefansson considered sufficient provisions for the three of them for the winter (300 lb. of rice, sugar, and oatmeal, most of which was cached twenty miles away). Stefansson promised to send more provisions from Camden Bay so that my father could remain with these Eskimos until June, but those supplies never arrived. One of my father's two assistants was Jimmy Asetsaq, who had accompanied Stefansson's hunting party from the *Karluk*. The other was a newcomer, Alfred (Brick), the teen-aged, half-native son of Brower's cook, Fred Hopson. Stefansson had hired him to serve as my father's interpreter while he wintered with the two local Eskimo families.[19]

After the departure of Stefansson, my father and his two young assistants took down the tent they had been sleeping in, cached it on a rack with their supplies, and moved into Aksiatak's house, depositing their sleeping bags and skins in the passageway to the house. The crowding this created soon necessitated the construction of an addition to the house, with which my father assisted. Meals were prepared by the two Eskimo women and usually consisted of frozen fish, rice, tea, and a baked pancake-like food locally called *mukpaurat*. Sundays were days of rest, sometime including prayers, reflecting the influence of the Protestant missionary at Cape Smyth.

Taking stock of his situation, my father, not yet twenty-eight years old, found himself confronted with surviving the cold and unfamiliar Arctic winter with two Eskimo families and

---

[17]In the 1920s and later, Anutisiak became well known in the central Canadian Arctic as the trader, Ikey Bolt.

[18]Unbeknownst to my father at the time, he would not see Stefansson again for the duration of the expedition, and indeed, not until 1920.

[19]Aksiatak's family had been joined by Aluk and his wife (Aksiatak's sister), and their two young children.

two inexperienced youths—only one of whom knew a little English. They were more than ninety miles east of Cape Smyth, the nearest settlement. To make matters worse, he was in Alaska, which was part of the United States of America, not even the right country in which to carry out the work he had been assigned. Nonetheless, with Brick's assistance, my father diligently acquired an elementary understanding of the local language, deliberately jotting down each new word and its meaning as the start of a preliminary Eskimo dictionary he later published.[20] Later, when he had a better grasp of the vocabulary, he wrote down folk tales, songs, and descriptions of string-figure games he was taught by Aksiatak's brother-in-law, Aluk, and prepared descriptions and drawings of their various handmade tools. Having left his camera on the *Karluk* and unable to obtain a replacement that first winter, my father sketched in his diary the various native objects that interested him. Of course, a camera would have been of little use to him during the dark, sunless winter months.

Fish and game were scarce that winter, forcing my father to draw heavily upon his limited supply of provisions, not only for his own three men and dogs, but also to augment the meagre provisions of his Eskimo hosts. While the men (including Jimmy) were off hunting, fishing in nearby Teshekpuk Lake, or trapping every day, my father spent his time with the two Eskimo wives and their children. It was a splendid opportunity for him to commence his Arctic ethnographic studies with these people, who had some contact with and influence by the white man. With Brick acting as his interpreter my father would ask the two women how and why they prepared the food in certain ways, about the utensils they used, and how they clothed their families. At other times he sat and played games with the children, or wrote descriptions of the activities he had observed during the day. Each day he observed and made extensive notes on the daily activities and relationships of the two wives, of their children, and of the treatment of the children by their parents. He was especially distressed to observe the deep dislike shown her second oldest child by Mrs. Aksiatak. The latter had wanted a son when her daughter was born and thereafter neglected her constantly. As a result, the 12-year old Kukpuk went about with sad eyes and a face that lacked the normal joyfulness of other Eskimo children, burdened unduly as she was with many of the family's chores.

Towards the end of January, conditions in the little Eskimo camp had deteriorated to the point where my father decided he must head west to Cape Smyth or starve. His food supply was almost exhausted, his dogs were starving, Jimmy had quit hunting for him to trap white foxes full time for himself, and Brick's interpreting duties had become less than satisfactory. My father, therefore, set off with Brick on February 3, reaching Cape Smyth seven days later, after a particularly uncomfortable and difficult journey. Again my father lodged with store-keeper Charles Brower while he awaited the arrival of someone from the Southern Party's base camp at Camden Bay. Fortunately he had to wait only nine days, for Stefansson's secretary, Burt McConnell, arrived on February 19. During the period before McConnell's arrival, and for some days thereafter, my father worked on his notes and Eskimo vocabulary and examined a collection of Eskimo artifacts Stefansson had purchased earlier from Brower, sketching many of them.[21] He also wrote correspondence, including letters to the mothers of

---

[20]Stefansson left on the *Karluk* an unfinished dictionary of northern Alaskan vocabulary he had been compiling, which was lost when the *Karluk* sank.

[21]Some of the artifacts from this collection are housed at the Canadian Museum of Civilization.

two of the scientists on the *Karluk*, McKinlay and Beuchat, to give them what little news he had of their sons.

At the end of February, my father, McConnell, and the latter's Eskimo companion, Fred Adluat, headed east with two well-laden sleds and well-rested dogs. The three-hundred-mile journey proved both challenging and tiring, and my father was greatly relieved to finally reach Collinson Point in Camden Bay on March 20. There they joined the men of the Southern Party, who were living in a log house that had been abandoned by a trader the previous year.

Just a few days earlier, in the crowded expedition headquarters, there had been an unpleasant confrontation between the scientists and Stefansson, the repercussions of which were felt for decades.[22] However, all was calm now, because Stefansson had departed on March 16 on the first of several bold exploration trips with sled and dogs over the frozen Beaufort Sea. In the months that followed, he demonstrated his remarkable ability to survive, located the North American continental margin, discovered a few inconse-

Figure 11 Diamond Jenness in winter attire at Collinson Point, northern Alaska, April 1914.
Photo by G.H. Wilkins, CMC 50806

quential uninhabited islands, and determined that no unknown continent lay north of Alaska. He even succeeded in interfering with the operations of the Southern Party without seeing any member of it again for years.

Meanwhile, several of the scientists had gone east from Collinson Point to undertake some early field work before the summer navigation season arrived. These scientists were to rejoin the men on the two expedition schooners at Herschel Island early in August.

My father took advantage of the next month at Collinson Point to work quietly over his winter's notes, struggling to make order out of his interpretation of Eskimo grammar, and transcribing folk tales told him by Jennie, the Alaskan native wife of Charles Thomsen, one of the expedition's sailors. For a short period, my father was the only scientist at Collinson Point, and had to maintain law and order among the crew of the two nearby ice-bound schooners who fretted about the lateness of the spring.

Late in April, a small party of men returned from Stefansson's ice trip, one of whom bore written instructions from Stefansson for my father to move east to Barter Island at the end of May to excavate a number of Eskimo ruins on the east and west ends of that island. After

[22]Jenness, S.E., 1996.

several months of ethnological studies of Eskimo linguistics, folklore, social anthropology, and games, he was now to try his hand at archaeology, another branch of anthropology. It was a subject in which he had little experience other than the brief study he had undertaken with Stefansson's collection of specimens at Cape Smyth, and his summer's work in the Dordogne cave region in southwestern France in 1910.

My father moved to the west end of Barter Island at the end of May. From then until July 24, despite the frozen condition of the ground, occasional snow and freezing temperatures, he worked diligently at two sites on that island and a third site on nearby Arey Island, excavating and making detailed notes on 103 long-abandoned Eskimo houses and other structures. During most of that time he was ably assisted by the Eskimo helpers he had hired, Aiyakuk and his stepson Ipanna, but was without an interpreter.

Excavation proceeded slowly because of the permanently frozen ground. To chip the frozen soil with pick axes would have destroyed many artifacts and rendered the results less than desirable. Accordingly, my father, Aiyakuk and Ipanna would strip off the surface layer of earth with shovels (over an area of less than 240 square feet—the maximum size of the dwellings), let the newly exposed surface thaw for two or three days, then carefully peel that layer away with special scrapers made from flat files. Two or more such layers had to be peeled away before the desired layer of artifacts on the original floor of each dwelling was reached. It was slow and tedious work, but by carrying out this procedure of stripping and scraping on several dwellings at a time, my father was able to excavate virtually every structure in the three sites over a period of some six weeks.

Figure 12 Eskimo ruin No. 12 (Thule culture, circa A.D.1450), west sandspit on Barter Island, northern Alaska, July 1914. Jenness' Eskimo helper, Oyeraq, on right.

Photo by D. Jenness, CMC 37154

My father made good use, in his spare moments, of a government-issued camera he had brought to Barter Island from Collinson Point, taking fourteen photographs of the Barter Island ruins at various stages of his excavation work on them. He finally completed his excavations on July 21, spent three days packing his specimens and equipment, and then sailed west in Aiyakuk's whaleboat, arriving at Collinson Point only a few hours before the *Alaska* and the *Mary Sachs* started east for Herschel Island. Wearily, he placed his boxes of specimens on the *Mary Sachs* and rested, wondering what adventures lay ahead.

His tireless and meticulous efforts daily without let-up yielded a remarkable collection of 3,300 artifacts from the three sites on and near Barter Island, which he later shipped to the Victoria Memorial Museum in Ottawa. Subsequent events prevented him from ever studying his collection, and it was not until the 1960s that their examination by an American archaeologist, Edwin Hall Jr., established that the three sites had been occupied by the whale-hunting, Thule-culture people some five hundred years earlier.[23] Tragically, hasty construction by American military personnel of a Distant Early Warning (DEW-line) station on Barter Island in the mid-1950s destroyed all three archaeological sites. As a result, my father's early archaeological efforts have left us with the only significant collection from that part of northern Alaska.

He once jokingly dismissed his Barter Island work as merely that of a "scrounger in the earth" because of his lack of practical archaeological training at the time.[24] Nevertheless, the Barter Island work helped lay the foundation of his knowledge that enabled him to make two outstanding archaeological advances barely a decade later: (1) the recognition of an early Eskimo culture in eastern Canada, to which he gave the name "Dorset culture;"[25] and (2) the recognition of a pre-Thule culture in northwestern Alaska, to which he gave the name "Old Bering Sea culture."[26] Years later, he was hailed as the "father of Eskimo archaeology" for these two discoveries.[27]

The Second and Third Years: Northern Canada

The two expedition schooners, *Alaska* and *Mary Sachs*, left Camden Bay for Herschel Island on July 25, working their way slowly through the broken ice to reach their destination on August 6. My father travelled on the *Mary Sachs*. At Herschel Island, he found Wilkins with the 10-ton schooner, *North Star*, which Stefansson had purchased in the spring from a trader near the Alaska-Canada International Boundary. Wilkins was waiting for a last-minute consultation with Dr. Anderson before leaving with the *North Star* for the west coast of Banks Island to meet or search for Stefansson, as per the latter's instructions in April. Also at Herschel Island were Chipman, Cox, and O'Neill, who had been mapping the delta of the Mackenzie River since the spring. There was no word of Stefansson and his two companions, although they were long overdue from their exploratory ice trip over the Beaufort Sea.

My father and the other members of the Southern Party were eager to proceed east immediately to Coronation Gulf to commence the work they had come north to undertake,

---

[23]Edwin S. Hall, Jr. (1971, 1987).

[24]D. Jenness to Edwin S. Hall, Jr., letter dated April 9, 1967 (quoted in Hall, 1987, p. 18).

[25]Jenness (1925).

[26]Jenness (1928b).

[27]Collins (1967).

but the arrival of mail from Ottawa via Fort McPherson delayed their plans. It also caused quite a bit of confusion, as conflicting instructions had been sent north by two government departments, and one of the two expedition leaders, Stefansson, was missing. A letter from the Department of the Naval Service instructed Dr. Anderson to send a search ship to Banks Island to look for Stefansson. These instructions counteracted those given him in the spring by Stefansson to send two ships to Banks Island—one for Stefansson's exploration work, the other to rescue the survivors of the *Karluk* in case they had reached Banks Island. Acting on Stefansson's instructions, Wilkins was about to start for Banks Island with the *North Star*, expecting the *Mary Sachs* to follow.

Shortly before Wilkins could depart, however, the trading ship *Herman* arrived at Herschel Island from the west coast with the news that the *Karluk* had sunk in January and its survivors were on Wrangel Island off the Siberian coast. This news eliminated the need for a ship going to Banks Island to rescue the *Karluk* survivors. After consultation with his fellow scientists, Dr. Anderson decided that the ship sent to search for Stefansson should carry supplies sufficient for two years in case there was another bad summer for navigation like 1913. The *North Star* was too small for that purpose, so he asked Wilkins to take charge of the *Mary Sachs*. Such a change necessitated unloading the one vessel and reloading the other, a task now made difficult by the unexpected drunkenness of most of the expedition's crewmembers, thanks to the whisky they had purchased from someone on the *Herman*. The *Mary Sachs* and Wilkins headed for Banks Island on August 11, leaving the *North Star* for the use of the Southern Party.

While at Herschel Island, my father packed his Barter Island artifacts for shipping to Ottawa, took physical measurements of some Mackenzie River Eskimos who happened to be at Herschel Island, helped move the supplies from the *North Star* to the *Mary Sachs*, and then assisted in the reloading of the *North Star*. He sailed east on the *North Star* on August 18 under the command of the assistant geographer, John Cox. The *Alaska* had gone east two days earlier. Although my father had little or no experience in sailing, he lent a helping hand during the voyage, mostly as helmsman. After an uneventful trip, the schooner reached the small harbour chosen by Dr. Anderson as the Southern Party's home on August 27. Dr. Anderson and the rest of the Southern Party had arrived on the *Alaska* three days earlier.

Once the two vessels were unloaded, Dr. Anderson returned to Herschel Island with the *Alaska* to collect much-needed coal and other expedition supplies that he hoped would have arrived there on the Hudson's Bay Company supply vessel from Vancouver. He also wanted to send news to the government and others from Herschel Island about the new location of the Southern Party.[28] Once the needed supplies were on board, the *Alaska* commenced its return trip, but ran aground at the Baillie Islands and was forced to winter there. Dr. Anderson and most of its crew sledded east to the base camp after freeze-up, arriving Christmas Day.

During their absence, the men at the camp constructed a cabin, laid in a supply of driftwood for fuel, and settled in for the winter. My father, being the only scientific member who could conduct some of his work year-round, had been studying the small number of natives that

---

[28] The Royal North-West Mounted Police personnel stationed on Herschel Island sent a patrol south to Fort McPherson during the winter with mail, and from there it was taken by other patrols to Fort Yukon and Alaska or south by way of the Mackenzie River to Edmonton.

soon appeared around their camp. He also initiated trading with them. Although their language differed somewhat from the Eskimo language he had been learning in Alaska, he was soon able to communicate with them with modest success. He thus became the camp's spokesman.

Within a few weeks, he started undertaking small trips afield in search of other natives. Several such forays took him across the then-frozen Dolphin and Union Strait forty-five miles to Simpson Bay on Victoria Island. There, he expected to find people Stefansson had two years previously called "Blond Eskimos." Stefansson had suggested that the physical features of some individuals he had seen in the region in 1911 indicated their possible ancestry as a Nordic people from Greenland who were known to have disappeared in the fifteenth or sixteenth centuries. The supposed Nordic features—blue eyes and reddish hair—were not apparent to my father during his visits in 1914 and over the course of the next two years, when he met far more Eskimos than Stefansson had seen. However, his trips allowed him to meet a fine couple, Ikpukhuak and his shaman wife Higilak. Both were in their forties, Higilak being a few years older than her mate, and both had been married previously. Higilak had two children from her first marriage before being widowed, Ikpukhuak had none of his own. My father soon established a strong and lasting bond with them and subsequently acquired a considerable amount of information from them about their people.

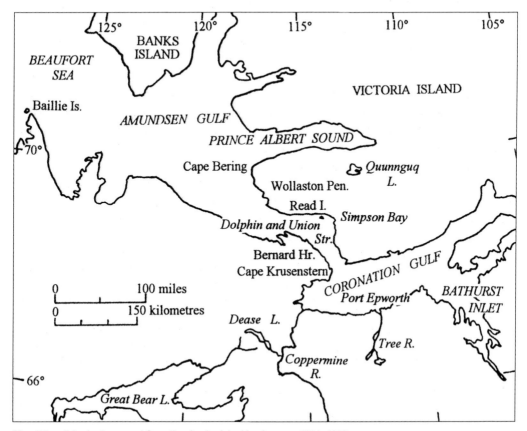

Map 5 Localities in the central Canadian Arctic visited by Jenness, 1914–1916.

Figure 13 Jenness' "adopted parents," Ikpukhuak and Higilak, with her son, Avrunna, Bernard Harbour, July 1916. Photo by R.M. Anderson, CMC 39415

During the winter months, when travel was discouraged by the cold and sunless days, my father spent part of his time conversing and trading with the Eskimos who visited the Southern Party's base camp at Bernard Harbour.[29] In February, he accompanied Dr. Anderson to the Coppermine River and ascended it for many miles,[30] seeking the Eskimos who were thought to live in that region. He found none up the river, but ultimately came upon a large group camped on the ice in Coronation Gulf, several miles north of the river mouth. They were hunting seals by their customary technique of locating the seals' breathing holes in the ice. Here with the assistance of Palaiyak, his young Mackenzie Delta interpreter, my father learned about their seal-hunting techniques and their other winter activities. Here, too, he first encountered the young shaman, Uloksak, with whom he had several subsequent experiences. After a brief stay, during which he again saw no convincing evidence of a Nordic ancestral link, my father returned to Bernard Harbour. Uloksak's people followed him there, curious to visit the strangers in their region and eager to trade with them. Shortly after their arrival, Uloksak held a séance to determine the cause of an Eskimo man's recent death. The natives apparently considered my father a prime suspect, but he cleverly worked with the shaman to remove any suspicion from himself. [31]

Having failed to find any real evidence of Stefansson's "Blond Eskimos" between Bernard Harbour, Simpson Bay, and the western part of Coronation Gulf, my father decided to go north across the Wollaston Peninsula in southwestern Victoria Island to Prince Albert Sound,

---

[29]This was the name given the locality where the camp was established. Originally, the name was assigned to the small sheltered bay in which the schooner *North Star* was icebound close to the base camp in 1914, to honour the early trader, Captain Joseph Bernard, who had informed Dr. Anderson of its existence. This bay lay along an otherwise shelter-less strip of coast northwest of Coronation Gulf. Dr. Anderson first used the name in a report to the Geological Survey of Canada, which was published in 1915, but when the expedition's final geographical report was published in 1924, the name had been assigned to the larger bay outside the entrance to the small bay. (For a more detailed discussion of the origin of the name Bernard Harbour, see Jenness, 1991, footnote 1 for Chapter 18, p. 772.)

[30]A female wolf invaded their temporary camp early one morning and pestered the tethered dogs. My father attempted to drive it away and was bitten on the wrist by the wolf. Details of this incident are given in Chapter 22 and in S.E. Jenness (1985, 1989, and 1991).

[31]A fuller account of this séance is presented in Chapter 4.

Figure 14 Jenness' "adopted sister," Jennie Kanneyuq (on left), and her friend, Kila, Bernard Harbour, July 1916. Photo by R.M. Anderson, CMC 38997

where Stefansson claimed he had actually seen blue-eyed and fair-haired Eskimos in 1911. Such a trip entailed spending an entire summer on Victoria Island, however, since the Eskimos could only safely cross Dolphin and Union Strait from Victoria Island to the mainland on the ice between November and May. His friends, Ikpukhuak and Higilak, agreed to "adopt" him for the summer and to bring him safely back to Bernard Harbour when the strait was again frozen over. My father's possession of a rifle and his skilled marksmanship[32] probably helped ensure his Eskimo companions would make every effort to keep him healthy during the seven months he was away from the base camp. There were also additional incentives to ensure his safe return, for Ikpukhuak had been promised several coveted expedition items as a reward when he brought my father back.

As an "adopted" son, my father slept on one edge of Ikpukhuak's sleeping-platform and stored his supplies inside the snow wall encircling Ikpukhuak's tent. He also acquired a delightful, eleven-year-old "sister," Jennie, as well as a older "brother," Avrunna, and "sister-in-law," Milukattuk. Being a part of Ikpukhuak's family, my father was made welcome by other families in Ikpukhuak's band as well. Together they headed across Dolphin and Union Strait

---

[32]My father possessed one of the two rifles among the group of Eskimos that accompanied him to Victoria Island. He had won prizes in marksmanship while at Oxford University.

on April 13, 1915, to join a seal-hunting group, accumulating seal oil and skins for a month and occasionally making brief forays to Victoria Island in search of caribou. Towards mid-May, they established a cache on the shore of Victoria Island, opposite Read Island, and commenced their trek inland with their sleds. Periodically they would halt for a day or two to fish through the ice of a lake they knew contained fish in order to augment their food supplies for them-selves and their dogs. While some jigged for fish, others in the group would scour the neigh-bourhood for caribou. When warmer weather melted the ice around the shores of the lakes, they moved farther inland, slowly northward in the direction of Prince Albert Sound, and focused their attention more on the hunting of caribou and ptarmigan. Game was scarce, however, forcing the nomadic group to split up and go separate ways. Late in May, Ikpukhuak informed my father that they would not be able to go as far as Prince Albert Sound, but would wait at a large lake (now called Lake Quunnguq, but mistakenly identified as Lake Tahiryuaq by my father at the time) midway across the Wollaston Peninsula, where they customarily met Eskimos from the sound. My father was greatly disappointed by this unexpected change in their itinerary, but quite unable to change the decision.

Early in June, seven Eskimos did appear from the north and joined Ikpukhuak's group for several days of feasting and dancing. During that time, my father took special note of their physical features, clothing, and activities, but even though they were the Prince Albert Sound people he had come to meet he saw little in their features to confirm Stefansson's claim that they were "Blond Eskimos."

After the two groups parted, my father and his "adopted" Eskimo family turned back south to a particular lake where they camped, fished, and hunted while waiting for the snow to disappear from the land. When it was gone at last, they cached their sleds and heavy equip-ment, strapped on back packs and, with their dogs, wandered like nomads from fishing lake to fishing lake in the region until the end of July. In mid-July, however, my father developed severe diarrhoea and a constant pain in the side, accompanied by an unquenchable thirst. Raw fish seemed to aggravate his symptoms, but the prevalence of fog at this time of year kept the vegetation constantly damp, rendering fire-making and cooking impossible most of the time. As the pains continued and his strength diminished, he treated himself with a laxative and expedition-supplied pills of iron and arsenic from a small medical kit he had with him, with but little improvement. Higilak held a séance on July 16 to determine the cause of his trouble, but that was of no help. On July 21, growing ever more worried, he took some lead and opium from his little medical pack, which provided a little relief.

"For a week," he wrote in a letter to V. Stefansson twenty-one years later, "I ate nothing but some 'Hudson Bay' dog-pemmican I had cached with my sled; I mixed it into a paste with a little cold water and swallowed a couple of spoonfuls every three or four hours. This I seemed able to digest without discomfort." [33]

In spite of his desperate medical condition, my father somehow managed to write essays he hoped someday would be published in one or other magazine. On July 25, for example, in spite of the cold, wet, and entirely inappropriate surroundings, he wrote, "I began to make

---

[33]Jenness to V. Stefansson, letter dated May 20, 1936, Jenness Correspondence, Box 658, Folder 41, Archives, CMC.

notes on the N. Alaskan Eskimos today and started the essay at the back of this diary, for want of paper." This essay pondered over the effect of civilization on the Northern Alaskan Eskimos and the possible effect it would soon have on the natives in the central Canadian Arctic. It was published three years later in the prestigious journal, *Geographical Review*, almost word for word as he originally wrote it on Victoria Island.[34]

Three days later, on July 28, amidst snow showers and a cold north wind, he added in his diary, "My essay on the Alaskan Eskimos has come to a standstill till I can think it over more. Meanwhile, I am jotting down some of my experiences in Papua; they should make interesting magazine articles with photos to accompany them, but I don't know whether I shall ever have time to write them up or if it would be fair to Oxford [University] to publish them if I do."[35]

My father and his companions finally headed south to the coast on July 31, where he obtained some of the rice, sugar, and man-pemmican he had cached earlier. Heather was plentiful at the coast, the fog disappeared, and they were able to cook their food once more. My father even managed to shoot a caribou.

"The diarrhoea gradually diminished and I regained my strength, though the pain in the side irritated me at intervals for a year or more and my digestion has been troublesome ever since."[36]

Thus partly recovered, he was able to carry on. This was fortunate, for as matters stood, he had no other choice. Dolphin and Union Strait was open water, and there was no way he could get back to Bernard Harbour until it froze over again, sometime in November.[37]

For the next two months, my father accompanied Ikpukhuak and his much-reduced party—other members having gone their separate ways—as they moved slowly west, a few miles inland from the southwest coast of Victoria Island, in search of the scarce caribou. By the end of August, they had almost reached Cape Bering at the west end of the Wollaston Peninsula, and it was time to turn back. Their journey back to their shore cache took them two weeks. There they remained until mid-October, supplementing their dwindling supply of caribou meat with occasional fresh seal meat. And there they were rejoined by the other small groups of relatives and friends from their original number, whom they had not seen for two or more months.

There was now sufficient snow to build snow-houses, commonly called igloos, so they cached most of their equipment and made a quick trip north to retrieve their sleds and other

---

[34]S.E. Jenness, 1991, p. 487 and pp. 806–807, notes 22 and 23; Jenness, 1918.

[35]These entries may have provided the basis for one or more of the following articles he subsequently published: "Along old cannibal trails" (1919), "The play hour in New Guinea" (1923a), and "The singing people of the South Seas" (1924). It is interesting, too, to find him so concerned about his alma mater in spite of his wretched circumstances.

[36]Jenness to V. Stefansson, letter dated May 20, 1936, *op. cit.*

[37]To my knowledge, his stomach trouble was never medically diagnosed, but I know that he had a sensitive stomach for the rest of his life. Mother occasionally explained to me that she did not dare cook anything but dreadfully bland meals lest his stomach act up. Told of his symptoms and his self-treatment, one medical doctor recently suggested to me that he might have contacted parasitic worms from the eating of raw fish. Years earlier, Stefansson had wondered if my father's symptoms might have been related to the malaria he had contacted in Papua-New Guinea (Stefansson to Jenness, letter dated May 22, 1936, Jenness Correspondence, Box 658, Folder 41, Archives, CMC).

items that they had cached inland during the summer. Then they sledded slowly back to the coast, where they remained until Ikpukhuak deemed the sea ice safe for travel, at which time they crossed Dolphin and Union Strait and reached Bernard Harbour on November 8.

In the seven months he was with Ikpukhuak and his family, my father gained a unique knowledge of the language and way of life of the Copper Eskimos. He also acquired a great admiration for their basic intelligence and wisdom, their routinely cheerful nature, and their ability to survive in such a harsh environment. From these experiences with his "adopted" parents and with other Eskimos in the Coronation Gulf region, he soon emerged as Canada's leading authority on the Copper Eskimos.

Originally, the study of the Canadian Eskimos by the Canadian Arctic Expedition had been assigned to the two ethnologists, Henri Beuchat of France as chief ethnologist and my father as his assistant. Beuchat was to focus on the language and cultural and social activities

Figure 15 Diamond Jenness at Bernard Harbour, July 1916.
Photo by G.H. Wilkins, CMC 51236

of the people, my father on their physical features and archaeology. Beuchat remained on the *Karluk* when Stefansson and my father left to hunt caribou, and perished trying to reach land after the *Karluk* sank. My father was, therefore, burdened with the entire anthropological study.

For two months after returning to Bernard Harbour, my father focused his efforts to gathering Eskimo folklore and recording the Eskimo songs on his manual phonograph. These songs were later transcribed and published in one of his government reports.[38]

By the winter of 1916, my father had concluded that the Eskimos in the Coronation Gulf region and southern Victoria Island were all part of one group, even though well separated, rather than many small distinct Eskimo groups as Stefansson had asserted following his much briefer visits there in 1910 and 1911.

By that time, too, my father had met and studied all but one of the groups that Stefansson had written about—a relatively unknown group from Bathurst Inlet. Accordingly, in mid-February he decided to visit them. He was accompanied by the Reverend Herbert Girling (a Church of England missionary from England who had recently arrived in the north) and an interpreter, the teen-aged Patsy Klengenberg (whose father was a trapper and trader then living at the mouth of Darnley Bay, well to the west). Avrunna, the married son of Higilak, also joined them as hunter and guide.

After encountering a number of Coppermine River Eskimos near Cape Krusenstern, my father's little sled party headed across Coronation Gulf for the mouth of the Tree River. Some miles north of Cape Barrow, at the mouth of Bathurst Inlet, they came upon a small cluster of Eskimo snowhouses, which were occupied by seal hunters from Bathurst Inlet. Some of these people had never seen a white man before. My father quizzed and observed them for the next few days, gathering valuable comparative information to add to what he already knew about the Copper Eskimos. He and his companions then were forced to return to Bernard Harbour because their food was running short.

Thereafter, he remained largely at the base camp, consolidating his notes and collections.[39] However, he made a few brief trips, one to the west to examine an archaeological site (which proved unexciting), one north to Victoria Island to search for the naturalist Johansen (who had decided to do a little exploring on his own and was overdue), and one east of Bernard Harbour to investigate a curious stone structure near Cape Krusenstern. At the base camp, he counselled two members of the Royal North-West Mounted Police who had arrested

---

[38]Jenness and Roberts (1925). In 1989, I took four audiotapes kindly made for me by a member of the audiovisual unit at the Canadian Museum of Civilization from my father's cylindrical recordings, together with a copy of Father's government report on Eskimo songs, to Coppermine (since 1995 renamed Kugluktuk) as a gift for a local government administrator, Rosemary Meyok. Rosemary is a great-granddaughter of my father's "adopted" mother, Higilak. Within a day, taped copies of the songs were circulating about the community. A number of the elders remembered some of the singers and were delighted to hear again the songs of their youth, which, with the passage of time and circumstances, had become largely forgotten.

[39]As packing for the many Copper Eskimo artifacts he had obtained through trade and wanted to protect from breakage during shipping to Ottawa, my father used some of the Southern Party's huge surplus of rolled oats. Despite this usage, however, more than 2,000 pounds of rolled oats were cached at Bernard Harbour, along with other surplus supplies, when the Southern Party left the Arctic in July 1916.

and charged two Copper Eskimos with the 1913 murder of two French Oblate priests on the Coppermine River.[40]

On July 13, 1916, with his work in the region completed at last, my father bade farewell to his "adopted" Eskimo family, boarded the expedition's schooner *Alaska*, and headed west to Nome with the other members of the Southern Party. On board were twenty-six people, twenty-two sled dogs, a vast amount of equipment, and several large collections of bird, animal, fish, plant, mineral specimens, and Eskimo specimens and artifacts. One can readily imagine the clutter on and below the deck. As there was no room on board for the expedition's canoe, it was given to Ikpukhuak as a parting gift.

On route west, the *Alaska* welcomed on board the Klengenberg family at Pearce Point and took them to Baillie Islands, where Patsy Klengenberg was paid for his year of service as interpreter and hunter to the Southern Party, and Ikey Bolt (Anutisiak) for his two years. Ikey had intended to return to his home at Point Hope in Alaska, but during the brief voyage from Pearce Point had been smitten by the charms of Klengenberg's daughter, Etna, and remained with that family.[41]

The members of the Southern Party experienced a few incidents en route to Nome. At Herschel Island, they watched the Hudson's Bay Company schooner *Fort McPherson* sail east to establish a trading post at Bernard Harbour (which in turn led to the establishment of additional trading posts even farther east within a few years at Coppermine, Cambridge Bay, Bathurst Inlet, and beyond). The *Alaska* started leaking shortly after it left Cape Smyth, and the engineer refused to work when his engine room became flooded. After that problem was remedied, the schooner and its personnel had to ride out a vicious storm north of Cape Prince of Wales. Three years after leaving Nome, the members of the Southern Party returned to that settlement, reaching it on August 14, 1916.

My father had a close brush with death when he was leaving Nome, but left no record of it in his diary. The incident, however, was described in the diary of his fellow expedition member, G.H. Wilkins.[42] The coastal steamer that sailed between Seattle and Nome was forced to anchor quite a distance from the shore because of the shallowness of the near-shore water. The passengers were taken to the ship on a flat-bottomed craft and then hoisted onto the ship by means of an open platform attached by cable to one of the ship's cranes. My father and two other men were the last to be loaded this way. Just as the platform was nearing its peak elevation, the two other men suddenly lost their balance and fell to their deaths on the deck

---

[40]For details on the arrests and trials of the two natives, Sinnisiak and Uloksak (Avingak), see Moyles (1979) and Jenkins (2005). Author Moyles, however, confused the personal traits of the shaman Uloksak (Meyok) with those of the Uloksak involved in the murder of the priests. They were different persons (S.E. Jenness, 1992), both known by my father.

[41]Ikey and Etna were married at Bernard Harbour in August 1924 by Reverend G.E. Merritt, the Church of England missionary living there, and perhaps also earlier in 1917 by Oblate Father Francois Frapsauce in Coronation Gulf (S.E. Jenness, 1991, p. 825, footnote 11; MacInnes, 1932, p. 274). Together Ikey and Etna later established important trading posts on Victoria Island and became widely known throughout the Arctic, he for his business success and she for her clothing design skills and her efforts to improve the lot of infant Eskimo girls in the region.

[42]S.E. Jenness, 2004, p. 361.

of the loading craft below. My father, visibly shaken, stepped off the platform onto the deck of the steamer a few minutes later.

My father and several of his expedition companions disembarked from the coastal steamer at Seattle on September 9, proceeded to Vancouver to wind up their affairs, then entrained for Ottawa. They reached that city by the end of September. Canada was embroiled in the First World War at the time, and my father, deeply instilled with a sense of duty to his adopted country and the patriotic desire to help defend Great Britain and the British Empire, promptly sought permission from his employer, the Geological Survey of Canada, to enlist in the armed forces for overseas duty. His request was denied, and he was instructed instead to complete his work on his Arctic notes and the sorting and cataloguing of his large collection of Eskimo artifacts and photographs.

1915–1924:
THE TRIALS OF A POLYGAMIST[1]

Diamond Jenness

[My father first encountered the Copper Eskimo polygamist and shaman (called "Knife" in this chapter) in a large snow-house on Coronation Gulf, several miles north of the mouth of the Coppermine River. The date was February 24, 1915. They had many subsequent encounters over the course of the next year and soon developed a strange form of mutual respect. Knife was 5 feet 6 inches, which was tall for an Eskimo, of light build, with slightly wavy black hair cut close on the crown but falling to his chest. His eyes were light brown, and he sported a small black moustache. He did not have a beard.[2] My father also used the name Knife for this man in his book, People of the Twilight, *published in 1928. The man was, in reality, Uloksak Meyok, a Copper Eskimo from the Coppermine River area.*

From Knife, my father learned much about the ways of his people as well as a number of folklore stories. Knife became the first Copper Eskimo to be employed by the white man, when in 1915 the members of the Southern Party of the Canadian Arctic Expedition at Bernard Harbour provided him with a gun and ammunition in exchange for supplying them with some of the seal and caribou meat from his hunting efforts. As he was a skilled hunter, this initial arrangement proved generally satisfactory to both parties. In subsequent arrangements, however, where he was called upon to accompany and guide individual members of the expedition on brief journeys, he proved less satisfactory.

Most of the following story rightly belongs in the period covered by Chapter 3, but because my father originally placed it in a separate chapter in his manuscript and also since it includes events that happened several years after 1916 (the year when the Southern Party departed from the Arctic), I have left it as he intended. A few of the details as narrated in this chapter vary from those given in his Arctic diary, in his 1922 government report, and in other accounts. As this was a version originally written for and published in a popular newspaper whose audience knew little about the Arctic at the time and tended to enjoy extraordinary and imaginative stories about it, some story embellishment might be excused. Readers seeking more accurate details should refer to my father's serious accounts.[3]] [S.E.J.]

I knew a man who had two wives, and prospered. He added a third, and still prospered. But retribution, which always limped slowly behind, overtook him at the last, and he paid for his extravagance with his life.

---

[1]Republished with permission from the *Toronto Star Weekly*, Saturday, January 11, 1930, p. 5. [D.J.] My father made additions in the 1960s to that original account, and I added the footnotes and italicized notes at the start of the chapter in 2003. One picturesque paragraph in the middle of this chapter, in which my father describes the treatment he offered the shaman for his abdominal pain, was not included in the 1930 newspaper version, or in any of his other publications.

[2]Jenness, 1923b, p. B-15.

[3]Jenness, 1922; S.E. Jenness, 1991.

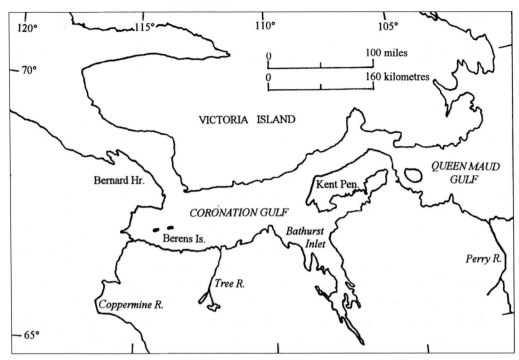

Map 6 Arctic localities mentioned in the story of the shaman "Knife."

He was an Eskimo named Knife, considered by his people a medicine man or shaman, for he fooled them with a few conjuring tricks until they believed almost anything. He could fly through the air like a bird, they said, go down into the sea like a fish, or murder a man with a knife and bring him to life again. And he performed all these marvels through the help of his family spirits, the bear, the wolf, and so forth.

My first meeting with Knife was rather dramatic. One February afternoon in 1915, while travelling by dog-sled along the Arctic coast of Canada, I came to a village of snow-huts built on the frozen sea fifteen miles from the nearest land. I set up my tent to one side and started out on a tour of inspection. Each family that I visited offered me a little titbit, some frozen fish, a piece of cold, boiled seal meat, or a tiny cube of seal blubber, and as I progressed down the line, I left a trail of matches as gifts in every home.

The last house was the largest. I crept down the long snow passage, crawled on hands and knees through the tiny doorway, and straightened up to meet the occupants. Directly in front of me, seated in great state on a low platform strewn with furs, was Knife, a broad-shouldered, haughty man barely in his prime.[4] And on each side of him, supporting his dignity, sat his two wives.

I stayed a few minutes only, but promised to return in the evening. He had the stage all set for my reception when I reappeared. The snow-hut was thronged with natives, and a big

---

[4]He was thirty years old (Jenness, 1923b, p. B-15).

Figure 16 The Copper Eskimo shaman, "Knife," and his three wives, Coronation Gulf, June 1916. L. to r., Haqungaq, "Knife," Koptana, and Kukilukak.
Photo by J.R. Cox, GSC 39690

stone pot filled with a concoction of tea and seal oil steamed over a lamp of burning seal blubber. The two wives sat together in a corner, relegated into the background, and Knife himself was dishing up the beverage in a pretty white teacup, which he handed to each man in turn. He offered me the cup, but I declined and sat down on the platform of furs. There, some of his other treasures were laid out to view—a Winchester rifle, a Hollis double-barrelled fowling piece, a few pages of an illustrated magazine, and a Roman breviary. Strange things these in the hut of an Eskimo who had seen not more than half a dozen white men in his life and knew no word of English. And there were stranger things still in this camp—a priest's cassock and a crucifix. Later, I discovered that they had belonged to two Roman Catholic missionaries whom the natives had murdered two years before.[5] Knife had not actually participated in the murder, but he had helped to plunder the missionaries' cabin.

At this time he possessed two wives only. In choosing the first he showed good judgment. White-tooth, who was a pleasant-faced woman about his own age, or perhaps a little younger, was the best seamstress in the country.[6] She tailored his clothes to perfection; the stitches, made

---

[5]The two missionaries were Fathers Jean-Baptiste Rouvière and Guillaume Le Roux, Oblate priests originally from France, operating out of a lonely mission post on the north shore of Great Bear Lake in 1913. They had traveled overland to the mouth of the Coppermine River with the intention of bringing Christianity to the Eskimos in Coronation Gulf, and were killed on their return trip.
[6]Her real name was Kukilukkak. She was from Coronation Gulf and about twenty-five years old (Jenness, 1923b, p. 28-B).

by hand with needles of beaten copper and with sinew instead of thread, were as close and even as if done on a sewing-machine, and the figures and insertions were all in excellent taste. Dressed in the finery she made for him, Knife was an Eskimo Beau Brummel.

He didn't ask White-tooth to specialize in cooking. The Eskimo—that is, the original Eskimo, not the native who has imbibed some of the white man's civilization—knows nothing of cakes and pastry and steamed puddings, and would not appreciate them if he did. He demands meat or fish, boiled for preference, frozen for second choice, and raw if necessary. White-tooth could boil salmon and meat as well as another woman, so that no one could find fault with her culinary powers. She could do more; she could provide the meat for the pot—nearly as well, in fact, as her husband.

When they stalked caribou together, she could shoot an arrow as straight as he could, and in winter, when food was scarce, she often harpooned a seal at its breathing hole when the other hunters returned empty-handed. She was neither a chatterbox nor jealous, two faults rather common among her countrywomen. In short, she was a paragon of all Eskimo virtues, and when he gained her hand, Knife certainly obtained a prize.

Still he was not satisfied. He and White-tooth between them obtained so much meat, and so many furs, that the labour of packing and dressing them was almost overwhelming. They needed another woman to take over part of the work. Besides, a second wife would enhance his dignity as the leading man in the country. So he searched through all the tribes for the prettiest girl he could find and selected Top-Knot, a rosy-faced cherub of about seventeen years.[7]

That was where Knife made his first mistake. Top-Knot had nothing but her good looks to recommend her. She was lazy and bad-tempered. Often, when Knife and White-tooth reached home after a long day's hunting, they would find no fire lit and the cooking-pot empty. The clothing that Top-Knot made for him, or for herself, fitted badly and ripped in the seams.[8] Instead of helping in the work, she increased it. Knife had to hunt more alone, and White-tooth cooked and sewed for three instead of two. He realized his mistake only too well, but he was helpless. If Top-Knot had not borne him a son,[9] he would have divorced her gladly; but only childless wives can be divorced in Eskimo land.

I met Knife afterwards in another village, where a young man had just died and the relatives were accusing me of murder.[10] I had bewitched the fellow, they said, because he had stolen a fox-trap from me. Other natives upheld my innocence, and the camp was divided until Knife appeared on the scene. Then they appealed to him as the greatest medicine man in the country, and he promised to summon his familiar spirits the next evening to discover the true cause of

---

[7]Her real name was Koptana (S.E. Jenness, 1991, p. 550).

[8]Here my father has taken literary liberties, for his Arctic diary on date March 12, 1915, states that both wives were good seamstresses (S.E. Jenness, 1991, p. 403).

[9]The baby boy's name appears to have been Kakovik (Chipman, 1913–1916, Nov. 2, 1915). The Canadian Arctic Expedition's photographer, George Wilkins, photographed the mother (Koptana) and baby on May 28, 1915 (CMC Photo 50902), during his visit to the Eskimos on the Berens Islands north of the Coppermine River.

[10]This was on March 4, 1915, after a small group of Coppermine River Eskimos, including Uloksak, arrived at the Canadian Arctic Expedition's base camp at Bernard Harbour to trade with the white men there and built snow-houses nearby.

the tragedy. It occurred to me that it would be wise to attend the séance and hear him deliver his verdict. I knew that he was shrewd. I knew, too, that he had no ammunition for his Winchester rifle and could obtain none except from me,[11] so that the chances were all against his placing the guilt at my door. But if he did accuse me, I ought to know the verdict at once, for the consequences might be very unpleasant.

Knife seemed rather embarrassed when I entered his hut, but, like a good actor, he quickly recovered his composure and set about his performance. He uttered a sharp cry, swayed heavily against a neighbour as though struck by a bullet, and staggered into the centre of the hut, his eyes bulging from their sockets and his face working convulsively like a man demented. A torrent of gibberish poured from his lips, gibberish that signified absolutely nothing, but his audience watched him closely, drinking in every syllable; and his aged father,[12] standing beside me, explained that the spirit of a white man had taken possession of his son's body and was speaking through his lips. "Surely you understand him," he asked. I saw through the trick in a moment and answered loudly, "Yes, I understand him perfectly." Knife, though apparently still demented, looked straight into my face and poured forth more gibberish, and I jabbered back at him in a similar manner. The poor deluded Eskimos were profoundly impressed. How wonderful was their medicine-man, who could bring the spirit-world under his control and converse with white men in their own tongue.

Knife was canny. Not knowing how far I would back him up in his deception, he ended the farce abruptly and summoned another of his familiar spirits, the spirit that could elucidate the murder. It spoke in broken Eskimo, in a squeaky, falsetto voice. "This white man," it said, "is friendly to you and plots no harm. It was not he who murdered your countryman, but another white man far away."

I was acquitted. Knife, the rascal, had turned a double trick. He had made a tool of me to increase his own prestige, and had then placed me under an obligation by absolving me of all guilt. The natives, of course, accepted his version without question. As for me, I gave him a Burberry overshirt the next morning, and traded him a considerable quantity of ammunition.[13]

Although Knife was shrewd, he overreached himself occasionally. I bought some dogs from a simple-minded old Eskimo, paying him with a rifle. Knife said that it was foolish to give a rifle to an old man who didn't know how to use it, and, a few days later, advised him to keep it outside his hut, on the roof, where it would be less likely to rust than indoors. The old man obeyed him, and when the rifle mysteriously disappeared came to me for help.

Knife and all the other natives in the village, he told me, thought that the dogs must have dragged it away and buried it in the snow. Could I not find it with my magic needle (a compass)? Now at this time, Knife was again short of ammunition. He came to purchase some, but I blandly informed him that I was not trading with anyone until the old man recovered his rifle. Naturally he protested that he knew nothing about it, that the dogs must have carried

---

[11]My father was the member of the Southern Party who carried out the trading with the Eskimos, their only source of ammunition at the time.

[12]He was Aneraq, aged about fifty years, from Coronation Gulf (Jenness, 1923b, p. 10-B).

[13]Accounts of this séance appear also in Jenness (1922, pp. 207–209; 1928a, pp.86–89) and S.E. Jenness (1991, pp. 399–400).

it away, no one knew where; equally naturally, I told him that he was such a wonderful medicine man that he could certainly find it if he would only invoke his guardian spirits.

He left me in a very sulky mood. For several days, I refused all overtures at trade, but nothing happened. Then, early one morning, a crowd of natives burst into my tent. The rifle was found. Knife, the great medicine man, had discovered it not a hundred yards from the settlement, buried in the snow by one of the dogs. Knife himself stood in the background, grinning. I congratulated him; he was a great medicine man.[14] Yet there were limits to his medicine power, as he well knew, and when his own health caused him a little concern he came to me, believing that I too was some kind of medicine man. "I have a pain in the pit of my stomach," he said. "Can you not rid me of it?"

He looked well, his eyes were bright, and he had eaten a large slab of seal-meat that morning. I told him not to worry, that a mischievous leprechaun had entered his stomach but that I would quickly drive it out, and I made him swallow a little blue pill. Half an hour later, a wild shout echoed down the line of snow-huts along the shore, and confused cries arose as a score of Eskimos hurried toward Knife's dwelling. I slipped on a parka and walked over. Yes, my medicine-power had succeeded. Summoning Knife to retire behind his snow-hut, it had driven out the goblin by way of his bladder. Every one could see it—a brilliant methylene-blue patch that was staining the whiteness of the pure snow.[15]

In the spring of the year, Knife's matrimonial affairs took another turn. He decided then to take a third wife who would perform most of the domestic drudgery, and fixed on a sturdy good-looking girl who had been married two or three weeks. The husband was an undersized youth much too feeble to defend his home, whether he wanted to or not. Knife simply ordered him to hand her over. If the youth had refused—well, Knife was a powerful man, handy with both gun and knife and not above using either.[16]

Now a man with three wives can never be very popular in a country where the men out-number the women. Bachelors who are compelled to remain unmarried look with envious eyes on their more fortunate neighbours, who can pull off their seal-skin boots at night and find them well chewed-over and repaired in the morning.[17] Knife's popularity waned nearly as fast as the good looks of this third wife, the drudge of the household, who had to chew the boots. For three years he strove hard to maintain his prestige, but the country was rapidly changing. Fur traders arrived to set up their establishments, and the Eskimos, abandoning their old communistic habits, became strenuous rivals of one another in the struggle for fox skins.

---

[14]This incident is mentioned also in Jenness (1928a, pp. 205–206) and S.E. Jenness (1991, pp. 559–560).

[15]This amusing story is not found in my father's scholarly report on the Copper Eskimos (1922), in his popular version (1928a), or in his original diary (S.E. Jenness 1991). However, he did include most of it in the 1930 newspaper article, and told it to me years ago on one or two occasions. He was obviously enjoying himself at the time and added with a bit of a twinkle in his eye that my mother had considered it quite unsuitable for inclusion in any of his scholarly works. She was quite right to try to protect his reputation, of course, but the story, told here in his own words, should not be lost, for it has anthropological value.

[16]Knife's third wife was Haqungaq, an adopted daughter of Ikpukhuak and Higilak, and sixteen years old or less at the time. She was married to Qikpuk when Knife (Uloksak) took her from him.

[17]Eskimo wives regularly chewed the sealskin boots at night to soften them for comfort and fit.

Rifles and shotguns completely ousted the bow and arrow, and younger men grew up who could use them as efficiently as Knife. Even his medicine-power, discredited and ridiculed by the white man, began to fall into disrepute.

Time worked his downfall. He imbibed a knowledge and taste for gambling, and one day, more in jest than in earnest, staked the eldest and best of his three wives. He lost. The winner, a younger man than himself, demanded his prize; kinsmen backed up his claim, and Knife, outnumbered, had to give her up. Worse than the loss of the woman was the blow to his prestige. No longer could he lord it over his fellow-tribesmen, seizing from them by force whatever he fancied. Rather, he dreaded lest they might turn against him and deprive him of the two wives that still remained to him.

In 1924, he migrated with his family eastward to the Perry River, but he could not escape his fate. The very thing he had dreaded happened to him there. He and his family became involved in a quarrel [with a stranger], and Knife, to protect himself, rushed for a gun. But his enemy got in a shot before him, and Knife, the great medicine man, fell dead in the snow.[18]

Verily, the path of a polygamist is strewn with thorns, and leads unto destruction.

---

[18]This account of Knife (or Uloksak) losing his wife and son, and subsequent events, differs somewhat from the account in the police reports filed by RCMP Inspector T.B. Caulkin at the time (RCMP, 1926, pp. 47–48; 1927, p. 70). According to Inspector Caulkin, Uloksak sold one of his three wives—White-tooth (Kukilukkak) according to my father's account—together with his six-year old son, to Sinnisiak (one of the murderers in 1913 of the two French priests, by then freed and employed by the RCMP at Tree River), the agreed price being a .22 calibre rifle. The boy was probably the one Koptana bore him in 1915, whose age would place the year as 1921 at the time of the exchange. (The name Royal North-West Mounted Police—RNWMP—was changed to Royal Canadian Mounted Police—RCMP—in February 1920.) Uloksak soon reclaimed his son, however, although not the wife he had sold, and moved east to the Kent Peninsula. The boy was subsequently picked up there by RCMP Constable Brockie of the Tree River police post and returned to Sinnisiak. Uloksak came back and seized his son again early in 1924, then moved farther east to the Perry River. There he was shot and killed that summer by another Eskimo, Ikayena, just as my father's account above states, after an argument over one of Uloksak's dogs. A patrol from Tree River, led by RCMP Constable F.A. Barnes, arrested Ikayena the following February (RCMP, 1926, p. 41), and he was taken to Aklavik, where he was tried for murder in 1926. Ikayena was acquitted and sent with his two wives (for he had taken Haqungaq as a second wife, along with her two children, after the shooting) to Cambridge Bay. There he was hired as a guide and snowhouse builder by the local RCMP detachment. Ironically, Haqungaq assisted Ikayena to commit suicide by hanging in the fall of 1929, inland from Perry River, when he was very sick with a swollen stomach, tongue, and mouth and unable to eat. A few months later she took another husband. (Report dated June 12, 1930, of Corp. A.T. Belcher, RCMP, Cambridge Bay detachment, RG 85, Vol. 767, File 5135, LAC).

1916–1922: THE FIRST WORLD WAR AND ITS AFTERMATH

5

Stuart E. Jenness

My father rarely spoke of his World War I experiences. The same silence applies in his reminiscences, where he included only the following statement:

> The scientific members of the [Canadian Arctic] expedition returned to southern Canada in the autumn of 1916, and the author spent the ensuing winter at the government museum in Ottawa, cataloguing and arranging his specimens and notes; but as soon as spring broke he enlisted in Canada's overseas' forces and served with a howitzer[1] battery until the armistice. The Ottawa museum then reclaimed him and assigned him the task of studying all the Indian and Eskimo tribes of Canada between the Atlantic and the Pacific.

The quotation above is a prime example of my father's disinclination to talk about himself. He was involved in many activities during those years, some of which influenced him or his thinking for much of the rest of his life. Two examples are: his marriage to Eilleen Bleakney, and his decision to live and work in Canada. He could also have mentioned completing the first of his two Papuan manuscripts in Oxford shortly after the armistice in 1918; his return to Canada in April 1919, immediately followed by his three-month honeymoon trip to New Zealand with his bride, Eilleen; his struggle to obtain permanent employment with the museum in Ottawa; his offers of other jobs; and writing about his Arctic studies. Thus, it seemed desirable to enlarge appreciably on his brief account about this busy period in his life.

The main sources of information about his World War I military activities in England and France are letters he wrote to his Oxford teacher (R.R. Marett), his New Zealand professor and mentor (William von Zedlitz), his friends in Ottawa (Marius Barbeau, Dr. R.M. Anderson and Mrs. R.M. Anderson), and his former expedition leader (Vilhjalmur Stefansson). Fortunately, all of these people saved his correspondence. He regularly wrote to his fiancée too, of course, and to his family in New Zealand, but those letters have not survived.[2] Sadly, too, he did not keep any of the letters he received, so that all of this known wartime correspondence is one-sided. Dr. Anderson's letters kept my father abreast of government and scientific matters at the Victoria Memorial Museum in Ottawa and elsewhere, and of the whereabouts of their former Arctic colleagues. Mrs. Anderson sent him news of local and family

---

[1] A howitzer is a short cannon with low muzzle velocity, firing shells in a relatively high trajectory.
[2] Several years after my father's death Mother told me that sometime in the 1920s, she and Father re-read all of their wartime letters and then burned them in the fireplace.

matters, as well as stationery and assorted items she had knit to keep him warm. My father regularly acknowledged the receipt of these letters and gifts, expressing his appreciation and frequently including light-hearted comments.

From my father's letters from France and one obscure document[3] we learn that after he reached France, he was initially assigned to be an officer's orderly and to look after the horses and mules that pulled the artillery pieces in his howitzer unit. Some while later, he became a gun spotter, peering out from a small concrete observation post mounted on a tower close to the German lines. Being small of build and gifted in powers of observation, he was well suited for this dangerous task. Thereafter he appears to have alternated his time between animal care and enemy-gun spotting. These were not exactly the sorts of wartime activities that might have inclined him to tell to his children or grandchildren years later, and he refrained from ever doing so.

One day towards the end of the war, while watching from his observation post near the northern French town of Lens, he had a surprise visit from his former Arctic companion, George Hubert Wilkins.[4] As all was quiet along that part of the front at the time, he obtained permission to accompany Wilkins to visit another Arctic friend, the geographer John Cox, who was with a nearby artillery unit. The three Arctic experts had a pleasant though brief reunion. Shortly thereafter, my father and his unit were involved in the Allied summer campaign of 1918 to push the German forces out of France and Belgium. He was stationed near Mons, Belgium, when the Armistice was signed. Our story is getting ahead of itself, however, so let us return to where we left off in Chapter 3.

After reaching Ottawa from the Arctic, late in September 1916, my father was assigned office space in the Victoria Memorial Museum building. Here for the next six months, while rooming in a house on Osgoode Street, he worked feverishly on his Eskimo notes, collections, and initial reports for the government.[5] The intensity of his involvement in his work triggered his first "run-in" with a government administrator. Some eight weeks after he reached Ottawa, he

---

[3]Nemo, 1918, p. 37.

[4]More than a decade after the war, my father revealed his locality (something he had not been permitted to do during wartime) and mentioned his encounter with Wilkins. Wilkins suddenly poked his head up through the trap door in the tiny concrete observation box my father was occupying on a tower overlooking the German-occupied town of Lens in northern France (Jenness, 1931).

[5]During this period he had many occasions to speak with his immediate superior, Dr. E. Sapir, the chief anthropologist at the Victoria Memorial Museum. In the latter's office, he thus met and was attracted to Dr. Sapir's secretary, Ottawa-born Frances Eilleen Bleakney, daughter of local Irish immigrants. Naturally reserved in manner and intensely focused on the overwhelming amount of work he faced, my father initially showed little indication of being attracted to the young lady. She was of a somewhat more impetuous nature, however. Many years later, she told me that one day, after receiving encouragement from her mother, she invited him to tea at her family home the following Sunday afternoon. This was the proper way in those days for a young woman to introduce a male friend to her family. When that Sunday came, however, my father failed to put in an appearance, apparently being so engrossed in his work at the museum that he completely forgot about the invitation to tea. His failure to appear distressed Eilleen so much that she burst into tears. Her sympathetic and understanding mother sought to comfort her with these words: "There, there, dear, don't let it trouble you so. All men are forgetful like that!"

received a letter from the office of the Deputy Minister of Mines, R.G. McConnell,[6] drawing to his attention that employees of the Government of Canada were required to sign daily in an attendance book or sheet. This, my father had evidently failed to do since his arrival. For four years, he had roamed at will in the wilds of Papua and the treeless wastes of the North American Arctic, risking life or limb in the name of science, without giving a thought to his attendance. Signing a daily attendance book had, therefore, never been one of his high priorities. He was excused for his gross neglect after explaining that he had not been informed of the requirement,[7] and signed religiously thereafter.

The disturbing war news from the western front in Europe troubled him deeply. Feeling a strong sense of duty to help Britain and its empire, he repeatedly sought permission from his employer for leave of absence to enlist. His requests were all turned down. To one of them McConnell replied bluntly, "The circumstances connected with your employment by the Department will not permit of the application being granted."[8] This note triggered a series of communications between my father and McConnell, my father asking for clarification of his employment status in the Geological Survey if he undertook military service. He mentioned that he possessed written statements from both the previous Deputy Minister (Dr. Brock) and from his boss, Dr. Sapir, which implied that he would be free to undertake military duty whenever he considered his overseas services were required, without prejudice to his position with the Geological Survey. My father's original contract with the Canadian government did not extend beyond the time required for him to write up his reports from the expedition. He was willing to go off to war now, asking in return only some sort of guarantee of on-going employment with the museum when he returned. The leave of absence he requested would ensure there was a job for him when he returned from overseas. In 1917, government regulations prevented the Deputy Minister from making that kind of offer, but my father was probably not aware of that.

My father ultimately grew so exasperated over the seemingly endless administrative obstacles that he enlisted, on April 2, in a Siege Artillery Draft for overseas. The next day, he notified McConnell of his action and again asked for a leave of absence, this time to permit him to proceed overseas with his military unit. This request, like all his previous ones, was denied, leaving him in a very awkward situation. My father then wrote McConnell on April 10 request-ing clarification of his status with the Geological Survey, adding that as he had not resigned from that organization, he believed he was entitled to the benefits of two Orders-in-Council, P.C.2553 and 3055, which would assure him of the continuation of his salary as a temporary staff member while he was in the army, minus the amount he would receive for military pay.[9]

He followed this letter with a visit to McConnell's office, probably at McConnell's request, to try to resolve the matter. During that visit, my father, perhaps in a state of total exasperation,

[6]R.G. McConnell was also Acting Director of the Victoria Memorial Museum. He had joined the Geological Survey in 1879, was its senior officer at the time he was made Deputy Minister in 1914, and believed that length of service was the only factor when promotions were made. He was considered "one of the 'stalwarts' of the old brigade of the Geological Survey." (Zaslov, 1975, p. 307).
[7]R.G. McConnell to Jenness, letter dated November 28, 1916, RG 45, vol. 49, File 3109, LAC.
[8]R.G. McConnell to Jenness, letter dated April 5, 1917, RG 45, vol. 49, File 3109, LAC.
[9]Jenness to R.G. McConnell, letter dated April 10, 1917, RG 45, vol. 49, File 3109, LAC.

Figure 17 Private Diamond Jenness, Canadian Expeditionary Force, May 1917.
CMC 67220

mentioned that he had just received an offer of post-war employment with the Australian Government at a much higher salary than that now being paid him by the Geological Survey. Quite possibly, he also added that if the Geological Survey could give him no assurance of post-war employment beyond the three years he needed to complete his Arctic work, he would likely accept the Australian offer.

McConnell replied two days later that, assuming my father returned to the museum to complete his reports, he would indeed come under the provisions of Order-in-Council No. 2553, "which permits (not obliges as you seem to think) the Government to continue civil pay to employees enlisting." However, he added sternly, in view of the fact that my father had apparently expressed his intention of accepting a position in Australia at the end of the war, his connection with the department would terminate when he left the Survey to assume military duties.[10] Consequently, he would not qualify under the special Order-in-Council for continuation of his government pay while he was overseas.

After receiving this unwelcome response, my father decided to take his problem to a higher level and wrote for assistance to a cabinet minister in the federal government, a former Oxfordian, the Honourable Sir George E. Foster. In this move, so out of character for my father, I suspect the guidance of his colleague, Barbeau, who in 1911 had enrolled the assistance of a federal politician to obtain his own appointment with the Geological Survey. Sir George wrote the Minister of Mines, Mr. Patenaude, for clarification of my father's case, which in turn led to the exchange of several letters between McConnell and M.F. Gallagher, the Private Secretary to the Honourable Mr. Patenaude.[11] The following statement from my father's letter to Sir George, quoted in a letter from Gallagher to McConnell, leaves one wondering why my father had told McConnell he intended to accept a job in Australia after the end of the war: "I wish to return at the end of the war and complete the work for which I was engaged and am willing to enter into an engagement to do so, provided I am granted the most elementary justice."

McConnell subsequently wrote Gallagher that my father was an able anthropologist and a keen student, one who could undoubtedly write up his Arctic work better than anyone else,

---

[10]R.G. McConnell to Jenness, letter dated April 12, 1917, RG 45, vol. 49, File 3109, LAC.

[11]M.F. Gallagher to R.G. McConnell, letter dated April 25, 1917; McConnell to Gallagher, letter dated April 28, 1917; Gallagher to McConnell, letter dated May 9, 1917; and McConnell to Gallagher, letter dated May 12, 1917. RG 45, vol. 49, File 3109, LAC.

and recommended he be offered a moderate advance on his present salary when he returned from overseas. It was the most he could do at the time. His action resolved the problem fairly satisfactorily for the time being, but the battle over my father's job permanency still remained to be fought. It was, in fact, not settled for another three years.

During the negotiations with McConnell, my father had not divulged his real reason for persistently seeking assurance of post-war employment with the Geological Survey. He wanted to marry his boss's secretary, Miss F. Eilleen Bleakney, and settle down in Canada. He wanted to propose to Eilleen before he went overseas, but did not feel he could do so without the assurance of continuing employment. Having already enlisted, he had very little time at his disposal to arrive at some mutual agreement with his employers and propose to his lady.

My father's wants were not fully met, but the government did release him for overseas duty after he signed a contract with the Geological Survey stating that he intended to return for three years after the war to complete his Arctic reports.[12] However, his appeal to the Member of Parliament had brought action, and on June 6, McConnell wrote the Deputy Minister, Department of Militia and Defence, stating that Mr. Jenness had been granted leave of absence from the Department of Mines under the provisions of P.C. No. 2553.[13] For the duration of the war my father was assured he would receive his government pay rather than the much lower pay of an Army private (his military status) and a salary for an additional three years while he completed his Arctic reports, but he received no assurance of continuing work at the Geological Survey after that.

My father accepted what the Survey offered, proposed to Eilleen, and was soon en route to England and the war. His Arctic companion, the geographer John Cox, also joined the same Heavy Siege and Artillery Draft unit, so the two friends went overseas together. They were soon separated after reaching England, but remained friends for the rest of their days.

My father received additional military training for two months (July and August 1917) at Shorncliffe in southern England before being shipped to France to serve with the 58th battery of 4.5 howitzers. Being short (five feet five inches) and light-weight (125 to 130 pounds), he was ill suited for heavy-duty activities, so was initially assigned to look after the horses and mules that pulled the guns and wagon trains. At some point he was taught to ride and thereafter permitted to undertake occasional brief solo explorations on horseback into the surrounding countryside well behind the front lines. He enjoyed dealing with the horses, but the mules were another matter. He found them mean-tempered and unpredictable creatures. About this time he wrote his friend Barbeau, "I'm not doing much towards winning the war—but at least it is all that I am able to do."[14]

Shortly afterwards he was made a forward gun spotter in a very small concrete observation post, watching for the locations and movements of enemy guns and men across the front lines and communicating his observations back to the gunners. It was an assignment that made more effective use of his intelligence as well as his keen eyesight than his work with the animals. He

---

[12]Nemo, 1918, p. 37.

[13]R.G. McConnell, Deputy Minister of Mines, to Surgeon-General Sir Eugene Fiset, Deputy Minister, Department of Militia & Defence, Ottawa, letter dated June 6, 1917, RG 45, vol. 49, File 3109, LAC.

[14]Jenness to Barbeau, letter dated October 9, 1917, Barbeau Correspondence, Box 206, Folder 27, Archives, CMC.

also served as orderly for an unidentified officer.[15] He continued to serve in this fashion until just before the Armistice in November 1918.

Little is known about where in France my father served with his howitzer battery during the war. Military combatants were instructed to refrain from identifying their geographic locations in their letters home lest the information fall into the hands of the enemy. Thus most of my father's wartime letters are simply headed "France" or "Somewhere in France." Just before the Armistice in November, 1918, however, following weeks of relative inactivity over the winter and early spring, his location, "Somewhere in France," was evidently close to the Belgian border north of Paris, because he mentioned in a letter to Barbeau[16] that his gun outfit had been hard on the heels of the Germans since the Allied offensive around Amiens during the summer. In an earlier letter[17] he mentioned that he hoped to get leave to go to Paris, where he would visit the mother of Henri Beuchat, his anthropologist friend on the Arctic expedition who had perished after the sinking of the *Karluk* in 1914. Had he managed to get to Paris he also intended to visit the Trocadero Museum in order to examine its collections of North American ethnographic material. However, I do not believe he was able to make either of these visits.

My father somehow came through the war without serious injury or lasting ill effects— other than a partial deafness of his left ear. His war record in Library and Archives Canada (formerly the National Archives of Canada) reveals little information other than that he was hospitalized for three days in France. His medical problem on that occasion was not the result of a war injury or battle stress, but eye trouble somewhat akin to the snow blindness he and other members of the Arctic expedition had experienced in the north. A few of his letters from the war zone mention that he also suffered occasional bouts of what he called rheumatism.

It is more than likely that my father all too frequently saw sickeningly destructive artillery action, but he never spoke about it to me, probably because he had no desire to recall those horrifying experiences. Once, when I asked him about that period of his life, he did, however, tell me two war-time stories, neither of which had anything to do with actual combat. His first story concerned his promotion from private to lance corporal. With a slight smile on his face, he commented that this promotion did not last long because shortly afterwards, he accidentally stepped on his sergeant's bowl of soup, which was cooling on the steps outside the mess hall. He was quickly demoted! I doubt this event was ever recorded in military files.

The second story was about an ill-tempered mule, one of a team that was hauling the howitzer guns for his unit. A few weeks after reaching France, my father was plodding alongside the mule team as they moved along a muddy dirt road when something frightened one of the mules, and it lashed out with its back hooves. One of its hooves struck my father squarely on the chest, he told me, and sent him flying over the low hedge that bordered the dirt road. Fortunately, he had shortly before received a thick bundle of letters from his fiancée, Eilleen, in Ottawa and had tucked them carefully into his breast pocket. The letters, he said, absorbed

---

[15]Nemo, 1918, p. 37.

[16]Jenness to Barbeau, letter dated November 7, 1918, Barbeau Collection, Box 206, Folder 27, Archives, CMC.

[17]Jenness to Barbeau, letter dated February 18, 1918, Barbeau Collection, Box 206, Folder 27, Archives, CMC.

much of the blow from the mule's hoof and saved him from severe injury. This story was largely confirmed in a letter to Barbeau,[18] wherein he mentioned that an ill-tempered brute had nearly sent him back to Canada with a broken sternum. Nonetheless, although the sternum was not broken, it was extremely painful for several days afterwards. His supposed flight over the hedge following the kick may have been a slight embellishment of the story for my amusement.

These two wartime stories are mild examples of my father's playful but gentle sense of humour, a kind of humour that surfaced when he was in one of his infrequent, less-than-serious moods. This same form of humour surfaces in some of his letters from the war front. For example, in a letter written to Barbeau a few weeks after reaching France, he commented "I have attended church more often since I joined the army than at any time since I left Oxford—though I must admit that in each place it was compulsory."

He then added a little dig at his friend, "Still it is excellent training for the future—for I remember Mrs. Barbeau makes you attend."

Although my father apparently proposed marriage to Eilleen Bleakney[19] shortly before he went overseas in July, 1917, the matter was kept secret in order (he wrote Barbeau later) to spare her from any office embarrassment or teasing. She was Dr. Sapir's secretary at the museum but also assisted Barbeau with his West Coast Indian and French-Canadian folklore studies.[20] However, the news of their engagement ultimately leaked out. Almost the first to learn of it was Barbeau. My father mentioned in several subsequent letters to Barbeau how very much he and Eilleen had enjoyed a picnic they had shared with Barbeau and his wife at a place called "Catfish Bay," shortly before my father went overseas in July 1917, and how much he looked forward to returning there after the war. From his frequent reference to that occasion, I suspect that was when he proposed to Eilleen. I do not know its exact location, but assume it was somewhere on the Ottawa or Gatineau rivers or on one of the many lakes in the Gatineau Valley within easy reach of the city. On November 25, 1917 my father wrote Barbeau, "I think you have found out already that Miss Bleakney & I are engaged. (This is confidential, however.)"

---

[18]Jenness to Barbeau, letter dated October 9, 1917, Barbeau Collection, Box 206, Folder 27, Archives, CMC.

[19]My mother's full maiden name was Frances Eilleen Bleakney. While my father was overseas, she published her first article with the assistance of Barbeau. In this she omitted her first name and initiated the use of the spelling Eileen, with only one "l," which she continued to use thereafter when she published, in preference to the correct spelling. She never offered any explanation.

[20]Sometime in 1917, Barbeau recorded Miss Eilleen Bleakney singing the English children's folk-song "Little Sally Waters" (Barbeau recordings, song MN 481, CMC). Miss Bleakney (who later became my mother) published this song and others the following year (1918) in *The Journal of American Folk-Lore* (vol. 31, no. 120, pp. 148–169). She sang the last six lines of the song to a different melody, one commonly known as "Here We Go Gathering Nuts in May," and neglected to sing two more lines, the words for which are given in her article. The part of the song with the second melody is listed as song MN 481A. (incorrectly identified as "The Mulberry Bush"), and may well be from a different song. The existence of these songs among the many recordings made by Barbeau and now in the Canadian Museum of Civilization's collections was discovered by chance in 2006 by the museum's reference archivist, Benoît Thériault, and the Audiovisual Archives Technician, Jonathan Wise, through whose kindness I subsequently obtained copies of the article as well as the two songs on a CD recording.

He then added, somewhat teasingly, "I hope you are truly remorseful, for you were the guilty agent who set the ball rolling in the first place."

When he went overseas, my father entrusted the management of his personal effects (clothing, books, etc.), his banking arrangements, and other business affairs to Barbeau's care. Later he added the care of his fiancée to his friend's responsibilities until his return from the war.

Other examples of my father's gentle humour appear in letters now housed at Library and Archives Canada, which were written to Mrs. R.M. Anderson during the war. My father's letters written to Barbeau during the early 1920s are now housed at the Canadian Museum of Civilization. This kind of humour continued after the war, for in an exchange in 1931 with his Arctic leader, Vilhjalmur Stefansson, from whom he had just received a book, he wrote, "Some day I hope to return the compliment with another book of my own, which you will probably not read."[21]

Stefansson promptly replied in a similar light-hearted manner, assuring my father that he had read my father's Arctic reports from cover to cover except for the two volumes on Eskimo songs and on string figures. He then added he would certainly read my father's next book thoroughly, unless it was about Eskimo songs or string figures.[22]

My father's sense of humour may have been dampened by distressing events in the years that followed his promotion to Chief of Anthropology, such as the end of his friendship with Barbeau (about which more will be said in Chapter 8), the frustrations he experienced in that position, and the worries and tragedies of the Second World War. Nevertheless, readers will encounter vestiges of his special sense of humour throughout these pages. When something amused him, he would take on an air of quiet enjoyment, rather like the one captured so delightfully in Figure 55.

In one wartime letter he even expressed concern for the safety of the German forces, an indication of his feelings towards other human beings whom he knew were simply trying to do their duty as he was himself, even if they were the enemy. He wrote: "Heaven help them if they don't [give up, because] all that they have done to France & Belgium is likely to be visited on their own heads tenfold."[23]

On December 4,[24] he wrote Barbeau that he had been at Mons, just inside the Belgium border, when the Armistice was signed (November 11) and would still "be grooming horses & cleaning stables" had he not had the good fortune to have recently transferred to the Canadian Corps Topographical Section, which was stationed in the same region.[25] His new

---

[21]Jenness to Stefansson, letter dated February 3, 1931, Jenness Collection, Box 658, Folder 41, Archives, CMC.

[22]Stefansson to Jenness, letter dated February 5, 1931, Jenness Collection, Box 658, Folder 41, Archives, CMC.

[23]Jenness to Barbeau, letter dated November 7, 1918, Barbeau Collection, Box 206, Folder 27, Archives, CMC.

[24]Jenness to Barbeau, letter dated December 6, 1918, Barbeau Collection, Box 206, Folder 27, Archives, CMC.

[25]It is a curious coincidence that my father served, albeit briefly, with the Canadian Corps Topographical Section during the First World War, when he was only a lowly private, and then created and headed an Inter-Service Topographical Section during the Second World War as a civilian (see Chapter 15).

unit had granted him leave, and he had just spent a pleasant seven days in Rome and three days in Florence before returning to the unit. His visit to Rome undoubtedly satisfied some of his curiosity to see the Roman ruins and other ancient features he had learned about in university. His visit to Florence might have been encouraged by the urgings of his fiancée, who had been taken there by a rich aunt shortly before the war and spoke glowingly of its beautiful paintings and buildings many times during my growing years. In the short period of time he was on leave, my father's unit had moved into Germany and was located near a small, unidentified countryside village between Bonn and Cologne. Unfortunately he was not permitted to visit Cologne because that city was out of bounds to the Canadian troops owing to the recent misconduct of some of their men. He regretted this restriction because he had wanted to visit the city's ethnological museum.

Following a suggestion made to him in a letter from his Oxford teacher, R.R. Marett, my father subsequently applied for a month's leave from military service to return to Oxford to complete his Papuan manuscript. He was granted that leave late in January 1919.[26] As a result, with Marett's assistance, he corrected and completed his report within the allotted leave time, and it was published the following year.

While at Oxford, my father received a letter dated February 20, 1919, from his former Arctic Expedition leader, Vilhjalmur Stefansson. My father's reply included this interesting comment: "I must thank you also for your kindness in attempting to accelerate my return. It so happens that my unit will be one of the earliest to be sent back, and I am expecting to sail for Canada about the middle of March."[27]

He had not seen Stefansson since 1913. From a letter dated November 26, 1918, written by Sapir to Stefansson, I learned that Stefansson had visited Sapir in Ottawa some days earlier. I think it highly probable that he urged Sapir on that occasion to see if he could do something to speed up my father's early return to Canada. Stefansson would probably have argued that it was justified because of the importance to Canada of Jenness' Arctic work and the great need for Jenness to prepare his extensive reports of that work as soon as possible. I suspect, however, that his real reason was that he was preparing to write his own popular account of the expedition and wanted to know what my father would be writing about his Arctic experiences, especially those with the Copper Eskimos. In any case, Sapir wrote the Directing Geologist, William McInnes, a day or two later, "Now that the war is over to all intents and purposes, it would seem a pity that Mr. Jenness should be withheld from the persecution of his anthropological work any longer than is absolutely necessary.... I therefore respectively urge that immediate steps be taken to request the military authorities to grant Mr. Jenness his discharge."[28]

While it may have been entirely coincidental, the suggestion appears to have brought results, for my father's unit was certainly one of the early ones to return to Canada. He reached

---

[26]Jenness to Barbeau, letter dated January 28, 1919, Barbeau Collection, Box 205, Folder 27, Archives, CMC.

[27]The letter is in the Jenness Papers, Stefansson Collection, Box IV, Folder 26, Rauner Library, Dartmouth College, Hanover, New Hampshire. Stefansson's letter to Jenness dated February 20 was not preserved.

[28]Sapir to W. McInnes, memo dated November 20, 1918, Sapir Correspondence, Box 625, Folder 1, Archives, CMC.

Ottawa in mid April 1919, married Eileen Bleakney on April 30,[29] and left with his new bride a few days later for New Zealand and his first trip home since 1913.[30]

Figure 18 Wedding couple, Diamond Jenness and Eileen Bleakney, Ottawa, April 30, 1919.

Figure 19 The happy honeymoon couple, Diamond and Eileen Jenness, on shipboard, 1919.

---

[29]Although my father had been brought up Methodist, my mother had come from several generations of Baptists (on both sides of her family), originally from Ireland. Neither parent attended church during my lifetime, although both held strong religion-based beliefs. They were married in my mother's church, the small uptown First Baptist Church at the corner of Elgin Street and Laurier Avenue in Ottawa. Thirty-six people signed the guest book. Of these, fifteen were my mother's relatives. Museum friends of my father included Dr. Rudolph M. Anderson and MaeBelle A. Anderson, Kenneth and Marjorie Chipman, J.J. and Lillian M. O'Neill, Harlan and Helena Smith, Dr. Edward and F. Olga Sapir, M. Macoun, S. Clifford, Edith M. McLean, and Frits Johansen. Also present was Ida C. Tavernier, the concert-pianist sister of the Museum's bird specialist Percy A. Taverner (note the different spelling of the last name of these two). Ida later married John McLeish, who became Chief of the Mines and Geology Branch in 1936.

[30]Under government regulations then in effect, Miss Bleakney was required to resign from her secretarial position at the National Museum when she married.

One of the gifts the newlyweds received was a poem for their boss, Dr. Sapir. Sapir enjoyed writing poetry,[31] and created this tender poem for their special occasion:

FOR LOVERS WED, FAREWELL AND HAIL[32]
(To D.J. and E.J.)
You slipped out with your hearts on fire,
We melted in the night,
You saw by the day that streamed from your eyes
We stood in the starlight.
You will come to us with the sun in your hearts
And sunlight in your eyes,
You will find us waiting by the door,
Standing at sunrise.

Edward Sapir
April 30, 1919

When the newlyweds returned to Ottawa early in August,[33] my father immediately set about writing his final reports on all aspects of his Arctic work. He worked steadily on this project for almost four years, producing, in all, eight reports in five volumes, more than one-third of the fourteen government volumes published on the Canadian Arctic Expedition. His first and principal publication, *The Life of the Copper Eskimo* (Part A) came off the government press as part of Volume XII in January 1922, after being delayed for about two years by Stefansson's demands that my father change some of its contents.[34] Part B of the same volume appeared

---

[31] He was a member of a poetry circle in Ottawa that included the well-known poet, Duncan Campbell Scott.

[32] A copy of this original poem was sent to me in the early 1980's by Professor William Cowan of Carleton University, Ottawa, who was editing the poetry of Edward Sapir at the time for a book he subsequently published (Cowan and Foster, 1986).

[33] My mother confessed to me long after my father's death that the New Zealand trip had been "perfectly beastly." Of course she was probably seasick on the voyage to New Zealand and back, and the rather staid in-laws she encountered there would have had a marked influence on the feelings of this lively and somewhat liberated woman—she had been a cultured working lady, not a homebody. She never returned to New Zealand, although my father asked her to accompany him there in 1947 when he took three months leave of absence towards the end of his government career.

[34] A letter from my father to Stefansson, dated December 27, 1919 (Jenness, 1919), reveals that the manuscript for this report was expected to be ready for the printers within three months. Stefansson somehow obtained a copy of at least part of the manuscript, for in June he sent my father a number of frank criticisms on it. My father agreed to rewrite part of his chapter on food to include some of Stefansson's observations (Jenness, 1920), but apparently disagreed with other criticisms made by Stefansson at that time and would not change the text in question. Stefansson then pressured the Deputy Minister of the Naval Service (G.J. Desbarats), whose department had agreed to publish the report, to delay its publication until my father modified the statements he (V.S.) considered unacceptable (Anderson, 1921; as editor-in-chief of the entire series of Canadian Arctic Expedition reports, Dr. Anderson would certainly have been aware of my father's problem with the manuscript at the time). My father stoutly refused to alter the views he had expressed, but after numerous exchanges between senior personnel at the Geological Survey of Canada and the Department of the Naval

in 1923. The other four volumes followed at irregular intervals thereafter: Volume XIII in 1924 (Parts A and B); Volume XIV in 1925 (with Helen Roberts of New York); Volume XV in 1928 (Part A),[35] with part B of that volume in 1944; and finally Volume XVI in 1946. These last two manuscripts had actually been more or less completed in the 1920s,[36] but their publication was delayed because of the severe money restrictions during the depression years and the Second World War.

A year and a half after my father's return from the war, in September 1920, the Canadian government finally initiated action to make his position at the Victoria Memorial Museum permanent.[37] It advertised for an Associate Ethnologist with special knowledge of the Eskimos. There were only two applicants: my father and a Montreal man named Vaillancourt.[38] My father received the appointment.

Following that appointment, my father was soon assigned to study many of the Indian tribes of Canada. As the record shows, he carried out his task sufficiently successfully that, within a decade, he was the Canadian authority on the fifty or so tribes between the Atlantic and the Pacific oceans. Before he could embark full time on his Indian studies, however, he was instructed to complete the writing of the remaining volumes on the Copper Eskimos. He essentially accomplished that task by 1923, but by then, the government's Editorial Board, whose responsibility it was to see the expedition's manuscripts through to publication, had been disbanded, and the work of the Canadian Arctic Expedition was fast becoming forgotten.

Service, finally agreed to insert footnotes about the controversial items, and the manuscript was finally published in January 1922. Stefansson later interfered with and delayed the publication of Part B of Vol. 12, *Physical Characteristics of the Copper Eskimos* (Anderson, 1923).

[35] Jenness, 1928c.

[36] At least three draft-copy manuscripts of Indian folklore prepared by my father in the 1920s and 1930s were still unpublished in 2006, initially largely because of the lack of funds prior to and during the Second World War, but also because other work prevented my father from getting them into acceptable condition for publication.

[37] Since his return from the north in 1916, my father had been on yearly contracts until he completed his Arctic reports. Now a war veteran, married, thirty-four years old, and wanting to start a family, he was seeking more security than the government had previously offered him. About this time, he was offered a teaching job at the University of Washington in Seattle and another job as Government Ethnologist in Papua for the Australian government, and had already turned down one from his alma mater, Victoria University College in Wellington, New Zealand in 1919. Dr. Sapir had written the Honourable Arthur Meighen, Minister of Mines, urging him to make Jenness' position permanent as he was "one of the best equipped men on the staff." He added that Jenness wanted to remain in Canada because of his Arctic work and for family reasons, but if not made permanent he would be forced to accept the offer he had received from the Australian government to become Government Ethnologist in Papua (Sapir to Meighen, letter dated May 3, 1920, Sapir Collection, Box 625, Folder 2, Archives, CMC). Barbeau also claimed a hand in obtaining the appointment for Jenness, stating in his memoirs, "I remember having gone to the office of the Minister, Mr. Coderre, to urge his [Jenness'] appointment as a permanent member of our staff and he was appointed very soon after" (C.M. Barbeau memoirs, 1957–58, Carmen Roy Collection, Box 622, Folder 4, p. 86, Archives, CMC). However, Barbeau's memory apparently misled him, for Mr. Louis Coderre was Minister of Mines only between 1913 and 1915, when my father was in the Arctic.

[38] Jenness to Barbeau, letter dated August 20, 1920, Barbeau Collection, Box 206, Folder 27, Archives, CMC.

1923–1924: ON A BRITISH COLUMBIA FRONTIER[1]

6

Diamond Jenness

[From a short while after his return from the war in 1919 until 1923 my father spent most of his time completing his research and writing on his eight detailed reports on the Copper Eskimos (Jenness 1922, 1923a,b,c, 1924a,b,c, 1928c, 1944a, 1946). Ultimately totalling 1368 pages, these reports were published in five volumes, three of them between 1922 and 1928, and the final two in 1944 and 1946.

In July 1920, my father took his wife, Eilleen, on a three-week camping trip with tent, canoe, and fishing tackle to Rock Lake in Algonquin Park. That trip confirmed their mutual enjoyment of quiet, private camp life alongside water, shaping some of the rest of their lives. When he returned to his office, he found a letter offering him a teaching position at the University of Washington in Seattle. He probably would have accepted this offer had not the Canadian government made his appointment permanent shortly thereafter. One cannot help but wonder in what direction Canadian anthropology might have developed had he left Ottawa at that time!

The following summer (1921), he embarked on the first of his field studies of Canadian Indians, studies which over the next several years took him all across Canada from Vancouver Island to Newfoundland. That summer he spent two months investigating the social organization and history of the Sarcee Indians on their prairie reserve near Calgary, Alberta. As was the case with his collections of Copper Eskimo material, his timing was right, and he acquired many valuable specimens for the National Museum of Canada, which but a few years later would no longer have been available.

He continued his Indian studies over the winter of 1923–1924 with the Carrier Indians in the Hazelton area of northern British Columbia. His museum colleague, Marius Barbeau, had worked around Hazelton during the summer of 1923, investigating the Tsimshian Indians and thus helped to "break the ice" for my father's visit. In October, my father boarded a train with his wife and twenty-month-old son John, and headed for Hazelton. In the following two chapters, he relates some of his experiences in that interior part of British Columbia. From them, one obtains an insight into my father's special talent for inspiring confidence and trust among the people he encountered there.] [S.E.J.]

---

[1]This is a somewhat expanded and modified version of an article my father published in 1933 under the title "An Indian Method of Treating Hysteria," *Primitive Man*, vol. 6, pp. 13–20. It is regrettable that because of editing and financial limitations within the Geological Survey of Canada at the time, the two lengthy reports my father wrote on the Carrier Indians as a result of his studies in 1923–1924 were published not by the National Museum of Canada but in the United States ("Myths of the Carrier Indians of British Columbia" in the *Journal of American Folk-Lore* in 1934, and "The Carrier Indians of the Bulkley River, their social and religious life" in *Bureau of American Ethnology Bulletin* no. 133 in 1943).

Human beings, like the birds and the trees, must adapt themselves to their environments or perish, and Canada's vast expanse offers them several well-defined environments that contrast very sharply with one another. Even today, it is not difficult to distinguish a Nova Scotia fisherman from an Alberta cowpuncher, or a Toronto merchant from a Vancouver longshoreman, although the grandparents of all four may have reached this continent from the same country. Nature in her mysterious way stamps men and women with the speech and mannerisms of the regions in which they are born and raised, and they bear her markings to their graves.

So it was, too, among Canada's Aboriginal population before any European set foot on this continent. The Indians who roamed her eastern lakes and rivers spoke languages, wore costumes, built dwellings, and inherited social customs and traditions quite unlike those of the buffalo-hunters on the prairies, the natives in the Mackenzie River basin, or the visibly Mongoloid, highly artistic peoples on the Pacific coast who harpooned seals, sea lions, and sea otters in the ocean, and trapped the immense shoals of salmon that every summer fought their way up the swift rivers of British Columbia to spawning beds in streams and lakes at their headwaters.

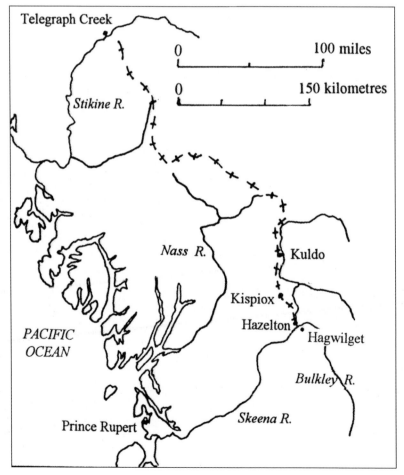

Map 7 Hazelton and adjacent communities, and the route of the Yukon Telegraph Line, Northern British Columbia, 1923–1924.

My duties at Ottawa's Victoria Memorial Museum demanded that I acquire a detailed knowledge of all the Canadian tribes between the Atlantic and the Pacific. By 1923, I had spent three years among the Eskimos of the Arctic, and one summer with a prairie tribe, the Sarcee.

For my next field trip, I chose a Rocky Mountain tribe, the Carrier, whose westernmost village at Hagwilget on the Bulkley River lay only four miles from Hazelton, the most northern British Columbia town then served by the government's transcontinental railway. Before the building of that railway, Hazelton had been the head of navigation on the Skeena River, and the hundred-mile stretch of country downstream to the sea was the still unchallenged domain of the Gitksan Indians, an offshoot of a coastal tribe which was slowly imposing its complex organization, its customs, and its religious beliefs on its less advanced neighbours at Hagwilget, although the latter spoke a language as unlike the Gitksan tongue as English or Japanese.

The two tribes frequently met at Hazelton which, in October 1923 when I stepped off the train there with my wife and two-year old son, counted a population of approximately three hundred whites and four hundred Indians. This population was enough to support two stores—one a fur-trading post of the Hudson's Bay Company, the other an independent enterprise—a tiny bank, a Methodist church, and a makeshift jail guarded by a lone policeman. There was also a small ramshackle hotel, which had survived the stirring days before 1911, the year in which the railway spiked its last rails and the paddle steamer ceased chugging defiantly up the Skeena to a dock hard by the river's confluence with its tributary, the Bulkley. Just beyond that dock, the Skeena bent sharply eastward, as if long centuries ago it had attempted to cut through the four hundred acres of flat land that were blocking its

Figure 20 Canyon of the Bulkley River near Hazelton, B.C. at low water in the autumn, 1923. The road over the bridge goes to Hagwilget village. At the foot of the cliff are Indian cabins for drying salmon and four totem poles.
Photo by D. Jenness, CMC 60589

union with the smaller river, but changed its mind and resumed its almost parallel course for another half mile. The Gitksan Indians then pre-empted the flat, and generation after generation of them levied a heavy toll on the salmon that migrated past its banks. You can still see traces of their main fishing site near the junction of the two rivers. Later came the invading whites, who constructed a road from their newly built railway to the settlement, dispossessed the Gitksan Indians of their flat land, and forced them to build new homes behind it on the side of a steep ridge, bisected diagonally by a dirt road to Hagwilget.

We deposited our bags in Hazelton's primitive hotel and endured that rat-infested shelter for five days, each day more convinced than ever that its Chinese proprietor was deliberately perverting the noble art of cooking to our discomfort. Desperate after one noon meal, we hired a horse and buggy and drove out to Hagwilget to reconnoitre the layout of its Indian village and assess the friendliness of its inhabitants. The road itself was lonely and uninteresting, without a house or other sign of life to break the monotony of the thin, second-growth woods of poplar and kindred scrub that lined its sides. When we reached the canyon of the Bulkley River, however, the scenery changed. The woods disappeared behind us, the landscape broadened, and a narrow, high-level bridge spanning a deep chasm invited us into a village where a score of frame dwellings, picturesquely scattered over a grassy terrace, faced the entrenched river and the western sun. None of the houses were painted. Two were unpretentious cottages, most of the others large, barn-like structures unrelieved except by two or three sash windows in each long wall and a rough platform instead of a veranda at the doorway end. Behind them stood the white church of a Roman Catholic mission, and on the left edge of the settlement, a one-roomed schoolhouse.

A woman dressed in black leisurely tended a small fire outside one of the dwellings, and a hundred yards away, an elderly man stood on the edge of the canyon, drinking in the warmth of the afternoon sun. They were the only persons in sight.

We pulled up beside the sun-worshipper and introduced ourselves. He informed us that two weeks earlier, all the active inhabitants of the village had departed for their hunting grounds around Eutsuk Lake seventy miles to the south, where they would be trapping beaver and other fur-bearing animals all winter. Only four men and about a dozen women and children remained in Hagwilget to guard the empty homes until their owners returned in March with the season's catch.

Old Felix   that was the name of our new acquaintance—spoke fluent English without undue regard for its grammar; and he became quite relaxed and communicative as we stood side-by-side on the cliff, gazing down at the river foaming under the bridge, the huge rocks that partly blocked its channel, and the row of four tall totem-poles planted like sentinels on a narrow ledge twenty feet above the water's autumn level.[2]

---

[2] This was my father's first encounter with totem poles, the unique, mystical, carving creations of some Pacific Coast Indians. During that winter he enquired about several totem poles, hoping that the museum in Ottawa might purchase one or more. The owner of a particularly good specimen at Skeena Crossing, fifteen miles from Hazelton, told him that he wanted $500 for his fifty- to sixty-foot long totem pole. My father passed the information along to his museum colleague, Marius Barbeau, who was the museum's authority on totem poles, but the museum was unable to pay that much. (Jenness to Barbeau, letter dated January 7, 1924, Barbeau Correspondence, Box 206, Folder 27, Archives, CMC.)

"A century ago," he mused, "more shoals of salmon than a man could count used to battle through this canyon every year and ascend the river another twenty miles to Moricetown. Then a terrible landslide filled the torrent's bed and barred their passage. Today the river has washed away most of the rocks, and the more vigorous fish occasionally work their way upstream, but very few shoals now turn aside from the Skeena River into the Bulkley, and their number seems to be growing smaller every year. You see that ledge with the line of totem poles? Standing there, our grandfathers used to trap and spear enough salmon to feed the entire village all winter, but today only the luckiest Indian can store away enough fish to last his family until Christmas."

The countryside was so peaceful, and the air so balmy that we chatted with Felix a full half-day.

"We are spending the winter in Hazelton," I told him, "and are looking for a suitable home. Your country and its people interest me greatly, not its whites alone but its Indians. You have lived here more than half a century and must have seen many changes. Will you tell me about them if I visit you a few days hence?"

He agreed without hesitation and pointed out his home, one of the large barn-like houses on the slope above. I then drove my family back to Hazelton, and two days later moved it from the hotel into a furnished cottage surrounded by a white picket fence. Its front gate looked across the street at the Methodist church, the community hall, and the trading store of the Hudson's Bay Company; its back gate opened on to the boulder beach of the Skeena River, whose rushing waters murmured day and night through every room of the house. We now possessed our own kitchen with a cast-iron, wood-burning stove, a modest dining room warmed by a small Quebec heater in the middle of the floor, and two front bedrooms, one on each side of a large hall furnished with a four-foot high barrel-stove, which our landlord guaranteed would keep the house comfortable all night long for the expenditure of two birch logs, even when the outdoor thermometer registered thirty degrees of frost. A government geologist and his young wife occupied a similar cottage next door to us, and beyond them, at the corner of the street, stood the little bank, staffed by a young bachelor, who slept on the premises to protect the district's wealth.

So we settled in and became semi-permanent residents of British Columbia's northernmost town. Four or five days weekly during the next three months I shuttled back and forth to Hagwilget astride a nervous bay horse, which shied and bolted every time a breath of wind or a partridge rattled the hard dry leaves in the woods at the roadside.[3] The first morning,

---

[3]Years ago my mother told me the following story about this nervous mare. Sometime during that winter, my father, mother, and their baby son went for a sleigh ride, possibly along the road to Hagwilget. All went well until a sudden noise frightened the mare, and it took off down the road at a speed that threatened the safety of them all. My mother was holding their well-bundled son tightly when this happened. My father immediately ordered her to throw their son into the snowbank, then jump after him. Meanwhile, he was tugging desperately on the reins trying to get the frightened mare to stop before the sleigh capsized and injured or killed them all. Without argument, my mother did as she was told. In quick succession the well-bundled child flew through the air and landed safely in the soft snow, followed immediately by my mother. Finding herself uninjured she hastily brushed herself off and retrieved her precious and unharmed offspring some yards back alongside the road. My father meanwhile struggled valiantly for several minutes before he was finally able to halt the horse and get it to calm down. He then turned the horse and sled around and returned to collect his two passengers. His quick thinking may have prevented a serious accident.

before I learned my steed's peculiar habit, it nearly entombed me in the leaves. Duty drove me from home about 8 a.m. and seldom allowed me to return until dusk.

Felix proved a veritable gold mine of information concerning his people, and my notebooks filled apace.

Winter's first frost touched us in November, when a white bonnet hid the summit of Rocher Deboulé, the argentiferous mountain fifteen miles south, which blinked at us each morning when we opened our front door. At Christmas, snow three inches deep carpeted the entire countryside, but at no time did the temperature drop below 10° Fahrenheit or the wind attain a velocity greater than ten miles an hour. Every day, or nearly every day, the sun shone brightly, the crisp, transparent air tingled the cheeks without freezing them, and the murmuring Skeena carried away every film of ice that threatened to delay its journey to the sea. Nature strove her utmost to give us a winter in paradise.

Alas, an Apple of Discord flourishes wherever human beings congregate. Like the population of certain islands in the West Indies, Hazelton's three hundred whites were graded. At the top floated an "upper ten" (the number fluctuated), led in 1923 by the wife of one of the two storekeepers. Local protocol ordained that this first lady of the town should delay her arrival at every party or function until all other guests had put in an appearance. Accordingly, one Saturday evening in late February, when my wife and I entertained all our white acquaintances in the community hall, the storekeeper's wife arrived in full regalia at 11:30 p.m., exactly one half-hour before the hall's puritan custodian preserved the holiness of Sunday by turning off all the lights.

At the bottom of Hazelton's social ladder stood the "dirty dozen," also a variable number which included our two best friends, Angus Beaton, a doughty Nova Scotia frontiersman, and his companion-in-arms George Beirnes, a veteran of the '98 gold rush to the Yukon, who had been stranded in Skagway at the time Soapy Smith and his gang of ruffians were terrorizing that half-way port. Beirnes had now purchased a ranch twenty-three miles north of Hazelton at the head of the Kispiox Valley, and was maintaining there a large train of pack horses to service the first nine stations on the Yukon Telegraph Line, which ran north through rugged, uninhabited country to Telegraph Creek on the Stikine River, thence to Whitehorse and Dawson in the Yukon. Once a fortnight throughout the winter, he would drive down to Hazelton to replenish his supplies; and on those occasions, he notified the townsfolk of his arrival, and at the same time saved his neck, by lashing a heavy log to the axle of his brakeless Model T Ford before committing the loudly complaining vehicle to the steep descent.

I cannot recall how we first became acquainted with these two men, but I well remember the first evening they spent at our house. We sat around the Quebec heater in the dining room, and for nearly an hour, our guests, embarrassed by the presence of my wife, shuffled uneasily in their chairs and replied to our remarks with monosyllables. By chance, I mentioned a hunting strategy practised by Arctic wolves. Angus stirred in his seat, pulled himself upright and, looking into the far distance, began to relate an experience of his own in the timberless Groundhog country between the Skeena and Stikine rivers, a virgin region abounding in grizzly bears, caribou, mountain sheep, and mountain goat, in which he had hunted and trapped alone for eleven months. He was crossing a series of ridges to reach his cabin, he said, and had stopped on a crest, as usual, to scan the landscape for game when he sighted below him, far to his left, a solitary wolf, which was scouring the slope of the ridge facing him. As he watched, four other wolves came into view, running in parallel courses up the valley bottom; and right under Angus's eyes the five animals, in crescent formation, swept the entire length of the valley and disappeared over the horizon. He saw no other game that day. Even the groundhogs had scented their enemies and prudently remained inside their burrows.

Angus's story struck a responsive chord in George Beirnes, and from that moment until past midnight our guests played off one tale against another, while my wife and I sat with eyes a-goggle. About 1 a.m., Angus mechanically pulled out his watch, gasped, and sprang to his feet like a startled hare, stammering an apology for the lateness of the hour. Beirnes jumped up likewise, and the two men fairly flew through the front door together. But they revisited us two weeks later and reminisced as before into the wee small hours of the morning.

The Indians lived in a world completely outside Hazelton's stratified white society. At the Methodist church, they sat on the left side of the aisle, and the whites sat on the right. My wife may have jeopardized her place in heaven during Christmas week by entering the church a few minutes late and slipping into a vacant seat on the Indian side. Etiquette permitted two whites, or two Indians, to walk side by side along the main street, but the Indian who accompanied a white man had to follow him like a dog. I sinned as grossly as my wife one morning by taking over the task of a sick Indian boy and guiding his blind old grandfather from his home on the ridge down to the one-room log cabin that I had leased as an office. Several Indians opened their doors as we passed and anxiously called to my companion "Where is the white man taking you, John? Is he taking you to the klink (jail)?" But Old John, having previously discovered my harmlessness, merely smiled and shook his head. As for Hazelton's shocked white community, it excused my unseemly conduct on the ground that I was an outsider from distant Ottawa, who had probably lacked any opportunity to learn good manners.

Yet Felix knew good manners. The old men of his tribe had taught him during his boyhood, when the only white man in this part of British Columbia was the factor of the Hudson's Bay Company. Like the Englishman of Chaucer's day, the Indians believed that Manners Makyth Man, and that good manners were inseparable from good morals. Lacking books or any knowledge of writing, they trained their children through folktales, related by the old men at bedtime in the big, pre-European, plank dwellings that housed from four to six families. And many of these folktales concluded with a moral.

Let us imagine ourselves back in the early years of the nineteenth century, living as guests of an Indian family on the banks of the Skeena River. All day long, our host's quarrelsome boy Wilat has been bullying little Satik, and no one has paid any attention, although Satik is a fatherless child whose mother is very poor and unhappy. Evening descends with its autumn chill and, retiring into our host's big house on the riverbank, we join his family around one of the half-dozen fires in the middle of the building and eat our dinner of boiled fish in his private cubicle. The hour grows late, and one inmate after another, tired from a day spent in fishing or hunting, stretches out on a rush-covered wooden platform in his doorless "apartment" and protects himself from the keen night air under a deerskin blanket.

From the back of the house rises the quiet voice of an old man reciting a tale of long-past days, when animals and men understood and respected one another more than they do now, and the unseen rulers of the sky and the thunder, of the trees and the waters, meted out rewards and punishments to the doers of good and evil. He recounts the misdeeds of the unsociable Destan, who supported himself and his family by robbing lone hunters of their hard-won booty, and a tense silence falls over the house as the story unfolds and approaches its dénouement. Of a sudden the old man pauses, then in a voice that echoes from the raftered roof he cries "Wilat, was it you who knocked down little Satik today?" The startled Wilat hangs his head and refuses to answer, but the old man repeats his question, and a babel of voices from all sides urges the boy to confess. The psychological pressure is tremendous; Wilat cannot help but yield. Then the old man quietly picks up the broken thread of his narrative and relates how the great sky-god Sa, who watches everything that happens in this world, endowed a poor abused orphan with magic strength and sent him forth to destroy the villain who preyed on his neighbours instead of helping them.

The Hagwilget Indians inculcated with their folktales the same virtues as we Europeans try to teach our children. First and foremost came loyalty to kith and kin, for when that lapses, society, whether human or animal, disintegrates. In common with every people that depends for its daily food on fishing and the chase, they placed a high value on courage, fortitude, and enterprise. In his younger days Felix had considered mere routine a caribou hunt which demanded two or three days of hard travel without food, often, too, without rest except when darkness drove him to stretch out on the bare ground and patiently await the return of daylight. Respect for the aged was another trait which the Hagwilgets shared with other Indians. Even the Eskimos of the Arctic clung until the last moment to the old and infirm who could no longer keep up with the wandering band, and only when relentless nature left no alternative did they abandon their helpless relatives to a lonely death.

Universal in Canada, too, was the obligation to care for widows and orphans, although so pliant is mankind everywhere that the Indians may have shirked this duty as frequently as the whites who have taken over their country. As far as my experience allowed me to judge, the Hagwilgets paid homage to the same high principles as whites, and observed them as much— and as little. For neither skin colour nor any other heritable trait which distinguishes one race from another influences man's moral nature. The chocolate-coloured New Guinea cannibal clad only in a G-string may conduct himself as nobly—or as basely—toward his fellow men as the white-skinned European who wears the robes of a nobleman.

Every human race, the American Indian no less than the African, looks back over thousands of years of history, during which Nature subjected it to special vicissitudes and demanded from it special adaptations. It should not surprise us, therefore, that in 1923, after less than a century's contact with white civilization, the Hagwilget and Hazelton Indians still interpreted the world around them differently from their white neighbours, and saw forces in nature, both good and evil, which were not visible to European eyes. Among them, Felix told me one morning, was a vague, formless, unseen force, *kyan*, which afflicts a man or woman with intermittent hysteria or dementia, accompanied at times by a craving for human flesh. For this mysterious malady, he said, Indian medicine men had devised a protracted but highly successful cure which allowed the patient to remain in his home and lead a normal life in the intervals between his paroxysms. But the Roman Catholic missionary had denounced their treatment as gross superstition, and white doctors who did not understand Indian psychology had despatched two Hagwilget patients to the mental hospital in New Westminster, where they died within a few months.

Yet under Indian care, Felix's own wife had recovered completely, as had also Old Sam, the Hagwilget's principal medicine man, who was now treating two women in the village. During the past week, the disease had attacked Old Sam's elderly wife. Paroxysms of hysteria were wracking her every day at sunset. Her husband had enrolled her with his other two patients and was applying group therapy to all three, but the noise of his drumming and singing had disturbed the village's white school teacher who—through a messenger, since he himself was afraid, or at least unwilling, to enter any Indian home—had peremptorily ordered the medicine man to "stop his humbug." Old Sam ignored the order, but then the man complained to the white policeman in Hazelton, and the Indians were afraid that the authorities might confine all three patients in the New Westminster hospital, whence they would never return. Old Sam therefore wanted me to observe their treatment, and to substantiate their protest that it was neither improper nor harmful.

At 6 p.m. that evening, the medicine man sent word that his wife was showing symptoms of disorder and that he would be treating her within the next half hour. Felix and I immediately went over to his house, accompanied by Mrs. Felix and her brother, who were to assist in the operation. We found the old woman lying on a pile of blankets against one wall of her living room, and in a corner, oblivious to everything around her, another old woman, blind and helpless, whose husband was dying in the district hospital. In the middle of the floor stood a camp stove under which someone had pushed an enamel basin half filled with water. Six kitchen chairs had been lined up against the wall facing Mrs. Old Sam. There was no other furniture.

Before we had time to sit down, a middle-aged Indian arrived with his wife. The latter, dressed in black, was one of the two patients Old Sam had been treating for several months. She at once pulled down the blind on every window, lit a hurricane lantern, and went to summon a third patient, a Hagwilget woman who had married a Chinaman and was living just over the boundary of the reserve. The two women entered together ten minutes later.

Excluding myself and the blind woman in the corner, there were now four men and four women in the room waiting to take part in the coming ritual. Mrs. Felix handed each of them a headband of red cedar bark, which she extracted from one of the corner chests, and then installed me on an end chair against the wall, with her husband beside me to interpret everything that happened. Next to him sat her brother, then the woman-in-black's husband, and finally Mrs. Felix herself. Old Sam pushed in front of them two long planks and four or five sticks, handed his tambourine to the woman-in-black's husband, and sat down on the remaining chair, a little aloof. All four women then removed their moccasins, and the three patients, shuffling out into the middle of the floor, sat one behind the other, Mrs. Old Sam in front and the Chinaman's wife in third place. Their heads drooped as in deep gloom, and at intervals they emitted whistling sounds and the long-drawn-out howls of far-off wolves, *hu-hu-hu*.

The stage was now set, the actors ready for their cue. Suddenly the air quivered with the shriek of a real whistle, blown doubtless by Old Sam, who began to chant one of his medicine songs while his assistants beat the tambourine and pounded the long planks with their sticks. The whistle, Felix shouted in my ear, had brought *kyan* into the room, the mystic force which was already tormenting the women and driving two of them to wave their arms and sway their bodies up and down, and from side to side, while sighing loudly *hu-hu-hu*. The Chinaman's wife reacted differently. Flinging her head toward the floor with a wild shriek, she alternately beat a tattoo with her hands on the bare boards and rhythmically clawed the air in front of her. Old Sam shouted his song again and again until it seemed never-ending, and the drum and planks intermittently swelled their thunder to augment the frenzy of the women on the floor. Several times, the Chinaman's wife raised her head, gazed at the singer in passionate adoration and tried to sing with him, but succeeded in uttering only shrieks, whistles, or haunting wolf-howls.

The din continued for a quarter of an hour. Then Old Sam broke off his first song and, with scarcely a pause, struck up a second, whose words Felix translated "A big beaver's nose goes inside the mountain," although he could not explain what they meant. The women resumed their frantic motions. They swayed their bodies, waved their arms, and began to execute a kind of squatting dance in front of the tambourine. Thereupon, Mrs. Felix dropped her stick and, dancing forward on her toes, pulled Mrs. Old Sam to her feet, braced her with one arm, and led her round and round the room in a slow, rhythmic dance, during which the older woman mechanically bobbed her head over a short wand held horizontally in both hands. The woman-in-black rose and danced behind her, flinging her own short wand now to one side, now to the other. And trailing behind danced the Chinaman's wife, her head bowed, her face concealed by her hair, and her hands waving gracefully to right and left alternately. As the women passed me, so close that I had to move back my chair, I could see their fingers quivering as with palsy, but the music seemed to be controlling them, for their feet and hands moved in perfect time with its beat.

Round and round the room they danced in an act that lasted nearly half an hour. Then at last Old Sam stopped singing, Mrs. Felix returned to her seat, and the three patients dropped to the floor, still breathing their wolf howls. But the medicine man allowed them little rest. Scarcely had his wife pushed back her hair and mechanically washed her hands in the basin of water beside the stove—to remove some of the invisible *kyan*, Felix said—than he began his third song, which provoked the squatting women to wave their arms and sway back and forth as before, but more languidly.

Two new songs, one after the other, Old Sam now turned on, so to speak, and the women swayed their arms and bodies, shuffled a little, but hardly moved from their places on the floor. At the sixth song, Mrs. Felix led them around the room in another dance. Standing in front of them like a band conductor, she waved her own arms to the beat of the music and forced the patients' feet to keep time with it. They were visibly tiring, but the treatment was taking effect. Even the Chinaman's wife seemed to be controlling herself, although every now and then she continued to breathe the wolf howl as though the mysterious force still lingered inside her. Only once more, therefore, did Old Sam make them dance, and when they finally sank to the floor he expelled all remaining traces of *kyan* by himself sighing *hu hu hu* into their ears and beating their chests and backs with a bundle of eagle feathers. A cloud then seemed to lift from their minds, leaving them fully normal but very weary, for their treatment had lasted more than two hours. The medicine man put away his planks and his tambourine, the women replaced the cedar-bark headbands in the chest, and all of us united in collecting from the floor the telltale wisps of eagle down. Then the woman-in-black revived the fire in the stove and refilled the kettle so that we might partake of a light supper before dispersing, and while we waited, the men gathered around me to enquire whether I did not judge their remedy for the "mountain sickness" both sensible and proper.[4] I told them that I could see nothing improper about it, but suggested that they muffle their tambourine a little and hold their sessions beyond the earshot of the querulous schoolteacher.

As I rode home that evening along the silent road to Hazelton, my thoughts revolved insistently around the drama I had just witnessed, and its significance to the Indians who had taken part in it. The malady from which the women suffered may have been purely psychological, but it was neither fictitious nor consciously self-induced. People who roam in wild and lonely places, whatever their race and upbringing, frequently hear strange noises which they can neither locate nor interpret, and when darkness descends, rocks and trees assume fantastic shapes which seem to appear and disappear at will. Can we wonder, then, that the Indians, believing as they did that our world is haunted by supernatural beings and mysterious forces which are continually obtruding in human affairs, sometimes experienced traumatic hallucinations that brought on periodic attacks of hysteria or paranoia, especially at the hour when daylight fades into night. The medicine man's remedy for the hysteria seemed equally intelligible. As a surgeon exposes a wound before he attempts to dress it, so, with his shrill whistle and deafening drum, Old Sam had deliberately provoked the women's paroxysms so that he might control them through the rhythms of music and dancing, whose discipline, his theory told him, maintained over many months, would ultimately remove or overcome the conditions that induced the illness. Relatives, convinced that the malady was temporary, contributed to the cure by refusing to isolate the victims, or impose any social restraints on them; instead, they maintained the patients' morale by encouraging them to continue their daily chores as if their paroxysms were no more serious than spells of coughing. And this treatment, Old Felix assured me, always succeeded.

The ancients Greeks, familiar with religious hysteria in the Dionysian and Orphic rituals, would have understood and approved the Indian remedy, for they too attributed great therapeutic value to music and dancing. But our medical profession today holds these agencies in little esteem. Is it so certain that large numbers of white mental patients would not benefit from them?

[*Around Christmas time, my father gave up the little office he had rented in Hagwilget, his work there done, and rented one in Hazelton, from which he continued his study of the local Aboriginals for a few more weeks. That January, a "grippe" epidemic swept through the district and my mother came down with it, requiring my father to take care of both her and their son. The combination of her illness, the unhappy behaviour of their son, who was suffering from teething discomfort, and a badly leaking roof on their rented house added to my father's problems. Fortunately he and son John were spared from coming down with the illness.*] [S.E.J.]

---

[4]This is probably a mythical use of the term "mountain sickness." The term today is customarily used for the feelings experienced by mountain climbers above an elevation of 10,000 feet because of the deficiency of oxygen. The Skeena valley in the Hazelton area is only about 900 feet above sea level, and the mountains on either side rise to elevations less than 6,000 feet.

1924:
TREKKING THE YUKON
TELEGRAPH LINE[1]

7

Diamond Jenness

By early February, my work at Hagwilget[2] had advanced so far that it seemed advisable to supplement it with studies in other Carrier Indian villages along the railway line east to Prince George, then in June to travel from that town down the Parsnip River and up the Findlay through the heartland of the Sekani Indians, the Carriers' northern neighbours. Winter, however, still gripped the countryside, and the cool, mild weather offered perfect conditions for a trip on snowshoes before spring burst in upon us at the end of the month.

So one evening, I slyly mentioned to Angus Beaton that I would like to see the country north of Hazelton and inspect the remains of Old Kuldo, a half-legendary Indian village that had been sacked and burned by its enemies around the middle of the nineteenth century.[3] The veteran frontiersman instantly rose to the bait and exclaimed, "I'll go with you. Tomorrow morning I'll arrange everything." And he did.

Here is the story of that trip.

In February 1924, I made a short trip of about eighty miles along this Telegraph Line on the upper waters of the Skeena River. My guide was a Scotch-Canadian, Angus Beaton, who had lived for twenty-five years in this region, trapping, hunting, and prospecting for the elusive gold mine. For four years, he had been an operator on the telegraph line itself, and he knew every telegraph station, or "cabin" as it is called, within a radius of two hundred miles. As most of our journey had to be made on snowshoes, packing what equipment we needed on our backs, he arranged with the operators along the line that we might sleep in their cabins and thereby reduce our outfits to a minimum.

Before many years, probably, the Canadian government will discontinue part of the famous telegraph line connecting British Columbia with the Yukon and replace it by wireless.[4] This

---

[1] This is a slightly modified version of an article entitled "The Yukon Telegraph Line," published by my father in the *Canadian Geographical Journal*, vol. 1, no. 8, pp. 695–705, 1930, and is reproduced here with the permission of the Directors of the Royal Canadian Geographical Society. In his manuscript, my father included this anecdote at the end of the previous chapter. I have made it a separate chapter.

[2] Discussed in Chapter 6.

[3] My father particularly wanted to examine old totem poles known to exist at Old Kuldo to see what condition they were in, for the Canadian government was contemplating a program of preservation and restoration of these unique objects. Towards that goal, it had established a Board of Preservation of Totem Poles. Harlan I. Smith, an archaeologist with the museum, would commence salvage and preservation work the next year.

[4] The federal government closed down the section between Hazelton and Telegraph Creek in 1936. [D.J.]

Figure 21 Typical winter scene on the Yukon Telegraph Line north of Hazelton, B.C., 1924. The telegrapher's backpack conceals the base of a broken-off telegraph pole. Photo by D. Jenness, CMC 60633

telegraph line, begun in 1899 and finished within three years, gave the rich gold fields around Dawson City their first all-the-year-round communication with the outside world, and its passing will end one of the first chapters in the development of that broad interior stretch of British Columbia which lies between the Rocky Mountains proper and the ranges that skirt the coast.

The telegraph line follows the Skeena River from the little town of Hazelton, on the Canadian National Railway, to Kispiox, an Indian village nine miles above, which at that time had two white residents, a missionary and his wife. The natives belong to the Gitksan tribe, which is closely allied in language and customs with the Tsimshian Indians around Prince Rupert, and their village has long been noted for its well-carved totem poles, though the number of these has been somewhat depleted of late years by the ravages of time and the demands of various museums. At Kispiox the Skeena River curves slightly to the eastward, and the telegraph line abandons it in favour of the Kispiox River, a small tributary coming in from the northwest. Twenty-two miles farther on, it abandons the Kispiox River, which now heads too far west, and strikes over the mountains to the Skeena again.

One cannot help thinking that the constructors of the line would have been wiser to keep to the Skeena the whole distance, even though the route is slightly longer, because the heavy snowfall in the mountains breaks down or uproots whole trees in the dense forests through which the line passes, and renders exceedingly difficult the keeping of unbroken communications.

In fact, between the beginning of November 1923 and my trip at the end of February 1924, only twenty telegrams had gone through to Dawson without long delays, owing to breakages of the line through windfalls. The wire itself is of No. 8 fencing, strung at an average of tweve feet above the ground on poles 225 feet apart—twenty-four poles to the mile. Here and there, tripods have replaced a fallen pole, which could not be re-erected by one or two men without proper tackle.

The cabins from Hazelton north are known by numbers—First, Second, etc.—and spaced about thirty-two miles apart. Each is occupied by two men, an operator and a linesman, who patrol the wire for sixteen miles both north and south, connecting with the operator or lineman of the next cabin at a "Half-Way" house, built of logs, and fitted with a stove, a table, bunks for two men and provisions sufficient to last four or five days. Since the heavy snowfall during the winter months (there is sometimes twelve feet of snow at the head of the Nass River) often makes it impossible for a man to travel the whole sixteen miles in one day, there are "Quarter-Way" cabins ("Quarter-Way North," "Quarter-Way South") between each "Cabin" and the "Half-Way," outfitted in the same manner as the "Half-Way," but smaller, and usually with one bunk only.

The telegraphers at these lonely cabins have no visitors except an occasional Indian or white trapper en route to his hunting grounds, and a summer pack-train that brings in their year's supplies. In the summer they overhaul their cabins and lay in a stock of firewood for the winter months.

When the snow comes, most of them set traps for fox and marten along their lines of patrol, for the country is rich in fur-bearing animals and a sixteen-mile jaunt, always along the same trail, becomes less monotonous when there is hope of picking up a $50 pelt. Each day for five minutes, the outside world comes near them, at 8 p.m., when an operator in Vancouver clicks over the wire [in Morse code] the headlines in the daily newspaper. Otherwise, the weeks creep wearily by without the sight of a new face or the sound of a new voice—with nothing to talk about except the weather, the condition of the trail, or the incidents of some magazine story read and re-read for the twentieth time. Pencil scrawls on the walls of the cabins testify to the dreary monotony. Some we read at the "Quarter-Way" house near Third Cabin run thus:

Snowbound, Dec. 9,10,11.
F.B.D.
This is a cold Point

Two cords of wood cut and stacked here

on 29th August, 1916
MX (Maxwell, the operator's name)

and, beneath a blackened smudge and blood-stains where a mouse had been shot with a .22 rifle:

This shot pulled off by Sniper Dowling.

Two men isolated together for twelve months cannot always endure each other's company, and at one cabin a lineman had moved out early in the winter and built for himself a separate hut several hundred yards away across a deep ravine.

The valley of the Kispiox River, north of Hazelton, is one of the beauty spots of British Columbia. It averages about a mile in width, being bounded on the west by the rugged Nass Mountains, and on the east by a lower range, some 4,000 feet high, that separates it from the

Skeena River Valley. The rough wagon road constructed by the government runs through avenues of poplar, cottonwood, birch, and spruce, with snow-clad peaks closing in the view. A few settlers, some of them Scandinavians, have taken up land and commenced farming, for the soil is fertile and the climate comparatively mild. But at the present time, the lack of markets close at hand, and the high cost of transportation by rail and boat to Vancouver, renders farming here hardly profitable.

My guide drew my attention to two historical buildings along the road. One was the "Dominion Post Office," five miles north of Kispiox village, opened some twenty years ago and now closed indefinitely. It was a tiny log cabin, about ten feet square and six feet high, with a slit in the door for the insertion of mail. It was surely one of the quaintest post offices in Canada.

Four miles beyond was the site of an ancient farm with the ruins of a church in the centre. Old-timers know it as "The Cock and Bull Ranch," and relate how a missionary arrived here many years ago to establish an Indian mission. His outfit comprised, among other things, a bull and a cow, a cock and a hen, and a cooking stove. To cross the river he made a raft, and placed his stove in the middle, with the cock and hen on top inside a wooden crate. He then attached the cow to the stove by a stout rope, leaving the bull to swim across unaided.

All went well until he reached mid-stream, when the raft struck a submerged crag and up-ended. The stove sank to the bottom, drowning the cow and the hen. The cock escaped from the crate and drifted ashore unharmed, and the bull crossed without misadventure. Supported by cock and bull, the missionary established a ranch and built a church, but soon he converted the church into a barn. A year or two later, his bishop arrived to inspect the new mission and opened the church door. Only one worshipper met his gaze—an angry bull.

Twenty-three miles from Hazelton, and only eight miles from First Cabin, where the telegraph line finally begins its ascent of the divide from the Kispiox to the Skeena River, lay the last inhabited and at the same time the largest ranch in the Kispiox Valley. It belonged to George Beirnes, who outfitted parties of hunters going north in quest of big game. For several years, he had held a contract from the Canadian Government to freight in supplies once a year to nine of the fourteen cabins that were strung out between Hazelton and Telegraph Creek, two hundred and fifty miles north on the Stikine River. The remaining five cabins were supplied from Telegraph Creek, since the country between Ninth and Tenth cabins is impassible for horses.

Beirnes maintained on his ranch nearly a hundred head of horses, for his pack train had to carry provisions, telegraph wire, and other articles sufficient to last the cabins until the following summer. He traveled north every August, making the three-hundred-mile journey in regular stages from one camping ground to another. These camping grounds could be distinguished by the blazes on the trees, such as the one we observed between First and Second Cabins inscribed:

August 4, 1923
Hamhlock [hemlock] Camp
Packtrain camp here going up to the 9th Cabin
Forte Grou-n [writer's name?]

They are not the only marks along the line. Some of the prospectors who selected this route to the Yukon during the Gold Rush of '98 also left their blazes, most of them as unintelligible as the one near Second Cabin which reads:

H M H
K
I A

Then there are blazes made by Indians, for in this area a face formed by cutting two notches for the eyes and a notch below for the mouth is the characteristic sign of an Indian camp.

At First Cabin, the end of the wagon road, we put on our snowshoes and followed the telegraph line over the divide to the Skeena River Valley. The trail led us through a dense forest of poplar, birch, cottonwood, and spruce, with a sprinkling of jack pine, hemlock, and balsam, but as we climbed higher and higher, the poplar and cottonwood disappeared, balsam and hemlock became more frequent, and cedar made its appearance.

Balsam seems to ascend higher than any other tree in the mountains of this district; hemlock and larch survive a little lower down; then comes spruce, and finally toward the valley levels, birch, cottonwood, and other trees. The divide between the Kispiox and the Skeena rivers is about 1,800 feet above the level of each river, and the Half-Way house between First and Second Cabins, where we spent the night, three hundred feet lower. In its vicinity are many lagoons, all except the very smallest well stocked with trout, and all draining into Salmon Creek, which in turn empties into the Kispiox River.

Four miles beyond the Half-Way is Boneyard Camp, a boggy beaver meadow strewn with the bones of horses and mules shot here in the early winter of 1901. That was the year when the line running south from Dawson was spliced to the line running north from Ashcroft, thus establishing continuous communication from the south of British Columbia to the Yukon. The construction party continued its operations late into the fall to avoid carrying over the work into another field season. By that time, however, nearly all the pack horses and mules were played out or had lost their shoes. New shoes ordered up from Hazelton failed to arrive and many of the animals had to be shot before the party reached Second Cabin on its way out. The surviving twenty-three horses floundered through the snow as far as Boneyard Camp, only to collapse in a heavy snowstorm. Not one succeeded in gaining the valley of the Kispiox River, although all the men of the party reached Hazelton without mishap.

Dropping down into the valley of the Upper Skeena through the snow-laden firs that flanked each side of the telegraph line like palisades of Christmas trees, we skirted the west bank of the half-frozen river up to Second Cabin and later pushed on to Old Kuldo, a deserted Indian village eleven miles farther north. On the opposite bank rose the last ridge of the Atna Mountains, covered with heavy stands of timber not yet despoiled by the lumberman's axe. A constant snowfall kept most of the game under cover, but, even during our hurried progress, we repeatedly crossed the tracks of coyotes and foxes, and in one place saw where a fisher had been chasing a rabbit.

Foxes are very plentiful in this district, marten and wolverine by no means rare, and beaver dams common on the many small streams. Both black and grizzly bears abound during the summer months, when the ground is black with fallen huckleberries, and every summer, one or more mountain goats are shot between Second and Third Cabins, although their real home is with the mountain sheep on the Atna Mountains. Moose seem to be increasing in number every year, and a few miles to the northward roam enough caribou to content the most insatiate hunter. Altogether, this is one of the richest hunting and trapping grounds in the whole of British Columbia.

The deserted village of Old Kuldo, which was the goal of our trip, has an interesting history. During the first half of the nineteenth century, and probably for generations before that time, it was an intermediate station on a native trading route that led from the mouth of the Nass River to Kisgegas, a village on the Babine River that flows out of Babine Lake.

The Indians from the mouth of the Nass carried overland boxes of grease from the *oolaken* or candlefish, a near relative of the Newfoundland capelin, but so much richer in oil that when dried it burns like a taper. The grease that dripped from the boxes saturated the leaves and tree-trunks along the trail (whence it became known as the "Grease Trail"), but whatever survived the journey brought a rich reward in furs from the interior Indians, who used it as a condiment with their meat.

The people of Kuldo tried to levy tribute on the traders who passed their doors, and aroused so much ill will that the Nass Indians attacked their village. Some of the inhabitants perished in the burning houses; others were forced to leap over a high cliff to the rocky bed of the Skeena. The few who escaped the massacre sought refuge with their kinsmen in Kispiox and Hazelton. Today, their descendants have built two or three new houses on the site of the old settlement, and half a dozen more at New Kuldo, overlooking the Skeena seven miles farther south, which they occupy only during the summer months.

Old Kuldo itself still preserves some traces of its past history. One must still walk carefully there on account of the numerous holes in the ground, some of them merely pits for storing salmon, others, much larger, places of refuge where the women and children concealed themselves from their enemies. There is a canal about a quarter of a mile long—the only canal, perhaps, ever dug by Canadian Indians on their own initiative—which diverted the water of False Creek three hundred yards out of its course to bring it nearer to the Indians' doors. And in addition to two small totem poles that retain their upright positions, there is a well-carved, forty-foot specimen rotting to pieces on the ground.

A few trees in the vicinity, it is said, retain the marks of stone axes, indicating how recent has been the introduction of civilization into this corner of British Columbia.

[*Early in March my father bid farewell to his friends in Hagwilget and Hazelton and took his wife and son to Prince Rupert and then to Vancouver, which they reached on March 9. There he was provided with an office in the Vancouver section of the Geological Survey of Canada to continue his aboriginal studies. Each afternoon until the end of the month, he worked in this office with a Kaska Indian from Dease Lake, a Mrs. Arnot, who was then living in the Vancouver area. She was fluently bilingual and thus an immense help to him working over the Carrier Indian vocabulary he had compiled in Hazelton, but to his disappointment she was not familiar with the old customs of her people. Around the end of the month, when his wife had finally recovered from the flu she had caught in Hazelton, she and son John headed east to Ottawa by train.*

My father then spent a week in Seattle working with a group of Alaskan Eskimos who were receiving training from the Alaska Bureau of Education. With one of them he checked the vocabulary of Barrow words he had compiled while on the Canadian Arctic Expedition, and with another he compiled a parallel vocabulary of several hundred Cape Prince of Wales words. The training in phonetics he had been given by Dr. Sapir proved most helpful, as his university courses had not included linguistics.

Returning to Vancouver, he proceeded by steamer north to Prince Rupert and then inland to Prince George. From there he visited Carrier Indians at Fraser Lake and the Stony Creek Reserve for about two weeks, where he took anthropometric measurements and obtained specimens for the museum. By pre-arrangement, a former overseas wartime friend, F. Salter, joined him at Prince George to serve as his cook and assistant. Salter was at the time an English instructor at the University of Alberta. Together they journeyed to Fort McLeod by way of Summit Lake and the Crooked River in May, utilizing the scows of the Hudson's Bay Company for transportation. At Fort McLeod, my father studied a considerable number of Sekani Indians, whose culture was quite different from that of the Carrier Indians. To his disappointment, however, much of their culture had been forgotten or lost through contact with the white man. From there, my father and Salter used Hudson's Bay Company transportation to proceed down the Parsnip River and up the Findlay River to Fort Grahame, in order to visit another band of Sekani Indians. They then travelled by canoe downriver, visiting members of the Beaver Indians at Hudson Hope before Salter returned to Edmonton and my father returned to Ottawa early in July. My father's trip had been an ambitious undertaking, but was completed without mishap, and he obtained much information on five separate bands for his Indian studies.

My father's compilation of Carrier Indian myths was published in an American journal ten years later (Jenness, 1934).] [S.E.J.]

1925–1926:
A FRIENDSHIP LOST

8

Stuart E. Jenness

In the spring of 1925, Dr. Edward Sapir decided to relinquish his position as Chief of the Division of Anthropology at the National Museum of Canada to become Associate Professor of Anthropology and Amerindian Linguistics at the University of Chicago. Under his direction, the anthropology division had expanded rapidly following its creation in 1910, so that by 1914 it included six anthropologists (Edward Sapir, Marius Barbeau, Diamond Jenness, Francis H.S. Knowles, J.A. Tait, and F.W. Waugh) and two archaeologists (Harlan I. Smith and J.W. Wintemberg). By the summer of 1925, four of these men (Sapir, Knowles, Tait, and Waugh) had departed for various reasons, but J. Douglas Leechman had been added as a museum preparator in 1923. At the start of 1926, the division contained only Barbeau, Jenness, Leechman, Smith, and Wintemberg.[1]

Sapir was entitled to leave with pay when he moved to Chicago early in September, which kept him on the government's books until November 23 and prevented his position from being advertised or filled before that date. Senior government appointments in the 1920s were customarily made by promotion from within departments. At that time only three members of the anthropology division qualified as candidates for Sapir's position: Marius Barbeau (on staff since early in 1911), Harlan I. Smith (on staff since 1912), and my father (on staff since 1913, although only as a temporary employee before 1920).[2] If none of these three would take the position, or if none was considered sufficiently qualified, the departmental administrators would have to look elsewhere. That would prove time-consuming, for candidates would have to be sought in the United States or Great Britain, there being no departments at any Canadian universities then graduating students in anthropology.[3] Meanwhile, someone must attend to the division's routine day-to-day activities until the new division chief was appointed.

My father was the division's only professional anthropologist in Ottawa when Sapir left, as both Barbeau and Smith were away on fieldwork. The museum's Acting Director, L.L. Bolton, therefore asked my father to serve as *chief pro tem* and take care of the division chief's day-to-day duties until the new chief was appointed. Father agreed, but only after Bolton accepted his two conditions: (1) that he (my father) would only have to carry out the temporary duties until the end of November, by which time Barbeau and Smith would have

---

[1] Smith retired in 1936, Wintemberg in 1940.

[2] The other active field man in the anthropology division at that time, William John Wintemberg (1876–1941), had carried out valuable archaeological field work but was largely self-educated, and thus inadequately qualified academically, so was not considered a candidate.

[3] T.F. McIlwraith taught the first undergraduate courses in anthropology in Canada in 1925 at the University of Toronto.

returned, and one of them could take over the duties; and (2) that Bolton would not consider my father in the running for Chief of the Division unless both Barbeau and Smith had turned it down.

My father mentioned this agreement in a letter early in October to Barbeau, explaining his reason for insisting on the second condition thus: "... if I took the position over your heads I should feel that I had stabbed two of my best friends in the back."[4] He then added the comment, "I don't think any of us cares for the position very much as a matter of fact; I certainly do not." Since he was the most junior member of the three candidates, salary-wise, position-wise, and in years of service, he took for granted that either Barbeau or Smith would be offered the position, but even before that had happened, that one of them would relieve him of his Acting-Chief duties on their return to Ottawa.

Sapir was carrying out some research in the eastern United States when he decided to resign his position at the museum and move to Chicago. From Boston on June 25, he wrote confidentially of his pending departure to Smith, who was doing field work that summer in the Hazelton area of British Columbia. His letter no longer exists, but from Smith's reply we can conclude that Sapir indicated he would prefer having Smith replace him as chief and hoped Smith would consider taking the position if it was offered to him. Smith's reply, dated June 29 and sent to Sapir care of the Department of Anthropology at Columbia University, professed his misgivings about being placed in charge of the division, his preference for working in the field, especially in the west, his long-held belief that if Dr. Sapir left the museum Barbeau would be his logical successor, and his surprise that Sapir "would prefer me in charge to men both of us I believe consider much better educated."[5] He did not mention Jenness by name in his letter.

In a second exchange late in July, Smith assured Sapir that he would not mention the latter's departure to anyone,[6] which Sapir had evidently requested. Smith then thanked Sapir for wanting him to be his successor, but added that he would probably not be offered the position. Again he refrained from mentioning Jenness.

Just why Sapir sounded out Smith secretly like this is something of a mystery. Smith was a capable archaeologist, but, by his own admission, was ill-suited for the job for a number of reasons: he regarded both Barbeau and my father as better educated than himself; he was already "an old man" (he was fifty-three years old, eleven years older than Barbeau and fourteen years older than my father, with life expectancy for men at that time of less than sixty years); and he was miserable and unhealthy when he was confined to desk work in Ottawa, and dreaded rows, debates, or arguments. Smith, like Sapir a protégé of Franz Boas, was also an American, which could have made approval of his appointment by the government's Civil Service Commission difficult when a Canadian-born candidate, Barbeau, was available. In September 1910, when Sapir was appointed, his American citizenship was not a problem because there had been no qualified Canadian-born anthropologists. One cannot help but wonder if Barbeau might have been appointed the National Museum's first anthropology chief if he had hastened

---

[4]Jenness to Barbeau, letter dated October 7, 1925, Jenness Correspondence, Box 206, Folder 28, Archives, CMC.
[5]Smith to Sapir, letter dated June 29, 1925, Sapir Correspondence, Box 633, Folder 41, Archives, CMC.
[6]Smith to Sapir, letter dated July 25, 1925, Sapir Correspondence, Box 633, Folder 41, Archives, CMC.

back to Canada following his graduation in the spring of 1910 instead of touring about Europe for the summer.

Might Sapir have thought it preferable to sacrifice Smith to the time-consuming duties of the division chief's position for the next few years in order to keep the two younger men, Barbeau and Jenness, actively pursuing their field work and research? Or was he simply probing to determine Smith's interest in the position? We can only speculate what his reasons were for contacting Smith, because he left no written explanation. Also, it is not known if either Jenness or Barbeau ever learned about the exchange of confidential letters between Sapir and Smith. In any case, shortly after that exchange, Sapir returned to Ottawa and in due course informed Bolton that the choice was most probably between Jenness and Barbeau.

As November approached, Bolton was faced with a strange and difficult problem: whom to recommend to the Deputy Minister as the candidate to replace Sapir. Having done his homework, he knew of the respective qualifications of Smith, Barbeau, and Jenness, and had Sapir's views on all three men. He also had solicited by mail Barbeau's views on the vacated position, had Smith's views either through correspondence or from discussions with Sapir, and had my father's views by direct conversation. Therein lay his problem. None of his three candidates had expressed any desire to be offered the appointment.[7] In fact, all three of them seemed to be doing their utmost to avoid being appointed, hoping one of the other two would take on the unwanted administrative responsibilities.

On October 7, my father wrote a personal letter to Barbeau, who was still busy collecting French-Canadian folks songs on the Ile d'Orléans, near Quebec City, telling him about the difficulties the administrative officers were having in deciding whom to appoint as Sapir's successor. Having for years been perfectly open with Barbeau, my father mentioned in this letter that Sapir had informed him, before moving to Chicago, that he had told Bolton he favoured my father for the position if seniority was not the deciding factor in the appointment. In addition, if my father were selected, Sapir would recommend Smith being put in charge of exhibits. My father had replied to Sapir that even if he were offered the appointment, he would not take it unless both Barbeau and Smith had refused it.[8] This information, too, he mentioned to Barbeau.

It is easy to imagine some of Sapir's reasoning here. Barbeau had been an ongoing problem to him because of his unwillingness to conform to departmental policies and directions. Barbeau had definite ideas about what he wanted to do and how and when to do them, which was often a valuable asset but one that was better suited for the more liberal academic world than for the strait-laced federal government of the day. Federal government anthropologists were "constrained by the Division's official scientific and educational mandate to document and preserve evidence of indigenous (i.e. unacculturated) native cultures, and by the vagaries of what sitting politicians considered in the public interest."[9] Unfortunately for Barbeau, there

---

[7] So stated by the Honourable Charles Stewart, Minister of Mines, to the Honourable Rodolphe Lemieux, Speaker of the House of Commons, in a letter dated December 18, 1925, Barbeau Collection, Box 213, Folder 65, Archives, CMC.

[8] Jenness to Barbeau, letter dated October 7, 1925, Jenness Correspondence, Box 206, Folder 28, Archives, CMC.

[9] Richling, 1995a, p. 52.

were no anthropology departments at any Canadian universities at that time. Whoever became chief of the division, if not Barbeau, would likely encounter the same problems Sapir had had with him. Sapir evidently felt that Barbeau's work habits and interests rendered him less adaptable to the administrative demands of the division chief than either Smith or my father. If my father were appointed to the position, however, perhaps his friendship with Barbeau would lessen the risk of the sort of friction between them that Sapir had experienced.

On October 8, my father again wrote to Barbeau, more confidentially this time, alerting him that Bolton was much annoyed by Barbeau's apparent inability to apportion his field-money allotment. Barbeau had a habit of requesting additional money during the field season to purchase special collections of French-Canadian artifacts he had come across or to extend his field season. In this letter, my father also alerted Barbeau that Bolton had remarked that Barbeau's French-Canadian studies were not part of the Native peoples' studies the Anthropology Division was authorized to undertake. By spending taxpayers' money and official time doing fieldwork that was not within his official instructions, Barbeau was putting himself in a position to be disciplined. "You can read between the lines as well as I [can]," my father warned him. Then he added:

> I don't know whether anything is being done, or planned, regarding a successor to Sapir, beyond what I told you in my letter, and what you write to me about Bolton's request for your ideas on the subject. But I do know that it ought to be either you or Smith, and I will be loyal to whichever one of you is appointed. It will be a rotten job for whoever gets it; I find that trifling routine matters even now take up to 3/4 of my time, and I can give very little time to my scientific work. I certainly don't want it myself, and don't want to be taken into consideration at all in connection with it. I am younger than you both, and your junior, and in many ways, I think, less competent. All I hope is that the matter can be settled without friction. I'd rather have you my friend, as now, and Smith, than be Director of the Museum or Deputy Minister.[10]

My father then added his own views on the position, "I am not finding this business of Acting Chief any pleasure, and the sooner you can get back and take my place, or Smith, the happier I shall be."

I believe we have here a clear statement of how my father truly felt about the division-chief's role: serving in that capacity had been for him a total frustration because of the amount of time he had to spend attending to divisional matters. In less than two months as acting-chief, he had become completely disenchanted with the daily tasks he had been required to do, many of which he considered trivial and even time-wasting, and was eager to return to his own research. He felt safe to voice such feelings in his letters to Barbeau because of the close friendship he believed they shared and because he had no expectations of being selected to replace Sapir. As a close friend, however, he wanted to alert Barbeau to the feelings he could expect when he (Barbeau) was selected, as I am certain my father believed he would be.

---

[10]Jenness to Barbeau, letter dated October 8, 1925, Jenness Correspondence, Box 206, Folder 28, Archives, CMC.

If my father were alive today, I suspect he would have disapproved of my discussing this subject any further, since airing "dirty laundry" was an activity for which he had little use. But today we live in a much more open world than the post-Victorian world of my parents. Many subjects that one would not dream of discussing during the first half of the twentieth century are now commonplace. What has prompted me to pursue this subject here was the implication, given in a biography of Barbeau published by Laurence Nowry in 1995, that my father deliberately deceived Barbeau on the matter of Sapir's job in order to obtain the job for himself. Knowing my father as I have, I regard Nowry's implication as both highly offensive and totally inaccurate. I therefore consider it essential to offer a different interpretation of my father's role in the Jenness-Barbeau relationship than that presented in Nowry's book.

Two statements in particular in Nowry's book gave me the impression that he thought that my father had deliberately deceived Barbeau. The first is in connection with his discussion about several letters my father wrote Barbeau in the fall of 1925, the last two of which I have already mentioned. Nowry wrote "Neither [Jenness nor Barbeau] wanted the administrative burdens. Or so Jenness said and at length, in three letters to his friend [Barbeau]...." [11] A few paragraphs farther along in his book, Nowry quoted the following passage from my father's October 8 letter, "Whatever happens, I shall be happy whichever is appointed, and shall be a loyal friend and assistant to you both." My father here is referring to both Barbeau and Smith, one or other of whom he expected to become the new division chief. It is, I believe, an honest statement of exactly how he felt. Nowry, however, obviously questioned the honesty of the statement, for he added after the quoted sentence the single word, "*INDEED!*" in italicized capital letters to emphasize his disbelief.

It was Barbeau who finally revealed details of his shattered friendship with Jenness, speaking of the incident to ethnologist Carmen Roy in 1957, while the latter was tape-recording Barbeau's memoirs.[12] Insofar as I am aware, these unpublished memoirs are the original source on the subject, and probably the only one, for my father would not have talked or written about the wretched affair, and I would be surprised if Barbeau had done so other than during his taped reminiscing. In his memoirs, Barbeau recalled his sudden angry outburst in my father's office on a morning in [April] 1926 (thirty-one years earlier). Since that day, he had deliberately avoided all further contact and cooperation with my father, and was unwilling to speak to him except when absolutely necessary, although their offices were separated only by the room housing the divisional secretary.

Barbeau's biographer, Laurence Nowry, had been interested from 1950 in Barbeau's work with totem poles of the North Pacific Coast, Haida myths, and folk music of eastern Canada.

---

[11]Nowry, 1995, pp. 264–265.

[12]Barbeau reminisced to Carmen Roy about his early days at the National Museum and his work over the years. He spoke in English for parts of the many tapes he recorded, in French when he described his work in French Canada. Two typescripts were then created from the tapes, one comprising the parts of the tapes spoken in English, the other comprising the parts spoken in French. The English transcript was subsequently translated into French and added to the French transcript. The French transcript was not translated into English. Thus only the French memoirs are complete. The passages from Barbeau's memoirs quoted in this chapter are from the English transcript, which Barbeau had taped in English. The memoirs, unpublished, are in the Carmen Roy Collection, Box 622, Archives, CMC.

The two men finally met, and early in 1965, Nowry dined and conversed with Barbeau, then collaborated with him in tape-recording some of his reminiscences, especially about his French-Canadian studies. These reminiscences add to those recorded in 1957 by Dr. Roy. In this way Nowry became well acquainted with both Barbeau and his work. To my knowledge he never met my father, however, nor did he approach any of the Jenness family for information about my father. And he did not have a comparable interest in my father's work. His understanding of my father and his character was thus very limited.[13]

Nowry drew upon Barbeau's 1957 memoirs when he prepared his biography of Barbeau, as well as upon the tapes he had made of Barbeau reminiscing in 1965. Nowry's account of the circumstances leading up to Barbeau's explosive confrontation with my father is as Barbeau had recorded them, but I take strong exception to his intimation that my father deliberately deceived Barbeau in order to obtain the appointment for himself.

To counter the picture presented by Nowry, I have chosen now to discuss the relationship of the two men in considerably more detail than has heretofore been published. In this way, interested parties will have two interpretations and thus the opportunity to form a more balanced understanding of the whole unfortunate affair.

My father's friendship with Barbeau commenced in the fall of 1908 when the two men met at Oxford University shortly after my father's arrival from New Zealand. Barbeau was then in his second year. He and an American student, Wilson Wallis, who like Barbeau was a Rhodes Scholar, persuaded my father to join them in a class on Social Anthropology given by R.R Marett, a kindly scholarly individual originally from the Island of Jersey in the English Channel. Marett was of Norman-French ancestry, as was Barbeau, and in fact looked a little like Barbeau, as Barbeau observed, although Marett was slightly taller.[14] The friendship between Barbeau and my father blossomed as they took Marett's course and other anthropology courses together during the next two years.

After Barbeau graduated in 1910, they kept in touch by mail until their paths crossed again in the fall of 1916. In the interim, Barbeau had joined the Victoria Memorial Museum in January 1911 to work for Dr. Sapir, while my father had completed another year at Oxford to obtain his B.A. in Classics, followed by a year of ethnological fieldwork in Papua-New Guinea, and three years studying the Eskimos in the Arctic. They again corresponded between 1917 and 1919 while my father was overseas with the army, and between 1920 and 1925 when one or the other was conducting fieldwork away from Ottawa.

Barbeau saved my father's letters during those years,[15] for he was the kind of person who saved almost everything, to the great joy today of interested researchers. My father, on the

---

[13]Nowry, L., 1995, pp. 264–265.

[14]Barbeau was only five feet five inches tall, the same as Jenness. Marett was particularly interested years later when Barbeau wrote him about the number of people he had encountered in Canada's Gaspé region whose ancestors had come from Jersey. Marett occasionally spoke Norman French with Barbeau, which the latter considered funny and called a "patois." (Marius Barbeau interviewed by L. Nowry at the National Museum of Canada, 1965. Transcribed by R. Landry, 1982. Collection Radio-Canada RC 166(1), Coll. Acq. 2002-10030, Box I-122, p. 5, CMC.

[15]Jenness' letters to Barbeau are in the Barbeau Collection, Box 206, Folder 27, Archives, CMC.

other hand, regrettably saved none of Barbeau's letters,[16] for unlike Barbeau, he was not a "saver." Each went about achieving his goals differently, but both men were intensely keen about their work in the emerging field of anthropology, and encouraged the other (prior to 1926) in a variety of ways. The warmth and depth of my father's feelings towards Barbeau are readily apparent in almost all of the letters he wrote him between 1911 and 1925: letters from Papua (1911–1912), from the Arctic (1913–1916), from France during the First World War (1917–1918), and thereafter until the autumn of 1925.

My father's trait of saving little to nothing, apart from a few scholarly books and journals, may have been the result of early home training, or possibly it developed as a result of his years of near-spartan living at Oxford, in Papua, in the Arctic, and during the First World War. The result is that virtually all that remains is his official correspondence, dutifully saved by his various secretaries at the National Museum of Canada commencing late in 1925 after his appointment as division chief.

As Barbeau's early letters to my father no longer exist, one has to interpret his feelings towards my father from his actions, as mentioned in some of my father's responses. From these I have concluded that while he liked my father sufficiently to share a lot of ideas and time with him in those earlier days, he did not share the depth of friendship my father felt towards him.

My father trusted and admired Barbeau completely in those pre-1926 years. When he went overseas with the Canadian Expeditionary Forces in 1917, for example, he asked Barbeau to take care of his small amount of personal belongings and, more importantly, of his banking affairs. Somewhat later, he even asked Barbeau to look after his fiancée, Eilleen Bleakney. From his letters to Barbeau, we gather that my father and Eilleen socialized with Barbeau and his wife Marie Ernestine on several occasions during the months before my father went overseas. Not only did the two men enjoy each other's company in those days, according to those letters, but the two women developed a warm bond of friendship as well.

After my parent's wedding on April 30, 1919, they and the Barbeau's continued to exchange visits to each other's dwellings as well as letters when one or other was out of town. Jenness' letters generally included greetings to Mrs. Barbeau and her new daughter (after 1921 her two daughters). A postscript my father added in a letter to Barbeau in 1920 is particularly revealing. After mentioning that his wife Eilleen was seven-months pregnant, my father added half-jokingly, "I have decided that it will be a boy, so the two ladies can arrange for a wedding some 25 years hence!"[17] Alas, no wedding was ever to be.[18]

---

[16]Jenness' official correspondence was saved following his appointment as Division Chief in 1926, but that was largely after Barbeau ended their friendship, so includes only a few inconsequential notes from Barbeau. Jenness Correspondence, Box 206, Folder 28, Archives, CMC.

[17]Jenness to Barbeau, letters dated September 13, 1920, Barbeau Collection, Box 206, Folder 27, Archives, CMC.

[18]The baby was a girl, tragically stillborn according to my father, and the doctors offered no explanation (Jenness to Barbeau, letter dated November 18, 1920, Barbeau Collection, Box 206, Folder 27, Archives, CMC). Years later, mother informed me that the baby actually lived for three days, and that its loss had been extremely distressing to her. The unnamed infant girl was buried in the Bleakney family plot at Beechwood Cemetery, Ottawa.

The financially better-off Barbeau lent my father money on at least two occasions when there was a need: once, in 1920, to cover unexpected expenses when my father decided to buy his first house,[19] and again in the summer of 1925, to cover unforeseen emergencies when my birth was imminent. On neither occasion did my father have to use the money, however. He returned the first cheque, thanking Barbeau for his kindness and foresight, adding, "A man has not many friends in this world who would do the same."[20] He tore up the second cheque rather than mail it back to Barbeau, who was out-of-town, but wrote him of his action, promising, "Some day, I hope we shall be able to offer you help as you have us, and I know that you will not hesitate to ask any time you need it."[21] The amount borrowed in each instance was in the neighbourhood of $200, seemingly small by today's reckoning, but equivalent to about one month of my father's salary at that time.

And just as Barbeau offered help financially to my father, so my father, too, helped Barbeau from time to time, but with deeds. During Barbeau's many absences from Ottawa on fieldwork in the early 1920s, generally with his family in tow, my father regularly and voluntarily checked Barbeau's residence to ensure that it was without damage from fire, water, vandalism, or even moths.[22] And during the severe coal shortage in the summer of 1922, a shortage caused by a coal miners' strike in the United States, my father visited many local coal dealers around town in order to ensure that Barbeau received a sufficient supply of the scarce fuel for at least the first part of the winter, even at the risk of being short on his own supply.[23] Additionally, he regularly shared with Barbeau ethnographic information he had gathered in the field, some of which he collected specifically for Barbeau, and he voluntarily edited more than one of Barbeau's non-government manuscripts to improve their English before Barbeau sent them off to a publisher. When Barbeau was in the field and my father remained in Ottawa, the latter regularly sent Barbeau items he requested, and wrote accompanying notes saying how much he looked forward to his return from the field and to evenings chatting in front of the fireplace or to sharing picnics again with the Barbeau family. When Barbeau established a Canadian branch of the American Folklore Society, both my father and my mother became members, the former helping Barbeau by serving for some years as treasurer. No records exist about their conversations during visits to each other's offices or residences, of course, but one can be certain that there was much exchange of stimulating ideas between the two scholars.

---

[19]Jenness to Barbeau, letter dated October 6, 1920, Barbeau Collection, Box 206, Folder 27, Archives, CMC.

[20]Jenness to Barbeau, letter dated August 24, 1925, Barbeau Collection, Box 206, Folder 27, Archives, CMC.

[21]Jenness to Barbeau, letter dated October 7, 1925, Barbeau Collection, Box 206, Folder 28, Archives, CMC. Although written on museum letterhead, I suspect that this letter was typed by my father (it has a few typographical imperfections and no secretarial initials) because of its personal content and therefore probably did not have a carbon copy for filing.

[22]Moths were a common household worry in those days, when wool was far more widely used than it is today. My father killed several moths at Barbeau's house while checking it one day in the latter's absence (Jenness to Barbeau, letter dated August 3, 1922, Barbeau Collection, Box 206, Folder 27, Archives, CMC).

[23]Jenness to Barbeau, letters dated August 3, 1922, and September 29, 1922, Barbeau Collection, Box 206, Folder 27, Archives, CMC.

With their shared university experiences, anthropological interests, enjoyment of philosophical discourse, and the friendship of their two wives, it is safe to say that up to the end of October 1925, my father and Barbeau were good friends, perhaps even very good friends. And judging by how few other men my father saw regularly and knew well in those days, I think it safe to conclude that he regarded Barbeau as his best friend. Working in offices that were virtually next door to each other, sharing ideas and interests, my father and Barbeau had the potential for collectively bringing much fame to the museum during their lifetimes.

The two men, however, differed considerably from each other. My father was three years younger than Barbeau and, I suspect at least initially, somewhat in awe of him. My father knew far fewer people, made friends less easily than Barbeau, and in contrast to Barbeau, had no friends in political and legal

Figure 22 Diamond Jenness, Chief of Anthropology, National Museum of Canada, 1926.

circles. Nor did he seek any. Furthermore, here in Canada he was in a foreign land, far from his family and roots.[24] Barbeau, on the other hand, was Canadian-born, had many friends, including politicians, and lived only a few hours from his family home for his entire life.

My father, although born in Wellington, was brought up in Lower Hutt, a small settlement on the Hutt River a few miles upstream from Wellington in ultraconservative, Victorian New Zealand. He was the tenth of fourteen sons and daughters of strict Methodist parents. His father was a watch- and clock-maker and jewellery-store owner, modestly well-to-do in spite of having a lot of children to feed and clothe, who hoped his sons, including his academically inclined son Diamond, would go into business like himself. His mother was a kindly homemaker who encouraged Diamond's scholarly studies. He always felt a closer bond to her than to his father. During his youth he spent some time on a sheep ranch, acquiring a love for the outdoors and a skill at hunting wild pigs and rabbits, but basically he was strongly focused academically. He walked or rode his bicycle daily from his home in the suburbs to school and later to college in Wellington. In college, he specialized in the classics and was influenced and encouraged by his Oxford-educated professors at Victoria University College to continue his studies at Oxford University. He had little money for that purpose, but upon graduating with a Master of Arts degree with first-class honours, he was awarded a small New Zealand

---

[24]He was the only Jenness in Canada for many years. Even today most if not all Jenness families in Canada are his direct descendants. From recent genealogical research, we now know that his grandfather went to New Zealand from New Hampshire, where today there are still lots of distant relatives, all traceable to one Francis Jenness, who came out from England to New England in 1662 as an indentured servant.

scholarship to attend Oxford, where he lived frugally, with the assistance of occasional small financial contributions from his mother.

His father probably could have assisted him financially but was apparently not inclined to do so. In the one instance I know about, where my father had to ask his father for money to pay his travel expenses from New Zealand to Canada in 1913 to join the Arctic expedition, he was expected to pay it back. He did so by arranging promptly upon his arrival in Victoria, British Columbia, to have the Canadian government send all the pay he would earn while in the Arctic ($500 per year) to his father. Thereafter he made every effort to keep within his financial means, always living carefully, though never stingily. It was a trait that served him well years later with his carefully administered government field and division finances, and still later when he and mother lived on his small government pension, which in those days did not have an annual cost-of-living increase as is provided today.

Barbeau was brought up in the small, French-Canadian and Roman-Catholic community of Ste-Marie-de-Beauce, south of Quebec City, the oldest of three sons and one daughter in a reasonably well-to-do family. During his earliest years, he was greatly influenced and home schooled by his religiously educated and musical mother. At age fourteen, he was sent away from home to receive several years of classical education and religious training in preparation for the priesthood. Six years later, just before his graduation in 1903, however, he decided that he did not want to be a priest. In this decision, strangely enough, he followed the pattern set years earlier by his mother, who decided after seven years as a novice that she did not wish to be a nun and left the convent. He decided instead to study law and went to Laval University in Quebec City. While there, he had frequent contact with politicians. Three years later he obtained a Bachelor of Science degree and was awarded a Rhodes Scholarship to Oxford University, one, as it happened, that had first been offered to and turned down by his good friend Louis St-Laurent.[25] He was the first French Canadian to be awarded that much-desired English scholarship.

Barbeau developed expensive tastes and desires in his youth, frequently forcing him to request money from his stern father, who regularly berated him for his reckless spending habits. Later, while at Oxford, he managed quite satisfactorily financially as a result of the fairly lucrative Rhodes Scholarship and several thousand dollars he inherited from his grandmother. Accordingly, he was able to afford quite a lot of social life, seldom needing to exercise financial restraint. During holiday breaks, he lived as he pleased, touring Europe taking in concerts, operas, museums, and other cultural and social activities, as well as attending classes at the Sorbonne. His free use of money caught up with him years later when he was spoken to severely a number of times by the museum's senior administrators for overspending government funds allotted him for his field expenses and for not conforming to the rather regimented rules of operation for field parties required by his government department.

My father and Barbeau thus reached Oxford with different cultural, educational, religious, geographical, and financial backgrounds. My father arrived in 1908, a year after Barbeau. They

---

[25]St-Laurent chose marriage and a legal profession to three years at Oxford. He was very successful in his legal profession and through it met many politicians. This led in due course to him entering politics, and in 1948 he became Canada's twelfth Prime Minister.

resided in different colleges, but somehow their paths crossed and Barbeau, as already mentioned, persuaded my father to take a course in social anthropology taught by R.R. Marett. Another of their shared courses was with Professor J.L. Myers, a founder of the School of Anthropology at Oxford.[26]

Professor Myers participated some months later in the formulation of a detailed resolution by the British Association for the Advancement of Science at its meeting in Winnipeg, Manitoba in 1909, which led to a petition being forwarded to Ottawa urging the Dominion government to create and house an anthropological unit in its Victoria Memorial Museum, a building then under construction in Ottawa. Similar petitions had reached the Canadian government from other scientific organizations, including the Royal Society of Canada, and the anthropology division was finally established at the museum in Ottawa in 1910 under the administrative direction of the Geological Survey of Canada. The actual beginnings of this anthropology division can be traced back many years farther, however, to the early efforts of several men and scientific groups.[27] Quite possibly Professor Myers had his student Barbeau in mind as a future employee in the proposed division when he was at the Winnipeg meeting in 1909, for Barbeau graduated from Oxford the following year.

In 1908, anthropology in England was in its early stages of development as an important new science. That year Marett had only three students in his social anthropology class at Oxford, all from overseas: Jenness from New Zealand, Barbeau from Canada, and Wallis from the United States. In Marett's words, they were "... a trio of which our nascent School of Anthropology might well be proud."[28] All three men received their Diplomas in Anthropology from

---

[26]Cambridge University got its first Professor of Anthropology in 1893, Oxford University in 1896. The first professor of anthropology in Canada was appointed by the University of Toronto in 1925.

[27]See Dyck, I., 2001, pp. 16–20 and Vodden, C. and Dyck, I., 2006. Two modern descendants of the National Museum of Canada (the Canadian Museum of Civilization and the Canadian Museum of Nature) celebrated their 150th anniversary in May 2006. The former resides in two modern eye-catching buildings on the north shore of the Ottawa River overlooking Canada's Parliament Buildings, while the latter has offices in a building on the western edge of Gatineau, Quebec, and presents its exhibits in the historic Victoria Memorial Museum building in Ottawa, which was the original home of the National Museum of Canada. That impressive castle-like limestone building, opened in 1912 and fast approaching its 100th anniversary, has undergone two major interior renovations since the Second World War, including extensive foundation work because the building rests upon the unstable sediments of an ancient lakebed. Indeed, a large central tower on the original building had to be removed in 1915 because of the structural damage its weight had wrought upon that part of the building's foundations. To justify their claim to 150 years' existence, the two museums had to trace their origin back to the mid-1800s and the Geological Survey of Canada, then located in Montreal. In 1856, the pre-Confederation government of Canada authorized the Survey's first director, Sir William Logan, to establish a museum to display appropriate items from the Survey's collections. In those days Logan and his few assistants collected rocks, minerals, fossils, birds, mammals, plants, and aboriginal artifacts. Some of these soon were displayed in the Survey's modest headquarters building in Montreal and thus formed the start of Canada's first national museum. The Canadian Museum of Civilization now houses a vast collection of aboriginal artifacts from across Canada, while the Canadian Museum of Nature houses a vast collection of birds, mammals, and large fossils including dinosaurs. The Geological Survey of Canada retained the rocks, minerals, and small, largely invertebrate fossils.

[28]Marett, R.R., 1920. Preface to *The Northern D'Entrecasteaux*, by D. Jenness and Rev. A. Ballantyne, p. 5.

Oxford in the spring of 1910, only the second group to do so. The Diploma was the document granted students then for completing the various anthropology courses, as Oxford did not offer a formal degree in anthropology until some years later.

Barbeau and Wallis obtained their B.Sc. degrees from Oxford in 1910, whereas my father, having reached Oxford a year later than his two friends, remained for another year. Following his graduation, Barbeau travelled about Europe for the next few months, enjoying museums, concerts, and operas, before returning to Canada in the fall. He was subsequently hired to work with Dr. Sapir in the newly created Division of Anthropology at the Victoria Memorial Museum in Ottawa, commencing at the start of 1911. He was the first Canadian ethnologist appointed to its staff.[29]

My father completed his course requirements at Oxford the following year, graduating with a B.A. with honours in Classics. Lacking funds, he could not consider spending a few holiday weeks on the continent as Barbeau had done the previous year. Instead he left Oxford soon after his graduation with two hundred and fifty pounds sterling in his pocket, an amount of money donated by individuals and colleges at Oxford to enable him to undertake a year of anthropological fieldwork among some little-known natives in Papua-New Guinea. He followed this work with three years among the Eskimos in the Arctic, then proceeded to Ottawa in September 1916. There for the first time in six years, he again encountered Barbeau. After nine months of renewed friendship, my father went overseas in June 1917 with the Canadian Army for two years at the war front. He returned to Ottawa shortly after the war ended, married, and took his bride Eilleen to New Zealand for three months. Thereafter, he and Barbeau saw each other regularly and their friendship continued. Following his marriage, my father was drawn socially into his wife's family circle for the first few years, but as the older family members died off or moved away he did not replace them with new friends; instead, he grew more immersed in his work and involved with his own growing family.

Barbeau's unpublished memoirs state repeatedly that he played an influential role in the early part of my father's life and career. Three significant occasions, already mentioned, bear repeating here: (1) in 1908, Barbeau (with some input from fellow classmate, Wilson Wallis, according to the latter)[30] effected a major change in my father's academic direction by persuading him to take anthropology classes at Oxford; (2) in 1913, Barbeau helped launch my father's profess-ional career in anthropology by recommending him to the explorer Vilhjalmur Stefansson for anthropological studies of the little-known Copper Eskimos in the central Canadian Arctic, studies which in due course formed the backbone to my father's professional career; and (3) in 1920, Barbeau's request to a high-ranking political friend on behalf of my father may have played a role in finally obtaining for him a permanent appointment with the government in Ottawa.

---

[29]Barbeau mentioned in his memoirs that at this early stage in his career, he was helped by "political" connections to obtain this employment, through a series of correspondences involving Sir William Osler, who was then a well-known Oxford Professor of Medicine, and also the Honourable S.A. Fisher, who was the Minister of Agriculture in Ottawa, and Dr. R.W. Brock, the Director of the Geological Survey of Canada in Ottawa (C.M. Barbeau memoirs, 1957–58, Carmen Roy Collection, Box 622, Folder 1, p. 21, Archives, CMC).

[30]Wallis, 1957.

We now return to the autumn of 1925 and events leading up to the appointment of the replacement for the departed division chief, Edward Sapir. As already mentioned, my father wrote two letters to Barbeau early in October of that year, the first reporting on the difficult problem the administration faced in selecting Sapir's replacement, the second stating my father's view that the appointee should be either Barbeau or Smith, that he did not want the job himself and pledging his loyalty to whichever of his two colleagues received the appointment, and expressing his heartfelt desire that "the matter can be settled without friction," for he valued their friendship too highly.[31]

Barbeau's memoirs state that his reply to my father's October 8 letter set forth his view on the appointment quite clearly. Unfortunately, my father did not keep that letter, forcing us to rely upon what Barbeau recalled of its contents thirty-one years later. I have itali-

Figure 23 Marius Barbeau, about 1954.
CMC J-4099

cized the sentences I consider most significant in view of subsequent events. Barbeau recalled writing, "We are good friends, you and I; I have had you appointed to the Museum, I had you selected by Stefansson for the Arctic Expedition, we are old fellow students at Oxford, I have confidence in you. *If they want to appoint you chief of the Division I gladly accept. I don't care to go into administrative work and the kind of thing that Sapir used to do. I am interested in my work, I have chosen it, I like it and I want to go ahead with it.*"[32]

As my father had found the duties of administering the division both time-consuming and tedious during the few weeks he had served as Acting Chief, he could readily understand his good friend's declared lack of interest in assuming those duties. Barbeau's memoir next claims, with apparent anger, that upon receipt of Barbeau's confidential letter, my father "took the letter at once—because he thought it served his own purpose—took it to Boulton [sic] and said 'Here' and Boulton appointed Jenness chief."[33]

---

[31] We have here a hint that my father anticipated some animosity over the appointment, possibly indicating that he suspected Barbeau really wanted the appointment in spite of his protestations to the contrary. My father may have had some indication from Bolton or Sapir that he (Jenness) was the likely candidate, even though he was junior to the other two. His two concerns at the time were that there be no bad feelings resulting from the appointment, and that it be made as soon as possible so that he could get back to his research. He did not relish being stuck with the Acting-Chief's duties much longer.

[32] C.M. Barbeau memoirs, 1957–58, Carmen Roy Collection, Box 622, Folder 3, p. 77, Archives, CMC.

[33] *Ibid.*

Barbeau's accusation is incorrect for several reasons. (1) Never in his entire life, to my knowledge, did my father ever deliberately deceive anyone, let alone a best friend; it was not in his make-up to do so, his strict Methodist parents having instilled in him a very strong aversion to anything dishonest or deceptive. (2) My father did not want Sapir's position, exactly as he had stated several times, because he had less seniority than the other two, because he had no desire to shoulder the long-term burden that went with the appointment, and because he much preferred pursuing his research interests. (3) He did not want to be the cause of the trouble that he suspected would likely ensue with his two more senior colleagues if he were leapfrogged over them to become their supervisor. (4) He valued his friendship with Barbeau too highly to treat him in such an underhanded fashion. He valued also his friendship with Smith, but I think that was more the result of professional respect than personal closeness. (5) My father may not have gone to Bolton, as Barbeau claimed, with or without Barbeau's letter. If he did go, however, it would have been in the role of Acting Chief, to suggest to Bolton, who had already heard from Barbeau about his disinterest in the position, that steps be taken to offer the position to Smith as soon as possible. My father's eagerness to be relieved of the division chief's duties was sufficient motive for any speed he may have shown to see Bolton.

Barbeau's accusation is incorrect for one other reason: Bolton could not make the appointment on his own. Following normal government procedures, his preference of candidate would be routed through the offices of his Deputy Minister and Minister, where the selection of the successful candidate would be finalized, and ultimately reach the Civil Service Commission, which would formally appoint the applicant recommended by the Minister and Deputy Minister.

No further letters passed between my father and Barbeau at that time because Barbeau returned to Ottawa at the end of October.[34] Soon after his return, Barbeau made a sudden and unexpected move to obtain political assistance. It was the initial of several moves, in fact, which totally contradicted his assertions to my father that he did not want Sapir's position. Of course, I do not imagine that Barbeau mentioned these moves to my father, nor did he mention them in his memoir. To start with, he wrote the Honourable Charles Stewart, Minister of Mines, expressing his desire to be appointed Chief of the Division of Anthropology and requesting the minister's assistance towards that end. Stewart did not respond immediately to Barbeau, but on November 25 wrote of Barbeau's request to the Honourable Ernest Lapointe, Minister of Justice.[35]

On December 8, Barbeau, having grown impatient over the apparent lack of action, wrote to the Honourable Rodolphe Lemieux, then the Speaker of the House of Commons, whom he had known since 1916, asking his assistance in obtaining the position of Chief of Anthropology. Lemieux acknowledged receipt of this letter the next day, saying he would recommend him with pleasure to the Minister of the Interior, and wishing him "tout le succès que vous méritez."[36] On December 15, Lemieux wrote about Barbeau's request to the Minister of Mines, the Honourable Charles Stewart. The latter promptly (and correctly) responded that the three senior officers in the division (i.e., Barbeau, Smith, and Jenness) had agreed among themselves that

---

[34] *Ibid.*

[35] Nowry, 1995, p. 265.

[36] "All the success that you deserve." Lemieux to Barbeau, letter dated December 9, 1925, Barbeau Collection, Box 213, Folder 65, Archives, CMC.

none of them would press a claim for the position, leaving the decision to Bolton, who was both Acting Director of the Victoria Memorial Museum and Assistant Deputy Minister of the department, and to Dr. Camsell, the Deputy Minister of the department. In this letter Stewart also pointed out that there was no increase in remuneration attached to the position and that the appointee would have to give up a good deal of his research time to administrative duties.[37]

Following a departmental decision reached late in December, my father was formally asked by the Minister of Mines (Stewart) and his Deputy Minister (Camsell) to accept the position of Chief of the Anthropology Division, effective January 12, 1926. Faced with such a high-level request, however, my father had little choice but to accept the appointment. His acceptance then created the somewhat awkward administrative situation where he, the lowest-paid of the three candidates, would now oversee the work of the other two more senior men. That was rectified four months later when my father's salary was increased to the level of his colleagues.[38]

What, then, of my father's repeated assertions that he would not accept the position unless his two older colleagues had had first refusal? I have found no evidence that either Smith or Barbeau was officially offered the position. (Sapir's expression of offer to Smith has to be construed as probing, not a formal offer.) My father was inclined to stand firm on some fundamental principles, especially where they involved the Golden Rule by which he sought to live, and I doubt that he yielded easily on this one. Yet, he was the obvious choice. He had demonstrated his ability over the previous several months to handle the divisional duties satisfactorily, his views about the future course of the museum were commendable, and his friendship with the somewhat uncontrollable Barbeau bode well for the future. Inevitably, the arguments of Camsell and Bolton, as well as his qualifications, collectively overrode his concern about his assurances to his colleagues.

Whatever the means used during the discussion my father apparently had with Camsell and Bolton, he finally accepted the appointment, although no doubt with misgivings, rather than be the one causing a further lengthy delay of the division's activities. The die was thus cast for what followed.

To start with, Barbeau was considerably upset by the appointment, and remained so over the years. In his memoirs he stated that he had replied to some friends who had written him, angry that he had not been appointed chief, "I didn't care. I thought to myself now with Jenness I'll do what I please."[39]

After my father was appointed to Sapir's position, he wrote Sapir to let him know about the selection. "Your recommendation concerning the succession was carried out, somewhat to

[37]Stewart to Lemieux, letter dated December 18, 1925, Barbeau Collection, Box 213, Folder 65, Archives, CMC. It is curious that this original letter from the Minister of Mines ended up in the Barbeau Collection. The explanation appears to be as follows. Across the upper left corner of the letter, in blue pencil, is written, in large letters "Compliments R.L." As the initials match the writing of Lemieux's signature on earlier letters to Barbeau, it would appear that Lemieux deliberately forwarded this original letter (or original duplicate of the letter) to Barbeau.
[38]A letter from Bolton to Jenness refers to a memorandum from Dr. Camsell, dated January 9, 1926, which advised that "it was the desire of the Minister of Mines and himself that you [Jenness] assume the duties of Chief of the Division of Anthropology." Bolton to Jenness, letter dated February 6, 1926, Jenness Correspondence, Box 641, Folder 2, Archives, CMC. This was virtually a command.
[39]C.M. Barbeau memoirs, 1957–58, Carmen Roy Collection, Box 622, Folder 3, p. 77, Archives, CMC.

my dismay; but I will do the best I can."[40] That last clause was so typical of my father's attitude towards life's many problems. (I recall several times during my working years, when I was wrestling with some problem or other, he would counsel me, "Just do the best you can, old man." For some unknown reason, he frequently addressed me and also my brothers individually as "old man," which he used as a congenial term. Perhaps it was akin to the friendly English expression "old chap" and had nothing to do with age.) Sapir promptly responded to my father's news, "... let me congratulate you heartily on your appointment. It is by far the best they could have done."[41]

Within three months of my father's appointment, the matter of Barbeau's unwillingness to conform to routine government policies and procedures under my father's direction came to a head. Barbeau had overspent his field budget, and his field-expenditure statement for the previous season (1925) had been extensively questioned by the treasury office. Bolton returned the account to Barbeau via my father, along with a memorandum from Bolton reprimanding Barbeau for excesses in many of his expenditures and instructing him to submit a revised version, eliminating some of his expenses in order to keep within his field budget.[42] Barbeau's hastily written response to Bolton, which has not been preserved, prompted an even stronger reprimand from Bolton.[43]

At this point, Bolton evidently instructed my father, as the new chief of the division, to take care of the matter, straightening the financial problem with Barbeau, and at the same time making it quite clear to Barbeau that he was henceforth to attend to his Indian projects and to cease using government time and money on his French-Canadian cultural studies.[44]

In matters of personnel discipline, the federal bureaucracy functioned somewhat like the armed forces. Instructions for the periodic enforcement of discipline were passed down the ranks

---

[40]Jenness to Sapir, letter dated February 2, 1926, Sapir Correspondence, Box 656, Folder 37, Archives, CMC.

[41]Sapir to Jenness, letter dated March 11, 1926, Sapir Correspondence, Box 656, Folder 37, Archives, CMC. In 1930, Sapir moved from the University of Chicago to Yale University, where he died unexpectedly of a heart attack in 1939. My father wrote an obituary (Jenness, 1939).

[42]Bolton to Barbeau, memorandum dated April 14, 1926, Jenness Correspondence, Box 641, Folder 2, Archives, CMC.

[43]Bolton to Barbeau, memorandum dated April 16, 1926, Jenness Correspondence, Box 641, Folder 2, Archives, CMC.

[44]At a meeting of the Anthropological Association in New York in 1913, Barbeau met Columbia University's Anthropology Professor Franz Boas, who urged him to collect French-Canadian folklore, needed to shed light on some American Indian folklore, which reflected French and Spanish influences. Barbeau discussed the idea with Sapir, but was told there was no government authority or money to undertake such studies, as the Anthropology Division's government mandate covered only native studies. Barbeau thereafter proceeded to collect the French-Canadian folktales anyway and soon added the collecting of French-Canadian folk songs and other French-Canadian ethnology to his activities, often at his own expense, spending office and field time on such matters in spite of his instructions to the contrary. Boas encouraged him by appointing Barbeau French editor of the *Journal of American Folk-Lore*. Sapir then translated into English many of Barbeau's French-Canadian folk songs and published with Barbeau in 1924 a book in the United States of such songs with his translations (C.M. Barbeau memoirs, 1957–58, Carmen Roy Collection, Box 622, Folder 2, pp. 28–36). Sapir's departure the following year left the awkward problem of Barbeau's continuing to undertake French-Canadian studies in defiance of his official instructions from Sapir's successor, which, as we have seen, was my father.

as we see here, with my father having to carry out the disciplining. My father did not like meting out discipline to anyone and, as I recall, was not particularly adept at the task. He must have anguished, therefore, when instructed to speak severely and sternly to the man he had long considered his best friend. His effort at carrying out that distasteful task, about which he never spoke in my presence, produced an agitated encounter and troubling results.

The only first-hand report of that encounter, to my knowledge, is the one in Barbeau's 1957 unpublished memoirs, which is both incomplete and strongly biased. In addition, it does not mention the problems concerning Barbeau's field expenses that must have been discussed that day, nor does it mention the date on which the encounter took place. That is unfortunate, for there does not seem to be any other record of it. It is reasonable to assume, however, that it was close to April 21, a few days after Bolton's second reprimanding memorandum.

Here is how the encounter with my father was recorded by Barbeau in his memoirs.[45]

> Things went along for a little while—in our offices until one day, Jenness called me in his room—we had offices next to each other.[46] He looked angry and said, "Now, Barbeau, there will be a show-down here today...." I was most surprised, I didn't expect anything of this kind. He said, "The Anthropological Division has been established on the lines of our studies at Oxford and then later developed here into the studies of Indians, and nothing else. From now on, you will do work on the Indians, and leave that other work you have been doing aside and forget it." Well, my surprise was deep, to say the least. I don't remember what happened immediately afterwards, but almost at once I said, "I have selected my work for my life. It has developed gradually, it is legitimate here, it is needed, it is justi-fied, and I am going ahead with it." And I slammed the door in his face, and went away. For ten years, we didn't speak to each other—ten years and more, almost to the present. We meet occasionally, somewhere, I don't know where, but we never were friends surely....
>
> I went through this crisis cheerfully. I was probably the only one who was cheerful about it. In a way, I felt that I had gained my independence, which had been cramped through a sort of friendship I always had for Sapir, and Sapir never opposed me squarely. Right now I had met one who would fight it up, and I had picked up the glove.... What resulted of this in actual facts? For the ten years that followed, ten, fifteen years really, from 1925 to 1939—the beginning of the war—what happened is this: I worked independently under the remote direction of the Director of the Geological Survey and the Museum, practically had never any dealings with Jenness, the chief who was reduced by that much in his own activities and authority over the Division. And I suppose that he must have been humiliated too; but he could do nothing.[47]

These words, spoken so many years after the incident and his avoidance of my father for so many years, suggest that Barbeau may have retained his anger against my father for the rest of his life.

---

[45] The reader is reminded that this account was recorded by Barbeau thirty-one years after the event.

[46] This was, strictly speaking, not quite true. The divisional secretary occupied an office between the two scientists.

[47] C.M. Barbeau memoirs, 1957–58, Carmen Roy Collection, Box 622, Folder 3, p. 79, Archives, CMC.

My father may have been briefly angered by Barbeau's rude response and his refusal to obey the Assistant Deputy Minister's instructions, but he was not one to remain angry for very long. However, I am sure he was deeply hurt and disappointed by Barbeau's actions, which I suspect he never fully understood nor forgot. Working in such relatively close proximity, and having to share the services of the same secretary daily for nearly twenty years, the two former friends could not help but encounter each other occasionally in her office, or in the halls, which would only have added to the discomfort of their strained relationship.[48]

My father would have been required to report the results of his disciplinary efforts to Bolton, or more probably to Dr. W.H. Collins, who had taken over the duties of Acting Director of the National Museum from Bolton on April 8, 1926.[49] My father probably also discussed the matter with Dr. Camsell, the Deputy Minister of Mines. I have found no record of such a meeting or meetings, however, but this does not really surprise me. Even if my father had been temporarily angered by Barbeau's actions, I am confident that he would have played down the severity of the incident out of continuing loyalty to his friend.

Barbeau ultimately realized that his defiant outburst in my father's office was quite inappropriate and deserved stern disciplinary measures, although he claimed that he did not realize it at the time. In his memoirs he commented, "There was only one thing to do, in those occasions, for Jenness and Bolton. They silently probably agreed about it. It was to dismiss me for insubordination or whatever they would call it. It didn't occur to me. Anyway, I would have found my way elsewhere, I trust."[50] But Barbeau was not dismissed.

Some years later a friend of his, Dr. C.T. Currelly, brought up the subject while they were having lunch together. Currelly was the Director of the Royal Ontario Museum in Toronto, a man for whose museum Barbeau had obtained totem poles and other Indian artifacts in previous years. As Barbeau recalled their discussion in his memoirs, Currelly said, "Do you know, Barbeau, had you not been a French Canadian, you would have been dismissed from the museum long ago." Barbeau then commented to Carmen Roy, who was recording his reminiscences:

> I was most surprised at this remark, because I knew that French-Canadians didn't exist on the staff of the Museum and the Mines Branch. Why not a little chick like me thrown out very indifferently, it was an easy thing to do, the most easy, because I was a French-Canadian—that might have been one reason to dismiss me. Well, Currelly was telling the opposite—that because I was a French-Canadian I could not be dismissed and what he means is this, I understood, there would have been reactions here in Parliament and other places had they heard that myself, who already was well-known for my work, had been thrown out of the Museum because of a reason they could not themselves allege, because of my work [e]specially, the work I was doing in French Canada. [51]

---

[48]It must have been most difficult and uncomfortable for the secretary as well, for she still had to work for both men.

[49]C. Camsell to Jenness, letter dated April 8, 1926, Jenness Correspondence, Box 641, Folder 29 (Camsell/Jenness Folder), Archives, CMC.

[50]C.M. Barbeau memoirs, 1957–58, Carmen Roy Collection, Box 622, Folder 3, p. 79, Archives, CMC.

[51]C.M. Barbeau memoirs, 1957–58, Carmen Roy Collection, Box 622, Folder 3, p. 80, Archives, CMC.

Dr. Currelly was obviously aware, even then, that French-English differences and the importance of Quebec votes were sensitive matters to the federal politicians and their bureaucratic representatives in the government.

Barbeau thus credited his French-Canadian origin and studies for saving him from being fired. While there might be some truth in that, I suggest there was another reason. My father, out of loyalty to the man he still regarded as his friend, may have urged Dr. Collins, Mr. Bolton, and Dr. Camsell to refrain from disciplining Barbeau for his insubordination, but instead to remove him from my father's administrative responsibility. He knew that Barbeau was a competent ethnologist, virtually irreplaceable in those days, and capable of greatly enhancing Canada's cultural and historical knowledge of French Canada in addition to its Indian knowledge when the opportunity presented itself for him to do so. Trying to force Barbeau to conform to departmental regulations was rather like trying to force a thoroughbred horse to pull a hay wagon. Better to put up with his unconventional ways and reap the benefits of his great enthusiasm for his specialized studies. This suggestion is purely hypothetical, of course, without any concrete supporting evidence, but it makes a great deal of sense when one recalls the intensity of my father's feelings of loyalty towards his adopted country of Canada as well as towards England in the First World War (and as revealed in Chapter 15 again in the Second World War). I believe he felt that same intensity of loyalty towards Barbeau at that time.

In any event, Barbeau was quickly removed from my father's line of authority and thereafter reported directly for the next ten years to Dr. Collins, who, in April 1926, assumed the duties of Acting Director of the Museum in addition to his role as the Director of the Geological Survey of Canada. Bolton then was able to resume his duties full time as Assistant Deputy Minister, thereby no longer having direct administrative dealings with Barbeau, an arrangement I feel certain pleased both men. Within days of his angry outburst with my father, Barbeau was largely set free to steer his own course, answerable only to Dr. Collins.

A year later, my father was asked by Dr. Collins to comment on a memo from Barbeau urging the museum to purchase a significant French-Canadian collection of cultural objects. In his reply my father stated that he did not think the museum should buy them, indicating thereby that his views on the role the museum should be playing had not changed since he first voiced them in May 1926[52]—namely that the museum should concentrate its time and money on obtaining and housing the finest possible collection of Indian and Eskimo objects. With regard to the French-Canadian material Barbeau had discovered, my father wrote, "I do not think our museum now or at any period that I can foresee in the near future, can handle a representative collection of French-Canadian technology, including furniture, statuary, textiles, etc. owing to restrictions of space and labour. I have always felt, too, with Dr. Sapir, that our primary work was among the fast disappearing Indian and Eskimo tribes, and with our limited resources we should concentrate mainly on them...."[53]

He did agree, though, that any French-Canadian objects offered without charge should be accepted. In taking the position he did, my father was simply sticking to Sapir's vision for

---

[52]Jenness to W.H. Collins, letter dated May 31, 1926, Jenness Collection, Box 652, Folder 1, Archives, CMC.

[53]*Ibid.*

the direction of the Anthropology Division. Some people might regard it as showing spiteful retaliation against Barbeau or an anti-French-Canadian prejudice, or both, but neither interpretation would be correct.

Over the ensuing months my father made a few efforts to dismantle the wall of silence Barbeau had erected between them.[54] In the first of two letters to Barbeau (who was doing fieldwork in Usk, Skeena River, British Columbia) in late September of 1926, shortly after my father's return from Bering Strait, my father mentioned that he had field money left over from his summer's work and had asked the financial officer to transfer some of this to Barbeau to supplement his field budget. My father knew that Barbeau could always use more field money. The unwillingness of the financial officer to do so did not diminish the genuineness of my father's gesture. In the October 1926 letter, he included a postscript bearing a similar tone to those he had frequently inserted in his letters to Barbeau before their office confrontation, in which he passed along Mrs. Jenness' kindest regards to Mrs. Barbeau, to Barbeau himself, and to their children, and his own also to Mrs. Barbeau. This personal gesture, revealing that he retained no hard feelings, was not reciprocated.

Glimmers of similar friendliness appear in the handful of communiqués that passed between the two men thereafter, but all were from my father to Barbeau; there were no more chatty, personal letters like those before 1926. In the spring of 1948, my father acknowledged receipt of a copy of Barbeau's *Bio-Biographica*, then added, "Such an account of your work has been long overdue and will be invaluable to all folk-lorists. I am delighted to see it appear at last."[55] The last communiqué in the Barbeau-Jenness correspondence file at the museum is a note handwritten by my father on a letter he had received from a man at the Pitt-Rivers Museum, Oxford University. In that note, which my father forwarded from his home to Barbeau at the office he still occupied at the museum, my father asked if Barbeau would answer the enquiry and added, "May I congratulate you also on your Honorary Doctorate from Oxford. It has been well earned."[56]

This chapter would not be complete without some attempt to explain why Barbeau turned on his friend of nearly twenty years and remained unfriendly towards him for the rest of their days. Only Barbeau could have provided the correct answer, but he refrained from doing so. His actions created years of strained relations within the small anthropology division and increased tensions between that division and the none-too-friendly administrators of the Geological Survey who controlled the division's finances. One day forty years ago, I sought an explanation from my father for their lost friendship, but his response was a gruff "I don't care to discuss it." Thus one can only speculate.

Here is my suggested explanation. Barbeau learned after his return to Ottawa in the fall of 1925 that Sapir had approached Smith about the position of division chief during the summer and was offended that he had not been asked first, for he was the more qualified of

---

[54]Jenness to Barbeau, letters dated September 30, 1926 and October 13, 1926, Barbeau Collection, Box 206, Folder 28, Archives, CMC.

[55]Jenness to Barbeau, letter dated May 12, 1948, Barbeau Collection, Box 206, Folder 28, Archives, CMC.

[56]Jenness to Barbeau, note dated February 9, 1953, Barbeau Collection, Box 206, Folder 28, Archives, CMC.

the two. He was also angered when he first suspected that my father had discussed the contents of his last letter with Bolton (if, in fact, this actually occurred). A few weeks later he was further upset when my father was appointed chief of the Division, because this was the second time Barbeau's efforts to obtain that position through his political connections had failed.[57] And then, finally when my father, acting on instructions from Bolton or Dr. Collins, reprimanded Barbeau on that eventful day in April 1926 over his poor handling of his field expenses, Barbeau's pent-up anger and frustration burst his mental dam and spilled all over my father's office. My father had apparently turned into another "by-the-rules" bureaucrat like Bolton, whom Barbeau heartily disliked.[58] Quite possibly also, the situation recalled hostile feelings from Barbeau's distant past, for Barbeau had long resented the frequent berating he had received from his father years earlier about his money needs and reckless spending habits. And Barbeau was not prepared to tolerate taking disciplinary orders from his younger colleague. As he said in his memoirs, "We may say that the Anthropological Division had split up in two parts at the time because of what I realize only now was my non-recognition of Jenness' authority over me."[59]

After my father's appointment, I suspect that Barbeau adopted the attitude that he could use Jenness' friendship to do the kind of work he was most interested in doing even more than when Sapir was chief of the division. In his words, "...with Jenness I'll do what I please."[60] My father had no intention of being manipulated, however, and Barbeau quickly discovered a strict, military side to him that he had not previously known. Being told by my father that he must cease work on his French-Canadian folk studies, which he had aggressively pursued for a decade in spite of occasional administrative objections from Bolton and Sapir (although the latter did in time become interested and even somewhat involved with Barbeau's unauthorized French-Canadian work), was a bit too much for Barbeau. It is also possible that being reminded on that occasion by Jenness that the policies of the museum's Acting Director Bolton and his departmental superiors restricted the anthropology division's investigations to Canada's Aboriginal peoples and left no room to consider French-Canadian folk studies as a legitimate part of its mandate may even have stirred up cultural, anti-British resentments in Barbeau dating back to the defeat of the French by the British at Quebec City in 1759.

In short, I suggest that my father's promotion to division chief, his reprimand of Barbeau over his uncontrolled spending habits, his firm instructions to Barbeau to cease his French-Canadian cultural studies, Barbeau's mistaken assumptions that my father had both deliberately deceived him in order to obtain the promotion and was in league with Bolton, and Barbeau's disappointment dating from 1910 when he was not offered Sapir's position, collectively brought about both his explosive outburst in my father's office and his continuing resentment towards, and unwillingness to cooperate with, my father thereafter. Perhaps it was his way of getting even with my father, who had suddenly become a new authority figure obstructing Barbeau's determination to have French-Canadian folklore given a significant role in Canada's national

---

[57]Sapir had been appointed instead of Barbeau in 1910 (Nowry, 1995, p. 90).
[58]Nowry, 1995, p. 264.
[59]C.M. Barbeau memoirs, 1957–58, Carmen Roy Collection, Box 622, Folder 4, p. 90, Archives, CMC.
[60]C.M. Barbeau memoirs, 1957–58 , Carmen Roy Collection, Box 622, Folder 3, p. 77, Archives, CMC.

Figure 24 Victoria Memorial Museum of Canada before removal of central tower in 1915 because its weight caused structural defects. Arrow points to Jenness' office when he was Chief of Anthropology.
CMC 18806

anthropology program.[61] Whatever the true reasons for his behaviour towards my father, it precipitated what I consider to be a truly personal tragedy, which played a role of its own at the museum over the next two decades.

This unfortunate incident in 1926 cost my father the friendship of the one person outside his family he had long trusted and admired. Indeed, he may have felt the loss as grievously as one who is bereaved. He may also have been disillusioned by the realization that the man he had so greatly admired over the years might not always have been quite above board with him.

There are still many unanswered questions about the Barbeau-Jenness relationship. For example, did Barbeau not want Jenness to be appointed chief of the division because Jenness was both junior to him in seniority and younger than him? (I would argue "yes.") Did Jenness in turn not want Barbeau to be appointed chief because he was confident Barbeau would prove unable to keep up with the tedious day-to-day duties, since his interests lay elsewhere and the

---

[61]Dr. Sapir had originally established four main fields of study when he became Chief of Anthropology in 1910—Ethnology, Archaeology, Physical Anthropology, and Linguistics. All national museums my father was familiar with in the mid-1920s were organized in this manner. With his almost constant pressing for more studies of French-Canadian folk culture, Barbeau was, in effect, trying to force the Museum to create a fifth field, one in Folk-Culture Studies. In the long run he was successful, but the new field was not formalized until well after the Second World War, by which time both he and his "opponents" had retired.

division would suffer? (I would say that Jenness fully expected Barbeau to receive the appointment, but had misgivings about how well he would deal with the assorted duties.) Did Bolton favour the appointment of Jenness because of his dislike for Barbeau? (I would say quite possibly, but there is no proof.) What was Smith's view about the appointment? (If it had been offered him, I suspect he would have accepted it, but would have been concerned that he would hate the work and not do a satisfactory job.) Was he offered the appointment? (I have seen no information on this.) Was he even considered for promotion by anyone other than Sapir? (No information on this.) Was Barbeau offered the promotion to chief of division before it was offered to Jenness? (No information on this.) Did Jenness accept the promotion without Barbeau or Smith already having refused it, a condition Jenness had said must be met before he would accept the appointment? (I have found no direct answer to this specific question, but because of his loyalty to Barbeau at the time, I cannot imagine my father doing so unless he was pushed by Bolton, Camsell, or the Minister, Stewart. There is, in fact, evidence that the decision for the appointment came from both the Minister and the Deputy Minister,[62] which would have forced my father to over-ride his principles. Questions still remain, however.)

With regard to his appointment as Division Chief, I believe that my father accepted it principally out of duty to the museum (i.e., he knew that it was a miserable job, but someone had to do it) and loyalty to his colleagues (i.e., he would do it to spare the other two from the frustrating experience). He certainly did not accept the position out of any concerted desire for the power and prestige it might offer. He may even have entertained the hope that he could help lead the museum to the wider recognition he sought for it. However, I am certain that he would far rather have pursued his Indian and Eskimo research and avoided losing Barbeau's friendship.

To put it another way, out of loyalty to both Smith and Barbeau, I believe my father knowingly sacrificed some of his own scholarly ambitions, interests, and career at that time to retain their valued friendships and to spare them from the frustrations of the chief's responsibilities. He certainly never anticipated Barbeau's reaction and subsequent behaviour.[63] Sadly, there was no one to whom either of these two proud men could have turned to help them resolve their differences in order to restore the lost friendships.

The museum may also have suffered because of Barbeau's actions. Had these two outstanding ethnologists continued to work cooperatively as they had done before 1926, and as I am sure my father hoped they would continue to do when he became chief of the division, they might have elevated the reputation of the museum to newer and higher levels of success in the days that followed. Each, operating independently brought fame to himself in due course, and some to the museum. But how much more might they have achieved marching side by side during those years? Instead, by Barbeau's actions, the anthropology division "was split in two parts" (as he stated it), withered in spite of my father's strenuous efforts to maintain and develop it, was unable to get the support of the Geological Survey, and was almost wiped out by financial restrictions during the great depression of the 1930s and during the Second World War. My father did, however, keep the division alive until better days arrived some years after that war.

---

[62]So stated in a letter from Bolton to Jenness, dated February 1, 1926, Jenness Correspondence, Box 641, Folder 2, Archives, CMC.

[63]Smith's reaction to my father's appointment remains unknown.

Only Barbeau seems to have felt no significant loss, apparently remaining untroubled by the termination of their friendship. As he recalled in 1957, "I went through this crisis cheerfully.... I felt that I had gained my independence...."[64] Four years before his death in 1969, Barbeau recorded the following comment, "... I had a happy career here because I succeeded in what I thought I should do, you see, and I had the best judgement in the case because I was a specialist in these subjects, you see. But the other people, the Geologists specially, [who] were in charge of the Museum for so many years, were people of another mentality. They opposed my work, and it is gradually overcoming that opposition that is satisfactory to me and I see with great pleasure and satisfaction now the fact that folklore, linguistics and folk arts are accepted in the Museum at the core of its very existence and activities and programme."[65]

Egged on originally by Franz Boas, Barbeau had set his mind and career in 1913 upon establishing French-Canadian folklore as a major new branch of Canadian anthropology; and by sheer determination, hard work, and an "administration-be-damned" attitude he succeeded, leaving a few casualties along the way.

From the day of his temper outburst in my father's office in 1926 until after the retirement of both men in 1948, Barbeau spent much of his time on his French-Canadian culture studies, working largely independently, doing exactly what he wanted to do, and reporting to the Director or Acting Director of the Museum. Most of his voluminous flow of manuscripts was published outside the museum, because the Department of Mines, which controlled the administration and funding of the museum, could not justify publishing studies on a culture it was not then ready to add to its native studies. Not until the 1950s was the anthropology division permitted to expand both its staff and activities, and folk-culture studies were then added to its program.

Today, the small division of anthropology that my father struggled to keep alive from the mid 1920s to the late 1940s has emerged from under the direction of the Geological Survey of Canada (in 1959), as he had urged be done in 1930, and evolved significantly. After brief periods under the names Human History Branch of the National Museum of Canada (1956–1968) and National Museum of Man (1968–1986), it has expanded and flourished independently under its present name, the Canadian Museum of Civilization. It now has two handsome buildings, claims to be the largest museum in Canada with the greatest number of visitors, and boasts an extensive list of fine publications. To its original subdivisions of archaeology, ethnology, physical anthropology and linguistics were added folklore and history after the Second World War. History was later merged with archaeology. My father wanted to help develop the National Museum into a world-class organization, but he could never have envisioned its current eye-catching form or status.

---

[64]C.M. Barbeau memoirs, 1957–58, Carmen Roy Collection, Box 622, Folder 3, p. 79, Archives, CMC.
[65]Marius Barbeau interview by L. Nowry at the National Museum of Canada, 1965, Collection Radio-Canada. RC 166(a), transcribed by R. Landry, 1982, Coll. Acq. 2002-10030, Box I-122, p. 73, CMC.

1926: SEARCHING FOR EARLY AMERICANS

9

Diamond Jenness

[*On February 17, 1926, my father wrote a brief letter to Professor A.C. Haddon, a founder of British anthropology, at Cambridge University, mentioning two recently recognized early native cultures in North America's Eastern Arctic, the Thule people and the "Dorset culture,"[1] and his proposed field investigations in Bering Strait, where he hoped to find evidence of an Asian origin for the early Arctic dwellers of North America.*

> *Eskimo history grows more and more complex the more we learn, and every new theory seems to go a year later into the wastebasket. Just at present I have this feeling, that 1,000–2,000 years ago there flourished two Eskimo civilizations. One (Thule culture) extended from N. Alaska to Hudson Bay & N.W. Greenland; the other (C. Dorset) centred around Hudson Strait, reached to the north of Baffin Island & even to Ellesmere Land, probably extended throughout the Labrador Peninsula. While peculiar in many respects, this C. Dorset culture shows strong Indian (Algonkin etc.) affiliations, and probably represents the legendary "Tunnit" of modern Eskimo traditions. I have other wild notions and theories floating in my head that I dare not put to paper. But this summer, if all goes well, I hope to visit Bering Strait and do a little digging. Who knows what luck I shall have?"*[2]

Here are my father's recollections of those investigations.] [S.E.J.]

In the first quarter of the twentieth century, most students of human history agreed that man had been roaming the three continents of the Old World for a quarter, perhaps even half a million years, but the two continents of the New World less than 50,000. They agreed, also that he first reached the New World, not over the Atlantic or the Pacific Ocean—though the winds and the waves may have carried a few castaways across one or both of those vast stretches of water during the long procession of the centuries—but over the Bering Strait, which separates northern Alaska from northeastern Siberia, a narrow strait that freezes over so solidly in severe winters that parties of Eskimos have frequently crossed from one continent to the other on foot. From Alaska, ran the accepted theory of the day, the first immigrants and their descendants

---

[1]The Thule people and their distribution across North America were first recognized in the early 1920s by T. Mathiasson, the archaeologist on the Rasmussen-led 5th Thule Expedition 1921–1924 (Rasmussen, 1924; Mathiassen, 1927). The "Dorset culture" was recognized by my father in 1925 (Jenness 1925). Mathiassen believed his Thule culture was the oldest and disagreed with Jenness' conclusions that it was preceded by the Dorset culture.
[2]Jenness to A.C. Haddon, letter dated February 17, 1926; in possession of S.E. Jenness, 2006.

Map 8 Bering Strait region, 1926.

gradually moved southward to warmer regions, supporting themselves on the abundant fish and game in the virgin continent; and as the centuries passed, they multiplied and spread farther and farther south until a small vanguard finally halted at the southernmost tip of South America, almost in sight of Antarctica.

Book after book elaborated this theory, and archaeologists in both North and South America searched intensively for remains of those early peoples who had occupied both the Americas before the Old World's inhabitants ever dreamed of the existence of a western hemisphere. In the jungles of Mexico and Peru, they discovered the ruins of cities long dead, and in every region from the Arctic to Tierra del Fuego, from the shores of the Atlantic to the shores of the Pacific, they unearthed traces of human dwellings and camp sites, and the tools and weapons of prehistoric man. Some of these remains were much older than others. They lay buried more deeply under the surface of the soil, or they had disintegrated more from the sun and the rain, and from the chemicals in the earth and the atmosphere. But because only Central America had left us written records, and no one had succeeded in deciphering Central America's Maya script, it was very difficult to determine the relative ages of the various archaeological sites and deduce from them consistent histories. So scholars were groping in inky darkness, faintly lighted here and there by jack-o'-lanterns of what they hoped was solid knowledge.[3]

Strangely enough, in spite of so much digging and delving before the First World War, no one had investigated the two sides of Bering Strait, the theoretical gateway through which the earliest Americans presumably entered the New World. Certain scholars conjectured that the Aleutian Islands might have provided an alternate or additional route to North America, and a U.S. archaeologist had tested this theory by probing a number of shell heaps there.[4] But while his specimens proved that man had inhabited the archipelago for many hundred years, they proved also that it had been a dead-end refuge from mainland Alaska rather than a stepping stone from Asia to the New World or *vice versa*. Later excavations have confirmed his conclusions; they have uncovered no evidence of any direct contact between the Asiatic mainland and the Aleutian Archipelago before the arrival of Russian fur-traders in the eighteenth century. Evidently, Japan was not following any traditional invasion route when she seized the outermost Aleutian Islands, Attu and Kiska, during the Second World War.

Bering Strait, on the other hand, has been an intercontinental highway for untold centuries. Throughout the Christian era, and probably for centuries before that, Eskimos were living on both its eastern and western shores and travelling back and forth to attack or trade with one another. And in the long centuries before the Eskimos or their forebears settled there, when men in all parts of the world were still wandering Ishmaels, ignorant of agriculture and constrained to roam unceasingly from place to place in search of fish and game, who can say how many non-Eskimo peoples crossed Bering Strait and then moved on to milder homes in North and South America? If we accept the theory that the ancestors of America's Indians came from the Old World in some period or periods before man acquired the ability to build transoceanic boats, what possible route could they have taken except the one through Bering Strait?

It was not the problem of the origin and migrations of North America's two million Indians, however, that first awakened my interest in the Bering Strait region. It was the vicissitudes of that small fraction of hardy folk, the Eskimos, who had so persistently clung to America's Arctic and sub-Arctic in preference to more temperate lands. In 1913, as a member of the Canadian Arctic Expedition commanded by the explorer Vilhjalmur Stefansson, I had sailed through Bering Strait on the expedition's ill-fated flagship *Karluk*. And in 1916, when returning from a three-year sojourn among Eskimos scattered along the Arctic coasts of Alaska and Canada, I and my ship-mates had sheltered from a storm under Wales Mountain, which towers on the Alaskan side of the strait above the Eskimo village of Wales, and on favourable days offers from its summit a clear view of the two small Diomede Islands to the westward, and beyond them the coast of Siberia from East Cape to Indian Point.

---

[3]Radiocarbon dating, now indispensable for archaeological dating, was not developed until the late 1940s.
[4]The shell-heap prober was William Dall (1877). I do not know to whom my father was referring as "Certain scholars."

Six years later, in 1922, the Danish Fifth Thule Expedition, led by the Greenland explorer Knud Rasmussen, announced that in the northern part of Hudson Bay it had uncovered irrefutable proof that the Eskimos of Canada's Eastern Arctic and their cousins in Greenland were descendants, in part at least, of Eskimos who had migrated from Arctic Alaska about a thousand years ago and crossed the top of North America to their present homes. This remarkable discovery immediately posed the question: if the forefathers of most or all of today's Eskimos once lived in Alaska, where did the Alaska Eskimos come from? Assuredly, they were not living in that region during the ice age, when almost the whole of Alaska and Canada was buried under immense ice sheets and as little habitable as central Greenland today. Did the ancestors of Alaska's Eskimos live somewhere in Asia during that period, and drift across Bering Strait as soon as the ice sheets melted away? Or did they linger in Asia until relatively recent times and not colonize America's Arctic until perhaps the Christian era?

In central Eurasia, man survived the various phases of the Ice Age by sheltering in caves, and by hunting the reindeer and other animals which had adapted themselves to the intense cold. We can read the record of his struggle in the paintings with which he decorated many caves in France and Spain. When the climate at last ameliorated, the ice sheets retreated northward or into the high mountains, and the reindeer, following them, occupied each new grazing area as it opened up. Some herds, we conjecture, spreading from the plains of Eurasia into the tundra of northeast Siberia, spilled over Bering Strait into North America, and the ancestors of the Eskimos may have pursued them across the strait and unwittingly entered the new continent. If that is what happened, may not those early migrants have left recognizable traces of themselves in that region? Not perhaps still visible dwellings, since time would have obliterated them, but more durable arrow-heads, spear-heads, knives and other implements of stone and bone similar to those made by Old World reindeer-hunters 15,000 years ago? In 1914, on the shores of the Arctic Ocean near the Alaska-Canada boundary, I had excavated half a hundred old dwelling-sites; but they had proved disappointingly recent, not older perhaps than four hundred years.[5] Might I not find much more ancient sites if I searched around Bering Strait?

That raised a difficult problem. Would my employer, the Victoria Memorial Museum,[6] finance such a search? Its administrators had ruled, less than ten years before, that museum scientists should restrict their fieldwork to studies of the natural and human histories of Canada, leaving the similar histories of foreign countries to the nationals of those countries. Canada's fieldworkers, that is to say, should study the fauna and flora of Canada, but not those of countries outside her borders. Nature, of course, pays no attention to human regulations, or the national boundaries marked out by her puffed-up offspring, man. Her plants and animals, even her mosquitoes and viruses, cross the forty-ninth parallel with impunity. Only the museum's scientists lacked that freedom, if they strictly adhered to their administrators' regulation, and to the latter's interpretation of that regulation. The ornithologist, for example, should dutifully study

---

[5]These were the three sites on Barter Island and nearby Arey Island, some five hundred years old, mentioned in Chapter 3.

[6]The name of the active museum was changed in January 1927 to National Museum of Canada. The original name Victoria Memorial Museum thereafter was retained for the building.

his birds all summer in Canadian woods and fields, but when the cold nights of autumn sent them migrating south, he should sadly wave them good-bye, commend them officially to the tender care of his ornithological colleagues in the United States and Mexico, and himself hibernate, or semi-hibernate, until the spring. Similarly the museum's archaeologists and anthropologists should study the Iroquois Indians north of Lakes Erie and Ontario and the St. Lawrence River, but not south of those geographical boundaries. And when investigating the origin and movements of Canada's Arctic Eskimos they should forget the brothers and cousins of those Eskimos in Alaska and Greenland.

There seemed little likelihood, therefore, that my superiors would sanction any sortie of a museum archaeologist into Arctic Alaska. However, desperation lends courage even to the most timid. In 1926, when submitting to my immediate chief the summer field program of my staff, I boldly requested for myself a modest sum—$3,000 I think it was—to cover the expenses of a field trip to Bering Strait to search for traces of ancient Eskimos. Miracle of miracles, the authorities sanctioned the request. How did it happen?[7]

In Canada as elsewhere, a veil impenetrable even to newspaper correspondents often conceals the deliberations of government administrators. Rumour whispered, however, that when the all-powerful member of the museum's hierarchy observed the $3,000 item in his organization's estimates, he asked, uncertainly,

"Bering Strait? Where is Bering Strait?"

"It is north of the Yukon, sir," replied the adviser at his back.

"Ah yes, the Yukon," murmured the Great one. "The Yukon, our darling at the turn of the century and our headache ever since. We must certainly do what we can for the Yukon," and he ticked off his approval.

My reader will understand that I cannot attest the accuracy of this rumour, but will he deny its credibility? In any case, what mattered was not how the project came to be approved, but that it was approved, and at bureaucracy's top level. Only then was I free to work out detailed plans.

No air service criss-crossed Alaska or northern Canada at that date. Throughout the summer, a passenger steamer plied monthly from Seattle to Nome, in the Bering Sea, whence a small schooner carried mail to Wales and to Kotzebue Sound. The navigation season opened at the end of May, after the U.S. revenue steamer *Bear* had certified that the Bering Sea's ice-mantle had broken up and unstrengthened vessels might safely navigate its waters. Well before the opening of spring, I booked a passage to Nome, but postponed further travel arrangements until I could consult U.S. officials and other residents of that port.[8]

Wales[9]

On June 12, the first passenger steamer of the season landed me in Nome. From there I travelled on to Wales in the mail schooner, a forty-foot motor vessel which generally made the trip in thirty-six hours, but on this occasion required six days, four of which it spent at the little settlement of Teller, in Port Clarence, waiting for a change of wind to carry away block-

---

[7] The explanation that follows is almost certainly an example of my father poking fun at his administrative personnel.

[8] My father left Ottawa May 24, travelling by train west to Seattle, then by coastal steamer to Nome.

[9] I inserted this heading and the one that follows to clarify the organization of the chapter. [S.E.J.]

Figure 25 Eskimo village of Wales, Bering Strait, northwestern Alaska, 1926. In the middle, at left, is the U.S. schoolhouse. In the distance on the right is the mound excavated by Jenness.
Photo by D. Jenness, CMC 67734

ading ice floes. At Wales, the U.S. school teacher[10] welcomed me and provided me with a comfortable room in his schoolhouse, which two weeks before had closed its doors for the summer vacation.

Wales at that time was a village of two dozen one-roomed log cabins, scattered higgledy-piggledy just above high-tide mark along a sandy beach, which stretched west–northwest about two miles from the foot of Wales Mountain to Cape Prince of Wales, the nearest point of the American continent to Asia.[11] Mountains sheltered the village's roadstead from easterly and northerly winds, but gave it no protection against westerly or southerly ones. When those winds raised a sea, vessels ran for safety to Port Clarence. Half a mile of level tundra separated the village from the mountains behind it, and across this tundra meandered a small stream, which supplied the community with drinking water. Near the eastern end of the beach, right under Wales Mountain, was the schoolhouse, and on the rising ground at the foot of the mountain, two inhabited log cabins and the ruins of several older ones. The settlement's winter

[10]The school teacher's name was C.M. Garber (Jenness, 1928b, p. 72). He secured native labour to help my father with his excavating and himself participated in all phases of the work (Camsell, 1926).

[11]In the nineteenth century, this community may have been the largest Eskimo village in Alaska. It was also the southernmost bowhead whaling station on the Alaskan mainland (Morrison, 1991, p. 3). Alaska and Asia are separated here by fifty miles.

population, all Eskimos save the school teacher and his family, numbered over one hundred, but in summer it dropped to below seventy-five, for nearly all the men left home to seek employment at a tin mine in the hinterland, or to tend the reindeer herd that roamed the Wales peninsula. The only workers who could help me excavate, the school teacher informed me, were an old man and half a dozen boy scouts.

After carefully reconnoitring the village and its surrounding terrain, I decided to excavate a dozen rectangular depressions, partly filled with water, on a low mount in the tundra, three hundred feet behind the modern houses on the beach. They seemed to mark the sites of dwellings, judging by their dimensions and the many protruding whale-ribs whose bone had outlasted the wooden parts of the walls and roofs. But the ground was frozen hard, to what depth I could not guess, for Wales, though a little south of the Arctic Circle, lay within the region where the earth's surface is perpetually frozen, often down to several hundred feet, and never thaws out from one year's end to another save for an inch or two at the surface. In the gold-bearing gravels on the outskirts of Nome, placer miners were driving iron pipes into the permafrost and forcing water through them to thaw out the ground and permit the use of dredges, but in archaeological excavations no such device seemed practicable, because it would damage or displace too many specimens. In any case, I lacked the necessary equipment. One method, and one only, seemed feasible, viz. to scrape away the inch or two of surface that had thawed out, expose to the atmosphere the still-frozen under-layer and let nature continue the thawing, two inches or less daily according to the weather. It was a laborious way to remove the three feet of earth covering the floors on which we expected to find most of our specimens, but we reached floor level in eight of the depressions, and in five found treasures in abundance.

Each passing day, however, made me more anxious. The ruins we were digging clearly dated back several hundred years, but they were not nearly as ancient as I had hoped to discover in this locality. Our progress, too, was depressingly slow. Mid-July, the brief summer's turning point, had already overtaken us, almost unnoticed. When formulating my plans in Ottawa, I had reckoned on discovering and sampling several sites in this general region, not at Wales only, but on the two Diomede Islands and perhaps also on the Siberian shore west of them, where a French-Canadian fur-trader[12] had observed, around 1916, scores of stone, bone and ivory implements protruding from the face of a high cliff overlooking the sea. The Canadian government had requested Moscow's permission for me to excavate there, and although no authorization had reached Ottawa at the time of my departure, I was still hoping that it would catch up with me before the end of summer. But my plans had been too ambitious, and the funds at my disposal too exiguous.

Unable to charter or purchase a motorboat that would be available at all times, I was dependent on local transport, and that had failed me. The mail schooner which had landed me at Wales on June 20 had undertaken to call back for me on July 6 and convey me to Little Diomede Island twenty-two miles away, but the vessel never reappeared, prevented from stopping at Wales or anywhere else, I learned later, by a contrary wind and high seas, which drove it straight to Nome, with no expectation of returning north for three or four weeks. Early in

---

[12]The fur-trader was probably Captain Joseph Bernard, then sailing out of Nome, with whom my father was acquainted.

July, nine or ten Siberian Eskimos unexpectedly crossed the Bering Strait from East Cape, slept overnight on the Wales' beach under their upturned *umiak* or skin boat, and pushed on to Nome the next morning, hoping to buy badly needed supplies with their furs. Four days later, they returned and spent another night on Wales' beach. I might have hired them to ferry me as far as Little Diomede, but a slight change of wind could easily have driven their overladen boat off course, and I disliked the idea of landing in a Soviet settlement without proper papers, especially as some White Russians, our Eskimo visitors told us, were still resisting the Reds in this remote corner of northeastern Siberia. Very reluctantly, therefore, I passed over that chance of bridging the eastern half of Bering Strait.

Except for this unscheduled visit from Siberia, Wales had been completely cut off from the outside world ever since my arrival. Even the school teacher was worried. He had been treating as best he could a local Eskimo woman who desperately needed expert medical attention and hospital care, but because there was no telegraph line in this part of Alaska and as yet no radio anywhere, he was unable even to communicate with the authorities in Nome.

Temporarily, therefore, I was marooned, but I could still keep on digging. Leaving undisturbed a few of the mound depressions so that future archaeologists could check my interpretations, I shifted my operations to the brow of a bank at the foot of Wales Mountain, where two house ruins seemed to be resting one on top of the other—although this first appraisal of their relationship needed to be confirmed by careful digging, since the ground had slipped a little. Nearby was a third ruin, which appeared to be of equal antiquity. I instructed my now trained workmen to begin excavating these three sites while I myself scoured the edge of the tundra for possible remains from a hypothetical period when the relative levels of land and sea differed from their present levels, and nature had not yet created the tundra plain because the ocean's tides were lapping the bases of the mountains.

I found no remains at the tundra's edge as ancient as those we were unearthing, but I did discover that the present-day Arctic can conjure up for the archaeologist some very unusual labour difficulties. Mine originated not from my hired workmen, whose diligence and discipline were exemplary, but from the neglected women and children in the village, who could see no reason why they should not profit from the southern interloper who was rifling the homes and property of their ancestors. At the outset, they did no more than rake over the rubbish heaps beside their dwellings and the greasy floors of the earth cellars in which they stored their meat and blubber, and vie with one another in selling me whatever specimens they found in those places. This was agreeable to every one, even though what they brought me was of little or no value. But when some of them stole out at midnight, which was nearly as bright as midday, and despoiled the floor of a ruin my workmen had just exposed, I felt decidedly aggrieved.

Yet what could I do? It was their village, not mine. I could perhaps bribe them not to disturb the sites on which I and my crew were working. That would not be difficult. But would they honour the arrangement and police one another?

Memory then brought back a tale about an Alaskan Eskimo who had thrown a stone at a graveyard and with difficulty escaped the attack of a skull which emerged from its grave and pursued him down the hill-side. It suggested to me that I might *taboo* my sites, as the natives of Melanesia and Polynesia used to *taboo* their coconut trees against robbers. I might invoke the ghosts of long-dead Eskimos to protect them, call in supernatural guardians whom no villager would dare to provoke. It seemed a brilliant idea. Accordingly, one evening after my workmen had returned to their homes, I surreptitiously planted, in the thawing floor of a dwelling which they were excavating, two skulls that I had picked up on the tundra. Glancing back at my handiwork, I fairly glowed with satisfaction at the sight of the two grisly faces peering at me out of the dark earth. "No Eskimo woman or child will dare disturb those ghosts," I said to myself, and that night I slept the sleep of the conqueror.

My confidence was short-lived. It might have been justified fifty years before, but times had changed. The white man had undermined the old religion of the Eskimos, ridiculed their ancient superstitions and the medicine men who upheld them, and destroyed all respect for age and wisdom. The Alaskan natives, like their fellow citizens farther south, had been undergoing a social and intellectual revolution, and the young were in open revolt against the outmoded ways of their parents and grandparents. When I examined my house-site the morning after I tabooed it, I found its floor systematically pillaged, and its two skull guardians ignominiously lying at the bottom of the bank over which the marauders had kicked them.

I consulted my old Eskimo foreman, as I should have done perhaps at the beginning. "It is the children," he sighed. "No adult woman would dare meddle with the dead, but the children no longer respect anyone or anything. Perhaps they will stop molesting us if you refuse to buy any more specimens from them."

The sudden arrival of the U.S. Revenue steamer *Bear* solved my problem. It brought me permission from the Soviet government to dig at East Cape and Utan, on the Siberian shore, but stipulated that before proceeding to those places, I must report to the Soviet authorities at Petropavlovsk, a thousand miles to the south, and immediately after my return transmit all my notes and specimens to the same authorities. Obviously, it was no longer possible to comply with these conditions, or at least with the first of them. I therefore abandoned the Siberian part of my program and applied to the captain of the *Bear* for passage to Little Diomede Island, whose school teacher he was transporting to a village in Kotzebue Sound.

The Diomede Islands[13]

We crossed to Little Diomede [Island] that night. By noon the following day, I had installed myself in its empty schoolhouse and the *Bear* was disappearing over the horizon, carrying the island's ex-teacher and his family to their new post.[14] Just before he sailed, the captain promised to call for me again about twelve days later when he would be returning from Alaska's most northern community, Barrow, and I programmed my work accordingly. Little Diomede Island was a grim home even for its ninety-four Eskimo inhabitants, most of whom left it during the summer to work in Nome and other places. The original island had been an immense crag of

---

[13]Jenness, 1928b, 1929. The two Diomede Islands lie midway between Alaska and Siberia in Bering Strait. The smaller island lies on the Alaskan side of the international boundary, the larger one, some four miles to the west, on the Siberian side. Big Diomede Island is twenty-one miles from Siberia, Little Diomede Island is twenty-two miles from Alaska (E. Jenness, 1933). The international date line runs between the two. Both islands are rocky, barren, and bleak.

[14]The departing school teacher was Mr. Charles Menedelook, who offered accommodation to my father and obtained native labour to assist in the excavation work (Camsell, 1926).

granitic rocks two miles long by one wide, permeated with tabular blocks of recrystallised limestone, but when time weathered away the limestone the crag broke down into a mass of breccia. Today, its shore-line presents a succession of steep precipices, broken only in the southwest corner, where the mountain slopes down less steeply and one can land from a boat in calm weather on a narrow boulder beach, about nine hundred feet long, which every southerly gale pounds with heavy breakers. Just above the breaker line stands (or stood in 1926) the two-story U.S. government schoolhouse, and above that building, along a narrow pathway, ten one-roomed huts built of beach boulders laid one on top of another without mortar, seven of them entered through frame porches. Over that tiny village towered the mountain, rising here at a sixty-degree angle to a height of 1,300 feet, and culminating in an almost level tableland strewn with lichen-covered rocks and sedgy pools. An uncanny apprehension gripped the adventurer who clambered up over the breccia to this tableland; he felt that if mother earth should shiver ever so slightly, the whole mountain would disintegrate and collapse in ruins under his feet.

No land animals made the island their home, although a few foxes and polar bears visited it during the winter. On every cliff, however, nested multitudes of sea-fowl—murres, cormorants, kittiwakes, and puffins—and the huge rocks in the breccia sheltered thousands of auklets, which at dawn and dusk moved between the mountain and the sea in dense flocks, like starlings attacking a grain field. The Eskimos hid among the rocks and caught them on the wing in large hand-nets similar to those of butterfly hunters.

Auklets, however, were a minor delicacy in their diet. Their main food came directly from the sea, for great numbers of whales and walruses migrated through the strait each spring and fall, and both hair and bearded seals abounded within the strait all the year round. It was these mammals which made the island permanently habitable for its small population. They supplied the natives not with food alone, but with that very useful article, walrus ivory, which the Eskimos prized for tools and weapons in the centuries before they acquired iron, and in 1926 eagerly sold to white traders, who paid them $2.50 a pound for the fresh ivory, and $3.00 or $3.50 a pound for the fossilized or discoloured ivory commonly found in old ruins. The island's position in the middle of the strait favoured its occupation by a people who would act as middlemen in the trade between the two continents. During my twenty five days of residence there, a boat-load of Chukchee natives from Siberia called in, bought what they needed from the inhabitants, and immediately returned to their homeland, or perhaps spent the night at the Eskimo settlement on Soviet-owned Big Diomede Island four miles away. Very few Eskimos in this region understood a word of the Chukchee language, or *vice-versa*, yet in pre-European times[15] a boatload of Chukchees frequently crossed Bering Strait during the brief summer and proceeded up the Alaskan coast to attend a regional trading mart in Kotzebue Sound.

After the Chukchees visited us, two white men, one an American and the other a Russian who spoke little or no English, landed on Little Diomede from a chartered Alaskan motorboat, rested half a day, then engaged my two workmen to ferry them across to Big Diomede

---

[15]That is, prior to the arrival of Europeans on the Alaskan coast.

Figure 26 An Eskimo catching auklets with a hand net, Little Diomede Island, Bering Strait, 1926. The live captives are strung on a line by their beaks to decoy others.
Photo by D. Jenness, CMC 67798

Island in an *umiak*. Who they were, how they fared on Big Diomede, and what became of them afterwards, I never learned.[16]

Nearly as mysterious as these two men were a Norwegian missionary and his wife who occupied a small frame dwelling at one end of the Eskimo village. They had refrained from

[16]The American my father mentions here was probably a newspaper man named Hammond who chartered a boat at Nome and went to Little Diomede Island that summer. Early in September, V. Stefansson wrote my father that there had been a sensational account in the *New York Times* of my father's recent discoveries on Little Diomede Island, dispatched by a Mr. Hammond, newspaper correspondent, from Nome. Because of the abundance of errors it contained, however, Stefansson had felt it necessary to respond with his own interpretation of my father's work and discoveries (Stefansson to Jenness, letter dated September 8, 1926, Jenness Correspondence, Box 658, Folder 41, Archives, CMC). My father replied that the man was certainly more after sensation than facts, and that he had no idea he was a newspaper man at the time of the visit (Jenness to Stefansson, October 1, 1926, Jenness Correspondence, Box 658, Folder 41, Archives, CMC).

visiting the *Bear* or associating with any of its crew during the three hours that vessel lingered at Little Diomede, and when I called on them after it departed they seemed strangely aloof and uncommunicative. At no time did I see them talking to any of the five Eskimo families who spent the summer on the island, and my two workmen knew nothing about them except that they had arrived just after the opening of navigation and spoke only five or six words of Eskimo. I suspect that they were apostles of a Pentecostal faith which invaded the Kotzebue district about this time and Canada's eastern Arctic twenty years later, but, whatever may have been their religious affiliation, one could not but admire their fervour and courage in choosing this desolate and lonely island for their mission.

Level ground for building existed nowhere except on the island's summit. Every dwelling on the slope above the beach appeared to cover an earlier one, and wherever a space lay empty, enormous rocks such as frequently tumbled down the mountainside concealed every trace of ancient ruins. All the small rubbish heaps in front of the houses had been overturned for their ivory, but one large heap seemed worth investigating, although it too had been ransacked to a depth of about two and a half feet. I marked out a rectangle fifteen feet by twelve feet on its frozen surface, and carefully worked over the soil as it thawed out, but because the temperature never exceeded 45°F in the shade, or 70°F in the sun, in twenty-one days we were unable to carry down our pit more than a scant three feet. At that depth, several inches below the level reached by the ivory-hunters, specimens became much more numerous, and a few of them differed in shape and also in the designs etched on their surfaces from any that I had found at Wales.

The rubbish heap seemed to extend down a further two feet, and I am sure would have revealed other differences had we been able to complete its excavation. But the brief summer had ended, and I had to suspend operations and return to the mainland. The villagers probably deepened the pit after my departure to reclaim the abundant ivory in its lower levels; and if they did, their uncritical disturbance of the strata will have destroyed whatever value the site retained for later archaeologists.

Like the mound at Wales, this rubbish heap on Little Diomede yielded large numbers of rectangular slats of ivory and antler, which the islanders had lashed together in rows and worn as breastplates or coats of mail. They confirmed the tradition, current in Siberia as well as in Alaska, that peaceful trade between the continents had alternated with hostile raids, and suggested that the middlemen in the strait, both the Diomede Islanders and the Eskimos at Wales, had been no more scrupulous or popular with their neighbours than were the German barons who, from their castles overlooking the Rhine, used to raid or levy toll on the traffic that passed their gates. I saw many stones on the western face of Wales Mountain that had been set on edge to shield the local warriors from the arrows of their enemies; and Wales' legends told of frequent battles with Asiatic invaders, and even of a flight of the Wales natives five hundred miles north to Point Barrow.

Old habits die hard, especially evil ones. In the middle of the nineteenth century, when American whaling vessels began to pursue the bowhead whales north of Bering Strait and at the same time trade with the Eskimos of both coasts, the Wales natives tried to maintain their traditional role of middlemen and tax-collectors; and on more than one occasion, they attacked vessels resisting their extortions and massacred some or all of their crews.

Retribution came swiftly. One noon, a rather small whaling ship dropped anchor in Wales roadstead and awaited visitors from shore. A crowd gathered on the beach, launched a large *umiak* and approached the vessel. Its captain, knowing the reputation of the natives, scrutinized the heavily laden boat through his telescope and observed that all the rowers were women, but all the passengers men. Forewarned, he ordered his crew to drop only one rope ladder over the side and to arm themselves against a possible attack. The *umiak* drew alongside, the Eskimo men climbed aboard one behind the other, each concealing a long knife under his clothing, and pretended to look innocently around the deck. One of them stealthily approached the bridge, pulled out his knife and rushed on the captain, but a vigilant seaman knocked him down with a belaying pin. Fighting then became general, but the crew of the whaler soon gained the upper hand. Four of the Eskimos jumped into the sea and were picked up by the *umiak*; others fled below deck, where the seamen hunted them down, struck them over the head and tossed their bodies overboard. The *umiak* tried to escape to shore, but the captain trained a gun on it and killed or drowned all its occupants. About ten percent of Wales' population perished in this disaster, which so cowed the surviving inhabitants that never again did they molest an American vessel.[17]

Every time I looked up from my Little Diomede pit I could see Big Diomede Island four miles away beckoning me across the water, and the desire to prowl along its shore for traces of early man became irresistible. There was a measure of risk in the escapade, of course. I would have to keep out of sight of the Eskimo settlement on the south end of the island, lest some Soviet official stationed there should suddenly intercept me in his motorboat, and dampen my curiosity in an uncomfortable jail while he awaited instructions from Moscow. A Soviet gunboat, too, the *Krasnyy Oktyabr'*, was patrolling this northeast corner of Siberia to prevent another invasion by the aggressive imperialists on the American side of the strait who had occupied Wrangel Island a few years earlier.[18] We had seen the steamer's smoke one clear afternoon between ourselves and East Cape. Might it not suddenly round the end of Big Diomede Island, "rescue" me and my crew from the perilous waters on the western side of the International Boundary, and carry us off to Petropavlovsk, or even Vladivostok, for a conference with political and juridical experts in those strictly administered ports?

To be sure there were risks, but my Eskimos knew little or nothing about them, and I myself deemed them so light that they merely strengthened the temptation to undertake the excursion. So on two days when our frozen pit discouraged any immediate attention, my workmen and I light-heartedly skipped over the intervening water in a small *umiak*, breaking the "time barrier" on both the outward and the return journeys. For between the two islands passes not only the International Boundary but the International Date Line, so that when we left Little Diomede at 8 a.m. on a Wednesday morning, it was 9 a.m. of a Thursday morning one hour later when we landed on Big Diomede; and when we pushed off from Big Diomede at 6 p.m. that Thursday evening, the day mysteriously changed to Wednesday again before we disembarked at 7 p.m. on Little Diomede.

---

[17]This story appears to refer to a well-known incident that took place July 5, 1877, when Prince of Wales natives attacked the crew of the whaling ship *William H. Allen* and its captain, George Gilley, and were shot or clubbed to death (Bockstoce, 1986, pp. 189–191).

[18]Arctic explorer Vilhjalmur Stefansson sent an unauthorized expedition of four men and an Alaskan Eskimo woman to Wrangel Island in the summer of 1921 to claim the island for Canada. Only the woman, Ada Blackjack, survived (Stefansson, 1925; Niven, 2003).

On our first visit to Big Diomede, we reconnoitred its eastern side, a rocky coast as we anticipated, where the land rose fairly steeply from the sea to a height of perhaps a thousand feet. After skirting it for a mile without finding a landing place, we came upon a very small, gravelly beach on which we pulled up our boat, and, climbing a shadowy path to a narrow terrace eighty feet above sea level, discovered the ruins of two houses and a small rubbish heap half buried under a shallow layer of earth.

We excavated the entire site during this and a second visit a few days later, and from the specimens we retrieved, [I] deduced that it was either coeval with the mound dwellings at Wales or a little younger. What really puzzled us, however, was why the Eskimos had troubled to build any houses in a spot that offered them neither fresh water, apparently, nor adequate protection for their boat; for they must have brought all their supplies by sea. Could the settlement have been just a temporary sentinel post from which Siberian natives had maintained a watch against enemies approaching from the American mainland under cover of Little Diomede Island?

August 7, the day I expected the *Bear* to arrive from the north, was very stormy, and neither then nor later did the vessel put in an appearance. For the second time I was marooned, and realized more than ever the truth of the remark a sourdough had made to me in Nome: "You can easily arrange to be landed on Little Diomede in July, or even in June, but whether you can escape from it again before winter sets in may prove more doubtful." I could do nothing but wait patiently and keep digging, but most of the days were foggy, and the fog was accompanied by a cold drizzle that seemed to slow down the thawing of my pit. To make matters worse, I myself was indisposed physically, the result doubtless of my diet, for the survival rate from my cooking has always been very low.

No boat regularly visited Little Diomede, and the chances of a stray motor-launch dropping in before the freeze-up were extremely slim. So the outlook seemed clouded. For some unexplained reason, however, the Arctic breeds fatalism rather than gloom, and I felt no special anxiety as the days flowed peacefully by. *Tout est pour le mieux dans le meilleur des mondes.*[19]

Then, in the late afternoon of August 18, the unexpected happened. A small motorboat chugged around the southwest corner of Little Diomede and drew in to the beach. Two Canadian botanists stepped ashore, A. Erling Porsild and his brother Robert, the former even at that day an outstanding authority on the plant life of the American Arctic. The Canadian government had commissioned them to study the possibility of purchasing a herd of domesti-cated reindeer in Alaska, driving it a thousand miles along the Arctic coast to the Mackenzie River delta, and establishing it there on Canadian soil as the nucleus of a profitable reindeer industry.[20] Finding themselves at Teller with three free days on their hands before travelling inland to

---

[19] "All is for the best in the best of possible worlds." This well-known quotation from Voltaire's famous novel, *Candide*, written in 1759, is highly appropriate here. The novel's main theme is optimism; its main char-acter, Candide, was taught that when something bad occurs, something happens to make things work out all right. That philosophy came to mind when my father wrote of his stay on Diomede Island. Voltaire applied his wit and his knowledge in his writing, often incurring the wrath of the French government. My father uses the same tactics in parts of this chapter, even poking fun at the Canadian government.

[20] The Canadian government hoped in this manner to provide employment for some of the Native people around the mouth of the Mackenzie River as well as a continuing supply of meat and furs for them, as had been done in Alaska years earlier.

inspect the local reindeer herds, they had hired this small boat and its engineer to transport them to Little Diomede, whose botanical relations with its continental neighbours still awaited investigations. They knew that I was somewhere in Alaska, but whether north or south of Bering Strait, whether on the coast or in the interior, they had no idea, and their surprise at meeting me on Little Diomede was as great as my own. That night, they shared my quarters in the schoolhouse while the engineer slept on his boat.

Early the next morning, the two botanists climbed to the plateau on the island's summit and filled their field herbaria with samples of every species of plant that met their eyes. The sea appeared calm that day, but the following morning when we packed our bags and boarded the motorboat, a strong north wind was blowing, just how strong we did not realize until we reached the open sea. The boat pitched and rolled, and, every now and then, the heavy spray completely concealed the figure of our helmsman, Robert Porsild, who, bareheaded and wrapped in an oilskin, triumphantly slid our little craft down the biggest waves to prevent any heavy pounding. He was a magnificent seaman, well-trained on Greenland's stormy coast, and we entertained no fears for our safety so long as our boat held together, but twice its engineer, better acquainted that we were with its antiquity and the rottenness of its planks, thrust his head out of the engine-room and shouted "If she pounds once again like that she'll break in two." By good fortune she held, the waves subsided as soon as we ran under the lea of the Wales Peninsula, and before midnight we moored our worn-out vessel at the peaceful dock in Teller harbour and found dry beds for ourselves in the settlement's tiny inn.

After thus rescuing me from a long, chilly winter on Little Diomede,[21] the Porsilds resumed their reindeer investigations[22] in the Teller district while I awaited the schooner to Nome. Bad weather delayed it for five days, during one of which I hired a small motorboat to run me seventeen miles up the Tuksuk River to check a rumour of rock paintings, which are common enough in Indian regions farther south but had never been signalled in Eskimo territory. We came upon fourteen or more rude figures of human beings drawn roughly half-size

---

[21]Unknown to him at the time, he could have left the island on the U.S. Bureau of Education motor ship *Boxer*, which reached Little Diomede Island a few days after his departure. On board was a young German immigrant and student, Otto Geist, who was collecting various kinds of specimens for the newly opened Alaska Agricultural College and School of Mines. While the ship was at anchor, Geist obtained assorted archaeological specimens from some of the natives and spent some time at the diggings my father had just vacated, then proceeded with the ship to St. Lawrence Island, where he carried out further collecting (Keim, 1969, p. 94). It is interesting to speculate that if my father had been picked up by the *Boxer* and visited St. Lawrence Island that summer, he might have wanted to excavate on St. Lawrence Island instead of suggesting the American archaeologist, Henry Collins, do so. Collins subsequent archaeological work on St. Lawrence Island confirmed the early culture my father identified tentatively on Little Diomede Island (Collins, 1931).

[22]Their investigations later took them east to the Mackenzie Delta, where Erling Porsild determined the location of the best grazing sites for the reindeer that his brother Robert subsequently helped drive east from northwestern Alaska. Erling later became chief botanist at the National Museum of Canada in Ottawa, and he and my father continued for the rest of their lives the friendship they started on Little Diomede Island. In the late 1940s, Porsild purchased the house of Percy Taverner after the latter's death. Taverner was Canada's bird authority and worked on the floor above my father at the Victoria Memorial Museum. He and my father knew each other well. Mrs. Taverner was my piano teacher during the last half of the 1930s and first half of the 1940s.

in black and red paint on a vertical block of chlorite schist that dipped down into the water on the river's north bank. All were greatly weathered, some indeed almost indecipherable, but there was no other clue to their age. My Eskimo boatman thought that they represented a battle with Siberian natives, but I myself could see no relationship between the individual figures, no attempt to portray a scene or outline a composite picture, and suspect, therefore, that he was giving over-free rein to his imagination.

That pleasant excursion ended my archaeological researches in Alaska, apart from a short run by car a few miles east of Nome to inspect a house site which had yielded a small number of potsherds, similar in type to the pottery the Bering Sea natives were fabricating at the time of their first encounter with Europeans.

The season was now too advanced to wander afield and attempt any further digging, since the steamer to Seattle was scheduled to arrive in two weeks. I spent that fortnight, accordingly, in Nome, tracking down Eskimos from various districts in Arctic Alaska, analysing their dialects, and trying to work out a "Grimm's law" of the phonetic changes their language had undergone in the course of the centuries. North and south of the trade and migration gateway at Bering Strait, I discovered, the Eskimo language had diverged in two distinct directions, a phenomenon which explained why Knud Rasmussen, the Greenland-born explorer, had been able to under-stand and, after a few days, converse with any Eskimo between his homeland and Point Barrow, at the northern tip of Alaska, why he encountered increasing difficulty from Point Barrow south to Wales, only half understood the Bering Strait dialect, and required an interpreter for every dialect farther south. It was unfortunate that I failed to locate at Nome any Eskimos from south of that port except one Nunivak Islander, for if the dialects between Wales and the Aleutian Archipelago have changed as progressively—albeit in a different direction—as those from Wales northeast to Barrow and along the Arctic coast to Hudson Bay and Greenland, they might shed a bright light on the place of the Aleut language in the Eskimo family, and furnish one more clue to the past history of the unfortunate islanders who spoke that tongue.

A grim tragedy marred my departure from Alaska. Nome has no harbour, only a long gravel beach exposed to every gale. The shallowness of the coast compels the Seattle steamer to anchor a mile offshore, and from that distance to disembark and pick up its passengers in flat-bottomed dories. The sea was so choppy on embarkation day that the vessel had to lash to its lea side a spacious lighter, to which it transferred us from the dories before hoisting us on a platform, three dozen at a time, up to its deck forty feet or more above our heads. The ship rolled heavily when the deck crane was hauling my group up, the platform packed with its human freight gyrated alarmingly, and, fearful of being pushed overboard, I gripped with both hands the rope that encircled us. Suddenly a man standing beside me lurched, dropped to the floor in a heap and disappeared over the edge before any one could clutch him. He struck the lighter with his head and died instantly. The steamer's officers would give out no information about him, but a fellow-passenger told me that he was a miner who had worked all summer in the interior of Alaska, and was returning to his home in the United States on this, the next to last boat of the season.[23]

---

[23]This tragic incident is so similar to the one recorded by George H. Wilkins in his diary on August 29, 1916 (Wilkins, 1913–1916; S.E. Jenness, 2004, p. 361) that I suspect my father unintentionally assigned his earlier experience to this departure from Nome.

I reached Ottawa on September 20, after an absence of four months. Before long I was asked what had I achieved for the Yukon during those four months, that "headache" region for which the "Great One" in my department had expressed such deep concern. What had I accomplished to justify the expenditure of nearly $3,000?

No man can judge impartially his own achievements, or his own shortcomings, but I feel confident that time will justify the following assessment of my field trip to Bering Strait.[24] When I left Ottawa on May 24, I prayed Dame Fortune to grant me the luck to discover traces, not of the first immigrants into America—that would have been too presumptuous—but of immigrants who reached this continent centuries and perhaps millennia before the Christian era. But the fickle lady scorned her unworthy suitor and granted me no such luck.

Yet she did take pity on me, and allow me to blaze a trail for the more highly trained archaeologists who came after me. She even permitted me to stake out the first mile of that trail by revealing, in that shallow pit on Little Diomede Island, traces of an Eskimo culture that pre-dated any uncovered up to that time in Arctic America—an "Old Bering Sea" culture (brilliantly elucidated during the next five years by the Washington, D.C., archaeologist Henry B. Collins).[25] This culture flourished some two thousand years ago and fathered all subsequent Eskimo cultures and sub-cultures in northern Alaska, including the "Thule" culture that spread, between A.D. 800 and 1000, from the Barrow region right across the top of the continent to Greenland and Labrador.

And Dame Fortune bestowed on me another mark of her favour. From my summer field trip to Wales and Little Diomede Island developed the fruitful collaboration of Canadian, United States, and Danish archaeologists, which has endured to the present day. It has carried the history of man's occupation of Greenland and Arctic America back to 2000 B.C., and of Arctic Alaska perhaps to 3000 B.C. And it has promoted cooperation in other Arctic enterprises, including the establishment of an Arctic Institute of North America in which the nationals of Canada, United States, and Denmark participate.

[*Over the course of but a few weeks, my father collected almost eighteen hundred artifacts from the sites at Wales and about twelve hundred from Little Diomede Island. These two 1926 collections of Alaskan Eskimo artifacts, like my father's 1914 collection of some three thousand artifacts from Barter Island on the north Alaskan coast, remained in storage for many years at the National Museum of Canada without study, description, or photographing. In the 1960s, American archaeologist Edwin Hall Jr. studied and reported on the Barter Island collection,[26] and nearly a quarter of a century later, Canadian Museum of Civilization archaeologist David Morrison studied and published on the Wales and Little Diomede Island collections.[27] The Barter Island studies provided absolute evidence for the*

---

[24]Indeed it did. Sixty-five years later, Dr. David Morrison, curator of anthropology at the Canadian Museum of Civilization, described my father's Alaskan collection as "aesthetically magnificent" and his field investigations as "the first systematic archaeological work in Alaska," laying the groundwork for later archaeological investigations (Morrison, 1991, p. iii).

[25]My father introduced the term "Old Bering Sea culture" for this pre-Thule culture in a National Museum of Canada Bulletin (Jenness, 1928b). Collins' edifying work was done on St. Lawrence Island (Collins, 1931), 160 miles south of Bering Strait and the Diomede Islands.

[26]Hall, Edwin, Jr., 1971.

[27]Morrison, D., 1991.

eastern migration of the Thule culture, whereas the Bering Strait studies confirmed the presence of an older culture stratigraphically beneath the Thule culture level, to which my father gave the name Old Bering Sea culture.

My father did not succeed in discovering any evidence of actual migrations of tribes from Asia to America or vice versa, but he did find ample evidence that such migrations were highly probable. In the summer, a trip by skin boat across the strait is possible within two days, with an overnight stop on one or other of the Diomede Islands. In the winter, a strong current usually keeps open a lane of water on the east side of Little Diomede Island, prohibiting passage over the ice in most years. But Eskimo traditions and numerous remains of armour in both ancient and modern dwellings in northwestern Alaska indicate raids by Siberian peoples during many centuries.[28]

In addition to his significant archaeological accomplishments that summer, my father also managed to gather about one thousand Eskimo words from the villagers of Wales, and three hundred to four hundred words each from East Cape (Siberia), Inglestat in Norton Sound, and Nunivak Island off the mouth of the Yukon River. These he later incorporated in a manuscript on Eskimo vocabulary from Wales to Coronation Gulf.[29] *From the summer's studies and during his three years in the Arctic a decade earlier, he was able to conclude that the Eskimo dialects from Wales east to Greenland showed only minor changes. My father did not have the opportunity to study the dialect of the Diomede Islanders, but noted that it appeared to be intermediate between that of Wales and East Cape. The East Cape dialect differed greatly from those north and east from Wales. From St. Michael south, he established a significant change in the Eskimo language.*[30] *He collected this information for the linguistic specialists, who sought to trace origins and migrations of peoples through the commonalities of their languages.*

My father's field expenses were well spent.[31]] [S.J.]

---

[28] D. Jenness, 1928b, p. 78.

[29] D. Jenness, 1927b, 1928c.

[30] D. Jenness, 1927b, 1928b, p. 79.

[31] My father actually spent only $1,750 of the $3,000 he had budgeted for his summer's work. Upon his return to Ottawa in September he tried to have some of the unused $1,250 transferred to Marius Barbeau's field accounts in case he needed extra funds, but his request was turned down (Jenness to Barbeau, letter dated September 30, 1926, Barbeau Collection, Box 206, Folder 28, Archives, CMC).

1926–1939: ADMINISTRATIVE TEDIUM

10

Stuart E. Jenness

My father was fully aware when he accepted the position of Chief of the Anthropology Division that he would have to sacrifice a high percentage of his time to the day-to-day tasks of the job. He had, after all, been attending to these tasks for nearly four months, so was well acquainted with how little time was left for his own research and writing. He had seen the large amount of routine correspondence that required responses, the memoranda from the Acting Director of the Victoria Memorial Museum, notes from other administrative personnel in the Geological Survey, and the various requests of his staff. These he could generally deal with calmly and logically, although they were time-consuming. What he had not anticipated was the petty haggling he would encounter with some of the administrators, sometimes because they considered his division and its activities and reports less important than those of the Geological Survey, under whose jurisdiction his division and the museum came, and sometimes for personal or other reasons. He could deal well with honest problems and individuals, but had low tolerance for individuals he considered were trying to throw their weight around. He had no way of anticipating all the challenges that lay ahead. Nor could he have foreseen the two events that severely dampened his efforts to develop the Anthropology Division over the course of the next fourteen years: Barbeau's sudden unfriendliness and Canada's economic woes of the 1930s.

My father officially took over the duties of Chief of Anthropology on January 12, 1926, succeeding Dr. Sapir, the division's first chief, but did not actually move into Sapir's office until the following month. Sapir, a former student of Franz Boas (the widely known anthropologist at Columbia University), developed and steered the division extremely well following his appointment in 1910. Within four years, he had added four professional men (ethnologist Marius Barbeau, 1911; archaeologist Harlan I. Smith, 1911; ethnologist Diamond Jenness, 1913; and physical anthropologist, F.H.S. Knowles, 1914), and two academically less qualified but highly capable men (social anthropologist F. W. Waugh, 1913, and archaeologist W.J. Wintemberg, 1913). He also oversaw the activities of a small group of professional men located elsewhere in Canada and the United States, whom he hired on short-term contracts. Under Sapir's capable leadership, the museum's reputation grew. Most of that growth occurred, however, during the first few years when Dr. Brock was the Director of the Geological Survey of Canada. Brock encouraged the development of a fine national museum in Ottawa with a strong ethnology division, patterned somewhat after the Bureau of Ethnology in the United States. Successive Directors of the Geological Survey did not have Brock's interest in either the National Museum or the Anthropology Division.

My father greatly admired Sapir and the work he accomplished during the fifteen years he had been Chief of Anthropology. When he took over Sapir's duties, he fully intended to continue moving the division along the same course Sapir had set. The real policy for the museum, as he understood it in the spring of 1926, was "to build up in Ottawa a truly national museum ...," one with "the most representative collection ... of objects used or made by the Indians and Eskimos of Canada."[1]

The first setback in my father's new administrative role came three months after he assumed his duties, when his disciplinary confrontation with his colleague, Barbeau, resulted in the latter's removal from my father's administrative responsibility. Barbeau's actions thereafter severely cramped the performance of the Anthropology Division until both he and my father retired in 1948. My father was left administering a staff of just three archaeologists: Smith and Wintemberg (both in their fifties), and J. Douglas Leechman, an English archaeologist whom Sapir had hired in 1923. Gone were the division's physical anthropologist (Knowles, through early retirement in 1921 because of ill health), and its social anthropologist (F.W. Waugh, who disappeared under mysterious circumstances near Montreal in 1924). My father was the only one left qualified to undertake studies in social or physical anthropology, and he was tied to his office desk. Had he been able to employ new, well-qualified men, things might have fared much better. As events unfolded, however, he was prevented from hiring any new professional staff during his entire stint as division chief!

One of my father's many administrative duties as division chief was to evaluate, edit, and accept or reject anthropological manuscripts submitted for publication by members of his staff, as well as by persons contracted to undertake anthropological fieldwork for the division. It was a thankless, time-consuming task, but one my father took very seriously in his efforts to ensure that all reports published by his division were of the highest quality. On numerous occasions, he brought manuscripts home to edit in his study during the evenings. In those days before computers and electronic mail,[2] corresponding with the contracted authors was done by regular postal service, which in itself was time-consuming.

Museum publications in those days were issued as memoirs and bulletins of the Geological Survey of Canada, and thus required pre-publication evaluation and editing not only by my father but also by the editor of the Geological Survey as well. Accordingly, once my father was satisfied with the quality of a manuscript submitted to him, he would take it to the editorial office of the Geological Survey, which was only a few doors away from his own. Occasionally he became embroiled in arguments with the Survey's editor, defending the merits of the descriptions and conclusions of his authors against the editor's objections. The Geological Survey controlled the use of the funds for the museum's publications, and these funds always seemed in shorter

---

[1]Jenness to W.H. Collins, letter dated May 31, 1926, Jenness Correspondence, Box 652, Folder 1, Archives, CMC.

[2]Telephones existed at that time, of course, but I seem to recollect that my father's division was granted only one line, which was in the secretary's office, with extension phones in my father's and Barbeau's offices and probably also Smith's. A buzzer system was used to signal for whom the phone call was intended. This combination of extension-phones and buzzer system was still in use in 1954 when I worked briefly across the hall from the room that my father's secretary had occupied. Long-distance calls were extremely costly and not always assured of clear connections, so that typewritten letters and postal service were the normal means of communication. Letters provided a valuable historical "trail," no longer commonplace in today's electronic-communication world.

supply when museum reports were involved than for Geological Survey reports. During the Great Depression of the 1930s, virtually all publication funds for the museum were cut off, and were not renewed for several years. Of course, this was not just the museum's problem; all federal government departments experienced severe cutbacks in their budgets at the time.

My father found it particularly frustrating to spend many hours reading and editing manuscripts so that he could recommend them for publication, only to have them set aside for one reason or another by the Geological Survey's editorial office. Such documents would then become unfinished business that had to be accounted for from time to time, and generally necessitated repeated correspondence with their authors concerning when the reports might be published.

Two ethnological reports submitted by temporary workers originally contracted by Dr. Sapir caused my father an extraordinary amount of frustration with both the editorial office and the Director of the Geological Survey. The first of these was a report on the Sweet Grass Cree Indians of Saskatchewan, written by an American professor, Leonard Bloomfield. The original study and its follow-up report had been done at the suggestion of Sapir some time before his departure for Chicago. Bloomfield had lived on the Sweet Grass Reserve for five weeks in the summer of 1925, and submitted his lengthy manuscript early in 1927. Anticipating strong resistance from the editorial office to the length of the manuscript, my father laboriously reduced the original 1,800 pages to 600 by removing the last two-thirds, which would normally have been published as a second part of the report. To the author he suggested that this second part be submitted to an American scholarly journal for publication, and forwarded the reduced manuscript to the editorial office with his recommendation for publication.

Some while later, during a meeting with my father about the Bloomfield manuscript, the chief geologist questioned the need to publish the manuscript at all. The entire document was worth publishing, my father responded indignantly, but the first part, which was the material he had submitted for publication, was the cream of the manuscript. Furthermore, the Linguistic Society of America, to which the foremost philologists and anthropologists on the continent belonged, had recognized the value of the remaining 1,200 pages, and was going to publish them. If the merits of the anthropology manuscripts he approved for publication were going to be judged by geologists, he later wrote heatedly in a memo to the Director, W.H. Collins, then "the geological reports of the Department should be submitted in like manner to the biologists and anthropologists [at the Museum] for rating before publication."[3] Needless to say, his suggestion was not put into practice.

Another troubling manuscript, equally as long as Bloomfield's, was submitted to my father in 1926 by Professor Thomas F. McIlwraith of the University of Toronto, who had been employed on contract by Sapir between 1922 and 1924 to carry out ethnological studies of the Bella Coola Indians of the west coast.[4] After spending several months editing McIlwraith's manuscript, my father recommended it for publication and submitted it in its entirety to the editorial office. The lengths of the Bloomfield and McIlwraith manuscripts and the latter's descriptions of the

---

[3]Jenness to Collins, memo dated July 9, 1928, Jenness Correspondence, Box 652, Folder 2, Archives, CMC.
[4]T.F. McIlwraith was, in 1925, the first anthropologist appointed to a Canadian university to teach anthropology, then still a relatively new science.

Bella Coola's sexual activities troubled the Survey's editor so much that a high-level meeting was called on January 29, 1929 to discuss how to deal with the problems my father was giving the editorial unit. Involved at the meeting were the Deputy Minister of the Department of Mines (Camsell), the Assistant Deputy Minister (Bolton), the Geological Survey and Museum Director (Collins), the chief geologist (Young), the editor-in-chief (Nicholas), and my father. A memo about the meeting reveals that it commenced with a veiled criticism of my father for recommending the publication of unsuitable reports. The extraordinary lengths of the Bloomfield and McIlwraith reports put an enormous strain on the Survey editor's time as well as on the funds available for museum publications. However, the Survey was prepared to publish the initial 600 pages of the Bloomfield's manuscript—if funds became available. They did.[5]

McIlwraith's manuscript, however, raised quite a different problem. As summed up by Camsell, the problem lay in the descriptions that would probably get the Department of Mines into trouble, specifically passages detailing sexual activities among the Bella Coola Indians. The Geological Survey had been berated by politicians some years earlier for publishing Indian folktales that included sexual matter, material the politicians did not consider appropriate for government publications. The editor-in-chief (Nicholas), understandably, had no desire for a repeat performance lest the department's government funds be reduced. He claimed that much of McIlwraith's report would offend the general public and recommended that it not be published at all.[6]

Once again, my father's ire was aroused, and like David against Goliath he challenged the editor's recommendation. Speaking on the McIlwraith manuscript, he declared that "he believed it was the finest report ever presented on an Indian tribe in either the United States or Canada. The tribe is the most interesting in Canada." He agreed that McIlwraith loved details, and the report did include much about sexual activities of the people, but nothing that would embarrass anthropologists for whom the manuscript was written. Someone in the group remarked that my father, as Chief of the Anthropology Division, should "realize pretty well the limit to which he should go in scrutinizing manuscripts before recommending them for publication." Although my father must have found this slur on his scientific judgment highly offensive, he somehow managed to reply that the report "was much too valuable a one in the anthropological field to be released for publication by any organization other than the National Museum,"[7] and offered to try to work with McIlwraith to render it more acceptable for a museum publication. His offer was accepted

After a year, Collins reported to the Deputy Minister that my father had diligently "cleansed" the first 400 pages of McIlwraith's manuscript during the previous months, and had sent it to McIlwraith with the hope that he would continue to treat the rest of his manuscript in the same manner. However, McIlwraith responded indignantly that to reduce the manuscript to a level suitable for a twelve-year-old schoolgirl would require both considerable rewriting and the

---

[5]The Bloomfield manuscript was published by the museum the following year (Bloomfield, 1930).

[6]John Barker, p. xxv in Introduction to: T.F. McIlwraith, 1992, *The Bella Coola Indians*, 2 vols., University of Toronto Press, Toronto, 763 pp. and 672 pp.

[7]C. Camsell to Jenness, memo on conference held January 29, 1929, Jenness Correspondence, Box 641, Folder 29 (Camsell/Jenness folder), Archives, CMC.

drastic elimination of valuable information, the end result being that its scientific value would be lessened. He was not prepared to undertake the revision until every other option was exhausted.[8]

Some time thereafter, Collins recalled that neither the previous director of the museum, William McInnes, nor Sapir had ever actually guaranteed to McIlwraith that his manuscript would, in fact, be published. Thus provided with a clear excuse, the senior officers, to my father's complete exasperation, agreed to place McIlwraith's manuscript back on the shelf (or perhaps, considering its bulk, on two shelves). The manuscript and its problems were thus taken out of my father's hands. It was finally dusted off by the Geological Survey some twenty years later, turned over to the University of Toronto Press, and published in two thick volumes by that organization in 1948.[9]

Insufficient secretarial assistance proved to be a different kind of administrative headache for my father. Frances Eilleen Bleakney was the division's first stenographer, having been appointed as Dr. Sapir's secretary in 1911, but was required to resign in accordance with government regulations when she married my father in 1919. At the time of his employment in 1912, the archaeologist Harlan Smith had arranged with Dr. Brock, the Director of the Geological Survey, that he would be supplied with a full-time secretary, part of whose duties would be to help Smith in maintaining the division's considerable archaeological files. Barbeau then insisted on having the services of a bilingual secretary to help him with the many projects he always had underway, but the Geological Survey would not provide the Anthropology Division with a third secretary. As a result, the time of the divisional secretary had to be shared between Barbeau and the Division Chief. This arrangement worked reasonably well during most of the years when Sapir was in charge of the division, for either he or Barbeau was regularly away from the office several months a year. However, after my father became chief, and more especially after Barbeau's temper outburst a few months later, the arrangement was never without tension. The awkwardness of the arrangement can be deduced from the schedule drawn up for the work of the division's secretary (Miss Ethel Kenny) in 1934:

> Mon. – Fri. 9:00 a.m. – 12:30 p.m. (Jenness and divisional work)
> 2:00 p.m. – 3:30 p.m. (Smith, archaeology files)
> 3:30 p.m. – 5:00 p.m. (Barbeau, folklore)
> Sat. 9:00 a.m. – 11:00 a.m. (Jenness, divisional work)
> 11:00 a.m. – 1:00 p.m. (Barbeau, folklore).[10]

My father requested additional full-time secretarial assistance on more than one occasion thereafter, to deal with both the heavy workload and the stress on the division's secretary. His requests were always refused, but a French-Canadian stenographer from the Survey's stenographic pool was assigned to spend a few hours a week with Barbeau.

---

[8]Collins to Camsell, memo dated November 19, 1929, Jenness Correspondence, Box 641, Folder 29, Archives, CMC.

[9]McIlwraith's book, *The Bella Coola Indians*, was reprinted in 1992 with a new introduction by John Barker, wherein he provided some of the background story of the manuscript and the struggle to get it published.

[10]Jenness to Mr. Daly (Accounts), memorandum dated November 6, 1934, Jenness Correspondence, Box. 661, Folder 38, Archives, CMC.

During his first five years as Chief of Anthropology, my father also had disagreements with Collins about other administrative matters. One item concerned Collins's plan to move the archaeological collections from the basement of the museum to storage facilities in a building several blocks away in order to make room for a new laboratory for the Geological Survey. The archaeological specimens would be endangered, my father wrote Collins, because the storage building under consideration lacked adequate heating, which would also seriously hamper the study of specimens during the winter. He suggested an alternate solution involving the more efficient use of rooms in the basement of the museum building. Sensing that the Geological Survey was trying to squeeze his division out of the museum building, my father added that he had the highest regard for the work of the Survey, but had an equally high appreciation of the work of the National Museum[11] and saw no reason why "the two institutions should not advance together side by side, *helping, and not crushing* each other."[12] His suggestion was ignored, and the archaeological specimens were moved to the inadequately heated building on nearby Frank Street.

Another subject of disagreement concerned the spending of and accounting for government funds allotted to the Division of Anthropology. My father argued that, as Division Chief, he was closest to the financial needs of his division, and it should therefore be his responsibility to oversee how the money was spent. Collins' view was that as he (Collins) had to account for how the taxpayer's money was spent, he had to maintain control of it. I believe that trust and responsibility were at the heart of my father's argument, not power, but Collins refused to change his view.

Some months later, in response to the Great Depression, the Canadian government imposed severe financial restrictions on all of its government organizations, including, of course, the museum. These restrictions remained in force for several years. Government employees were forced to take a ten percent salary cut (my father told me), and both museum publications and fieldwork were terminated. The addition of these unpleasant conditions to the increasing frustrations my father encountered with the Geological Survey's administrators, in particular with its director, Collins, finally drove my father to appeal to the Deputy Minister (Camsell) at the end of 1930 to relieve him of his duties as Chief of the Division of Anthropology and allow him to return to his ethnology position. He had much to do in his ethnological capacity—not only ethnographic reports to write but also organization preparations to make for the

---

[11]From its opening in 1910, the museum was known as the Victoria Memorial Museum until the end of 1926. From January 1, 1927 until 1968, it was known as the National Museum of Canada, although in 1956 the anthropology division was split off as the Human History Branch, adding in 1958 the Canadian War Museum. The establishment of the National Museums of Canada Corporation in 1968 was accompanied by a change in name for the Human History Branch to the National Museum of Man, which in turn was renamed the Canadian Museum of Civilization in 1986 following the repeal of the National Museums Act of 1968 (Vodden and Dyck, 2006). The greatly understaffed and underfunded Division of Anthropology my father faithfully nursed through the depression years of the 1930s and the Second World War had finally reached maturity, although perhaps not in the form he had envisioned so many years before. In its most recent capacity, the museum acquired full autonomy, but retained administrative control over its "little brother," the Canadian War Museum.

[12]Jenness to Collins, letter dated February 2, 1928, Jenness Correspondence, Box 652, Folder 2, Archives, CMC.

5th Pacific Science Congress scheduled for Victoria and Vancouver in 1933. (He had been asked by the President of the National Research Council of Canada to chair the anthropology section at that congress, solicit authors and papers, and edit them through to publication.)[13]

Camsell apparently asked him under what conditions he would remain as Division Chief. In due course he received my father's written responses with more than half a dozen suggestions. My father grasped the opportunity to voice his considerable dislike for the museum's inferior role within the Geological Survey of Canada, and stated as one of his terms that the anthropological operations at the National Museum should be severed from the control of the Geological Survey to enable it to make any future progress.[14] Camsell then asked my father to discuss his complaints further with Collins in hopes that the two men could reach a workable solution. My father did as Camsell requested, but reported to him afterwards that neither man would budge from his previous position on the various aspects of the Division Chief's duties and responsibilities. As a result, he saw no alternative but to step down.[15] He was formally relieved of his duties on March 1, 1931.

For the next five years, Collins served as Acting Chief of Anthropology in addition to his already weighty duties as Director of the Geological Survey and Director of the National Museum of Canada. Ironically, although Collins was officially in charge of the divisional duties, my father apparently continued to do much of the division chief's day-to-day paperwork and other administrative activities. Perhaps he was allowed to step down from his administrative role on condition that he continue taking care of the division's day-to-day tasks. However, I suspect that his sense of loyalty and duty to the museum and the division were the reason he did so, without any fanfare. In any case, his official letters during that period were on museum letterhead, as before, but he merely signed them, without including the underlying title "Chief of Anthropology."

My father was "reappointed" Chief of Anthropology in November 1936, after Collins became too ill to work and was hospitalized.[16] The speed with which my father assumed his official duties clearly indicates to me that the chief reason he relinquished his division-chief's responsibilities in 1931 was his insoluble disagreement with Collins. For a person like my father, who considered himself an Englishman and a gentleman, resignation was the proper thing to do when personal differences with his superior officer could not be resolved.

---

[13]Jenness to Camsell, letter dated December 5, 1930, Jenness Correspondence, Box 641, Folder 29, Archives, CMC.

[14]This was a visionary suggestion at that time. The separation of the National Museum from the Geological Survey took place in the government reorganization of 1950, although the two organizations remained in the museum building until the Geological Survey moved into its new building in 1959. Further changes since then separated the Anthropology Division and the Biology Division, which today occupy independent buildings, and are distinct, internationally renowned museums —the Canadian Museum of Civilization and the Canadian Museum of Nature, respectively—the headquarters of both located in Gatineau on the Quebec side of the Ottawa River from Ottawa. The exhibition part of the Canadian Museum of Nature remains in the original Victoria Memorial Museum building in Ottawa, where my father spent so many years.

[15]Jenness to Camsell, letters dated December 3, December 26, and December 27, 1930; memorandum from Camsell to Jenness, January 3, 1931; and memorandum from Jenness to Collins, January 8, 1931; Jenness Correspondence, Box 641, Folder 29, Archives, CMC.

[16]Collins died two months later.

In 1932, my father was suddenly burdened with an unexpected task. A long-retired member of the Geological Survey, palaeontologist Henri Ami, died early in 1931, leaving in his office an enormous collection of mostly unlabelled archaeological artifacts. Ami's executors asked the director of the museum to have the specimens sorted and collections distributed to museums and universities in Canada that wanted them. The long-retired Ami had years before become fascinated with early man, and with some guidance from Sapir had undertaken, from time to time, independent archaeological diggings in Canada and the United States, accumulating specimens from various localities. At some time between 1920 and 1926, my father met Ami, and over the next several years they exchanged discussions and correspondence. I suspect that, during one of their early meetings, my father mentioned how he had enjoyed some rather amateurish diggings for early man in the cave-ridden Dordogne region of central France in 1910 (while he was a student at Oxford University). He may then have suggested that Ami seek permission to dig there. Ami subsequently succeeded in incorporating in 1926, under the auspices of the Beaux Arts of Paris[17] as well as the Royal Society of Canada, a "Canadian School of Prehistory in France," of which he was the director and virtually sole member. For the next five years, he spent several months each summer digging with a few students and local work-men at a site near Les Eyzies-de-Tayac in the Dordogne, "the Paleolithic Capital of France," amassing and shipping to Ottawa during that time an estimated 300,000 specimens.

The task of sorting, identifying, and distributing that enormous collection fell to my father, at the request of the museum's acting director (Collins). Working several days a week for more than a year, starting in the summer of 1931, my father and/or a colleague managed to identify and salvage roughly one quarter of the specimens and distribute representative collections to museums and universities around the country. It was "rather disappointing to have a great many specimens, but of a very few types only," my father wrote R.C. Wallace, the President of the University of Alberta,[18] to which a large collection of Ami's specimens was sent. My father willingly undertook this frightfully tedious work out of loyalty for an old friend. And of course, the National Museum retained a good collection of largely Mousterian material.

Over the years, the never-ending flow of correspondence received by his office kept my father and his secretary busy many hours each week. Some of the letters were serious in content and required library search and considerable thought before dictating a response. Others were unusual. One enquiry came from our family's former pediatrician, who asked if there was originally an Indian name for the Rideau River, which flowed quietly through the nation's capital city. After some library research and checking with the Canadian Board of Geographic Names, my father responded that he had found no indication of an Indian name for the river prior to its being named by Champlain or one of his contemporaries early in the 1600s.[19]

Some enquiries were truly strange, such as the one my father describes in the next chapter.

---

[17]Ami, H., 1927. Memoirs of the Royal Society of Canada, 1927, p. LXII–XLIII.

[18]Jenness to R.C. Wallace, letter dated January 20, 1932, Ami Correspondence, MS 80-1743, Archives, CMC.

[19]Dr. George Campbell to Jenness, letter dated October 19, 1944, Jenness Correspondence, Box 641, Folder 28, Archives, CMC.

1934: ANTHROPOLOGY RESCUES AN IMMIGRANT

11

Diamond Jenness

[*At Oxford University, my father was taught to measure heads, heights, arms, legs, and even noses of natives, using special instruments, as a means of determining their race and origin. Other features were taken into account as well. He, therefore, carefully measured these features of some of the native people he encountered in Papua in 1911–1912, and followed this by measuring many of the Eskimos in northern Alaska (1913–1914) and in the central Canadian Arctic (1914–1916). The interested reader can learn more about this in Jenness (1923b). He applied this technique of physical anthropology two decades later in the curious incident recorded here.*] [S.E.J.]

The day began badly. I walked into my office, emptied my pipe, stuffed it into my pocket, and took my usual place in the swivel chair behind my desk. A moment later, a burning pain jerked my body to my feet and my hand to my right hip-pocket, where the loose matches I was carrying had ignited as I sat down. At that critical moment, there came a gentle knock on the door, and my secretary entered with the day's mail, which she dropped into my in-basket. "Not much mail this morning," she said, glancing at my face with a puzzled smile. I thanked her, and as the door closed again, swiftly investigated the extent of the damage produced by the conflagration, then gingerly sat down in my chair once more and picked up the mail.

A book catalogue. I thumbed over its dozen pages and threw it into the waste basket. A Smithsonian report. Ah yes, Henry Collins's report on his Southampton Island excavations; a nice piece of work that.[1] What's this? The program for the Chicago meeting, to which I am to contribute a paper? I'll look it over later. And here's a letter from Massachusetts. Who can that be from?

I opened it. The letter was typewritten, but on private, not office paper, and the address at the top named a town I had never heard of. Then came my name and official title, both quite correct, but the signature at the end, a woman's, was unfamiliar, so she must have culled my address and title out of some book. I began now to read the letter, rapidly at first, but slowing down more and more as I proceeded. It concluded on the second page and, laying it on the desk, I sat back and reflected.

---

[1] Henry B. Collins was an archaeologist at the Smithsonian Institution in Washington, D.C. He conducted archaeological field work in the late 1920s on St. Lawrence Island south of Bering Strait, which confirmed and augmented my father's recognition of the "Old Bering Sea Culture" (Collins, 1931). Collins later worked at Wales, Alaska, adding to my father's 1926 work, and subsequently, after a suggestion by my father, on Southampton Island in Hudson Bay.

What a strange request! Who is this imperious woman—a Hebrew evidently—who requests, indeed demands, my help and gives me such implicit instructions how to render it? She and her husband, she writes, have just returned to the United States from India. I wonder then why is it she who writes me and not her husband, but the letter offers no explanation. She mentions a servant, stranded in Montreal and denied entry to the United States by the immigration authorities because he was born in Cochin, India, and therefore should come under their Indian category, whose 1934 immigrant quota is exhausted. He is not an Indian, she insists, but a Semite. A pretty tangle! She asks me now to examine him personally, to measure his head and other physical features, and to testify that he really is a Semite and not an Indian.

As if racial type and legal category bear any relation to each other, are identical twins which exactly coincide with one another. What a pity she had not attended that lecture on genetics given at Oxford in my student days, the lecture in which Professor Bates, the famous Cambridge scientist, threw on the screen a photograph of three beautiful ladies born on the same day to the same mother, and solemnly announced, as he pointed to two of them who were indistinguishable, "These two are identical twins, but this third one who shows so little relationship to the other two (he paused, and a breathless silence fell over his mixed audience), she is an added ovum."

"This is a queer business," I said to myself as I let my thoughts wander. "I am an anthropologist employed by the Canadian government. What right have I to meddle with the operations of the U.S. immigration service?"

But then the plight of the poor Hindu, Semite, or whatever he was, threatened to haunt my mind—that lonely stranger waiting helplessly in a strange country for persons unseen to decide his fate. What his mistress had asked me to do was not difficult, even though there seemed hardly one chance in a million that it could help him. Could I stand cynically by and refuse to lift a finger?

I called in my secretary and dictated this letter to the lady in Massachusetts.

Dear Madam:

   If your servant Joseph will present himself at my office at 11 a.m. on the morning of Wednesday, August 7, I will examine him physically, as you request, and inform you later of my judgement concerning his racial type.

I am, Madam, etc.

My secretary laid the typed but unsigned letter in front of me a short while later, discreetly concealing any evidence of curiosity. She knew as well as I did that it is impossible for a man to hide his demeanours and misdemeanours from his secretary—which is the reason, by the way, why so many high executives hasten to marry their personal attachés. At this particular period, the secretary whom the museum authorities had attached to my office happened to be a gem of purest lustre, loyal, intelligent, and far more capable than they realized until another government department lured her away to a post two grades higher than the museum was willing to offer. I explained to her what I intended to do, and how she might help me, and we awaited the fateful day—fateful, that is, for our unfortunate client Joseph. Meanwhile I borrowed from the museum library the standard work on racial types, perused it carefully, and tabbed the relevant pages.

At the stroke of 11 a.m. on the appointed day, my secretary ushered into my office a dark-skinned gentleman with jet-black, slightly wavy hair, dark eyes, a prominent Semitic or Jewish nose, and ingratiating hands which seemed to indicate his social status. I shook hands with him, offered him a seat, and asked if his mistress had informed him what she wished me to do with him. She had. My secretary then brought me my callipers and graduated rod, and I measured the length and breadth of his head, of his face, and of his nose, and also his stature, standing and sitting. From these figures I quickly calculated the related indices and asked my secretary to bring me the book on racial types, which the librarian had carefully laid to one side.

Turning to the author's description of the Semites of Mesopotamia, I examined his mean figures for the physical traits that I had just measured on Joseph. The correspondence was amazing. Joseph could have been their archetype. What was his history?

I questioned him. He knew very little except that there had been a large colony of Jews in Cochin since time immemorial, and his parents and grandparents had been members of that colony. I remembered then that around A.D. 700 many Jewish traders had settled there and established a flourishing community which isolated itself from the indigenous population by strictly adhering to its old religion and forbidding marriage outside its own closed circle. If its members ever lost contact with western Judaism they renewed it, although relations remained very tenuous until quite recently,[2] when the new state of Israel has sought to strengthen them.

I now dictated another letter to my secretary, heading it with the words: *"To Whom it may Concern."* It ran:

> I hereby certify that I have this day subjected Joseph Y. to a rigid anthropometric examination. I find that his cephalic index is _____, his facial index _____, and his nasal index _____. These indices coincide almost exactly with the mean indices of the Semitic peoples of Mesopotamia, as recorded in the standard text-book Martin, R., *Lehrbuch der Anthropologie*, Switzerland. I have no hesitation, therefore, in attesting that Joseph Y. is of Semitic descent.
>
> (signed) Diamond Jenness
> Chief, Division of Anthropology
>
> National Museum of Canada
> Ottawa, Canada
> Aug. 17, 1934

I said to my secretary: "Please make two carbons of that letter. We will give the original to this gentleman, one copy you will send to his mistress in Massachusetts, and the other you will place in our files."

"How much must I pay you," Joseph asked, as he pocketed his letter, and I answered:

"There is no charge. The Canadian Government renders you this service free." And I escorted him to the door.

---

[2]The state of Israel was established in 1948, which could be considered as "quite recently" in the 1960s, when this chapter was written.

Five days later I received this one-line letter from Massachusetts:

"Joseph has arrived safely. Thank you."

For many months thereafter, I crossed the border into the United States with fear and trembling. I feared the immigration officials, who might accuse me of conniving at the smuggling of an illegal immigrant into the Land of Promise; and I feared my anthropological colleagues, who might ask me: "What do you mean by Semitic descent? There are Semitic languages just as there are Aryan ones. But whatever Hitler and his Nazis may say, you know perfectly well that there is no Semitic race, any more than there is an Aryan one."

To which I could think of only one answer: "But Joseph succeeded in reaching Massachusetts, didn't he?"

1936:
AN INDIAN MEDICINE MAN[1]

12

Diamond Jenness

[My father undertook his main field studies of Canadian Indian tribes in the fifteen years between 1921 and 1936 (Table 1). The following account of Old Pierre and shamanism derives from his work with Coast Salish near Vancouver in 1936.

Old Pierre's story was included in a manuscript on the Coast Salish that my father wrote sometime in the late 1930s. Like two or three other ethnographic manuscripts he prepared on specific western tribes, it fell victim to the federal government's financial priorities during both the depression years of the 1930s and the war years that followed. By 1948, when father retired, those unpublished manuscripts were largely forgotten and gathering dust in cabinets at the National Museum of Canada. In the fall of 1951, my father chanced to mention them while lecturing at the University of British Columbia. His remarks greatly interested Wayne Suttles and Wilson Duff of the British Columbia Provincial Museum, together with Professor H.B. Hawthorn of the University of British Columbia's Anthropology Department, who soon requested permission of the National Museum of Canada to publish my father's manuscript on the Old Salish Indians. Suttles' ethnographic notes on the Indians near Katzie were published with my father's manuscript. According to Suttles, Old Pierre's son, Simon, was my father's interpreter during his many conversations with the old medicine man. Old Pierre died in 1946, nine years before my father's manuscript on the Coast Salish was finally published.] [S.E.J.]

"Ask Old Pierre, the medicine man at Katzie. He is the only man who can answer your questions," said Old David, my friend on the Saanich Indian Reserve near Victoria, British Columbia, who could remember the long past days when he and his kinsmen had hunted whales in dugout canoes off the coast of Vancouver Island. "Old Pierre knows more about the ancient traditions and the early religion of our people than any other Indian in this region. Ask him."

I left Old David and wandered north to Indian reserves near Cowichan Bay and Nanaimo. Everywhere the natives gave me the same advice, "Ask Old Pierre."

Indians on the Musqueam Reserve in Vancouver echoed it too, and since the Katzie Reserve was only twenty-five miles up the Fraser River from Vancouver I resolved to motor out to Old Pierre's home and interview this medicine man whom natives for a hundred miles around held in such high esteem.

It was early February 1936. A few patches of snow blotched the highway out of Vancouver, but the weather was clear, and after I passed New Westminster, no traffic impeded the road

---

[1]Much of this chapter appeared originally in Ch. 6 of The Faith of a Coast Salish Indian, by Diamond Jenness (1955). It is reproduced here with the permission of the publisher, the Provincial Museum, Department of Education, Victoria. B.C. [D.J.]. The published passages are indented in this chapter.

Figure 27 Old Pierre (Peter Pierre), at Katzie, British Columbia, about 1895.

Photo PN 9522 courtesy Royal BC Museum, BC Archives

except a few Japanese children cheerfully straggling along to school. I found the reserve without difficulty. Its fifty inhabitants were dwelling in a row of frame cottages a quarter of a mile off the highway on the north bank of the Fraser River just one mile west of Port Hammond. In the middle of the row stood a tiny church, and a short distance behind it, a small schoolhouse. Old Pierre's house was the second cottage beyond the church.

A woman of perhaps thirty years answered my knock on the door. She was the youngest of Old Pierre's children and spoke English fairly fluently. "Yes, he is at home," she said and, inviting me into a dingy living room, offered me a chair while she summoned her father from a room behind.

A short, thick-set man well into his sixties then entered, sat quietly down on the opposite side of the table, turned on me a broad, rather introspective face, and waited to learn the purpose of my visit. His daughter interpreted for us, since he understood very little English.

I told him that I had been writing down everything his Vancouver Island countrymen could remember about the early history of their people so that it would never be forgotten, and that every Indian I had interviewed had counselled me to consult him because he was better informed than anyone else in the region. He questioned me about the individuals I had interviewed and what they had told me, but after a few minutes he seemed to lose interest, said that he himself had forgotten many things his elders had taught him and no longer felt any desire to recall the vanished past. I nodded my head in understanding and dropped the subject.

But instead of hurrying away, which would have been discourteous, I asked him about the salmon and sturgeon in his river, told him how I had learned to jig for trout with a barbless hook through the ice of far northern lakes, and drew from him two fishing experiences of his own. Then I apologized for troubling him and said that I was travelling thirty miles farther on to Chilliwack, where I hoped to visit Old Silas, a man he probably knew quite well. His face brightened at the name, and he asked me to carry his greetings to Silas, after which we shook hands and, waving goodbye to him as he watched me from his doorway, I drove on up the Fraser Valley.

Chilliwack held me for a week as I gleaned from Silas and one or two other old Indians what little they could tell me of the "days of long ago." In our last interview, Silas said to me, "If you stop at Katzie on your way down to Vancouver, greet Old Pierre from me. We were good friends in childhood, and now we have grown old together."

Leisurely, I drove down the Fraser Valley, pondering whether it would be worth my while to turn off the highway and visit Old Pierre again. He had stated so positively that he did not want to talk about the past, so why awaken old memories which might cause him pain?

Then I began to wonder whether his daughter had interpreted him correctly, whether perhaps she had given too much weight to words that had expressed just a fleeting impulse. Should I not sound him out once more now that he had been granted a whole week for reflection? Silas, his friend, had joined the chorus of acclaim for the old medicine man, had spoken with deep respect of his knowledge and integrity. Surely it was worth my while to try again to enlist his cooperation.

I called in at the Port Hammond country store and bought a dozen oranges, a luxury greatly appreciated at that date in every Indian household, then I drove down the muddy dirt road that led to the Katzie settlement on the river's bank. The same young woman answered my knock and summoned her father from a back room. This time, Old Pierre greeted me with outstretched hand and a welcoming smile.

"Did you go to Chilliwack?" he asked as we sat down. "Did you meet my old friend Silas?"

"Yes," I answered, "and he returns your greeting. He would like to see you again and talk with you, but Chilliwack is many miles away and his feet will no longer sustain so long a journey. His grandsons own an old Ford motorcar, but the jalopy breaks down every two miles, he says, and in any case they are not interested in reviving the old traditions of their people, but only in motorcars and other contraptions of the white man. So he spends his days quietly indoors, or sits outside in the warm sunshine."

Old Pierre then asked me what I had learned from his Chilliwack friend, and we conversed for about twenty minutes on the beliefs and customs of the Indians before the coming of the white man. When at last I rose to leave he said, a little hesitantly,

"Some of the things Silas has told you are not quite correct. If you care to come back tomorrow morning I will correct them for you."

I returned the next day, and the day after, and the day after that again, spending with him on each occasion the whole morning. His memory seemed inexhaustible, and he was the soul of honesty. No historian could have thirsted more for accuracy. I think he must have lain awake every night during the five weeks our association lasted, preparing, like a conscientious professor, the lesson that he would give his pupil the next morning.

He described to me his boyhood, and his life in the long shed-like dwelling on the river-bank that housed a dozen families; and he told me how his mother, herself a medicine woman, had trained him for the healing art as it was understood and practised by his ancestors before any white man reached the shores of British Columbia. It was a grim training, grimmer than the training our white physicians receive today, because it was founded on a different conception of man and his universe, of human nature and human diseases. The Katzie Indians believed that the "Lord-Who-Dwells-Above" had endowed every living thing, and some things which to white men are not living—e.g., the sun—with some special quality or power which under certain circumstances the individual man or woman could enlist into his service. They believed, too, that there dwelt in realms invisible to human eyes mystic beings which might reveal themselves to men and women who underwent long and strenuous training, suffered intense hardships, and diligently sought them through prayer and fasting; and to these human beings they granted the power to heal diseases, subject always to the will of the "Lord-Who-Dwells-Above."

Old Pierre was one of these favoured individuals. I did not directly question him concerning his training, for one does not probe the secrets of a friend. But one morning, three weeks after I began my daily visits, he said, "This morning I am going to tell you how I became a medicine man." And all that morning I wrote his story:

When I was only three years old, my mother, who was herself a medicine woman, made me bathe in the river and scrub my limbs with spruce-boughs before breakfast, even though there was ice on the water. And one morning, after I had scrubbed myself—I was still only three—she clothed me with her blessing or power, what we call in our language *swiam*. Every living creature, you know, possesses its special strength or power, something invisible to normal eyes that dwells inside it, and yet can issue from it, giving it power to do the things it wishes to do. Well, that morning, she clothed me with her power; she passed her hands over my body, from head to feet, draping her strength over me to shield and fortify me for the trials that she projected for me later. Thereafter, she would never allow me to creep into her bed on cold dark mornings, or to receive food from anyone who might be ceremonially unclean. Every night, I slept alone in my own little bed, and every morning, I bathed and scrubbed myself with spruce boughs that I might be pure and without taint in both mind and body. By day, I played with the other children, and I helped my kinsmen at home and in our hunting camps. My uncles (for my father died soon afterwards) taught me to handle a fishnet, to trap small animals, and sometimes to fire off their guns. Yet always I felt that I was different from other children, though in what way I could not understand.

Thus I grew to the age of about eight. Then at intervals throughout one winter my mother called in three of her oldest and best-informed relatives to teach me the ancient history of our people, and the commandments which He Who Dwells Above had imposed upon us when He established us upon this earth. I still bathed night and morning, winter and summer, but so also did other boys of my own age and many of the men.

Two more years passed uneventfully, and I reached the age of ten. Then one morning, my mother roused me from my bed and said: "Pierre, it is time now that you trained to become a medicine man. Go back into the woods, but be careful no one sees you. Whenever you come to a pool, bathe and rub yourself with spruce-boughs, then walk on again. Stay out as long as you can. Remember that He Who Dwells Above has given you power. Pray to Him as you walk along; ask His help, plead with Him to strengthen you for the trials you must now undergo. Don't be afraid or imagine that you will die. Be of strong mind."

I dressed and stole away into the woods. No one except my mother knew where I had gone, or that I was training to be a medicine man. I was hungry and cold, for there was snow on the ground and she had sent me away without breakfast, but I remembered what she had told me, and I prayed to He Who Dwells Above for strength. Twice when I came to pools of water, I bathed, rubbed my shivering limbs with spruce-boughs, and hurried on again. But by noon I could bear the cold and the solitude no longer. My mind became weak, my feet turned uncontrollably homeward, and I ran as fast as I could to the house.

It was afternoon when I entered, but my mother paid no attention to me; neither then nor at suppertime did she offer me any food. I crept into my bed, worn out with fatigue and hunger, and fell sound asleep.

At daybreak she woke me again and said: "Pierre, you must go back into the woods. Go farther than you went yesterday, and don't come back so early. You are hungry; drink all the water you wish, but don't nibble anything, not even a blade of grass. And remember to keep praying to He Who Dwells Above."

I cried bitterly and thought that she was terribly cruel to me, but it was of no use; I had to go. I don't remember how far I walked that day or how many times I bathed, but it was late in the afternoon when I reached home. Although I was famishing, my mother gave me very little to eat and immediately sent me to lie down. Then at dawn, she drove me back into the woods, without breakfast, and with orders to stay away longer even than the day before.

That third day it was almost dark when I returned. I thought that now she would surely give me a full supper, but she sent me to bed fasting, and drove me, still fasting, into the woods again the next morning. This time I did not return until it was really dark. Then she gave me a scanty supper, but half an hour after I had eaten she handed me a feather, saying: "Go and bathe in the river and, after you have bathed, tickle your throat with this feather so that you give the water what you have eaten. For the river is holy; it journeys day and night, coming no man knows whence and travelling no one knows whither. Pray to it. Tell it that you are striving to become a medicine man, that for a long time yet you are going to fast, and ask it to help you. Then come back into the house."

I obeyed her instructions and went back into the house. She led me to one side so that no one might overhear us and said: "Tomorrow morning you must go back into the woods and stay away as many days as you can. Be sure not to nibble at any of the shrubs or trees, but bathe often and rub yourself with the boughs of evergreens. Drink copiously from the pools in which you swim, then give back the water by tickling your throat with fine twigs of the vine maple. Remember that when you are pure in mind and body and lie down to sleep, you will hear voices singing. Pay no attention to them. They are the voices of the evil medicine men who live around us, medicine men who bewitch their fellow-men and cause sickness and death. Do not listen to them. Put their songs out of your mind because, if you think of them, they will stay with you for ever and you will become an evil medicine man as they are. Think always of He Who Dwells Above and pray continually, 'I would help the people when they are ill; I would gain power to heal sickness.' Now lie down and sleep."

In the morning she examined me to see that I was warmly clad, gave me some matches but no blankets, and sent me out to continue my fast. I do not remember how many days and nights I stayed away on that occasion, only that before darkness descended I would kindle a fire and gather branches for a bed. But when I did return home, weak and exhausted, my mother fed me very sparingly and sent me out again as soon as I seemed able to endure another trial. So I continued all through the winter. Each time I went out my sufferings seemed a little less, until after the first hour of walking I felt light and vigorous, and was conscious of neither hunger nor thirst.

Spring came, and my mother said to me: "Stop fasting now, Pierre. The sweet briars are budding, and the berries will soon be ripening. They would tempt you to eat, and you would be unable to resist the temptation. Bathe in the woods as often as you wish and scrub yourself with fir boughs, but do not try to fast."

So from spring to autumn, I fished and hunted and played with the other boys of our village. But when winter came again, I resumed my fasting. I roamed the woods, bathed in its icy pools, rubbed myself with the boughs of the evergreen trees, ate nothing, but drank water copiously and gave it up again. After each bath, I prayed to He Who Dwells Above, and I danced until I fell to the ground exhausted. Then at night, I slept on beds of branches or in the hollow of some tree. Gradually, my skin became hard like the bark of the trees with which I scrubbed it. No cold could penetrate it; the rain and the snow that fell on me seemed warm.

I remember well how I returned to my home one morning, exhausted by many days' fasting, and stretched myself out on my bed; and how an old priest, one of my early teachers, came up to me, thinking that I had lain there all night, and said in a voice of scorn: "My boy, a wonderful medicine man you will become, lying there with your head covered by your blankets, pampering your miserable flesh. If you cannot endure fasting in the woods, take some meat and tea with you; and if you cannot bear to scrub your body with branches and stones, rub it with soft flour."

He taunted me until I rose from my bed and said bitterly: "You wish me to die. Well, I will die. I will go farther into the woods than I have ever gone before. I will stay away longer than ever." Then I walked out of the door and stayed in the woods for three weeks.

Four winters I endured this penance. Then at last my mind and body became really clean. My eyes were opened, and I beheld the whole universe.

I had been dancing and had fallen to the ground exhausted. As I lay there, sleeping, I heard a medicine man singing far, far away, and my mind travelled toward the voice. Evil medicine men seemed to swarm around me, but always there was someone behind me who whispered, "Pay no attention to them, for they are evil." And I prayed constantly to He Who Dwells Above, asking for power to heal the sick, not to cause sickness as did these evil ones.

I reached the place where the medicine man was singing, a house unlike any that I had ever seen before. He who was behind me whispered: "Go inside. This is he for whom you are seeking, the true medicine man for whom you have undergone penance all these years."

I entered. The medicine man was kneeling on the floor, and beside him was his water, in some mystic vessel that was neither a dish nor a basket. He turned and looked at me. "Poor boy," he said. "So you have come at last. Kneel down beside me."

I knelt beside him. In front of us appeared every sickness that afflicts mankind, concentrated in a single human being. "Wash your hands and wrists in this water." I washed them. He grasped them in his own and massaged them, giving them power. "Now lay your hands on that sickness and remove it."

I laid my hands to the patient and cupped his sickness out with them. He rose to his feet, cured. "That is how you shall remove every sickness. You shall chant the song that you have heard me sing and cup out the sickness with your hands. Now go."

My mind returned to my body and I awoke, but now in my hands and wrists I felt power. I rose up and danced until I fell exhausted again, and my mind left me once more. Now I travelled to a huge tree—the father of all trees, invisible to mortal eyes—and always behind me moved the same being as before, though I could not see him. As I stood before the mighty trunk he said, "Listen. The tree will speak to you."

For a long time I stood there waiting. Finally the tree spoke: "O poor boy. No living soul has ever seen me before. Here I stand, watching all the trees and all the people throughout the world, and no one knows me. One power and one only I shall grant you. When you are treating the sick, you shall see over the whole world. When the mind of your patient is lost, you shall see and recapture it. Remain here for a while till someone comes with a noise like the rushing of a great wind, someone who always rests on top of this tree. Do not look until I bid you."

I waited. There came a sound as of a great wind at the top of the tree. "Now look," said the tree. I looked. On its summit stood a great white horse. Its hoofs were red, and two persons sat on its back. "That horse flies all over the world," said the tree. "I shall not give you its power, for you would not live long."

My mind returned to my body. I awoke and bathed again in the pool at my side. After my bath, I drank copiously of its water, and tickled my throat with a twig of maple. They I prayed to He Who Dwells Above, and I danced till I fell and lost consciousness. My mind travelled forth again over a beautiful prairie until something tripped me, something hard like a stone, and a voice said to me: "Poor soul, go no farther. This is the leader of all things that are upon this earth. You are the first who has come here."

The being who had tripped me stood up and chanted a song. "Take this stone that I use for a pillow," he said. "Hold it in your two hands and kneel down. For a long time I have been watching you, watching your struggles."

As I knelt down, holding the rock in my hands—it was different from all other rock—the being mounted the back of my head and rubbed my jaw. "You shall heal the sick. Place your lips to the rock and suck it. Suck it once only, but suck it hard." I laid my lips to it and sucked. It became soft like flesh, and something—it was blood—issued from it and entered my mouth. "Don't eject it on to the ground, but swallow some of it and rub the rest on your hands." He came down from the back of my head and took the rock from me. "That is how you shall heal the sick. That is how you shall suck away their illnesses. Now go."

I awoke and found myself lying on the ground. Now I had power—power in my hands and wrists to draw out sickness, power in my mouth to swallow it, and power to see all over the world and to recover minds that had strayed from their bodily homes. I was a medicine man. I could heal the sick, I could banish their diseases, even as my mother had foretold me. But not always. Whenever He Who Dwells Above decided to take away someone's soul, I could do nothing. That also my mother had foretold me.

I rose from the ground and returned home. My years of fasting were ended. I think my mother knew what had happened, for she asked no questions, nor did she urge me to stay in the woods again. So I remained at home, and as soon as I recovered my strength, I joined my uncles in the fishing and hunting.

Thus it was that Old Pierre, at the very beginning of his adolescence, graduated as a medicine man, a professional healer of diseases. At that period, his tribesmen commonly ascribed sickness to one of three causes. The patient might have lost his consciousness or mind, either because it had wandered away and failed to return, or because an evil medicine man had stolen it; or he might have been infected by some supernatural agency, might have been touched, for example, by an evil spirit or ghost; or a sorcerer might have magically implanted some harmful object in his body, or brought on him some grievous misfortune.

The treatment provided by the medicine man was largely psychological. He massaged or sucked at any place where the pain seemed localized and at times succeeded in removing a tumour or other swelling. Should it not discharge, he extracted, or feigned to extract, a mysterious hair or other object not visible to the eyes of the laity because it had been implanted by a sorcerer. If his patient was wholly or partly unconscious, indicating that his mind had strayed, he pretended to recover and restore the missing organ by cupping his hands over the sick man's head and blowing through them. To enhance the psychological atmosphere he washed his wrists and hands in warm water or smeared them with melted fat, chanted a hymn or song to the rhythm of his drum, and shading his eyes with his hand, stared into space as if he were peering into another world.

Faith healing is not restricted to the white man's world, and no one will question that Indian medicine men effected many cures. Whatever deceit they practised was nearly always unconscious, for they were themselves deceived no less than their patients and onlookers. There were a few charlatans, no doubt, who were not deceived, who acted like wolves in sheep's clothing and tricked their audiences deliberately; but even they generally believed in the genuineness of other practitioners.

Old Pierre certainly exercised his profession in good faith, and with a sense of responsibility toward his fellow men equal to that of any white physician. His first patient, a woman older than himself, happened to visit him during one of my morning lessons and on her own initiative confirmed his description of her cure.

> A few months after I had obtained medicine power, when I was still only 14 years of age and Mary 17, my mother came to me one evening and said: "Mary is very ill from a large tumour in her side. I have tried to cure her, but without success. Did you receive power when you fasted?"
>
> "Yes," I answered. "I have power. But I do not want the people to see me the first time I use it because I may fail, and then they would laugh at me. Hang some mats around her bed and I will come."
>
> I entered Mary's room unseen, and my mother set a basin of water in front of me. First I washed my hands, as I had washed them in my vision, and I chanted the song I learned at that time. Power flowed into me; I could feel it in my wrists and fingers. I laid my hands to Mary's side just where the tumour was situated and manipulated it. Then I set my lips to the place and sucked. It palpitated, but my mouth remained empty. Drawing back, I said to my mother: "I must go to the woods and obtain more power. Tomorrow evening I will come back." Without food or drink I went into the woods, although it was dark, and as I stumbled along I prayed:

"O You Who Dwell Above, Holy One, You have made me. You have made the trees and the animals. You know how I have tried to obey the rules that You laid down for us. You know that for four winters I fasted and purified my mind and my body, that I might gain power to heal the sick. Help me now to heal this girl; give me power to wrest the sickness from her."

"O Holy One, You who gave my hands power to draw out sickness, give me that power now, that I may draw away the tumour from her body and restore her to health."

"O Holy One, You who gave my lips power to draw blood from the hard stone, give them the power now, that they may suck out the infection from her body. Do not hold back Your gift. Help me to cure her.'"

Finally I lay down, and as I slept, my mind travelled away to the Holy One it had visited at the close of my fasting. Once again I sucked at the hard stone, and once again I filled my mouth with its blood. When I awoke, it was already light. I wandered throughout the day from pool to pool, bathing and rubbing myself with spruce branches, and all the time I kept praying to He Who Dwells Above, and to the Holy Ones who had given me power.

At evening, I returned to Mary's room, washed my hands, and chanted my song. My power flowed strong within me, and as I laid my lips to her side I knew that this time I could not fail. Once and once only, I sucked; then the tumour suddenly collapsed, filling my mouth with its fluid, which I ejected outside the house. Then I said to my mother: "She will recover now. But I will come again if she needs me." They did not send for me again. She began to recover immediately, and, as you see, she is now an old woman.

It was probably because his mother also was a medicine woman that Old Pierre undertook his first case at an unusually early age; most Indians waited for several years after their visions before they ventured to practise. Their profession was an honourable one that to many brought considerable profit, despite the custom of "no cure, no pay." Old Pierre stated that he himself never set any price on his services, but accepted whatever was offered him. It always disturbed him when the relatives of the patient offered him money or blankets beforehand, because his power had been given him to help his people, not to benefit himself.

The Cowichan Indians once sent for me to cure their chief Modeste. Dozens of wagons lined the roads beside the chief's house, and his doorway was so crowded that I could hardly squeeze my way in. While I was washing my hands and summoning my power, an old man stood up and addressed the crowd as follows: "My friends, be liberal with your gifts. You know that our chief Modeste is very ill. Here is the great medicine man Pierre of whom you have all heard, though he has never visited us before. He has come to heal our chief. Be liberal, all of you."

Immediately, one man came forward with $10, and another with $5. Money began to pour in from all sides. I shivered. My mind was concentrated on the sick man; power was already flowing into my hands, and it disturbed me to see the money. I turned around and shouted to them: "Take away your money. I did not come here for money, but to cure your chief. If I cure him, you shall always remember me and hold my name in honour. Take your money away."

They took back their money, and I chanted my song again. My power came back to me, and I laid my hands on the patient, whose gall was spilling over into his liver. He fainted, being so weak that he was ready to die. I treated him for three days. On the fourth, I bathed him and helped him to rise to his feet. His sickness was cured.

That is the way of the true medicine man. When he is treating a patient he pays no attention to the amount of money or blankets that the people offer him; and if his patient dies, he returns everything that has been given him.

1926–1939:
FIELD WORK, BOOKS, CONSULTING, AND CONFERENCES

13

Stuart E. Jenness

In Chapter 10, I stated that my father's years as Chief of Anthropology were extremely challenging, and that administrative duties demanded most of his time, energy, and attention. He did, however, manage to find some time to continue pursuing his ethnological research, fieldwork, and writing.

In the summer of 1926, following his initial appointment as Division Chief, my father undertook what proved to be highly important archaeological investigations around Bering Strait (Chapter 9). The next March, while he debated whether to remain in Ottawa during the coming summer or go to Newfoundland to undertake some archaeological work, he received an unexpected enquiry from the National Geographic Society asking him if he would lead an archaeological expedition to the Bering Sea that summer, one sponsored jointly by that society and the Smithsonian Institution in Washington. He agreed to do so provided he could get official approval from the Canadian government. To Dr. Sapir, by then at the University of Chicago, he wrote, "… it seemed impossible to turn down the Alaskan project if only for the prestige of the Division."[1] Before official permission was granted him to head the expedition, however, the entire project fell through. The National Geographic Society withdrew its offer of funds after the two organizations failed to reach agreement on what to name the expedition![2]

With the Bering Sea project out of the picture, my father reverted to his previous plans to undertake several weeks of exploratory archaeological investigations in north-central Newfoundland, which in 1927 was still a British colony with a Governor. He took mother, my older brother and me by train as far as Nova Scotia, where he left us with mother's aunt and uncle[3]

---

[1]Jenness to Sapir, letter dated March 16, 1927, Jenness Correspondence, Box 656, Folder 37, Archives, CMC. His interest in advancing the prestige of the Anthropology Division rather than his own is noteworthy.

[2]Jenness to H.D. Skinner, letter dated March 29, 1927, Jenness Correspondence, Box 657, Folder 44, Archives, CMC. The following year (1928), an American archaeologist, Dr. Henry Collins, led a Smithsonian expedition to St. Lawrence Island in the Bering Sea that confirmed the existence of the Eskimo culture my father had termed the "Old Bering Sea culture," (Collins, 1931) and initiated a life-long friendship with my father.

[3]Mother's uncle was Cooper Boville, federal Deputy Minister of Finance during the First World War. Following the end of the war he retired to the coast at Chester, N.S., where he soon became active among the local sailing enthusiasts.

at Chester, then continued on to Newfoundland. He spent almost nine weeks working around Notre Dame Bay, searching for burial mounds and sites of the little-known Beothuk Indians, the last of whom had died in the 1800s. He discovered two unpillaged gravesites and carefully collected the remains for the National Museum in Ottawa. These, along with artifacts recovered during his reconnaissance, provided him with finite, rewarding evidence that there had been contact in the past between the Beothuk Indians and the Labrador Eskimos. His findings also enabled him to plan further archaeological investigations in Newfoundland for another member of his staff.

On the completion of his fieldwork in Newfoundland, my father sent a telegram to my mother asking her to "meet him in Paradise." When he told me this mildly amusing story years ago, it meant little to me until he explained that Paradise was the name of the railway junction where mother would meet his train from Sydney, Cape Breton. I do believe that this anecdote reveals a little romantic streak in him. United once again, our family enjoyed a pleasant two-week's vacation on the Bay of Fundy at Port Lorne near Digby before returning to Ottawa.

In the summer of 1929, my father spent two months with the Ojibwa Indians on their reserve in the Parry Sound region, gathering much information on their ancient beliefs and customs.[4] He took mother, my older brother Pete, and me with him. Pete remembers being taken fishing by one of the local Indians; as I was scarcely four years old, I recall little about the summer except that we lived in a tent.

The Anthropology Division received no fieldwork funds between 1930 and 1935 because of government cutbacks during the Great Depression. Money for divisional publications likewise was unavailable. During the summer of 1935, however, the government's financial restrictions eased slightly, and my father utilized the small amount of government field-expense money his division was allotted to have his colleague, Harlan I. Smith, film Algonquin Indians northwest of Ottawa demonstrating some of their rapidly vanishing activities. At Golden Lake, Smith filmed Chief Matthew Bernard and his wife constructing a birchbark canoe. My father took me to Golden Lake in our car for a brief visit one day, along with some of the native objects (borrowed from the museum's collection) to be used as props in the film. The visit gave my father the opportunity to assess how the project was going and to ensure the safety of the Indian artifacts we took with us in the car, which saved the government shipping charges. I was instructed to watch quietly as the chief went about his work. Later in the summer, Smith filmed the same couple gathering wild rice at Rice Lake near Peterborough. The resultant 35-mm film, now housed in the Canadian Museum of Civilization, was entitled *Cheenama the Trailmaker*.

The appearance of darkening political clouds over Europe in 1935 gave my father some concern, with good reason. Germany took over the coal-rich Saarland that year, repudiated the Versailles Peace Treaty of 1919, reintroduced compulsory military service, and recreated its air force. From these militant moves, Father sensed (correctly) the likelihood of another war with Germany sometime in the next few years. Not wanting his son John (Pete) to be as ill-prepared as he had been, nor to serve as a private in the Army as he himself had done in the First World War, he arranged to have him attend a private school near Munich, Germany, for

---

[4]Jenness, 1935a.

a year to learn German. Pete was only thirteen years old and the only English-speaking student in the school. He did learn German as Father hoped, the war did commence in 1939 as Father anticipated, and Pete did qualify as an officer in the Canadian Army in 1942. However, the army units to which he was subsequently attached served in Italy, France, Belgium, and the Netherlands in the Second World War, but not in Germany, and he made only limited use of the German he had learned during the winter of 1935–1936.

Mother felt she should be somewhere near Pete that winter (1935–1936) in case he got sick or otherwise into trouble, so bundled my younger brother Bob and me off to Munich with her, where we settled into a comfortable boarding house. While a German nursemaid looked after Bob each weekday, Mother and I visited museums and art galleries, attended concerts, took private piano lessons, and studied German. Pete was permitted to visit us at Christmas and again at Easter. We all returned to Canada late in the spring. Looking back seventy years later, I cannot understand why my father sent his oldest son to Germany at such an early age and at that uncertain time, and then allowed the rest of his family to go there as well.

Left behind in Canada, my father spent the winter of 1935–1936 investigating the Coast Salish Indians on Vancouver Island and in the Fraser River Valley near Vancouver. It proved to be his last field assignment among Canada's Native people. He divided his time during the first part of the winter on reserves near Sydney and Duncan, on Vancouver Island, then visited a well known elder, Peter Pierre (Old Pierre as reported in Chapter 12), on a reserve at Katzie in the Fraser Valley near Vancouver.[5] During the winter, he lectured in Victoria and at the Universities of British Columbia, Washington, and Toronto.

After being separated from his family for so many months, my father sought to have a special surprise for his wife upon her return from Germany. He contacted her best friend, a talented pianist, and enlisted her aid in finding a good second-hand piano that he could buy. One was found, and it was delivered to our cottage before mother and we three boys reached Ottawa. Father soon had the immense pleasure of seeing her surprise and joy in discovering it against a wall in the cottage and hearing the music that was performed on it for many years afterwards.

My father always knew that he must publish to establish his reputation. Whether he learned this from one or more of his university professors, through discussions with Vilhjalmur Stefansson in the Arctic, or reached that conclusion on his own, I cannot conjecture. He published twenty-one books between 1920 and 1968, but his two best-known, *People of the Twilight* in 1928 and *The Indians of Canada* in 1932, appeared within the first six years of his assuming his administrative duties as Chief of Anthropology, a tribute to his focus, literary talent, and industriousness.

His eight reports on the Copper Eskimos (volumes 12A, 12B, 13A, 13B, 14, 15A, 15B, and 16 of the Reports of the Canadian Arctic Expedition 1913–1918) were all written in the 1920s, but publishing-fund restrictions delayed the last two until the mid-1940s. The first of these various expedition reports, *Life of the Copper Eskimos* has been called "the best description of any Eskimo tribe" and "one of the classics of ethnographic literature."[6]

---

[5]Jenness, 1955.
[6]Collins, 1971, p. 10.

When his Canadian Arctic Expedition report on *Eskimo Songs* was published in 1925,[7] my father mailed a copy to his former colleague, Sir Francis Knowles, in Oxford. In his letter of thanks, Knowles may have planted a seed that led to the writing of father's charming account of the Copper Eskimos, *People of the Twilight*, with his remark, "I hope that someday you will write an account of your life with the Eskimo family, especially with reference to their daily life & employments; it would be of the greatest interest—popular as well as scientific. Have you anything of the sort in preparation?"[8] My father published *The People of the Twilight* two years later. He wrote that book largely at home and dedicated it to his mother in New Zealand, who had encouraged him so much with his academic studies. When he completed the manuscript for the book, my father sent a copy to Sapir and asked for his comments. Sapir found it "exceedingly interesting and remarkably well told," but suggested that my father "contrive to give a somewhat livelier sense of the Eskimos as differentiated peoples, also of the more serious aspects of the personalities of your companions." He also criticized my father for depending too much on whimsical anecdotes in the manuscript in order to give a feeling of humaneness.[9] My father made some modifications to his manuscript in response, but replied, "There are one or two jokes (?) which I absolutely refuse to cut out even for you; my perverted sense of humour forbids."[10]

The book was "written for the layman as well as for the scientist," he later wrote his former Arctic leader, V. Stefansson, after it was published, "in the hope that it will awaken sympathy and interest especially in Canada for these people whom you and I admire so greatly, and thereby promote whatever measures Canada may undertake for their future welfare."[11] My father asked Fridtjof Nansen to write a preface for the book "because he is a great Arctic explorer, a keen student of the Eskimos, and a champion of distressed peoples as shown by his well-known work on behalf of the League of Nations."[12]

The book sold for two dollars, so his royalties were small. It was originally published in 1928 with an incongruous bright-orange hardcover by Macmillan and Co., and was soon out of print. The University of Chicago Press printed several paperback versions commencing in 1957, with a poignant Epilogue added at that time by my father. The book remained in print until the late 1980s, and received much praise, perhaps the finest of which came from the late William E. Taylor, Jr., the first Director of the National Museum of Man. In 1990, Taylor wrote that *The People of the Twilight* was, in his view, "... the best single book on the traditional Canadian Inuit."[13]

---

[7]Jenness and Roberts, 1925

[8]Knowles to Jenness, letter dated May 17, 1926, Jenness Correspondence, Box 647, Folder 55, Archives, CMC.

[9]Sapir to Jenness, letter dated June 7, 1927, Jenness Correspondence, Box 656, Folder 37, Archives, CMC.

[10]Jenness to Sapir, letter dated October 22, 1927, Jenness Correspondence, Box 656, Folder 37, Archives, CMC.

[11]Jenness to Stefansson, letter dated March 15, 1928, Jenness Correspondence, Box 658, Folder 41, Archives, CMC.

[12]Jenness to Sapir, letter dated April 12, 1927, Jenness Correspondence, Box 656, Folder 37, Archives, CMC.

[13]Taylor, W.E., Jr., 1990, p. xvi in S.E. Jenness, 1991. Taylor greatly admired my father.

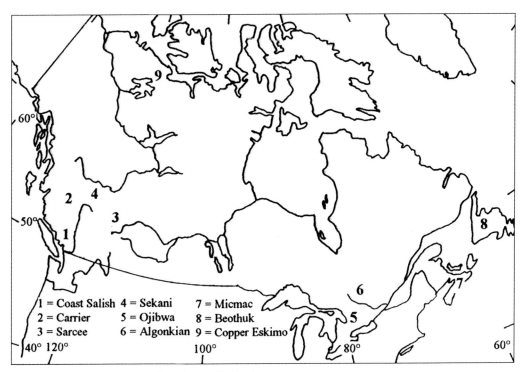

Map 9 Distribution of the main Indian tribes studied by Jenness.

One of the "stars" of this book was the Copper Eskimo man, Ikpukhuak, who agreed to "adopt" my father in 1915 for a summer of nomadic living on Victoria Island. My father developed a high regard for Ikpuk, as he called him, and admired the abilities of Ikpuk's jolly shaman wife, Higilak. He was also especially fond of Higilak's daughter, whom he regarded as his "little sister" Jennie. The feelings were evidently reciprocated, for in 1930, fourteen years after my father left the Arctic, he received a message from Ikpukhuak and Jennie (Higilak had died three years earlier) urging him to come back to see them. It had been sent by a young radio operator named Richard Finnie from a newly erected radio station at the two-year-old settlement of Coppermine (now known as Kugluktuk), at the mouth of the Coppermine River. My father sent back the compassionate reply by radio, "I shall never forget my father and my younger sister. Though I would like to see you, it cannot come to pass. It is too far away. I am getting old. Do not be frightened. When we die we will meet each other. We will be happy all together."[14] This message was translated for Ikpukhuak and Jennie by the Church of England missionary at Coppermine, Reverend Harold Webster.[15] My father was forty four years old at the time, so he was not old by the life expectancies of males in southern Canada, but he was

---

[14]Finnie, R.S., 1940, p. 169. Reproduced also in S.E. Jenness, 1991, pp. 633–634.

[15]Archdeacon A.L. Fleming to Jenness, letter dated February 10, 1932, Jenness Correspondence, Box 644, Folder 29, Archives, CMC. Archibald Laing Fleming later became Anglican Bishop of the Diocese of the North.

old by the life expectancy of the Eskimos of the Coronation Gulf region at the time, and expressed the point in words that Ikpuk could understand. His statement in this message about death and the after-life is one of only two places I know of where his expression of that belief is on record.[16]

Another similar message came from Ikpukhuak in 1931, by which time the "little sister" Jennie had died painfully of spinal tuberculosis.[17] This time my father responded by sending a parcel to his "adopted father," together with a covering letter addressed to Corporal G.M. Walls, who was in charge of the newly established RCMP Detachment at Coppermine. The letter read: "I am sending you, for my adopted Eskimo father, Ikpukhuak, the binoculars that he and I used on Victoria Island nearly twenty years ago. I think he will appreciate them more than anything else that I can send. Will you please give them to him and tell him that, although it is not possible for me to visit him again, he is not forgotten."[18] Ikpukhuak died two years later, reportedly at or near Basil Bay at the west end of Coronation Gulf. He has not been forgotten.

While my father was working on *The People of the Twilight*, Collins, the Acting Director of the National Museum of Canada, asked him to prepare a "text book on Aborigines, for the use of colleges and teachers."[19] It was also intended for the general public. My father started writing this important work in 1927 and completed it four years later. It was given high priority and published in 1932, although other scientific reports in his division had to be set aside because of the lack of government funds for publication at the time. When he submitted his completed manuscript for departmental editing, it bore his more accurate title, "The Aborigines of Canada." This title was changed to "The Indians of Canada" during the editorial stage, although I expect not without his objections at the time, for it included a chapter on Canada's Eskimos.

The original 1,600 hardbound copies of *The Indians of Canada* were printed in 1932, priced at three dollars, and sold out within two years, a best seller by Canadian standards and almost unprecedented for a government report. Since then six more editions have been published, the most recent one in 1977. A noted Canadian historian has called it "one of the great works of World anthropology."[20]

In 1930, while he was still busy preparing *The Indians of Canada*, my father was asked to solicit anthropological manuscripts for a special book entitled, *The American Aborigines — Their Origin and Antiquity*, which was to be published and disseminated at the meeting of the 5th Pacific Science Congress, in Vancouver in June 1932. (The date of the congress was later changed to June 1933.) In the spring of 1929, he had attended the 4th Pacific Science Congress in Java

---

[16]The other is in a letter to his long-time friend John Cox, written in April 1967, seven months before my father died. The letter was in my possession in 2006.

[17]She was buried in the Church of England cemetery on a small island at the mouth of the Coppermine River.

[18]Jenness to Corporal Walls, letter dated June 8, 1932, Jenness Correspondence, Box 644, Folder 29, Archives, CMC.

[19]Jenness to D.C. Scott, Superintendent General, Department of Indian Affairs, letter dated May 17, 1930, Jenness Correspondence, Box 643, Folder 3, Archives, CMC.

[20]J. Granatstein, 1998, p. 40.

as one of two official Canadian delegates,[21] and thus was a logical person to undertake the special volume. My father succeeded in getting important papers from well-known anthropologists at the American Museum of Natural History, at Harvard and Columbia universities, and in Sweden, and added his own paper, *The Problem of the Eskimo*. He edited these papers and nursed them through publication on behalf of the government sponsor, the National Research Council of Canada, in time for the meeting.[22] He also successfully organized and chaired the anthropological section at the meeting.

That same year (1934), he somehow managed to find time to prepare a report for publication on the Carrier Indians of northern British Columbia, a report for the Justice Department contrasting the social organization of the Indians and Eskimos, and a map for the Department of the Interior showing the location of Indian tribes in northeastern North America in 1774.[23]

One year earlier, an enquiry came from the Deputy Minister of the Department of Justice to the office of the Deputy Minister of Mines, seeking clarification on whether Eskimos were to be considered as Indians under the terms of the British North America Act. Personnel in the Justice department evidently held the view then that the Canadian Eskimos should not be regarded as "Indians" under the act. Father was asked to provide the desired clarification. I suspect that he sensed a desire on the part of the federal government to avoid what he regarded as its obligation to its northern people, for his 6-page response concluded with the comment, "Today all the leading anthropologists agree that the Eskimo are but a specialized sub-type of American Indians, and include them in the general term 'Indian'."[24] The Department of Justice was busily looking into what responsiblities the federal government had assumed over Indian affairs when the British North America Act was passed in 1775. My father, on the other hand, wanted to make sure that the Eskimos were not left out.

A change of government in 1936 resulted in the termination of the federal Department of the Interior and the subsequent transfer of that department's Indian Affairs Branch to the Department of Mines and Resources. That August, Father submitted an important memorandum to

---

[21]Professor C. McLean Fraser, a zoologist at the University of British Columbia, was the other delegate. My father left Ottawa by train late in March, and sailed to Batavia, the largest city and principal seaport on the island of Java, stopping briefly en route at Yokohama, Kyoto, Shanghai, Hong Kong, Singapore, and Johore. From Batavia he proceeded by train with the other delegates to Beutenzorg, where they visited two museums and a rubber experiment station, and then to Bandoeng, where the meetings were held. In addition to the various scientific sessions he attended, my father accompanied eight other delegates on an airplane flight to a nearby, recently active volcano. The pilot circled around and inside the rim of the crater before returning to the airport. My father expressed much pleasure in what was undoubtedly his first airplane ride. (D. Jenness to Mrs. D. Jenness, letter dated May 22, 1929, from Bandoeng, Java, in my possession in 2005.)

[22]Jenness, 1933b.

[23]Jenness to C. Camsell, memo dated March 8, 1934, Jenness Correspondence, Box 641, Folder 29, Archives, CMC. A map in this folder shows the location of the several dozen Indian tribes known to inhabit the region south of James Bay and east of the Mississippi River in 1774. I recognized the inked names of the tribes on the map as in my father's handwriting. The map bears a Geological Survey Photographic Division stamp dated October 12, 1933.

[24]Jenness to C. Camsell, memo dated August 14, 1933, p. 5, Jenness Correspondence, Box 641, Folder 29, Archives, CMC.

Charles Camsell, the Deputy Minister of Mines,[25] in which he criticized the condition of the native-reserve system, stating that the reserve system had been downgraded into a system of permanent segregation. The people on the reserves felt like outcasts, their morale was destroyed, their health was poor, and the reserves were breeding grounds for serious diseases. "The most crying need today," he wrote, "is to restore the reserve system to its original purpose, i.e., to make it a purely transitional phase of education and training leading to full citizenship."

Towards that goal, he submitted six suggestions for action to remedy the problems on the reserves: (1) the gradual closing of separate Indian schools and compulsory involvement of Indian children in regular provincial primary schools; (2) the creation of many scholarships to enable the more intelligent and diligent Indian children to attend high schools, technical schools, and, in special cases, universities; (3) the establishing of a system of following up on Indian children after they left school to ensure, whenever possible, that they had steady employment and did not drift back into idleness on the reserves; (4) not enforcing the Potlatch Law, expecially in British Columbia, until it was clarified; (5) measures involving closer collaboration between federal and provincial offices with regard to Indian health services; and (6) the protection of native trapping and hunting grounds. Sadly, his suggestions appear to have had little influence, for today, more than seventy years later, the conditions of many of Canada's native reserves are still described as deplorable, in spite of the spending of billions of dollars by the federal government in recent years in its efforts to remedy the situation. His well-expressed concerns, however, may have helped bring about the following activity.

In the fall of 1936, Father was placed on contract with the Indian Affairs Branch as a part-time consulting anthropologist.[26] Several high-level communiqués were exchanged between the Department of Mines and Resources and the Civil Service Commission before agreement was reached that permitted my father to be paid a stipend of $500 per year by that branch in addition to his regular salary from the National Museum as Chief of the Division of Anthropology. The Governor-General's Order in Council creating a part-time consulting position for him with the Indian Affairs Branch was effective April 1, 1937. He retained this part-time status until April 6, 1950, although it was dormant between 1941 and 1947 when his duties with the Air Force kept him too busy to attend to Indian Affairs matters.[27]

In March 1936, my father received an unexpected invitation to be an expenses-paid guest of the British Association for the Advancement of Science at Blackpool, England, the following September and to deliver a paper to its members. The British Association was then the senior scientific organization in the British Empire. He promptly accepted the invitation, subject to being able to obtain official permission to attend, and added that he considered it an honour not only to himself but also to the National Museum of Canada. In his request to the Director of the National Museum for official permission to attend the meeting, my father asked that he be advanced a sum of $613 for travel and accommodation money, and he would reimburse

---

[25]Jenness to C. Camsell, memo dated August 25, 1936, Jenness correspondence, Box. 641, Folder 29, Archives, CMC. Jenness left Ottawa to attend a scientific meeting in England very shortly after submitting this memorandum.

[26]Jenness to C. Camsell, memorandum dated November 26, 1936, RG 32, Vol. 137, File 1886-02-10, LAC.

[27]Civil Service Commission, RG 32, vol. 137, File 1886-02-10, LAC.

the government whatever funds he received from the British Association for his expenses. In that sum he included $100 for unforeseen expenses, which he explained he wished to use to visit a few museums in London and elsewhere in England to examine their early Canadian Indian collections with a view of initiating exchange arrangements with Canada's National Museum. To his surprise and delight, three months later he was granted both the permission to attend the meeting and the funds he had requested. He was also granted permission to present his paper entitled "The Indian Background of Canadian History" at the Blackpool meeting.

A story lies behind that paper. My father had originally written it early in 1934 and read part of it that spring at a meeting of the Royal Society of Canada. He had expected the museum to publish it but "the authorities turned it back on to my hands at Christmas time because it is not 'popular' enough to justify publication in a time of economic stress."[28] The paper was in two parts, the first entitled "Backwardness of the American Aborigines and its Causes," a rather controversial title, as indeed were its contents; the second part was entitled, "Prehistory of the Canadian Indians." For the Blackpool meeting, he chose to read the first part, which included philosophical ideas he had pondered for some time about the wave-like progress of civilizations, rising and falling in various parts of the world. The second part, which focused on early Canadian Indian history, he sent to L.H.D. Buxton, a friend of his in Oxford, for inclusion in a collection of essays to mark the seventieth birthday of his former teacher, R.R. Marett.[29] The National Museum of Canada subsequently published the two parts in its Bulletin series.[30]

Early in 1935, my father read with much interest the third volume of British historian Arnold J. Toynbee's monumental work, *Study in History*, wherein Professor Toynbee attempted to analyze history in terms of the growth and decline of civilizations. My father and Toynbee had been residents of Balliol College at Oxford at the same time. So enthusiastic was my father with the ideas presented in Toynbee's book that he wrote to him, extending his congratulations and offering some philosophical ideas and questions of his own for the professor's consideration in subsequent volumes of his book.[31] He also enclosed a copy of his two-part manuscript, "The Background of Canadian History." Professor Toynbee replied, "I always remember our going au pair to read essays to McKinnon Wood ..." and remarked that the third volume of his book, to which my father had referred, benefited by information from father's book on the Coronation Gulf Eskimos (i.e., *Life of the Copper Eskimos*). My father had raised too many points in his letter to deal with by correspondence, Toynbee added, but he was particularly interested in the suggestion "that general decline may be accompanied by creativeness along certain lines and that art, philosophy and religion may rise at certain times of social decline, economic misery, and general unhappiness. I am sure this is profoundly true and in fact it is one of the main ideas which I am trying to put forward in a part dealing with 'Declines' which I am now writing."[32]

[28]Jenness to A.J. Toynbee, letter dated March 18, 1935, Jenness Correspondence, Box 659, Folder 53, Archives, CMC.
[29]Jenness, 1936b.
[30]Jenness, 1937a.
[31]Jenness to A.J. Toynbee, letter dated March 18, 1935, Jenness Correspondence, Box 659, Folder 53, Archives, CMC.
[32]A.J. Toynbee to Jenness, letter dated April 16, 1935, Jenness Correspondence, Box 659, Folder 53, Archives, CMC.

Before leaving for England in the summer of 1936, my father revived an idea he had con-templated for more than a decade, namely to visit several museums throughout Europe in order to examine their Canadian Aboriginal collections and discuss the possibilities of trading specimens with them. He had first voiced the idea in a letter to Barbeau in 1922.[33] He requested permission to spend several weeks in Europe after the Blackpool meeting, but his request was turned down.

My father sailed to Southampton on the *Empress of Britain*, and read his paper at the Blackpool meeting. While in England, he managed to spend sufficient time at Oxford with his former colleague, Francis Knowles (by then, Sir Francis Knowles, having inherited his father's title), to help him complete a long-outstanding manuscript on the physical characteristics of the Iroquois Indians, which the National Museum of Canada subsequently published after my father had carefully edited it. In addition, he managed brief visits to a few museums, notably in London, Oxford, Cambridge, and Paris before returning to Canada. He was overwhelmed at the kindness and hospitality he received at Blackpool and elsewhere in England that summer, from both long-time friends and new acquaintances. After his return to Canada, he wrote to R.U. Sayce, recorder of Section H of the British Association for the Advancement of Science, and revealed an interesting internal longing, one I do not recall ever hearing him express: "England has never felt so truly a home to me, although I once spent three years there and from childhood was taught, like other New Zealanders, to consider it 'home'...."[34]

Within two months of his return from Britain, my father was offered an appointment as Professor of Social Anthropology at Cambridge University at an annual salary of £1,200.[35] This would have been a salary increase of about $1,500 per year, a considerable amount in the 1930s. There is no way to estimate the value of the added prestige involved. In view of the feelings he had about England at that time, as already mentioned, and the unhappy state of his division at the National Museum, I feel certain that he was greatly tempted to accept it, even though he sensed the likelihood of war with Germany in the foreseeable future. Nevertheless, he

[33]Jenness to Barbeau, letter dated September 16, 1922, Jenness Correspondence, Box 206, Folder 27, CMC. I have no doubt that the two men discussed this idea in the months that followed. Several years after he ceased talking with my father, Barbeau requested leave and funds to study Indian materials in Paris and neighbouring museums "particularly from the point of view of the French renaissance designs and crafts with any relation that may exist between them and arts of the North American Indians. This is a subject I have been working on for some years." He also asked to go to London, Oxford, and Cambridge for the same purpose. One might be forgiven for thinking he was deliberately trying to make first use of my father's idea; however, to give him credit, the purposes of the two men differed, Barbeau wishing to compare the designs and artwork in Europe with that of North American Indians, whereas my father was seeking pre-1880 Canadian native artifacts he might acquire for the National Museum through trade (Barbeau to Director, NMC, letter dated March 3, 1931, Barbeau Collection, Box 182, Folder 21, Archives, CMC.

[34]Jenness to R.U. Sayce, letter dated October 27, 1936, Jenness Correspondence, Box 641, Folder 15, Archives, CMC.

[35]Dr. Charles Camsell, Deputy Minister, Department of Mines and Resources, to C.H. Bland, Chairman, Civil Service Commission, letter dated February 12, 1937, RG 32, Vol. 137, File 1886-02-10, LAC.

turned down the offer, perhaps because he felt that such a move would have been too much of an upheaval for his family.[36]

---

[36]During a conversation I had with Mrs. Graham Rowley in the early spring of 2005, she suddenly exclaimed "You know, it is really a great pity your father never accepted the offer to teach at Cambridge!" I confessed having no knowledge of such an offer and asked how she knew. "He must have told Graham" was her response. Graham was her husband, a Cambridge graduate in archaeology, and a good friend of my father's since they first met in the 1930s. "Do you have any idea why he didn't accept it?" I then enquired. "Your mother refused to move!" was her prompt response, adding that Graham had told her this. He must have heard that explanation from my father during one of their many conversations.

1938: EUROPE IN THE SHADOW OF IMPENDING WAR

14

Diamond Jenness

[*Late in 1937, my father revived his long-held idea to visit a number of European museums known to hold Canadian Aboriginal collections, especially those with holdings older than 1880, for most collections made in Canada before that date had ended up in British or European museums. During his visits, he would observe and make a record of the material they possessed and discuss exchange possibilities. He particularly hoped to find some specimens collected by Captain Cook or Captain Vancouver, and perhaps others who had visited the west coast of Canada in the 1700s.*

Two years earlier, he had sought permission to visit these particular museums in Europe after he attended the meeting of the British Association for the Advancement of Science at Blackpool, England. On that occasion, his request was turned down. Nevertheless, he did succeed in visiting several British museums and even one museum in Paris before returning to Canada from that meeting.

This time, in the spring of 1938, when he requested official leave to attend the International Congress on Anthropological and Ethnological Sciences in Copenhagen from August 1–15, to which he had been invited to present a paper[1] and participate, he again asked permission to visit European museums before and after the congress. Fully aware of the financial restrictions under which the Canadian government had been operating for several years, but eager to grasp what seemed a wonderful opportunity, he volunteered to pay his own expenses. He was granted permission to attend the congress and also leave on official duty for up to two months while he visited the museums around Europe—partly prior to the meeting in Copenhagen, partly after—as well as his expenses both at the Congress and to visit the museums.[2]

My father quickly set about contacting the directors of some two dozen museums on the continent to learn if they had Canadian Indian and Eskimo artifacts, especially items older than 1880, and whether they would permit him to examine their collections, stating approximate dates he could be there. He received encouraging responses from at least eight museums, notably ones in Antwerp, Leiden, Munich, Budapest, Brunn (or Brno), Prague, Berlin, and Leipzig. He subsequently enjoyed friendly visits at several of these museums, but political events that summer prevented him from visiting them all.

As my father wished to take Mother to Europe with him, he had to make arrangements for the care of his three sons. John (Pete) went to a French-language camp north of Montreal for part of the summer and to Mother's youngest brother's house for the rest of it, while Bob went to the Niagara

---

[1] Jenness, 1940.

[2] J. McLeish, Director, Mines & Geology Branch, to F.C.C. Lynch, Chief, Bureau of Geology & Topography, memo dated March 18, 1938, copy in Jenness Correspondence, Box 652, Folder 6, Archives, CMC. McLeish was married to Ida Tavernier, the sister of the National Museum's bird specialist, Percy Taverner.

Peninsula to stay with Dr. Ellis Hurlburt, a medical man whom my father had known overseas during the First World War. I was to spend the summer learning German at the home of a German family in Wiesbaden, Germany, having been promised that Mother would buy me an accordion when we got there. Father had to preside over anthropological sessions at a meeting of the American Association for the Advancement of Science in Ottawa late in June, so could not head for Europe before that meeting was over. As a result, Mother and I preceded him to Germany, travelling from Montreal on the Norwegian freighter, S.S. Brant County. *My father's account of his European trip follows.*] [S.E.J.]

In the autumn of 1937, I received a notice stating that the biennial International Congress of Anthropological and Ethnological Sciences would meet in Copenhagen in early August 1938, and that one section of it, under the direction of Dr. Kaj Birket-Smith of Denmark's National Museum, would devote its meetings to Arctic America. About the same time, Dr. Birket-Smith himself wrote to me, inviting me to open the meetings of his section with a paper on "Prehistoric Culture Waves from Asia to America."[3]

I accepted his invitation, subject to the approval of my employers, the administrators of Canada's National Museum, and forwarded a copy of both the invitation and my reply to those administrators, along with a request for permission to attend the congress and defend my paper in person. I pointed out, furthermore, that the journey to and from Copenhagen would provide an excellent opportunity to visit a number of museums in Europe known to possess old and rare ethnographical specimens from Canada, and to negotiate for the redemption of a few of them, perhaps, by offering, in exchange, surplus specimens from Canada's National Museum. The American Association for the Advancement of Science was holding one of its rare Canadian congresses in Ottawa in June 1938, and being a Vice-President as well as a section chairman of that organization, I would have to preside at some of its meetings, but I could attend the Copenhagen congress after the American one ended, and spend the remainder of the summer visiting European museums, instead of hastening back to Canada before winter closed in to work, as usual, on one or other Indian reserve.

The fullness of time brought the administrators' reply. The government would grant me leave of absence to attend the Copenhagen conference at my own expense and to read a paper there, and it would defray the cost of my travelling afterwards to various European museums to examine their Canadian ethnographical collections and negotiate for such as seemed valuable and recoverable.[4] Elated at this extraordinary concession, I prepared my paper with enthusiasm.

The European trip that I now outlined for myself appeared to offer a splendid opportunity to place my 12-year-old son Stuart, who would shortly be entering high-school, in the bosom of a German family where the new language would root itself painlessly in his subconscious, and strange customs and unfamiliar sights stimulate his curiosity and broaden his horizon. Probably, as I flitted from museum to museum, I could drop in two or three times to observe his progress, perhaps even take him to a few places particularly interesting to a boy of his age.

---

[3]My father read his paper at the Copenhagen meeting that summer. It was published two years later (Jenness, 1940).
[4]The department later compensated him for his expenses at the Copenhagen conference.

With these ideas in mind, I began to make enquiries, and discovered that a Miss Herta Hartmanshenn, German instructor in the University of Toronto,[5] was planning to spend the summer at her parents' home in Wiesbaden, in the Rhineland, where her family would gladly accept Stuart as their guest.[6] To keep the boy from loneliness, my wife decided to accompany him to Wiesbaden, and to remain near him until I arrived three or four weeks later, after which she would attend the Copenhagen conference and travel through Europe with me. We booked passages for all three of us, therefore, with a Norwegian freight line which ran a monthly service between Montreal and either Antwerp or Rotterdam, and was accepting six to ten passengers on its vessels at the extraordinarily cheap rate of $75 each—an important consideration to a civil servant whose government post provided him with a salary less than one third the amount the same post carries today [mid-1960s]. My wife and Stuart secured berths on the early June boat, the S.S. *Brant County*, I on the boat that would be sailing at the end of that month, three days after the American Association for the Advancement of Science terminated its Ottawa meetings.

The freight vessel that carried my family to Europe faithfully adhered to its schedule. It landed them on the advertised day at Antwerp, whence they travelled by train to Wiesbaden by way of Brussels and Köln [Cologne] without incident. But the freighter which transported me displayed the characteristic unreliability of its breed on the very morning of its departure by changing its first port of call from Antwerp to Bordeaux, and by engaging to stop at Dunkirk en route from Bordeaux to Antwerp, thereby delaying its arrival at this last port two or three days. In consequence, I too changed my plans, for my European schedule had little flexibility. I therefore disembarked at Bordeaux, travelled on the night express to Paris and, after verifying my train schedule in the morning, wired my wife to meet me at 7:30 that evening in the Wiesbaden railroad station.

The railway authorities in Paris informed me that their French train ran no farther than Saarbrucken. At that frontier town I would have to transfer to a German train, and then

---

[5]I do not know how my father learned about Miss Hartmanshenn, but suspect it was through one of his scientific acquaintances.

[6]Some financial agreement was undoubtedly made between my father and the Hartmanshenn family for my accommodation at their small but tidy house on Fasanerie Strasse in the suburbs of Wiesbaden, but of its terms I have no knowledge. The family consisted of a retired father and a partly crippled mother, twin daughters Herta (who patiently taught me German for ten weeks) and her unmarried but working sister Gerda, and a young Schnauzer dog that was not housebroken. Mother bought me the accordion I had been promised and the Hartmanshenn family suffered daily but silently while I learned to play it. Herta taught in Toronto during the following winter and returned to Germany in the late spring of 1939. The start of the Second World War that summer forced her to remain there. She and her family apparently suffered many hardships during the war, so when my father received a request from Herta in 1946 for permission to translate his book *People of the Twilight* for publication in Germany, he not only granted his permission immediately, but also assigned to her any royalties that might arise from the book's publication. The book was self-published in Wiesbaden under the title *Schneehütten Völkschen* (Jenness 1947) and Herta sent father a few copies. By the merest chance, a used copy of the translated book that I purchased over the internet in 2004 turned out to be a copy my father had originally given its vendor in the late 1950s. This vendor, to my great surprise, was Nansi Swayze Glick, who published the first biography of my father (Swayze, 1960).

change a second time at Mainz, in the Rhineland, for a local train to Wiesbaden. They assured me, however, that it was all very simple, and that I would not experience any trouble any-where. I pocketed my ticket, therefore, found my carriage and took my seat. People boarded and left the train at every stop, but I paid no attention until, at the last French town before the frontier, I became aware of a general exodus which left me the only passenger.

Somewhat surprised at my privileged status I kept my seat, and the train, steaming on, deposited me in Saarbrucken station. There a porter carried my suitcase into the customs office, a soldier escorted me to a waiting room separated from the customs office by a glass partition, and two army officers carefully examined my passport.[7] Finding no flaw therein, they closed it again without comment, but instead of handing it back to me, they kept it, and detained me also. Meanwhile, through the glass partition, I could see the customs officials meticulously scru-tinizing every item in my suitcase, just why I could not imagine, and presently six or seven officials began to circulate between the two rooms and converse with one another in low tones. Wonderingly, I waited.

The French train returned to its homeland, the German train I was scheduled to board pulled out soon afterwards, and still I awaited the return of my passport and the release of my baggage. Finally, two ramrod-straight army officers approached me, thrust under my eyes a small package which had been extracted from the suitcase, and barked, "What is this?"

"Those are my pipe cleaners," I answered, and drawing my pipe from my pocket, I demonstrated their use.

My interrogators sagged. What? Those little white sticks are pipe cleaners, not fuses for time bombs?

They turned their backs to me, spoke to each other rapidly, then ordered another uniformed man to return me the passport. I could now depart, they told me, and take my bag-gage. They even smiled at me, expressed their regret that I had missed my train, and directed me to another train that would carry me to Wiesbaden by a different route.

The new route proved to be faster than the old one, bringing me to Wiesbaden a little before the hour I had notified my wife, who in consequence failed to meet me at the station. I knew her address, however, and summoning a taxi, drove to the Hotel Neroberg, on the summit of a steep, thickly wooded hill. The manager looked surprised when I signed the register and asked about my wife. "She left the hotel an hour ago to meet you," he said. "Did you not see her?"

She returned an hour before midnight, having met not only the train I had specified, but another from the west three hours later. The manager came forward to greet us as we entered the hotel together, and my wife formally introduced me to him before leading me to our bedroom on the top floor, a large room whose French windows, I discovered in the morning, overlooked not the city but a wide, cultivated plain. Hardly had we settled down to talk,

---

[7]My father had requested and been provided with a diplomatic visa by the Canadian government to accompany his passport for this European trip (Laurent Beaudry to Jenness, letter dated May 28, 1938, Jenness Correspondence, Box 646, Folder 27, Archives, CMC). The modest appearance of both himself and his luggage with such a passport and his being alone may have aroused the suspicions of the German customs officials during those somewhat tense pre-war months.

however, when the doorbell rang and a maid brought in a heart-warming supper, and with it a little note carrying the manager's compliments—an unexpectedly thoughtful gesture which we greatly appreciated, the more so as neither of us had eaten since noon.

The hotel was a large, castle-like structure occupying a glorious situation within the city, but secluded from it by the forested hill. At the end of the Second World War, the United States army of occupation requisitioned it for a staff headquarters, but in 1938 it was still a tourist hotel under the supervision of the government. Tourists had been very scarce that summer, however, and during the three previous weeks, my wife had been its only resident guest, although from time to time a few visitors lunched or dined on its broad, gravel terrace and threw crumbs to the friendly finches that hopped around their tables. Both the manager and his small staff of maids had been extremely kind to her, but they appeared unhappy and apprehensive, and made no attempt to conceal their state of mind. Naturally, we could not ask the reason, but we encountered many Germans that summer, both in Wiesbaden and elsewhere, who seemed weighed down with anxiety.

During my two days at the Hotel Neroberg, I visited a large farm outside the city and, some miles beyond, the museum in Frankfurt, two of whose staff were planning to attend the Copenhagen meeting. Their institution contained a few specimens from Canada, but none of any special value. The farm interested me because it was employing one of the many thousand Italian families whom Mussolini was despatching to Germany each spring, under an agreement with Hitler which aimed at relieving both the Reich's desperate shortage of agricultural labour and the chronic unemployment that was crippling the Italian peninsula, especially the region from Naples south. This German farm had accepted a man, his wife, and their four small children, all of whom seemed comfortably housed and reasonably content. Their pay was small; what percentage of it, if any, they could expect to take home at the end of the season I did not ask. But at least they were self-supporting and healthily employed at a time when half a million of their countrymen, through no fault of their own, were rotting in idleness the whole year round.

From Wiesbaden, my wife and I went on to Berlin, whose museum possessed a large collection of Indian specimens from the Pacific coast of Canada, and a smaller collection from the prairies, the former acquired in the 1870s or 1880s, the latter about thirty years earlier. Unfortunately for me, or rather for my Canadian museum in Ottawa, this museum's director had studied North American history and, being well aware of the rarity of Canadian ethnographical material from the early years of European settlement, was by no means disposed to exchange any of his old specimens for twentieth century ones, however authentic the latter might be. In any case, as he politely explained, most of his institution's collections were stored in a building on the western outskirts of the city and at that moment were not readily accessible.

Disappointed, we did not linger in Berlin, but arranged to return at the end of summer when conditions might be more favourable. Before leaving the city, however, we hired a taxi to drive us through the sector in which Hitler was confining its Jewish population. The blond, fair-haired children playing in its streets seemed indistinguishable from those elsewhere in the city, but our taxi driver spoke of them contemptuously, and expressed his hearty approval of Hitler's anti-Semitic measures and of his insistence on the dominance of the master "Aryan," i.e. Germanic race. Neither we nor our taximan, of course, could foresee the calamities that the mad dictator's policies were bringing not to Berlin alone, but to the whole Reich. Fate spins her web slowly, but what she spins is irreversible.

Berlin pointed the way to Scandinavia. In Copenhagen, old friends from both the university and Denmark's National Museum came to greet us. We broke saucers with them at Tivoli,[8] the city's playground, admired and laughed at one another in the hall of distorting mirrors, and we pored over a collection of archaeological specimens from Greenland which had just reached the National Museum—a collection that linked the earliest inhabitants of that island with those of Canada's eastern Arctic and widened the vista of a mysterious branch of the Eskimo race that seems to have evolved in Canada's north during the second or third millennium before Christ.

My museum friends showed me one of their Indian treasures from North America, an Iroquois stone-headed tomahawk that had been presented to the King of Denmark in the six-teenth century, about the same time as a similar weapon passed into the possession of the King of Sweden. These two specimens, they told me, were the only genuinely Aboriginal tomahawks from North America that had survived the centuries, and because of their uniqueness, Denmark was stamping the image of her weapon on the metal buttons she planned to distribute to all registered delegates at the approaching congress.

Educationalists have long recognized that moving exhibits attract more attention than motionless ones; that parks and zoos in which living animals roam in replicas of their natural environments interest and instruct both old and young far more than museums of musty cases filled with lifeless skeletons and stuffed skins. It was not until the nineteenth century, however, that a noted French architect and antiquarian, Violet-le-Duc, sought to apply this principle to the teaching of history, and through it to stimulate the pride of his countrymen in the achieve-ments of their ancestors. When he restored the shattered walls and buildings of Carcassonne, the mediaeval fortress near the eastern end of the Pyrenees, he deliberately provided the old houses with feudal-age furniture and peopled them with men and women who could actively pursue the arts and crafts of the same period.

Denmark and other Scandinavian countries then copied his techniques. They erected villages of old, or at least old-style, dwellings in which they fostered the illusion of rolled-back centuries by settling peasants clad in the same costumes as their forefathers, and engaged in the same occupations. If today's Scandinavians, they hoped, can see with their own eyes the past from which they have emerged, they will march with greater confidence and courage into their unknowable future.

We visited two of these "old villages" or "outdoor museums" in Denmark, one at Lyngby in Copenhagen and the other at Aarhus on the Jutland Peninsula. Then, travelling north, we spent a morning at the popular but too commercialized Skansen Museum in Stockholm, and another morning three days later at the less sophisticated but more satisfying museum near Helsinki, which convincingly reproduces the simple life of rural Finland four or five centuries ago.

We had scheduled Helsinki as merely a stopping-place on the way to the Soviet Union, for during the preceding winter an unconfirmed rumour had reached me that the Leningrad

---

[8]"Breaking saucers" refers to the "game" of paying money to throw two or three balls at a dish set upright some distance away, at an amusement booth in order to win a prize—a stuffed bear or other animal, for example.

Museum held a large collection of ethnographic specimens which the eighteenth-century English navigator Captain James Cook had deposited with the Russian authorities in Petropavlovsk as security for some ship's chandlery he purchased in that Kamchatkan port.

Captain Cook is best remembered today for his discoveries in Polynesia. During my New Zealand boyhood, indeed, I had shot several "Captain Cookers", or tusked boars, wild descendants of the domestic pigs which the great navigator had released there, not to perpetuate his name, but to provide the chivalrous if cannibalistic Maoris with other meat than one another, or the less beefy whites whom they were sure to encounter in the years ahead. For in Cook's day, New Zealand's only indigenous animals, besides human beings, were rats and bats. But Cook did not limit his researches to Polynesia. He explored, among other places, parts of the northwest coast of North America, and any collection of ethnographical material he pledged in Kamchatka was likely to include Canadian specimens from British Columbia. Why not visit the Leningrad Museum prior to the Copenhagen congress, I said to myself, and see what exactly it does contain? It is only a few hours' train ride from Helsinki, and the Soviet Embassy in Ottawa has validated my passport so that I can cross the Finno-Soviet border without hindrance.

I had discussed such a trip with friends in Copenhagen, but they warned me that I would merely waste my time. That spring, they informed me, a Danish botanist who had been corresponding with Soviet colleagues had visited Leningrad to discuss certain problems with them, but Soviet officials would not permit them even to meet. In addition, a distinguished U.S. archaeologist had been cooling his heels in Leningrad for nearly three months without succeeding in either consulting his Soviet confreres or viewing the scientific material that had prompted his journey. "The Soviet Union is alarmed at Nazi expansionism," my friends said, "and wary of any contact with foreigners or the outside world. You will accomplish nothing."

A scientist in Helsinki corroborated their opinion. I therefore abandoned all thought of travelling on to Leningrad and, with ten free days before the opening of the Copenhagen congress, concentrated on seeing a little of Finland itself, which had greatly intrigued me from the moment the Stockholm ferry-boat landed me in the little port of Turku. Our greatest stumbling block was the language, for neither my wife nor I could speak Finnish or Swedish, and very few people we met seemed to understand a word of English or French. To avoid the pain of being restricted to conversation with one another, we resorted to German, which we discovered many Finns understood (or misunderstood) as much as we did. Yet language caused us less difficulty than we had expected, for the Finnish people were so friendly, and so transparently honest, that it never entered our minds to mistrust anyone. And nothing happened during our stay in their country to weaken this sense of complete security.

There were more signs of poverty than in either Denmark or Sweden: more unpainted houses and farms, fewer articles of luxury in city stores, and more women performing heavy labouring jobs such as cleaning streets and carrying hods of mortar.[9] Yet the people seemed industrious, and we saw no marks of squalor. City streets were clean, and the poorest farms that were visible from the train were scrupulously tidy, their yards free from litter and their woods cleared of fallen brush. Life might be hard, we concluded, but it was not sordid, and Finnish

---

[9] A hod is a tray or trough with a pole handle that is borne on the shoulder for carrying mortar, brick or similar loads (Webster's Third International Dictionary of the English Language, 1965, p. 1076).

men and women, being individuals of worth and dignity, possessed the strength to withstand its rigours. Wherever we went, the keynote seemed to be respect—respect for oneself, respect for one's neighbour, respect for the forests and the waters which nature had furnished for man's use, and respect for the buildings and other creations of man himself. Orderliness prevailed everywhere, not from compulsion but from choice. Railways and streetcars operated efficiently, roads and buildings were in good repair, and forests and streams well managed.

The Finnish tongue is said to be related to Hungarian, and Hungarian people have a reputation for gaiety and laughter, but the Finnish people seemed serious and reserved, qualities which they may have acquired during the long centuries of Swedish rule. Yet they were not philistines. Their modern paintings and sculptures in the Helsinki Art Gallery seemed more virile, more truly imaginative, than any we saw elsewhere in Western Europe. In the field of music, Sibelius ranked among the greatest of twentieth-century composers, and in architecture, Saarinen and at least two other Finns had won world renown.

After spending two days in the lake district north of Helsinki (which reminded me strongly of Canada's Lake of the Woods region), we travelled on to Viipuri, a town of 40,000 inhabitants which boasted a competently restored mediaeval fortress, a railway station built by Saarinen, and a small library specially designed for the city by one of its native sons. This library was an architectural gem; its exterior form delighted the eye and harmonized perfectly with the landscape, and its interior was successfully utilizing the latest techniques in heating, lighting, and acoustics. Whether the building still exists, however, or whether it was destroyed during the Finno-Soviet war of 1939–40, when the Soviet Union annexed Viipuri and renamed it Vyborg, I do not know.

I can still picture the library's lecture hall, so pleasingly intimate and so restful. It was a small, rectangular room probably not more than sixty feet long by thirty wide, and one of its long sides was a wall of glass separating it from a cool, green conservatory. The wooden ceiling seemed unusually low and flat, surely the worst shape possible acoustically, I thought. But presently I noticed with astonishment how excellent the acoustics really were, and glancing at the ceiling again, observed that it was not flat at all, but mathematically broken up into a series of parallel vanes connecting two levels, one about a foot higher than the other. My description may be neither clear nor quite accurate, for I am not an architect, and the lapsing years which have erased so many memories and corrupted others may have dimmed my memory of this building. Yet I can recall my amazement at the ease with which I could follow from just inside the door a quiet conversation that was taking place at the far end of the hall. The speakers seemed to be standing only three or four feet from me.

The days passed quickly, and all too soon it became time to retrace our steps to Copenhagen. Only one incident brightened that long and rather tedious journey. Our timetable required us to spend a night in Stockholm, where the ferryboat from Finland deposited us late in the afternoon. After booking in at a hotel and window-shopping until sunset along two or three main streets, we entered an attractive restaurant to enjoy a quiet dinner. We knew that we were too early, but a waiter invited us to rest in a comfortable corner and enjoy the pleasant music that would be starting in a few minutes. So we stayed. Presently, three men arrived carrying musical instruments, which they deposited in a corner while they exchanged their street coats for formal jackets. They then thumbed over some sheets of music, tuned their instruments, and began to run lightly through a few modern scores.

A man and his teen-aged son now entered and sat down near us. With a two-table audience waiting to be entertained, the trio began to play more seriously, but still modern music only.

My wife leaned over to me and said: "That violinist is a virtuoso. Go over and ask him if they have any trios of Schumann, Brahms or Dvorak that they would play for us."

Reluctantly I pulled myself to my feet, walked over to the violinist, and in the best German my brain could muster conveyed my wife's request.

"Why yes," he said, and his eyes shone. "We have some classical music in the basement. We don't play it very often because the public seems to prefer modern music."

He disappeared downstairs, and returned quickly with a whole library. His companions pulled their chairs closer around him, and within three minutes we were listening to a concert which Bruno Walter might have conducted. When they finished, we both clapped enthusiastically, as did also the man and boy at the table near us, and our artists smiled and bowed and carried on.

An hour went by. Every table in the restaurant was occupied, and the waiters hastened from one to another filling their orders. Then at last the maestro laid aside his violin and, approaching us, said: "The restaurant if full. During the rest of the evening we must play modern music."

We thanked him warmly. He and the two other members of his trio, he told us, were refugees from Vienna who had found a temporary home in Stockholm. At the moment they were supporting themselves fairly well, but they hoped before long to move elsewhere.

International conferences generally conform to a set pattern and run their courses without strain, but from the day of its opening attendees at the Copenhagen congress seemed unusually nervous and ill at ease. Its Danish officials were as efficient and courteous as always, but some of the Central European delegates appeared jittery, while two were so arrogant and overbearing that they spoiled the enjoyment of the rest. Our acquaintances from the Frankfurt Museum

Figure 28 Diamond Jenness (on right) and fellow delegate at the Copenhagen Congress, August 1938.
Photo by E. Jenness

remained two days only, driven out by starvation, one of them confessed to us as she was depart-ing, because her country's regulations prohibited anyone from carrying more than ten German marks over the frontier, and ten marks did not purchase many meals. Groups of two and three people furtively gathered in quiet corners and looked embarrassed, or changed the conversation, when outsiders approached. A Danish friend of many years' standing[10] introduced us to his daughter, a young actress who had just arrived unexpectedly from Berlin. She had participated in an escapade there which had seemed to her no more than a joke, but her friends, alarmed lest it blow up into a police-court affair with international overtones, had shipped her post-haste home to Denmark. Many other stories about strange happenings in the Reich circulated through the congress halls, for the clang of Hitler's marching legions had echoed all through Europe, and the watchdogs of every nation were stirring uneasily.

As soon as the congress closed, I resumed my circuit of mid-European museums, planning to comb the Rhineland, Switzerland, Austria, and Hungary, then move north to Czechoslovakia and west through North Germany to Holland and Belgium. In the Rhineland cities, factories were working full blast, and the civilians who thronged the streets were quietly pursuing their usual occupations, but on the new highways there seemed to be many more military vehicles than a month before, and many more soldiers on the side roads. Of course, such an increase in military activities might have resulted from a delay in staging the annual manoeuvres, and that, in fact, was the explanation Herta Hartmanshenn gave me when we arrived back in Wiesbaden. She discounted the fears of an imminent war which had been current in Denmark, brushed aside—though not without embarrassment—and labelled as vicious exaggerations foreign rumours of unmentionable brutalities in over-crowded concentration camps, and said that she herself felt so confident all would be well that she had notified the University of Toronto to expect her at the opening of the autumn term. She acknowledged quite frankly, to be sure, that neither she nor her friends knew very much about what was happening in Germany and the rest of Europe, or were qualified to judge whether or not events were approaching a crisis, but everything around them seemed undisturbed and prosperous, and no sane individual wanted a war. Why then conjure up calamities that would probably never happen?

Yet her optimism could not dispel the oppressive atmosphere that seemed to be brooding over every city we visited, or to banish the feeling that a terrible storm was impending. Museum officials were courteous to us, but so preoccupied with concealed thoughts as to seem disinterested in their ethnographical collections. Could it be that they, too, felt the approach of a storm?

The rushing from city to city, and the heavy atmosphere in every one of them, so wearied us that after ten days we fled for a long, weekend rest to the Schwarzwald, the Black Forest, accompanied by Stuart and his new piano accordion. Two miles from Todtnau, near the Swiss border, we discovered a very attractive inn five hundred feet up the side of a mountain where fat cattle grazed quietly on the grassy slope, three red-cheeked maidens in the field below rhyth-mically scythed the season's third crop of hay as if they were dancing to Schubert's violin, and the knickerbockered, knapsacked hiker we encountered on the road dutifully raised his arm and muttered "Heil Hitler" as we approached, then smiled from ear to ear and responded with the

---

[10]Quite possibly Fritz Johansen, the naturalist who was on the Canadian Arctic Expedition with my father in 1913–1916.

hearty "Grüss Gott" when we disregarded his Nazi salutation and greeted him with the time-honoured Bavarian one. Stuart wandered one hundred and fifty feet from the inn with his accordion and began to play some Strauss waltzes, whereupon our little maid dashed out the door and danced in the courtyard, and that evening our dining table fairly creaked with the weight of veal cutlets, cherry pie buried in rigid whipped cream, and other Bavarian specialties.

And so for three days, here in the mountains of southern Germany, we enjoyed the beauty and peace of which the poets sing, a peace that was not disturbed by war's alarms, the rattle and dust of armoured cars, and the disciplined tramp of marching troops. And each night, the fresh clean air that streamed silently in through our casement windows brought back the dreamless sleep of long-lost childhood.

From the Black Forest my wife and Stuart travelled straight across country to Munich, a city in which they had lived for several months three years previously, but I circled around through Switzerland, stopping in Basel, Bern, and Zurich. It was late in the day when I reached Bern, and as I booked in at my hotel, I asked the clerk whether there was an opera or a concert on the list of the evening's entertainments. He replied that it was Bern's annual festival week, and that each evening Switzerland's best singers and actors were staging a mediaeval mystery drama, "Death comes to Everyman," in front of the city's fine Gothic cathedral. The performance began at nightfall, 8 p.m., she added, and if I dined immediately I could easily reach the cathedral on time.

Darkness had already descended when I arrived at the cathedral square, half of which had been curtained off by a high canvas fence. I bought a ticket near a gap in this fence and was admitted to an open-air amphitheatre facing a long, wide stage to which the half-illumined facade of the great cathedral formed the backdrop. The play, which was sung, not spoken, contained seven scenes, each of which concluded with the entry of Death carrying a scythe to mow down his victim—a king on his throne in one episode, a maid dancing at a harvest festival in another. As the last scene ended, a thousand electric bulbs lit up the cathedral's entire front from foundations to spire, proclaiming to the world Death's final conquest by the God of Light. The actors played their parts with great sincerity, and the magnificent voice of the leading tenor resounding through the dark square under the starlit sky carried more than earthly authority. But the sombreness of the subject and its uncanny parallelism with the current political situation in Europe left in me, and I suspect in a large part of the audience, a presentiment of impending disaster.

The same presentiment obsessed me four days later when I travelled with Stuart from Munich as far as Stuttgart,[11] where he was to transfer to another train that would carry him to Wiesbaden. Many soldiers got off our train at the same time we did, and many others were

---

[11] In his manuscript, my father mistakenly gave Nürnberg as the city we went to from Munich. The city was Stuttgart, as I noted in a little pocket diary I kept that summer. We each enjoyed a delicious midday wienerschnitzel (veal cutlet) dinner outdoors underneath a shade-supplying umbrella at a hotel across the street from the railway station. After finishing our dessert of ice cream, we visited a local museum where my father saw several Canadian native artifacts he wished to obtain through exchange for the National Museum in Ottawa. In later years, we often reminisced about that sunny day in Stuttgart and the wienerschnitzels. Later in the afternoon, he saw me safely on the train to Wiesbaden, where Herta Hartmanshenn met me when I detrained.

roaming the flag-strewn streets near its railroad station as if they were mustering for some event. But why were they being called up so late in the summer, I wondered, after the children had returned to school and the universities were preparing to unlock their doors?

II

The Munich newspapers, like all others in the Reich, were heavily censored. The man in the street knew that relations between his country and Czechoslovakia were strained, but since all Germany had been living under stress for a full decade and in some way or other had weathered every crisis, he was quietly going about his business. The Swiss newspapers that I saw during my three hurried days in that country had expressed grave alarm, but assured the public that the great powers would compose their differences without resorting to open conflict. At Vienna, our next stop, Austrian newspapers printed only what their Nazi masters wanted the public to know.[12] They seemed even more cautious than the German papers. Not until we reached Hungary, therefore, did we learn that the international situation had deteriorated very greatly, and that war might break out at any moment.

This put us in a quandary. Our travel arrangements scheduled us to go from Budapest to Prague, and from Prague back to Berlin, whose museum director, I hoped, might be more inclined to open up his Canadian specimens than he had appeared to be in midsummer. If the international situation was as precarious as the Hungarian newspapers depicted, however, it would be foolhardy to linger in Central Europe, or indeed anywhere east of the English Channel.

Since Canada maintained no representative in Budapest at that period I consulted the British consul. He was courteous, and also frank.

"You are a Canadian," he said, "and I cannot advise you officially. But if I enjoyed your freedom of action, I would catch the first train out of Budapest and take my wife and son west of Germany as fast as I could."

Within two hours, we had readjusted our travel arrangements. I then wired Miss Hartman-shenn to pack Stuart's bags and meet me at the Wiesbaden railway station the following afternoon.

Our express to Brussels left Budapest that evening at 10 p.m. The railway platform was crowded, and nearly half the people were weeping. Wives seemed to be parting from husbands, young people from parents and kindred, as if they expected never to see one another again. A porter carried our bags to the eight-place compartment in which our tickets gave my wife one of the two corner seats on the corridor side, and myself a seat next to her. Two men occupied the other seats on our side, and opposite us sat a grey-haired man and his wife, a tall thin youth, and, in the far corner, a soldier in uniform.

For an hour after the train had rolled out of the station, no one stirred. Once or twice, the grey-haired man whispered to his wife, and I to mine, but the rest sat in brooding silence, seemingly afraid to look at one another. Then the ticket collector came round, and behind him an officer in uniform who scrutinized our passports and silently passed on. Soon afterwards, we reached the Austrian frontier, where the soldier left us, and with him the two men who had been sitting beside me. No one came near our compartment, however, and as we moved on again, our three remaining fellow-passengers seemed to breathe more easily. Presently the woman

---

[12]German troops had invaded and taken control of Austria on March 11, 1938.

opposite my wife pulled down the curtain of her window and smiled, and her husband said to me, in German,

"You are Canadians?"

Clearly he had seen the word "Canada" on the covers of our passports.

"Yes, we come from Canada," I answered, and my wife, who spoke German more fluently than I did, added smilingly,

"We are returning home."

The couple talked together quietly for several minutes, after which the woman leaned forward and opened up a conversation with my wife, who told her where and why we had been travelling in Europe and what arrangements we were making for returning to Canada. Our fellow-passengers then became quite friendly and told us about themselves. Her husband, she said, had been a pharmacist and had owned a good business in Budapest, but she was Jewish, despite her fair complexion and red hair, and they feared a war in which Hitler would certainly overrun Hungary and arrest every Jew he could lay his hands on. They had therefore sold the business and invested part of their capital in jewellery, which they could carry on their persons if they succeeded in emigrating, as they hoped, to the United States, for the Hungarian government, like the German, had prohibited the export of capital without a special permit and was imposing heavy penalties on the smuggling abroad of Hungarian currency. Several hundred dollars of their capital they had paid to an underground agency which had undertaken to slip them over the German–Belgian border after the train on which we were travelling passed Köln; its guides would meet them at a certain stop and conduct them over the heavily guarded frontier during the night. When my wife asked whether the agency was reliable, she replied that they did not know, but that their plight had become so desperate (in what way she did not explain) they could do no other than trust it blindly. If the guides betrayed them and they were caught by the border guards or the police, they intended to commit suicide together, and, opening a small handbag, she showed my wife a length of rope. The tall youth seated beside them, she added, was Jewish also, and fleeing Hungary for the same reason as they were, but he had made separate arrangements for entering Belgium.

Throughout the dark night, our train sped on across Austria, rarely stopping, and when it did stop, for two or three minutes only. At intervals we dozed, all of us rather fitfully. In the case of the fugitives this was understandable, for within the next twenty-four hours, fate would spin out their destiny—security in a foreign land, if they were lucky; if unlucky, sudden death from a border guard's bullet or arrest and confinement in a German concentration camp.

My wife and I confronted no such grim alternatives, but we too faced a small problem of our own, for we had not yet worked out any new plan to replace the carefully organized tour we had so abruptly cancelled. For the moment, our thoughts were focussed on three cities: Wiesbaden, where Stuart would be awaiting us; Köln and the American Express Company's office there, to which my wife had mailed numerous packages of musical compositions purchased in various music stores; and Brussels, the temporary refuge towards which we were speeding. Delay anywhere short of Brussels was dangerous, but how could we pick up Stuart and retrieve the music in Köln without lingering inside Germany an extra eighteen or twenty-four hours? In the end, we decided that I would drop off the train at Wiesbaden, but that my wife would continue on to Köln and there engage two rooms at a certain hotel near the station, collect her music from the American Express before that office closed, and await Stuart and myself. All three of us would then take the first available train to Brussels and in that city, with fuller knowledge of what was happening, mature our future plans.

Our train meanwhile was rolling onward. By mid-morning it was approaching Nürnberg. Hitler was holding a rally there the next day, and also—although we did not know it—meeting Britain's Prime Minister Neville Chamberlain to discuss the question of Czechoslovakia. Through the windows of our carriage, we could see that every road leading to the city was black with marching troops, and our train, when it halted at the station, disgorged hundreds of additional soldiers who were to take part in the parades. But we five civilians sat quietly in our compartment until, fifteen minutes later, the train started up again and carried us far away from the city's menacing legions.

About 3 p.m. we reached Wiesbaden, where both Stuart and Miss Hartmanshenn greeted me as soon as I entered the waiting room. The latter, at my request, checked the time of the next train to Köln, after which we adjourned for a tête-à-tête at a neighbouring café. There she told me that, as arranged before the Copenhagen meeting, she had booked berths for herself and Stuart on the Canadian Pacific liner *Empress of Britain*, which was scheduled to sail from Cherbourg on September 17, only a few days hence, and to reach Quebec six days later. So rapidly had the international situation changed during the past week, however, that she was greatly alarmed, knowing that if it worsened before they left Germany, Stuart might very well be interned and she herself conscripted for special duties. On receiving my telegram, therefore, she had immediately packed his bags and begun to pack her own, since no one could predict what the morrow might bring, whether war, or a continuation of the uneasy peace.

We agreed that she would hold to her plan of sailing on the *Empress of Britain*, travelling from Wiesbaden to Paris and taking the boat train from that city to Cherbourg, but that Stuart would depart from Germany immediately and go with me to Brussels, where there was no risk of his being interned. She would telegraph me the hour that the boat train would be leaving Paris, and he and I would meet her on the Paris platform. With this arrangement clinched and four hours still to wait before the train to Köln, she returned home to check Stuart's baggage. He and I, meanwhile, went on a spending spree to rid ourselves of our German money, which otherwise would have been taken from us by the German authorities at the border.

We emerged from the Köln station at midnight. A surprising number of people were walking the semi-darkened streets, and several newspaper boys were shouting as they pounded their beats "Extra, extra! Czech atrocities. Down with the Czechs!" At the hotel, the night clerk asked me, "Do you think war will be declared before morning?" and I could only shrug my shoulders and answer, "Who knows?" My wife, worn out by the long train journey, lay fast asleep, but we wakened her to assure her that we were all together again, and ourselves lay down to snatch some sleep before daylight.

All was peaceful in the morning, the newsboys silent and the streets crowded with people going quietly to their work. With our music and other impediments, we caught the early train to Belgium, where the government had ordered a general mobilization, which, as in Germany, filled both town and country with marching troops. By late afternoon, we were comfortably lodged six hundred feet from Brussels' Gare du Nord in a hotel whose name and address we had discovered in a U.S. guidebook endorsed by the Travellers' Aid Society, the Y.M.C.A., or some other organization of unimpeachable reputation. My wife and I were allotted an almost luxurious room on the top floor overlooking the Botanical Gardens, and Stuart a smaller room alongside us. A kindly old lady who might have been a duchess' serving woman waited on us in the dining room that evening and served us an excellent meal. We seemed to be the only guests, except for a red-headed girl of some indeterminate age between twenty and forty, who sat alone at a table in the far corner, whether a guest also or an employee of the hotel we could not determine.

Two new guests entered the hotel the next morning as we were going out the front door. They, too, were Canadians from Ottawa, the Dominion Statistician and his wife, just arrived from Prague, where an international Statistical Congress had abruptly ended its sessions and dispersed. We gazed at one another in amazement and asked simultaneously, "Where have you come from? How did you happen to choose this hotel?" It appeared that, fugitives like ourselves, they had selected it more or less at random from the same guidebook as we had, but they left it again the next morning, whereas we lingered on for four days until it was time for Stuart to join Miss Hartmanshenn in Paris.

We were extremely comfortable in this Brussels hotel, the view from our bedroom window was beautiful, and the old lady who waited on us at dinner and brought breakfast to our room each morning could not have been more charming. Yet there was an aura of mystery about the place, an eeriness that seemed real to both of us, although it could have been just a figment of our imaginations. Once we left Belgium, the aura vanished, and we thought no more about it until after the Second World War, when a lady who had lived all her life in Brussels, learning that we had once spent a few days in her city, asked us in what hotel we had stayed. She seemed rather startled when we told her its name and address, then quietly remarked, with an amused gleam in her eyes, "Yes, I know where it is, but we Brussels' people do not usually recommend it to our friends."

After seeing Stuart safely on his way from Paris to Canada with Miss Hartmanshenn, [I returned to Brussels and] my wife and I enquired about boat passages for ourselves, since Chamberlain's forthcoming conference with Hitler in Munich merely postponed the danger of war without abolishing it. And while tension remained so high, there was little or nothing I could accomplish from further peregrinations in Central Europe. The regular passenger liners to Canada had been booked up since early summer, so heavy was the westward traffic across the North Atlantic, but we secured a cabin on a small Norwegian freighter that was leaving Rotterdam for Montreal in ten days time. Those ten days would give us ample opportunity to visit the two Dutch museums on my list, one in Rotterdam and the other in Amsterdam. Accordingly, we paid our bill at the Brussels hotel and moved on to Rotterdam.

The short journey proved more exhausting than we had expected. The weather was warm and summer-like, and being alone in the compartment, we were able to open both the outer windows. Our tickets had told us that we would have to change trains at a small Dutch town just across the Belgian border. As soon as we entered the town, but were still about a quarter of a mile from its station, I reached up to the rack to pull down our two suitcases, and the heavy bundle of music on top of one of them. The train was running along the edge of a very picturesque canal and at that moment, slowly crossing a street protected by a small guardhouse. Absorbed by the scenery I absent-mindedly pulled on the wrong suitcase, and a full half-hundredweight of music crashed down on my unprotected head, bounced on to the windowsill and disappeared into the canal, while I dropped back into my seat, barely conscious.

From a far distance came the voice of my wife:

"Oh, I'm so sorry. Are you hurt? But (in a crescendo) where is the music?"

"Outside, in the canal," I muttered savagely.

By now, the train had reached the station. Before it stopped, she wrenched open the door, leaped out, and in French, then English, then in both languages together told a station workman what had happened. The man understood neither language, singly or together, but from her manner and torrential words he knew that some dreadful tragedy had occurred and concluded that her baby had fallen into the canal. He rushed her to the stationmaster. That dignitary, fortunately, understood English. Also he was a cultured diplomat who knew exactly how to soothe a distressed foreign lady ready to perish from the loss of her music. He promptly ordered the workman to accompany us back along the track and probe the canal with a long pole.

Slowly we walked back, the blue-smocked workman in front carrying a long pole. From time to time, he stopped to push aside the thick mantle of weeds and scum that concealed the canal's surface, then walked on again. A crowd of people, mostly children but a few adults also, gathered on the far side and kept in step with us, wondering what could have happened, and nearer and nearer we drew to the crossing without detecting any sign of the music. The babel of voices reached the guard in the canal-house, who looked out his doorway and shouted something to our workman. The latter shouted back, whereupon the guard entered his little house again and reappeared, carrying in his two arms our precious bundle, which he had observed as it fell from the train and dutifully rescued.

We had recovered our bundle, but its outside, perhaps too its inside, had been soaked with the canal water, and we feared that its sheets might stick together or the dye of the covers render the notes illegible. Hastily we unwrapped it and discovered to our joy that virtually none of the books was seriously waterlogged. The gratified guard brought out a sheaf of old newspapers, friendly bystanders gathered around to help, and on hands and knees we inserted sheets of newspapers to dry out all the pages that showed signs of dampness. Today [in the mid-1960s], thanks to our Dutch benefactors, not a page is missing. One volume lies open on our piano, the others are resting in their shelves. Only one book is gravely stained from the red dye of its cover, and even in that one, all the musical notes are clearly legible.[13]

A hurricane that had ravaged the eastern regions of the United States and Canada swept out to the mid-Atlantic before it died away, and so buffeted our little freighter that the vessel fought for three days just to keep its head into the gale. It carried five passengers only, my wife and myself, a German lady and her young son who had spent the summer in the fatherland and were now returning to their home in Montreal, and a talkative woman who carried a Polish passport, claimed to be an Austrian, and declared her small mongrel dog a pure-bred Saturnian, if I correctly interpreted its fantastic designation. Fearful that the immigration authorities might question the purity of its descent or raise some other objection to its entry, she and the German lady spent several hilarious hours composing an elaborate pedigree for it, which they cheerfully allowed us to peruse before the vessel stopped at Father Point to take

---

[13]It was a red cloth-covered album of Chopin etudes, waltzes, and mazurkas.

on a pilot and two customs' officers. Their document—or the bottle of whisky which happened to rest beside it at the inspection hour on the table of the ship's dining room—won immediate acceptance as a valid passport, and our Polish-Austrian-New Canadian fellow-passenger walked proudly down the gangplank in Montreal, snuggling under her arm an invaluable addition to Canada's canine stocks.

[*While attending the Copenhagen meeting, my father spent many pleasant moments conversing with several archaeological friends and admirers, including Henry Collins from Washington, Graham Rowley from Cambridge, Frederica de Laguna from Bryn Mawr College near Philadelphia, and Kaj Birket-Smith and Therkel Mathiassen from Denmark. "We were a jolly family at the Congress, weren't we?" he wrote Miss de Laguna two months later. "It would be hard to find two more splendid men than Mathiassen and Birket-Smith in any country."*[14] *Miss de Laguna, a former student of Franz Boas, had first contacted my father for advice in 1930, when her plans to assist Birket-Smith on an archaeological site in Alaska were cancelled suddenly because he had fallen ill. Father had provided archaeological counsel to her on several other occasions over the next decade and been quick to congratulate her when she established the Department of Anthropology at Bryn Mawr in 1938. At the Copenhagen meeting, his "spur of the moment" offer to donate much of his personal anthropological library to her college left her almost speechless. Later in the fall he clarified his thoughts about his offer, "I have always intended, when I dropped out of the museum here, to donate my anthropological books to some institution that could use them. My days, I hope, are drawing to an end; even though I may stay in the museum for a few years longer I have a more complete library alongside of me. Consequently, I may as well get rid of my books now, except the few that I constantly refer to. Since a large proportion of them came from the United States as free gifts (e.g., the reports of the Univ[ersity] of Col[orado]), it seems only right for them to go back there, and Bryn Mawr is as good an institution as any....Your library is very welcome to all, except some personal gifts which I treasure, like Rasmussen's works, some Eskimo books I constantly use, and perhaps half a dozen others."*[15]

Aided by a list she sent him of her college library's anthropological holdings, he slowly packed up the journals and books he would donate to her school and shipped them to Bryn Mawr by freight collect the following June.

What I find interesting here is the direct evidence that he was starting to shut down his active career in anthropology as early as 1938. He was apparently restless and ready for a change of career—to geographer as it turned out to be—which, unbeknownst to him at the time, lay immediately ahead.]
[S.E.J.]

---

[14]Jenness to F. de Laguna, letter dated October 25, 1938, Jenness Correspondence, Box 648, Folder 12, Archives, CMC.

[15]Jenness to F. de Laguna, letter dated November 18, 1938, Jenness Correspondence, Box 648, Folder 12, Archives, CMC.

1939–1948:
THE SECOND WORLD WAR
AND EARLY RETIREMENT

15

Stuart E. Jenness

Soon after the outbreak of the Second World War in August 1939, rumours circulated at the National Museum of Canada that it might be closed and its staff laid off. Seeking to protect the museum's staff from possible job termination, the chief administrator for both the Geological Survey and the National Museum, F.C.C. Lynch, arranged to lend my father and Barbeau to the wartime Dependents Allowance Board for a year. This government agency had been hastily created to oversee the assignment of allowances for the wives, widows, and families of men in the armed forces. Its offices were located in a newly erected temporary building on Wellington Street about a mile north of the museum, but it was arranged that both my father and Barbeau would do their Dependents Allowance Board work at their own offices in the museum and would be allowed to attend to any urgent matters relating to their museum duties. At age fifty-four, my father was too old for armed combat but wanted to "do his bit for his country."[1] Still, this new assignment was not one he would normally have chosen. He and Barbeau commenced their new jobs early in 1940, soon finding that the work was unreward-ing and their abilities wasted. Ever the idea man, Barbeau dreamed up a scheme he thought would get him released from the wretched task he had been given and promptly wrote about his idea to the Department of National Defence; by August, that department had responded by arranging his release from his temporary duties to prepare a booklet of French-Canadian folk songs for the soldiers overseas. My father faithfully continued on with his temporary duties until January 1941, meanwhile making enquiries in the hope of obtaining more challenging and worthwhile wartime work.

He was ultimately successful, being permitted to transfer to the Royal Canadian Air Force in January 1941 as civilian Deputy-Director of Special Intelligence. He worked initially for Wing Commander R.A. Logan, the Director of Intelligence, then six months later for his successor, Group Captain H.R. Stewart.[2] The Director of Intelligence was responsible to the Joint Intelligence Bureau within the Department of National Defence. Father's work was secret, so he could not and did not speak about it at home.

---

[1] Some of the same patriotic feelings that had led my father to the battlefields of France in 1917 must still have remained in his blood. In a letter to archaeologist F. de Laguna shortly after the outbreak of World War II, he wrote "I love Germany, and many of its people. Yet if it were possible, I would enlist tomorrow" (Jenness to de Laguna, letter dated January 24, 1940, Jenness Correspondence, Box 648, Folder 12, Archives, CMC).

[2] RG 24, Vol. 5216, File 19-6-4, LAC.

How my father arranged to spend most of the war years working as a civilian for the Royal Canadian Air Force remains unexplained. Ottawa was not a large city in 1940, with the offices of the senior government officials concentrated within a relatively small area, bounded on the north by the parliament buildings. My father knew a few senior officers in the RCAF then, one of whom, F. Vernon Heakes, comes especially to mind. Air Vice-Marshall Heakes, an original member of the permanent RCAF, had been a Staff Officer in Ottawa from 1926 to 1934, then returned in August 1940 for sixteen months, before being posted to Newfoundland and then as Air Officer Commanding Western Air Command in 1944. My father may have been in contact with Heakes sometime in the fall of 1940, with his subsequent attachment to the RCAF resulting from that discussion. The RCAF certainly found a worthwhile assignment for my father and greatly benefited by his addition. According to mother, my father "was known far & wide during the war" for his ability "to work under real pressure."[3] As for his civilian status, I understand he requested that as a condition of his secondment to the air force, in order to ensure his greater personal freedom to concentrate on his work.

My father's new boss, the Director of Intelligence (AIR), worked at that time in the Jackson Building on Bank Street, Ottawa, but was unable to find office space there for my father. As a result, my father remained at his museum office, where he had ready access to secretarial help as well as a large library. This arrangement soon created a minor bureaucratic problem regarding his daily attendance, however, which he resolved by signing regularly on the museum's attendance sheets and submitting a monthly memorandum on his attendance to the Camp Commandant, RCAF.[4] After a number of months, he was moved to an office between Elgin Street and the Driveway, probably in the former Ottawa Normal Model School on Lisgar Street, which the RCAF had occupied at the outbreak of the war. He shared this office for several months with two other men, Lieutenant Gordon R. Taylor, Royal Canadian Navy, and J. Ross Mackay, an officer soon to be assigned to a new Army Signal Intelligence Unit, with both of whom he developed a lasting friendship. These two men, the sons of Canadian missionaries who had lived in China and Formosa (now Taiwan) respectively, were bright, intelligent military men whose knowledge of the language and geography of those regions proved to be of considerable help to the intelligence unit after the Japanese entered the war. They were just two of several people with knowledge of the Far East who were combed from the Canadian armed forces about that time to work with my father.

Mackay, the only one of the three still alive in 2006, informed me that he, Taylor, my father, and several other men similarly knowledgeable on the Far East would meet occasionally during the war years for lunch at a Chinese restaurant they could reach easily on foot from their offices.[5] Mackay, later Professor of Geography at the University of British Columbia, at some stage in the early 1940s proposed the names "Confucius" for Taylor and "Socrates" for my father, from which one may gather that the intellectual level of their conversations was fre-

---

[3]E. Jenness to S.E. Jenness, letter dated February 12 [1960] from Manzanillo, Mexico.

[4]The man with whom my father dealt concerning his attendance was a Flight Lieutenant Hawkins; he may have been the same man who moved into a house a few doors from ours on Broadway in the mid-1940s and after the war renovated our house.

[5]J. Ross Mackay to Stuart E. Jenness, letter dated March 4, 2006.

quently philosophical. Both nicknames were apparently used regularly among these military friends at the time, and I well recall my father speaking fondly many years later about his good friend "Confucius."

I first learned that my father had been called "Socrates" only after I had contacted Professor Mackay in 2006 asking if he could tell me anything about the days he worked with my father during the war. He mentioned in his reply that he had coined both names, although none for himself, but did not remember his reasons for suggesting that name for my father. I suspect that it was on the basis of my father's early love for Greek philosophy and history. Whatever the reason, the name was especially apt. Both Socrates and my father had keen senses of humour and no interest in politics, would not compromise their principles, had distinguished records for endurance, and were true patriots. Furthermore, both men married fairly late in life, had wives with rather quick tempers, and fathered three sons. In one respect, however, they differed markedly. My father passed into virtual obscurity after his departure from his government position and lived quietly the rest of his days. Socrates, on the other hand, was found guilty of some serious political misdeed and forced to drink hemlock, a nasty poison, as his punishment.

In his job as Deputy Director of Special Intelligence, my father found the wartime challenge he sought, and felt that he was finally making a worthwhile contribution to his adopted country. The following brief memorandum entitled "Activities of Dr. D. Jenness, D.D.S.I., June 1 – Sept. 30, 1942," which may have served as a preliminary report for the developers of the Alaska Highway, offers a good indication of the intensity, scope, and productivity of his work during a four-month period at that time:

> Dr. Jenness, who earlier had furnished a substantial report on "Military Targets in Japan" accompanied by photographs and maps, accumulated a little further material on the same subject; and he cooperated with Lieut. Gordon Taylor, of the Navy Department, in the compilation of two further reports of a similar nature, one on Formosa and the other on Korea. RCAF Intelligence forwarded copies of all this Far Eastern material to both the U.S. Army and the U.S. Navy Intelligence services, at their special request. In addition to these activities, Dr. Jenness submitted an appraisal of the "Far Eastern Strategy of the Soviet Union," and prepared a report on the "Practicality of Supplying Yukon Basin Airfields with Gas from Norman Wells, Mackenzie River.[6]

Long after his retirement my father told me about an interesting wartime problem the Director of Intelligence suddenly thrust upon him. Starting in mid-November 1944, a few large incendiary balloons suddenly appeared from the Pacific along the west coast of North America between Alaska and Mexico, most of them between Southern British Columbia and California. No one knew initially from whence they had come nor why. The numbers of balloons sighted slowly increased. Most of them ultimately crashed and were considerably damaged; a few were shot down by aircraft of the U.S. or Canadian air forces; and a small number simply disappeared, their ultimate whereabouts remaining largely undiscovered. All that were subsequently examined were found to carry small incendiary bombs or anti-personnel

---

[6]Jenness Correspondence, Box 656, Folder 14, CMC.

bombs, which set off a few forest fires when they crashed in the heavily timbered mountains of British Columbia, Washington or Oregon, but caused very little damage in return for the time, effort, and money put into their manufacture and launching. Fears arose, however, that they might start carrying toxic bacteria intended to create biological havoc, and the task of determining their country and place of origin quickly received a high priority. In addition, a total public blackout of information about the balloons was imposed by the military in both Canada and the United States to deprive the enemy of learning anything about their ultimate fates.

My father was asked to determine where the balloons were coming from and called for samples of the ballast sand carried by these balloons to be recovered and examined. Japan seemed the likely source, and the Japanese were known to have several well-trained bacteriologists. There may have been some concern, therefore, that the balloons were carrying harmful bacteria. Today, Library and Archives Canada holds a thick government file of formerly secret documents about the mysterious balloons.[7] Other government scientists were asked to examine the bombs and the mechanical components of the balloons for clues. The "cloth" that housed the gas that kept the balloons aloft was found to consist of small connected pieces of thin paper, layer upon layer, made from mulberry bark. The ballast yielded sands, small sea shells, twigs, and seeds, all of which were of varieties or species known to occur on some Japanese islands. By the spring of 1945, various clues led to the locations of the actual balloon launching sites, and they were subsequently destroyed by American aircraft.[8]

During the early 1940s, my father made suggestions that proved useful to the U.S. Army engineers during the construction of the Alaska Highway from Dawson Creek, British Columbia,

---

[7] "Japanese balloons," RG 24, Vol. 5195, File 15-13-9, LAC.

[8] Two seemingly unrelated incidents appear to have a connection with my father's story. The first involved Dr. Clarence S. Ross of the U.S. Geological Survey, who was asked, late in 1944, to determine the mineral composition of a sample of sand from one of the incendiary balloons. His mineral identifications led to five possible localities in Japan from which they could have come. Subsequent U.S. Air Force reconnaissance and photography revealed a manufacturing plant at one of the five suggested localities, outside of which were several balloons being readied for launching. Their incendiary menace was quickly "terminated by military measures" (Hurlbut Jr., 1952, pp. 14–15). It would appear that Ross and my father (and no doubt many others) were involved in solving the same problem. It was learned after the war that, over a period of six months commencing in mid-November 1944, Japan had launched 9,000 of these incendiary balloons into the high atmosphere, where they were carried rapidly eastward at heights of 20,000 to 30,000 feet. Few of them did much damage, however, probably because of the speed with which the Canadians and Americans found out their source (S.E. and J.M.S. Jenness, 2003, pp. 148–149).

The second incident was a news item carried over the radio by the Canadian Broadcasting Corporation on February 7, 2005. An elderly farmer in southern Saskatchewan had just revealed, after more than 50 years' silence, that early in 1945, a lone incendiary balloon had destroyed a section of his barbed-wire fence near Minton, Saskatchewan, set a small fire, and then dumped several sandbags and small bombs. The balloon had then lifted and disappeared. Local people were told to keep quiet about the incident so the enemy would not learn of it, and they had done so until the farmer revealed his long-kept secret. Only a few of the incendiary balloons managed to travel over the mountains to reach the Prairie Provinces, one as far as Manitoba. The Director of Intelligence (AIR) in the RCAF—my father's boss—was regularly kept up-to-date on the balloon problem.

to Fairbanks, Alaska.[9] He also played a role in the planning of the Canol Pipeline,[10] which within two years carried oil from the newly expanded oil field at Norman Wells on the Mackenzie River southwest over mountainous terrain to Whitehorse, where it was refined for fuel for military trucks and aircraft en route to defend Alaska (and Canada) from anticipated Japanese attack. I understand also that my father had input on the selection of sites for several new airports in the Canadian northeast, including those at Frobisher Bay (now Iqaluit) and Coral Harbour. These northern airports served both as defence bases against any foreign invasion by air, and also as refuelling posts for fighter aircraft and bombers being flown to England during the war.

On November 14, 1944, my father changed jobs once again. This time he was appointed chief of a newly established Inter-Service Topographical Section (ISTS) in the Department of National Defence. This Section was a geographic unit within the Joint Intelligence Bureau of the Department of National Defence and was patterned after a similar military intelligence organization known as the Inter-Service Topographical Department (ISTD) in Great Britain. His salary, still to be paid by the Air Force, remained at $5,000 per annum, unchanged since 1937. His ISTS unit was located in the "Lisgar Building," an old grey limestone building on Lisgar Street, between Elgin Street and Lisgar Collegiate in Ottawa. Prior to the Second World War, this was the home of both the Ottawa Normal School, where schoolteachers trained, and the Ottawa Normal Model School, an associated semi-private grade school (kindergarten to Grade 8, which was then first-year high school). My two brothers and I attended that school until the RCAF took charge of it in 1939. The much-renovated building today (2007) forms part of Ottawa's City Hall. His ISTS office was close enough for my father to pay occasional brief visits to his office at the museum. During such visits, he endeavoured as before to keep up with his anthropological administrative duties, responding to accumulated correspondence, and consulting with his meagre staff and with senior officials as situations dictated.

---

[9]My father was contacted for advice by Professor Froelich Rainey, a University of Alaska anthropologist who had been asked by the U.S. War Department to make an archaeological survey along the route of the military highway (now Alaska Highway) they were constructing so that archaeological material unearthed during that activity could be preserved (F. Rainey to D. Jenness, letter dated June 23, 1942, Jenness Correspondence, Box 652, Folder 8, Archives, CMC).

[10]Shortly after the war ended, Richard S. Finnie, the official photographer for the Canol Project, presented my father with an inscribed copy of his abundantly illustrated, limited-edition book, *The Canol Project*. When the Japanese entered World War II in December 1941, the Americans had few military bases in Alaska, and the ones they had could be supplied only by air and sea. With the sea routes now threatened—there were Japanese troops in the Aleutian Islands a few months later—the U.S. Army started building the 1,600-mile Alaska Highway in March 1942 from Dawson Creek, British Columbia, to Fairbanks, Alaska, linking a chain of airports along the route for the use of fighter planes, bombers, and transports. To acquire the fuel needed for the vehicles using the new highway and the aircraft sent north to defend Alaska, the U.S. War Department created a plan to develop the known oil field at Norman Wells on the Mackenzie River, and transport the crude oil by pipeline they would construct over the intervening mountainous region to Whitehorse, Yukon, on the Alaska Highway, where the oil would be refined. This major pipeline project became known as the Canol Project—short for Canadian Oil. Construction by more than 2,500 U.S. Army Engineer troops started in June 1942, and by April 1944, crude oil flowed into Whitehorse to the completed refinery. Together, the Alaska Highway and the Canol Project were considered to be the greatest construction jobs since the Panama Canal (Finnie, 1945, pp. 1–9).

For his new job, my father had to have the personal knowledge of where to seek specialized information, a staff of capable research people to gather the needed information quickly, and a small but readily accessible reference library with skilled personnel operating it. He set out to establish an invaluable military information unit with an operating staff ultimately of twenty-four highly qualified persons, largely drawn from the three military forces (army, navy and air force). He envisioned his section having four parts and aims: (1) books and reports covering the various countries of the world; (2) 50,000 maps on different scales, covering the various countries of the world;[11] (3) about 100,000 photographs of foreign countries, appropriately catalogued and indexed; and (4) a set of information files giving up-to-date topographical information on foreign countries.[12]

After an initial shaky start, his ISTS unit functioned efficiently throughout the remaining war months and was visited by many senior Canadian, British, and American government and military personnel seeking information on all manner of northern geographical problems. I learned some years after the Second World War that one of his military visitors was U.S. Army Major Richard F. Flint, a glacial-geology specialist. Flint may have discussed with father possible sites for the construction of new air bases in northeastern Canada to be used for servicing American fighter planes flying to Great Britain from the United States during the war.[13]

From time to time throughout the war, my father would call Mother early in the afternoon to ask if he might bring a distinguished foreign visitor home for tea. Father was never a regular restaurant frequenter, and since restaurants were almost non-existent near his office in those days, it seemed reasonable to entertain his visitors at home. This arrangement also ensured that confidential information they might exchange in my father's study did not reach unwanted ears. On one such occasion, according to Mother many years later, my father telephoned her to say he was very busy with a gentleman from England but would like to bring him out for tea at half-past three. She dutifully prepared a pot of tea and a plate of cookies or cake for that hour, but the two men failed to show up on schedule. By four o'clock she had placed the teapot on the back of the stove to keep it warm until they arrived. (Tea was one of the many items rationed in Canada during the war, so she could not spare more tea leaves for a new potful.) The men finally arrived about five o'clock, still deeply immersed in conversation, and mother surreptitiously reheated the pot of tea for them. The visitor took a sip and told mother that it was absolutely the best cup of tea he had tasted since leaving England!

Early in the war, our family acquired its first radio, purchased from a friend leaving town. It was a large console radio-phonograph with several short-wave radio bands, reputedly a radio that had been available for the use of Great Britain's King George VI and Queen Elizabeth during

---

[11]The map collection later became the foundation for a federal depository of well over 200,000 maps.

[12]RG 32, Vol. 137, File 1886-02-10, LAC.

[13]Flint became Director of Graduate Studies in the Department of Geology at Yale University after the war, and his admiration for my father's abilities may have influenced the acceptance in 1951 of my application to become a graduate student in that department. He mentioned to me on one occasion that he had met my father during the war. My father provided a chapter entitled "Ethnology and archaeology" for a book entitled "A Program of Desirable Scientific Investigations in Arctic North America," compiled by Flint, and published in 1946 as its first bulletin by the newly formed Arctic Institute of North America.

their May 1939 Royal Visit to Ottawa and Canada. Once he had installed it in his upstairs study, my father spent some of his limited spare time listening to the BBC news coming by short wave from London to keep abreast of the latest war news.

When the war ended in the summer of 1945, my father continued as Chief of the ISTS rather than returning to full-time duty at the National Museum of Canada. He was still Chief of Anthropology, however, so continued visiting his museum office regularly to keep up with the division's correspondence and other administrative matters. Sometime during 1946, he was offered the post of Acting Curator of the museum, the senior administrative position in that organization, but declined the offer.[14] Indeed, why would he want to return? The museum was in bad shape. In March 1946, my mother wrote a friend in Budapest whom they had visited in 1938, "... though in theory he [Mr. Jenness] is Dominion Anthropologist, the Museum has been allowed to go to such appalling neglect during the war, that I doubt if he will ever go back."[15]

The months following the end of the war proved somewhat tumultuous for ISTS. Father's staff, being largely military personnel and still a part of the Department of National Defence, were fast being demobilized and leaving his section, and there were no provisions to replace them with qualified civilians. The termination of the section seemed unavoidable, but the Air Force Branch held out for its continuation. Father was asked to submit a report on the civilian staff he required to continue as a peace-time organization, and in February 1946, he asked for twenty-four employees—primarily geographers, two librarians, and clerical support. Over the objections of the Air Force chiefs and my father, the Army Branch was suddenly assigned responsibility for maintaining the Section, a decision that merely recognized the fact that some of ISTS had been moved from Air Force headquarters to the new Army Building to alleviate space problems. As the summer dragged on without decision, my father found himself down to only nine staff, his activities severely handicapped. The Air Force Branch was again assigned responsibility for the Section, pending further discussion. The ISTS Section had become rather like an orphan, with father caught in a tangle of administrative fumbling as the Chiefs of Staff Committee pondered what to do with his unit.[16]

In November 1946, my father received a top-secret communiqué from the chairman of the Joint Intelligence Committee expressing concerns over defence measures against surprise attacks against North America through Canada. The problem was stated bluntly: "By 1950, a limited

---

[14]My father told me of this offer more than forty years ago. In February 1947, Dr. Frederick J. Alcock, a geologist with the Geological Survey, was appointed Acting Curator of the museum; he was promoted to Curator in September of the same year (National Museum of Canada, 1949, Annual Report of the National Museum of Canada, 1939–1947, Bulletin 112). At about the same time, the Air Force requested the creation of a permanent position for my father (H.F. Gordon, Deputy Minister of National Defence for Air, to the Secretary, Civil Service Commission, letter dated April 2, 1946, RG 32, vol. 563, file Jenness, D., LAC).

[15]E. Jenness to Mrs. Norah Drewett de Kresz, copy of a letter dated March 20, 1946, in my possession in 2006.

[16]The stresses and frustrations my father must have experienced during the turmoil and uncertainty over the future of his ISTS unit in 1946 and 1947, an organization he had developed and directed with feelings of accomplishment after years of troubled direction at the museum, may have played a significant role in bringing on the heart attack he had a short while later.

offensive may be carried out against North America by a major power."[17] The Joint Planning Committee of the three armed forces had recommended the collection of strategic information for the whole of Canada and Newfoundland. One agency should be assigned the task, and ISTS was the appropriate choice. Could it take on the task? Northern Canada was of particular concern, for so little information was available on it. The opinion of the Joint Intelligence Committee was that if ISTS did not compile the strategic information on Northern Canada, "the United States will expect to be given facilities to carry out the work in the near future."[18]

My father responded that ISTS would require a considerable increase in qualified personnel (but warned that such persons would not be quickly available), would need twice as much working space (which the Air Force administrators could not provide), and would need the authority to contract-out tasks. In December 1946, the responsibility for administering his unit was unexpectedly handed to the Defence Research Board, another branch within the Department of National Defence. Two months later, tentative approval was given to develop ISTS more or less as my father had proposed, and Dr. Trevor Lloyd, an English geographer then teaching at Dartmouth College in New Hampshire, was recommended to become Head of the Topographical Section, as the civilian unit that would replace ISTS was slated to be called.

The months of uncertainty over the future of ISTS culminated on June 5, 1947, when the federal government abruptly approved the establishment of a new geographical information-and-research unit within the Department of Mines and Resources, to which it gave the name Geographical Bureau. A large number of the books and maps my father's ISTS unit had accumulated formed the nucleus to the new geographical unit, while the confidential military documents and military personnel remained with the Department of National Defence.

The Geographical Bureau experienced a rough road for the next several years, being moved rather ruthlessly from building to building. It was housed initially in a building long since replaced at the northwest corner of Elgin and Slater Street, then in 1948 in a temporary building in Cartier Square, located where the Court House now resides, where it shared space with the library and other parts of the Defence Research Board. After that, it was moved to the Militia Stores Building on the Driveway at Laurier Avenue. It ultimately found an ongoing "home" when new government buildings on Booth Street were completed in 1959, but by then my father had been retired for a decade.

My father steered the non-military parts of his former ISTS unit through the summer and early fall of 1947,[19] wishing to retire at the earliest opportunity, but serving unofficially as

---

[17]G.G. Crean, Chairman, Joint Intelligence Committee to Jenness, letter dated November 14, 1946, RG 24, Vol. 6167, File 15-9-103, LAC.

[18]Lt. Col. J.A.K. Rutherford, Secretary, Joint Intelligence Committee to Secretary, Chiefs of Staff Committee, letter dated December 30, 1946, RG 24, Vol. 6167, File 15-9-103, LAC.

[19]My older brother Pete commenced work as a geographer with the Geographical Bureau early in the summer of 1947 right after he graduated from Cambridge University, having been hired on the recommendation of the bureau's first chief, Dr. Trevor Lloyd. For a time, he was the only person in the office of the new bureau, as Dr. Lloyd did not commence his duties until October of that year . Pete does not recall seeing my father at the office during that summer. That may have been when father was hospitalized as a result of his first heart attack. I left Ottawa in mid-June of that year for field work at Great Bear Lake with the Geological Survey, just about the time father's ISTS unit was dismembered. His heart attack may have occurred shortly after my departure.

the bureau's Acting Chief until the arrival of Dr. Lloyd, its first chief, in October 1947.[20] By that time, my father was 61 years old, physically exhausted from years of stressful wartime duties and the recent confusion over the future of his geographic information unit, and not desiring to return to the National Museum to resume his responsibilities as Chief of the Anthropology Division full-time. He thought of retiring and pursuing other interests, but on the urging of Dr. Lloyd, agreed to stay on at the Geographical Bureau for a while, until it was able to muster a functioning staff. From then until his last day of work a year later, my father held the title of Director of Research and was responsible for planning and directing the Geographical Bureau's Arctic research studies.

In December 1947, a month after Dr. Lloyd took charge of the Geographical Bureau, my father took four months leave of absence and flew to New Zealand. Both of his parents and several of his siblings had been dead for many years, but he did visit a few members of his once large family. He wanted to take Eilleen to New Zealand with him, but she preferred to remain in Ottawa, not eager to make the long airplane trip to New Zealand. He then asked me to go with him, but I chose to remain at university to complete my senior year and graduate. He therefore travelled alone, flying on a Pan American Airways Clipper (flying boat) from San Francisco to Auckland.

He carried two government letters with him. The first was a copy of a letter sent by Dr. Hugh L. Keenleyside, Deputy Minister of the Department of Mines and Resources, to the Deputy Minister, Department of Native Affairs, in Wellington, requesting information about New Zealand's educational policies with regard its native people (the Maoris). Canada's Indian Affairs Branch was especially interested in obtaining such information because the Canadian government was in the process of revising its Indian Act. The second was from Dr. Trevor Lloyd requesting information about the organization of geographical work in the New Zealand Government, which had done outstanding land utilization studies, and in the universities. Such information was expected to be very useful for the planning of future activities by Canada's new Geographical Bureau.[21]

My father was well received on his return to New Zealand after an absence of nearly thirty years. He presented Dr. Keenleyside's letter to the Prime Minister of New Zealand, the Right

---

[20]As the first department of geography at a Canadian university had only been established in 1935, there were no well-qualified Canadian geographers to fill the appointment as first chief of the new Geographical Bureau. Professor Lloyd had been educated in Great Britain. He stayed in the job for only about a year, however, and for several months, a geologist, Dr. F.J. Alcock, the Curator of the National Museum of Canada, served also as acting chief of the Geographic Bureau. Dr. J.W. Watson, Head of the Department of Geography at McMaster University, was appointed chief of the Geographical Bureau on June 1, 1949. In January 1950, his status was elevated to that of Director after the Geographical Bureau was renamed the Geographical Branch. These changes came about as a result of a re-organization within the department, which also brought about the change in the departmental name from the Department of Mines and Resources to the Department of Mines and Technical Surveys. The Geographical Branch was abolished in 1968 and its geographical responsibilities were returned to the Surveys and Mapping Branch in the same department, where they had been for many years prior to 1947.

[21]H.L. Keenleyside to Deputy Minister, Department of Native Affairs, Wellington, New Zealand, letter dated December 4, 1947, RG 10, vol. 8587, File 1/1-10.2, LAC.

Honourable Peter Fraser, who was also the Minister of Native Affairs, and also met the Minister of Education. The latter arranged for one of his native-school inspectors to escort my father around the North Island, permitting him to observe many of the native schools in operation. The Canadian High Commissioner supplied my father with an official car and chauffeur for the tour. My father also visited several communities on the South Island. He submitted a report of his observations to the Indian Affairs Branch soon after his return to Canada in May 1948.

Much of the old way of life he remembered from his youth had changed considerably in the years since he had last been in New Zealand, which left him with a distinct feeling of sadness. His trip was evidently not a particularly happy one, for he seldom spoke of it after his return to Ottawa or showed any desire to visit his homeland again. "It is no longer the same," he said rather wistfully to me one day. Canada was now his home.

After his return from New Zealand, my father continued briefly at the Geographical Bureau. His duties in the spring and summer of 1948 involved the planning and direction of geographical studies in Northern Canada, one of which involved Keith Fraser's investigation of the conditions of coastal harbours along the Arctic coast that summer. With the bureau operating satisfactorily under Dr. Lloyd's guidance, my father finally retired on October 8, 1948.[22] He had dutifully served his adopted country, Canada, for 35 years and was 62 years old. His retirement was noted in the Department of Mines and Resources annual report with a single sentence: "Dr. Diamond Jenness, recognized world authority on the Indian Tribes of Canada and on the Eskimos of the Canadian Arctic, also retired on superannuation."[23] (The word "also" had been included because the previous sentence had ironically mentioned the retirement of fellow anthropologist and former friend, Marius Barbeau.)

---

[22]This was the date he ceased going to work. With six months retirement leave, his actual employment termination date was April 7, 1949. His monthly superannuation thereafter, until a cost-of-living increase was supplied by the Canadian Government in the 1960s, was $3,681.29 (Minutes of Meeting of Treasury Board, 27 April, 1949 RG 32, Vol. 137, File 1886-02-10, LAC).

[23]Annual Report of the Department of Mines and Resources for the Fiscal Year ending March 31, 1949, p. 121. My father had been granted an honorary Litt.D. from his Alma Mater, the University of New Zealand, in 1935, justifying the use of the title "Dr."

1948–1965: POST-RETIREMENT WANDERINGS

16

Stuart E. Jenness

Following his retirement from the government, my father was free to travel and renew his early interests in such subjects as Greek and Roman history and philosophy. The main factor governing his choice of winter's destination was its climate—it had to have an appreciably warmer winter climate than that of Ottawa. (He was content to live during the rest of each year at home in Canada.) It is not surprising, therefore, that he chose to spend many of the next twenty winters in countries bordering the Mediterranean and Caribbean seas. With few exceptions, he was accompanied by his wife.

During those years, his travels took him to eleven countries (see Appendix 1) and provided him with the opportunity, ideas, information, and motivation to undertake a variety of writing projects. These projects in turn led to the publication of several scholarly articles, a popular book about his first year in the Arctic (*Dawn in Arctic Alaska*), a scholarly book on the historical use of the land in Cyprus under various political regimes (*The Economics of Cyprus to 1914*), his five-volume series on Eskimo administration, several lectures, at least one radio talk, and three chapters in the present book. In this manner, he made very creative and productive use of his retirement years.

In 1948, he purchased a compact 35-mm Kodak Retina I camera with which, over the course of the next twenty years, he took many hundreds of pictures (coloured slides). He later discarded many of them, but painstakingly labelled the ones he retained. The surviving collection, now catalogued and currently in the family's possession, provides a useful guide to where he and my mother went and the things that interested them. The information provided by the slides, together with details from published and unpublished articles, chapters in this book, odd notes, family recollections, and a few surviving letters (mostly from my mother), were used collectively to assemble the following compilation of my father's winter haunts from 1948 to his death in 1969. He and mother spent their summers at their cottage north of Ottawa until the mid-1960s.

When they drove to Florida or Mexico for the winter, my parents followed a daily driving routine. They would get up early, have a cup of coffee each, and then drive about two hours before stopping in mid-morning for breakfast. They then continued on their way, sometimes having a light picnic lunch (my mother always arranged to have coffee in thermos bottles, some fruit, and snack food, such as dried prunes or apricots), and driving until about 4 p.m. My father was a calm and careful driver, observant of speed limits, and generally did all the driving on such trips. Mother knew how to drive, of course, but was always somewhat nervous about it. By stopping mid-afternoon, they could always obtain a room without difficulty in a clean and reasonably priced motel for the night. According to my mother, they deliberately chose a motel "... quite far off the main road, where we had no noise, and often a nice back road nearby where we could have a good and very pleasant walk before our supper."[1]

1948–1949: Bergeggi, Italian Riviera

Late in the fall of 1948, my parents took a freight boat from Montreal to Antwerp for the first of many winters they would spend in warmer climates. From there they entrained for Brussels and thence to southern France, winding up ultimately in a small apartment in the little coastal village of Bergeggi on the Italian Riviera. Without an automobile and the freedom it would have given them to explore the region, they lived quietly in the rocky village, exploring the hilly surroundings on foot, enjoying the sunshine and the blue Mediterranean Sea, resting, and studying Italian. In March, they headed west by train to Toulouse, where they settled for about two weeks in a small but tidy hotel, visiting old churches and other historic sites, attending lectures at the university during the daytime, and going to concerts or operettas during the evenings. From there they returned to Paris and then to Brussels, where they visited the parents of their new daughter-in-law, Eliane, the post-war bride of their eldest son Pete, before catching their freight boat back to Canada.[2]

1949–1950: Italy and Sicily

(See Chapter 17.)

1950–1951: Mérida, Yucatan

My parents drove to New Orleans before Christmas, stopping en route to visit me and my (first) wife Joan in Allentown, Pennsylvania. Leaving their automobile in New Orleans with a university friend, they flew to the Yucatan, settling for much of the winter in an apartment in Mérida, a city with more than one thousand windmills, each of which drew drinking water from deep wells. Using Mérida for their base, they made bus trips to the archaeological sites of Chichen Itza, Uxmal, Kabah, Palenque, Mitla, Teotihuacan, Tula, and Tenayuca, all of which my father, as an anthropologist, examined with much interest, and photographed. Mother later told me about the buses they rode on to get to the various Mayan sites, mentioning especially the confusion that arose occasionally when local peasants boarded their bus with chickens, ducks, pigs, or goats that they were taking to sell at some nearby market. My father did not bother to mention such incidents, however, probably because he had had many strange experiences during his lifetime and took that sort of confusion in his stride. During the course of their travels about the Yucatan, my father evidently made mental and pictorial note of some of the churches he observed, whose architecture reflected Spanish influences of earlier times, for he mentioned the subject years later in an article (see Chapter 19). In March, they flew back to New Orleans, retrieved their automobile, and drove home to Ottawa.

---

[1] E. Jenness to S.E. Jenness, letter dated February 12 [1961], from Manzanillo (in possession of S.E. Jenness in 2006).

[2] E. Jenness to S.E. Jenness, letter dated March 26, 1949, from Toulouse (in possession of S.E. Jenness in 2006).

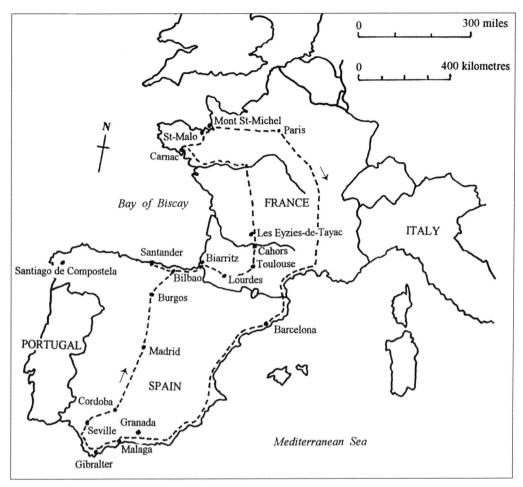

Map 10 Route taken by Jenness to and from Spain, 1951–1952.

1951–1952: Málaga, Spain

My father rented a small English automobile (a Hillman Minx) in Paris, and with Mother, drove south through France to Málaga, northeast of Gibraltar, on Spain's Mediterranean coast. Here they obtained an apartment for the winter and lived quietly overlooking the sea. Mother wrote and subsequently published an article about their Málaga sojourn.[3] During the winter, my father studied Spanish, translated articles in a local paper to sharpen his vocabulary, and read. Early in the spring, they drove inland to visit the old Moorish city of Granada, giving my father the opportunity to see the influence of Moorish architecture in that part of Spain and assess the economic and geographic conditions of the region.

When it came time to return home, he deliberately chose a different route from that by which they had first reached Málaga. Coming south early in the winter, they had travelled down the Rhone Valley and along the Mediterranean coast by way of Barcelona. Now, with

---

[3]E. Jenness, 1953.

spring approaching, they drove west past Gibraltar to Seville, where they toured its Gothic cathedral, then north via Córdoba to Madrid, visiting en route a primitive pottery works at Bailén. Both parents were keenly interested in pottery and porcelain manufacture, so it is possible they stayed a day or two at Bailén, enjoying the relative comfort of a new government-sponsored tourist house or *parador*, facilities they later praised when speaking of their winter travels. In Madrid, their mutual interest in art drew them to view some of the wonders on display at El Prado. Leaving Madrid, they proceeded north to Burgos in northern Spain, which they reached in time to observe and photograph Palm Sunday festivities. They then continued to Bilbao, on the Bay of Biscay, and briefly turned west towards Santander. At nearby Onuno, a fine old Roman bridge attracted my father's attention briefly. I suspect that the Santander trip was to allow them to visit the Altamira Caves nearby, known since 1879 for their prehistoric paintings of bison, boars, and deer. He may have wanted to compare the paintings there with the ones he had seen in 1910 in the Dordogne Valley near Les Eyzies. While they were in the Basque country, father purchased a navy-blue beret of the kind worn by local fishermen. It suited him nicely, kept his head warm, and he wore it for many winters thereafter.

From Bilbao, they drove along the coast to Biarritz, then turned southeast for a brief visit to the village and shrine of Lourdes, just north of the Pyrenees. Here they were probably appalled by the religious commercialization of the small community (described in a modern guide book as "an affront to any instinct of veneration")[4] and very likely departed hurriedly after my father took a couple of pictures. They proceeded farther east to the very old city of Toulouse in order to examine the famous brick-built basilica of St-Sernin, the largest Romanesque building in France. Begun between A.D. 1075 and 1080, its plan is nearly identical to that of the cathedral of Santiago de Compostela in Spain, construction of which was commenced in the same year. From Toulouse, they headed north by way of Cahors to the limestone cave region in the Dordogne River Valley. It is easy to suspect that my father returned to that part of France to show mother one or more of the archaeological sites he had examined and places he had stayed, in or near Les Eyzies-de-Tayac, many years earlier. He took several photographs while he and Mother were in this region. Next, they headed northwest and visited the ancient aligned stones near Carnac, Brittany, then Mont-St-Michel and St-Malo, as mentioned briefly at the end of Chapter 1, all places my father had visited by bicycle in the summer of 1909 after his first year at Oxford. This return trip from Spain seems to have been a special journey of remembrance for my father, as well as an opportunity for him to gather information to feed his interest in mediaeval church architecture.

1952–1953: Guadalajara, Mexico

My parents drove to Mexico for the winter, staying for a time in Guadalajara near some Ottawa friends. My father evidently took no pictures while there, but later in the winter, took a few pictures in Mexico City, where he and Mother visited museums, the National Palace, and parks, before making brief trips to the nearby communities of Taxco and Toluca.

---

[4]Robertson, Ian, 1984, p. 470.

1953–1954: Alassio, Italian Riviera[5]

Early in November, my parents took a Swiss freight boat from Montreal to Bremen, Germany. Almost all of the passengers spoke German, which enabled both my parents to refresh themselves on their vocabulary before they reached Germany. My father had pre-arranged the purchase of a small German Volkswagen automobile, of which they took possession a few days later, after all the necessary papers had been completed. They intended to drive to the French Riviera and look for a small house or villa they could buy for about $2,000, either there or farther east in the Italian Riviera, a place to which they could return each winter.

Their route took them south through part of Germany, then into France near the Saar border and on through central France, where my father sought out a considerable number of Romanesque churches to visit, ones that fit into his "evolution scheme of church architecture," as Mother wrote at the time. A week later she wrote "Dad is a wonder for working out his routes," after they had passed through Arles and reached the Mediterranean Sea. Once there, they stayed briefly at a little French inn in the Grasse Valley, just north of Cannes, where they had stayed four years earlier. They found it just as pleasant as the previous time. The sunshine and blue Mediterranean were a welcome change after three weeks of foggy weather farther north, weather which deterred my father from taking many photographs during their trip south. After searching the Grasse Valley for a house to buy, they decided they really wanted to be able to see the sea, so continued east to the Italian Riviera and quickly found a suitable one-bedroom apartment with balcony overlooking the sea at Alassio, southwest of Savona, and close to a long white sandy beach. The ease with which they found this apartment and its reasonable rent quickly convinced them to forego their previous notions of buying a villa.

Within two weeks of settling into their apartment, they arranged to receive daily lessons in Italian conversation from a former professor of Greek who had turned local landowner, in exchange for my parents helping his twenty-some-year-old daughter with her English. My father soon devoted much of his time to reading the Italian newspapers, for which his knowledge of Italian was adequate. As a challenge, he would translate geographical articles in the papers to send to my brother, Pete, who was then a newly appointed associate professor of geography at the University of Pittsburgh. Father also commenced writing a book about his first year in the Arctic, *Dawn in Arctic Alaska*.

That winter proved to be almost the coldest on record on the Italian Riviera, and their apartment was desperately cold after sundown and on cloudy days. That may have been why both of them came down with the flu in February. When the weather improved, they took walks along the narrow stone donkey paths that led to tiny inland villages, some dating from early mediaeval days, sometimes having a picnic but always enjoying the scenery and the fresh air. They also visited a local museum that contained a fairly recently discovered and restored ancient Phoenician or Greek sailing ship, which had sunk a short distance offshore from their village about 100 B.C., scattering amphoras of many sizes and shapes about the sea floor. Indeed, they occasionally wit-

---

[5]Information on the Jenness activities during the winter of 1953–1954 derives from twenty-one letters from E. Jenness to S.E. Jenness, dating from November 15, 1953 to May 19, 1954, in the possession of S.E. Jenness in 2006.

nessed the fishermen retrieving one or more of these amphoras in their nets. In mid-March, my parents made a small tour of an assortment of northern Italian towns—Florence, which Mother had visited as a young woman and Father on a short vacation at the end of the First World War, Pisa, Lucca, and Ravenna, where rain prevented my father from getting any decent photographs of the Byzantine basilicas. While in Florence they attended a concert by the Peruvian soprano Yma Sumac, whom the Italian audience greeted with emotional extremes, from bravas to hissing, clapping, and cat-calls. They also visited the hilltop town of Assisi, which fascinated Mother so much that she persuaded my father to stay for three days. Then they explored Etruscan ruins near Tarquinia. Shortly after they returned to their apartment, my father headed by train for Venice and Padua to attend an international geographical congress.

Mother also mentioned that before they left Alassio to return to Canada, they were invited to assorted tea parties by several elderly village ladies, including three marquises, and that my father spoke Italian sufficiently well by then that he liked practicing it by flirting and joking with the ladies. That was how Mother perceived his behaviour, at any rate. He even seemed to enjoy himself, much to Mother's surprise, for at home in Canada, she added, he would have been bored to tears at such a social event. They left Alassio early in May, amid tears and well wishes, and drove back to Paris, taking back roads and visiting many early churches en route. They stored their new Volkswagen inexpensively just outside Paris for the summer and returned to Canada on the S.S. *Atlantic*.

Figure 29 Diamond Jenness (on left) and artist friend, Giacomo Raimondi, enjoying the Mediterranean sun at Albisola, Italian Riviera, 1955.

Photo by E. Jenness

1954–1955: Albisola, Italian Riviera

After spending the summer at their cottage at Ramsay's Crossing, my father and mother returned to Paris late in the fall (probably by airplane from Montreal), picked up their Volkswagen from its storage site, and drove via Geneva, Grenoble, and Cannes to the Italian Riviera. Once there, they obtained an apartment in the village of Albisola, about three miles east of Savona. There my father spent much of the winter quietly writing the last part of his book *Dawn in Arctic Alaska* and discussing with a local impoverished artist details concerning the creation of drawings (based on an assortment of old Arctic photographs) for his book.[6] No letters survive from this winter, so details have been reconstructed from my father's colour slides. When it came time to return north, they proceeded north

---

[6]His book was published in 1957 (Jenness, 1957), with illustrations by Giacomo Raimondi. My father may have enjoyed the company of this local artist. Mother commissioned him to create a pastel portrait of my father (*see* Figure 71b), but was not satisfied with the finished work.

through the Brenner Pass, pausing long enough by the roadside for my still-romantic father to photograph mother picking some alpine flowers, thus preserving a happy moment from that part of their trip. They stayed overnight in the picturesque Austrian village of Pettnau in the Inn River Valley before continuing to Freiburg and then on to the Volkswagen head-quarters. That company, as a marketing ploy at the time to encourage the introduction of their automobiles into Canada, offered an arrangement with new owners like my parents whereby it would ship their vehicle to Montreal (or New York) for them for a price much cheaper than they could arrange on their own.

1955–1956: Kyrenia, Cyprus
(See Chapter 18.)

1956–1957: Daytona Beach, Florida
Breaking their routine of going to Europe early each winter, my parents stayed at home for Christmas in 1956. In January, they set off in their imported German Volkswagen to Florida, renting a large apartment overlooking the Atlantic Ocean in Daytona Beach. The town and beach proved too commercial for their tastes, but their location was close enough to Ottawa and Pittsburgh to attract visits from their children and grandchildren. They returned to Ottawa late in March after a relatively uneventful winter.

1958: Almogarve, Portugal
After my father recovered from a near-fatal automobile accident shortly before Christmas 1957 (see Chapter 22), he and my mother flew to Portugal in January. There they rented a furn-ished apartment in the coastal resort and fishing town of Almogarve, south of Lisbon. The absence of colour slides from that winter makes me suspect that my father either forgot to take his camera or deliberately left it in Canada. There is also no preserved written record of that winter, which I believe they found pleasant but somewhat chilly.

1959: Fort de France, Martinique
Late in January, my father and mother flew to Fort de France on the Caribbean island of Martinique. It was a curious choice of winter haven for them, but it gave my father the oppor-tunity to brush up on his French, which he put to good use the following winter. For most of their two-month visit, they stayed in a small hotel near the outskirts of town, relaxing, swimming, enjoying the island's music, colourful costumes, and folk dances, especially during the Carnival celebrations at the start of Lent. Before returning to Canada they arranged to rent an automobile and chauffeur to take them on a tour around the island. They were thus able to see most of the towns around the coast as well as the ruins of the former town of St. Pierre, which was buried by hot volcanic ash during the violent eruption of Mt. Pelée in 1902.

1959–1960: France
(See Chapter 19 for an account of my father's winter activities.)

In the spring of 1960, following his return from France, my father commenced work on his last major research and writing project, a series of comparative reports on Eskimo Administration across the Arctic from Alaska to Greenland. Initially, he envisioned writing what he called a "trilogy," consisting of reports on Alaska, Canada, and Greenland, respectively. In time he added a report on Labrador, which preceded Greenland as the third report in the series, and ultimately a fifth volume, wherein he summarized, analyzed, and reflected upon the entire project. He spent over six years on the project (1960–1966), encouraged and financially supported by the Department of Northern Affairs and National Resources and its Northern Co-ordination and Research Centre.

A chance enquiry by my father that spring concerning possible funding for his Eskimo Administration project to help defray his travel and other expenses triggered a flurry of official letters reminiscent of the exchanges in 1936 when he asked about funds for taking on the duties of part-time consulting anthropologist for the Indian Affairs Branch (discussed in Chapter 13). What to him undoubtedly seemed simple enquiries forced administrators to pore over thick regulatory books for answers. To their credit, they found legitimate means to fund my father's investigations in both cases, and thereby obtained, both for the government and for Canada, excellent value for their money. In the earlier instance, the Indian Affairs Branch of the Department of Mines and Resources benefited by more than six years of my father's careful responses to enquiries and assorted reports in the 1930s and 1940s for the paltry total cost of $3049.91; in the latter instance, the Department of Northern Affairs and National Resources benefited from the publication of five carefully researched, no-punches-pulled reports, the result of six years work in the 1960s, for the sum of $24,000. But just as in the earlier instance, when my father's enquiry triggered much concern because an employee of one department was getting two government pay checks, the later one raised considerable alarm because the government was paying money to one of its superannuates.

Most of his Eskimo Administration writing and research were carried out in an office at 150 Kent Street, Ottawa, supplied by the Department of Northern Affairs and National Resources, but he did make two trips, one in the summer of 1963 along the Labrador coast, the other in the summer of 1964 to Denmark and then the west coast of Greenland. All of the five reports he ultimately submitted were edited by Mrs. Graham Rowley and published by the Arctic Institute of North America. The first volume ("Alaska") appeared in 1962, the last ("Analysis and Reflection") in 1968.[7] These were his last professional works. They were followed by only two minor articles and the manuscript that inspired this book.

1960 (Summer): Labrador Coast

My father took passage on a coastal steamer to visit a number of settlements along the Labrador Coast in eastern Canada and gathered first-hand information for the report he was preparing on the federal government's Eskimo administration in that part of Newfoundland. He left the steamer at Fort Chimo and flew back to Ottawa.

---

[7]Jenness (1962b, 1964, 1965, 1967a, 1968a). Chapter 2, "The hour of crisis" (pp. 40–59) in the fifth and final volume of *Eskimo Administration*, was reprinted three years after its original publication in 1968 as the final chapter in the first American edition of the book *Eskimos* by my father's long-time Danish friend Kaj Birket-Smith (Crown Publishers Inc., N.Y., 1971, pp. 237–259).

1960–1961: Manzanillo, Mexico

My parents drove their Volkswagen to Mexico for the winter, finding accommodation in the friendly seaport of Manzanillo until early March. There my father devoted his time mainly to preparing one of his reports on Eskimo administration.

1961–1962: Gandia Playa, Spain

(See Chapter 20.)

1963: New Smyrna Beach, Florida

My parents drove to Florida this winter but chose to stay at New Smyrna Beach, a less popularized community than Daytona Beach and a few miles south of it. They had a quiet winter, but again father took no photographs.

1964 (Summer): Denmark and Greenland

(See Chapter 21.)

1963–1964: Ottawa

This winter my parents rented an apartment in Ottawa. The building had a swimming pool, which attracted visits from grandchildren and their parents. My father worked on one of his Eskimo administration reports during the winter.

1964–1965: Albufeira, Portugal

My parents flew to Lisbon after Christmas and rented a furnished apartment in the picturesque coastal community of Albufeira along the southern coast of Portugal. There are no colour

Figure 30 Eilleen and Diamond Jenness, 1964.

Photographer unknown

slides from this trip, so I suspect my father left his camera in Canada. While there, he suffered his third heart attack the month after they arrived, but the quick action of a local doctor and a lengthy convalescence pulled him through.

1965–1966: Daytona Beach, Florida

My parents drove to Florida one last, uneventful time. There were no further trips.

1949–1950: WANDERING THROUGH ITALY[1]

17

Diamond Jenness

[*On November 12, 1949, my father boarded the 7,500-ton freighter* M.S. Stegeholm *in Montreal, destined for Antwerp, Belgium. Mother remained in Ottawa for the winter, encouraging my younger brother Bob to finish high school. There were only four passengers on the freighter. It took on a load of zinc and lead concentrates and a little asbestos at Quebec City and after a rough ocean crossing, reached Antwerp on November 27. In Brussels, my father visited the parents of his oldest son's Belgian wife and sought to buy or lease a small used automobile for the winter. Unable to obtain one within his means, he proceeded by train to Paris, where his luck proved no better, and then to the small coastal village of Bergeggi in northwestern Italy, where he and my mother had spent some time the previous winter. In Bergeggi, he remained briefly at the Hotel Miramare, intending to spend the next ten weeks touring Italy by car to study its social recovery from the Second World War. His account of that journey follows.*] [S.E.J.]

For several months, I had toyed with the idea of hiring a small motorcar and roaming around Italy at my leisure, without having to stand in line for hours on end to purchase bus and train tickets. In 1949, however, that country was still struggling to pull herself out of the wreckage of World War II, very few Italians could afford private motorcars, and anyone who could raise the money to buy a new vehicle had to enter his name on a long waiting list. To hire a car, therefore, even a second-hand one, was quite difficult. So when a friend relayed to me an offer of a tiny Topolino, I immediately closed the deal in a lawyer's office and set out.[2] A Topolino, I should perhaps explain, was a two-seater Fiat, at that time the smallest car on the market. My

---

[1] In this chapter my father has used a mixture of metric and British Imperial units for distances—kilometres for the distances he drove, because both his road maps and the speedometer and odometer of his little Italian automobile were calibrated in kilometres, and feet, yards, and miles for his other, more casual measurements. Although metric units had been in common use in Europe for well over a century, they were not in use in everyday practice in Canada in the early 1950s when he toured Italy nor even in the late 1960s when he wrote this chapter. Even today, more than a quarter of a century after the official introduction of metrification in Canada in 1971, Canadians still waver in their everyday usage of the two systems, as is readily evident in the labelling of items in our grocery and hardware stores and on the speedometers of Canadian automobiles. And our American neighbours still stoutly resist the introduction of metrification in almost any form outside of scientific and medical laboratories.

[2] The arrangement called for my father to pay 50,000 lire (approximately 90 Canadian dollars) per month for the three months he expected to use the car (D. Jenness to Mrs. D. Jenness, letter dated December 20, 1949, in S.E. Jenness' possession).

Map 11 Route taken by Jenness around Italy, 1949–1950.

Topolino was an early model; it belonged to the "first series" and had travelled 47,119 kilometres [29,266 miles], but it had been newly overhauled, reportedly, and was said to be in excellent shape to carry me the length and breadth of the Italian peninsula. Its four tires certainly looked fairly new, even if the fifth, the spare, was decidedly questionable; and though it lacked a trunk or roof carrier, there was ample space behind its two chair seats for the suitcase, the portable typewriter, and the haversack of books that constituted all my luggage. I took delivery of the car at eleven o'clock one morning, drove it around all afternoon to familiarize myself with its four gear-shifts, and its signals for right and left, then, gaily packing my suitcase, I said goodbye to my village friends and started bright and early the following morning, December 23, 1949.

An easy run of eight kilometres along the Riviera highway brought me to Savona, a small but active port from which I proposed to strike north over the mountains rather than continue on seventy kilometres more to Genoa, because I was a little doubtful of my ability to behave properly in the narrow streets of that large city. At Savona, I dropped my Italian friend, whose conscience had been so troubled by similar doubts that he had insisted on accompanying me at least that far on my journey; and, rejoicing in the clear atmosphere and bright sunshine, I headed northward toward a rather narrow valley. The car rolled smoothly along over the asphalted highway at close to the maximum speed, fifty to fifty-five kilometres, but no sooner had I entered the valley than the curves became sharper and sharper, and the gradient, though hardly visible to the eye, forced me to change into third gear. Even so I made good progress for about ten kilometres, when I noticed a slight fogginess in the atmosphere around me and patches of snow on the mountain slopes above. Soon the highway itself bore a covering of snow, deep enough in the narrow streets of one village to make me drop down into first gear for a few yards. Just beyond this village, the fog thickened and, turning on my headlights, I crawled along, now in third gear now in second, just as one does in Vancouver on certain winter days. In one place, a huge truck loomed up suddenly in the gloom, and forced me out of the ruts into deep snow that bogged me down completely; but a friendly peasant who came along a few minutes later helped me push the car onto the roadway again. For whatever its weaknesses, a Topolino has at least this merit, that it weighs little more than a motorcycle. So on and on I crawled until after some forty kilometres, the road steadily descended, the snow disappeared completely, and

Figure 31 The troublesome Topolino and a farmhouse near Parma, Italy, 1950.
Photo by D. Jenness

the fog thinned out to an innocuous haze. Finally, I emerged altogether from the mountains into the broad level plain of the Po River basin and, turning eastward, sped along a three-lane highway through several small towns to Piacenza, the city in which I had planned to spend the night.

In Italy, as in other countries, highway engineers were beginning to avoid the denser traffic centres by routing the through roads around the edges of the cities instead of through their centres. This had not been possible at Piacenza, apparently, and as I nosed my car into one of its narrow arteries I wondered how far I would get without running someone down. But in Italy you blow your horn ferociously and keep moving, no matter how many people seem deliberately to block your path, and somehow or other, the throng always melts a little in front of you, leaving you just enough room to slip through without actually striking any one. Streetcars and bicycles are a nuisance, of course, but the police are exceedingly efficient and polite, and every narrow lane you negotiate successfully doubles your confidence with the next. So by the time I finally parked my car in the little quadrangle in front of the Croce Bianca hotel, I felt completely certain of my ability to drive it anywhere.

From Piacenza, the highway was nearly as smooth as a billiard table, and the flat land on either side occupied by prosperous-looking farms. I picked up my first hitchhiker on this run. He approached me at a red light on the outskirts of Reggie and asked me to give him a lift to a small village eleven kilometres farther on. When I agreed, he dashed across the road to recover two huge bundles of vegetables, which we managed, not without some difficulty, to pile into the car behind us. Italian hitchhikers, I discovered, never held up just a thumb to beseech a ride, but stretched out the whole arm; and they never looked very optimistic, hitchhiking being still a somewhat rare phenomenon along the highways.

On this day also, I experienced that deliberate fleecing of the foreigner which occurs in all countries, but was particularly prevalent in Italy after the war, doubtless because of the misery occasioned by that war. I had stopped for lunch in what seemed to be a very respectable restaurant in Reggie, and ordered (partly for safety's sake, not being certain of the meanings of some of the items on the menu) exactly the same meal as a man at a neighbouring table. What his bill came to I could not see, but I will swear that my own was double, and that the waiter deliberately "upped" the prices because I was unable to check them properly. It was not only the restaurants that cheated, but the taxi-men and bus drivers, the little shopkeepers and even some of the big ones. Many Italians lamented this exploitation on both moral and economic grounds, for they realized that it discouraged a considerable number of tourists from visiting their country, and, of course, the practice was not universal, Florence and many other towns being almost free of the taint. By and large, however, it was so widely spread, especially in southern Italy, the poorest part of the country, that the foreigner really breathed a sigh of relief when he crossed the frontier into France and Switzerland and no longer felt it was necessary to remain perpetually on his guard.

Halfway between Bologna and Ravenna, I stopped for a short time in Faenza to visit some of its world-famous majolica works; but the town had been greatly shattered during the war and hardly any factories seemed to be operating again. Reconstruction appeared to be going forward a little more rapidly at Ravenna, which had been another anchor of the German line. I arrived there about noon on the day before Christmas, when the market square and all the narrow streets leading into it were so crowded that I abandoned the Topolino and made my way to the local tourist agency, the *Ente Tourismo*, on foot. That agency, with its usual efficiency, provided me with a list of hotels and a small guidebook, then along with all other business places, closed its doors in order to prepare for the imminent celebration. Even the market square cleared magically away within half an hour of noon, and the town assumed the peaceful, leisurely aspect that one associates with a Sunday morning.

No one except myself seemed to be travelling over the Christmas season, and I would have been the only guest in the hotel had not a very handsome setter dog kept me company while I ate dinner. It squatted on the floor beside my chair and looked at me so appealingly with its big soft eyes that, willy-nilly, I offered it various tidbits, which it accepted very gently, almost without touching my fingers. Suddenly, the door swung open and there appeared in the entrance a portly figure clad in a hunting suit and feathered hat. He marched jovially over to the lady hotelkeeper, kissed her loudly on each cheek, and handed her a spray of some seaside flower much esteemed at Christmas in certain parts of Italy, though its name has escaped my memory. Then this descendant of Sir John Falstaff looked at me, and in his booming voice said "Good evening, sir. I wish you a good appetite. I just came in to look for my dog. Ah, there it is, I see." "Yes," I remarked, "a most intelligent animal." And he answered, as he stalked out of the door again, "Yes, most intelligent." I noticed, however, that the dog paid very little attention to him, and showed no inclination to follow his departing footsteps, from which I conjectured that it spent more time, perhaps, in the hotel dining room than at home with its master.

Ravenna lies on the edge of the Po River delta, and though its climate is damp and probably rather unhealthy, the rich soil of the surrounding plain yields very abundant crops. Beside every farmhouse were several stacks of hay, the grapevines trailed neatly along the wires from pole to pole and from tree to tree, and the whole aspect of the countryside outside the war-damaged city gave an impression of prosperity and contentment. Belying this impression, however, were the miserable hovels I saw in one or two villages, and the wretched clothing of some labourers whom I met on the road. And in Ravenna itself, an ex-soldier who stopped me to ask the way to the public baths complained bitterly of his inability to find work and wished he could emigrate to rich America.

I shall not attempt to describe the ancient churches and other treasures of Ravenna, nor those of the many other Italian cities that I visited, for there are guidebooks enough on these places to satisfy the curiosity of every reader. From Ravenna, my course lay south along the Adriatic coast, past well-known watering-places like Cattolica whose beaches, black with people during the summer months, now lay deserted, and the hotels and pensions behind them barred and shuttered until the spring. At Pescara I had the definite feeling of passing out of northern Italy into the southern half of the country, the *meridiana*, where people wander the streets more aimlessly and the stranger draws uninvited looks and sometimes questions from an ever-inquisitive crowd. However, I did not linger in Pescara, but pushed on to Ortona, not realizing that, next to Cassino, it had been shattered more than any other city in Italy, and that while most of the rubble had been cleared away, reconstruction in any real sense had hardly begun.

It was almost dark when I reached the town and slowly nosed my way past ruin after ruin, vainly looking for some hotel in which to spend the night. A passing couple informed me that there was no hotel, and directed me to a restaurant just below the main square on the top of the hill. I found the restaurant in a narrow alley, and, two doors from it, was offered a room by a middle-aged man and his wife who had evidently known better days, judging from their educated speech and cultured manners. The walls of the room were splattered with bullet marks, and there were no panes in the Venetian doors or balcony outside them, though the shutters had been repaired; but the place seemed clean and the couch comfortable, and I was promised a jug of warm water in the morning.

I became better acquainted with my hosts in the course of the evening. Between the two wars, Signor Salomone had been a newspaper reporter in Milan and his wife a schoolteacher; but because they were anti-fascist and did not hesitate to say so, Mussolini had banished them to Ortona. There they had supported themselves and their two children by setting up the restaurant to which I had been directed; but when an allied bomb crashed into their home, they leased the restaurant to help build a new roof over their heads. Their daughter had been an interpreter for the Canadian forces, and Mrs. Salomone herself had worked in the Salvation Army canteen and other Canadian organizations. With dignified pride, she showed me letters of commendation that she had received, one of them from an army chaplain who had since become, she said, Professor of Christian Education in Emmanuel College, Toronto. She described, too, how her son had beckoned into their house a Canadian soldier who was peering through a shattered window on the ground floor while a German was still firing from the roof. Both she and her husband were very despondent about the future, but now that their daughter was married, they hoped more than all else that their son, twenty-five years old and training to be an agriculturalist, might be allowed to emigrate to peaceful and prosperous Canada.

At the edge of Ortona, I picked up another hitchhiker, this time a travelling salesman who had thumbed his way from Lucera and wanted to return home. Before the war, he had been a government clerk; but the Germans had taken him across the Alps to work for five years in a prison camp, and now that he was free again, the only job he could find was selling candy. Sales were not good, but somehow or other he was making a living and even supporting an eighteen-year-old bride.

My new acquaintance, like most Italians, had breakfasted on a small cup of very black coffee, highly sweetened with sugar, but without even a piece of bread to swallow with it. Since the highway was almost deserted, and any grades we had to climb were both short and gentle, we decided when we reached Termoli to stop and have lunch. I suppose that somewhere in that little town there was a restaurant, but my companion suggested that it would be much cheaper to buy a little bread, cheese and bologna, then adjourn to a wine tavern with which he was familiar. We bought the cheese and bologna in a shop on the main street, the bread in a low, one-roomed brick bakery at the end of a blind alley, after which we drove into a rather muddy court-yard and entered a concreted cellar divided into three rooms, two fitted with tables and benches, the third filled with wine barrels and bottles. There he ordered a medium-sized bottle of wine for the two of us, and from somewhere or other obtained a bowl of very appetizing soup; and we ate our lunch at one of the tables. The place was immaculately clean, though rather dingy, and the whole meal cost us only half the amount we would have paid in a restaurant, although we had bought twice as much food as we needed. It showed me one way in which the Italian workingman was coping with the high cost of living, for certainly he could not afford to eat many meals in a restaurant.

After lunch, we drove on to Foggia, where my companion guided me to a comfortable hotel and then, with many expressions of thanks, went off to catch a train to Lucera eighteen kilometres away. At Foggia, I changed my route; instead of following the coast south along the Adriatic highway, I struck west over the mountains to the Tyrrhenian Sea and the coast below Naples. I crossed, first, the broad Foggia plain, which is almost waterless and needs irrigation to increase its fertility, then entered the winding valley of the Cervaro River and slowly climbed upward to a nearly level plateau. Here a few white farmhouses dotted the land, about half of which was in pasture, the remainder planted with wheat and other crops. The landscape was so attractive that I stopped to take a photograph; and at the same moment, a shabbily dressed youth who was riding a bicycle fifty yards in front of me dismounted to converse with another youth who was walking along the side of the road. The two lads approached me as I was snapping my camera, and the taller, who may have been twenty-one-years-old, asked me what I was doing, where I came from, where I had acquired an Italian automobile, how much I had paid for it, how did I like Italy, and a number of other questions I had been asked several times before, and was to be asked again and again almost everywhere I stopped. The younger lad broke in at this stage and said, "Do you think America will make war on Russia?"

I answered truthfully "No, I do not think so. The newspapers may talk a great deal about it, but the American people themselves do not want another war."

The lad turned instantly to his companion and exclaimed, "Isn't that what I told you? No people wants war. It is only the generals and the newspapers that talk about it all the time."

That same question I had been asked by other Italians, but always by persons much older. That two peasant lads in the mountains of central Italy should also be preoccupied with the topic clearly indicated how heavily the dread of another war weighed upon the minds of the whole nation.

We chatted a few minutes longer, then went our separate ways; they smiled and waved to me cheerfully as I passed them. Stretches of almost level ground now alternated with steep slopes, two of them so steep, indeed, that even in first gear, my little Topolino laboured heavily and I was afraid that it might not reach the summit. I climbed up to the hilltop town of Ariano, where scores of tiny children were playing in the narrow street; and I passed another hilltop town called Prado, some of whose houses were poised on precipices and ready to fall into the abyss whenever a strong rain loosened their foundations. Except on a few large estates, every patch of cultivable ground was planted to crops, with which were mingled olive trees and grapevines. Soil erosion was severe, and it was aggravated in one or two places by cultivation across the contours, although this seemed exceptional. Altogether the chief impressions I received were the heavy pressure of a population, amazingly dense for a mountainous region, on the meagre land resources, the dearth of farm machinery, and the evident cheapness and abundance of hand labour.

Pressing on, I descended early in the afternoon the switchback highway down the western slope of the mountains, and, passing through the coastal city of Salerno, arrived at Paestum in time to park my car outside the government hotel and visit the ruins of the Greek temples while they were still bathed in sunlight. As I gazed at the huge stone blocks that made up the pillars and their capitals, I could not help wondering how many hundreds of slaves had spent their lives in quarrying and hoisting them into position, slaves who lacked all those mechanical aids which today's engineers can command for such work. Of course, time was not so pressing when these temples were erected, five or six centuries before the birth of Christ; and slaves were not paid for their labour by the hour or the day. Perhaps, too, the plain of Paestum, while just as damp then as it is now, was not quite so unhealthy, since the anopheles mosquito and malaria did not spread to southern Italy until two or three centuries later. For Paestum is another area that, like Foggia, needs large improvement works, in its case not irrigation but drainage, much of the plain being now too wet to serve for anything but pasture.

II

A fairly good road, much of it asphalted, runs down each coast of Italy to the straits of Messina, but the national highway turns inland at Battipaglia, half way between Salerno and Paestum, and winds through the mountainous interior of the peninsula almost to its toe. In winter, this route is often blocked by snow, but the season was still so early that there seemed every prospect of my getting through without trouble. The car itself seemed to disapprove the proposal, for it balked at starting in the morning and delayed my departure until 10 a.m. However, after letting the engine warm up for a few minutes, I ran out to the main road and stopped to consult my map.

A man who was loitering at the corner walked over to the car window and asked where I was going. When he learned that I was heading for Battipaglia he requested a lift. I hesitated

Figure 32 Temple of the Corn Goddess, Ceres, at Paestum, near Naples, Italy, 1955. It was built by the Greek colonists about 500 B.C.

Photo by D. Jenness

for a moment, but finally told him to jump in. He was about forty years of age and quite rough-looking, but his face seemed open enough and, after all, what danger could there be in carrying a passenger for twenty kilometres over an open road in broad daylight? He began to chat as we started off, using a dialect of which I understood very little, though he seemed to understand me; but I gathered that he was a woodcutter, and that throughout most of the war he had kept out of the way in the high mountains. He wanted to treat me to a cup of coffee when we reached Battipaglia, but it was late, and I was anxious to push on. I therefore excused myself as best I could and shook hands with him very warmly; but as he turned away, I could not help feeling that he was a trifle hurt.

Actually, I didn't leave Battipaglia for another half hour, because when I filled the tank of the car at the nearby service station, I saw gas spouting out of a small hole in the cup of the fuel pump. Luckily, a garage down the street was able to put in a new cup for me. With everything then in order again, I turned southeast up a wide valley into the mountains, passing, but not entering the town of Eboli, which Carlo Levi has called Italy's last outpost of Christendom as one travels south. The road, well paved and wide enough for two and in some places three cars, climbed slowly and evenly, while oaks and chestnuts began gradually to replace the vineyards and orange groves of the lowlands.

After an hour or so of steady travelling, I dropped down into a small village and began to climb the long ascent beyond it. The grade here was a little steeper than usual, but the car was moving steadily forward in second gear when suddenly the motor died away and refused to start again. I blocked one wheel with a stone to keep the vehicle from sliding downhill, and rather hopelessly—for I am no mechanic—was proceeding to investigate the spark plugs when a car coming from the opposite direction pulled up beside me and three men jumped out to ask what was the trouble. Now I can talk of the weather and of the condition of the highways in moderately fluent Italian, but to explain the inner workings of an automobile is quite beyond my capacity in any language. As I was groping for words, however, one of the men said to me in passable English, "Do you speak English, or French? My brother is a mechanic. Can we help you?" The mechanic at once took over, while my new acquaintance asked me where I had bought the car and where I was going. When I told him that I was on my way to Sicily, he paused and, glancing first at the car, then at me, said smilingly "You are very courageous." I thought at the time that he was just being courteous, but before three days were over, I realized that he meant not courageous but foolhardy.

The mechanic quickly diagnosed the trouble in the distributor, and within a few minutes had the engine running smoothly again. "Now you can go," said his brother, "and good luck on your journey." And almost before I could thank them, the three men had shaken hands with me and sped off. As I climbed into my Topolino again, I could not help remembering a similar incident twelve years previously, when a Californian motorist held up a score of cars on the highway outside Albany, New York, and dragooned their occupants into lifting my Chrysler out of a ditch.

I now drove on for an hour without incident until, at the foot of a long incline, I overtook three road workers who were holding out their arms for a ride. To accommodate them all was impossible, but one man appropriated the seat beside me while a second squeezed in at the back beside my luggage. The third man we left behind to climb the hill on foot, somewhat to my regret, because he had been a prisoner of war in England for several years and spoke gratefully of the kind treatment he had received from the English people.

My two passengers climbed out near some houses at the top of the hill, and I was rolling cheerfully along, with two hours of sunlight still ahead of me, when I heard an ominous thumping from the engine. Prudence warned me to stop for the night at the little town of Lagonegro just ahead of me and to seek the advice of a mechanic. I drove slowly into the town as far as the broad main street in its centre and, seeing no hotel, stopped to ask a youth about twenty-one-years-old where I could find one. He directed me back a few yards to the narrow street along which I had come, and learning that I needed a mechanic also, pointed to himself and said that his garage was almost opposite the hotel door. I invited him to drive the car back and tell me what was wrong with it, which he did, discovering the trouble almost immediately. It was in the frame, which had cracked at the welding and allowed the motor to tilt down on one side. Had I driven another mile, the welding on the opposite side would probably have broken also and sent the whole engine crashing to the ground.

Obviously, the frame had to be re-welded; but before that could be done it was necessary to remove the engine. This the youth proceeded to do without delay, calling to his aid another youth of about the same age; and before the sun had set, I saw them trundling the motorless frame of the car along the street to a welding shop, from which it returned at dusk. They then set about putting the engine in place again, but the poor illumination of their garage—it had only one twenty-five-watt light bulb—forced them to postpone part of this operation until the morning.

Lagonegro lay in a deep hollow entirely surrounded by mountains. One part of the town, the oldest apparently, covered the summit of a semi-detached hill; the rest sprawled halfway up the face of one of the mountains, the last house being accessible only by steps. The scenery was very austere, for the only trees in numbers were oaks and chestnuts, and now that it was winter, the chestnuts stood naked without leaves, and the leaves of the oaks were brown and withered. Near the bottom of the main street, the highway turned sharply left and, crossing a deep ravine, zigzagged upward among scattered chestnut trees, being protected on its outer edge by a stone wall. As I walked up this road in the gathering dusk, I met a number of shepherds driving home their sheep and goats, and women and children, some with bundles of firewood on their heads, others with baskets of laundry. One little girl of about seven years was sitting rather forlornly at the roadside, her back against a stone wall and a bundle of firewood bigger than herself on the ground at her side. The air was distinctly chilly, for the heights above were covered with snow; and during the night, there was a heavy frost.

I rose at seven the next morning, but my young mechanic was already working across the street. By 10 a.m., he had tested the car in a trial spin and declared it satisfactory. I left immediately, and at the last house in the town, was flagged by an old pensioner who wanted a lift to the next village. Shortly after I had dropped him at his home, I crossed a wide valley, on whose far side stood a large sign stating that the road for twenty-five kilometres ahead was under repair and that motorists would proceed at their own risk. I looked at the sign, then at my Topolino, and frankly had no liking for the risk; but it was too late to turn back.

Actually, the road was not nearly as bad as I had anticipated. It carried neither mud nor potholes; but for the whole twenty-five kilometres, it was covered with very coarse stone, and for about half that distance, ran uphill through rather dense scrub. Of houses I saw only four, and met only one car and two road workers. It was not a stretch of road that one would choose for a breakdown, but my Topolino never faltered.

The landscape changed after I struck the pavement again. The trees vanished, and for kilometre after kilometre I was surrounded by high, naked hills of a dolomitic rock whose fragments covered so much of the valley bottoms as to leave only one or two patches of cultivable soil. In one of these patches stood two miserable houses, side by side, and from one of them, a middle-aged woman rushed out and waved a basket at me as I passed. I stopped to see what she wanted, and discovered she had six eggs, which she was eager to sell me for any price I would pay her. I explained to her, gently, that I could not use them; but, discovering that she had also three children, I emptied my pockets of the small change they contained and left her well satisfied.

A long ascent to a pass over the mountains led me out of this stony waste and brought into view another valley that was refreshingly green and fertile. The descent here was as full of hairpin curves as the climb up had been, but as usual, every curve was well banked and the gradient mathematically uniform; also, numerous signs gave the motorist adequate warning. Halfway down, I ran into a gang of about twenty roadmen who had just broken off work for the day and were returning to Morana, a small village that was visible five or six hundred feet below us. They crowded around my car, very cheerful, and two of them came in with me, both ex-soldiers who had gladly accepted road work at 750 lire ($1.35) a day rather than join the over-swollen ranks of the unemployed and unemployable. They answered my questions frankly but rather quietly, and when I dropped them in the village each of them shook my hand and raised his cap.

Fifty yards farther down the road, a little knot of people had watched me drop the workmen, and when I drew nearer, a man and a girl signalled me to stop. If I was going to Castrovillari, they asked, would I take the girl with me? There was no question of refusing, for the town was directly on my route and only seven kilometres away. The girl was about twenty years of age and neatly dressed; in her arms she carried a live kid, tightly trussed, which she had just bought in the village and was taking home for the New Year's dinner. She told me, in pure Italian, not in dialect, that both she and her younger sister were attending a teachers' training college, and that she hoped to graduate in another year and then secure a position, even though she was engaged to be married and expected the wedding to take place in late spring or early summer. In addition to two sisters, one of them married, she had an older brother, a lawyer, who had emigrated to Barranquilla in [Colombia], South America, and was succeeding very well. She added that several young men with whom she was acquainted also wanted to emigrate to South America, where the opportunities for employment were much greater than in Italy, but there seemed to be many obstacles in their way.

At Castrovillari, she invited me into her home, which was a neat white house at the entrance to the town. There she introduced me to her mother and two sisters (her father, I gathered, was dead), and left them to entertain me in the drawing room with some excellent vermouth while she delivered the kid to the butcher. I loitered there very pleasantly for an hour, being in no hurry, since Cosenza, the capital of the province, was now only fifty kilometres away, and there were no intervening mountains to slow my progress. The drawing room was comfortably but not expensively furnished, and the place had all the appearance of a respectable middle-class home.

Cosenza lies in the middle of a fertile but greatly dissected plain and, like many other Italian towns, has two parts, an older part with narrow streets built on a small hill, and a newer part with wider streets on the flat land below. After booking a room at the Imperial Hotel in the newer part, I drove my car to a garage to have the carburetor cleaned, since the motor had suddenly begun to stall every time I took my foot off the accelerator. Half a dozen men and youths who were loitering in the entrance gathered round me while I was explaining my needs to the chief mechanic, and one of them, a tall, rather sinister-looking individual, planted himself in front of me and exclaimed "Who are you? Where is your car licence?" The mechanic, who was an elderly man, said to him "Oh, it's all right. Can't you see he's English?" But the fellow retorted, "He may have stolen the car," and shouted more and more loudly "Where is the licence? Where is the licence?" I paid no attention to him at first, but finally walked round to the far side of the car, unwrapped the licence and held it out, saying "Here is the licence. Perhaps you want to read it?" "No, I don't want to read it," he answered. I then turned away and paid no further attention to him; but I noticed a minute or two later that he was no longer in the garage.

Erosion has caused much gullying in the soft red earth to the south of Cosenza, and the process was being intensified in some places, where steep slopes that should have been left in woodland or pasture had been ploughed and planted to wheat—not from ignorance, perhaps, but through the pressure of a dense population and the need for a maximum production of grain. About fifty kilometres from the city, I abandoned the National Highway in favour of a well-paved road over a mountain range to the town of Nicastro; and, meeting a road worker not far from the turn-off, drove him to his village, Cappanzora, on the hilltop above. There he insisted on my taking some refreshment, so we left the car in the narrow main street under the watchful eye of a small boy and entered his house, which seemed to consist of a single room on the ground floor, a cellar beneath it and one or possibly two bedrooms above. After introducing me to his young and rather astonished wife, who was carrying a year-and-a-half old baby in her arms, he made me sit down at their small table and placed before me a bottle of red wine, some bread, grapes and apples. I was afraid there would be no limit to his hospitality, for when my appetite failed to correspond to his wishes he wrapped up a fresh bottle of wine, two bunches of grapes and a dozen apples, and insisted that I carry them away with me. Payment, of course, was out of the question, but I slipped his wife a 500-lire bill (90 cents) to buy something or other for her baby.

The mountain range that divides the Cosenza plain from Nicastro had been left in forest, and with a well-powered car the trip across it must be very beautiful during the spring and summer months when the chestnut trees are in full leaf. But my little car began to shimmer badly as I descended the far side, so that I was relieved when I reached Nicastro and could turn in at a garage on one of its main streets. Here I observed what I had noticed already from Battipaglia down, that while the establishment was owned or at least operated by an old mechanic, all the workers were young lads ranging in age from twelve to about twenty-two years. In Nicastro, the mechanic and one of the older lads were working on the motor of a large bus, but he turned my car over to another senior youth and assigned two small boys of twelve or fourteen to work with him.

The sky had been clouded all day, and a drizzly rain was now falling, but having nothing to do for two or three hours, I lunched in a restaurant and then strolled about the town, which was remarkable for one thing only, the peculiar dress of some of its women. I lacked the courage to examine it minutely, but it resembled the fantastic bustles that were so fashionable toward the end of the nineteenth century. Over a scarlet underskirt bordered with a white band was a dress, black in the older women, green or some other bright colour in the young, that seemed to be cut short at the waist in front, and at the back to be either padded or gathered into a fold about four inches thick, after which it hung down over the underskirt. One had to admit that the costume was very striking, but it seemed a little ungainly compared with the neatly tailored blouses and skirts, also brightly coloured, of the other women on the streets.

From Nicastro south, there are several long inclines, but no high hills or mountains. I had expected to reach the Strait of Messina, therefore, without stopping, but the mishap to the car delayed me so long that darkness overtook me when I was still about a hundred kilometres from my goal. Since there was no advantage in driving on at night, I turned aside from the highway and descended the escarpment to the little coastal town of Pizzo. It proved to be a rather dingy place, as far as I could observe it that evening, having nothing to recommend it except a beautiful green sea; consequently I was quite content to leave it again early the next morning. The highway now traversed or skirted four or five villages, and passed some olive plantations where the trees, favoured apparently by the rich soil and warm climate, were fully twice the height of the olive trees in north Italy. On one plantation, a team of white oxen was ploughing the spaces between the trees, which elsewhere had been planted to wheat and beans; for not one inch of soil seemed to have been left uncultivated. I was told later that all or most of these plantations are worked on a share system, the tenant turning over half the annual produce as rent.

The car ran perfectly for about sixty kilometres, but then a steady hammering sound in the rear warned me that something was wrong. Seeing a little garage at the roadside and a mechanic working on a car outside it, I stopped to ask his judgment. He told me that a ball-bearing in the differential had broken, and advised me to seek a mechanic in the town of Palmi five or six kilometres farther on, since he himself handled ignition troubles only. It was a Sunday morning, and every garage in Palmi was closed, but after I had searched the town from one end to the other, a small boy found me a mechanic who had no scruples about throwing off his fine Sunday clothes and opening up his workshop. He was comparatively young, thirty-three years old perhaps, but without question he knew his job perfectly, for he made not a single superfluous movement. Even a little three-year-old child who called him daddy and played with his tools never seemed to fluster him. From time to time, he merely offered her another tool to play with or gently moved her a little to one side.

This child, with its blue eyes and fair hair, so little resembled him that I have no doubt its real father was an English or Canadian soldier of the invasion army. I had already noticed three very fair children of about the same age at Lagonegro, where a British unit spent an entire winter; and in Nicastro I saw still another "ugly duckling." Probably there are scores of them throughout the length and breadth of the Italian peninsula. Happily, they are not treated as ugly ducklings, as far as I could discover, but receive the same affection and care as the more olive-complexioned children in the communities.

The mechanic not only put in a new ball bearing, but also replaced a broken bolt in another part of the car. As it was then mid-afternoon, instead of continuing to the Strait of Messina, I engaged a room for the night in a small hotel and drove eastward through vegetable gardens, orange groves, olive plantations and a little woodland to the small town of Taurianova fifteen kilometres away, for unlike Palmi, which is a popular summer resort, Taurianova and its surrounding plain have no resources except agriculture, and I was hoping that, even in the short space of an hour, I could gain some impression of the social conditions in that purely agricultural centre. The main street of the town was rather sordid, though not more so than other places through which I had passed, but the streets behind it were malodorous slums, crowded with barefoot children clothed in mere rags. How many individuals occupied each room in their houses, on the average, I could only guess, but I would estimate not less than three or four; for it seemed to be the rule in southern Italy that wherever one encountered the greatest poverty, there also one found the most babies.

At noon the next day, I finally reached the Strait of Messina, passing the rock of Scilla, which has lost most of its terror since Homer's age. The highway there skirted the coastline, and the slopes were clothed with grapevines instead of with olive trees, possibly because they were very steep. A big Lancia car raced by me soon after I passed Scilla, and when I drew up at the ferry station and began to enquire about tickets, its driver came to my assistance and piloted me aboard the boat.[3] He told me that his name was Diego Scopelliti, that he was a chauffeur-mechanic at the Lancia agency in Messina, and that he had just driven down from Turin in two days. When he learned that I intended to spend the night in Taormina he suggested that I follow him through the city of Messina, since his home lay five kilometres beyond it on the Taormina road. Very generously, too, he offered to help me whenever I returned across the ferry, or to have another workman in his firm secure my tickets for me if he himself were not free. When the time came for me to return to the mainland [from Sicily], however, I was afraid my Topolino would break down for good and all on south Italy's mountains; so I took the night boat from Palermo to Naples, and never re-crossed the Strait of Messina or saw my friend again.

III

Mediterranean winters are wholly unpredictable. One will be almost rainless, the next so wet that the land is virtually inundated. You start out for a walk at 10 a.m. under a cloudless sky, and at 11 a.m. you are deluged by a thunderstorm. It was not at all surprising, therefore, that all through northern Italy I had enjoyed continuous sunshine, whereas in the southern mountains the sky was perpetually overcast and on both sides of the Strait of Messina it rained heavily.

South from Messina for some fifty kilometres, each village seemed to overlap with the next, and the motorist emerged from one narrow street only to run into another. The highway followed the coastline, but at intervals turned inland for two or three hundred yards in order to cross some stream that came down from the Pelorian Mountains. When I crossed them in early January 1950, these streams were almost dry, but their wide stony beds showed what torrents could foam down them after three or four days of heavy rain at their sources. On every

---

[3] The Strait of Messina where the ferry crosses to Messina on the Island of Sicily is about four kilometres wide.

hand were orange trees laden with golden fruit, but much of the landscape was obscured by the growing darkness, and by a windshield dripping with rain. By the time I reached Taormina, I was really groping in the darkness, knowing only that I had climbed uphill for a kilometre or more with a wall on one side of me and trees or another wall on the other.

The tourist season was in full swing at Taormina, and there was hardly a vacant room in its more than a score of hotels. Villa San Pancrazio, where I stayed two nights, provided the maximum of comfort for a very reasonable price, but the conversation was entirely in English, all its guests having their homes somewhere between the Rio Grande and the Canadian border. The sky cleared the morning after my arrival, enabling me to explore the ancient Greek theatre and other sights of the town, and to visit also its greatly overrated beach. Some of the pebbles on this beach were of white marble streaked with red bands, the same marble that the Greeks—or their Roman successors—had used in their theatre and temples. I did not discover the source of the stone, but suspect that it was some distance back in the mountains.

The colour of the sea, too, was intriguing. In the shallow water close to the beach, it was a beautiful shade of light green, streaked inshore by white combers and flecked here and there with patches of purple that, in some cases at least, marked the presence of submerged rocks. Farther out it was the familiar Mediterranean blue. The same three colours, pale green, blue, and purple, prevail along part of the Riviera coast west of Genoa, but east of that city, at Santa Margherita Ligure and Rapallo, the sea is dark and rather forbidding. Since the sky seems the same everywhere, I wondered whether the difference could be caused by geological factors, for the rocks and beaches at Rapallo and Santa Margherita Ligure are of black slate, whereas west of Genoa and in Sicily they are for the most part some form of white limestone.

As I wandered up from the beach into the town again, I passed an open workshop in which an elderly man was chiselling a nude figure out of a block of white chalk. I stopped to talk to this small-town Praxiteles,[4] and he showed me the dozen or so pencil sketches that he was following in his work. They were in classical style—he disliked what he called modern futuristic sculpture—and, on the whole, quite pleasing, though the anatomy was a little sketchy. Standing in the corner of the workshop was the complete figure of a nude boy about one-metre high, and two small bas-reliefs were hanging on the wall. I omitted to ask him what market he found for his statues other than perhaps a church or a park, for with the change in houses and fashions during the last century a one-metre statue would certainly seem out of place in most of our modern homes.

It was an easy run from Taormina to Siracusa [Syracuse in English], only one hundred and thirty kilometres, and almost exactly halfway lay the city of Catania, sprawling out over its wide plain and still licking its war wounds. I lost my way in this city; instead of turning left off its long main street I kept straight on, to find myself at last in nearly open country where three centuries ago a grim river of molten lava from Mt. Etna had lapped against the backs of the houses on one side of the road. Seeing a priest come out of a tiny white church that had barely escaped the fiery flood, I asked him whether I was travelling in the right direction. He answered very courteously, in a voice unusually soft and gentle, that I should circle back at the next crossroad, and proceed down a parallel road until I came to a great arch and a sign reading

---

[4]A fourth-century B.C. Athenian sculptor.

Siracusa. Then he walked on, and I saw him enter one of the most dilapidated of the houses, after exchanging a few words with a little girl outside its door.

This road, or street, running down to the archway was a scene of dire misery. It was wet and muddy, lined on both sides with houses that had lost much of their plaster, and were so crowded with women and little children, many of them in rags, that I could hardly work my way through. Their number was really so excessive, even for Sicily, that I suspect that many bombed-out families had found shelter on this street among relatives or friends, for there was evidently a great housing shortage in the city.

At a right-angle turn just outside Catania, a peasant woman joined me and kept me company as far as an orange farm thirty kilometres farther on. She talked incessantly in high-pitched cadences that sounded strangely like laughter, but she guided me very efficiently through a rather intricate hilltop village, and she did her best to teach me the art of cultivating oranges. I gathered that orange trees need a considerable amount of water, which in this country of limestone hills surges out of the rocks in odd places and flows down narrow ravines to the valley floor. The orange farmers plant their trees not only at the bottoms of the ravines (if they contain any soil) but in terraces up their sides, and they pump the water into wells above them so that it can drain down from one terrace to the next. Near Siracusa, later, I saw what in old England would be called a dingle[5] that had been hollowed out in the level plain by a small stream. Here a fine crop of oranges was being harvested, while a grove of almond trees was flowering on the drier ground above.

Siracusa is bounded on the north by a wide limestone ridge on whose highest part the ancient Greeks built a strong fortress, from which they ran a stone wall, five miles long, to the sea. The north side of the ridge rises up rather gradually from the plain, but the side facing Siracusa drops more abruptly, in some places forming perpendicular cliffs in which the early Christians dug catacombs. Several centuries earlier, about 470 B.C., a Siracusan ruler excavated in one spot a large theatre, still so well preserved that old Greek plays are sometimes enacted in it, not in their original tongue, of course, but translated into modern Italian. The highway, evenly graded, traversed the ridge and descended into the newer part of Siracusa, then crossed a bridge into the old town on the little island of Ortygia, which jutted out from the mainland to enclose a wide and almost circular bay.

In this old part of Siracusa, I found a comfortable room that faced the afternoon sun and the bay, where boats of all sizes passed to and fro in front of me. Whenever I sat on my little balcony and looked northward along the esplanade below, I could see two or three vessels tied up at the docks and, beyond them, if the weather was clear, Mt. Etna high in the sky belching smoke from its summit. As elsewhere in the Mediterranean, the air chilled rapidly at sunset, but the climate was so much warmer than farther north that many almond trees were flowering by the middle of January, a month earlier than on the Riviera. I was told, too, that in exceptional years, a few dates actually ripen on their palms, something that has never been known to happen on the Italian mainland.

The townspeople, too, were friendly, and did not pester the stranger, as they do at Naples, by buzzing around him like flies on a pastry counter. Only once was I annoyed by an over-persistent

---

[5]A small, deep, wooded valley.

cabby, and he yielded without too prolonged an argument. There were practically no beggars, though the amount of unemployment, and of men idly loitering in the squares, was heart-breaking. As the allies discovered during the war, Siracusa is nearer to Tripoli than it is to Naples or Rome, and in Mussolini's day it had been the shipping centre for most of Italy's extensive commerce with her North African possessions. Those possessions had now been wrested from her, and the maritime activities of Siracusa had fallen away almost to nothing. To make matters worse, the city had been flooded with fugitives from Tripolitania [in northern Libya]. The government in Rome had assisted with the housing and unemployment problems by building an enormous apartment house for the refugees and by subsidizing the erection of other buildings, as well as by allocating large sums from European Recovery Program (E.R.P. or Marshall Plan) funds for the construction of a highway around the city and a hydro-electric project in the vicinity. But it could not possibly find work for all who needed it here and in other cities of this war-devastated, heavily populated land.[6]

Siracusa itself possessed no industries except a little fishing, a fairly large olive-oil refinery, a macaroni plant, and some tiny factories making tiles, cement, and orange crates. Inevitably, there was much distress. Scores of would-be workers applied for every available job, and the competition pushed down wages to a minimum. Often they were excessively low. In my hotel worked two elderly housemaids who took turns in bringing me hot water and in tidying up my room. One was a hunchback, the other a passionate singer of operatic arias. Both performed their duties cheerfully and well. They confided to me one evening that their wages were only 450 lire (80 cents) a day, out of which they had to pay for any meals. They had never seen the absentee owner of the hotel. He was a baron, they said, and extremely rich.

One outcome of the fierce struggle for existence was the prevalence of child labour, for not only were children paid less than adults, but every member of a family, however young, had to pull his or her weight. In the little coffeehouse that I often frequented after buying my evening papers, a boy of perhaps seven regularly washed the cups and saucers. And in the barber's shop next door, a boy of about eleven stood ready both to trim my hair and shave my beard. Half the workers in the orange-crate factories and the automobile garages were boys in their early teens, while everywhere girls of nine and ten seemed to take full responsibility for all younger children whenever the mother was away from home, which meant in some cases all or most of the day.

Nevertheless, one could not help admiring the brave show put up by nearly all the younger people, and indeed by most of the older ones as well, especially the women. You wandered down a narrow lane into a small, half-paved piazza or court, and suddenly, out of some miserable hovel, stepped a young woman who, to a man's eyes at least, looked surprisingly clean and smartly dressed, even though her coat and skirt might not be of the finest quality. You said to yourself that in every country, marriageable youths and girls always tried to dress smartly, for a very obvious reason. But then you observed a group of middle-aged women gossiping in a little bake-shop, and you thought how respectable they all seemed, just as respectable and tidy as a group of very poor women in your home town.

---

[6]While in Siracusa, my father wrote and subsequently published three articles that reveal some of his concerns at the time (Jenness, 1950a,b,c).

In every Siracusan street-crowd, the prevailing tone of the costumes was black; but some shade of bright red—especially a coat or a sweater of that colour—was very fashionable among the younger women, and, next to red, a bright blue, green, orange or yellow, in that order. Bright though these colours might be, an innate artistic quality in the people checked discordant combinations. You sensed this artistic quality in the designs painted on the sides of the small fishing-boats—floral patterns, usually, and rows of rising suns—and in the more elaborate but not always quite successful designs and historical pictures with which the country people decorated the sides and wheels of their donkey carts.

I was prowling along the limestone escarpment near the old Greek theatre one morning when I noticed two small caves in the cliff above me and, to my surprise, heard voices issue from one of them. Presently, a woman came out, spread on the rocks two or three articles of clothing, and called to some children who were playing at a spring about a hundred yards away. I turned back then, but a few minutes later the husband overtook me and asked if I knew where he might find work. He was a *bracciante* or day labourer who had lived and worked in the city during the war, but could find no job after the Allied forces overran Sicily. And when a German bomb destroyed his home, he had moved into this cave a mile out of town, where no one demanded rent, and plenty of good spring water bubbled up right at his door. There were four children in his family, all girls, the oldest fifteen and the youngest three. For these children the nuns provided four rations of soup each day, but otherwise he received no assistance, since he lacked the "worker's book" of the regularly employed and had never contributed to the social security fund. There seemed to be no way in which I, a foreign tourist, could help him, but I arranged to visit his cave between 10 and 11 a.m. the following morning.

Figure 33 Greek theatre, fifth century B.C., hewn out of a solid limestone ridge, Siracusa, Italy, 1950.
Photo by D. Jenness

No one was at home when I arrived there, about 10:30 a.m., but a pregnant dog, half starved, came up and barked at me, and presently the oldest girl and another about nine came running up from the spring. Their parents, they said, had gone to Mass (it was Sunday), but they should return at any moment and were expecting me. Would I enter the cave and wait for them? I entered and examined the place closely. On each side of the main tunnel, which ran into the hillside for about fifteen yards, were four small alcoves or rooms, two of which contained regular beds, while in a third two young pups were sleeping. The girls said that the cave was always dry and warm, and at the moment it was reasonably tidy, though I suspect it had been spruced up in anticipation of my visit. Still, there seemed to be no reason why it could not be made as comfortable as many Sicilian farmhouses, or indeed many homes in the cities. It may well be, however, that some stigma attaches to the troglodytic life, even in Sicily.

The father arrived a few minutes later and with him the two youngest children. All four girls were barefooted and wretchedly clad; the child of three wore nothing but a thin cotton frock that did not reach her knees. This child looked half-witted, whereas the girl of nine was very bright and vivacious, though afflicted with some eye disease. As for the oldest child, fifteen years of age, she appeared hard and very sophisticated. Probably she was, for to girls in her position here, virtually only one road seemed open: indiscriminate prostitution.

In Siracusa, as in other Italian ports, the foreign tourist must beware of a slick confidence racket which, judging by my own experience, generally runs to a set form. I encountered it first in Genoa. There a man stopped me on the street one morning and, after enquiring if I understood English, said that he was an engineer on a cargo vessel that had just come in from New York and was to leave again that afternoon. He had some goods to deliver to a Mr. William Armstrong, whose address he did not remember, and he hoped I could help him. I explained, quite innocently, that I too was a foreigner and knew nothing of any William Armstrong, and I was about to advise him to consult the U.S. consul when he interrupted me by saying "You speak Italian, don't you? Ask this man here." He then stopped an apparently chance passer-by. The new man, an Italian, using me as an interpreter, asked the "engineer" what goods he had to deliver, and learning that they included whisky, cigarettes, woollen cloth and other things, suggested that we adjourn to a neighbouring café and make a deal of some kind. The "engineer," of course, wanted to sell for dollars, which the Italian could not supply until late in the afternoon, but if I would go into partnership with him and lend him the dollars temporarily, he would buy some of the goods at cut-rate prices, sell them for double or triple the amount, and divide the profits with me. Needless to say, I too had no dollars on hand and the transaction fell through.

In Siracusa, I was accosted in exactly the same way, not by an "engineer from an American vessel," but by a "Polish seaman without a passport" who carried a large bundle of cloth under his arm. He and his passing friend tried to inveigle me into a café to talk business, but I referred them to the customhouse authorities farther down the street.

One or two Siracusan families made a little paper for the tourist trade from papyrus bushes brought to the town from Egypt and planted at the mouth of a small stream that flowed into the bay. Near it was another stream, the Anapo, which had cut in the limestone hills thirty-five kilometres inland a deep gorge in whose vertical cliffs prehistoric man dug about five thousand shallow receptacles or cells to house his dead. These tombs had all been excavated and their contents deposited in the Siracusan National Museum, where their examination had thrown a flood of light on the history of Sicily between 1100 and 700 B.C., before the Greeks established any colonies on the island.

The cells themselves still remained in the cliffs and appeared to be worth visiting. A railway ran below them at the bottom of the gorge, but no trains stopped near. However, my map indicated no difficulty in reaching the place by car. I started out, accordingly, about 9 o'clock one morning, taking with me a young Swiss woman who operated an orphanage in northern Italy and was vacationing for a few days in my hotel.

Six kilometres from Siracusa, our road began to climb, but so gently that I could keep the car in high gear. We passed through two villages and, beyond them, high in the hills, two very large farms with fields sown to wheat and dotted with fruit trees, mainly olives, carobs, and almonds. In one field, five men working side by side were hoeing up the weeds, a clear indication of the lack of machinery and the abundance of cheap day labour. Farther on, we met a road gang that was repairing the highway, which was very rough for the next five or six kilometres. We were then about eight hundred feet above sea level, and the land had become so stony that in many places it was difficult to see any soil at all. Yet there were humble farmhouses in the middle of small patches of cultivated ground, and here and there, the stone cabin of some labourer.

One such cabin, put together with little or no mortar, had been built apparently within the last year. It contained only one room, to which was attached a stable where a mule was feeding. Two bundles of firewood lay on the ground in front of the door, and behind the house, a man and a woman, working side by side, were digging out the stones and piling them in small heaps. They were too far from the road for me to guess their age, but both must surely have been quite young, for only youth could have possessed the courage and optimism to build a home in so hostile an environment.

By this time, we had travelled more than thirty kilometres, and there was still no sign of the gorge and its strange necropolis. Three roadmen whom we interrogated told us that we should have turned off the highway near the second village, but that having come so far out of our way we might better adopt an alternative route. Take the road that runs off to the right about two hundred metres ahead, they said, follow it down the slope for three kilometres, and you will come to the necropolis. And they added, perhaps because we looked a little doubtful, that it was quite a good road, which our Topolino could negotiate without hazard. We found this statement perfectly true—for two hundred yards. Thereafter, the road became very rough and so narrow that it was impossible to turn around. Lacking any alternative we kept going, gradually descending, all the time in second gear, until at the end of about two kilometres we came to a wide turn-around platform and a small stone shed. There the road ended, but just ahead of us a string of twenty to thirty labourers was building a long flume for the stream below, which was being harnessed for electric power. They told us that to find the necropolis we would have to proceed on foot down the hill to a cliff overhanging the river, whence some of the cells were visible on an opposing cliff. Actually to reach them, however, was impossible without ladders and other equipment, since the cliff was almost perpendicular.

The engineer-in-charge now appeared and suggested that we accompany him down the slope toward the river, he himself being on his way there to start a motor that pumped up water for the mid-day meal. He led us to a cliff divided by the river and the railway from another, one hundred and fifty yards away, which was so pitted with cells, some round and some square, that it looked for all the world like an enormous honeycomb, or a cluster of holes made by giant bank-swallows. Prominent above the cells was a large cave which some hermit had occupied during the early years of the Christian era. And visible farther up the gorge were more honeycombs, one beyond another, until they vanished from sight behind a hill.

When we returned to the car, the inquisitive workmen gathered around us as usual like a crowd of schoolchildren. They complimented my Swiss companion on the fluency with which she spoke Italian, and they introduced us to the inevitable veteran who had been a prisoner of war in England and spoke a few words of the English language. I have no doubt that they would cheerfully have dragged our car back to the highway had we needed their assistance, but luckily it climbed the slope again under its own power, after my companion lightened its load by walking, without actually pushing the vehicle, up some of the steeper places.

IV

Late in the autumn, many birds that had summered in Central Europe flew south for the winter, and some of them ended their migration in Sicily. Just after sunset one evening, as I stood idly under the last palm tree on the avenue in Siracusa that joins the old part of the city to the new, I heard a ceaseless twittering that completely drowned the noise of the traffic, and, looking up, observed several hundred birds fluttering from the telegraph lines to the eaves of some high buildings, from the eaves to the tree-tops, and from the tree-tops to the telegraph lines again. I thought that they were chaffinches, but was not at all sure of their species, and an Italian who was loitering near me could not enlighten me. He told me, however, that every winter night at sunset they roosted in the eight end trees of this avenue and that no one paid any attention to them, although they poured showers of leaf fragments on the people and the ground below.

It was now my turn to be questioned. "Where do you come from?" the man asked me. "You are not an Italian." When I replied that I had come from Canada he said, in slightly broken English, "I lived nine years in Canada, from 1914 to 1922. I was working in British Columbia for the Consolidated Mining and Smelting Company." He then went on to tell me that he had returned to his native Siracusa in 1922, intending to stay only a few weeks, but because the girl he had married during those weeks had been reluctant to leave her parents for a foreign land, he had bought a little store in the city and stayed on. Now he had four children, and his little store was earning him a modest livelihood; but he wished that he could return to Canada because the working hours in Italy were too long and government taxes almost unbearable.

Another evening, I joined a crowd of about 2,000 people who had gathered in the main square of Siracusa to hear a speech by the Sicilian senator Li Causi, ostensibly to commemorate the twenty-ninth anniversary of the founding of the Italian Communist Party. Like the official of the Italian Socialist party who spoke from the same balcony a week later—not by accident, I suspect, for there seemed to be little or no difference between the two parties—, he denounced the imperialism of England and the United States, denounced the capitalists of northern Italy, condemned the government for brutally using police to break up legitimate parades of striking workmen and prevent the occupation of disused land by destitute peasants, demanded the partition of all the large estates among the workers, and the establishment of a truly free and democratic government that would end unemployment and give the country lasting peace. He was an eloquent orator, and every now and then, the attentive crowd interrupted him with hand clapping and cries of *bravo*, but I noticed that only about twenty-five percent of the people joined in the applause, and that the rest appeared interested but distinctly sceptical.

A gathering of quite a different character took place the day before Li Causi's meeting. To mark the feast of St. Sebastian, the church authorities paraded through the streets of the old town a life-sized image of the saint, preceding it with a smartly uniformed and well-conducted band. When darkness set in, they illumined the image with candles and transported it to a church in the newer part of the city. Considerable numbers of women and children, and a few old men, joined the procession, but almost all the able-bodied men continued their usual pursuits or watched rather indifferently from the sidewalks.

These two nearly simultaneous incidents strengthened my earlier, half-latent impression that in this early post-war period, the hearts and minds of the Italian people concealed a great void. The rosy dreams of the old fascist regime had ended in suffering and want, and all the promises of the new political parties, including the Communist, struck their ears with a hollow ring. Disillusioned and sceptical of everything, they had lost faith in themselves and in their leaders, lost faith too in their church, which had failed to bring them hope and comfort in the dark days of defeat and invasion. Life had become weighed down with hardships. Blind victims of a blind and heartless fate, they were awaiting a new prophet, a new vision that would fill the inner void and lead them to a more secure and peaceful existence. A few individuals seemed full of hope, but the majority were apprehensive, fearing that a false prophet, a wrong leader, might once again lead the country into a bloody civil war.

I happened to be dreaming along these lines one day at the old Greek theatre—a place so sunny and peaceful that I spent many of my morning hours there—when a large crowd of tourists suddenly drove up to the entrance, accompanied by three young men from the quaestor's office, one of whom had helped me renew my driving license when I arrived in Siracusa. Noticing that I sat alone, this man came over to talk to me. His crowd consisted mainly of Italians, he said, but there were a few Swiss and French tourists among them, and even one or two English. The conversation gradually drifted around to the local labour situation and the great number of unemployed men who loitered all day in the Siracusan streets. Up to this point my companion had spoken very quietly, but now a dam seemed to break inside him and his words came with a rush.

"They put me in the army when I was twenty one," he said, "and I was a soldier for twelve years. I served in Italy, Tripolitania, Libya, and Somaliland. For five years, I was a prisoner of war in Uganda. When at last I returned to Italy, my parents were dead and my home had been destroyed by a bomb. They wanted to throw me out on the street without work, without money, without anything, and when I protested they told me that the only thing for me to do was to join the police. So I was given this job at the Questor's office because I speak a little English. But it is not a real job. I want to work, to make a home for myself and raise a family, and there seems to be no work for me here in Italy. The Christian Democrats promise us this and the Communists promise us that, but we can't believe anything the politicians tell us. I wish I could emigrate to Australia, for I've heard that there is room on the land there for half a million Italians."

The following morning, this man left a note at my hotel saying that he would call again at 3 p.m. and conduct me, if I wished, through the old fort at the entrance to Siracusa, which had been used as a barracks for many years and was therefore not open to the public without a special permit. Actually, it contained very little of interest, even architecturally, for it had been shattered and rebuilt several times without regard to style or beauty. Nevertheless, I enjoyed the fine view from its foreland, and appreciated still more the young man's friendly gesture.

The time arrived at last when I should move from Siracusa to another city. The evening before I left, I went as usual to buy my newspaper at a little store kept by an elderly lady who had been born and brought up in Venice, and who always seemed nostalgic for her old home. When I said goodbye to her, she thanked me for my steady patronage, wrote her name on a card, and asked me to send her a postcard after I returned to northern Italy, preferably one from Venice. I had never given her my name, or bought anything in her store except the daily paper and an occasional weekly, but Italians are very warm-hearted, and it is the little things of life that give pleasure and create friends.

The highway from Siracusa around the southeast corner of Sicily took me to Modica and Ragusa, two towns perched on the cliffs of limestone ravines, each with a few houses excavated in the rock itself. I noticed that every farmhouse on the plateau beyond Ragusa was a regular fortress; its windows were small and inaccessible except by ladder, and it was surrounded with a solid stone wall that possessed only one entrance.

From the plateau, the road snaked down to the depressingly slummy town of Comiso, in whose main square I stopped to replenish my car's fuel tank. Both the square and the streets

Figure 34 Stone farmhouse on stony land west of Siracusa, Sicily, 1950.
Photo by D. Jenness

leading into it were crowded with people, who looked curiously, first at the licence plate on my car, then at myself. But they asked me no questions, and even chased away a small beggar boy who sidled up to me with outstretched hand.

I had now passed out of the rocky area into a fertile plain green with wheat and vegetables, the latter mainly beans and peas, but in places also artichokes, cauliflowers, and fennel. Outside one of the farmhouses, a merchant who had been negotiating for its cauliflower crop signalled me and asked me to drive him ten kilometres ahead to Licata, the place where the Allied forces landed on the first day of their Sicilian invasion during the Second World War.

At the next small town, Palma di Montechiaro, I picked up another hitchhiker, this one a clerk in the government service who was going home for his weekend. He was more intelligent, or at least more talkative, than his predecessor, and expatiated at length on the land question, and on the many kilometres that the labourer had to travel each day, on muleback or in a mule cart, between his home in the town and the fields in which he worked. Certainly, there were hardly any houses in the rolling, badly eroded countryside between Palma di Montechiaro and Agrigento, and we passed numerous mules that were tied up at the roadside while their owners, usually in groups of from two to five, worked all day in the adjacent fields. My companion drew my attention to one cultivated area covering perhaps three or four square miles, and said that it belonged to a single individual, a very wealthy man who paid his labourers only 400 lire (about 72 cents) a day.

It was impossible to check his statement, of course, and I was warned later than many large estates registered in the name of one man belonged to a whole family. My companion may have been wrong in this particular instance, but he unquestionably laid his finger on one very important reason for the social unrest prevalent in Sicily, and in parts of the Italian mainland.

My host at Agrigento was an unusual type of hotelkeeper. From his appearance and dress, he could have been mistaken for an English squire, for he was tall and rather portly, and he wore knee breeks and a hunting jacket. Also, he spoke fluent English, with an accent that could hardly have come from anywhere except England itself. He told me that he had lived in London for a year and a half, and that he had many English friends. In fact, two or three artists from that country were represented in the score or more paintings that covered the walls of his private sitting room, paintings contributed by various people who had stayed at his hotel. He treasured, too, a case of Irish coins which an English friend had sent him in remembrance of some archaeological researches that they had carried out together.

But these were not his only acquisitions. He had owned and excavated, he said, an ancient Greek necropolis, and he let me handle some of his finds, which he kept in a glass-fronted cabinet. There were two large Attica vases, one that dated from the fifth century B.C. and the other from the fourth century B.C., some smaller vases also from Attica, two or three pottery lamps, several clay figurines, and a few other objects, any or all of which, except the two big vases, he was willing to sell me at a reasonable price. The bottom shelves of the cabinet contained fossil shells that he had collected in different parts of Sicily, and in another room he kept a few minerals.

Most remarkable of all, however, was the large album in which he had painted all the wildflowers of Sicily, and written beneath them their names in Latin, Italian, German, and in some cases English. For several years, he had spent most of his evenings making these watercolour sketches, which he had hoped a German firm in Dresden would reproduce in book form, but the war had interrupted his negotiations, and now he feared that his sketches would never see the light of day.

My Topolino found a resting place a few yards from his hotel in the workshop of a Signor Moschera, a wrought-iron artist who had fallen on evil days. Twenty years earlier, his work had won him a medal at the London Art and Industrial Exhibition, and earlier still, King Victor Emmanuel of Italy had created him a chevalier for making a magnificent iron wreath to decorate the tomb of Queen Margherita. He had fashioned a gate for a wealthy Englishman, and doorknockers and lamps for other clients.

Then the war came, and a bomb destroyed his home in Palermo, together with all his equipment. Now he was making automobile radiators, under the patronage, apparently, of my host the hotelkeeper. In 1949, he sent President Truman two wrought-iron flowers as samples of his workmanship, but all he received in acknowledgement was a courteous letter from the U.S. consul general in Palermo. "I should have sent them to Mrs. Truman," he said with a rue smile, "for of course the President himself would never have time even to look at them."

Agrigento was another of those towns that lay on a hilltop, looking out over a fertile plain at the distant sea. From my bedroom window, I could see the ruins of its famous Greek temples standing on a low ridge above orchards of olive and almond trees. They were not more than a kilometre away as the crow flies, but perhaps twice as far by the highway, which curved and recurved up the steep hillside. The sun rose over their white pillars on a cloudless sky, inducing me to dress hastily and ring the bell for an early breakfast. It consisted, as usual, of one small pot of black coffee and another of hot milk, some bread, two or three pats of butter and a tiny dish of apricot jam. What was not usual, however, was the return of the maid in less than twenty minutes, and her cheerful smile as she poured the dregs of the coffee into my empty cup and gulped them down, then ate the remainder of the jam, after smearing it on a small crust of bread which she had been keeping somewhere in her dress. I could not help wondering whether her employer made her pay for all her meals, as did my chambermaids in Siracusa, and whether this was her method of obtaining a breakfast for nothing.

After spending the morning at the temples, I wandered toward mid-afternoon along the hillcrest east of the city, where men were quarrying the soft, calcareous tufa into large building blocks. Farther on was a disused quarry, about eighty feet square and twenty feet deep, divided by low partitions into open stalls, one of which housed three goats, another two mules, and a third some poultry. Four caves in the walls sheltered other goats, and on top of one wall was a single-story dwelling whose iron balcony actually overhung the quarry. I could not see whether an inside staircase led directly from the house into the pit below, but as I looked down from the roadside, I had the curious feeling of seeing one of the roofless ruins in Roman Pompeii suddenly filled with life again.

Beyond these quarries, the road became a narrow pathway that led past a row of small dwellings to a high precipice facing north towards a wide valley. As I passed the last dwelling, which was merely a cave in a low bank, a sad-faced woman greeted me with a friendly "good evening" (*sera*: "evening," began for Italians about 3 p.m.). I walked on then for a few more yards, but turned back rather hastily when the path grew narrower and was skirting the very edge of the precipice behind two fenced-in houses. The sad-faced woman advised me to return, pass through the gate in the fence, and circle round in front of the houses instead of behind them. This I did, and arrived at a pinnacle which opened up a vast panorama stretching in three directions for several miles. So magnificent was the view that I felt grateful to the woman for her advice, and stopped to thank her when I retraced my steps down the path.

In this way began a conversation, on my part only half understood, since she used many words from the Sicilian dialect. I gathered, however, that her eldest son, twenty-one years of age, had been killed in North Africa, that her former home had been destroyed by a bomb, that her husband and a boy of fourteen had left her for some reason, perhaps to seek work, and that she lived in this cave with her two daughters, one eleven years of age and the other twelve, both of whom were attending school in the city. Their dinner that evening was to be the spinach I had seen her culling—no fish or cheese or figs, not even a crust of bread. She did not beg, or ask me to help her, but I could see tears in her eyes as she invited me to look over their dwelling. It consisted of two small rooms, both scrupulously clean, an outer one that contained a table, a large clay pitcher, and a tiny stove, and an inner one with two rag-covered beds and a collection of photographs on one wall. Nothing else. No cupboard, no scrap of food except the greenery on the table in the outer room. I asked her where she obtained her water, and she said that she carried it in her pitcher from a house one hundred and fifty yards away.

There was nothing I could do to help her. When I mentioned her circumstances to my hotel proprietor that evening, he merely shrugged his shoulders and remarked that there was much misery in the city. What he said was quite true, and I believe his attitude expressed not so much callousness as that feeling of helplessness which overwhelms the individual in the face of wide-spread suffering. One can find numbers of rich people in Sicily, but also scores of thousands who are living at the perpetual hunger level, and only far-reaching changes in the economy of the island can improve their lot.

For several years, Italian newspapers, and some foreign ones also, had been thrilling the public with accounts of a Sicilian bandit named Giuliano, a kind of Robin Hood, according to one group of writers, and a Jesse James according to others. In any event he was an outlaw who so far had successfully defied the Italian government and its police from his hiding-places in the mountains south and west of Palermo. It is not for a foreigner to say whether his "revolt" had a political as well as an economic aspect, as some Italians asserted. What is certain is that armed police patrols that had been scouring the countryside for months had clashed with members of his band on several occasions, and the casualties had been luridly headlined in the daily papers of both Sicily and Italy. Consequently, there was a widely spread feeling that the highways of western Sicily were rather unsafe for travellers, and the police chief at Siracusa, just before my departure, had advised me to consult the police in Agrigento prior to undertaking the next hop to Palermo. At Agrigento, however, and later in Palermo, people scoffed at the notion of any danger, and the police officer in the former city was quite surprised at my asking him whether it would be wise to take the direct highway overland to the north coast. I suspect, therefore, that distance and the newspapers had greatly magnified the trouble, and that for the ordinary traveller, the highways in western Sicily were just as safe as those in other parts of Italy.

Not all of them, however, were as good. The highway that ran northwest from Agrigento to Palermo was paved and fairly smooth for the first five or six miles, but from there on, paved and unpaved stretches alternated, and I found the unpaved stretches not only rough but muddied by a misty rain. It traversed a region of low mountains, irregular and completely treeless. In one rocky defile, the scenery was as savage as in the wilder parts of Wales. There were few villages, none large enough to be called a town, and long stretches of the highway lacked any habitations at all. Not even the most exacting traveller would have complained of the traffic. In a hundred kilometres, I met only one motorcar, although I passed dozens of men and boys travelling on mules or in mule carts, either to the villages—for it was Sunday—or to and from their fields, since even steep slopes had been planted to wheat and beans. Many of these men had swathed their faces in black shawls which concealed everything except their eyes and noses, giving them the appearance of highwaymen, but this derogatory comparison seemed ungenerous, for whenever I waved to them most of them waved back and a few smiled.

The bars of a railway crossing halted me in one place, but a train passed within three minutes and the bars immediately rose again. Not always does the traveller meet with such luck. I was once held up at a crossing near Siracusa, along with two other motorists and several carts. No train ever appeared, but after nearly an hour a very drowsy woman emerged from the house of the crossing-keeper, opened up the barrier without a word of apology or regret, and went indoors again to resume her slumber.

After driving for four hours through desolate mountains, it was almost exhilarating to arrive within sight of the sea again. But the sky was grey and the rain falling steadily as I turned west along Sicily's north coast and, cautiously threading my way through Palermo's eastern suburbs, drew up at last in front of the Villa Lincoln, just behind the Botanical Gardens.

V

The large city of Palermo lies on the northwest coast of Sicily on a small bay hemmed in by a semicircle of mountains. The local people affectionately called their coastline *conca d'oro* (Golden Shell), and indeed their harbour does present the shape of a cockleshell. But the bombs of the Allied forces had struck the city mercilessly during the recent war, because it was the jumping-off place for North Africa. They had made homeless, I was told, 40,000 people. Those who could, fled to the mountains, but the majority had to take refuge in the basements of their houses and in the air-raid shelters on or near every street. Now that peace had come, they were displaying wonderful resilience, but in spite of what they had accomplished, a short walk in almost any direction still revealed large open spaces and piles of shattered masonry. When I went to visit the National Museum it was closed for repairs. So also were two of the oldest churches, while several others were nothing but empty shells. Fortunately, one of the city's principal treasures, the twelfth-century Palatine Chapel with its beautiful mosaics and marbles, was untouched. And no bombs fell near the unique cathedral and cloister in the suburb of Monreale, which were built in the same century as the chapel, and in the same Norman-Arabic style. The guide who conducted me through the cathedral told me that he had been raised in Boston and trained as an electrical engineer in the Boston Technical School. "Here I am stuck in this dump," he added moodily, and I could well understand his discontent, for even in sunny Italy dependence on tips is neither pleasant nor very remunerative.

One building that happily escaped the war was the headquarters of the University of Palermo in the very centre of the city. About 12,000 students of both sexes, and from all the western part of Sicily, attended this university, which offered courses in law, medicine, engineering and agriculture, in addition to the usual arts and science subjects. I asked its rector what the average student paid for a year's tuition, including board and lodging in the city. He estimated about 30,000 lire [about 55 Canadian dollars], which was much less than what Canadian students were paying at that time in McGill University and the University of Toronto.

The term examinations were in full swing when I first called at his office, and a delegation of student veterans had gathered there to voice some grievance. Two days later, in another office, I found the head of the geography department pacing up and down in a mood of deep depression because some of his pupils had failed to answer the simplest questions. But that same day, outside the university, a crowd of students gaily marched along the street, one of them arm-in-arm with a smartly dressed young woman whose stride seemed remarkably masculine, for it was the first day of the pre-Easter carnival, and Sicilian students, like young people the world over, preferred the vivid realities of life to musty books and dull examinations.

Many boys and girls who were studying English frequented the British Institute a few doors away, which placed at their disposal a good library of English books and all the important English journals and newspapers. I, too, was welcomed there, and one evening attended a lecture, delivered in Italian, on English literature of the twentieth century. Another evening, four or five university students staged a puppet show in the same hall. It was an Italian rendering of Shakespeare's *Richard III*, and about two hundred people, all Italians except myself, listened with rapt attention as the players juggled the figures and declaimed their lines. Puppet shows are not as popular in this age of television and motion pictures as they were thirty and forty years ago, yet only a fortnight later, I heard a player's voice issuing from a shabby booth on one of Rome's main piazzas, and joined the score of people who watched him juggle his two dolls.

The itinerant organ grinder, on the other hand, still managed to hold his own, perhaps because Sicilians, and their cousins in South Italy, are unable to live without noise. I must have

Figure 35 Vegetable-laden donkey cart, its sides painted with scenes from Sicily's early history, Palermo, Sicily, 1950.
Photo by D. Jenness

seen a dozen organ grinders in Palermo alone, each of them attended by a small boy or girl to stretch out a hand to the passers-by. The monkey that once squatted on the organ had disappeared, but an oracular parakeet sometimes warned the petitioner of his fate by delivering to him a printed slip of paper.

The organ grinders generally kept to the broader streets. In the narrow slum lanes (and there were many in Palermo), the children provided their own entertainment. All boys from three years upward played football, of course, as they do everywhere in Italy. A laughing, shrieking, struggling mob of some two hundred children engulfed me one afternoon, while they were pursuing a fantastic figure mounted on high stilts. On another occasion, I followed a children's procession behind a six-piece drum-and-fife-band; the drums were broken buckets and the fifes small sticks of wood. Palermo's main streets were reasonably clean, but in these slum areas, muddy with the winter's thunderstorms and often littered with garbage, it was pathetic to walk beneath the lines of multi-coloured laundry that covered the fronts of all the houses from one end of the street to the other, and to observe the half-clad infants playing in the dirt while their care-worn mothers or older sisters ceaselessly scrubbed the family rags.

The harbour front had been completely shattered during the war, when Allied-forces' bombs destroyed not the docks alone, but all the streets leading to them. The piers themselves were rebuilt as soon as hostilities ended, and now reconstruction gangs were working in three places along the esplanade behind them. In each place was posted a large placard that described the work in progress, reported the name of the firm that had undertaken the contract, stated the amount of money involved, and acknowledged that the funds had been contributed by E.R.P. (European Recovery Program). This making known to all and sundry the amount of each contract seemed to me an excellent idea, and I wondered whether we might not profitably follow the same practice in Canada. As for the E.R.P., which was providing nearly all the funds, those three letters opened up another story of which I obtained a glimpse from the Lands Branch of the Sicilian government, whose chief generously authorized his officers to spread out their files before me and to answer any questions that I might ask them.

Many of the problems with which these officials were contending arose from the mountainous character of the island and the predominance of an impermeable clay in its soil. This clay prevented the winter rain from soaking deeply into the sub-soil, with the result that it rushed down the slopes in sudden floods, which washed away much of the top-soil, carved deep ravines and gullies, and stagnated when it reached the coastal plains, creating marshes that provided fertile breeding-grounds for the malaria-carrying mosquito. Yet enough of the water remained in the surface soil to render it sodden and greasy, especially at the end of winter, when steep slopes tended to break away in destructive landslides. Every year, for as long as people could remember, local newspapers had reported how some hilltop house or hamlet had been swept away by a landslide and its occupants buried in the abyss. And in Sicily alone, government officials had listed eight villages so endangered that they were to be evacuated as soon as new homes could be built for their inhabitants.

I myself did not fully appreciate this characteristic of Sicilian soil until I visited the picturesque town of Cefalu, eighty kilometres east of Palermo, to see its fine old cathedral. After spending three hours in the town itself, I followed its beach westward and tried to climb a grass-covered slope in order to take a photograph. The slope was not particularly steep, and its surface seemed perfectly dry, no rain having fallen for at least two days, but the ground was so water-laden and slippery that I was unable to climb more than a very short distance, and at every step on the way down, the whole bank seemed to be giving way under me. When I finally did reach the bottom again, I noticed that a considerable landslide had occurred a few hours before, a hundred yards farther along the beach.

The night boat from Palermo reached Naples in twelve hours, and the trip must be very pleasant on a calm summer night, with the flames of Stromboli's volcano visible on the horizon; but when I boarded the steamer just before 6 p.m., a cool stiff breeze was blowing, and along with all the other passengers, I gladly abandoned the deck for my cabin. Before 8 a.m. the next morning, my Topolino had been discharged onto the Naples dock, and I was heading northward along the Via Casilina in the direction of Cassino and Rome.

This highway ran through a broad, well-cultivated plain for some fifty kilometres, after which the country became more rolling, and hills high enough to be called mountains bound the view on either side. The traveller coming from Sicily notices the more even diffusion of farms and houses, and particularly the absence of donkeys and mules; not their complete absence, to be sure, but for every mule there would seem to be about twenty horses, whereas in Sicily the proportion was just the reverse. The soil, too, was well drained and well watered, evidently neither too sodden in winter nor so parched during the hot summer months as to check all growth. In short, it is a fertile, pleasant land that must have seemed a paradise to the early Greeks who colonized it several centuries before Christ.

Cassino, where I stopped an hour, resembled an Italian version of a Canadian mining settlement undergoing its first boom. Allied-forces' bombs and shells had razed to the ground the old town, which nestled on the hillside under the famous monastery. Nothing remained there

Figure 36 Shattered town of Cassino, Italy, spring 1944.
Photo by J.L. Pete Jenness

but rubble.[7] At the foot of the hill on both sides of the highway, however, there had sprung up a town of temporary shacks constructed not of wood, but of brick and stone—food-stores, restaurants, barber shops, and garages—and among them were rising a score or more of fine four-storey buildings, some of them already open for business on the ground floor and occupied as dwellings on the three floors above. Half a dozen large buses were parked outside a new bank on the main thoroughfare. They seemed too luxurious for workmen's buses, but I could see no visitors to account for their presence.

Beyond Cassino lay Frosinone, another of those hilltop towns that had found itself in a backwash and sprouted a new settlement on the plain below. One encountered them all through central and southern Italy as well as in Sicily, centuries-old communities that were desperately re-orienting themselves to meet the conditions of a new era. From the earliest times down to the middle ages and even later, life had been too insecure for farmers to live in the open country among their fields. Instead, they lived in towns that were surrounded with high walls so that they might serve as fortresses in case of need. And naturally towns built on hilltops were easier to defend than towns on the plains. But then came long-range artillery and more recently airplanes, which greatly diminished the value of hilltops and high walls. Furthermore, an industrial age demanded swift and easy communications, and first the railways, then the automobile highways, both of which avoid steep grades, by-passed the hilltop towns and left them in back-eddies. Some of their inhabitants vegetated, hoping for a return of the golden age; others, often the more enterprising, moved down to the railway and the highway, opened up new industries and built new homes.

Thus, new towns arose below the hills, towns that replaced the old narrow lanes and dark alleyways with broad streets and tree-lined avenues. A few gave themselves new names, but the majority retained the names of their mother towns and, if not too remote, united with them through a common administration.

This phenomenon was widely spread, but one observed curious variations of it in southern Italy and Sicily. Near the Strait of Messina, for example, the sea was once a more important highway than the land, and settlements on its shore more exposed to sudden raids. Both for security and to gain more agricultural land, therefore, some of the principal towns, e.g. Gioia Tauro, were built on the nearly level plateau overlooking the sea, and linked to their ports by short roads down the steep escarpment. The national highway ran on top of the plateau through or near the old towns; yet it is not they which are flourishing, but their ports, especially those with good bathing beaches.

Ragusa and Modica in southeast Sicily displayed a pattern peculiar to themselves; the new settlements they sprouted moved up to the plateau, not down. They were inland towns which, to gain security, had hidden themselves against the cliffs of narrow ravines below the level of the surrounding country, and the modern automobile highway passed above them. In all cases, however, the underlying principle seemed to be the same, and for the tourist like myself, it was one of Italy's greatest charms that a few steps from suburb to centre-town could carry him seven or eight hundred years backward from the modern industrial world into the Middle Ages.

---

[7]My father's natural curiosity may have drawn him to visit Cassino, for he was aware that his oldest son, Captain John (Pete) Jenness, had been involved in the heavy fighting that levelled that old community in 1944.

Fortified by a cup of coffee in Frosinone, I drove on to Rome, where Signor Nardizzi offered me the same room in his *pension* as I had occupied a year earlier. He told me that during January and February, the first two months of this Holy Year, or Year of Pilgrimage, the number of visitors to Rome had been disappointingly small, but that everyone was praying that in April and May the present trickle of tourists would turn into a flood. Both the city administration and the Italian government had spent large sums of money to ensure a proper reception for the anticipated crowds, and, quite apart from other considerations, the country stood to suffer a considerable financial loss if the hoped-for flood failed to materialize.

My arrival in Rome coincided with the opening night of Bellini's opera *Norma*, so before unpacking my bag, I rushed over to the theatre to purchase a ticket. My seat was not a good one, but I was lucky to get one at all, for the theatre was so packed that many people had to stand against the back wall. *Norma* has always been popular in Italy, and the audience was most enthusiastic. I heard people softly singing some of the airs before the curtain rose, and at the end of the first act the audience recalled the principals no less than six times. Two of Rome's newspapers the next morning were more discriminating, for they praised some features of the performance and criticized others with what appeared to be impartial pens.

The sky was overcast when I awoke in the morning, and by 9 o'clock the streets were wet with rain. I visited two of my favourite churches, and bought an old parchment sheet of Gregorian music in a bookstore; but late in the afternoon, when the rain showed no signs of abating, I took refuge in a cinema to see the Italian version of Lawrence Olivier's *Henry V*. One could not fail to notice, particularly in the first part of the movie, that the adapter had experienced great difficulty in devising an Italian translation terse enough to fit the movements of the actors' lips. It underscored the fact that in Shakespeare's own lines there is rarely a superfluous word.

The one day I spent in Rome was just a breathing spell before rumbling northward again. A few miles outside the city, two or three families were living in caves in a clay bank, but it was raining, and I did not stop to investigate. Soon afterwards, I came to rolling, rather infertile country where the farmhouses were spaced long distances apart. Two women stood talking near the gate of one of them, and when I drew near, the taller of the two stretched out her arm. "Would I take her as far as Spoleto?" she asked me, and, of course, I opened the door of the car and let her in.

She was about thirty years of age, and must once have been very attractive. Now her face was thin and lined, and there were deep hollows in her cheeks. She told me that her husband had died a few months before, leaving her without resources and with a six-year-old child to support. Her home lay near the farm where I had discovered her, but she was going to Spoleto because someone had told her that she might find work on a certain farm near that town.

Whether her story was true or not I cannot say, for there seemed to be so many widows floating around Italy's highways during this post-war period. Two days before, on the outskirts of Naples, I had picked up a peasant woman who was travelling to Formia, and a few days later, just north of Florence, I was stopped by a third who wanted to visit a friend in Bologna.

One thing I did discover about my Roman companion: she was desperately hungry; for after we had travelled a considerable distance in silence, she timidly asked me for a cigarette, and when I explained to her that I did not smoke, she murmured, "Smoking takes away one's hunger." Only then did I notice her shoes, which were paper thin and gaping in every seam. I asked her if she would lunch with me in Terni, a small town that we would reach about noon, and she accepted quickly. There, at the little restaurant, she gulped down her food so ravenously that I readily believed her when she said that she had eaten nothing for thirty-six hours.

We parted company about 2 p.m. at the farm near Spoleto, but whether she found work there or not, I do not know. Our fleeting encounter was just one more of the innumerable little incidents that make up the sum total of an individual's life.

I myself continued on through Spoleto, and on the other side of that town passed through a long gorge in the mountains that would have been desolate and forbidding in the extreme had it not been dominated by a huge castle, which gave it a picturesqueness lacking in the other monotonous passes we had crossed during the morning. The gorge ended in a wide, fertile valley on whose eastern side, perched on top of a high hill some distance from the highway, stood St. Francis' little town Assisi. A good paved road, lined in places with trees, wound in long curves up the hill, passed under an arch in the city wall, and opened out into an irregular square, one-third of which was occupied by a large church with a fine rose window. The view from the square was magnificent, as it was also from many other parts of the town. On that day at least, everything combined to create a feeling of peacefulness, of partial withdrawal from the restless, struggling world. The valley below with its noisy trains and motor cars seemed strangely remote, while Assisi's own streets and lanes were clean and quiet, unimpeded by wandering animals and traversed only at long intervals by a motor car or truck. Clear above all other sounds rang the bells of the three main churches, St. Francis' own great church partway down the hill, the church in the entrance square, and the cathedral nearer the summit.

The people whom I met, too, were leisurely and courteous. In one small store the "sisters" were examining some linen handkerchiefs embroidered in blue thread, a specialty of Assisi's nuns. "Beware of Florentine machine-made imitations," the storekeeper warned me. Other shops contained majolica from the factories of Deruta twenty-two kilometres or more away. Most of the ware reproduced more or less accurately the forms of seventeenth-century Deruta majolica. But life had changed since that century and the old pottery forms seem ill-adapted to modern homes, the abundance of yellow in the painting less appealing. I saw no tea sets or breakfast sets, for example, but many bowls and pitchers of old-fashioned shapes, and large service plates decorated with portraits in the style of Raphael and Mantegna. My hotel-proprietor told me that one of the schoolteachers in Assisi dabbled in the manufacture of majolica. He modelled, baked, and painted the local clay with his own hands. The few samples I saw of his handiwork, however, were uninspiring.

Assisi was one hill-town that had not declined in the industrial age or felt the need to hive off a new colony down in the valley. It held enough attractions within its walls to delay the stream of tourists travelling from Venice and Florence to Rome, and its aloofness from the highway and railroad, which pass three kilometres away, served to protect its charms. St. Francis sought peace and beauty on this hilltop seven centuries ago, and scores of pilgrims, not all of them his disciples, follow his example today, though most of them come from spring to autumn only. Even such an organization as E.R.P. recognized the special character of the town, for I came on a sign stating that it was contributing to the repair of the little "Church in the Broken Wall." Evidently, someone in that vast organization was great enough to realize that man does not live by bread alone, but that the things of the spirit may be more permanent than walls of brick or stone.

VI

A dark sky, strong wind, and frequent rain showers had followed me from Rome to Assisi, and they continued to dog me from Assisi northward. On the coast to the westward, a gale was raging, a gale so strong that it tore off the roof of the big theatre in La Spezia. In the mountains, however, it raged less fiercely, so that I had no hesitation in taking the highway to Florence. This highway, after skirting the city of Perugia, climbed a long ridge whose summit looks down on Lake Trasimeno, a rather shallow body of water bordered in most places with reeds, despite its being the largest lake in central Italy. On this day, the waves raised by the wind had stirred up the bottom, and, along the shore at least, the water was very muddy and the lake far from beautiful. I could not remember whether it was on its northern or its eastern plain that Hannibal met and defeated the Romans, but both plains are so small that the troops on each side could have done little manoeuvring, unless indeed historians have grossly exaggerated their numbers.

From Lake Trasimeno the highway continued to Arezzo, after which it crossed a high ridge and descended the valley of the Arno River, which flows through Florence (Firenze). Though rain fell steadily and obscured the view, this valley seemed greener and more wooded than others I had passed through, and the farms more like country estates.

I followed the valley down to Figlino, an overgrown village twenty-eight kilometres from Florence, and there, on the main street, met with my first and only accident. Without warning, a girl on a motorcycle suddenly roared out of a laneway to my right and tried to make a left-hand turn in front of me. My car was not travelling more than twenty-five kilometres an hour, but even so it was impossible to avoid her. The left fender struck her motorcycle squarely in the middle and hurled her to the roadway. Almost from nowhere, it seemed, a crowd of about a hundred people gathered around us and lifted her to her feet. Then, seeing that her ankle was swelling and she could not stand, they carried her to another car that happened to be parked nearby and whisked her away to a hospital. I looked around for a policeman to whom I could report the accident, but there was none. The crowd, insisting that I was in no way to blame, urged me to continue on my way, and even trundled my car along the street to start the engine again, but the wretched machine balked. A local mechanic then worked over it for three hours and succeeded in making the engine turn over, but it broke down a second time six kilometres from Florence, which I did not reach until nearly midnight. There it spent a day and a half in a garage undergoing a complete overhaul. As for the girl, I heard before I left Figlino that her ankle was not broken but merely bruised, and that the hospital had sent her straight home.

Normally, it would have been sheer pleasure to spend a day and a half in Florence, but it rained almost continually, and the rain was accompanied by a cold wind. The inclement weather blurred the exteriors of the churches and palaces, and so darkened the interiors that their paintings were hardly visible. Though the outdoors was gloomy, there was no gloom in the welcome I received from Signor Vannini, the leather artist who had exhibited in Paris and other cities. Leatherwork offers little scope for novelty, but he showed me some of his more recent creations, and said that he was looking forward to the spring and summer season of this Pilgrimage Year, when he expected the numbers of tourists would exceed all previous records.

The autostrada from Florence westward to the coast runs through a wide, flat plain intensively cultivated, but apparently rather wet, although its wetness may have been only the temporary effect of several days' rain. The highway had been blocked off at Lucca, presumably for repairs farther on, and motorists had to cross the mountains by an older road, less well graded and full of hairpin curves, but offering glorious views of Viareggio and the sea. From Viareggio, it ran northward parallel to the coast, but along the foot of the mountains, four or five kilometres inland. This was marble country, though Carrara, its most famous centre, lay a few kilometres off my route. I visited one marble quarry close to the highway, and lingered for a few minutes in stone-dressing plants at Pietrasanta, Massa, and one or two smaller villages. In none did I see any of the red, green, or mottled marble that is mined in other parts of Italy; ninety percent of the stone in this locality was white, and the remaining ten percent dun-coloured or streaked with dun-coloured lines.

At Massa, I picked up a mechanic who worked in the naval shipyard of La Spezia. Like so many of his countrymen, he was discouraged by labour conditions in Italy and wanted to emigrate to Buenos Aires, where he was sure that he could earn more money. His wages at the shipyard were 32,000 lire monthly (about $59 Canadian), on which he supported a wife and two children. How he managed to do it I cannot say, unless his wife also earned a significant wage, for food prices along the Riviera at that time seemed very little lower than in Canada.

It was only 5 p.m. when I reached the outskirts of La Spezia, and knowing that the daylight would last at least another hour, I pushed on, not realizing that the next sixty kilometres would be very slow travelling. Right from La Spezia, the road climbed steadily, thinly forested mountains gradually closed in all around me, and for kilometres at a stretch there were neither houses nor people. I dropped down into one small valley where there was a rather dingy village, then, some distance farther on, into a larger one through which flowed a fair-sized stream. Here, on the highway overlooking the stream, was a very humble inn, and on the slope above it the village of Carradano, which on my map had looked like a small but not unimportant town. Darkness was now closing in, and the highway seemed to climb endlessly up and up beyond the village towards some snow-capped mountains. Somewhat reluctantly, therefore, I decided to spend the night at the inn.

The ground floor contained three rooms—a bar with a kitchen behind it, a dining room, and a storeroom for wine flagons and other supplies. Each room opened into the next, and also onto the highway. I was the only guest, and my dinner, which consisted of a bowl of soup followed by a dish of mutton, carrots, and artichoke, was laid out on a small table in the dining room, in the middle of which stood a large iron stove. As soon as I had eaten, a young girl brought in an armful of wood and lit this stove, for the air was chilly, and the warm fire brought in from the bar five men, who pulled up some chairs and grouped around it. A young man in his twenties monopolized most of the conversation. He described some of his experiences during the previous summer in northern France, where for four months he had worked in a coal mine near Lille, in the company of Poles, Spaniards, and other foreigners, and he entertained his companions with smatterings of the various tongues that he had picked up. French, Spanish, and the rest, he explained, are strange languages because you pronounce them one way and write them another. Italian alone is really logical, since it is only in that language that you write words exactly as you pronounce them.

These villagers were friendly and mildly curious, but not as inquisitive as their countrymen in southern Italy and Sicily. One was a woodcutter; the occupations of the others I did not discover. They asked me many questions about Canada and the United States, including, of course, that inevitable one as to whether I thought there was going to be another war. I gathered that they were neither rightists nor leftists, but rather distrusted all political parties and programs, wishing for nothing but peace and enough work to take care of their needs and the needs of their families. Nor was this surprising, for their district had witnessed some of the worst excesses of the civil war of 1943, when the wives and children of Italian partisans, even babes in arms, were massacred without mercy by other Italians who had continued to fight for Mussolini and the Germans.

I felt a little dubious about my bedroom, which lay at the head of a long flight of concrete steps leading from the storeroom to the third floor. It contained a double bed with a good mattress and sheets, but with only one heavy blanket under a red cotton coverlet, a large cupboard, two cane chairs, and a washstand carrying an enamel basin and a jug of cold water. The floor was of concrete, and there were two windows, one tightly shuttered, the other not constructed to open. Everything looked clean, however, and by piling my coat and overcoat on top of me I was able to pass a fairly comfortable night, despite the heavy frost outdoors.

A long climb of about twelve kilometres next morning carried me to the summit of a pine-clad pass, and an equally long descent brought me to Sestri Levante and the Riviera coast. Italians coming here from the south, like Canadians when they cross the Rockies from Alberta into British Columbia, feel that they are passing into another country. One reason was that among themselves Riviera people spoke a peculiar dialect, *Genovese*, which sounded like a blend of French and Italian with a few Arabic words thrown in for good measure, and Italians from other regions hardly understood a sentence.

The climate, too, was different. By day, it could be nearly as warm as southern Italy or even Sicily, but the nights were cooler, the air in winter keener, and between November and March the coast was often lashed by a bitingly cold Alpine wind, which the French called *mistral* and the Italians *tramontana*. Spring came about a month later than in Sicily, for almond and peach trees that had shed most of their blossoms when I left Palermo were just beginning to flower at Sestri Levante and Chiavari. There were many small vegetable gardens, and in terraces on the hillsides, groves of dark-green olive trees, but one saw no large fields of wheat and beans, doubtless because there was seldom room for them between the mountains and the sea. Everything faced the sea: first, the bathing establishments and the palm-lined esplanades along the waterfront; next the rows of luxury hotels and pensions, most of which closed down at the end of summer; and behind these, and all around on the mountain slopes, other hotels and pensions, private villas both large and small, and genuine mansions, many of which also stood barred and shuttered throughout the winter, or were occupied by caretakers only. Finally, there were the exotic palm trees, and the eucalypti and sickly scented mimosas that had been introduced into both the Italian and the French Riviera from distant Australia. Apart from Genoa and two or three smaller ports, it was a tourist's paradise, where nature and man seemed to have vied with each other to satisfy all human desires.

Unfortunately, in our modern world no earthly paradise seems able to close the gate on business and business practices. All along the Italian Riviera were gaudy placards advertising the textiles of this firm, the brandy of that one, and the motorcycles of a third. I especially noticed one placard that had been erected two months earlier on an unusually picturesque headland near the town of Savona. It was a blue and white sign, nine feet wide by five feet high, which carried a large picture of a certain Canadian whisky bottle and the words "famous throughout the world," along with the name and address of its agent in Italy. As I looked at it, musingly, I could not help wondering whether among the numerous lesser sins of our capitalist society we should not also include this one, the almost universal defacing of nature's finest beauty spots.

I did not linger at Sestri Levante, Rapallo, or any of the other tourist resorts of the eastern Riviera, but continued straight on along the highway, stopping only at Nervi, a suburb of Genoa, in order to enquire my way. The man whom I accosted there happened to be a rather morose ex-soldier who had served five years in Albania. He immediately asked me to drive him to the centre of Genoa, and I consented gladly, because Genoa, like numerous other Italian towns, contained many narrow streets running off at odd angles, among which it was easy to wander around in circles. Moreover, it had been heavily bombed during the war, when its seven largest theatres, together with scores of other buildings, were razed to the ground, and the reconstruction that was still proceeding necessitated several detours. Luckily, part of my route lay along the wide waterfront where there was plenty of room to manoeuvre, despite the heaviness of the traffic, for Genoa was one of the busiest ports on the Mediterranean, and the harbour was filled with ships of all sizes and nationalities.

There were no good beaches of fine white sand along the rocky coast from Sestri Levante to Genoa. They began only at Arenzano, twenty kilometres west of that port, and continued from there halfway to the border with France. Each little bay along that part of the coast possessed a stretch of fine sand, separated from the next stretch by a rocky headland tunnelled for a railroad, and in places also for the highway. Small valleys traversed by mountain streams occupied the interspaces between the headlands, which were really spurs jutting out from the mountain chain that ran parallel to the coast.

In an unusually wide valley twenty kilometres west of Arenzano lay the little town of Albisola, which possessed not only an unusually fine beach, but half a dozen majolica factories that used a local clay and occasionally hired first-rate painters, among them Picasso. Their ware was lighter and more brittle than most majolica, and its glaze scratched more easily. Some of their smaller productions were very attractive, and now and then, they turned out large vases worthy to rank with their best creations in the Middle Ages. But as at Deruta, the industry was over-conservative, too many of its products being decorative pieces of old-fashioned shapes suitable only for large mansions.

I passed through Albisola without stopping, but returned to the town a few days later to revisit one of the majolica firms from which I had bought a set of dishes twelve months before.[8] In the little factory at the back of the store, an old man was carefully stacking two or three hundred vessels in a high oven, which he would afterwards brick up and fire for two days. Two men potters on the floor above were modelling small vases on their wheels, and in an adjoining room, four girls were painting some large plates under the watchful eye of the master painter, a man of about fifty. There was also a man to pack the goods, a girl to run the store, and a small boy, beside the two brothers who owned the establishment. In all, therefore, this tiny factory gave employment to twelve persons.

---

[8]The blue-and-white pottery dishes were a wedding present for son Stuart and his bride-to-be in 1949. Unfortunately they tended to chip easily and hence proved more decorative than utilitarian.

Just beyond Albisola lay Savona, an important ship-repair centre and cargo port, which, like Genoa, had been heavily battered during the war. Only two large vessels were moored at its docks as I passed by, but a third was approaching the harbour, a foreign vessel diverted to Savona under an E.R.P. shipbuilding and ship-repair program that was helping to put the city on its feet again. The comparative emptiness of the port had created some temporary unemployment, and several groups of men were gossiping idly on the waterfront, while others lounged in the city's squares.

At Vado Ligure, a much smaller industrial centre just beyond Savona, the people seemed to be celebrating some holiday, for scores of men and women were roaming the streets; but when I enquired at a service station, I learned that it was not a holiday but a strike. Two women had been caught the night before illegally painting political slogans on the stone walls that line the highway between Savona and Vado Ligure; "Down with Scelba" (the Minister of the Interior), read one of them; another, "Men, join the Italian Communist Party and fight for peace." And there were more sentences in the same vein. The police locked up the women for the night, and although it released them in the morning, the executive of the local labour union called a strike to protest against the government's violation of the right to free speech, and the workers faithfully obeyed.

Near the edge of the town was a concrete pool at which a woman and two girls were washing their laundry. I asked permission to photograph them, and after I had snapped their picture, lingered for a few minutes to talk. The woman lamented the high cost of living, and the recent rise in taxes, which had affected the prices of coffee, sugar, and tea. The price of clothing, she thought, had dropped a little in the past year, but feed was dearer. In Vado Ligure people were paying 40 lire ($7\frac{1}{2}$ cents) apiece for cabbages, which farmers around about were feeding to their animals because they could not afford to buy the market licenses requisite for selling their produce in the town. When I mentioned that I had heard a similar complaint in Sicily about oranges, she said "Yes, and the people there are much worse off than we are. Compared to them, we in northern Italy are living like lords." But then she complained of the difficulty in finding work, and asked if I couldn't place her in some Canadian household; she could cook and wash and iron, she added, and she was not afraid to work. Probably she would have made an excellent housekeeper, for most Italian women work very conscientiously. In southern Italy, in fact, they seemed to work much harder than the men.

Two kilometres from Vado Ligure, around a headland and a lighthouse, was the small village of Bergeggi, from which I had started out just ten weeks previously. Only the slowest trains halted at its station, whose platform, barely six carriages long, lay in an opening between two tunnels. A local bus based in Savona provided road transport three times daily, but all other Riviera buses sped by without stopping.

Being so weakly linked with the outside world, the village was unknown to any but northern Italians and to a few French people from across the border. Yet a recent broadcast over the Turin Radio Station had justly described it as the most beautiful spot along the entire coastline. In its new-moon, half-kilometre-wide bay, bounded at each end by a high cliff, the sandy beach occupied only a quarter of the waterfront. The remaining three-fourths was rocky, with reefs extending out a short distance from the shore. There was no flat land; even the highway along the water's edge had been cut out of the cliffs, but the houses were echeloned up the hill slope, and above them, a little to one side, towered a white church. Part of the hillside had been terraced and planted to fruit trees, mainly olives, around whose trunks grew wheat and vegetables. The only industries, if one could call them such, were a tiny bakery and an ancient stone mill, hand-turned, for crushing the olives and extracting their oil.

Virtually all the Bergeggi men worked in Vado Ligure. They left home at 7 a.m. and returned at evening. Throughout the day, therefore, Bergeggi was a village of women and children. Its small hotel accommodated six guests, and several families leased rooms or small apartments during the summer season, when vacationists arrived in droves. But for nine months of the year, the village slumbered, and the climate was so healthy that some of the old people kept on dreaming until they were nearly one hundred.

Here in Bergeggi, my vagabonding came to an end. Looking back, it had been wonderfully interesting, despite the occasional misadventure. Throughout both Italy and Sicily, the scenery had been varied and often beautiful, and the people friendly and helpful. A few, it is true, had been tempted to cheat the foreigner who spoke their language imperfectly, but others had gone out of their way to smooth my path or to show me hospitality. Ruined temples and old churches, ancient towers, and crumbling walls, had revived the sense of history that we inhabitants of the New World generally lack. It had seemed strange, at first, to hear people speak of the fifteenth century, the *cinquecento*, as though it were only yesterday. But history does not give men their daily bread, and I had seen, also, some of the problems of an underdeveloped, overpopulated land that possessed limited resources: ten people trying desperately to scratch a living from patches of ground that could support only five; half-naked infants crawling in muddy streets; squalid homes; women and children waiting around soup kitchens; and hundreds of men lounging idly in city squares because there was no work for them. Perhaps the chief impression I gained from my journey was a feeling of sadness that millions of people should have to struggle so hard to obtain the barest necessities of life, and a puzzled doubt whether for many of them life could have any real meaning.

One task still remained. The car had to be returned to its owner. I had hired it for three months, and was entitled to use it until the expiration of the contract; but now that it had brought me back to my starting-point, I was satisfied. It had been a regular jinx from the day I took it over, and it retained its character to the very end. The day before I intended to surrender it, the battery ran down because the generator had stopped functioning, and the next morning a spring broke in the door handle just five kilometres from the owner's home. Some day, perhaps, I may resume my vagabonding on Italy's highways and byways, but never, never again will I travel in a second-hand, first-series Topolino.

1955–1956: A WINTER IN TROUBLED CYPRUS

18

Diamond Jenness

[*Between 1948 and 1959, my parents rented their three-story duplex brick house at 108 Broadway Avenue, Ottawa, then spent their winters in warmer locales and their summers at their secluded waterfront cottage on the Gatineau River about eighteen miles north of Ottawa. The two apartments in their old house, created through remodelling in 1946, provided sufficient rental money when added to my father's government pension for them to winter abroad during many of those years. My mother, having been born in Ottawa, would have been content to winter in the upstairs apartment of their house, a house her father had purchased and in which she had lived since about 1910. However, in 1957, she arranged to have a small bungalow built overlooking the Gatineau River a mile north of their summer cottage, and two years later, my father sold the old house in town. Mother loved the view down the Gatineau River from her new home, and the peace and quiet that surrounded it, but I do not think my father found the same contentment there. He had grown up in subtropical Wellington, New Zealand, had suffered a heart attack in the 1940s that somewhat restricted his activities, and disliked the cold blowing winds and deep snowdrifts of Canadian winters. Now retired, he wanted to travel and study in warmer countries flanking the Mediterranean where he might renew some of his early love of the classics, including visiting the sites of ancient Greek and Roman settlements he had studied during his university days.*

By the mid 1950s, my father and mother had spent three winters in Italy, two in Mexico, and one in Spain. An unexpected but welcome grant of money in 1954 from the Guggenheim Foundation in New York, to work on any project to his liking, permitted him and Mother to winter in Cyprus, a British crown colony off the Turkish coast since 1925. Since his student days, he had envisioned spending several months in Cyprus, "studying its complicated ethnic background, and man's use—and abuse—of its uptilted and karst land surface."[1]

In the fall of 1955, however, Cyprus was far from peaceful. For a year, it had experienced increasing numbers of violent attacks between the majority Greek Cypriots, who were demanding self-determination for the island, and their long-time enemies, the Turkish Cypriots, who occupied the eastern end of the island. The organization promoting the Greek self-determination was known as EOKA. It was strongly encouraged by the government of Greece and the Greek Orthodox Church to pursue its disruptive tactics. The minority Turkish Cypriots, for the most part, tried to live peacefully, somewhat comforted by their proximity to Turkey and its protective military forces. Archbishop Makarios, the head of the Greek Orthodox Church in Cyprus since his election in 1950, had pledged to achieve self-determination

---

[1] This quotation is from an unfinished article on Cyprus by D. Jenness, in the possession of S.E. Jenness in 2006.

for his people on Cyprus. British military forces stationed on the island to maintain law and order between the two rival peoples and also to protect the Turkish minority, came under attack regularly from the Greek Cypriots, as my parents soon discovered. However, having been "reassured by Cypriot scientists that the troublemakers were only unruly school children who would quickly turn to their studies again,"[2] my father and mother set off from New York for Naples, Italy. While awaiting a ship to Athens, they explored Naples and nearby Amalfi and Paestum for several days. Their ship then took them through the Strait of Messina, across the Ionian Sea, and through the Corinth Canal before reaching Athens. From there they boarded another ship and sailed to Limassol, Cyprus, for another winter's adventure.]

I

The course of true love never runs smoothly, says the proverb. But neither has the history of Love's Isle, Cyprus, where in the world's first days, according to the fairy tale that ancient Greece handed down to us 3,000 years ago, Venus, the Queen of Love, rose from the foamy sea to complicate the hitherto tranquil lives of men and beasts. Today,[3] Venus—or perhaps rather her underground allies—is once again stirring up Cyprus's froth and foam, as my wife and I discovered ten years since, when we spent a winter on the island.

We went there not on our honeymoon, which we had relegated to ancient history more than thirty years before,[4] but after preparations more prolonged and less romantic than those which had preceded our earlier honeymoon voyage. A generous fellowship conferred on me by the John Simon Guggenheim Foundation of New York several years after I had been retired from the Canadian government provided me with unexpected funds to "conclude any unfinished business that weighed on my conscience," which meant—or I interpreted to mean—that I might expend them on any research my government duties had prevented me from pursuing.

Now ever since my college days, I had been haunted by a desire to learn why in recent centuries almost every island in the eastern Mediterranean, as well as large regions of the adjacent mainland, had become barren and rocky wastes, although many of them were heavily forested in the centuries before Christ. Cyprus, the largest and most isolated of the islands, had undergone more vicissitudes in the course of history than any other, yet it alone had escaped the general denudation.

Most of its inhabitants had spoken the Greek language for three millennia, though they were never ruled from Greece, but, in the pre-Christian era, by local kings and chieftains, and from the Dark Ages onward, by successive conquerors who spoke alien tongues: Egyptian, French, Italian, Turkish and, from 1878 until a few years ago, English. In the mid-1950s, about eighty percent of the population acknowledged Greek as its mother tongue, twenty percent Turkish, but nearly all spoke English also. And much of Cyprus's history has been recorded in English. Since that is also my native tongue, Cyprus was obviously the most suitable of all the Mediterranean islands on which to begin my studies.

---

[2]*Ibid.*

[3]In 1966, when my father wrote this chapter.

[4]My father and mother were married less than two weeks after he stepped off the troop ship in Halifax returning him from the First World War in April 1919. Four days after their wedding, they entrained for Vancouver and a three-month honeymoon trip to New Zealand.

In October 1955, my wife and I sailed for Naples, passing en route sufficiently close to the Azores Islands to photograph their smoking volcano. At Naples, we transferred to a small steamer, which carried us through the Corinth Canal to Athens, and from Athens to Cyprus. On this last leg of our voyage, we encountered so severe a storm that only eight passengers braved either the deck or the dining room. The rest took refuge in their cabins, among them, to our contentment, three young beatniks from California who were travelling on to Israel, whether as tourists or immigrants I did not discover.

Late in the afternoon of the second day out from Athens, our vessel arrived off the small port of Limassol, on Cyprus's south coast, and dropped anchor there about half a mile from the shore. The anchor's clang summoned two open motorboats, which shot out from behind a long mole[5] and raced toward us to unload our Cyprus-bound passengers and freight. Nearly twenty passengers then lined up on the deck to disembark, all except my wife and myself Greek-speaking Cypriots or Greeks from the mainland.

The disembarkation procedure was original, as was also our reception when we reached the shore. Our steamer, anchored in an unprotected roadstead, pitched and rolled so erratically that neither of the two motorboats dared approach it save with extreme caution. Each disembarkee descended a rope ladder to within six or eight feet of the tossing water; then, at a shout from below, he closed his eyes and leaped into the void, fervently praying that he would fall into the arms of the two stout seamen precariously balanced on the motorboat's prow. None of us, fortunately, had attained Falstaff's dimensions; what would have happened in such a contingency I shudder to contemplate. My wife was among the first to descend the ladder. She leaped through the air as coolly as if she expected to alight on *terra firma*, and I, her lifeguard for more than three decades, could do no less than follow her, whether the descent carried me to safety or to a watery perdition.

It was dark when the motorboat landed us near the immigration building at the base of the mole. There, a policeman ushered us into a large shed closely packed with other passengers, government officials, police, and soldiers in uniform. One official demanded our passports, a soldier frisked me carefully for concealed weapons, and a woman led my wife to a room at the far end of the building for a similar operation. Then a customs officer instructed us to sort out our bags from a mountainous heap against the wall and open them. We obeyed, and after he had minutely examined their contents, he gave us our *congé*.

"You will find a taxi outside the door," he said with cold courtesy. "It will drive you to your hotel."

We thanked him with equal courtesy. Like the passport official and the soldier who had frisked me, he had performed his duty efficiently and impersonally, and he was probably as relieved as we were to be spared any longer acquaintance.

Our troubles, however, were not yet over. Before we left Canada, the tourist agent who had booked our passage to Cyprus reserved us a room at Limassol's principal hotel, but when our taxi drove us to its door and we pushed through the score of soldiers and their ladies who were dancing in the lobby, the desk clerk blandly informed us that every room in the building was occupied. We might find accommodation in another hotel a short distance away. This second

---

[5]A stone barrier built in the water to serve as a breakwater.

hotel proved to be a shabby affair on the main street, but its proprietor was at least courteous and provided us with a quiet if somewhat rustic bedroom on the second floor. We might have questioned its cleanliness had we been less tired, but by now it was past midnight and, grateful for any roof that would shelter us from the chill night air, we deposited our bags on the rough plank floor and slept like tortoises until the morning.

A noisy rabble of men and girls thronged the lobby when we descended the stairs around 8 a.m., but the proprietor's wife served us an excellent breakfast at a benched table in the rear, facing a long counter and an open kitchen. While we were eating, a stranger approached us and, without waiting for an invitation, sat on the bench beside me and plied me with questions about our reasons for coming to Cyprus, what places on the island we expected to visit, and how long we intended to remain. His aggressive manner warned us to be careful. We knew that the islanders were restless, that the port of Limassol had recently elected a Communist mayor whose party was openly advocating close ties with the Soviet Union, and that a rival party, EOKA,[6] stronger and more active than the Communist, was already waging an underground terrorist campaign against the British authorities in order to bring about a political union with mainland Greece. Our interrogator, we suspected, was a spy for one or other of these parties, which one we could not tell. Forewarned, therefore, I deliberately ignored any enquiries which might carry some political overtone, told him that I was a retired university professor interested in afforestation and agriculture in the eastern Mediterranean, and, at every pause in his interrogation, questioned him on Cyprus's water supply, its soil erosion, and the depredations of goats on the forested mountain slopes. My problems seemed not to interest him, however. Indeed, he found me so boring that presently he turned his back on me, and after a few minutes walked away with the air of a man who was too busy to waste time on a harmless old crank and his female companion, an attitude so sensible that we could not but agree with him.

For our part, we felt no desire to waste our time on either him or Limassol, at least not until we became acquainted with the rest of the island. Accordingly, we hired a taxi to drive us the fifty-four miles to Cyprus's capital Nicosia, since we had missed the morning bus, and the island's only railroad—which in any case had never served the south coast—had been dismantled between the two world wars, a victim of the automobile.

Directly behind Limassol tower the Troodos Mountains, an igneous massif more than 6,000 feet high which forms the core of the island, and Nicosia lies northeast of it in the middle of an extensive plain.

Our narrow but asphalted highway ran eastward over barren foothills along the southern face of the mountains, then turned north and crossed a low spur to the capital, a city of roughly 45,000 inhabitants. We encountered very little traffic along the road. Much of the countryside, indeed, appeared depopulated, for we passed only half a dozen hamlets, all clinging to the beds

---

[6]EOKA is the abbreviation for the Greek words, ETHNIKI ORGANOSIS KIPRIAKOU AGONOS, literally "National Organization of Cypriot Struggle." It was a small underground nationalist movement of Greek Cypriots, organized in 1955 by an officer in the Greek Army, Colonel Georgios Grivas, and encouraged by Makarios III, the Orthodox Archbishop of Cyprus. The movement's goals were the expulsion of the British from Cyprus and the union of Cyprus with Greece (*New Encyclopaedia Britannica*, 2003, vol. 4, (*Micropaedia*) p. 513).

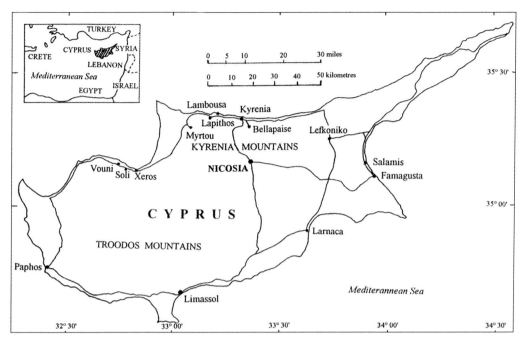

Map 12 Route taken by Jenness in Cyprus, 1955–1956.

of mountain streams that had dried up during the hot summer. In two or three valleys, we caught sight of terraces planted to vines, but nowhere an isolated house or farm, for Cypriots, like other eastern Mediterranean peoples, prefer to live cheek by jowl with one another. They may scatter each morning to cultivate their individual plots of land, but when evening approaches they invariably return to their villages to enjoy each other's company.

Our fleeting glimpse of Limassol had left with us the impression of a sprawling, untidy village of no particular interest or age, attached to the twentieth century only by the presence of a small, neatly kept park on its outskirt. Nicosia was different; it looked piquant even from a distance, with its minarets and Gothic steeples contending with one another for supremacy. Its heart still preserved the mediaeval town of narrow streets and lanes protected by a massive wall and gates, but now the expanding population had streamed outside the gates in every direction and replaced the old mud-brick huts of suburban villages with red-roofed bungalows of white-stuccoed stone or concrete. Nearly all the shops had lingered inside the city wall, nearly all the hotels and government offices were located outside it, and what survived of the ancient moat had become a sunken park that seemed to separate a Greco-Turkish fortress within from a dominantly English community besieging it from without.

The hedge-girdled hotel at which our taxi-driver deposited us illustrated the contrast with nondescript Limassol. At the latter town—or village—our lodging-place had been a rough, wild-west establishment on the main street, bare-walled, bare-floored, noisy, and impressively unclean. Our hotel in Nicosia, on the other hand, was spotless, and both outside and inside breathed the quiet atmosphere of a twentieth-century family hotel hidden among the trees of a peaceful square in central London.

Seasoned campaigners as we should be, but not always are, we spent the afternoon in reconnoitring our surroundings. Approaching the old city by way of Mataxas Square, where the British administration had torn down a section of the wall to make another entrance, we sauntered slowly down the full length of the main shopping artery, Ledra Street, recently modernized by the addition of a two-foot-wide pavement on each side from which every one-hundred-and-fifty-pounder cold-shouldered the puny hundred-pounders. Though not wide enough for two donkey carts, the street bisected the Greek-Cypriot part of the city in which everyone spoke Greek, and in most cases English also, and terminated in a cluster of shops operated by a small Armenian colony, descendants of one hundred to two hundred individuals who migrated to the island eight hundred years ago, carrying with them their special version of the Christian faith. During succeeding centuries, they suffered greater oppression from fellow-Christians of the Roman Catholic and Greek Orthodox faiths than from Turkish Moslems, and at the time of our visit, were planning to emigrate to America or Australia if Britain abandoned the island and left them to the mercy of a Greek hierarchy.

Beyond the Armenian enclave, lay a Turkish quarter, which appeared to live a life of its own. It pivoted around two places, a thirteenth-century French-Gothic cathedral which the Turks, who conquered the island in the sixteenth century, had converted into a mosque, and a square named Ataturk, after the national hero of modern Turkey.

From the Turkish quarter, we circled back to the city's Paphos Gate to visit the new Archaeological Museum, an attractive white building, half-concealed within dark-green shrubbery, which housed many of Cyprus's remarkable antiquities. Passing rather hurriedly through its exhibition halls, whose treasures we hoped to inspect at some later date, we introduced ourselves to its Greek-Cypriot director, a distinguished scholar who had made many notable contributions to his island's prehistory. He showed us his library, which contained an unrivalled collection of books on Cyprus, many of them exceedingly rare, and he graciously gave me permission to consult them for as long as we remained in the neighbourhood. Hesitating a moment, he asked us then where we were lodging, and advised us not to linger in Nicosia or its immediate vicinity because of the growing disorder, but to buy or rent a small motorcar and look for a home in Kyrenia, a pleasant little port and watering-place sixteen miles away on the island's north coast. There we would find many interesting ruins, he said, some of them dating from as far back as the bronze age two thousand years before Christ, and we could easily commute to Nicosia whenever business called us, or I wished to work in his library.

His advice was not lightly given. Even while we were talking to him, some fanatical member of the EOKA organization hurled a bomb through the open window of Cyprus Airways, a British European Airways affiliate which occupied an office across the street from our hotel. The explosion not only wrecked the office, but seriously injured its manager, who was carried to the city hospital unconscious. Police were still barring the street when we returned about 5:30 p.m. and stopped us to check our identity before they would allow us to proceed.

At the hotel, we learned that buses equipped to carry thirty-six passengers plied daily between Nicosia and Kyrenia on a three-hour schedule. We boarded one early the next morning. It rolled noisily northwest through a small suburb onto an open plain bordered by a few eucalypti, that useful Australian tree which was introduced into southern Europe during the nineteenth century and immediately adapted itself to the Mediterranean climate. Four miles from the city, we rumbled through a village whose Turkish-speaking inhabitants had painted on the asphalted highway three English words, "Down with Enosis,"[7] a slogan that left no doubt in the traveller's mind as to which side they favoured in the current political struggle.

From this village, the highway turned straight north through a treeless alluvial plain deeply gullied on both sides by the run-off of the winter rains, giving the appearance of what Americans would call "badlands." We skirted an irrigation aqueduct for half a mile, and on rising ground to our left, saw a shepherd's stone shelter alongside his rectangular stone sheepfold, both empty in this autumn season when the bare soil was bone dry, and shepherd and flock had migrated elsewhere in search of pasture. Mediterranean pastoralists have roamed from place to place seasonally ever since Biblical times, and for hundreds of years, no doubt, before the Christian era.

Within half an hour, we arrived at the foot of the Kyrenia Mountains and the entrance to a low pass. Here we passed a grove of trees under which a platoon of English soldiers had pitched their tents, doubtless because a small spring emerged from the rocks in this locality. Nature had built the Kyrenia Mountains of porous limestone, not of impermeable igneous rocks like those of the Troodos Mountains between Nicosia and Limassol, and water was a very precious commodity throughout the district, and indeed everywhere in Cyprus.

Our bus now began to climb steadily, rounding one serpentine curve after another until we reached the pass's summit at about the 2,000-foot level and could see the mountains of southern Turkey forty miles away across the strait. Descending then, we passed half a dozen lime kilns, and sighted on the top of a peak, Hilarion, the ruins of a castle erected by thirteenth-century French Crusaders over the remains of an earlier abbey to control what was the only vehicle road connecting the north coast of Cyprus with the interior.

At the beginning of the twentieth century, British authorities constructed two other motor roads over the Kyrenia Range, one at its western end and the other at its eastern end, both following old pack trails that had existed in Roman days. But the direct route from Kyrenia to Nicosia continued to be the most travelled, and the English soldiers who were garrisoning the southern entrance to its pass were employing exactly the same tactics as their French predecessors in the closing years of the Middle Ages.

Down and down we went until the road flattened out a little and, rounding a sharp corner, we found ourselves at the upper limits of Kyrenia village. Below, parallel with the shoreline, stretched the commercial centre. The village's eastern part terminated in an immense mediaeval castle towering over a tiny port, its western part at a large hotel standing in solitary splendour on a rocky promontory. Immediately in front of us, a uniformed sentry, stationed in the gateway of a high stone wall, guarded a two-story barrack and a road that disappeared within a dense pine plantation. And opposite the gate, at right angles to the highway, a wide, freshly gravelled street opened up a large field that had already been subdivided into building lots and was carrying a few scattered bungalows, one of which still lacked doors and windows. This was all we had time to distinguish as our bus sped swiftly down the slope between houses on one side and a school and miscellaneous buildings on the other, swung ninety degrees left onto the main street of the village, and stopped beside a small meat market. There we alighted and looked around us, while the vehicle drove on to its terminus in the village of Lapithos, nine miles to the west.

---

[7]Enosis was the Greek word for the union of Cyprus with Greece, much desired by the Greek Cypriots.

Noon saw us again at the meat market, awaiting a bus that would carry us back to Nicosia. We were jubilant. My pocket contained a receipt for the first month's rent of a fine new bungalow, unfurnished, but equipped with running water and electric light. It lay above the turmoil of the village on the freshly gravelled street we had observed from the bus, facing the doorless and windowless house but thirty yards beyond it. Built by an Italian architect, it was to have been the dowry of the local postmaster's daughter, Sophie, a primary-school teacher as fluent in English as in her native Greek. She was affianced to another teacher, Andreas, an extraordinarily handsome youth who had received part of his training in England, and was now principal of a small school two miles west of his fiancée's.

The young couple had hoped to marry during the previous summer, and had cooperated in planting a neat flower garden around two sides of their future home, but the bride's father, a widower, had fallen gravely ill, and the wedding had been postponed. All this we discovered later, of course, for as yet we had not met either of them, but only their agent in the village.

The ride back to Nicosia gave us an opportunity to plan our next manoeuvres, and after a hurried lunch at the hotel, we went our separate ways to carry them out. My task was to purchase a small used car which we could re-sell in the spring before returning to Canada.

I consulted, first, the manager of an export-import firm whose name I had extracted from a guidebook. He told me that one of his clerks was leaving Cyprus within a fortnight to take a position in the Belgian Congo, and that he was very anxious to sell his almost new Volkswagen for American dollars. Did I wish to see the car? He would have it brought to the door, and while waiting until it arrived, we would sip a little Turkish coffee in his office.

The owner himself brought the car. He was a young man, and this was his first automobile, he told me, as he drove me two or three miles into the country to prove that it was in perfect condition. Its speedometer registered 3,000 miles, but so lovingly had he handled the vehicle that it might have rolled off the assembly line that very hour. He was grateful that I could pay him in U.S. dollars instead of in Cyprus currency, but he desired one other favour.

Figure 37 The Jenness rented bungalow in Kyrenia, Cyprus, 1956.
Photo by D. Jenness

Would I permit him to retain the car seven more days while he wound up his affairs and finished his packing?

I returned to the hotel very proud of my achievement, or should I say my good luck, but I was prouder still of my wife when she related her adventures over the dinner table, for her task had been twice as difficult as mine, and her success little short of miraculous. Alone, with only twenty Cyprus pounds in her purse—the maximum she dared to carry in Nicosia's unfamiliar thoroughfares—she had set out to find and purchase the most essential pieces of furniture we would need in our empty bungalow. She had begun her quest on Ledra Street, retracing our route of the afternoon before. None of that street's shops, however, seemed to carry what she wanted, and, confused by the noise and jostling of the crowd, she had drifted toward the city market and entered the Armenian enclave. There by chance she passed an open doorway, and glancing through it, saw two large wicker chairs and other objects hanging from the ceiling of a dark corridor. Hesitatingly she entered, and was threading her way through the maze of furniture and bric-a-brac when a burly, middle-aged man suddenly appeared in front of her and asked, in excellent English, whether he could be of service.

She pointed to the wicker chairs that were dangling over her head and asked:

"How much are those chairs? Have you sofas and tables of the same material?"

"Most of my stock is at the back," the man answered. "Will you walk round with me and point out anything you wish to examine?"

His countenance was so open, his voice so respectful, that her trepidation vanished, and she followed him through all the recesses of his store. They passed from one dingy room to another, and her eyes opened wider and wider with astonishment. Here was everything she had been looking for—beds, mattresses, chairs, sofas, tables, rugs, even kitchen utensils. Her twenty pounds evaporated within a few minutes, and she committed herself to purchases that cost as much again. Suddenly panic seized her. How could she ever convey all her purchases sixteen miles across the mountains?

"Don't worry," the merchant reassured her with a smile. "When you have bought everything you need I will gather all the articles together and load them on the roof of your Kyrenia bus. They will travel with you."

She checked her list. Every item had been paid for or charged except a portable butane stove.

"I don't sell stoves," said her friend, "but there is a stove shop on the next street. Come."

"But I have no more money," she protested, "and I can't pay my debt to you until tomorrow morning."

"You can't set up house without a stove," he answered. "I will lend you the money. You are English, and English people always pay their debts. Come with me."

He guided her through a narrow lane, gently holding her elbow whenever the crowd pressed strongly on them, then led her up a moderately wide street to a wholesale establishment that imported stoves and other appliances. There my wife selected the stove she wanted, and her companion, tucking it under his arm, carried it back to his store. Again she checked her list, assured him that she would return in the morning, and rejoined me at the hotel.

Her victory called for another council of war. We agreed that I would catch the 9 o'clock bus to Kyrenia the next morning, pick up the front-door key from the agent who had leased us the bungalow, open up the house and await her arrival with the furniture. Meanwhile she would return to the Armenian store, purchase any further items she needed, pay her bill and climb into the noon bus after the merchant had loaded her furniture on its roof. All that night we tossed in our beds, dreaming of Volkswagens and butane stoves.

Morning dawned warm and sunny, for Cyprus's rains fall only during the second half of the winter; at every other season one can count on fine weather. I accomplished my simple task without a hitch. I opened up the bungalow and loitered in and around it until the fateful hour when my wife was due to arrive. Neighbours seemed to be watching me, intrigued no doubt by the lone stranger who was preparing to settle in their midst, but I paid no attention to them, being absorbed in the beauty of the surroundings. Our front door faced the long, imposing range of the Kyrenia Mountains, with Hilarion Castle gazing sternly down from one side, and our back door looked beyond Kyrenia village and the blue waters of the Mediterranean to Turkey's snow-capped mountains on the far horizon. The air was clear as crystal. That morning, the whole world seemed young and fresh again.

As I stood at the gate, scanning the scrub-covered slopes in front of me, a tiny crag seemed to tremble and move very slowly down the mountain face. I rubbed my eyes and looked again. Yes, it *was* moving: a vehicle of some kind, but the incredible height. Surely this colossus was not the bus with our furniture?

The juggernaut appeared and disappeared around successive curves. Finally it came into full view, approached the corner of our street, turned a cautious right angle and crept slowly to our gate. Strange faces stared at me through the windows, but at the door stood my wife, smiling triumphantly. Single-handed she had collected enough furniture for the whole house, and now she had delivered it, whole and undamaged, at our front gate.

Three male passengers alighted from the crowded bus after her, the driver mounted to the roof, and before I awakened to what was happening, a large wicker sofa brushed past me into the living room. Two armchairs and all the rest of the furniture followed quickly, the men re-entered their vehicle without waiting to receive our thanks, and we stood alone on the doorstep, as breathless as our departing benefactors.

Thus No. 6 Philemonos Street, Kyrenia, Cyprus, became our home for five months. We had reached our land of promise and entered upon a new life, a life of ease, study, and adventure all combined. But the first day of that life brought only abstemiousness, for the larder of our bungalow was empty and we had to lunch on crisp air.

II

Nature diverted our thoughts the next morning from furniture to provender, and, there being no telephone in the house, counselled us to explore on foot for any shopping areas in our vicinity. Turning our backs on the highway, therefore, we walked to the far end of Philemonos Street and swung left along a road that promised, like the highway, to lead us to the sea, but farther to the east. It carried us past a large olive grove and an unpretentious Moslem mosque to an L-shaped hamlet, which contained, so far as we then observed, only one shop, a grocery.

We opened the door, and at the tinkling of its bell a young girl appeared to wait on us, but when she discovered we did not understand Turkish she called her brother, who spoke English more fluently than she did. He was an intelligent youth of seventeen years, very alert, especially when he learned that we had rented the new bungalow on Philemonos Street, for both Sophie, its owner, and Andreas, her fiancé, lived in this hamlet. He offered to call at the house two or three times a week for our orders and to deliver the groceries the same day, or whenever we needed them, and he could supply us with nearly all the staple goods, flour, bread, cheese, canned foods, breakfast foods, wine and other things, but not fresh fruit or vegetables. The latter, he said, we could buy in Kyrenia village half a mile farther on. There and then, we placed a large order with him and continued our reconnaissance.

Hassan, for that was the boy's name, served us cheerfully and faithfully all winter. After we became better acquainted, we visited his mother and sister. They were true Cypriots, born and raised in the district, as had been their parents and grandparents, for Turkey conquered and colonized Cyprus three hundred years before England took over the island's administration. But they were also loyal Turks, though they knew nothing of Turkey proper except through that country's books and newspapers, and the letters of Hassan's older brother, who was studying medicine in Ankara. The English government had provided the Cyprus Turks with schools which taught in Turkish, using text-books from Ankara, and Hassan himself was hoping to study medicine in Turkey after his brother graduated. Meanwhile, his mother told us proudly, he was managing their small grocery, which supported the three members of their family in Cyprus and at the same time contributed to the older boy's maintenance at the university.

This **L**-shaped hamlet bore a Turkish name, but only the long arm of the **L** was Turkish. The short arm was the domain of Greek Cypriots, who mingled as little with their neighbours as oil does with water. Whether Hassan and his family could speak Greek I do not know, and if Andreas, our landlord, understood Turkish he would never have admitted it. Only fifty yards separated their homes, yet so great was their mental separation that they might have inhabited different continents and belonged to different branches of the human race. When they unexpectedly met in our living room one evening they turned their backs on one another and gazed out of opposite windows.

Hassan told us of an elderly Turk at the end of his street who quilted warm bed-coverlets from Cyprus' home-grown cotton, a plant that had brought the island great prosperity during the sixteenth century before cheaper cotton from America's slave plantations began to flood the markets of Europe and Africa. We found the old man busily hand-stitching a coverlet for another customer and, after examining his workmanship, ordered a similar one for ourselves. I think he must have been a rug-maker in his younger days, for the coverlet he made us was a genuine work of art. It was warm too, as warm as the eiderdown sleeping bags of Arctic explorers, though slightly heavier and more bulky.

Returning through the Greek-Cypriot section of the hamlet, we passed the outdoor brick-oven of a bakery, which not only sold bread, but for a small fee would cook any pie or cake we cared to mix and carry there. (The "we" of this last sentence, it will be noted, is singular, meaning my wife, for any cake I myself had mixed might have damaged the oven or imperilled our health!) My wife tested this Cyprus oven once during the early part of the winter and it baked her cake perfectly, but she decided that the bakery was too far away, and that it was easier to buy a small electric oven in Nicosia and "whip up" a cake or cookies in her own home whenever she needed them.

Kyrenia village contained three hotels for summer vacationists, a post-office, a bank, and more than a score of shops, all operated by Greek Cypriots. We introduced ourselves to a few of the trades people by purchasing meat at the market, fruit and vegetables in one shop, an English language newspaper printed in Nicosia at another, and in a third, a tank of butane gas, to be delivered later in the day. Having thus taken care of our immediate requirements, we hurried home and found, waiting at our gate, a diminutive Turkish woman aged somewhere between forty and seventy five, who declined the chair I offered her on our porch, but squatted on the floor and, from the recesses of a voluminous black dress, produced first one hen's egg, then a second. She made known to us, in English, how much we should pay for them, and as soon as she felt the money in her hand brought to light two more eggs.

Thereafter she visited us each week, sometimes with two eggs, sometimes with four, and once or twice with six. Where she lived, and where she obtained her eggs, we never discovered, for her English was too limited to question her. But we did learn two things: first, that the price we were paying her was satisfactory, and, second, that we were good, but that Greek Cypriots were the scum of the earth and she would gladly cut all their throats.

Satisfied with the stock of food we had laid in, we turned our thoughts to food's boon companion, fuel. The Italian architect who had designed our bungalow had built in the middle of the living room a fireplace so spotless and attractive that it cried out for us to use it, but there was no wood. Early that morning, however, a man had passed the house in a donkey cart laden with the trimmings of olive trees, presumably from the grove at the end of the street, and hard olive makes excellent firewood. As soon as we had finished lunch, therefore, we set out to investigate, and on the far side of the grove came upon the isolated home of a Greek-Cypriot farmer who was sawing up olive branches in his yard. He spoke flawless English, was delighted to sell us a load of his wood, and delivered it within the hour.

When night fell on that first day, and the post-sunset Mediterranean chill that penetrates right to the bones descended on us, we arranged our wicker armchairs, sofa, and table in a half-circle round the crackling fire, loaded the table with our choicest eatables, and dreamed that we were baron and baroness of a castle like the one which we had passed that morning at the foot of the hill.

An hour before the sun set, however, Sophie and Andreas visited us to find out how we had settled in. The girl was very shy at this first meeting, and scarcely spoke a word until we enquired about the plants in her garden. Then she became articulate, and led my wife around each flower bed to show her the jasmine and other fragrant shrubs, two or three of which were beginning to bud now that the long hot drought of summer had come to an end. Andreas and I, meanwhile, tagged along behind, discussing whether he would have time after school hours to teach us his modern Greek tongue. Within a few minutes, we struck a satisfactory bargain; he would come two afternoons a week to give us an hour's lesson, and Sophie might weed and water her garden any and every day in the week, at any hour that was convenient to her.

Two little tots from the windowless house on the other side of the street had been watching us, and decided now that there was no reason why they should be excluded from the visit. In the early morning, they had attacked us with stones, the Middle East's traditional method of informing a stranger that he is not wanted, but their assault had been ineffective because neither of them was quite old enough to stand firmly on its feet. Andreas and Sophie were their friends, and when they saw the four of us walking together in the garden they toddled over to help their compatriots. Sophie then explained to us that they were the children of a poor shoemaker who worked from dawn to dusk in her hamlet, striving to earn enough money to finish this house on Philemonos street, making one room his workshop. But the struggle had already lasted eleven years and was now quite hopeless, because some of his best customers had been English people who had left the island or were now embroiled in the political unrest.

All through this conversation, the children were standing beside her, listening with wondering eyes to the strange speech. My wife went indoors to bring them some biscuits, which, with a little encouragement from Sophie, they accepted and ate. After that, they followed us around, still puzzling in their little minds how their friends could associate with obvious enemies. At last Sophie told them to run along home, and gently pushed them through the gateway.

Pre-school children often acquire more wisdom than their parents suspect. They learn, for example, that a stranger may chatter unintelligibly like a songbird, yet be both friendly and a good cook. Next morning, while playing outside their home, these Greek-Cypriot children kept turning their eyes toward our house, and when my wife waved two biscuits at them, they toddled across somewhat timidly and took them from her hand. Thereafter, hardly a morning passed that we did not see them at our gate, and when Maroula, their mother, undertook to come over and houseclean our bungalow each week, they always accompanied her to visit their funny "granny" who greeted them with a smile but never learned to talk properly.

Next door to us lived a Group Captain of the Royal Air Force NATO command, with his wife and five-month-old baby, and farther down the street, on the opposite side, a Wing Commander of the same force, with two fair-haired children, a boy of seven and a girl of five. These English children had no playmates, for Maroula's toddlers were too young, and other Greek-Cypriot children who ventured into our neighbourhood were hostile, or presumed hostile, to be avoided or driven away with stones. Their mother allowed them to roam together, free and unrestrained, within a radius of about seventy-five yards from their home, and this area they regarded as their private playground, shared by Maroula's infants alone.

Strictly out of bounds was the Nicosia highway, but one day, just where Philemonos Street branched off from it, I witnessed a pitched battle. Who began it I never discovered, but three Greek-Cypriot youngsters had driven the English children behind a low stone wall, from whose shelter the seven-year-old boy was vigorously bombarding his besiegers with the stones his little sister feverishly handed up to him. Every child was fighting in deadly earnest. Luckily, none had yet been injured when I interrupted the battle and sent the combatants home.

Two days after our arrival, the Wing Commander's wife called on us informally and presented us with a bowlful of small cakes still hot from her oven. She was a young, warm-hearted extrovert who welcomed a third English-speaking family in her neighbourhood, since her husband had to drive away before 8 a.m. each morning with his Group Captain, and neither man returned until evening. It was a lonely and anxious life these two officers' wives were leading, marooned amid a people alien in language and religion, rent by dissension and strife, and resentful—thirty to forty percent of them at least—of English rule. A fanatical nationalism fathered by the Greek Orthodox Church had taken root among them during the First World War, and now the virus was rampant among little children, some of whom did not hesitate to throw stones at the Group Captain's baby, helpless in its perambulator as its mother wheeled it down the highway on a shopping expedition to the village. British soldiers closely patrolled the Kyrenia Pass, but the Air Vice-Marshal, whose secluded home among the pines to the west of us had to be guarded by Turkish sentries, travelled everywhere by helicopter; and the wives of our R.A.F. neighbours spent their days till evening in silent fear that their motoring husbands might be shot down by some hidden sniper and never return.

I must not forget one other neighbour, a Greek Cypriot who, nattily dressed and sporting a swagger-cane under his left arm, frequently passed our bungalow about 8:30 in the morning on his way to the harbour front. He never spoke to us, nor we to him, but he certainly knew that we were visitors from Canada, and we knew that he was the Kyrenia district's Chief of Police. When disorders first began to spread over the entire island, the English authorities had barricaded the entrance to Kyrenia Castle with barbed wire, and converted it from a tourist show place to a prison for political internees and a headquarters for the district police. There, our natty police chief maintained his main office. Gossip whispered that he prudently locked himself inside it, or vanished into some more remote hiding place, whenever any disturbance broke out or was brewing, and more than once, I heard a Cypriot insinuate, in veiled language, that he carried two hats, an official hat which earned him a good salary from the authorities, and a clandestine one which he wore only among his friends in the EOKA underground.

Perhaps they were right. All Turkish Cypriots were adjudged pro-British because they were anti-Greek, and under English rule had enjoyed equal status with Greek Cypriots. But the Greek Cypriots themselves were divided, some favouring the English who had delivered them from Turkish rule and given the island economic prosperity, others demanding the expulsion of the English and the union of Cyprus with Greece. The student generation, as usual, was the most fanatical. Fortunate was the Greek Cypriot who could distinguish his friend from his foe. Suspicion reigned everywhere, and men distrusted next-door neighbours whom they had known from childhood. Little wonder then that the Kyrenia police protected their stronghold with barbed wire, and that many churches in the district, even Kyrenia Church just outside the castle gate, bore crudely painted slogans on their outer walls that read "Long live EOKA," "Death to Traitors" (i.e., Greek Cypriots who opposed EOKA), and the like. Cyprus, the Isle of Venus, seethed not with love but with hate.[8]

---

[8]In 1960, Britain granted independence to the island of Cyprus, but retained two military bases on its south coast. The island became the Republic of Cyprus, with Archbishop Makarios as its first president. Its constitution provided that seventy percent of the ruling government members would be Greek Cypriots, the remainder Turkish Cypriots, but this proved unworkable. Greece staged an abortive coup of the president in 1974, prompting a military invasion by Turkish forces to protect the Turkish population on the island. Turkish forces overran thirty-seven percent of the island before United Nations intervention resulted in a cease-fire, a partition of the island, and the establishment of a United Nations buffer zone between the Turkish and Greek parts of the island, a zone that extended from west of Xeros on the northwest coast of the island southeast to the vicinity of Larnaca on the south coast. The Turkish control of the island thereafter included the region around Kyrenia, including Bellapaise, forcing the Greek-Cypriot inhabitants to leave. Nicosia remained barely within the Greek-Cypriot zone. United Nations forces have remained in Cyprus since 1974 while the United Nations sought a peaceful solution between the two Cypriot people. The Republic of Cyprus was scheduled to join the European Union on May 1, 2004, but only the Greek-Cypriot segment was admitted after a United Nations plan for the unification of the island was rejected by the Greek-Cypriot majority. The problem between the country's two peoples continues unsettled. The Republic of Cyprus is now a member of the United Nations and also of the British Commonwealth.

At Christmas that winter, during the celebration of a Sunday morning Mass, three masked men entered a Greek Orthodox Church just over the mountains from Kyrenia, marched down almost to the altar, shot the precentor [choirmaster], and marched out again without interference or protest from the officiating priest or any member of the congregation.

We ourselves were neither Cypriots nor connected with English officialdom or military, but Canadian tourists interested in the history and resources of Cyprus, not in its political intrigues and strife. Because Cypriots are Mediterraneans and very curious about strangers, we anticipated that those of the Kyrenia district would quickly recognize us and respect our neutral status, so that we could safely travel wherever we wished. For the moment, of course, we were crippled through having no motorcar in our laneway, but our Volkswagen was to be handed over within a few days, and meanwhile we could commute to Nicosia by bus or explore the immediate countryside on foot.

We did both. We strolled eastward one afternoon three miles past the home of our Greek-Cypriot woodcutter to the village of Bellapaise, which shelters the ruins of a thirteenth-century French-Gothic monastery that was sacked by the Turks in the sixteenth century and largely demolished. Fifty years ago, because it had been the finest French-Gothic structure in Cyprus, if not in the Levant, the government restored it as far as was humanly possible and made it a state monument. The dirt road which led to it meandered across the lower slopes of the mountains, and at the entrance to the village, skirted a circular patch of bare, hard-trodden ground on which the local farmers still threshed their sheaves of wheat, not with the flails that western

Figure 38 A corner of the Gothic cloister of Bellapaise Abbey, near Kyrenia, Cyprus, in 1956. The abbey was built by French crusaders in the thirteenth century and destroyed by Turkish invaders in the sixteenth century.
Photo by D. Jenness

Europeans were using before the machine age, but with a heavy "harrow" of flint-studded planks drawn by one or two oxen. The sharp flints shredded the grain stalks, and hand-wielded winnowing fans then separated the wheat from the chaff.

On another visit to Bellapaise two months later, we turned aside to follow a faint trail up the mountainside and came upon a water-driven flour mill that had ground the wheat between two enormous stones. Whether this mill was still being used I did not enquire, but its aqueduct was dry when we visited it and the building deserted.

The name Bellapaise is a corruption of Abbaye de la Paix and means "The Abbey of Peace," but we encountered only sour faces in the village, and even the custodian who unlocked the monastery gate for us seemed ill at ease and almost surly. We spoke English, of course, for our knowledge of modern Greek at that time was less than elementary. Rows of Greek flags strung across the nave of the village church publicly proclaimed the political attachments of the people, but no one was openly hostile. They were more friendly during our second visit, for this was the village in which Sophie taught school, and she had told her pupils about the elderly Canadians who had studied the poems of Homer and the histories of the wars between ancient Greece and Persia, and were now learning to speak modern Greek from Andreas. Nevertheless, we carried away a rather sad memory of the place, although the beautiful arches of the monastery's cloister, and the magnificent refectory with its lofty vault, deep windows, and glorious view over the sea, amply compensated us for our long walk.

I caught the noon bus to Nicosia one day before the end of the first week, and spent most of the afternoon poring over some books in the museum library. Dusk had fallen when I regained

Figure 39 Oxen turning up the soil of an olive orchard with a wooden plough so that wheat and beans can be planted between the trees, near Kyrenia, Cyprus, 1956. Very few farmers have tractors, and there is no pasture for horses.
Photo by D. Jenness

the marketplace and squeezed into the last vacant seat on the returning bus, and it was pitch dark when we reached the foot of the Kyrenia Mountains and began the ascent. We had gained the summit of the pass without incident, and were descending again, when suddenly the driver applied his brakes and stopped his vehicle. The door swung open, an English soldier with a rifle flung over his shoulder poked his head in and shouted: "All men out."

We clambered out. Across the road in front of us was a barbed-wire barricade and a squad of soldiers, some of whom carried flashlights. They lined us up at the side of the road and ran their hands over us to see if we concealed any weapons, just as had the police in the Limassol immigration office. They frisked us efficiently but politely, yet not so efficiently, I reflected, because they paid no attention to the women on the bus, and any terrorist among us could easily have passed his pistol to a woman. Only a few days later, indeed, the police arrested a high-school girl who was packing a loaded revolver. But perhaps the commanding officer was right and I was wrong, for Cyprus was at peace, at least nominally, and in peacetime, only a totalitarian government would dare allow its soldiers to frisk women travelling quietly in a public conveyance along the open highway.

The ex-owner of our Volkswagen duly delivered the car at our door on the appointed afternoon and returned to Nicosia by bus. We were now mobile, but I needed a Cyprus driving licence and some practice in attaching myself to the left-hand side of the road before venturing across the mountains and facing the confusion of Nicosia's narrow streets. For a time, it was safer to restrict my excursions to the north coast of Cyprus where the traffic was very light.

The licence gave me little trouble. I merely walked down to the police station in Kyrenia Castle, presented my passport and my Canadian driving license, and quietly waited for the constable to fill me out a new permit. The man led me into his office, offered me a chair facing him across the desk and closed the door.

He examined my passport first very slowly. The words New Zealand caught his eye.

"This is a Canadian passport," he said; "but you were born in New Zealand, and New Zealand lies near Australia. Do you know anything about that country?"

"I have visited it twice," I answered, "but that was long ago."

He hesitated a moment, then blurted out, "I want to emigrate there with my family. We do not belong to Kyrenia; we come from the (Troodos) mountains. I do not trust the people here. They smile at you by day, but when night comes, who knows? They could shoot you in the back. What is Australia like? Tell me something about it."

This policeman was not the only Cypriot who wanted to emigrate. I looked up the official statistics at the end of winter, and discovered that during the preceding six months, an average of three hundred and fifty Cypriots, almost all of them young men, had sailed away each month from the island's ports. A few, like this policeman, were deserting their native land on account of the political unrest, but the majority went away to better their fortunes, since it was becoming increasingly difficult to find satisfactory jobs on the island. Not that there was significant unemployment; indeed, Cyprus had seemed to us more prosperous than any other country in the eastern Mediterranean, judging from the clothing its peasants wore, the homes we saw and visited, and the number of bicycles and private motorcars we met on the roads. England had poured about a million dollars into the island since the Second World War, but Cyprus is so small, so poor in natural resources, that only with difficulty was it supporting its half-million inhabitants. Of the three hundred and fifty persons who emigrated each month during that winter, two hundred and sixty six went to England to find employment and from England some moved on to the United States; twenty-seven sought new homes in Australia. Only forty-three went to Greece, only fourteen to Turkey, and nearly all of these were students or businessmen who expected to return to Cyprus later. Not one intended to settle permanently in Greece or Turkey because those two countries were much less prosperous than Cyprus, especially Greece, where thirty percent of the labour force had been unemployed for several years.

Driving on the left-hand instead of the right-hand side of the road presented no problem on the quiet north coast roads, but several weeks passed before the habit became ingrained in me, and during those weeks we narrowly escaped at least one accident. We had surveyed that morning the almost uninhabited stretch of coast fifteen to twenty miles west of Kyrenia, and were returning home when, rounding a headland with a high bank on our right and a fifty-foot drop to a boulder beach on our left, we encountered an army jeep carrying three rifle-bearing soldiers, over and above the driver. It swept round the corner without warning, closely hugging the bank on its left. Automatically, I swerved to my right, as would have been the correct procedure in Canada. But it was not correct in Cyprus, and the two cars screeched to a halt within a foot of each other's bumpers.

"Americans?" roared the Jeep's sergeant, glaring at me.

"No, just Canadians," sweetly answered my wife. "We're awfully sorry."

A half-smile flickered over the sergeant's crusty face. "Drive on," he gruffly ordered the soldier at the wheel. The jeep backed up and drove on, while the two boys in the rear half raised their rifles in salute and grinned at us.

There were other perils on Cyprus's narrow roads. Greek-Cypriot truck drivers seemed to enjoy crowding off them any small cars that contained English people, so one quickly learned to pull over to the side as far as possible and wait until the truck passed. We ourselves almost ran down three camels loaded with firewood, which were being driven, caravan fashion, by a man half hidden on the back of the middle animal. In this case, also, no one entertained any doubt about who should yield. We drove swiftly to the side of the road and halted while the lordly beasts stalked disdainfully by, scorning even to glance in our direction. These three animals, and perhaps two score more, were all that survived of the numerous long camel trains which had freighted Cyprus's wheat to its seaports in the days before man invented railways and automobiles, before he had built any real roads in Cyprus except a rough wagon-track from Nicosia to Kyrenia. We had been warned that some Turkish Cypriots still kept a few camels, but we were not expecting so abrupt an introduction to them.

And there was a peril greater even than camels: the ubiquitous donkeys, for which the government had provided special paths at the sides of the roads, a safety measure which Denmark adopted later to protect her equally ubiquitous cyclists when the motorcar threatened to push them too off the highways. We once overtook a Cypriot farmer riding a mother donkey along such a bridle path, while its baby trotted quietly behind them. So charming was the sight, so idyllic and peaceful, that involuntarily I slowed down as I drove by. But the baby instantly lost its peacefulness; it took rapid aim, flung its two back heels high in the air, grazed my windshield, and nearly clipped off my ear. Only then did we learn that the gene which in human

Greek Cypriots was provoking so violent an antagonism towards English-speaking peoples had infected also their donkeys, and thereafter we gave the animals a wider berth.

One hazard we faced arose not from dumb donkeys, but from even less intelligent humans. Our neighbour the wing-commander dropped in to our house one evening to warn us never to leave our car unguarded, however lonely the parking place might seem. That afternoon, he and his family had picnicked on a secluded beach, leaving their car parked on the headland above it, and during their absence, someone, who must have been spying on them, deliberately smashed their windshield with a large stone. My friend was less well insured against such "accidents" than we were. The Greek Cypriot from whom we had bought our Volkswagen had equipped it with three or four Cypriot charms, one of which hung over the dashboard and protected it against the "evil eye." He had evidently found this supernatural insurance infallible, since not a scratch had marred the car's surface when he transferred it to us. We had retained the charm over the dashboard, therefore, feeling sure that the magic taboo which had protected him so effectively would work equally well for us.

By late November, I had completed my apprenticeship in left-hand driving and felt capable of negotiating any automobile road and circulating in any town that was marked on my 1″ = 4 miles map. Two days a week, I now drove into Nicosia and spent the mornings in the library of the museum, whose director had already set up a charcoal brazier under his desk to make his office more habitable, for the building was unheated, and the mornings distinctly chilly until about noon. There was no brazier in the library, and after I had thumbed over my books at a table for two hours I received a message from frozen feet and numbed fingers that it was time to seek the sunshine, turn on the heater of my car, and return home. Fortunately, in those two hours I was able to scribble out enough notes to occupy my thoughts for the next three or four days.

The evenings became shorter as the weather grew colder, and we needed portable lamps in our living room so that we might read around the fire. But lamps—at least portable ones—are furniture, and furniture, which in some strange way is related to art, came under the jurisdiction of my wife. She had always admired the shapes of Attic fifth-century trade vases, and hoped that she could discover something similar in Nicosia, or have a pair manufactured for her by one of Cyprus's small pottery factories. Andreas had mentioned in the course of one of his Greek lessons that there was a factory at Lapithos, the village nine miles west of us which had replaced Lambousa, a town of Roman date, whose ruined walls and shattered pottery fragments still littered the neighbouring seashore. Thither then we hurried, hoping to find some quaint art-pottery establishment such as delights the traveller in certain remote villages in Italy and Spain, some factory that has continued to work the ancient clay deposits and recreate the lovely shapes and designs of remote antiquity.

What we found in Lapithos, alas, was very different: a primitive drain and roofing-tile factory operated by four surly men who resented our English speech and would gladly have dumped us in the soupy sump in which they washed their clay. The experience somewhat dampened my wife's antiquarian enthusiasm. Despairingly, she sought in Nicosia's market-place the artistic earthenware jars that the Lapithos factory had never heard of, bought a pair that pleased her, wired them in an electric store that provided the necessary cord and sockets, and carried them to a humble handicraft shop, where a smiling girl fashioned for her two decorative lampshades.

With our olive branches crackling merrily in the fire-place, a burnished lamp glowing at each end of the mantelpiece and a large red pottery vase between them ready to receive such wild spring flowers as anemones, hyacinths, and cyclamens, we considered ourselves well prepared to entertain any twentieth-century princes of Serendip who might come knocking at our door.

III

The political unrest on the island intensified that December. Every second or third day, the newspapers reported a riot or a shooting incident in one or other locality. At dusk one evening, a patrol of English soldiers came upon a trio of Kyrenia high-school girls painting EOKA slogans on the Nicosia highway at the end of our street, and two weeks later, a bomb exploded harmlessly outside a house in that vicinity. Two hundred yards from us in the opposite direction, near the Turkish mosque, the asphalted road bore counter-slogans, "Union No" and "Up with Volkan," this last word being the name of the Turkish underground party that was opposing the EOKA and union with Greece. From our back door, we often saw two English gunboats anchored off Kyrenia harbour, or patrolling east and west along the north coast of the island to check gun-running from mainland Greece, and perhaps from Turkey.

But no patrol could be effective as long as civil and military authorities in Athens supported the traffic and the archbishop and bishops of the Greek Orthodox church in Cyprus openly encouraged it. Colonel George Grivas, one of Greece's most noted soldiers, was smuggled into Cyprus at this time to organize and direct the terrorist campaign against the English and their supporters, and a few of his terrorists established secret hideouts and arms caches in the limestone caves of the Kyrenia Mountains on both sides of us.

Despite the general unrest, the evil-eye charm that had protected us from malevolent camels and donkeys still dangled defiantly over the dashboard of our Volkswagen and lured us to further adventures. Intrigued by the name Pachyammos ("Deep sand"), we motored one noon to a crescent-moon bay twelve miles east of Kyrenia and lunched on the grassy cliff above its sandy beach. Kicking into the bare ground between scattered tufts of turf, we unearthed half a dozen flint arrowheads or knife blades. They were relics of Cyprus's first settlers 3,000–4,000 years before Christ, the Director of the Nicosia Museum told me, for of earlier remains the island had yielded no trace. Colocynth (gourd-apple) vines held together the face of this cliff and trailed down over the beach to trip unwary bathers, or to stub their toes with its hard green "apples," which Cyprus still exports to Europe's drug manufacturers, although their purgative qualities have failed to rid the island of its own internal disorders. This we discovered from a brief visit to a dozen or more Turkish families who were living in windowless, adobe huts on the small but fertile plain a mile beyond Pachyammos, whence they breathed fire and brimstone against their Greek-Cypriot neighbours. The latter breathed them back, and the consuming flames threatened to scorch us too as we ate our lunch on the cliff, for a Greek shepherd, accompanied by his wife and five-year-old daughter, drove his flock around us, mistaking us perhaps for invading Turks, and studied us with such manifest hostility that we could almost feel the fiery blast. But blessed be little children. They are the world's most successful peacemakers. My wife offered a piece of cake to their little girl, who liked both its appearance and its taste. Encouraged by a word or two we said to her in Greek, she begged for a second piece, and of course received it. Then the hard faces of her parents relaxed into smiles, and the flames of hatred subsided.

Another excursion carried us seven miles west of Kyrenia to the ruins of Lambousa, the ancient port that was founded in the eighth century before Christ, and destroyed by Arabs about eight hundred years after Christ. Its prosperity had rested on its proximity to a splendid perennial spring, which issued from the foothills behind it and irrigated the gently sloping olive orchards, orange groves and wheat fields that separated the mountains from the sea. Because of this spring the Cypriots did not abandon the district after Lambousa's devastation, but built a new and safer town a mile and a half inland, the present-day Lapithos, which supports about the same population—6,000—as its predecessor, judging from the area covered by the latter's still unexcavated ruins. Some archaeologist had uncovered one hundred square feet of a mosaic floor in a house of the Byzantine epoch, probably to determine its date, and many marble columns, or fragments of them, had been carried to Lapithos and other places, but there were shards of pottery everywhere, and a vast wealth of archaeological treasure certainly awaits the archaeologist's trowel and shovel.[9]

We followed the traces of ancient steps down the bank to the old harbour's stony beach, where some fishermen were drying their nets, and we noticed an ancient lighthouse there and an old fish-pond scooped out of the solid rock, probably by some Roman or Byzantine noble who demanded for his table a steady supply of fresh fish. When we asked the fishermen about these remains, however, and the abundance of fish in the locality, they surlily turned their backs and refused to answer us.

Just west of ruined Lambousa were two small churches and a monastery, all of different ages. One church, or rather chapel, St. Eulambios, had been carved directly out of the quarry which had supplied Lambousa's building stones. Niches in the chapel's three-foot-thick walls had served as tombs, but as in so many places, all had been rifled for their gold and silver many centuries ago. All but one, that is, for about 1900, a lucky prober discovered a niche that had escaped the tomb-robbers' hands and extracted from it a quantity of fine silver plate wrought in the sixth century A.D. Three museums now share his treasure, the Cyprus Museum in Nicosia, the British Museum in London and, thanks to the millionaire Pierpont Morgan, the Metropolitan Museum in New York.

The second church, St. Evalios, was built about 1500 A.D. and is therefore comparatively modern, but its graceful outlines, and its picturesque situation on the rocky cliff overlooking the blue sea, have made it a national monument. More interesting, historically, is the two-story monastery and chapel a few yards away, built at various periods from the fourth century onward. Legend declares that the monastery stood originally on the mainland of what is now Turkey, and that one night, to prevent its desecration by infidel Moslems, angels carried it intact across the Caramanian Strait and planted it on the coast of Christian Cyprus. Its name, Akhiropietos, commemorates the miracle. It means "not built by human hands." A few years before our visit the Cyprus government repaired the building and converted it into a summer hotel, closed and deserted during the winter months when the sea is too cold for bathing.

During these and similar excursions, we passed through many small villages, some of which were friendly while others glowered. All alike, whether friendly or unfriendly, possessed attractive

---

[9]Archaeological excavations were undertaken at Lambousa in the early 1990s by the Cyprus Department of Antiquities and a team of German archaeologists.

elementary schools either inside their boundaries or within easy reach, and every large village and town possessed also a modern high school. Some schools the government had just closed because the national flag of Greece had been hoisted over their roofs, and organized mobs of school children had stoned any police or soldiers sent to take the flags down. Greek-Cypriot school committees protested the government's action, Greek-language newspapers (there were three in Cyprus) declaimed against the outrage of denying Greek children an education, and the Athens and Cairo radios beamed abuse on the English administration for its barbarity, but the Department of Education stood firm, and toward the end of winter the turmoil died down, the Greek flags vanished from the school roofs as mysteriously as they had appeared, the buildings re-opened their doors, and the children cheerfully trooped back to their lessons.

Just after mid-winter, a Greek-Cypriot newspaper deplored the high incidence of juvenile delinquency on the island, and stated that ninety percent of all crimes were being committed by youths between the ages of seventeen and twenty-three. I myself heard anxious parents lament the lack of discipline of their children, not the high-school students only, but the younger ones in the elementary schools. There seemed to be little doubt that the educational system had backfired. All the textbooks in the Greek schools came from Athens, as did also some of the high-school teachers, and all the textbooks in the Turkish schools came from Istanbul or Ankara.

I could not read the Turkish textbooks, but the Greek readers I borrowed from our wood-cutter's children fell far below the standards demanded in Western Europe. They did not mention modern Cyprus, of course, but only Greece and its history, and that history they grossly distorted. Some pages were filled with puerile homilies. The reader for children eight to ten years of age taught these lessons:

"How wonderful is a walk in the country with your teacher," and

"How ashamed you will be one day if you don't say your prayers and wash your face and hands each morning."

Other lessons were more disturbing. Here is one that I have translated, from the same reader designed for eight-to-ten-year-olds.

Lesson 48

On each house floats today a flag. Young and old are full of joy. The bells ring. It is the day we celebrate our fatherland, Greece.

Everyone has gathered in the little village church. They sing a hymn of praise. There also is the school with its flag, the flag of Greece. The tallest boy, Liakos, holds it; he is the flag-bearer. They sing songs about heroes. Above, on the bishop's seat, is written *NO*; and, underneath, another inscription, *28 OCTOBER, 1940*.

The priest wears the sacred vestments and walks majestically. The chanters chant. The congregation makes the sign of the cross.

When the hour arrived, the schoolteacher mounted the bishop's seat to make a speech. His voice is like thunder; his eyes are shooting flames. He speaks about the fatherland, Greece, about the war that broke out there in 1940. He himself had fought in that war. He speaks of our enemies who came to make war on us, to enslave our fatherland, to seize our villages and towns, our seas and islands. All the Greeks then rose as one man. The whole world admired us in that war. Numerous were our enemies, but we conquered them, on the mainland, in the air, on the sea.

Among those who were in the church was a wounded veteran. The poor man had lost a hand for the fatherland. How sympathetically everyone gazed on him. And how proud he was at having made this sacrifice for the fatherland.

When the children returned to the school they said, enthusiastically: "We too, sir, when we become soldiers, we will make war and increase the might of Greece our fatherland, as our parents have done."

In Cyprus, a British colony, that is what three-fourths of the schools were teaching the young children.

While I was reading their schoolbooks in Kyrenia, the authorities in Famagusta, sixty miles away, were holding an inquest over a high-school youth, the official bearer of his school's Greek flag, who had been shot by an English soldier during a riot. The soldiers testified that the youth had been the ringleader of the riot; lawyers engaged by relatives declared that he was an innocent bystander. One English-language newspaper, but none of the Greek-language ones, mentioned another victim, a young English soldier whose skull had been cracked by a stone from a catapult.

A few days later I met a U.S. radio engineer who had been living in Cyprus for two years. He commented: "England has brought all these troubles on herself. If we Americans had owned the island we would not have tolerated separate education for Greeks and Turks. We would have made English the medium of instruction in all schools, with Greek and Turkish as second languages only. Then there would have been no divided loyalties on the island, no riots between Greeks and Turks and between Greeks and English." Perhaps he was right. It is easy to recognize one's mistake after the event.

We met English soldiers everywhere. They sped along the highway in trucks and jeeps, their rifles always at the ready in case of ambush. Nearly all were boys of from eighteen to twenty-one, good-looking youngsters who might relish a little excitement to relieve the tedium of national service, but who clearly hated some of the duties they were called on to perform. I was greatly impressed by their good humour and patience, and wondered whether our Canadian boys would be as restrained. Yet the Greek-language newspapers on the island, and even Archbishop Makarios, the head of the island's Orthodox Church, constantly charged them with brutality and sadism. The newspapers were especially indignant in January, just after a riot outside the Nicosia high school. They admitted that the students had gathered piles of stones, barricaded the street, and, from both the schoolyard and the roof of a neighbouring building, showered volleys of stones on the soldiers who came to clear away the obstruction. One paper even reported, rather indiscreetly, that two priests of the Orthodox Church had been urging on the students from the rear! No one was injured severely enough to spend a night in hospital, yet these Greek-language newspapers fairly screamed at what they called the "brutal handling of enthusiastic schoolchildren by savage British troops."

They failed to add that many of the troops were no older than the schoolchildren. Three weeks later, the same newspapers expressed no more than the mildest regret when a bomb hurled into the bedroom of two English infants blew off the foot of their mother, who had thrown herself over them on the bed to protect them with her body.

The English administration honestly acknowledged that its soldiers did occasionally mishandle the Greek Cypriots, and shortly before we left the island, it court-martialled and severely punished two officers who had beaten a Greek prisoner suspected of terrorist activities. The island's governor, General Harding, exacted strict discipline from his men, but it was impossible always to hold in check troops who knew that at any moment they might be stoned by schoolchildren, shot at from ambush, or blown to pieces with a bomb. Such incidents were happening two or three times a week. We heard the explosion of a bomb that had been thrown at the feet of four English soldiers sitting in front of a café in Kyrenia's main street. One of the soldiers quickly kicked it across the street, where its blast destroyed the front of a new store that was being erected for the island's most intransigent firebrand, the local bishop.

An ugly riot broke out at Lapithos during February, when the Greek Cypriots were celebrating the Independence Day of mainland Greece, their "fatherland." The local Turks blamed the disorder on drunken Greeks, and the Greeks retorted that some Turks had been insolent to a party of peaceful holidaymakers. About a dozen victims, the majority of them Turks, were carried to the Kyrenia Hospital, among them an old woman and two girls who had been thrown to the ground from an upper balcony.

When the news reached Nicosia, bands of angry Turks stormed through the streets beating up their Greek-speaking fellow citizens and breaking the windows of Greek shops. It required all the persuasion their elders could muster, backed by a company of British soldiers and half a mile of barbed wire, to restore an uneasy peace.

In Famagusta, too, Cyprus' second largest town, Turkish youths loudly called for vengeance. Kyrenia fortunately remained quiet, although no shops opened for two days and most of the people, Turks and Greeks alike, stayed anxiously indoors.

That same month, Kyrenia experienced a disturbance of its own making. Some youths carried a number of concrete building blocks up to the roof of the bishop's unfinished store, which occupied the inner corner of the right angle where the Nicosia highway entered the main street, and they began to hurl these blocks down on every English motorcar that turned the corner. They damaged six, and wounded an English captain so severely that he was carried immediately to Kyrenia hospital. A seventh car they crushed completely, but its owner-driver escaped with only slight injuries. By a stroke of irony, he proved to be a Greek Cypriot. Warned then that two jeeps of soldiers were approaching the youths fled, and no one in the village appeared to know their names or where they came from. My wife and I barely escaped being eyewitnesses—or victims—of this episode. We had been walking down the highway to shop on the main street, and had reached within one hundred and fifty yards of the corner when a woman stopped us and warned us to turn back, because some disturbance had just erupted ahead of us.

Three or four days later I entered Kyrenia's small stationery shop to buy my usual newspapers. Its Greek-Cypriot proprietress smiled at me, since I was one of her regular customers, but she continued to serve two other clients while I scanned the headlines of that morning's

Nicosia Greek-language journal. Presently the other customers left, and she said to me, in English, "Can you read that Greek newspaper?" I read the headlines aloud. It seemed to open a floodgate, for her words came pouring out: "Every morning I wake up afraid that I will never see my husband again. He carries supplies to the English soldiers in—, you know; it is the only job that he could find. But EOKA is angry with him, and I know that it will shoot him down one evening and leave his corpse at the roadside. What will become of us then, myself and our two children? What is to be the end of it all? Cyprus used to be such a happy place, and now we are all afraid of one another, afraid even to speak."

Her prediction came true. A month later he was dead, shot down in the dark as he was returning to his home. It was Ancient Greece that created tragic drama, and tragedy has never ceased to stalk that land or the people who speak its tongue. Is there some madness in their blood that passes on from generation to generation? At the same time as the Erinyes[10] were pursuing this man to his death another Greek-Cypriot woman, sitting beside her wounded husband in the Nicosia hospital, helplessly watched two masked men walk down the corridor, shoot him dead before her eyes, and escape through the hospital door. Youths still in their teens were committing some of these outrages, for the virus raged even among the children. The schools made no effort to combat it. They seemed rather to encourage it. Had we been transported to another planet?

Nominally, Cyprus schools were governed by elected committees, but the real controller of the Greek schools was the Orthodox Church, and it was the Orthodox Church—or rather its Archbishop Makarios, several Cypriots told us—that had organized the EOKA movement which was fighting to unite the island with Greece. For in Cyprus, as in mainland Greece, the Orthodox Church is a political as well as a religious organization. Ever since the collapse of the Roman Empire, it has held, or at least claimed, a leading place in the island's political life. During the three hundred years of Turkish rule, indeed, it was the archbishop and bishops of the Orthodox Church who really governed the island, because the Turks found it easier to let the clergy squeeze the taxes from the recalcitrant population than collect them through agents of their own nation. The Church lost much of its political power when Turkey handed over the administration to England, but past history certainly gave Archbishop Makarios solid grounds for claiming that he was entitled to speak for all the island's Greek-speaking inhabitants.

In Western Europe, the Roman Catholic Church had exercised similar political power during the Middle Ages. But it had also been the champion of civilization, because very few people outside its clergy could read or write, or knew anything about art or science. In Cyprus, the Greek Orthodox Church never undertook this mission. It acquired wealth, prestige, and authority; it was the centre of all social life, but it was not a civilizing force. It could not be, because most of its priests and monks were as ignorant as the peasants around them. In Turkish times, indeed—if we may trust the statements of contemporary travellers—many of them were illiterate. Very rarely were they able or permitted to travel abroad, and, isolated in their small island, they knew almost nothing of the world beyond their shores. It was not surprising, therefore, that until this last half-century, Cyprus failed to produce an artist, a writer, a musician or a scholar of even second rank, that its textiles, pottery and other handicrafts were inferior to

---

[10]In Greek mythology, the Erinyes were "black goddesses of wrath" who avenged crimes and bloodshed.

those of Greece and Italy, and that the mass of the people, even the kindest and most hospitable, were extremely backwoodsy in their outlook, and also extremely conservative. I am painting the picture in its broadest outline, of course. One must never forget that today there are many well-educated Cypriots, men of high attainments and wide horizons.

Graver in Western eyes than the ignorance and superstition the Cyprus Orthodox Church had fostered through the centuries was the low standard of ethics it had condoned. The island has never really belonged to the European world but to the Middle East, where truth means something very different from its connotation in the West. In Egypt and the Levant, it savours strongly of expediency. Cyprus's three Greek-language newspapers, each of which reflected some shade of EOKA opinion, were distorting the news with as little hesitation as newspapers in communist countries, and using language just as violent. Truth to them was pragmatical; it changed to fit the circumstances. So too did right conduct. If it seemed expedient, it was not wrong to be friendly with a man to his face and shoot him in the back when he was off his guard; or, if you were a schoolchild (I take this from the Greek-Cypriot school reader), to deny that it was you who scribbled on the school walls—provided no one saw you. The lies told by witnesses in Cyprus's law courts may have been no more flagrant than those told in Canada, but in Cyprus, the public condoned them, and applauded if they succeeded.

From the Greek-Cypriot point of view, Archbishop Makarios quite rightly refused to condemn EOKA's violence and assassinations because those acts promoted his own political program. And in January, when his young cousin Mouskos ambushed and killed the driver of an English army jeep, and was himself shot by the officer who was riding in the jeep, the Archbishop, according to the Greek-Cypriot newspapers, acted righteously when he presided at the funeral in the full regalia of his office and proclaimed the Cypriot youth a national hero, but scorned even to mention the unfortunate English lad who had fallen his victim. I am sure that had it been possible to take a poll of all the Greek Cypriots who had read Homer, and asked them who was the greater hero, Achilles the straight-forward warrior or Odysseus the crafty one, ninety percent of them would have chosen Odysseus.

Clearly, Greek-Cypriot schools and churches were teaching ethical values unlike those we of the Western world try to inculcate in our children. During one of our Greek lessons, I asked Andreas why he and his fiancée did not prepare better school readers, and he answered,

"A few years ago, the Department of Education did introduce new text-books, but the school committees and the mothers of the children protested so vigorously that the Department withdrew them again."

Everything we saw and heard strengthened our conviction that the clouds over Cyprus were darkening. A few years before, it had been counted a very happy island, but now it was being swept by a tide of unreasoning "nationalism" aroused by its Orthodox Church and encouraged by Athens. That tide seemed destined to run its course, and outsiders like ourselves could do no more than hope that wise statesmanship would guide it in a constructive direction and ward off some of its foreseeable ills.

The political union with Greece, which so many Greek Cypriots were demanding, threatened economic disaster. England had poured large sums of money into the island, not for military purposes only, but for roads, electricity, harbour works, water supply, reforestation, and agriculture, as well as for education, pensions, and medical services. Greece could not possibly maintain such a program. That country was virtually bankrupt, and plagued with widespread unemployment. It would inevitably take more from Cyprus than it could give. Furthermore, if Cyprus stepped outside the Commonwealth, she would lose her preferential market in Britain, which was now her best customer, and find great difficulty in selling elsewhere the lemons and oranges, the carobs, potatoes, barley, and wines that made up her principal exports, apart from a little copper and iron pyrites.

Many Cypriot businessmen and senior civil servants realized this, but an uncompromising fanaticism held the stage and they were afraid to raise their voices. The EOKA party had proclaimed, "Whoever is not for us is against us." And EOKA demanded that England go.

Many English people, even some who had lived many years in Cyprus, seemed willing to leave. Yet England could hardly wash her hands of the island without further concern. She had obligations towards the Turkish minority of 100,000 persons, nearly a fourth of the population; she had obligations to NATO; and she had obligations to the Greek Cypriots themselves, who should see the issues clearly before taking the final step. Many who were clamouring for union with Greece might want to pause and reconsider if that union suddenly threatened them with a depreciated currency, a loss of outside markets, higher taxes, unemployment and a lower standard of living. They and their church leaders might quickly cease their agitation if the Communist Party, which is exceedingly strong in Greece, should gain control of that country. And they would certainly change their minds if, as seemed quite probable, England's withdrawal sparked a bloody civil strife and either annexation by Turkey, or a division of the island into two halves which would disrupt the whole economy. An overwhelming majority of the Greek Cypriots, including their own church leaders, might then prefer self-government within the Commonwealth for an indefinite period, in the hope that world tensions might one day relax and nations find new and better ways of working together in harmony. One thing appeared clear, viz., that the permanent solution of the Cyprus question rested not with Greece and England, but with Greece and Turkey. If those two countries could lay aside their centuries-old enmity and work out an agreement, England would not hesitate to drop out of the picture.[11]

One other thing we discovered when we re-visited Lambousa after the late winter rains and the spring sunshine had revived the grass and the wildflowers. The stone throwing and the bloodshed so prevalent throughout the island had not extinguished the goodwill and hospitality for which Cypriots were famous during the nineteenth century. At the turn-off from the highway, it is true, we encountered hostile scowls from a group of men who were gossiping at the corner, but when we stopped a hundred yards down the lane beside an almond orchard and were picking some of the yellow oxalis blossoms that spangled the green grass beneath the trees, a very pretty high-school girl approached us, asked how long we intended to stay among the ruins of the old town, and suggested that we stop and rest at her home on the way back. She met us later at her gate, clasping in her arms a large bunch of wild cyclamens she

---

[11]On March 9, 1956, while my parents were living in Kyrenia, British soldiers swooped down on Archbishop Makarios and whisked him by airplane to the Seychelles Islands in an effort to rid Cyprus of one of its principal instigators of political conflict. Increased violence followed, to which was added the demand for the release of the Archbishop. He was released in March 1958, forbidden to return to Cyprus, and went to Greece. Ironically, he returned to Cyprus as its first president in 1960.

had just gathered for my wife. And her mother, who immediately appeared in the doorway, invited us to enter and partake of the wine and sweetmeats traditionally offered to honoured guests. Here at least was one family which had escaped the venom of pseudo-nationalism and the bitter hatreds engendered by the two world wars.

Then there was the Turkish shepherd boy, Enver, who fortuitously struck up an acquaintance with us and became one of our staunchest friends, without ever comprehending a word we said to him or uttering a word that we ourselves understood. He was a sturdy lad of perhaps fourteen, shabbily dressed in an old coat six sizes too big for him, and a pair of trousers tucked into long, loose, knee-high boots that clattered as he hobbled along. Our first encounter was unscheduled. He, his father, and his younger sister were shepherding through the vacant lots behind and in front of our house a small flock of the long-faced, longhaired, fat-tailed but deceptively athletic sheep that are so characteristic of the eastern Mediterranean. One of the animals somehow found its way into our garden, or more correctly, Sophie's garden, and was racing among the flower beds, vainly trying in one place or another to squeeze through the iron pickets of the encircling fence. Terrified for Sophie's plants—for the only creature more omnivorous than a Cyprus sheep is a Cyprus goat—I tried to capture it. Enver then came in through the front gate to retrieve his wayward animal. Between us we cornered the invader, threw it over the fence with a united heave, and turned to face each other. He looked glum, expecting at the very least a severe scolding, but when I smiled and held out my hand he grasped it in both his, smiled back, and sealed our blood-brotherhood.

A few days later he brought my wife a large bough of blossoms which I suspect he stole from some Greek-Cypriot's orchard. And nearly every week thereafter he presented her with a bunch of flowers or some other little gift which he thought would give her pleasure.

IV

Ever since the autumn harvest the farmers had been trimming their olive trees or ploughing their dry fields in preparation for the rains, and the flocks of the shepherds had been fertilizing those fields with their droppings, for artificial fertilizers were expensive. We saw only one tractor in our district. North coast peasants were too poor to buy power machines; even teams of oxen seemed scarce. The average farmer worked his land with a pair of mules or donkeys, or with a cow yoked to a mule or a donkey, and he used a homemade wooden plough with a pointed share crudely shod with sheet iron.

During the winter of 1955–56, the rains began in early February. Throughout that month black storm clouds swept across the Caramanian Straits every third or fourth day and lashed the Kyrenia range with drenching showers. Part of the rainwater penetrated the limestone rocks and burst out far below in unannounced springs, and part raced down the steep ravines, filled the water tanks and the irrigation ditches, overflowed the stony streambeds that had lain dry for nine months, and scored new erosion channels in the ploughed fields. There are no perennial rivers in Cyprus. Even in the rainy season, very little water reaches the sea, for the thirsty lowlands, parched by the scorching summer sun, drink up most of it and store the surplus in underground wells.

February passed, and with it the rainstorms. The sky became cloudless and gloriously blue, the transparent air was laden with the scent of the damp earth. Green grass sprouted everywhere, and, one after another, the spring flowers opened their blossoms. First of the fruit trees, the almonds burst into bloom. Slumbering nature had awakened in a fever of energy, and with corresponding energy, the farmers flung their seed bags over their shoulders and went forth to sow. Some of their seed fell on rich soil and some on stony ground, for outcrops of useless bedrock littered many of the fields.

We, too, succumbed to spring's fever and turned our thoughts, not to the traditional house cleaning, but to extended trips through the island. The first trip took us to Salamis, the old capital of Cyprus six miles north of Famagusta, which was founded about eight hundred years before Christ and destroyed by successive earthquakes a thousand years later. It had been the home of Barnabas, that disciple of St. Paul who, in the words of the *Acts of the Apostles,* "having land, sold it, and brought the money, and laid it at the apostle's feet." St. Paul and St. Mark sailed with him to Cyprus, converted the island's Roman governor, and left Barnabas to establish in Salamis Christianity's first foreign mission. But Barnabas suffered martyrdom at the hands of the city's Jewish colony.

Four centuries later, he appeared to the Bishop of Cyprus in a vision, and disclosed to that dignitary the cave in which he had lived and the grave in which he had been buried. Thereupon, the bishop, with great pomp and ceremony, uncovered both, and on the strength of the miracle in which he had participated claimed second place in the hierarchy of the Greek Orthodox Church, and received the Roman Emperor's privilege of wearing a purple robe on special occasions and of signing his name in red ink. Today's Archbishop of Cyprus, Makarios III, still enjoys these last two privileges, but his claim to rank second in the church's hierarchy, below the Patriarch in Constantinople (Istanbul) but above the Archbishop of Athens, has not ceased to provide fuel for controversy.

We left Kyrenia at 8 a.m., carrying in our car enough food for two meals each, and heading eastward, passed Pachyammos and the Turkish village, where an early-rising farmer was already pacing up and down his fields broadcasting by hand his seed wheat. Beyond, in the rolling land between the highway and the sea, were many sand dunes anchored down by the deep-rooted carob tree, which some one has nicknamed "the peasant's tree," because it provides his sheep and goats with nourishing food during the winter months, and himself with sustenance in times of famine, fuel for his oven, grateful shade in the hot days of summer, and protection for his land against eroding water and drifting sand. I do not think that, in this sparsely populated part of the coast, the Cypriots had planted these carob trees expressly to check the creeping sand dunes, but rather that the trees were survivors of cultivated carobs which their owners had abandoned during the troubled years of the sixteenth and seventeenth centuries.

Here and there on the landward side of the highway, the rising ground carried orchards of olive trees that grew on manmade terraces faced with dry-stone walls. This agricultural technique seems to have been unknown to the ancient Greeks and Romans, and may have originated in Syria or Lebanon during the early centuries of the Christian era, when the break-up of the Roman empire exposed the entire Mediterranean to piratical raids and made life particularly insecure along the shores of Asia Minor. During that period, farmers in many lowland areas abandoned their fields and moved their cattle and sheep into the mountains, where trees were scarce or non-existent, but the sun and the frost had split the surfaces of the limestone rocks into excellent building blocks which could take the place of wood. From the Levant, the Moslems, and perhaps some returning pilgrims and Crusaders, would have carried the new "stone-terrace" technique into the Western Mediterranean, where it spread along the rocky coasts of Sicily and Italy, and up the Rhone valley into the heavily wooded Cevennes. In recent centuries, farmers have abandoned many of these ancient terraces, and today they seldom construct new ones because of the heavy labour in transporting the stones and the earth, constructing the walls and maintaining them year after year in proper repair. However, in certain parts of Sicily, they are utilizing the old terraces to grow oranges instead of olives and grapes, and on the Italian Riviera they have substituted flowers which, shipped by plane, find profitable markets in Paris, Brussels, and London.

The highway left the coast about twenty-five miles from Kyrenia and turned south through a very low pass, which brought us out onto Cyprus's central plain near the large village of Lefkoniko. Here, dominating the main square, stood an ancient church which still retained its graceful shape, despite considerable remodelling during the nineteenth century. Being anxious to reach Salamis as soon as possible, we deferred its examination until our return and kept straight on, noting only that the villagers looked askance at us and seemed by no means friendly. They had good grounds for unfriendliness, for Lefkoniko was one of the "hot spots" in Cyprus, a nest of terrorists or patriots, depending on one's point of view. Just five days earlier, they had shot three English soldiers two miles south of their village, and the assassins had escaped scot-free because none of their countrymen would inform on them. Now suddenly here were we, two foreigners, prowling around their neighbourhood. Were we spies for the English government? Little wonder they seemed suspicious of our presence. No one molested us, however, as we drove slowly down the main street, crossed the square and followed the highway south. Could it be that the "evil-eye" charm on our windshield was faithfully diffusing its magic?

We reached Salamis without mishap. It had been a large city in the days of St. Paul, but most of what remained, after the earthquakes had shattered it and a tidal wave swept over it, lay buried beneath the sand or had been carried away to build the later city of Famagusta. The government had uncovered the pavements and some pillars of the forum, the gymnasium and the public bath, and it was slowly digging out some neighbouring ruins. But funds were limited, and the work, carefully done with hand labour, was slow and laborious. Aleppo pines, mimosa and eucalyptus trees had been planted to check the drifting of the sand, but though they provided pleasant shade and introduced a restful green into the arid landscape, the place seemed desolate and the ruins insignificant compared with those of Asia Minor, Greece, and Italy. The work-men, half of them women, came and went each day, and one or two shepherds pastured their flocks among the shattered walls and broken pillars that protruded above the ground, but the only permanent residents were an archaeological custodian and a fire ranger. The visitor felt that Nature had condemned to total destruction Barnabas's thriving city of over 100,000 inhabi-tants, and accordingly, it had disappeared almost without trace. Even the long aqueduct that had supplied it with water had crumbled into the dust. Two of its arches were still visible near Salamis, and we know that it began at Kythraea, thirty-five miles away, where a large spring, the second largest in Cyprus, issued from the foot of the Kyrenia Mountains, but its route was no longer traceable. *Sic transit gloria* [*mundi*].

Early in the afternoon, saddened by what we had observed, we headed home, and, crossing the dreary plain, arrived once more in Lefkoniko. Straight in front of us as we entered the main

Figure 40 Excavated Roman ruins of a gymnasium at Salamis, near Famagusta, Cyprus, 1956.
Photo by D. Jenness

square was the church we were planning to examine, but in front of us also, on a corner to the left, about twenty men were drinking and gossiping on a café sidewalk. What should we do? Where dared we park our car? And was it safe to enter the church, leaving the car unattended?

This was not the moment to hesitate. I drove direct to the café sidewalk, stopped the Volkswagen within five feet of a black-bearded, ferocious-looking "Blackbeard," and said to my wife,

"Get out and ask him, in Greek, if the church is open."

All conversation on the sidewalk had stopped. Every eye was watching us, every face alert to what might happen next. But my wife, calm and dignified, with head erect and silver hair gleaming in the sunlight, stepped in front of "Blackbeard" and asked him, in measured Greek, "Is the church open?"

Pandemonium broke loose before "Blackbeard" had time to answer her. From nowhere and everywhere a horde of schoolchildren bore down on us and took us prisoners. "Come with us, come with us," they shouted. Two girls seized my wife's hands, the boys surrounded me, and the shouting, laughing crowd led us to the church, pulled down its chandelier so that we could examine its sparkling crystal, lifted up a tombstone in the floor that we might marvel at its bones, lined up gaily outside the church door while I photographed them, then escorted us back to the café in triumph. The men still sat quietly at their tables, the car stood untouched at the sidewalk, and the only remark that reached our ears was "Blackbeard's" injunction to the children, "Don't pester the strangers." No one asked us who we were nor why we had come, but everyone smiled and waved his hand as we drove away. Out of the north we had appeared, unheralded, and back into the north we vanished, trailing behind us a cloud of good wishes.

A later excursion took us forty miles westward to a steep, conical hill overlooking the sea, around whose sides Swedish archaeologists discovered, fifty years ago, traces of a small town, and on its summit two ruins, a temple to Athena on the landward side and a sumptuous palace on the sea side facing Turkey. In the fifth century B.C., when ancient Greece reached the zenith of her glory and Pericles presided over a resplendent Athens, this place had been the capital of one of Cyprus's petty kingdoms, all of them dominated at that period by Persia. It may have been the pettiest of them all, for it lasted less than a hundred years and bequeathed to us neither its name nor the names of its rulers. Sheep were wandering through the ruins of its palace and sleeping in the bedchamber of its long-forgotten "King of Kings." And its citadel, the hill known today as Vouni, was deserted save by the government custodian and his family who dwelt at its foot.

Forty miles by car on a paved highway, even if that highway is narrow and winding, is a mere, after-breakfast jaunt, but there were so many interesting sights along our route that, although we set out as usual about 8 a.m., it was midday before we reached our destination. Lambousa with its Roman and Byzantine ruins did not delay us on this occasion, nor Lapithos, where night and day a Christian church and a Moslem mosque frowned defiantly at each other. But just where the Palaeomylus River emerged from the hills to bury its trickle of water in the coastal plain, we stopped to gather a few of the beautiful wild anemones that patterned both sides of the highway. Our road turned southward here around the end of the Kyrenia Mountains and entered a district of bright red earth, an infallible sign of low rainfall, and in the heart of this district, near a pine plantation, lay the village of Myrtou and an ancient monastery dedicated to St. Panteleimon, the patron of physicians. Ten years earlier, it had housed four monks and several destitute old men who, in Cyprus, as in Western Europe during the Middle Ages, traditionally turned to the monasteries for food and shelter.

But now that the English government had introduced pensions for the aged, more and more old people were remaining with their kindred in the villages, where many could still perform light duties and live useful and contented lives to the end of their days. That was probably the reason why we found at Myrtou Monastery only one monk and two pensioners, one of whom was dreaming away the years with his donkey in the shade of an arcade.

In Xeros, twenty-five miles beyond Myrtou, a line of trucks crossed the highway on a narrow-gauge railway and temporarily barred our passage. They were carrying copper pyrites over a long pier to a motor barge, which then transported it to a freight steamer anchored in deep water a mile off shore.

Cyprus is the Greek word for copper, and the island received that name because, from 2500 B.C. to A.D. 500, it was Mediterranean Europe's principal source of the metal. The ore that we saw being shipped from Xeros came from a mine that was operating in A.D. 166 when a Greek physician named Galen visited it and described the mining techniques of its Roman engineers, the cramped shafts that ran into the earth, the sulphuric acid and its salts that dripped through the ceiling onto the naked backs of the miners, and the terrible sufferings of these slave miners, some of whom were Christians condemned to this hard labour because they would not renounce their faith. Cyprus's copper mines were abandoned three or four hundred years after Galen's day, when Europe found richer sources for the metal in France and Spain, and none of them were re-opened until the beginning of this twentieth century, when a Los Angeles company, the Cyprus Mines Corporation, purchased the mineralized properties near Xeros, installed modern machinery, and engaged several hundred local workmen. In 1956, some 5,000 Cypriots depended for their livelihood on this one mine. The corporation was providing excellent working conditions, moderately high wages, good homes, reasonable pensions, and free medical care in a well-equipped hospital, which it had built on the seashore. No labour troubles had disrupted its operations until the year previous, when some political agitators infiltrated into the working force, incited a few men to acts of sabotage, intimidated others, and fomented strikes and threats of strikes. The agitation was very short-sighted, for the ore body was approaching exhaustion, and no adequate reserves were in sight. The main result of the unrest, indeed, was to hasten the mine's abandonment.

We did not visit either the mine or the concentration plant, but after watching the loading operations for a few minutes, drove on two miles to a well-preserved Roman theatre, practically all that remains of the once important city of Soli, whose ruins had supplied neighbouring villages with a convenient stone quarry, and de Lessop's engineers with excellent stone blocks for constructing the quays at Port Said. Like the builders of Egypt's pyramids, Greek and Roman architects erected public buildings to outlast the centuries. But all their knowledge and skill could not prevail against man's own ravaging hands, which have been the most destructive agency our world has ever known.

We ate our picnic lunch under an olive tree near the Soli theatre, then pushed on two miles to Vouni, where the custodian's young daughter guided us up the steep trail to the ruined palace on the summit. It was not the palace, however, that we saw first when we peered over the summit rim, but two flourishing carob trees, which were being systematically trimmed by a flock of sheep. The athletic animals leaped up all around the trees, tearing off every leaf and branch within their reach and leaving, above six feet of naked trunk, two symmetrical circles of dense foliage that might have been marked out by a landscape engineer. They reminded me of Holland's well-trained kine [cattle] which, tethered to stakes, steadily mow down that country's lush pastures in progressive semi-circles; and I wondered whether undulating lines and circles, symmetrical curves and faultless rotundities, possess the same irresistible appeal to cattle, sheep and other animals as they do to human beings.

The site of Vouni's palace was an eagle's eyrie, the view from it breathtaking. At our feet lay the blue sea. From the edge of the abrupt cliff, eight-hundred-feet high, it seemed possible to leap straight into the water. Behind us stretched a line of low mountains separated from us by a green valley almost narrow enough to constitute a gorge. With but a feeble stretch of the imagination, one could see a band of soldiers armed with long spears marching up this gorge behind a two-horse chariot in which a corseleted, bronze-helmeted Ajax stood erect and guided his charioteer. The very plan of the palace, as its excavators had pointed out, heightened the illusion of being transported back to the Homeric age, for, despite its date, the fifth century B.C., this building was not constructed for the elected ruler of a democracy similar to contemporary Athens or Thebes, but for a despot who possessed the power of life and death over his subjects and lorded it, perhaps, over the adjacent sea. Here was the great megaron or hall in which he dispensed justice (or injustice), there his bedroom and his hot-water and cold-water baths. And yonder were the quarters of his servants and the kitchens. On the opposite side of the summit stood the temple of his tutelary deity, and below, around the hill slopes, the rude habitations of his subjects or the tenements of his troops. Perhaps he was not a Greek at all, but an oriental satrap of a lilliputian kingdom that perished with its protector, the mighty empire of ancient Persia.

Our homeward drive was uneventful, but this excursion into the Homeric age had over-taxed my heart. For several days afterwards I was plagued with fainting spells, and the local Greek-Cypriot physician we eventually called in, Dr. Thales, ordered me to bed for several weeks. That cancelled all plans for further expeditions, whether afoot or by car. Even my table in the Nicosia Museum the doctor decreed out of bounds, although he allowed me to sit up in bed and read or write at my pleasure. To curb my impatience he admonished me one day, half humorously,

"Your age[12] should have cautioned you not to pursue ancient Cyprus too vigorously. Now you are paying the penalty. You're a typical disciple of Epimetheus; you act first and repent later."

Dr. Thales himself, trained in Athens and London, was a faithful disciple of the father of his profession, Hippocrates. He treated all his patients with equal care, regardless of their nationality, their religion and their political faith. At this period, they included, besides myself, the child of an English air force officer, and the leader of the Greek-Cypriot terrorists, Colonel Grivas, who had been wounded in an encounter with English soldiers. But this we did not know until later. We never discussed politics with him, but talked of Cyprus's history and its legends, peasant handicrafts, and some quaint old customs that still survived in out-of-the-way places. He was a well-educated man and a highly trained physician from whose numerous visits we derived both profit and pleasure.

During my period of enforced leisure, Enver, the Turkish shepherd boy, came to our gate every few days with a spray of flowers or some other token of his friendship. And once, he brought his little sister. My wife called to me one drowsy afternoon that a gentleman on the street was trying to attract my attention, and she bade me look out of my window. I looked out, and there was Enver, proudly bestriding a fine donkey that his father had purchased for him that morning. He had hurried around to our house so that his foreign friends might admire it with him.

Reading, writing, and visitors caused the days to pass fairly quickly, and my wretched heart to beat more normally. After three weeks, Dr. Thales permitted me to dress and walk around the house slowly and quietly, and one day Andreas drove me over the mountains to observe how swiftly the sprouting grain was veiling the brown plains with a film of green. Maroula's children played around my chair on the patio, the Wing Commander from across the street dropped in from time to time to discuss the political situation and Middle East intrigues, and one Sunday, the museum director and his wife drove out from Nicosia, bringing two rare books from his library for me to browse over.

Spring leaped almost instantaneously into early summer, and the sun became more fiery. It warned us that Canada's snow would have melted, that her rivers would have thrown off their covering of ice, and that it was time for us to wind up our commitments in Cyprus, pack up our belongings, and fly home. Dr. Thales rigorously examined me and gave his consent, blend-ing it with a stern warning against any future indiscretion. Then my wife, though gravely burdened by her useless husband, cheerfully undertook the necessary preparations. By good fortune, Andreas's brother was Kyrenia agent for Cyprus Airways, and he undertook to reserve passages for us from Nicosia right through to Ottawa.

---

[12]70 years old on February 10, 1956.

The day of our departure drew near. Our neighbours knew and spread the word that we were selling out, and very quickly we disposed of our Volkswagen and most of our furniture. The remainder we gave away, reserving only a number of useful articles for Maroula, who would clean up the house after we moved out. On the eve of our departure, my wife put the finishing touches on her packing and a few friends dropped in to say goodbye. By nine o'clock, all was quiet. I had already retired to my bed, and my wife was preparing to retire also, when the doorbell rang violently.

Sitting up in bed, I heard the strange voice of an Englishwoman. She was introducing herself.

"I am Mrs. X.... We haven't met before, but I just heard that you are leaving for Canada tomorrow morning. I am the president of the local chapter of the Knights of St. John, and, as you know, your governor-general, Mr. Vincent Massey, is the world president of that organization. I thought it would be so nice if our chapter used the occasion of your return to send him a case of the famous Commanderia wine which the Knights of St. John cultivated during the Middle Ages on their feudal estate in southern Cyprus. I will send the case down to you in the morning, and we shall be most grateful if you will present it to Mr. Massey with our compliments."

"I am sorry," my wife answered coldly. "My husband, you no doubt know, is an invalid, and our flight to Canada will be very long and tiring to us both. I am afraid we cannot undertake your commission."

"Oh, I am sure it will cause you no trouble," expostulated the stranger, "and Mr. Massey will be so pleased."

A harder note crept into my wife's voice.

"I am very sorry," she said, "but it is quite impossible. You will please excuse me. I must finish my packing."

Poor Mr. Massey. To the best of my knowledge he still lacks his Commanderia. But Cyprus is today only a half-member of the British Commonwealth, so Mr. Massey may prefer to survive on the sherry of a full member, Australia.

At 10 a.m. the following morning a taxi arrived to convey us to Nicosia. The last person to say goodbye to us was Maroula, who flung her arms round me wife's neck and wept copiously. Her two children wept in sympathy, too young to know what was happening. Poor little tots. I'm sure that for weeks afterwards they missed the daily ration of cookies my wife had handed them through our gate.

When Andreas's brother delivered our plane tickets, he instructed us to report to the Ledra Hotel in Nicosia before noon on a certain date, but warned us that the weekly flight to London might be delayed for several hours and even days. Actually it was delayed only two days, which we spent very quietly and comfortably at the hotel, conscious that the postponement arose not from any inefficiency on the part of the airline, but from its concern for the safety of the passengers. Exactly two weeks earlier, a sister plane on the London run had crashed into the Mediterranean, torn apart by the explosion of a time bomb which some Cypriot terrorist had planted in its carriage. Not a single passenger or crewmember had survived the disaster. The English authorities immediately doubled the guard around Nicosia's airport, prohibited all unauthorized visitors from entering its gate, and informed the public that, for an indefinite period, times printed on flight schedules from Cyprus would be provisional only.

On the third day, a car arrived at the hotel to convey us to the airport, where a squad of soldiers instantly blocked our entrance. Now before we left Kyrenia, our neighbour, the R.A.F. Group Captain, had whispered to my wife that she was not to worry when we reached the airport gate, because he had arranged that we should be properly taken care of. Sure enough, there at the gate was a friendly officer, who checked our papers and sent us forward in a military car to the foot of the plane's gangway. This was guarded by two soldiers, one an ordinary private, the other a strapping sergeant nearly twice my height and weight. At the first step of the gangway, I paused, and was remarking to my wife that it seemed unusually steep, when the sergeant swept me abruptly into his arms, carried me *plonk, plonk, plonk* up the steps as if I were a sack of potatoes, deposited me in a seat that the hostess hastily pointed out to him, straightened up, saluted, and marched down the ladder again. He had obeyed the Group Captain's orders and taken proper care of me. But so fiery was my face, so stiffly bristling every hair of my head, that my wife, who had followed right behind, fearfully turned her eyes away and murmured,

"I was as surprised as you were. But wasn't that sergeant strong!"

The flight to Canada was unmarred by any further incident. In London, where we transferred to British Overseas Airways Corporation, a dear old Scottish nurse mothered us from the Cyprus plane to the transatlantic one. The latter stopped at Reykjavik, Iceland, to refuel, and all the passengers except our two selves disembarked and dined, or rather supped, for it was after midnight. There was some confusion at Montreal, where a British Overseas Airways Corporation official escorted us through customs and handed us over to a Canadian airline officer for transmission to Ottawa. The latter buried his face in his papers and ignored everyone and everything around him, although there was no place to sit and at times hardly standing room. For a quarter of an hour, we stood backed into a corner, resting as best we could against the wall. Then our BOAC friend caught sight of us and went into action. One minute later, the desk-loving Canadian apologetically trundled a wheelchair up to me and conducted us to a private waiting room, there to rest in comfort until he returned at the appointed time and escorted us to the Ottawa plane.

It was on this Ottawa leg of our flight that the last incident occurred. Another unknown woman—a journalist perhaps—approached us at the front of the plane and said to my wife:

"Do tell me, please, who you two are. I have been observing you all the way from London, and I know that you are very special VIPs. Please tell me who you are."

And my wife answered:

"We are just garden-variety Canadians who have been living in Cyprus. There an R.A.F. Group Captain and a British army sergeant—may Allah reward them—performed a great miracle. They wafted us back across the Atlantic."

[In 1962 the results of my father's many hours of research, reading, and writing both in Cyprus and in Ottawa came to fruition with the publication of his book, The Economics of Cyprus—a Survey to 1914. *This title was an eleventh-hour change by the publisher. My father had submitted the manuscript with the title* Cyprus through the Ages. *In this scholarly work, he attempted to show how man had used the island throughout nearly six thousand years under a number of political regimes, the changes that had emerged in that time, and what successes had accompanied his efforts to obtain a satisfactory living from the island's meagre resources.]* [S.E.J.]

1959–1960: A FRENCH PILGRIMAGE AND EARLY CHURCH ARCHITECTURE

19

Stuart E. Jenness

During the 1950s, my father published articles on many of the subjects and ideas he had found interesting since his retirement. By 1959, he had exhausted most of the topics he wanted to investigate, and while trying to think of a new project to research, recalled his earlier interest in mediaeval church architecture. He may originally have been attracted to the subject during his student days at Oxford University, but if so his interest appears to have remained largely dormant throughout his professional years. A decade earlier, following his retirement in 1948, he purchased a 35-mm camera and photographed churches as well as other subjects while wintering in Italy, Spain, Mexico, and Cyprus. During those years, however, he was generally more occupied with other research interests, so his photographs (more exactly, his 35-mm colour slides) accumulated and remained virtually unknown to anyone but himself and Mother.

At last, in 1959, with time on his hands, he delved into a number of books about European and Middle Eastern church architecture and decided to spend the following winter visiting many of the older churches in France. Through his reading, he had learned that Gothic architecture developed and flourished in France's Seine River valley in the twelfth and thirteenth centuries. It seemed reasonable to think, therefore, that a winter in France would give him an excellent opportunity to visit and study many historic Romanesque and Gothic churches. He did not spend the winter in the Seine River Valley, however, for the climate there was not to his liking.

The prime reason he went to France for the winter of 1959–1960 appears to have been to seek answers to some of the questions on Romanesque and Gothic church architecture that had challenged his curiosity over the years. He had evidently formulated several ideas about a westward evolution of Christian church structures, with its extraordinary development in France between A.D. 1000 and 1500, and wanted to find evidence to confirm or refute his ideas.

My father rarely spoke about his interest in mediaeval church architecture, perhaps because of the lack of a receptive audience. He did not publish on any aspect of it, nor did he mention it in any of his recollections in this book. My first awareness of it came late in 2004 while I was examining his 35-mm colour-slide collection and unearthed two manuscripts he had written on the subject together with a well-worn notebook crammed full of details about various parts of many European churches, complete with references to books from which he had obtained most (if not all of) his information. My two brothers were as surprised as I was to learn of his interest. Only my mother would have known about it, for she, too, had been interested in church architecture for many years, and he would certainly have shared his ideas with her.

It seemed appropriate, therefore, to mention this little-known interest of his, reconstruct his winter's pilgrimage through France hoping to answer his long-held questions about mediaeval church architecture, and to include his unpublished essay on the subject, "Reflections on Early Churches."

Lacking correspondence or other kinds of documentation that would have told of his activities during his winter in France, I have pieced together his probable itinerary from the three kinds of evidence he left us: (1) his 35-mm colour slides of mediaeval French churches; (2) his well-worn notebook containing details about numerous French, German, and English churches; and (3) his two unpublished manuscripts. These three items, collectively, offer a glimpse of the intensity and enthusiasm with which he pursued his architectural interests.

During the last year or two of his life, my father examined and organized all of his hundreds of 35-mm colour (mainly Kodachrome) slides, in the process discarding many of them. Thankfully, he then laboriously labelled those that he retained and divided them by country— Italy, Spain, Cyprus, Mexico, France, and Martinique. From the French group, he set aside a topical collection of eighty-eight slides—fifty-nine of Romanesque churches and twenty-nine of Gothic churches. Most of these he took during the winter of 1959–1960, but a few date from 1952, when he and Mother were driving north after a winter in Málaga, Spain.

My father's well-worn stenographer's notebook contains many details (in his neat but very small handwriting) about specific French churches, with references to several books from which he obtained his information. Accompanying these details are a number of sketches, mainly rough ground plans he drew of some of the churches he described. Stapled to the inside of the front cover of the notebook is a two-page typed list of the names of dozens of towns and villages along ten pilgrimage routes to northwestern Spain, mainly from northern France but with links to England and parts of Germany. An asterisk beside many of the names marks important sanctuaries, hostels, or Establishments of the Knights Hospitalers (i.e., Templars). The notebook also includes brief details about a number of Italian, German, and English churches, so was not exclusively related to his travels in France. It is undated, lending uncertainty as to when he made the notes, but I suspect he wrote them in preparation for his 1959–1960 winter in France.

His two unpublished manuscripts have somewhat similar themes, but were intended for different audiences. The one, entitled "Reflections on Early Churches" (reproduced at the end of this chapter), is a short essay about his conclusions, following years of quiet contemplation, on the migration of architectural developments in the Middle Ages from Constantinople westward. He apparently completed it in the spring of 1963, for enclosed within its cover when I found it was a letter of rejection from a Canadian magazine publisher dated June 1963. The other manuscript, entitled "French Mediaeval Churches," is more geographically specific and architecturally descriptive, and includes twenty-two photographs (some of which are commercial postcards). Judging from its contents, it was prepared as an illustrated lecture, which my father may have given as part of a seminar at Ottawa's Carleton University sometime in the 1960s.

Journeying through France

Late in the fall of 1959, my father set off alone for Europe, leaving Mother behind by her own choice in their new bungalow overlooking the Gatineau River. He travelled by freight boat

Map 13 Communities in France with mediaeval churches visited by Jenness.

from Montreal to the Netherlands, where he purchased a new Volkswagen on a buy-back arrangement with its Dutch dealer.[1]

After taking possession of his automobile he drove to Paris and found accommodation in a hotel near the Gare de L'Est. He had been to Paris several times previously, but on this visit, he particularly wanted to see two churches: the Abbey of St-Denis in the northern suburbs, and Notre-Dame Cathedral. The Abbey of St-Denis is best known for being the burial site of many of the French kings, and hence is in that respect comparable with England's Westminster Abbey, the burial site of many English monarchs. What interested my father more, however, was the church's mixed architectural style. It had been erected about A.D. 1144 on the site of earlier churches dating back to A.D. 475, and had several structural features unknown to the

---

[1] A new Volkswagen at that time cost less than $2,000 U.S.

Romanesque style of the day, such as pointed arches and flying buttresses. After it collapsed in A.D. 1231, the damaged parts of the church were reconstructed in Gothic style, leaving it an unusual mixture of Romanesque and Early Gothic. In the years following its renovation, the Abbey of St-Denis aroused tremendous interest, which resulted in the construction of a dozen or more emulations in northern France, especially in Paris, Chartres, Amiens, Rhiems, and Bourges. Each of these other churches, of course, had its own special features.

Paris's Notre-Dame Cathedral, in contrast, was erected between A.D. 1163 and 1250, and is entirely Gothic in style. It features some of the most daring flying buttresses ever constructed and three remarkable thirteenth-century rose windows. My father noted that the rose window over the south transept of Notre-Dame was possibly the finest ever built. Coloured glass was known in Roman days, but its placing in lead frames to form pictures dates only from the tenth century. Stained-glass picture windows and rose windows made their first appearance in early Gothic churches.

From Paris, my father drove slowly southward, often following the routes of the Crusaders and pilgrims who had tramped laboriously southward in the eleventh to thirteenth centuries, as they headed to the shrine of St. James at Santiago de Compostela in northwestern Spain, the graves of saints in Rome, or holy places in Jerusalem. I do not know his actual route to the Mediterranean coast, but his colour slides include pictures of the following churches or cathedrals, which may have been taken on this southern trip: the Cathedral of St-Étienne at Sens, one of the earliest Gothic churches, whose architect also rebuilt Canterbury Cathedral in England after its destruction by fire in A.D. 1174; St-Étienne church at Auxerre, which shows the beginning of the flamboyant phase of Gothic architecture; the church at Vezelay, which claims to possess the remains of Mary Magdalene; the tenth-to-eleventh-century chapel at Le Puy, so curiously perched on top of an eighty-metre-high volcanic pinnacle; and the abbey church at Conques, dating from A.D. 1050. He also visited the Benedictine church in Beaulieu-sur-Dordogne to examine the tympanum[2] over its south door, which features one of the earliest carvings of the Last Supper and the prototype of the one at the Abbey of St-Denis in Paris. Before reaching the Mediterranean coast he examined the pink brick, fortress-like cathedral at Albi, considered the most impressive late-thirteenth-century church in France. Brick was used for that church's exterior because of the scarcity of stone in the district.

My father stayed most of the winter in the small French town of Mandelieu, on a hillside about five miles northwest of Cannes. From the road in front of his boarding house, the Pension Blanche Neige, he could see Cannes and the Mediterranean beyond, yet enjoy the smell of the flat-topped Mediterranean pines (which may have reminded him of the smell of the tall white pines at his Gatineau River cottage north of Ottawa) and the quiet of the surrounding countryside. During the winter, he took brief trips in his Volkswagen about the region, visiting various sites that interested him, such as the Romanesque churches in the ancient towns of Arles[3] and St-Gilles near the mouth of the Rhône River, and the fortress-church of Les Saintes-Maries-de-la-Mer at the mouth of the Rhône, where legend states the Holy Family

---

[2]A semi-circular space above a church door and enclosed by an arch, often ornamented with a sculpture.
[3]St-Trophime Church in Arles is said to be "perhaps the finest Romanesque church in Provence" (Robertson, 1984, p. 820).

landed after they fled from Herod. Yielding to his classical interests, he also visited the ruins of the Roman theatre at Arles, and Roman arenas at Arles and Nîmes. The well-preserved arena at Nîmes was originally capable of seating about 20,000 spectators. While in Nîmes, my father also examined that city's excellently preserved Roman temple.

I have been able to trace my father's route back to Paris in the spring by means of the identifying marks on some of his slides. Setting out from Mandelieu, he proceeded west and stopped briefly to view the remains of the Malpasset Dam, which had burst a few months earlier, tragically flooding parts of the city of Fréjus and drowning four hundred and twenty people. Bypassing Marseille, he continued to Montmajeur, near Arles, where he visited the ruins of a Benedictine abbey founded in A.D. 949. He then turned north and followed the valley of the Rhône River past the old fortified town of Avignon, with its twelfth-century bridge popularized in French song, and stopped briefly at Bourg St. Andreol to examine its Romanesque church with later-built spire and flying buttresses. Continuing past Lyon, France's second largest city, he turned west at Mâcon and proceeded to Cluny to examine the remains of the Romanesque abbey church, originally the largest Christian church until St. Peter's was built in Rome. Founded in A.D. 910, this abbey "became in the eleventh-to-twelfth centuries the influential base of an Order with some three hundred dependent houses,"[4] which had organized great pilgrimages to Santiago de Compestela, Rome, Jerusalem, and lesser shrines, and promoted the building of pilgrimage churches along the routes. His next stop was Paray-le-Monial, whose Romanesque church is considered a superb example of monastic architecture. It is also a pilgrimage place, but only since the 1870s. Continuing north, he paused briefly in Autun to examine the twelfth-century Romanesque Cathedral of St-Lazare with its sculptured "Last Judgement" (dating from A.D. 1135) over one of its doors, and then proceeded to Fontenay Abbey, northwest of Dijon. The plain Romanesque style of this abbey, dating from A.D. 1118 is a good example of the austerity of the Cisterian monks who occupied it. Nearby at Pontigny, northeast of Auxerre, he viewed another Cisterian abbey, the structure of which, being somewhat less old, was Gothic in style. His journey then took him west to the Loire River valley, where he visited several churches near Orléans. One of these, at Germigny-des-Près, bore remnants of its original Byzantine form, dating from A.D. 806, but later generations had greatly modified its appearance. Proceeding on his way, my father stopped at Chartres for several days, revelling in the beauty of its magnificent cathedral, which is considered by many to be the finest of all Gothic churches.

From Chartres, he proceeded north to the Netherlands, where he returned his automobile to the dealer as pre-arranged and then boarded a ship to Canada.

Sometime in the months that followed he prepared the two manuscripts on mediaeval churches mentioned previously. One of these is reproduced below.

Reflections on Early Churches
(by Diamond Jenness)

Many people hold the opinion that the most beautiful building man has yet constructed, the building with the most perfect form, is the ancient Greek temple. Its interior was relatively unimportant because the common people did not enter to meditate on the Divine, as we do

[4]Robertson, 1984, p. 527.

in our churches; instead, they gathered outside and awaited in the open air whatever message they expected to receive from their priest. For this reason, the Greek architect devoted most of his attention to the exterior of the temple; and since his fellow countrymen cherished very precise and clear-cut ideas about man and his place in the universe, he built for them an edifice that was equally clear-cut and devoid of mystery. So too did the Roman architects, who simply copied the temple architecture of the Greeks when their nation took over the hegemony of the Mediterranean.

A profound change came over the ancient world, however, within four or five hundred years of the death of Christ. The Roman Empire that had ruled it with apparent stability for several centuries collapsed and divided into two, an eastern empire and a western one, and it was the eastern empire, with its centre in Constantinople, that proved the mightier. Vanished was the old Greek faith that man could guide himself through life by the might of his reason alone. Man had grown to distrust his reason. No longer did the universe seem to him an open book, but mysterious and irrational, and philosophers both pagan and Christian began to search for the reality behind outward appearances, for the invisible, the mystical, and in many cases the magical. The mysticism that pervaded the old Orphic cults of the near east—the Eleusinian mysteries at Athens, the cults of the Great Mother and of Mithra—profoundly influenced their search. It influenced, also, the architecture of the churches that the early Christians built, for these Christians assembled inside their sacred edifices, not outside them, as had been the custom previously; and their architects, disregarding in large measure the external appearance of the buildings, concentrated on the interiors, and the effect those interiors would produce upon the congregations.

Early Christian churches fall into two main types.[5] In one, the building was constructed around a large octagon, from which it expanded outwards on all sides while remaining permanently centred on the high altar. Theologians of the period interpreted its form as symbolizing the universe centred on the Christian faith. France contains a few ruins of these central churches, but the principal surviving examples are Santa Sophia in Istanbul, and San Vitale in Ravenna, North Italy. San Vitale was gravely damaged during the Second World War, but is now completely restored.

The second type of church, the type that finally predominated over the whole of western Christendom, was the basilica, which derived its form either from Roman law courts, or from late Roman palaces. This type normally had a long high nave flanked on each side by a considerably lower aisle, from which it was separated by a row of colonnades. More rarely, it had aisles of equal height with the nave (i.e., it was an aisled hall rather than a basilica), or a nave with two aisles on each side (as in Notre-Dame de Paris), or even with no aisles at all. At the far end was the apse, which at first was merely a place for the high altar, but later was expanded into a choir and an ambulatory. The earliest churches appear to have possessed no transepts separating nave from apse; but when the transept did emerge, the faithful regarded the church as a

---

[5]A third type, much rarer, has the shape of a Greek Cross. San Marco of Venice bears this form: built in the ninth century A.D., it copied a sixth-century church in Constantinople. Later, the French copied San Marco when they built the Abbey of St-Front in Perigueux and St-Benoit-sur-Loire; but succeeding generations have reshaped those churches. [D.J.]

symbol of the cross. The nave was the foot of the cross, the apse its head, and the transept its two arms. The even lines of the columns down the nave, and the dim light from the narrow windows in the clerestory, drew the worshiper mystically eastward to the altar at the head of the cross. Until perhaps the ninth or the tenth century, there were no chapels to delay his progress, probably not even any sculptured figures; for the magnificent life-sized statues so characteristic of Greco-Roman art had passed completely out of fashion. Instead, from the dim walls, there shone down on him flat polychrome figures of virgins and saints patterned in glass mosaic, an art that the Byzantine Empire inherited from the Greco-Roman world, but applied much more widely and carried to greater perfection.

The exteriors of the earliest basilica-type churches seem to have been plain and unadorned. They even lacked towers, and when these were added in later times they were frequently built alongside the churches instead of over them, particularly in Italy. Perhaps the oldest basilica still virtually intact is San Apollinare in Classe near Ravenna; the church itself was built in the sixth century, the campanile beside it some two centuries later. Incidentally, this campanile is slightly off the perpendicular, though not as much as that other campanile, the Leaning Tower of Pisa.

Wars, trade and pilgrimages kept western Europeans familiar with Byzantine art and architecture, and their knowledge was deepened in the eighth and ninth centuries by the flight of many eastern monks to Northern Italy, France and Germany, where they could disregard the ban against the setting up of images that had been imposed by the emperors in Constantinople. These monks stimulated the worship of saints throughout the western churches just at the time when the bones of the Apostle James were uncovered, reportedly, at Santiago de Compostela in northwestern Spain, and that tiny village began to attract as many pilgrims as Rome and Jerusalem. The crowds of pilgrims required larger and statelier churches for their processions, churches that would be suitable also for the increasing worship of saints; and it was largely to satisfy their needs that there arose, before A.D. 1000, a new style of church architecture, one that the French call Roman and English-speaking people Romanesque. Some of its finest examples lie along the old pilgrimage routes from France to Spain. The church of St-Sernin, at Toulouse, is one of them, but there are many others, scattered all the way from England to Spain, from Germany to Italy, and even to Palermo in far distant Sicily.

Romanesque architects, all or nearly all of them monks, possessed unlimited funds, because the Benedictine abbeys and monasteries which financed them possessed domains as large as those of the nobles. In most of Western Europe, they retained the basilica plan for their churches, but gave special attention to the western facades. In many places, deep, rounded portals led into the nave and the aisles, each portal carrying sculptures of men and beasts around and above its door. The sculptures above the central door commonly depicted Christ in Glory with the four beasts of the Apocalypse, or the Last Judgement with Christ sitting above and the saved and the condemned beneath Him. Rows of arcades or lines of sculptured figures relieved the plainness of this front façade; towers over its corners gave height and dignity to the building; and very often additional towers—or in a few cases domes—emphasized its other architectural features, viz. the apse, the crossing, and the two arms of the transept. Inside, the nave was sectioned into square or rectangular bays, and the aisles were extended beyond the transept to give a larger ambulatory. Both the ambulatory and the transept were then flanked with chapels so that the processions of pilgrims could pause and worship before the images of the saints.

Such, in broad outline, was the Romanesque style in western Europe, although each region so modified it that it varied greatly from one country to another, and even in different parts of the same country. It lasted roughly one hundred and fifty years, from A.D. 1000 to about A.D. 1150, during which period western Europe built an amazing number of imposing churches, churches whose architecture and adornment breathe the fervour of the pilgrim throngs that drifted slowly and solemnly down one aisle to the eastern end, circled the high altar, and slowly drifted back along the other aisle to the main entrance again. Often, instead of a drift, it was a militant march of armoured knights and their retainers, for between the tenth and twelfth centuries, the Christian world of Western Europe, flanked on the east by pagan Slavs and on the south by non-Christian Moslems, was swept by a wave of stern fanaticism. Men interpreted the sacred texts literally, and girded themselves day by day for a Second Coming of Christ and a Judgement Day that would separate the faithful from the unfaithful, bestowing bliss eternal on the former and consigning the latter to the awful torments of Satan's demons in hellfire. Dante mirrors their fanatical intolerance in his Divine Comedy; but the Romanesque builders themselves revealed it in the harsh, almost savage sculptures with which they adorned the portals of their churches outside, and the capitals of the pillars within.

The architects of that day faced some very difficult problems. Consider, for instance, the roofs of their churches. Structural steel, such as we use, was, of course, unknown. The Greeks had their temples with ceilings of wood protected from the weather by pottery tiles; but these were extremely vulnerable to fire. The immediate predecessors of the Romanesque church builders also made their roofs of wood, except when the nave was so narrow that it could easily be spanned by a simple vault (a "barrel" vault) of stone. Some of the Romanesque architects constructed wooden roofs, especially in Normandy and England, but the majority preferred to cover their churches with a barrel-shaped stone vault, strengthened with semi-circular stone ribs each running from the top of a pillar on one side of the nave to its counterpart on the other side. Yet even this did not solve the roofing problems completely. First of all, the nave still had to be quite narrow. Secondly, the weight of the heavy roof fell evenly along the whole length of the side walls and tended to spread them, even though they were built very thick and were supported by contreforts or buttresses running perpendicularly from ground to roof. Openings weakened the walls still further, so that Romanesque windows were quite small and the churches rather dark and gloomy.

It was not until the twelfth century, and then first of all in Northern France, that architects, now mostly laymen, not monks, succeeded in overcoming these difficulties. Instead of the old round arch that had been employed since Roman times, they adopted for their naves the much stronger pointed arch, which was adaptable to uneven spaces; and they underpinned the roof vault with diagonal ribs, or cross ribs, instead of just transversal ones, thus causing practically the whole weight of the roof to fall upon the pillars of the nave instead of upon the walls. From these nave pillars they carried the stress through flying buttresses to the pillars of the aisles, and from there through a line of external buttresses to the ground. In this way the walls of the church ceased to be functional, but served simply as fillings between its pillars. Diagonal ribs underpinning stone roofs, pointed arches and flying buttresses thus became the characteristic features of the new-style Gothic church, which was not nearly as dark as the Romanesque church, despite the introduction of stained glass to fill window frames.

Structural details, however, tell only half the story. The old Greek temples, despite their beauty, had been immobile, solidly bound to mother earth. Romanesque churches pulled the worshipper eastward toward the altar. They had a forward movement, as it were, the architectural expression, perhaps, of the resolute march of the mediaeval pilgrims towards their goals. Though the buildings were still tied to earth, they no longer seemed static, at least internally. In the great French Gothic churches of the twelfth and subsequent centuries, churches like Nôtre Dame de Paris, Chartres, Bourges, and Amiens, there is still an eastward pull, but now this pull is subordinated to a pull skyward. The eyes are drawn upward insensibly, along the tall slender pillars of the nave to the glorious stained-glass windows in the clerestory that transmit so diffused and mysterious a light.

This is not the only difference between the two schools of architecture, Romanesque and Gothic. Even before we enter the great Gothic churches, we notice the soaring steeples and pinnacles that have replaced the low square towers of earlier times, and we remark a new quality in the scenes sculptured on the portals, which are gentler and more serene than those on Romanesque churches, even when they depict the same subjects. They tempt us to believe that Romanesque may have evolved into Gothic not so much through a conscious change in architectural style as from an unconscious change in outlook, that men's minds were becoming more free and soaring upward, filled with a greater hope in human destiny and in the benevolence of the Powers above. Nor can we doubt that this change in outlook reflected, in its turn, a change in the social life, a slow breaking-down of the old feudal system, the increasing emancipation and improved status of the serfs, the gathering of men into cities and the rise of a prosperous middle class.

From its birthplace in the Seine River basin, Gothic architecture quickly spread over the whole of France and Belgium. It held the stage in those countries for about three centuries (until A.D. 1500 approximately), during which period many Romanesque churches were remodelled to conform with it. Naturally, it underwent a number of changes, as art must do if it is not to stagnate and disappear altogether. In the case of Gothic architecture, however, the changes affected the decorative features of the buildings more than the purely structural. They led to pillars without capitals, pointed arches with leafy ornamentation, net-work and star-work in the vaulted roofs, and, in and around the windows, a flame-like tracery from which the French-Gothic derived its name Flamboyant.

Some writers look upon the Gothic churches of England as merely variations of Norman churches, seeing that it was from Normandy that the Gothic style reached the British Isles. Once it had established itself there, however, it underwent a slightly different development. Thus it is that English churches often seem narrower and loftier than French ones because their naves are longer in proportion to their breadth (a common ratio is 6:1) and France has nothing quite resembling the enormous, flatly pointed windows conspicuously divided by vertical parallel bars, that characterize the late or "perpendicular" phase of English Gothic.

The Gothic style invaded Germany east of the Rhine, Italy, and Spain as a foreign French fashion, which in those countries failed to strike deep roots. Already, in the twelfth and thirteenth centuries, Venice, Genoa, Pisa, and other Italian cities were expanding their trade with the eastern Mediterranean and feeling the first stirrings of the Renaissance. The friars of the newly founded orders of Dominicans and Franciscans disliked aisles in their churches, or at least aisles

that were not of the same height as the nave and really a part of it, because they made preaching more difficult; and the friars' influence was strong enough to cause both Italy and Spain
to reject the basilica form in favour rectangular hall-like church with a plain exterior, and an
interior so wide open that it formed just a single room. Even when such a church had pointed
windows and a Gothic vault, its interior lacked the upward surge, the characteristic skyward pull,
of the true French Gothic, although for many worshippers it might be more restful and conducive
to quiet meditation.

A.D. 1500 or a little later marks the end of the great church-building era in the Old World.
Commerce and population had been growing side by side from about A.D. 1100, and the
countries of Western Europe, which in Romanesque times had known very few settlements
larger than the village, found themselves four centuries later dotted with thriving cities. The
religious fervour that had inspired the pilgrimages and the Crusades had declined, and the vast
sums of money that had once been lavished on churches and cathedrals were being diverted more
and more to the construction of city halls (e.g., the magnificent Hotel de Ville in Brussels) and
the building of private mansions in town and country. Such church-building impetus as remained
passed largely to the New World, where Spanish missionaries sought to wean the Indians from
their superstitions by demolishing the pagan temples and erecting Christian churches with
their stones. Living among sullen populations that had just been reduced to serfdom, these
missionaries favoured the undivided preaching hall with thick walls, solid buttresses extending
from ground to roof, very narrow windows set high beyond reach of assault, and a flat roof,
parapetted at times like a mediaeval fortress. Later, when the danger of revolts had ended and
conditions were relatively secure, they modified this form by covering the preaching halls with
domes; or they introduced other styles of architecture from their native Spain, the Baroque,
and the Ultrabaroque or Churrigueresque.[6]

One may remark, in conclusion, that two features borrowed from the Moorish architecture
of Spain found more favour in the New World than they did in Spain itself. One was the
dome, for today there are probably more domes in Mexico alone than in the whole of Western
Europe. The other was the use of brightly glazed tiles for the roofing of churches, so that their
multi-coloured gleam, visible from a dozen miles away, would draw the faithful to worship.

[*Father's journey about France and his article raise a variety of questions. For example, was his
interest mainly in the variations over time of the structural forms of the Gothic churches? Was he
perhaps looking at them with wonder because they had been constructed without the use of structural
steel and other modern-day building materials, without the aid of today's lighting and other electrical and
mechanical devices, and using such devices as wooden scaffolding, block-and-tackle rope pulleys, and simple
hand tools that were far more primitive than what today's builders use? Or was his interest perhaps
centered more upon the historical influences the remarkable churches soon had upon contemporary western
cultures? He certainly was aware of the connection between many of the French churches and the Christian
pilgrims who paused briefly at them on their long journeys to and from holy places in northwestern
Spain, Rome, or Jerusalem. Or was he contemplating even more profound topics such as why man was
on earth and why the earth was so full of unhappiness, pain, and suffering? "Is there any purpose in
human life?" Father wrote my brother Pete that April from somewhere in France. "Does the mind,*

---

[6]Named after the Spanish leader of the architectural trends of the day, José Churriguera (1650–1725).

the soul, the personality, or whatever you call it, perish completely when the body perishes; or has it an existence independent of the body, that continues after the body dies?" Plato thought so. We know, too, that Father's thoughts wrestled with other historical and philosophical subjects as well, for Pete has told me that during several of their conversations following Father's return from France in 1960 he touched briefly on the Crusaders and the Knights Templar. Perhaps he also reflected on their role in the civilizing of man. Sadly, we will never know where his thoughts were trying to lead him at that time.]

1961–62: ADRIFT IN SPAIN

20

Diamond Jenness

[*In one of his last public activities, at a "Resources for Tomorrow" Conference in Montreal in October 1961, my father presented a paper which the news media reported offered "an extremely bleak picture" of the future of the Canadian Eskimos. He criticized the manner in which the Canadian government administered to the Eskimos and proposed that the brightest ones be brought south for education and training. This drew a sharp rebuttal from senior government officials, who favoured taking the education and health facilities north to the people.*[1]

Three years later, the Arctic Institute of North America published his detailed report on the Canadian Government's actions with its Eskimo population, entitled "Eskimo Administration: Canada." In this report, he expanded on the theme in his 1961 paper. Although it was the most comprehensive and thoughtful assessment of the government's handling of its considerable problems with its northern Aboriginal population at that time, it was not, I understand, greeted with grateful appreciation by the government's northern administrators.

My father and mother had spent the winter of 1960–61 on the west coast of Mexico. After enjoying the summer months in the Gatineau Hills north of Ottawa, they returned to Europe for the next winter.] [S.E.J.]

My wife and I decided that we would spend the winter of 1961–62 among the sunlit orange groves of Valencia, Spain's second largest port on the Mediterranean coast. There, in the balmy climate of a cultured city, we would erase every memory of Canada's icy roads and howling blizzards, would stroll by day along sandy beaches dabbling our feet in a tepid sea, visit art galleries and museums of world-wide renown, study Spanish literature at a Spanish university and, at night, listen to the music of Beethoven and Brahms whenever my masculine instincts did not drive me forth to one of the numberless cinemas or frequent bullfights.[2] Motor excursions into mountain villages up and down the coast would dispel any incipient homesickness or ennui, and a pocket dictionary supplemented by a Berlitz conversation book could be counted on to untangle any language snarls that might mar an otherwise perfect holiday.

So we dreamed and, buoyed by faith, shouldered our flight bags at Montreal's airport, waved goodbye to our family and climbed into a trans-Atlantic plane. Promptly at 11 p.m., the advertised time, its propellers clanked and turned over; and as soon as we were airborne, a smiling steward emerged from the galley to trundle a wagon of liquid refreshments down the aisle. Up and down he trundled it, slaking and re-slaking the thirst of the passengers around us, but my

---

[1] Grottke, 1961.
[2] This reference to cinema and bullfights is an example of my father's sense of humour. He rarely went to the cinema, and I cannot recall him ever expressing any interest in watching a bullfight.

Map 14 Localities in northeastern Spain visited by Jenness, 1961–1962.

wife and I, who had supped just before embarking, declined his thoughtful ministrations, wrapped ourselves in a pair of blankets, and settled down for a much needed rest.

Exactly one hour later, a violent push jolted me abruptly upright—too abruptly, for my face sank, most embarrassingly, into the broad soft back of one of the stewardesses, who was swaying above me brandishing a small syringe. Facing her, and struggling with two teen-aged children who were trying to hold her down, staggered a wild-eyed, 180-pound woman brandishing a lighted cigar, who had sampled too liberally the airline's whisky selection and now harboured an aspiration to soar through space under her own power. The plane rocked dangerously. Two stewards raced up to help the frightened children, but it was not until the stewardess had deftly plunged the hypodermic needle into the arm of the inebriated mother that she subsided and, dropping heavily into her seat, forgot her aspirations until we reached Paris's Le Bourget airport the next morning.

Paris resembled a human beehive enveloped in a depressingly wet fog, but within forty-eight hours, we had acquired a brand-new Volkswagen and were heading south to find the Mediterranean sun. France resented our neglect of her capital by molesting us with frequent snow flurries, which checked our speed and brought on the evening darkness an hour before we expected it, but she relented overnight and gave us three days of warm and cloudless weather. Sprawling Barcelona then bewildered us, and in a street somewhere behind the docks, wedged us into a mile-long caravan of trucks; but, one by one, the trucks disappeared, the traffic thinned out, and we regained the coastal highway unscathed. From then on, we rumbled along triumphantly through Tarragona and several smaller towns until Valencia's imposing gate rose up in the distance and cautioned us to slow down.

Valencia is a fairly large city where the traveller very easily goes astray, but a young boy guided us to a modest hotel hidden away in a lilliputian square near its centre. The staff was courteous and obliging, the cuisine excellent, and the price astonishingly reasonable, but the place was too dark and confined to provide a comfortable home for more than a few days. We confided our problem to its friendly manager and, on his advice, armed ourselves at the City Hall with a list of real-estate agencies, which we optimistically canvassed, one after another, about leasable apartments and bungalows. Each agency in turn assured us that there were none, or, if there were, it had no record of them on its books. Ever since Spain's civil war [1936–1939], the city had been plagued with an acute housing shortage, which the authorities were now deliberately aggravating by tearing down mile after mile of good buildings to make room for a superhighway. The country had just awakened to the economic advantages of a healthy tourist traffic, and was plotting to capture a major share of it from France and Italy.

For three days, we besieged every housing bureau on our list without success. Finally, a sympathetic agent said to us, "There is really no hope of finding what you want in Valencia. Why don't you motor forty-five kilometres[3] down the coast to my hometown of Gandia? There you'll discover plenty of empty houses and apartments, if not in the town itself, then at Gandia Playa (Beach) just three kilometres away."

We thanked him for the suggestion and drove down to Gandia. It was an old town of 40,000 inhabitants, built over a small stream that issued from the hills and meandered to the sea through a swampy, lagoon-dotted plain. Gandians of an earlier era had dredged the stream's mouth, walled its banks and protected them with a long breakwater, thereby creating a small port capable of docking two vessels of 2,000 or 3,000 tons. They then built a narrow causeway—later asphalted—to link their port with the coastal highway two miles inland and with the town of Gandia on its upper side. During the mid-winter orange harvest, crate-laden trucks rattled down this side-road to the dock, while during the months of July and August thousands of motorists sped back and forth over it, attracted by the broad sandy beach which stretches northward for several kilometres, and by the new summer resort of Gandia Playa, which was rapidly spreading along it. That resort already boasted three long rows of white, blue and pink stuccoed bungalows, as well as a few two-storey houses. And beyond these private dwellings, entrepreneurs were building two seventy- or eighty-roomed hotels, one so nearly finished that its manager was sitting at his desk every afternoon inside the open doors, ready to welcome the tide of vacationists whom the Government Tourist Bureau had promised to send him the coming summer.

---

[3]As in Chapter 17, my father mixed metric and British Imperial units when he mentioned linear measurements (kilometres, miles, and feet). I have left most of these unchanged as they reflect his thinking in the days before Canada "went metric."

It was still only December, however, when we reconnoitred the Playa, and at that season it seemed a charming, sunlit village of ghost houses with shuttered windows and padlocked gates. Barefoot, we wandered along its beach. The clean white sand was warm and dry, and no living creature was in sight except two seagulls, but our thoughts of bathing disappeared at the unexpected chill of the water. Whispering wavelets gently caressed the shore, and the tranquil sea merged imperceptibly into the far horizon. Landward, beyond the picture-book houses, placid lagoons were lapping the feet of the grey-green hills, and beyond the hills rose snow-capped mountains to puncture the cloudless sky.

"How beautiful," we exclaimed to one another, "and how peaceful! Why should we look for a stuffy apartment in the noisy town?"

Brooding over this idea, we retraced our footsteps and began to examine the shuttered houses more carefully. One in particular attracted our attention. It was a rectangular, two-apartment building of white stucco surrounded by a stone wall, and separated from its neighbours by a vacant lot on each side and a large open field at the back. Round pillars along its front supported an unusually wide balcony accessible only through a folding glass door on the upper floor, and from the same floor, but on the building's south face above a gravelled laneway, projected a much smaller balcony likewise accessible through a glass door from some room or corridor behind. The sun was shining brightly on this smaller balcony, but had moved away from the larger one, which looked eastward over the street to the beach and the sea. Several shrubs, among them two large cacti, grew in front of the house, and the gravel laneway at its side ended in a tall tree encircled by a low stone bench. A padlocked gate prevented us from inspecting the place more closely, but the stucco seemed so clean, and everything in such perfect condition, that we wondered whether its apartments had ever been occupied.

While we were still loitering at the gate, the woman caretaker of a bungalow farther down the street approached us and, seeing that we were foreigners, asked us very politely what country we came from. We replied that we were Canadians, and that we were searching for a quiet place in which to spend the winter. This house had pleased us, and we wondered whether it would be possible to lease its upper apartment.

She did not know, but she told us the owner's name, Juan Lucero, a local mechanic. He and his family, she said, had occupied the house during the summer, but had moved into an apartment near the Gandia railway station when autumn set in.

By this time it was nearly noon, and we had parked our car half a mile away. We quickly retrieved it and hastened into the town to interview Señor Juan before lunch. We found him not at his home, but on a side street two blocks away outside his "garage," which was a large barn-like structure without any identifying sign, and so tightly shut and barred that it was impossible to see within. A bystander directed us to its proprietor, who was talking with some man on the opposite side of the street. He appeared startled and rather suspicious when we two strangers accosted him, but soon regained his composure when we explained the purpose of our visit and agreed to meet us at the Playa as soon as he had disposed of some pressing business.

Half an hour later, he drove up to the apartment house in a small truck, bringing with him two large keys, one to unfasten the padlocked gate, the other to open a door off the laneway which led by a stairway to the second floor. On the landing was a bathroom equipped with cold-water taps for the basin and the shower, but with no provision for hot water. From the bathroom,

Figure 41 "Las Vegas," the Jenness rented house in Gandia Playa, south of Valencia, Spain, 1962. Photo by D. Jenness

a dark corridor with three doors on each side ran the full length of the house to the double glass door that opened onto the front balcony. The first room on the right was a modest dining room with a round table in the middle, three chairs, and, in place of a window, the glass door that gave access to the balcony over the laneway. The second room was the kitchen, outfitted with two stoves, an old-fashioned one for burning charcoal and a new, portable stove for propane gas. The last door on that side led into a large bright bedroom with a double brass bed in the middle, a huge cupboard in one corner, two upholstered chairs, and two windows, one facing the sea and the other the midday sun.

The three rooms on the opposite side of the corridor were bedrooms also, but much darker and colder, since their windows faced the north. Tables, chairs, beds, mattresses, and other furniture filled two of them from floor to ceiling, but the middle room across from the kitchen was empty and could serve as a storeroom for fruit and vegetables. The building lacked central heating, of course, and its tiled floors were not encumbered with troublesome carpets—useless luxuries, Señor Juan called them, because all Spanish people wear felt slippers, which protect the feet even in the coldest weather. Yes, he replied to my question, Gandia did sometimes experience cold weather, when icy winds swept down from the Pyrenees and wrecked the tomato crop, in exceptional years also the oranges. But this winter would probably be very mild, seeing that it was now mid-December and the days remained unbrokenly warm and sunny. Should we wake up some morning to an icy wind or a chilling frost, however, we could always make ourselves very comfortable in the dining room. To reassure us on this point, he led us back to that room and showed us, under the trailing tablecloth, a brightly polished brazier filled, not with the usual charcoal, but with a very low-powered electric ring that plugged into a wall-socket. "This heater," he said, "may be less economical than charcoal, for electricity is very expensive in Spain, but it will certainly keep any water on the table from freezing. Also it will be more convenient for you, since you Canadians are not accustomed to our charcoal braziers."

I felt some misgivings about Señor Juan's electric gadget, and so too did my wife, as she confessed to me afterwards. But we were incorrigible optimists, and we liked both the apartment and its owner. He was indeed a very pleasant young man, thirty years of age perhaps, and bubbling over with joy at the prospect of winter tenants. And he was shrewd enough not to lose them by demanding an exorbitant rent. How could we know that he was a *contrabandista* who had filled his "garage" with automobile tires and other goods smuggled into Spain without benefit of customs? He promised us bedclothes enough for the Arctic, and I cannot remember what else besides. And we, very contented, paid him three-months' rent on the spot, arranged to take possession of the apartment the next day, and returned to Valencia to pick up our baggage, while Juan and his wife put the rooms in order and furnished them with whatever necessities were lacking.

At noon the next day, they handed us the keys. Every room was immaculately clean, the kitchen equipped with a bewildering variety of pots and dishes, including a tank of propane gas in one corner, the brass bed ready for immediate occupancy, and extra blankets neatly folded and stored away on the cupboard shelf. Señora Lucero had even decorated the two balconies with potted geraniums and other plants, which she guaranteed would blossom within three weeks and supply my wife's breakfast-table with a never-failing succession of fresh flowers.

We thanked them warmly and settled in. Straight away, the weather, which had been awaiting this signal, deteriorated. The days remained warm only as long as the sun shone brightly. Its retreat behind a cloud sent a shiver through the atmosphere, which made us scurry for our overcoats. Then two calm, moonlit nights blanketed the ground with frost, which blighted all the tomato gardens between Gandia and Valencia and warned the orange growers to hurriedly gather in their crop. The following week, workers on foot, bicycles, motorcycles, and trucks were crowding both the main highway and the road to the port, and a few days later a steamer was loading oranges at the dock. Soon there were two steamers at the dock, and a third waiting at anchor in the roadstead. The whole countryside was in turmoil. Everyone knew that the incomes of hundreds of families depended on the hour-to-hour vagaries of the weather, and innumerable candles burned day and night in the churches, wordlessly beseeching a bountiful harvest.

Like the oranges, we too opened out and mellowed whenever the sun shone warmly, then shrank within ourselves and patiently endured the chill of the nights until morning dawned. Our bathroom became a place of torment, its temperature never changing from midnight to midnight. We lacked the courage to experiment with the shower, but once a week, around the noon hour of a day when the sun poured in through the kitchen window, we heated a little water on the propane stove and feverishly sponged ourselves before the tiled floor completely numbed our feet.

Day followed day imperceptibly, as in a dream, but a dream very different from the Canadian one which had lured us to this Mediterranean land. Each morning, we roamed the empty beach for an hour or more, depending on the state of the weather. There were rare days when it became again the haven of beauty and peace it had seemed on our arrival, but too often now, a bitter wind swept down it, lashing our faces with sand and spray until we cursed the inhospitable climate and fled for our chilly home. Frequently, we took refuge in our Volkswagen and drove inland to some picturesque village in the windless hills, or we wrapped our legs in the rust-coloured tablecloth and thawed them out in the brazier's feeble glow, washed the sand from our throats with hot coffee or warming Málaga,[4] and refreshed our minds with the delectable conversations in Mr. Berlitz's Spanish primer.

Gandia supported no university, art gallery or museum, no opera or symphony orchestra, but we discovered a cinema house conveniently situated next to the town hall and relaxed in that place of refuge all one stormy afternoon. Before dark, however, we returned to our apartment, sadly disillusioned, not by the picture—for that was interesting enough—but by the inadequacy of Mr. Berlitz's instruction and our own stupidity in not understanding more than a fraction of the dialogue.

Gandia Playa naturally offered even less entertainment than the old town. Excluding our two selves and four employees of the new hotel, which had opened its doors a few days before our arrival, its permanent population numbered exactly four: three elderly people, and an eleven-year-old girl. The girl generally passed our house when running errands for her grandmother and lingered long enough to learn from my wife several English nursery rhymes. A peripatetic shepherd haunted our neighbourhood for about a month. His two dozen sheep cropped the vacant fields and, in unguarded moments, all the garden shrubs that they could reach through the fences. The man himself disdained to watch them. Indeed, he seemed to slumber even when he was walking. But his small white dog, a blend of every breed on the Spanish mainland, knew its duties better than its master and never for a moment closed its eyes. Each of the vacant lots beside our house merited a two minutes' pause in the group's slow circuit. When the last second expired, the shepherd automatically grunted, his dog sprang to its feet and, rounding up the scattered flock, steered it skilfully along the street to the next pasture while the master mumbled and maundered in the rear.

The days flowed silently by, too silently for my wife, who is constitutionally incapable of dreaming away the weeks on a sandy beach, idly soaking in the warm sun. She announced one morning that our life was becoming monotonous and, surveying the suit I was wearing, informed me that it was dreadfully shabby and that I must get a new one right away. I had myself noticed that a front button of the coat was missing, that its sheen had faded, and its elbows had become a trifle thin, also that the knees of the trousers were slightly rounded from the hardships of four consecutive winters. But these imperfections, I pointed out to her, were bagatelles; the suit had grown into me and was now so comfortable that it would undoubtedly last two more years. Strangely, none of my arguments seemed to convince her. She declared that her own suit, too, was growing shabby, and that we must drive into Gandia that very afternoon to look for new cloth and a competent tailor.

---

[4]A warm, sweet Spanish wine from Málaga, which my father apparently had enjoyed a decade earlier. He was not averse to an occasional glass of wine, and enjoyed sampling the many varieties available while on his European trips, but he never over-indulged.

We found both, and for three weeks. our world hummed with activity again. As a master of a very distinguished craft—and every one in Gandia acclaimed him a master—our tailor was more dignified than the local nobleman. He scrutinized very closely the cloth samples we had selected at the principal haberdashery in the town, pronounced them downright shoddy, and undertook to procure choice qualities of similar goods from Valencia. He would then make my suit first, he said, to allay any misgivings we might entertain about Spanish tailoring techniques and skills. Afterwards, he would proceed with her costume.

My suit, fashioned of the heaviest dark-green corduroy, gave him little trouble, for men's clothes differ very little from one western country to another, and a well-tailored Spanish gentleman may easily be mistaken for an exceptionally well-dressed American. Women present another problem. Their garments hid subtleties that are not apparent to the uninitiated male, and which vary from one country to another. At this particular juncture, Spain's couturiers had decreed a notable accentuation of the mysterious allure that Providence imparted to the first female figure in the Garden of Eden; and not only Spanish women, but a considerable number of women in the United States, particularly movie stars, had signalled their allegiance to that decree. Canadian couturiers, however, had never heard of it, for that country had not yet emerged from her backwoods, and her women continued to linger behind the rest of the civilized world.

Was it surprising then that our tailor, a Spanish gentleman patriotic to his fingertips, should see in our patronage a golden opportunity to spread his nation's culture into a North American wilderness? My wife could be his emissary. The costume she would carry back from Spain would teach her under-privileged countrywomen how a lady of charm and distinction should be attired when she needed a discriminating public.

Her first fitting for this costume was tranquil; the second nearly caused an international incident. Well-primed beforehand, I attended the third, which called into play every skill I possessed as an art expert and professional conciliator. The aesthetic tailor argued his case with vigour, but after a long and at times animated discussion he changed his stance and agreed with us that in Canada's dull climate the pinched waists and voluptuous curves that dazzle men's senses in sunny Spain would flatten out and devolve into harsh and discordant lines. Under these circumstances, the costume he was making for my wife should challenge attention by its subdued—very subdued—contours, gracefully harmonizing with her dignified deportment and silvery hair. The master craftsman gallantly accepted this challenge, changed his design to give full rein to his artistry and sartorial skill, and fashioned for her the noblest costume she had ever possessed. Wherever she later went in Canada or the United States, it never failed to elicit glances and sighs of admiration and envy from every feminine acquaintance. A near tragedy thus reached a happy conclusion. But it taught us an important lesson. During those critical days when we were negotiating with the tailor, as earlier at the cinema, Mr. Berlitz's Spanish instruction had utterly failed to prepare us for the stark realities of Spanish life. It was imperative for my wife to obtain practical lessons in the language from some local expert. We enquired from this person and from that, and finally interviewed the principal of a private school, whom we engaged to teach either or both of us privately, three evenings a week, for a very reasonable fee. I myself, alas, could not take advantage of this heaven-sent opportunity, because I had contracted to finish a book by a certain date, and that date was fast approaching.[5] But because my wife ought not to suffer from my misfortune, I promised to drive her to the school for each five o'clock lesson and to call for her again at 6:15.

By an unexpected stroke of luck the schoolteacher proved to be also a landscape painter, and he was delighted to discuss Spanish art and Spanish literature with his new student while I struggled at home to meet the deadline of my editor. The lesson-hour was not altogether convenient, for darkness descended before 6 p.m., stores and offices closed at that hour, and Gandia's narrow streets overflowed with workers hurrying to reach their homes. Nevertheless, everything went swimmingly. My wife, long an enthusiastic student of international art and world languages, quadrupled her Spanish vocabulary and was talking like a native Española; and meanwhile I was making excellent progress with my book. Both of us forgot the family gremlin who had followed us from Canada, and that faithful retainer cautiously refrained from making his presence known.

But not for long. He was merely biding his time, and that time came three weeks later, when all Spain was celebrating the feast day of Saint Silvestre.

I called for my wife that day at the usual hour and drove slowly back through Gandia's narrow streets to its outskirts. There, turning right onto the coastal highway, I found my way blocked by the fast bus from Valencia to Alicante, a run of over one hundred miles. The vehicle had stopped fifteen feet out from the pavement, where a score of men were gossiping and laughing at the door of a café. Without warning, it started up again, and a man with long dishevelled grey hair detached himself from the group and raced after it, shouting with all his might. We trailed behind him, expecting the bus to stop again at the edge of the town a hundred yards ahead. Instead, it gathered speed, and its unhappy pursuer, utterly exhausted, abandoned the chase and staggered toward the sidewalk.

"Oh, the poor man," exclaimed my wife. "Pull up alongside him and let him in."

We had just arrived at the turn-off road to the Playa. Should I disobey her and turn left? Unthinkable! I drew up alongside him, and my wife, opening wide the car door, leaned forward and cried, "Jump in."

The man turned to stone, immobilized by the sudden call, which seemed to come from heaven. She called again, "Jump in."

This time he did not hesitate. Climbing past her into the back seat he stretched his arm out between us and shouted, "The bus, the bus."

I pressed the pedal hard, and the Volkswagen shot forward. Gandia fell behind immediately, and, in pitch darkness, we sped along a two-lane highway between two solid walls of workers plodding wearily to their homes. The walls came together in the distance, and, from time to time, one or two human shadows flickered momentarily in the middle of the headlights and disappeared as we bore down on them and roared by. Far in front shone the bus's tail lights, now in, now out of view. *Mas rapido, mas rapido*, our passenger murmured behind me, and my wife answered him soothingly, but I was too preoccupied to pay any attention to them.

The walls of pedestrians thinned out and finally ended. I speeded up, but so also did the bus. Fifty, sixty, sixty-five miles an hour it was travelling, and still I held grimly on, my mind blankly reciting "Overtake that bus, come hell or high water." My wife gripped the plastic handle on

---

[5] Probably Volume II in the five-volume series of reports on Eskimo administration that he ultimately prepared, all of which were published by the Arctic Institute of North America between 1962 and 1968.

the dashboard, and in the seat behind us, our passenger sat silent, conscious that a power greater than human now controlled his fate.

A few lights glimmered in the distance, and one behind the other we raced through a small village. Then came the open highway again, now without pedestrians. Mile after mile we sped, until I wondered whether the bus would stop this side of Alicante and whether the tank of my car carried enough gas for that distance?

Fifteen miles, twenty miles. Then came more lights. The bus slowed down and swerved right. I overtook it and was almost touching its rear bumper when a series of heavy jolts jerked my foot from the accelerator and knocked my head against the roof. We had entered a narrow, cobble-stoned street in which half the cobbles were missing, and while the huge tires of the bus carried that vehicle smoothly over the craters, the engine of our little Volkswagen was being jolted nearly out of its frame. Of necessity, I slowed down to a snail's pace and tried to skirt the largest holes in the road. Meanwhile the bus, not needing to slacken, pulled farther and farther ahead until its tail-lights disappeared around a corner. With a bitter sense of defeat we crept on, and at last we too rounded the corner. There, just a few yards ahead, was the bus, halted at the entrance to a small square. Our passenger seized the door handle, leaped from our car before it had fully stopped and, pushing his way through the crowd that surrounded the bus, triumphantly retrieved a large suitcase from the vehicle's roof.

Our mission had been accomplished. Now to head for home again. In this narrow street, it was impossible to turn around even a Volkswagen. I squeezed it past the bus, therefore, circled the unlighted square and approached the parked vehicle again. The glare of my head-lights caught our grey-haired friend gesticulating in the midst of an entranced audience, spell-bound apparently by the miracle of his rescue in Gandia and his translation to his hometown. His jaw fell, his eyes started from their sockets as we drew alongside, and he shouted, "Look! They have come back."

A score of astonished eyes turned to gaze on us, a score of mouths opened wide, and two men raised their arms in blessing, or perhaps in prayer. My wife, framing her silver-crowned head in the open window, smiled on them and waved her hand, while I flung them a hasty salutation and stepped on the accelerator. Thick darkness enveloped us once more, but behind us floated the reverent cry: "*Oh Virgen Santísima. Oh bendito San Silvestre.*"

We drove home in silence over the empty highway, and the pounding of my heart gradually subsided. Myriads of frogs croaked in chorus as we entered our laneway. Bringing the car to a halt, I turned to my wife and said, gruffly, "Never open that car door again for any unfortunate human. You may be a blessed angel from heaven, but I'm no miracle-working saint, just a highly nervous motorist."

1964:
IN GREENLAND

21

Diamond Jenness

[*In the summer of 1964, with the assistance of both the Canadian government and the National Museum of Denmark, my father spent several weeks researching books and government documents in Copenhagen, conversing with local authorities, and then visited most of the main settlements on Greenland's west coast. It was his first and only trip to Greenland, and his last trip to Europe. While he was in Greenland, a talk he had prepared for broadcast was translated and delivered in Danish (by another man) over the Godthaab radio station, on July 30, 1964. His studies and observations that summer provided the information he needed to write the fourth volume in his series of reports on Eskimo administration for the Arctic Institute of North America, this one on Greenland. It was published in 1967. He did not keep a diary nor did he write any account of his visit to either Denmark or Greenland. Only the text of his talk survives, which follows.*] [S.E.J.]

It was the isolation of Greenland in the North Atlantic, the dangers of navigation in its unknown waters, and the fact that it was an island remote from the European mainland and world centres of trade and commerce, which allowed Denmark to experiment with Greenland in a way that was not possible for Canada and the United States in the Arctic regions of mainland America. She could quarantine Greenland from all other countries, even from her own people. She could train and educate its inhabitants as much or as little as she thought fit, without interference from the outside world. Greenland was her adopted child, and she could raise it as she liked.

From the very beginning of her rule, she laid down the principle that her traders and colonists should deal with the Greenlanders justly, should try to give them all the benefits of a Christian civilization. That principle she has faithfully obeyed for two hundred and fifty years. She has raised her child, Greenland, with the care and affection that a human parent tries to give his offspring. And she can rightly be proud of her record.

She has made mistakes, of course, in bringing up her adopted child, just as you and I have made mistakes in bringing up our children. Particularly in the eighteenth and early nineteenth centuries, she sometimes let trade take precedence over the welfare of the Greenlanders, just as you and I have sometimes thought of our businesses first and our families afterwards.

Later, she failed to foresee how quickly the world was changing, once the industrial revolution began to grip every civilized nation. She failed to foresee how suddenly these changes would destroy the isolation of Greenland, and did not fully prepare the Greenlanders to take their place in our shrinking world. But has any nation been far-sighted? Has any nation prepared its people for the space age that lies just around the corner?

To me, the wisdom and humanity of Denmark's rule in Greenland shines out most clearly in the Criminal Code which she proclaimed for the island in 1954. Nowhere in its pages does it speak of "punishment" for any offence; instead, it talks of "re-socialization," of the redemption of offenders through compulsory labour and other means, and their return to society cured of their weaknesses. That is Christianity in its most enlightened form. That is the essence of humanity.

Here in Godthaab I have seen the Criminal Code in action. I have visited Greenland's only jail, a "modern" jail, erected just a few years ago, which looks like an ordinary house except that it is surrounded with a high wire fence of the kind we use in Canada for confining chickens. It holds six prisoners, I am told; but I could not count the number because the gate was wide open and the "chickens" had flown away to perform their daily tasks, from which they would not return until evening. In this jail they sleep each night until their sentences expire. Then they return to their homes without a blemish on their names, and are welcomed by their families and kindred just as if they are patients returning from a hospital, cured.

I realize that this idyllic method of enforcing Greenland's laws cannot last forever. The world is becoming more crowded, and man has too many flaws in his nature to dwell quietly and contentedly in a Garden of Eden. Already, the gathering of Greenland's inhabitants into towns, the growing amount of money that is circulating, the temptations of all the showy goods in shop windows, these and the faster pace of life are beginning to subvert people's minds, especially the minds of the young, and even Greenland is not the peaceable country it was before the war.[1] No doubt she will have to find new ways of enforcing her laws, of governing the country and training her boys and girls. But I for one carry away with me a picture of a beautiful land, inhabited by a people that has always smiled, and will never cease to smile. And it has been well worth the journey to visit them.

I have travelled over many parts of Arctic Canada and Alaska, and when I meet old friends I can say, in the dialect of the Alaskan Eskimos, *alienarksilekpaktunga*, "I am very happy to meet you." For many long years I have dreamed of visiting Greenland, and now I am here in Godthaab. You have uncovered your sun for me, and given me some warm bright days, and you have shown me your fog and a very little mid-summer snow. I thank you for both.

---

[1] The Second World War, 1939–1945.

RECOLLECTIONS OF "A SPLENDID LITTLE CHAP"[1]

22

Stuart E. Jenness

The previous twenty-one chapters have dealt with my father's life more or less in chronological order. In this chapter I depart from that format in order to set down a variety of largely family-related facts, incidents, and items of general information about him which will not be found in any other discussion about him and should expand our knowledge and understanding of "Jenness the man."

Biographers seeking information about my father, as well as an understanding of him, have access to only a few kinds of sources.[2] The main ones are his letters and his publications. As more than thirty-seven years have passed since his death, there are few persons still living who knew him and can impart hitherto unrecorded information about him. For that reason, I have included here an assortment of personal recollections, observations, and anecdotes known only to myself and to some of his family. These include a picture of his family life not otherwise available to the general public. My respect and admiration for the man whom I have had the privilege of calling my father increased appreciably while I was preparing this book, and I hope that some of those same feelings may permeate my readers as well. He was not perfect, for no one is, but he was certainly the best father I could have wanted.

Origin and Pronunciation of his Names

The question most frequently asked me about him is "How did your father get the name 'Diamond'?" Even Canada's Governor General Adrienne Clarkson asked me that question some

---

[1] My father's Oxford teacher, Mr. R.R. Marett, described him in these words in a letter to Marius Barbeau dated January 26, 1913, Barbeau Collection, Box 218, Folder 37, Archives, CMC. The description seems most apt.

[2] These include his published and unpublished reports; copies of his professional correspondence after 1925 (Archives, Canadian Museum of Civilization); a few short biographies; personal recollections of those who knew him; and his letters in a few private collections. Although I have not made an exhaustive effort to ferret such collections out, I have determined that there are letters by my father in: the Harry Hawthorn collection, Archives, University of BC; the Henry Collins papers, Smithsonian Institution; the Frederica de Laguna papers, Bryn Mawr College; the Committee on Anthropology papers, UDC/C/2/4, Bodleian Library, Oxford (Jenness letters to R.R. Marett); Henry Balfour papers, Pitt Rivers Museum, Oxford; Professor W. von Zedlitz papers, Hocken Library, University of Otago, New Zealand; R.M. Anderson and Mae Belle Allstrand (Mrs. R.M. Anderson) correspondence, LAC; C.M. Barbeau and E. Sapir collections (pre-1926), Archives, CMC; V. Stefansson correspondence, Special Collections, Dartmouth College; Professor George Quimby correspondence, U. Chicago; Franz Boas papers, American Philosophical Society Archives, B:B61, Philadelphia; the William A. NewcombeCollection, GR 111, Box 7, Archives of British Columbia, Victoria, B.C.; and the Society of American Archaeology, Smithsonian Institution.

years ago when I was introduced to her. On that occasion, however, it was her second question. Her first was one I had never previously been asked. "Was 'Diamond' your father's nickname?" "Diamond was his true and only given name and definitely not a nickname," I responded. I then explained that his father was a watch-and-clock-maker, owned a jewellery store in Wellington, New Zealand,[3] and had fourteen children, of whom my father was the tenth. In the 1880s when Diamond was born, the three jewels commonly used in watches were diamonds, rubies, and pearls. For some reason, no longer known but undoubtedly linked with the business, these names were given to my father and two of his younger sisters.

"Where did the name 'Jenness' come from?" is another question I have been asked. Many years ago, I asked my father about the origin of our family name, for I knew it was uncommon. (No others with our surname were listed in the Ottawa telephone book then, nor for that matter in any other Canadian telephone books. Even today, years later, all or almost all persons listed in Canada's telephone books with our surname are related to my father in some manner—sons, grandchildren, or in-laws.) My father replied that he knew almost nothing about the origin of the name and little about his ancestry. All he knew was that his own father, George Lewis Jenness, had been born in Wellington, New Zealand, and was the son of Nathaniel Jenness, who had come to New Zealand about 1840 from New England in the United States.

Genealogical investigations in the 1980s and 1990s by my older brother John (more commonly known by his nickname, Pete), and by a few distant relatives in the United States and New Zealand have since revealed that Nathaniel Jenness, a carpenter in New Hampshire, had arrived in New Zealand on a whaling ship in 1839.[4] He remained there and two years later married Hannah Haynes, who was newly arrived with her widowed mother and siblings from southern England. Six generations of ancestors preceded Nathaniel in New Hampshire, mostly farmers, all of whom descended from the earliest-known ancestor, one Francis Genings. This oldest-known ancestor's name was spelled "Genings" on the passenger list for the sailing ship on which he sailed from Bristol, England, in 1663,[5] but someone other than him had written it on that list because he was illiterate. He always marked his name with an "X" on the few existing documents that he later signed in the colony. Some of his grandchildren, however, were listed in New England documents with the spelling Jenness. We have concluded, therefore, that Jenness is the correct spelling of the name, not Genings or even Jennings.[6] No connection with the well-known Jennings family in England or the United States has ever been proven.

Where in England Francis came from originally, who his parents were, or why he left England to come to New Hampshire remain largely unanswered questions. It is known, however, that he came to the New World as an indentured servant, required to serve someone for three years before obtaining his freedom. After that, he was a baker, serving customers for miles along the coast of what is now New Hampshire. Given the political turmoil in England at the time, it

---

[3]My father showed my mother his father's jewellery store when they visited New Zealand on their honeymoon in 1919. (E. Jenness to H. Hawthorn, letter dated March 13, [1970], H. Hawthorn collection, Box 7, Folder 2, University Archives, UBC).

[4]J.L. (Pete) Jenness and Mary A. Jenness, 1998.

[5]Michael Tepper (Ed.), 1977, *Passengers to America*, p. 153.

[6]When I was about six years old my father taught me an easy way to remember how to spell our name. "Two n's, two s's, two e's, and a j / Put them together and say them right away."

is possible that he might have served in the army of Oliver Cromwell and felt it advisable to leave the country after Cromwell was defeated and Charles II was crowned king.

My brother Pete suspects that the Jenness family originally came to England well before 1650 from northern France, where the names Genes and Genis were (and still are) common. I have noted, however, that the name Jenness was recorded at least as early as the 1700s in the region known as Friesland, in the northeastern part of what is now the Netherlands, and feel that that region, with perhaps a linkage to Denmark, needs to be looked into someday as a possible early source of our family name.

The pronunciation of our family name seems to have originally been JENNess (with a slight emphasis on the first syllable), but JenNESS (with the emphasis on the last syllable) is now a common variant, especially in Massachusetts and most of the mid-western American states, where the name is much more plentiful than in Canada. In New Hampshire, where many descendants now live, the pronunciation is commonly JENNess (or even JENNiss). The JenNESS variant may have arisen after the influx of large numbers of French Canadians to the manufacturing regions of New England in the late 1800s, for I recall hearing the French-Canadian ladies in my mother's music club during the 1930s pronouncing her name that way. My father once told me his father had pronounced his name with the emphasis on the first syllable, and that is how I remember Father pronouncing it. My mother, for some reason, chose to pronounce it with the accent on the last syllable. Her younger brother, George, once suggested to me (with a smile) that she thought it sounded more important that way. There may have been some truth in that, for certainly, when a teacher in school called out my name in class to answer a question, I felt more comfortable when the JenNESS pronunciation was used, as did my older brother Pete.

Appearance

My father was short (five feet, five inches), slightly built (125–130 pounds), with gentle blue eyes, fine straight brown hair, and a narrow short-cropped moustache, which he originally grew while in the Arctic. His hair remained brown to his death, although by then it had greyed around the temples, and was thinner than in earlier years.[7] His moustache turned white some years before his death. His eyesight was always good, though he wore glasses for reading in his later years. He had both small hands and small feet (size 8, if I remember his shoe size correctly). "You have a larger understanding," he sometimes remarked to me with a smile when I commented on having larger feet than he had.

He did not possess a lot of clothes, nor did he feel the need to. On weekdays when he went to the office, he generally wore a three-piece, single-breasted, grey wool-tweed suit, tie, white shirt, and brown leather brogue shoes. Such was the customary attire for one in his position in the first half of the twentieth century. Men's shirts were not sized as today, and since he had short arms, his shirtsleeves were always too long. For years he shortened them to the proper length by using a white elasticized armband or an ordinary elastic band on each arm. He also wore garters to hold up his socks (elasticized socks were invented years later).

---

[7]Mother's brown hair, in contrast, turned white when she was in her 40s. She kept it long but always tidily folded up in a perfect "French roll."

During the winter months in the 1940s, he wore a wool scarf, wool overcoat, and galoshes with clasps. To top off his attire, he customarily wore a soft grey or brown fedora, as did most men before the Second World War. (Men stopped wearing fedoras, which were felt hats with a curved brim and a crown creased lengthwise, sometime after that war, supposedly because President John F. Kennedy would not wear one.)[8] A few years after my father retired, he commenced wearing as his head covering of choice a navy-blue woollen beret that he purchased in northern Spain.

For years, he carried an inexpensive Westclox pocket watch in his vest pocket. When men's vests went out of style he kept his watch in a small pocket on the front of his trousers until wristwatches became popular and watch pockets in trousers disappeared.

After his retirement he generally wore more casual-looking grey flannels or khaki trousers and a tweed or corduroy jacket over a white shirt and tie. His cottage attire was even more casual, however, as I note later in this chapter. When he travelled alone, he used a money belt for his cash, traveller's cheques, and passport. When Mother was with him she generally carried the money belt, passports, and other valuables. In Canada, he kept his money loose in his trouser pocket, for I do not recall him ever owning a wallet. Plastic identification cards for banking, shopping, health insurance, car driver's licence, and social insurance, all of which fatten my wallet today, did not exist then. He kept his paper driver's licence and insurance identification paper in the pocket of his car, once cars started to include dashboard pockets.

Father smoked a pipe for many years, a habit he probably commenced in the Arctic, where most of his scientific companions on the Canadian Arctic Expedition smoked pipes. He invariably lit his pipe after meals and had the occasional smoke between meals as well. At home, he kept a six-holed pipe rack complete with three or four straight pipes, and a can or glass jar of Hudson's Bay Company pipe tobacco on a side table in his study. When he went to work, he filled a tobacco pouch with pipe tobacco and tucked this and one of his pipes into the side pocket of his coat. A slowly developing cough that troubled him by the 1940s prompted his family physician to insist that he cease smoking, which he did, "cold turkey," never to smoke again.

Character

My father was a gentleman, serious-minded, compassionate, thoughtful and wise, thoroughly dedicated to his work and at the same time totally loyal and devoted to his family and his friends. He was a modest, quiet, gentle, soft-spoken individual by nature, yet not afraid to stand up for his or another's rights whenever necessary. His view on life was positive and optimistic, yet realistic. He accepted adversity with stoicism, and acclaim and praise with extreme modesty (he was "too damn modest," one admirer remarked to me one day some years after my father's death). He let his accomplishments speak for themselves.

My father's brilliant contributions to the field of anthropology are well known to anthropologists. "Diamond Jenness was a pioneer and a giant," stated his good friend, archaeologist William E. Taylor, Jr., "He was Canada's greatest anthropologist and one of the world's two or three outstanding Arctic anthropologists—and none expect to see his like again."[9] Few know,

---

[8]Steinberg, 2005.

[9]William E. Taylor, Jr., Director of the Museum of Man, in a speech on June 26, 1976, at the unveiling of a historic plaque dedicated to Diamond Jenness at the entrance to the Victoria Memorial Museum building in Ottawa.

however, that his intellectual interests extended well beyond the boundaries of anthropology. From an early age, he had a natural curiosity to learn about many things and continued that love of learning all his life.

My father had the sort of personality that suited anthropological fieldwork—quiet, observant, respectful, industrious, and co-operative. This asset was recognized early in his life by at least one of his teachers at Oxford (Professor J.A. Smith) who wrote in 1910 that "Jenness will do credit to Balliol as a field Anthropologist ... [he] struck us as remarkably observant and level-headed, the two main qualities needed in an explorer."[10] He also had a special talent for establishing confidence and trust with the native people from whom he sought to obtain information, successfully gathering thereby and helping preserve vast amounts of valuable anthropological data for future generations. In this, Dame Fortune frequently smiled upon him, however, for he often chanced to be in the right places at the right times to make priceless collections of information, folklore, and artifacts.

He displayed the above qualities as well as tact and patience in the office when he was called upon to edit the manuscripts of the men under his direction before recommending them for publication. With his excellent classical training and knowledge of the English language he was good at such work; his criticisms were constructive and valid, and his prose was superior.[11]

Father was not averse to offering praise for work well done, but he had no use or tolerance for devious or incompetent individuals, nor for lazy individuals at his office or at home, "slackers" or "loafers" as he called them.

He lived and travelled modestly, taking with him only basic clothing, a toothbrush, shaving equipment, a small manual typewriter, paper, note pad, pen and pencil, a small pocket knife, and a few scholarly books. His reading interests focussed largely on anthropological and geographical subjects and current world news, and did not include popular novels. His favourite book was evidently Homer's *The Odyssey*, a copy of which he carried with him throughout the Arctic in 1913–1916.

He was infinitely patient with his family, seldom arguing with Mother or raising his voice towards any of his three boys, even though we had a propensity for getting into mischief and testing his patience.[12] He was quietly proud of his family, devoted to his wife, and pleased with his sons' accomplishments in music, art, and sports, and later their successful acquisition of

---

[10]Nemo, 1918, p. 36.

[11]My father would have been surprised to learn that his excellent example as an editor served unwittingly as a role model for me (with many years of editing scientific papers behind me as well as the editing of this and other books since my retirement), and for both of my children, who have demonstrated the same aptitude and patience and are continuing comparable editorial activities in their respective parts of the world.

[12]On one occasion during the 1930s, my older brother Pete and some of his friends were caught by the police playing football in a small city park near our Broadway Avenue home and were driven to the police station. When the police contacted Father, he hastily drove to the station, where instead of assuming an apologetic air with regard to his son's behaviour, he lectured the sergeant about the stupidity of pulling in young teenagers who were causing no harm and were keeping healthy and off the streets out of harm's way. Startled by my father's sharp rebuke, the sergeant growled at the boys not to get caught again and let them return home.

advanced university degrees and government positions. He shared their successes proudly, but did not boast about them.

With his grandchildren, he was gentle and playful, seldom strict. Sometimes he told them interesting or amusing stories or went for short walks with them in the countryside around his country home, encouraging them to be curious about the life and nature that surrounded them.

Beneath his serious-minded veneer lay an impish sense of humour. This occasionally surfaced in the form of whimsical observations or mildly amusing stories, which were frequently about himself.[13] His stories were never offensive or vulgar. One of his guiding principles was, if you cannot say something nice about a person, better to remain silent.

Father was a generous man, willing to share what little he had with family or friends if they were in need, or on occasions even with an honest-looking person begging money on the street. He gave me my first automobile (his fifteen-year-old Dodge, which still ran well) following my graduation from university in 1954, and a year or so later, spent days with me cheerfully putting up a picket fence around the large back yard of my first home. During the depression years of the 1930s, unemployed men came occasionally to our door asking for something to eat. If Father was home and judged their needs to be genuine, he would have them clean our yard or basement for an hour or so, then have Mother feed them and finally give them a note to the head of the men's shelter where they could get a meal and a bed for the night, authorizing that organization to bill my father for one night's accommodation. I recently learned that his generosity also extended in an unusual direction. A year before the outbreak of the Second World War, he voluntarily offered to house and finance the education of a young son of each of three European anthropological friends until the war clouds blew over: Professor Alfred C. Haddon of Cambridge University, Sir Francis Knowles of Oxford, and Dr. Kaj Birket-Smith of Copenhagen, Denmark. For reasons not now known, none of the three boys came to Canada. Apparently, they were not the only European friends to whom he made his offer, for in July 1940, the teenage son of a long-time English medical friend of Father's in London arrived on our doorstep, resided with us briefly, then went off to a private boy's school in Brockville, where my father had arranged his attendance until the end of the war.[14]

Although perhaps a little shy, Father genuinely liked people and may have trusted them more than he should have. He was not afraid to ask travel directions of complete strangers, nor to pick up lone hitchhikers and chat with them when he was driving alone in his car, whether in North America or Europe. In a crowd, however, whether at a scientific conference or in a public street, he generally let others do the talking.

He had only a small circle of close friends, almost all of whom were men he had been associated with either during university days, the Arctic expedition, the First World War, or

---

[13] A good friend of my father, fellow New Zealander Professor Harry Hawthorn, wrote shortly after my father's death, "It is tempting to think of writing about Diamond Jenness through the anecdotes which are going to be told about him wherever his friends and associates meet. But they should never be the ones he told about himself, which were witty but over-modest. The revealing ones are those that others tell which illustrate his unfailing generosity, warmth, and courage" (Hawthorn, 1970, p. 95).

[14] This was Bill Bourdillon. I do not know how my father came to be a friend of Bill's father, a medical doctor in London.

through his anthropological work. He generally commenced his letters to them using their surnames ("Dear Cox," or "Dear Newcombe" or "Dear Collins") rather than using their first names, and evidently preferred to be addressed in a similar manner when among his professional friends or in correspondence.[15] Vilhjalmur Stefansson, for example, always started his letters to my father with the salutation, "Dear Jenness." My father, however, probably because of his irritation with Stefansson stemming from incidents in the early 1920s (mentioned in Chapter 3) always replied more formally with "Dear Mr. Stefansson," until the late 1940s, by which time he decided they both had mellowed sufficiently that he could address him as "Dear Stef." Relatives or close friends, of course, used my father's given name, Diamond, when they communicated with him.

If I were asked for a single word that best described my father's character, I would probably say loyalty—loyalty to his King or Queen (he was exceptionally patriotic), loyalty to his country and adopted country (and indeed to the British Empire), loyalty to his friends, and loyalty to his family.

Religion

My father was, I believe, a deeply religious man, but he kept his beliefs largely to himself. These beliefs were unrelated to church attendance, for neither he nor my mother were churchgoers during most if not all of my lifetime. I know that he sometimes shared his views on religion and philosophy with my first wife, Joan (now deceased), who had studied both those subjects at university and could discuss them intelligently with him. However, I believe that she, rather than my father, initiated such discussions, and she did not relay his views to me.

Early in 1960, my father wrote an extraordinarily revealing letter to my brother Pete and his (second) wife, Mary, from which they have graciously allowed me to quote.[16] In it, he mentioned that, after a strict Methodist upbringing, he had had a painful religious disillusionment when he was about nineteen years old. He was then in his first or second year at university in New Zealand. (What brought it on, he never did divulge, although he might have mentioned it to his wife years later.) Why, he had asked himself, would an almighty and all-good God create a world in which every creature had to live by destroying other creatures or plants? Why did He create a world so full of pain and suffering? My father ceased at that time to have any faith in Christian doctrines, he wrote, but did not become an atheist. Instead, he concluded that each thinking person had "to steer his own life." He chose as his guiding principle "the aim of decreasing as much as I could the pain and suffering that seem inherent in life. No individual, however hard he tries, can do very much; all his efforts hardly cause a ripple on the surface of the ocean. But at least he can try, and thereby keep his own life on an even keel...."

He then mentioned our two worlds, the material world we see and feel, and a mysterious non-material world about which we know virtually nothing, but which the mind can sense in such matters as the beauty about us and the emotions we experience. This led him to a discussion of life after death, which he said practically all people have believed in, adding, "You

---

[15]Hawthorn, 1970, p. 93.

[16]D. Jenness to Pete and Mary Jenness, letter dated April 1960, in their possession in 2006. He was in France at the time.

cannot prove that life continues after the death of the body, any more than you can prove that 2 and 2 make 4; but the world hardly seems intelligible unless life does continue."

He also felt that the world was full of mystery. "We don't know where we come from, why we are here, or where we are going." Life as he perceived it was rather like Pandora's box, out of which so much evil flew, yet Hope remained in the bottom of the box. He had always thought, however, that the box contained one other element besides hope, namely Curiosity. To him, "Curiosity is the basis of all science, of all learning." Hope and curiosity had always guided him along his way, and he made the best of whatever situation he found himself in. He had always tried to diminish the amount of suffering and pain in our material world, in the belief that, when our time on earth was finally up, there would be a better, although entirely different, afterlife.

In another letter, dated April 7, 1967, this time to his lifelong friend John Cox, my father again broached the subjects of religion, life, and death. Cox had been the assistant geographer on the Canadian Arctic Expedition in 1913–1916. Following his stint in the Arctic, he had spent several years in India, Indonesia, Africa, and South America, returning to Ottawa during the 1930s. Here he found the climate too severe for his health (I believe that he suffered greatly from asthma), so sought relief by moving to the hot, dry climate of Arizona in the 1940s. My father corresponded with him periodically thereafter until his own death, after which, Mother continued the family connection until she was no longer able to write because of failed eyesight. Thereafter for several years, I continued the family ties by occasional correspondence with Cox's younger daughter Penelope, who looked after her father and remained in Arizona after his death. I obtained my father's 1967 letter from her during a visit in 1991.

In his letter, my father wrote, "I do not know whether you still adhere to the Christian faith we were saturated with in our childhood. I don't, but I still strongly feel the mystery of life, & am sure that we have not (and never can as long as we are human beings) unravell[ed] even a minute fraction of what our world is and means. Yet my reason tells me that the world must have some meaning, that what we call matter and mind are inseparable, and that our lives continue in some way after we are dead, as we call it, since otherwise all our aims and aspirations and efforts would be meaningless. So what we know as death is just turning a corner, as it were, rounding a bend in a river and finding a new landscape ahead of one. And having been gifted (by Mother Nature?) with an insatiable curiosity, I wonder sometimes what is around that corner and whether it won't be an 'enjoyable adventure' to find out."

Elsewhere in this letter, he commented, "I often think that a man's life is very much like dog-sledding in the Arctic: you grow very tired towards the end of the day, your dogs are dead beat, yet you carry on." Obviously this described how he felt as his life drew to a close.

Family Photographs

Historians, when seeking to create a realistic picture of the people they write about, look for pictures. Prior to the mid 1800s, when photographic techniques first evolved, sketches and paintings were the main sources of such pictures, but these were seldom plentiful. Today we have ample opportunity to take large numbers of photographs of our family members, for cameras are widespread and picture-taking techniques are relatively simple, but few of us actually take advantage of such developments. Our family was regretably of the latter kind. There were two or three cameras in our house when we grew up, all relatively simple models, but they were rarely touched, let alone put into use. No family album of photographs of my parents and their three sons was ever assembled. Father had no objection to having his picture taken, but we rarely thought to do so. Mother tended to go out of her way to avoid having her picture taken. As a result, when I commenced gathering family pictures for this book, I soon realized that there were few to collect. I know of no single photograph of Father with his wife and three children. We have even fewer pictures of Mother. The better pictures of those available appear in this book, some published for the first time.

Professional Life

My father's professional life has been the subject of a number of scholarly articles since his death, notably his obituary by Henry Collins and William E. Taylor Jr., and several more recent articles by anthropologist Barnett Richling.[17] Richling is also completing a scholarly biography of my father, which may get into print before this manuscript. In addition, I have been approached for information in recent years by several other persons who were writing about one or other aspect of my father's professional life. The archivist at the Canadian Museum of Civilization has informed me that she receives many enquiries about my father's life and works, enquiries from far and wide. In the preceding chapters my father has provided some information on his professional life and activities, and I have provided other details, quite a bit of it not heretofore known outside of our family. Neither of us has endeavoured to comment upon the success or failure of his professional efforts, however, nor to evaluate the impact of his work, leaving those interpretive matters to others.

His Museum Office

Prior to 1926, my father occupied an office somewhere in the Victoria Memorial Museum building on Metcalfe Street, Ottawa, but its location is not known to me. In February of 1926, he moved into the office vacated several months earlier with the departure of the chief anthropologist, Dr. Sapir. The division chief's room was located on the third floor in the east wing of the castle-like, beige-coloured limestone museum building. It was a large, rectangular room, measuring about sixteen by thirty feet , with a high ceiling and two tall windows that looked northwards along Metcalfe Street towards the Parliament Buildings. Though heated in the colder months by large hot-water radiator coils under the windows, the room was drafty and chilly. The thick stone walls provided some insulation against the summer heat, but the only air-conditioning available during my father's time at the museum was obtained by opening the large windows. The room in the 1930s contained a desk, two tables, and several chairs and bookcases.

My father preferred to enter his office by way of a door from his secretary's room, keeping his door to the hall closed for added privacy. Fellow ethnologist Marius Barbeau's office was immediately east of the secretary's room, hence two doors along the hall from my father's office. East of Barbeau's office lay the National Art Gallery, which occupied the easternmost part of the building. The other members of the anthropology division had offices elsewhere in the building, possibly in one or two of the nearby rooms. The room across from my father was, I

---

[17]Richling, 1989, 1990, 1991a,b, 1995a,b, 2004a,b and 2005.

think, occupied by a geologist. My father retained his same office until he ceased going to work in October 1948, although after 1939 he spent very little time there. The offices he and Barbeau occupied for so many years disappeared during the museum renovations of the 1960s and 1970s when the entire east wing of offices on the third floor became a new exhibition hall.

During the mid 1930s, before I was a teenager, my father sometimes took me to his office on Saturday mornings to give my mother more time to take care of my younger brother. Regularly, I would be seated at a table in my father's office and supplied with paper and coloured pencils to create artistic masterpieces while he worked. Equally regularly, my attention span was insufficient to fill the hours before we could return home, so when I became restless and annoying, he would take me along the hall to the library and ask the librarian, a kindly, motherly lady named Mrs. F.B. Forsey, to keep me interested with books that included pictures of birds and dinosaurs.

On two or three such visits to the museum, he drew my attention to a white Arctic wolf on display opposite one of the old cage-type elevators on the main floor, and remarked that it had bitten him many years ago when he was in the Arctic. Some fifty years later, I read in a newly published book that wolf attacks on humans in North America were extremely rare; indeed no wolves were known to have ever attacked humans without provocation,[18] and recalled my father's remarks years before about the wolf at the museum, as well as the scar he had shown me on his right wrist. By then, however, he had been dead for seventeen years and the wolf specimen was no longer on display. My enquiries revealed that the specimen was in storage, and the museum's records confirmed that my father had indeed been bitten by that wolf in 1915. Believing the incident worth reporting, I published an account of it in the journal, *Arctic*, boldly claiming that it was the best-documented account of a wolf attacking a human.[19] The wolf had gotten among some tethered sled dogs while my father and Dr. Anderson were camped along the Coppermine River, and when my father tried to scare it off by throwing a large stone at it, the wolf had rushed at him. In attempting to prevent the wolf from biting his leg, my father had suffered a nasty laceration on his right wrist. Dr. Anderson then shot the animal and subsequently preserved it for the museum. Four years after my first note, I published a second one in *Arctic* with two photographs of the wolf after it was shot. This second note also stated that the wolf was in heat, which I had in the interim learned after tracking down the field notes in Denmark of the biologist F. Johansen, who had been with my father on that trip. My two notes drew a pair of disapproving responses in later issues of the same journal, both authors arguing that my father had provoked the wolf to attack him.[20] Evidently, I had challenged a long-held conviction among some North American biologists and outdoorsmen that wolves were unlikely to attack humans.

There is a postscript to this wolf story. Sometime in the late 1930s, the editor of a major Winnipeg newspaper offered a sum of money to anyone who could show proof of a human being having been attacked by a wolf. My father wrote him about his encounter with the wolf on the Coppermine River, claimed the reward, and asked the editor to donate it to the Red

---

[18]Mech, 1981, pp. 291–292.
[19]S.E. Jenness, 1985; see also S.E. Jenness, 1989 and 1991, p. 386.
[20]*See* Stewart, 1990, and Streisinger, 1991.

Cross. He never received a reply, but told me years later that he felt that the editor's silence confirmed the validity of his claim. I do not know whether the Red Cross benefited or not.

Public Speaking

Commencing in 1912, individual staff members at the Victoria Memorial Museum were called upon from time to time to give lectures for children in the museum's auditorium on Saturday mornings during the winter months, followed by more serious versions of the same lectures the next Wednesday evening for adults. My father responded to the call on more than one occasion during the 1920s and 1930s, speaking on various aspects of Eskimo or Indian life, and illustrating his talks with lantern slides and occasionally with motion pictures.[21]

My father did not enjoy giving public talks and was not a natural-born public speaker. In the first place, his soft voice lacked the volume to permeate large auditoriums. He would have fared much better today with our lapel microphones, powerful amplifiers, and speakers. In the second place, he was always nervous about facing and addressing large gatherings of strangers, a condition reflecting his discomfort with the setting rather than any insufficiency of knowledge of his subject. As Chief of the Division of Anthropology, however, he was expected to give occasional public lectures, present papers at learned societies, and even make a few radio talks.[22] They were always a challenge for him. He was much more at ease with small gatherings, such as graduate-student seminars, where he could carry on a two-way exchange of information and ideas quite contentedly.

Social Matters

My parents seldom socialized with other couples during our growing years, in part because of the difficulty of meeting couples that both of them enjoyed. They also rarely dined out by themselves, partly because of the scarcity of restaurants at the time, partly, I suspect, because of financial circumstances or unwillingness to leave their three sons unattended. "Baby sitting" by teenagers had not yet become an accepted activity. Likewise, they did not attend sporting

---

[21] In the late 1980s while visiting the National Museum's photograph collection in a rented Walkley Road building in Ottawa, I noticed several dozen old lantern slides that were about to be discarded because they were unlabelled. I recognized a number of them as slides like the ones my father had used in his lectures, of photographs he or the expedition photographer, George Wilkins, had taken of the Copper Eskimos in 1914–1916. Some of them had been carefully hand-painted to bring out their natural colour. Now properly identified, many of these lantern slides are today preserved, catalogued, and stored at the Canadian Museum of Civilization.

[22] In June 2007, my brother Bob gave me a thin square box on which was glued a Canadian Broadcasting Corporation (CBC) label bearing the date 4/59. Inside was an old magnetic audiotape, which Bob told me he had possessed since the early 1960s. The tape is a recording of a CBC Radio talk entitled "History of the Eskimo" by Dr. Diamond Jenness, one of a weekly series of fifteen-minute scientific programs prepared then by the Northern Service of the CBC in cooperation with the Arctic Institute of North America. It is the only existing recording of Father's voice known to the Jenness family. Enquiries with the CBC archives in Toronto failed to reveal the exact date on which the talk was recorded, but available information suggests that it was probably sometime between September 1960 (when the series of radio talks commenced) and 1962. The audiotape (with both CD and typescript derived from it) is currently held in the archives of the Canadian Museum of Civilization.

events and rarely went together to concerts or to see a motion picture, although Mother attended frequent concerts held on Thursday mornings during the 1930s at the Chateau Laurier. Neither of my parents craved excitement or entertainment, and both seemed to expect to remain at home in the evenings.[23] Furthermore, my father regularly brought work home from the office to do in the evenings and usually retired to his study after supper. Mother then generally busied herself with some household chore, or played classical music on the piano, which she did rather well. Father had once played the flute equally well, but sometime in the 1930s it was damaged, possibly as a result of my attempts to play it without instruction or supervision, and he rarely played it again. He enjoyed good music, but we did not have a radio prior to the early 1940s, so that any music in our house had to be self-created, as it apparently had been in his and Mother's family homes when they grew up. He often encouraged me with my piano practising, but made no attempt to direct my playing.

My father thoroughly enjoyed the appreciation and respect he was shown when young university students visited him. On such occasions my mother was always the gracious hostess, serving afternoon tea, cookies, and bran muffins or homemade cake. One day in November 1937, for example, Anthropology Professor W.M. Fenton brought his entire class of thirty-five students from St. Lawrence University, in Canton, New York, to Ottawa to visit the National Museum and to meet my father. My father escorted them about the anthropology collections in the museum, delivered a luncheon lecture to them on the Eskimos, and then invited them to our Broadway Avenue home for afternoon tea. There they sat on the floor in a semicircle around his armchair in the living room for nearly an hour, totally captivated with his responses to their questions and his observations on an assortment of subjects.[24]

Twenty-one years later, Professor Frederica de Laguna of Bryn Mawr College, Bryn Mawr, Pennsylvania, a great admirer of my father for more than two decades, brought her anthropology students to Ottawa to visit the National Museum and my father, and they too were invited to tea in the Jenness home. By then, however, his home was the little two-bedroom house north of Ottawa overlooking the Gatineau River. There the students sat on the floor around my father in the small living room, listening to his sage responses to their many questions.

As a result of that visit, one of the students, Nansi Swayze, returned to visit my father in July 1959 to have him tell her about his life. She spent an entire day with him under the trees at our family cottage, she told me years later, asking him question after question, and a year later, published the first biography about him, one written for high-school students.[25]

Two other staunch friends and admirers of my father were A.S. "Scotty" McNeish and William E. Taylor Jr., both young and ambitious archaeologists at the National Museum in the late 1950s. My father would go to their offices periodically and discuss anthropological

---

[23]They acted differently when in Europe after my father's retirement, however, for Mother's letters in 1954 told of attending art galleries, concerts, and operas in Italy and France. Mother may have been the initiator of most of such activities.

[24]Jenness to W. Malcolm, memo dated October 26, 1937, Jenness Correspondence, Box 652, Folder 1, Archives, CMC.

[25]Swayze, 1960. This biography includes some information she obtained from him during that visit that is not available elsewhere. Ms. Swayze's book also includes short but interesting biographies of Barbeau and Wintemberg.

developments, and they, in turn, occasionally visited our cottage with their wives.[26] McNeish subsequently joined the faculty of Andover College in Massachusetts and conducted archaeological fieldwork that established the origin of corn in central Mexico and the likely presence of very early man (about 60,000 years ago) in New Mexico.[27] Taylor went on to become, in 1967, Director of the National Museum of Man, an offshoot from the National Museum of Canada. He was also the driving force behind five projects to show appreciation for my father: (1) the painting of Father's portrait as an 80th birthday gift for him in 1966; (2) the naming of a large peninsula on the west coast of Victoria Island after my father;[28] (3) the naming of certain volumes in the museum's Mercury Series as "Jenness Memorial Publications;"[29] (4) the installation of a handsome red and gold plaque about Father at the front of the Victoria Memorial Museum Building where Father worked for so many years; and (5) the issuing of a postage stamp in 1986 to commemorate Father's 100th birthday. Only this last project failed to materialize in spite of Taylor's strong urgings to Canadian postal officials.

Family Life

My Earliest Recollections

My earliest recollection of my father dates to the spring of 1929, when he drove Mother, my brother Pete, and me to the railway station. Being not quite four years old, I did not understand why my mother was so ill at ease; all I understood was that my father was going away for a long time. In the days preceding his departure, he had given Mother a few hasty driving lessons in our new car, his first automobile, a two-door Chevrolet sedan. Thanks to those lessons, she was able to get us home safely following his departure on the train to Vancouver, and around Ottawa from time to time during the ensuing months until his return.[30] It was not until many

---

[26]About 1987, Bill Taylor enthusiastically encouraged me to complete the editing of my father's Arctic diary with a grant from the Social Sciences and Research Council, where he was President, and two years later helped me get the diary published by the Canadian Museum of Civilization.

[27]Human hair radiocarbon-dated at 19,000 years B.P. and with DNA unlike any North American Indian hair has been found in a layer above a layer enclosing charred firewood, burned animal bones, chipped stone tools, bones with imbedded stone points, and other evidence of man in the floor of a cave near Orogrande, New Mexico, radiocarbon dated at about 60,000 years B.P. (Nelson, 1992; Chrisman and others, 1996).

[28]A small dignified ceremony was held in the office of Dr. William Taylor, Jr., Director of the National Museum of Man, on April 5, 1972, formally announcing the naming of a large peninsula in the western part of Victoria Island in Canada's Arctic as "Diamond Jenness Peninsula." My mother, my two brothers and I were present, and a framed copy of the topographic map showing the peninsula with its new name was presented to Mother. It was in my possession in 2006.

[29]Many of the volumes so dedicated were MA or PhD dissertations in anthropology that were considered to be valuable contributions to studies in Canadian anthropology. Sixty-five volumes were issued between 1976 and 1986 as Jenness Memorial publications.

[30]His journey took him by steamer from Vancouver by way of Japan to Batavia, thence by train with the other delegates to Beutenzorg, where they visited two museums and a rubber-experiment station, and then to Bandoeng, where the meetings were held. While there, my father had the opportunity to accompany eight other delegates on an airplane flight to a nearby volcano, the aircraft circling around and inside the crater before returning to its base. Father expressed much pleasure in what was undoubtedly his first airplane ride. (D. Jenness to E. Jenness, letter dated May 22, 1929, from Bandoeng, Java, in my possession in 2006.)

years later that I learned of the importance of his trip — he had gone for four months as an official delegate of Canada to the 4th Pacific Science Congress in Java. My father kept a diary telling of his activities on that trip to Java and also took many photographs, which he later placed and captioned neatly in a photograph album. Following Mother's death in 1993, I donated both the diary and the photograph album to the Canadian Museum of Civilization.[31]

City Residences

In the fall of 1919, my father rented a small apartment for his young bride and himself a few blocks from the museum. The following year he bought a double house on Fifth Avenue, not far from the home of his wife's parents. He owned this building only three years, then rented other accommodation from the fall of 1923 until the fall of 1926, when he bought the large house on Broadway Avenue previously owned by his father-in-law.

296 Fifth Avenue

My father purchased a small double house at 296 Fifth Avenue in 1920 for $6,200, painted and rented one half unfurnished for $25 a month, and lived with his wife in the other half.[32] He sold this house in 1923[33] shortly before he took his family to Hazelton, British Columbia. Between 1924 and 1926 he rented an apartment on Frank Street within walking distance of his office. He and his wife and son spent the summers at the cottage he purchased in 1921.

108 Broadway Avenue

After my grandfather's death in August 1926, Father purchased for $7,500 his large brick house on the southwest corner of Broadway Avenue and Torrington Place, and Grandmother Bleakney and her two unmarried sons moved to a house they rented on the next street. The Broadway house had been my mother's home since about 1910 and was the house where my two brothers and I grew up. It was well located, close to the southern limit of Ottawa at that time, with Dow's Lake two blocks to the west and the Rideau Canal and the Driveway one block to the south. The "Elgin" streetcar line of the Ottawa Electric Railway Company conveniently commenced its route one block from our house, near where Bronson Avenue crossed the canal, proceeded uptown to Queen Street, then south on Elgin Street past the National Museum.[34] My father undoubtedly took this streetcar regularly to work before he purchased his first car in 1929, and even thereafter, between December and March each winter when he stored his car in our garage.

---

[31] These items are in Box 760, Ethnology Documentation, Archives, CMC.

[32] Jenness to Barbeau, letters dated October 6, 1920, and Feb. 6, 1923, Barbeau Collection, Box 206, Folder 27, Archives, CMC. Jenness described it as "a miserable shack from the outside but very cosy within" and intended to keep it for a year or two, then sell it and buy something better. (Jenness to J.R. Cox, letter dated February 12, 1922, obtained from Cox's daughter Penelope in Arizona in 1991 and in possession of S.E. Jenness in 2006).

[33] The house no longer exists.

[34] The "Elgin" streetcar turned around near where the present Pretoria Avenue Bridge crosses the canal. In those days, a small swing bridge crossed the canal at that locality, leaving room for the street cars to make a circular loop on the bridge's west side in order to return along Elgin Street.

Figure 42 The Jenness house from 1926 to 1959 at 108 Broadway Avenue, Ottawa, July, 1959. D. Jenness' study was behind the left window above the veranda.

Photo by S.E. Jenness

Our Broadway Avenue house was large, three-storied, drafty, and poorly insulated (characteristic of older houses), and was built of local red brick on a foundation of thick blocks of local grey limestone. A large veranda fronted the house (and still does). Our centre front door opened into a small vestibule for hanging coats, hats, and umbrellas or canes, and thence into a slightly larger front hall facing stairs to the two upper floors.[35] The rest of the ground floor consisted of two living rooms (which we always called the front and back parlours), a dining room, and a large kitchen with attached pantry. Our front parlour had a brick fireplace, a couch, and upholstered armchairs. The back parlour contained an upright Heinzmann piano on which Mother and we three boys practiced, a large and heavy couch that my Uncle George told me once rested in Canada's first prime minister's final Ottawa residence,[36] a low, round,

---

[35]A telephone was attached to the wall in the front hall separating it from the vestibule. Prior to the renovation of the house into two flats in 1946, it was the only telephone in the house. To place a call, one turned a crank to obtain the service of a telephone operator, to whom one gave the telephone number of the person being called. Our telephone number in those pre-dial-phone days was Carling 106.

[36]Mother's father had purchased this couch at an auction of the household contents at the Cooper Street residence of Sir John A. Macdonald following the latter's death. Her brother George was with his father at the time, so I have no reason to doubt his statement. Our family offered the couch to the Government of Canada when the East Block of the Parliament Buildings was renovated in the 1980's to create a Sir John A. MacDonald room, but it was not accepted. It was given to a helpful neighbour of Mother's at Cascades, Quebec, in 1993, after Mother's death.

ornamented brass and carved walnut table that had come from India, assorted Queen Anne-style chairs, and a drafty bay window.

Our second floor had three bedrooms, one bathroom with a lion's-footed bathtub but no shower, and a study with a red brick fireplace. This study was where my father spent most of his evenings working when I was young, for it could be rendered reasonably comfortable in the winter with a brisk wood fire. It measured about twelve by fifteen feet, and, in the 1930s to early 1940s, contained an oak typewriter desk complete with a heavy manual Royal typewriter, a lamp, a bookcase, a side table, a chair or two, and a small antique lady's reclining couch. On the floor was a black-bear rug, the skin of which my father had purchased at Fort McLeod, British Columbia, in the spring of 1924.[37] My parents slept in the back west bedroom, I was in the front west bedroom, and the back east bedroom, overlooking the Driveway along the Rideau Canal,[38] was the "nursery," where my younger brother Bob slept during his early years.

Our third floor (the attic) contained two large rooms, each of which had front and side windows, a double bed, a clothes closet, a bureau, and a chair or two. The west room was occupied by our maid (we had several from the late 1920s through 1939). My older brother, Pete, slept in the east room of the attic until he went off to military college in 1940.

At the back of our house was a covered porch with steps leading down to the lawn and an unattached, wooden, single-car garage. This porch was replaced in the 1930s with an open veranda. The garage was located at the edge of a narrow lane that backed all the houses on the south side of our stretch of Broadway. It still stands there today, but looks like a strong wind would blow it over.

Our poorly lit, cramped, white-washed, limestone-walled basement with its low ceiling, contained, in addition to a large coal furnace with its massive heating ducts and the necessarily large adjoining coal bin, an unheated, eight-by-eight-foot cold-storage room. Here each winter we stored bagged carrots, potatoes, a barrel of Spy apples (that variety kept better than other apples then available), Mother's bottled jams and preserves, and our skis and skates, among other things. We boys were told not to take the good apples from the barrel if there were any bruised ones or ones starting to go bad, and so usually ended up eating nearly a barrel of partly rotten apples every winter! Understandably, Mother also made a lot of tasty applesauce, apple dumplings, and apple pies in those days.

In 1946, in anticipation of his pending retirement, my father contracted with a neighbour to convert the Broadway Avenue house into two apartments.[39] An upstairs veranda was also added to create a back exit from what had been my parents' bedroom, and was immediately above the regular back veranda. That bedroom was converted to a kitchen for the upstairs flat. During the renovations, my father also had the old, inefficient, forced-air, coal-burning system replaced by a more efficient oil furnace with hot-water heating. No thought was given in those days to air-conditioning, and the house would get wretchedly hot and humid during the summer months. I think Father contracted for these renovations primarily to provide

---

[37]Jenness to Sapir, letter dated June 12, 1924, Sapir Correspondence, Box 625, Folder 2, Archives, CMC.

[38]The Driveway is known today as Queen Elizabeth Drive.

[39]This neighbour was a retired RCAF officer named Hawkins. He may have been the same man to whom my father sent his attendance records in 1941–1942 after Father was attached to the air force but continued to work from his museum office.

reasonable accommodation for one or more of his sons when they married, for housing was in short supply in Ottawa during most of the 1940s. All three of us subsequently lived in one or other of the two apartments, for periods of time ranging from one month to two years. However, the renovations were also a means of augmenting the small monthly government pension he anticipated receiving upon retirement.

For the next two years, while my father was still going to work each day, my parents retained the upstairs apartment for themselves and rented the one-bedroom flat on the ground floor to my newly married, ex-army brother Pete and his Belgian wife Eliane. For several winters thereafter my parents rented their own upstairs apartment, spending the winter months in warmer climates and the summer months at their cottage on the Gatineau River north of Ottawa.

In 1957, my parents arranged to have a small bungalow built on a hillside overlooking the Gatineau River about a mile north of their summer cottage. They moved into this house just before Christmas that year, and sold the Broadway Avenue house two years later.

Maids, Mother, and Meals

Mother had a series of live-in maids during the 1920s and 1930s. The maid slept in the attic and received room and board and about $15 to $20 a month. She did not come to our cottage with us, so was apparently sent home each summer. We had several different maids during the 1930s, all of whom came from rural areas near Ottawa. After the start of the Second World War in 1939, however, the young women were able to work for higher wages in wartime industries or the federal government, and Mother had to manage as best she could without help.

It was not uncommon for senior government officials in Ottawa to have maids in the 1920s and 1930s, when large houses were the norm. Having a maid to cook, wash, and houseclean left Mother free to partake of social and cultural activities as her maternal grandmother had done.[40] She thus was able to be active with local amateur musical groups, to attend weekly morning concerts at the Chateau Laurier, to have some of her friends to our house for musical afternoons and tea in the back parlour, to go to auctions downtown where the contents of many Scottish castles were frequently sold in the 1930s, and to participate in other cultural activities. She also had time to write a few articles and one book, which were published during the 1930s. Her book was entitled *The Indian Tribes of Canada*,[41] and proved quite popular, being reprinted several times. It was a simplified version of my father's *The Indians of Canada*, prepared for use in the grade schools and written under his watchful eye.

---

[40]Mother's maternal grandmother, Mary O'Neill, was said by my mother and her brother George to have been Lady O'Neill, daughter of an Irish baron from County Antrim, near Belfast, in what is now Northern Ireland. I have been unable to establish such a genealogical link, but it is nevertheless possible that one existed. Mary married a commoner named Charles Rainey, bore him two children, was widowed, then married a carpenter named William Boville and had several more children. The Boville family left Ireland and came to Ottawa in 1874. If, by marrying commoners, Mary incited the wrath of her aristocratic Father, she might well have been disinherited and sent to Canada, not an uncommon practice in those days, and had her genealogical connections severed. Following her death, the *Ottawa Journal* on June 29, 1903, described her as "one of Ottawa's oldest and most estimable residents."

[41]E. Jenness, 1933.

Most of Mother's cultural activities ceased when the war commenced and our maid departed for other employment. Mother spent much of her time thereafter taking care of our big house and her family, but in her spare time, she undertook some volunteer work, helping refugees from Europe to get settled in the region, and knitting socks and scarves for the soldiers overseas.

After the departure of our last maid, Father was the parent who generally prepared breakfast for the family. In the winter, he made hot porridge; in the warmer times of the year, we generally ate a cold cereal (usually shredded wheat or corn flakes) and milk. We boys also had fruit juice, toast, eggs and jam, bacon, and a glass of milk, for both parents were determined that we started each day with a good breakfast. Perhaps that is why all three sons grew taller than their parents. Father and Mother drank tea rather than milk. Coffee for some reason invariably gave my father a pain in the side within two hours of its consumption, a problem stemming from his summer on Victoria Island,[42] so it was almost never served.

During the school year, we went home at noon to a hot meal, which we called dinner. The evening meal, supper, was a lighter meal, often with soup or egg dishes or macaroni and cheese and dessert. We followed a fairly rigid pattern of eating during our growing years: breakfasts before 8 a.m., dinners a little after 12 noon, and suppers about 6 p.m. Meals during the summer were different, for the distance to our cottage was too far to allow my father to come home in the middle of the day. Hence we usually had sandwiches for mid-day lunch and the hot meal in the evening, which we nonetheless called supper. Somehow, my father found an eating place in a private house a few blocks from the museum where a woman offered hot meals each noon hour very inexpensively to an assortment of people. He took me there with him on a number of occasions.

My father, being from New Zealand, was especially fond of roast lamb. As fresh Canadian lamb was plentiful in the shops in the 1930s and not expensive, Mother occasionally served roast lamb along with potatoes and vegetables at dinner. Mother always made lots of gravy whenever she roasted lamb or beef, and my father loved to eat a piece of bread smothered with her delicious gravy as a follow-up to the main course. Vegetables during the colder months of the year were such durables as potatoes, parsnips, turnips, and carrots, or assorted canned vegetables. Fresh vegetables were unavailable in Ottawa during much of the year in those pre–Second World War days. Soup, bread or crackers and cheese were common supper fare as well, Father particularly enjoying old cheddar cheese.

We had desserts at both dinner and supper. These included fruit Mother had preserved the previous summer, canned peaches or pears, stewed prunes, or some variety of cake, pie, or pudding (Mother made delicious bread puddings, rice puddings, custards, and apple dumplings).

As far back as I can remember, we had finnan haddie,[43] which Mother boiled and covered with an unsweetened white sauce and served us every Friday midday for years. I suspect it was a routine Mother had learned and continued from her Irish mother, because, not being Roman Catholics, we were under no obligation to eat fish so regularly. However, it was the thing to

---

[42]Jenness to Stefansson, letter dated May 20, 1936, Jenness Collection, Box 658, Folder 41, Archives, CMC.

[43]Also known as finnan-haddock, this was haddock cured with the smoke of green wood, turf, or peat earth. The word *finnan* probably came from the Findhorn River or the fishing village by the same name, on the coast northeast of Inverness, Scotland.

do in those days, and it was supposedly good for us ("brain food," Mother called it). Father always ate his fish without comment, but we boys generally complained when this dish appeared and were regularly chastised for doing so. I probably complained more than my two brothers, for I always thought I got the most bones on fish day. This repetitious routine may be difficult to comprehend today when there are so many varieties of fresh fish, whole, halved, and filleted, along with other kinds of seafood in our supermarkets. Fish were rarely filleted then, however, and Atlantic Ocean fish was several days old by the time it reached the small grocery shops available then in Ottawa. Nevertheless, our battle with the hated finnan haddie went on year after year, until one day we complained once too often, and Father reached the limit of his patience. Bringing his fist down hard on the dining-room table, he thundered, "That's enough! Henceforth there will be no more fish!" Mother got the message, and we were never again subjected to that hated fish dish.

Today, most families drive their automobile to fancy supermarkets or large grocery stores for provisions, fill large grocery baskets on wheels with the items they desire, and then drive them home. In my parents' day, however, there were no supermarkets, only small grocery stores here and there, with far less choice of products. During my father's working years (i.e., until the 1950s), Mother would phone one or other grocery store within a few blocks of our house and read them a list of groceries she wanted. Someone in the store would gather and pack the items into empty cardboard boxes and have an employee deliver them by bicycle or truck sometime later the same day. Men employed by local dairies and large bakeries followed regular routes through the streets, delivering milk or bread daily from their horse-drawn wagons in the summer, sleighs in the winter. I suspect that Mother would have been overwhelmed by the size of and variety of products in one of our large, present-day supermarkets, let alone contending with the number of different volumes and weights of packaged goods today. When the old ways started to change after the Second World War, she fled to the country and dealt mainly with small country stores thereafter. Father was more adaptable to change.

Music and Newspapers

Sometime around 1941, my parents were asked if they would like to buy a large, floor-model radio–phonograph owned by friends who were moving west and wanted to dispose of it. We had no radio at the time, probably because my father did not consider one an essential possession. More to help their friends than through desire, Father bought the radio and installed it in his study. It was a beautiful console model with walnut finish and four short-wave bands, a Rogers Majestic product if my memory serves me correctly. It was reported to have been used by King George VI and Queen Elizabeth during their 1939 visit to Canada. Thereafter, my father used it each noon hour and evening to tune in the latest news from the BBC London by short wave about the progress of the war in Europe. It served us well until it broke down during the 1950s, after which Mother had its cabinet converted into a writing desk!

During the 1930s, the two Ottawa newspapers (the *Ottawa Citizen* and the *Ottawa Journal*) were published in both morning and afternoon editions. My father had home delivery of the afternoon edition of the *Ottawa Citizen*. Politically minded individuals might try to perceive some political leaning on my father's part for taking that newspaper in preference to the *Ottawa Journal*, but I would suggest that his decision was more likely based upon which local youngster persuaded the family to take delivery than on the political leanings of the paper. He was not always pleased to find part of his newspaper spread around the living-room carpet when he got home from the office, with one or two of his sons' bottoms facing his entrance while they knelt on the carpet to read the latest comic strips or sports news. Fortunately those were not the parts of the paper in which he was interested. I am sure he would have preferred to have his paper intact on his arrival home, but fathers with sons had to adjust to such problems in those days. On Sunday afternoons, he occasionally drove downtown to obtain a copy of the Sunday edition of the *New York Times* for its coverage of world news. As it carried neither comic strips nor local sports news, it did not interest us as the local paper did, so Father had it more or less to himself.

In his later years, in the confinement of the little bungalow up the Gatineau, he did not get a paper delivered to him daily. Instead, he regularly heard the news on a small table-model radio, listened to classical music, read from the few scholarly books he had saved when he and Mother moved to the country, wrote letters, or worked on a manuscript or two. He never owned a television set.

Book Binding

In 1935–1936, during our winter in Germany, and again in the summer of 1938, Mother bought a considerable amount of piano music in that country. Much of it was second hand, and the paper covers were prone to damage with use. My father found out that Percy Taverner, the bird specialist at the National Museum of Canada, knew a great deal about book binding, and talked to him on several occasions to acquire a grounding in the specialty. Taverner's wife, Martha, was the piano teacher for my brothers and myself for several years. Soon our basement sported an assortment of binding equipment, including a heavy metal glue pot, which one heated on the stove when needed, and a much heavier metal press. During the winter months for the next few years, my father spent many hours in our basement carefully installing bound covers on some of our piano music as well as on some of his own anthropology books. He showed me the technique at the time and let me cover one or two books under his watchful guidance. Following Taverner's instructions, he used thin leather to cover both the spines and the top and bottom corners of the front and back covers, where the most wear would likely occur, and cloth or patterned paper in contrasting colours for the central parts of front and back covers. His binding activities ceased after he became heavily involved in wartime duties in 1941, and the equipment then sat idle in the basement of our house until the house was sold, at which time it was somehow disposed of. Today, most of the music he bound is gone, and the only example I have of my father's brief journey into the art of book binding is his Volume XV Part A report about the Canadian Arctic Expedition.

Summer Cottages

In the early 1900s, it was customary for many residents of Ottawa to seek refuge from the summer heat and humidity by moving to cottages on nearby lakes and rivers. Families moved to their cottages as soon as the schools closed in June and remained there until Labour Day weekend. Fathers then commuted to and from their work place in Ottawa by streetcar, automobile or train, or remained in town during the week and spent the weekends with their families.

Figure 43 The Jenness summer cottage at Ramsay's Crossing, Quebec, 1993.
Photo with permission of Century 21 McIntyre Inc., Wakefield, Quebec

Tenaga

My mother's two unmarried aunts (Lucy and Kate), both schoolteachers, owned a large, two-storied cottage at Tenaga, Quebec, where her family resided in the summertime during her youth. It was located about twelve miles north of Ottawa, between the Gatineau Highway and the scenic Gatineau River. My father purchased it from the elderly ladies in 1921[44] and our family spent the summers there until 1931. Members of Mother's family owned the two adjacent cottages. The property was large, with several towering pine trees and a tennis court, but was about a quarter mile from the river and not convenient for swimming. After 1931, my parents maintained it and rented it to summer tenants for extra income during the depression years until 1939, when they sold it.

Ramsay's Crossing

In 1930, a friend of Mother's told her about an acre of waterfront property for sale on a wooded peninsula several miles upriver from the increasingly populated Tenaga community. The property belonged to the Ramsay family—several middle-aged, unmarried brothers and sisters who for many years had farmed about ten miles farther up the Gatineau River. Forced off their

---

[44]Jenness to J.R. Cox, letter dated February 12, 1922, obtained from Cox's daughter, Penelope, in Arizona in 1991 and in possession of S.E. Jenness in 2006.

farmland because of flooding resulting from the construction of a dam on the Gatineau River in the mid 1920s, they had moved a few miles south, and by 1930, had established their new farm and were prepared to sell wooded waterfront lots suitable for summer cottages.

As my parents had purchased their first automobile the previous year, they could easily drive the extra few miles from Ottawa, so they bought the one-acre property in 1930 for $500. The property was somewhat triangular-shaped, with rocky waterfront on two of its three sides. It was heavily covered with small shrubs and mature pine and spruce trees, which required many hours of hard work to clear and make sufficient room for a cottage and a road leading to it. My father arranged with local workmen to undertake those tasks. The following spring a local carpenter built a small, one-room, clapboard-sided cottage on a smooth rock exposure near the shore, at a cost of $500, and our family moved in for the summer. We had a splendid view up the river, which delighted Mother, and it became our family's much-loved summer camp for the next sixty years. Mother appreciated its privacy and quiet. My father enjoyed it too, and was able to get to it within an hour's drive from his office. There he relaxed in peace and quiet during evenings and on weekends, or found some chores to keep himself busy.

There were lots of regular outdoor chores, such as chopping wood for the wood stove, breaking dead or fallen branches for controlled bonfires on the rocky water's edge, tending to our annual vegetable garden, and painting the rowboat, raft, and cottages, all of which gave Father physical exercise and undoubtedly took his mind off of his office problems during the unhappy 1930s.

For the first few summers, my brothers and I slept in two tiny, semi-partitioned rooms on one side of the cottage, Father and Mother on a wretchedly uncomfortable folding bed on an adjoining side. In 1935, Father arranged to have a small bedroom and a screened porch added to the back of the cottage, and my parents then moved a double bed into the new bedroom and slept there. In the hot weather, we ate inside the screened porch. About the same time, Father also had a small bunkhouse constructed behind the cottage near the property line. When completed, it held two bunk beds, an old dresser, and a kerosene lamp, with little room for anything else. Here my older brother found solace and some independence for a summer or two, but neither I nor my younger brother Bob slept in it regularly.

Two years later, in 1937, Father arranged for a local carpenter to build a two-storey, two-roomed wooden cottage with an open veranda on the water's edge opposite the railroad tracks. Pete and I thereafter slept in its upstairs for a few summers, as did also our occasional overnight guests, and later, our own children. We called it the "boathouse," because we stored the rowboat in it for the first winter (which proved more cumbersome than practical), and thereafter a canoe for many subsequent winters. (Father purchased a fifteen-foot canoe in 1939 for us boys to enjoy.) He had had experience with canoes while he was in the Arctic and when he visited Indian reserves, but these were both work-oriented activities. I do not recall either him or Mother ever using our canoe.

These three buildings and an outhouse partly hidden in the woods some distance from the main cottage, served the family well for several decades, although they required occasional painting and other maintenance. It was truly a primitive summer camp, but here every summer my father found a fair degree of peace, contentment, and space for quiet reflection, and Mother welcomed her privacy.

A cottage community soon developed around the peninsula on which our cottage and the Ramsay's farmhouse were located, and adopted the name "Ramsay's Crossing," the name derived from the crossing of the railroad tracks near the Ramsay's farmhouse by the access road from the highway. The Canadian Pacific Railway Company chose the same name for the stopping site of its passenger trains in the late 1930s. During the Second World War, a daily commuter train between Ottawa and Alcove, just north of Wakefield, stopped at Ramsay's Crossing regularly to pick up and drop off cottagers, for gas rationing prevented them from using their automobiles to drive regularly to and from work. My father frequently took this train to Ottawa during the war years, or else remained in town during the week. When the war ended, gas again became plentiful, commuters reverted to driving their automobiles to work, and in the 1950s the Canadian Pacific discontinued its Gatineau commuter train service.

Camp Life at Ramsay's Crossing

Our camp life in the 1930s and 1940s was, to say the least, primitive by today's standards—no running water, plumbing, electricity, or telephone. The nearest country store was at the village of Wakefield, several miles upriver to the north, but my parents depended mainly on bringing supplies from Ottawa. As a result, we lived simply, with food that came mostly from cartons or cans. Mother would give my father a grocery list on some of the days he drove to work, and he would pick the items up after work. Without electricity it was difficult to keep some food fresh, but its rapid consumption by three growing boys rarely allowed food to spoil. To minimize spoilage we initially kept perishables, such as milk, meat, butter, and eggs, in containers in a small, earth-covered, cemented enclosure with a wooden door, which my father had someone construct on the side of a slope alongside the cottage. This we called the "mud house." Although the interior of the "mud house" was a little cooler than the exterior, milk frequently went sour within three days in the really hot periods in the summer. Along about 1936, my father bought a used icebox to serve as a refrigerator, which held a large block of ice that the local farmer delivered every few days. Father replaced the icebox with a used electric refrigerator in 1947 after poles carrying a power line had been installed across our property to our two buildings. We continued to store the non-perishable canned and packaged goods on a single shelf on the screened porch and along the walls between the studs, and kept bread and cake in metal boxes.

Neither the main cottage nor the "boathouse" had running water for bathing or bathroom facilities, even in 1993 when the property was finally sold. Several cottage owners around the peninsula installed pumping systems to use the river water, but I feel certain that Mother saw no need for such an expense at our cottage with the river but a few yards away. For personal washing, there was the river, or alternatively an enamel bowl on a low wooden bench located just outside the back of the main cottage, with a pail of river water generally alongside. One of my jobs was to ensure that there was adequate water in this pail. My father routinely used the enamel bowl on the bench for shaving after breakfast, taking hot water from the stove, and making use of the mirror mounted on the wooden medicine cabinet above the bench. Indoor bathroom facilities were impractical, owing to the lack of space inside the houses and no reasonable place to install a septic tank, because both cottages were resting on bedrock. Years later thoughts were given to getting a chemical toilet or an electric one, but nothing came of either scheme, so we continued to use the old outhouse. My father and mother both cheerfully put up with such primitive conditions summer after summer, perhaps because they had grown up without all the modern conveniences.

The first year we stayed at the cottage, my father had a well sunk on our property, hoping to obtain a good supply of drinking water. The well did yield a relatively small flow of clear and probably safe water for a few summers, but within a few years, river water somehow seeped into the well and contaminated it so that we had to stop using it. Thereafter we obtained our drinking water from the pump at the Ramsay's farm about 1,000 feet away and carried the pails back to our cottage. Father insisted we chlorinate this water in case it was contaminated, which it might have been because the well was located downhill from two barns. Mother boiled the river water for washing the dishes, using a dishpan because there was no sink in the cottage.

For laundry purposes, my father balanced an old railroad tie he had salvaged from the river on some large stones near our swimming site, placed a large galvanized wash tub on the tie, and built a small stone fireplace nearby, where Mother could heat water in an old pail. She generally just used the cold river water, however, and let the dirty laundry soak with the soap in the warm sunlight for a while before rinsing the items in the river and hanging them up with clothes-pins on a couple of wire clotheslines strung between nearby trees. Frequently, she spread the sheets on the grass for the sun to bleach as well as to dry. Few of today's young people would put up with such primitive arrangements, but Mother seemed quite content to operate in this manner. She was probably employing laundering methods her own mother had used years earlier, and perhaps her grandmother before that.

For lighting in the evenings before we had electricity, we initially used inexpensive kerosene lamps with tall glass shields and shiny metal reflectors. The glass shields invariably blackened quickly from the sooty smoke given off by the cloth wicks, and hence needed frequent cleaning. We later used Coleman lamps, which produced much brighter lighting, but the delicate, mesh wicks were easily broken once they had been used, and were fairly expensive to replace. We sometimes used flashlights to walk between the two cottage buildings or to the outhouse after dark, but most of the time just found our way in the dark. With the long daylight hours of summer, Father and we three sons kept busy outdoors in the evenings until it was almost time for bed, so the lack of electricity before 1946 was missed mainly by Mother, primarily for cooking. She had to keep a fire in the stove, day and night, for any cooking activities. My father saw to it that she always had an adequate supply of both kindling and firewood. After a power line reached the cottage after the Second World War, my father obtained a small two-burner electric stove with which Mother could do light cooking on really hot days.

Our usual cottage attire was as primitive as the two cottages. Father was always happy to exchange his hot office clothes for his casual wear when he returned from work. The lack of government funds for fieldwork during the 1930s meant that he could enjoy evenings and weekends at the cottage. On hot weekday evenings, then, when no visitors were expected, he frequently went about stripped to the waist, with just khaki shorts, running shoes, and an old hat. The hat was usually a pith helmet he had purchased in Singapore in 1929 while en route to Java. This attire he jokingly called, his "walkabout" attire.[45] On weekends, when we sometimes

---

[45]My father was probably employing this word as it is used in Australia, where it refers to an Aborigine's temporary return to the outback to wander the bush and renew traditional skills and practices. It is also sometimes used in New Zealand. It was thus a most appropriate word for him to use.

Figure 44 The explorer Vilhjalmur Stefansson, Diamond Jenness, and son Stuart, at the Jenness summer cottage, Ramsay's Crossing, July 1931.

had visitors, he would dress up more formally by the addition of a clean white jersey. This was his "walka-walkabout" attire. Mother, meanwhile, generally wore white shorts, a sleeveless blouse, white socks, white tennis shoes, and a floppy white cotton hat. Both of them sported fine tans by the end of each summer, no thought being given to skin cancer in those days. We boys frequently went about all day in our bathing suits and also sported fine tans by summer's end.

From time to time, Father would invite friends to visit us for a swim and tea on Saturday or Sunday afternoons in the summer. Out-of-town guests were especially welcome. A few of these visitors were persons of some importance in connection with Father's work. As I recall, they included archaeologist Henry Collins from the Smithsonian Institution and his family, British anthropologist Beatrice Blackwood from Oxford University, anthropologist Cornelius Osgood from Harvard University, and the Danish-Canadian botanist Erling Porsild and his daughter Karen. Some of the guests enjoyed the swimming, and all who came enjoyed the privacy and quaint primitiveness of the cottage, Mother's tea parties under the tall spruce trees near the waterfront, and especially the stimulating conversations with my father. Most of our guests drove back to Ottawa the same evening.

A visit of historical significance took place on our property one weekend in the summer of 1931, shortly after my parents first moved into the cottage. A carload of visitors suddenly entered our gate and drove along the dirt road to a parking spot under the pine trees. From the car descended Richard Finnie, the photographer and radio operator who the previous year had sent my father from Coppermine the poignant radio message from Ikpukhuak and Jennie (mentioned in Chapter 13). After Finnie came his wife Alyce, the explorer Viljhalmur Stefansson, and Karsten Andersen, a young man who had been with Stefansson on the Canadian Arctic

Expedition between 1916 and 1918. Finnie was well aware that my father and three other scientists from that expedition (Chipman, O'Neill, and Dr. Anderson) had asked for a Royal Commission in 1923 to investigate inflammatory charges Stefansson had made about them in his book, *The Friendly Arctic*. The request had been refused and the scientists involved were left angry through being prevented from clearing their names. Stefansson had also interfered with and delayed for many months the publication of my father's book *Life of the Copper Eskimos* because of my father's different interpretation of Stefansson's so-called "Blond Eskimos" in the central Arctic and other statements in the book. Finnie had now brought Stefansson face to face with my father for the purpose of trying to smooth over their differences. As I was but six years old at the time, I am unable to comment on whether the visit was a success or not. Proof of the meeting is indicated by the photograph of Stefansson, my father, and myself at our cottage, taken during the visit. Finnie sent a copy to my father, and it has been in our family's possession for many years.[46] That was, to my knowledge, the only time Stefansson visited us.

My father started a vegetable garden in the mid-1930s near the back of the cottage property. Each May or early June, after adding cow manure purchased from the local farmer for fertilization, and turning over the heavy clay soil, we planted the seeds of beans, Swiss chard, beets, and carrots. Because of the heavy clay soil, our carrots assumed the most grotesque shapes. Some years, we also planted seeds of lettuce, asparagus, and green peas, but these did not grow very well. Father recruited and directed all members of the family in the gardening operations. Almost every hot night during the summer, he would rally us to draw pails of water from the small bay separating our property and the railway tracks so that we could water the garden. That was a chore we boys often grumbled openly at having to do, but we did enjoy the rewards of the fresh produce resulting from our efforts. One summer, my father also planted four apple trees near the garden, but all of them died within a few years before they bore more than one or two apples apiece. Neither parent ever showed any interest in planting and maintaining a flower garden, either at the cottage or in the city.

Wild raspberries grew profusely along the railway tracks opposite our cottage. After supper on nice July evenings when the berries were ripening, my father would have all family members arm themselves with empty honey pails, metal cups, and even a pot or two, proceed together across the inlet in our rowboat, and climb carefully about the rockfill that supported the tracks along that stretch of shore. Here we picked all the ripe berries we could find before dark and then returned to the cottage to check them for worms. That task completed, Mother would set aside a bowl of berries for eating at mealtime. The following morning, she would cook the rest of the berries and make jars of delicious raspberry jam and raspberry preserves, which served our needs all the following winter. My father generally picked the most raspberries, possibly just another indication of his dedication to the tasks at hand.

---

[46]Parts of the images of my father and Stefansson lie outside the camera's field of view in this picture, and the print is faded, probably because of improper development. These are faults the talented photographer, Finnie, would hardly have committed. I suspect, therefore, that this picture was taken by someone else, and somehow became a part of his collection, wherein it was inadvertently stamped "Photograph by Richard Finnie" Some years ago I saw two or three other photographs revealing my father with Stefansson, Finnie, and Karsten Andersen, which were taken on the same occasion. They were in the R.S. Finnie Photographic Collection at the Library and Archives Canada (LAC 1987-154).

Country living frequently brings the city dweller into contact with a variety of creatures they do not commonly encounter. Year after year, for example, my parents regularly battled unwelcome mice at our cottage, which sought to enjoy our food while we slept. As a result, we kept mousetraps in constant use every summer. The task of finding and disposing of carcasses fell on Father or one of his sons. Snakes occasionally surprised us around our property during the summer, but most of these were relatively small and harmless garter snakes. They did not worry Father in the least, and he assured us that there were no poisonous snakes in our part of the country. Green frogs bred in the shallow waters of the bay near my father's vegetable garden and serenaded us on warm summer nights, often disturbing the sleep of our visitors, but we easily got used to their cheerful noise.

On dark nights in August, bats flew silently around the cottages snatching insects on the wing. An occasional bat managed to crawl inside one or other cottage and then flew around in the rafters, causing Mother great distress. I recall several occasions hearing that my father had gotten up in the night, on Mother's insistence, to try to knock down with a broom a bat that was flitting among the low rafters of the "boathouse." I suspect Mother subscribed to the old wives' tale that bats liked to settle in women's long hair. Father told me on a number of occasions that he had developed a deaf ear during the war, presumably the one facing his howitzer, and that he slept on the other ear, thereby avoiding hearing noises in the night, such as the squeak of the bats, or, as he liked to add with a twinkle in his eye, "your mother's snoring."

Mother had little tolerance for animals, and always refused our requests to have a house pet while we were growing up.[47] I disturbed the cottage equilibrium in the summer of 1940 by bringing home a young white rabbit after spending a week at a farm near Prescott. Mother finally agreed to let me keep it provided I looked after it and kept it caged well away from the main cottage. Father patiently helped me construct a chicken-wire fence to enclose it, but showed less patience when he learned later that I was feeding it the young carrots and lettuce leaves he was growing in his garden for the family's consumption. When it came time for our family to move back to the city at the end of August, Father drove me and my well-fattened rabbit back to the farm at Prescott from whence it had come, where it no doubt later provided the farmer and his family with a fine evening meal.

And then there were our experiences with skunks. These curious creatures would appear early in August each summer, mostly after dark but sometimes in the daylight as well. Our most noteworthy experience with one occurred in August of 1942. On the night in question,

---

[47]Interestingly enough, when Mother was working at the National Museum in 1917, she one day arrived home with a small kitten, which she evidently convinced her mother to let her keep. I learned years later from mother's brother George that Mother largely ignored her pet after that, and it was taken care of by my grandmother. As it happened, this was a kitten with a famous ancestor. Its mother had been presented as a kitten to Dr. R.M. Anderson, the zoologist who had led the Southern Party of Stefansson's Canadian Arctic Expedition 1913–1916. The mother of Dr. Anderson's kitten was Nigerauruk, the mascot on the ill-fated *Karluk*, the flagship of that expedition. The ship's fireman, Fred Maurer, had brought Nigerauruk back from the Arctic to his home in Iowa in 1914, and three years later had visited Dr. Anderson in Ottawa, at which time he presented one of Nigerauruk's kittens to Dr. Anderson. That kitten in due course mothered the kitten my mother brought home as a pet. When the latter feline died years later, it was buried in the back yard at 108 Broadway Avenue, underneath where the garage is located today.

my parents were sleeping in the upstairs of the "boathouse" and I was in the bedroom of the main cottage, some two hundred feet away. The door to my bedroom would not close, probably because of some settling of the house. It opened into the screened back porch where most of the family's food was kept. Early one morning, just around daybreak, I was awakened by strange noises from the back porch. Mother had baked a white cake with chocolate icing the previous day, and most of that cake, covered by the round metal lid of a large roasting pan, was sitting on a large plate on the floor of the porch. Peering through my partly opened doorway I saw to my horror a full-sized skunk not more than eight feet from me, happily devouring Mother's cake. It had scratched its way through the rotting screen on the door and then had managed to remove the round metal lid from her cake.

As quietly as I could I exited the bedroom by way of one of the windows, and ran quickly to the "boathouse" to awaken my parents. Father had faced far worse dangers in the Arctic or during the First World War, so he calmly instructed me to return to the back of the main cottage while he got dressed, and to open the damaged screen door through which the skunk had entered. When I had succeeded I was to signal him with a hand wave as he approached the front of the cottage. Greatly comforted by his calmness as he prepared for the "attack," I hastened back to open the screen door. Father knew that at bedtime he or Mother always closed the solid wooden door that separated the porch (where the skunk was), from the main room of the cottage, which he was about to enter. Fortified with this knowledge, he marched noisily up the path from the "boathouse," prepared for battle. Much was at stake, for if the skunk became alarmed and sprayed, it was unlikely that we could use the cottage for the rest of the summer.

By the time he reached the upper cottage, I had succeeded in propping the damaged screen door wide open, observing to my relief that the skunk was still too busily engaged in consuming the cake to have noticed my actions, and waved to my father. He then opened the front door of the cottage and trod loudly inside, all the while adding a little drama to the scene by whistling the "Toreador Song" from Bizet's opera *Carmen*. I stood outside the corner of the cottage to see what would happen next. As my father stamped noisily about in the main room, a very guilty-looking but well-fed skunk darted out the open back doorway and headed for the next property as fast as it could go, periodically glancing over its shoulder and wondering what frightful beast was after it. Thankfully, it was in such haste to depart that it did not stop to spray. Together, my father and I had saved the cottage. Father seemed remarkably cool after the incident, but I think he was less so a little while later, after Mother's unrecorded response to his suggestion that we could salvage the small part of the cake that the skunk had not eaten!

I was the cause of one of my father's worst animal problems at the cottage. With gas and automobiles almost unobtainable during the war, I foolishly purchased a horse in the spring of 1944 so that I could ride on Saturday afternoons with several young friends from the National Research Council where I worked. Mike was a fine-looking, chestnut-brown gelding about seven years old, reportedly a "drop-out" from the RCMP training school, and since I knew nothing about horse maintenance, I arranged for his keep at the riding stable in Ottawa South, where my friends and I rode. Then our family moved to the cottage in the middle of June. Faced with no way of seeing Mike while we were at the cottage, I decided to ride him to the cottage and keep him there. My parents were not thrilled at the idea, but Father, perhaps recalling fondly the horses he had tended during the First World War, finally went along with the idea, having my assurances that I would take care of the horse.

The next Sunday morning, I rode Mike the thirty-five miles from the stable to the cottage, a tiring twelve-hour journey for both of us. After feeding him some previously purchased oats from one of Father's water pails, I led him to the back of the property, well away from the "boathouse," and tied him to a tree for the night with a rope attached to his bridle. Sometime during the night, Mike broke free from the tree and, for the rest of the night, roamed aimlessly about in the evergreen trees on Father's fenced property, frequently slipping on the rocks and whinnying in fright as he sought to find some comfort for his loneliness in this strange environment. Mother admonished me in the morning, after Father had gone to his office, saying that my horse had kept her awake all night and something would have to be done about it.

The next night was almost a repeat performance, but with a new slant. During the night while Mike roamed the property after getting loose, he caught one of his hooves in the wire fence near the gate to our property and, on being forced to stand immobile on three legs in the moonlight, sought to let the world know about his plight with his loud whinnies. Mother soon dispatched Father to see what the noise was all about, and he, after assessing the situation, came to waken me for assistance. Together we walked in silence to the gate, my father armed with pliers, wire cutters, and a determined look. Once at the scene, he instructed me to hold the horse's broken rope and soothe the animal while he undertook to cut the fence wire lodged firmly between the metal shoe and the hoof of Mike's left front foot. No sooner was Father successful than Mike unwittingly dropped his tired foot right on my father's shoe. At three o'clock in the morning, it seemed an appropriate time for the air to be rendered blue with language learned on the wartime battlefields of France, but my father was not that sort of person. I think, on reflection, that he may have muttered a strong "damn" at the time, but nothing more for the moment. We silently tied Mike up again, and fortunately he remained so for the rest of the night. In the morning, however, undoubtedly prompted by words from Mother, Father informed me somewhat testily that my horse was no longer welcome on his property, and I had to find somewhere else to keep it. That evening, after he returned from his office, he noticed where Mike had trod in his garden the previous night, pressing Father's young shoots of lettuce and carrots firmly an inch or two deeper than they were intended to be. It did not enrich his feelings towards my horse. Mike had to go![48] He spent the rest of the summer roaming forlornly around a back field owned by the local farmer. In the fall, after I went off to college, Mother somehow managed to sell him to a riding school on the outskirts of Ottawa.

---

[48]Curiously, after years of literally shunning both large and small animals, Mother took a great fondness in 1952 to small donkeys she first encountered near Málaga, Spain, and then later at Alassio, Italian Riviera. After writing about the fat little donkey that brought her jars of fresh milk each day in Alassio, she added, "Some day I really will bring home one of these dear little donkeys—they are the most wonderful little creatures both here and Spain; but Diamond says that one donkey is enough for him to tote all around Europe!" (E. Jenness to S.E. Jenness, letter dated February 5, 1954, in possession of S.E. Jenness in 2006.)

Figure 45 Diamond Jenness and his three sons on the course of the Larrimac Golf Club, Quebec, about 1937. L. to r.:
John (Pete), Diamond, Stuart, and Bob.
Photo by E. Jenness

Sports Activities

My father could not, under any stretch of the imagination, be described as an athlete, a sports-
man, or even a sports enthusiast. Having grown up in New Zealand, the games he was most
familiar with were cricket, soccer, and rugby, none of which were popular in Ottawa during
his lifetime. Nevertheless he did enjoy, at various times in his life, participating in a variety of
sports activities.

In the early 1920s, ably assisted by two of Mother's brothers and a local farmer with a team
of horses, he built a tennis court on his cottage property at Tenaga. For a few summers thereafter, both Father and Mother enjoyed almost nightly games of tennis, as did Mother's brothers
when they were there. By the early 1930s, however, when I was old enough to retain memories
of such activities, the tennis rackets were gathering cobwebs within the cottage and the clay
tennis court was covered with weeds.

In 1933 or 1934, my father joined the Larrimac Links (years later renamed Larrimac Golf
Club),[49] a rough but scenic nine-hole course located about half way between Tenaga and our
new cottage at Ramsay's Crossing. To Father's disappointment, Mother preferred to stay at the
cottage and attend to her many chores or read under the trees in quiet. Prior to the Second
World War, my father would play nine holes of golf on Sunday mornings, sometimes with Pete
and me. In 1941, Pete was away, so Father would sometimes bring my younger brother Bob

---

[49]This odd name derives from the first and last name of the club's founder, Larry McCooey, who for
   years was club champion. The club was founded in 1924.

and me to the course. He always treated us with much patience on those occasions, in spite of our periodic outbursts of offensive language over bad golf shots.[50]

My father also occasionally participated in the golf club's Saturday afternoon 9-hole tournaments during the 1930s and 1940s. In those days, these tournaments were more or less social events for both ladies and men, with afternoon tea being served, rather than being the highly organized and competitive tournaments of today. The golf club was not licensed then to serve beer or liquor. Two topographers from the museum—K.G. Chipman and S.C. McLean—were members of the club and had cottages nearby. Chipman had been with Father on the Canadian Arctic Expedition from 1913 to 1916. Father was only a mediocre player, never seriously competitive. He possessed only an inexpensive golf bag, some used golf balls he or we boys had found, and half a dozen unmatched clubs,[51] but he nonetheless managed to win two or three tournaments when paired with a lady member in a mixed 2-ball foursome match, a type of tournament then popular at the club. Chipman's wife, Marjorie, was his partner in one of those successful tournaments.

My father played golf for the exercise and the fun of the game. However, he had to give up playing in the late 1940s after suffering a heart attack, for the course was hilly, and there were no motorized golf carts then. His three sons continued his interest in the game, winning a variety of club prizes over the next several decades.

Our entire family enjoyed swimming at the cottage, and Father would frequently have a brief swim to enjoy the refreshing nature of the cool river after a hot day in the city. About 1937 we boys helped him build, paint, and launch a raft that had a ladder on one side and floated on four barrels. Once it was launched in late June, we three sons were able to swim around it and sunbathe on it contentedly whenever we liked. Father and Mother refrained from using the raft, preferring to swim quietly to one side.

Table tennis (or as we called it, ping-pong) was also a game Father played with his family. Sometime around 1940, we helped him construct a tabletop, painted it dark green, and set it upon wooden "horses" in a large open area under the trees near the main cottage. Evenings and weekends thereafter for several summers, we frequently had rousing games of ping-pong,

---

[50]I recall one memorable occasion in 1941 shortly after my younger brother Bob became a junior member of the golf club. He was ten years old. Father had taken the two of us to Larrimac for 9 holes of golf. On one hole, after hitting an especially bad shot, Bob threw his club after the ball and emitted some entirely unacceptable language. Father's seemingly infinite patience suddenly reached its limit and turning to Bob, he said,

"Bob, do you know what you sound like?"

"No," replied Bob, in a disgusted voice.

Our normally quiet, gentle Father then launched into a two-minute tirade of language he must have learned in World War I in France. It was the one and only occasion I heard him express any swear-words more offensive than "damn." Even that word seldom passed his lips. When he finally ran out of breath, Bob looked defiantly at him and responded, cheekily,

"Way to go, Pop!"

Totally deflated by this unexpected response, Father wheeled about and strode off in search of his ball.

[51]I donated his old golf bag and a few of his old clubs to the Canadian Museum of Civilization in 2003 for their collection of early golf artifacts. It still included one or two annual Larrimac Golf Club membership tags from the 1940s.

occasionally including visitors. Mother sometimes joined in. My father learned to play rather well, but the nimbleness of his three sons soon left him wanting. He was always a good sport about it, though, even when we beat him.

Fishing was not an activity my father showed any interest in at our cottage, probably because he did not care for the kinds of fish we could catch in the Gatineau River—pike, suckers, small rock bass, and perch. It was not because he lacked interest in fishing, however, for in July 1920, he had trolled happily for trout with Mother on a three-week canoe and camping trip at Rock Lake in Algonquin Park,[52] and he wrote enthusiastically of fishing in early letters to Barbeau, and later in several letters to fishing enthusiasts, U.S. archaeologist Henry Collins and fellow New Zealander, H.D. Skinner.[53] A long pole and a large wooden fishing reel with copper wire at the cottage may have been the fishing equipment he used to catch the trout at Rock Lake, and he may also have used it to troll for muskellunge (a very large pike) at Parry Sound when he visited the Ojibwa Indians there in 1929. I think the rod finally ended up being put to use as a pole for climbing beans in the vegetable garden at the cottage.

In any case, just as there were no guns of any kind, there were no usable fishing rods in our house until I was given a fishing rod and reel by a family friend on my eighth birthday in the summer of 1933. Thereafter on weekends, I would sit contentedly upon an old pine stump near the water's edge at our cottage, casting with my new rod and coloured lure, but rarely caught anything large enough to eat, nor anything one would particularly want to eat. Feeling squeamish about handling wet and writhing fish, I generally called to my father to remove any small victim I chanced to catch from my multi-hooked lure and to dispose of it, for it invariably was lacerated beyond survival and had to be killed and buried. He was always very patient with me, occasionally endeavouring to instil in me some philosophical attitude or understanding as a result of an incident involving an unfortunate fish. On the rare occasions when the bass or perch was of sufficient size to be worth cooking, my father had the luckless task of scaling and de-boning it before putting it in the pan, for Mother stoutly refused to prepare or cook it. Father had learned much about such matters while in the Arctic, if not in Papua or even New Zealand before that. He also was the only one who voluntarily ate the fish. I also recall that he may have grumbled a little at the time about the need for a certain person to learn to take care of what he caught, but the words had little impact upon me at the time.

There was one memorable summer day when our family lined up with makeshift fishing rods around the shore between the "boathouse" and the swimming area some yards away. Even Mother was involved, holding a long bamboo pole with a fishing line tied to the far end, but no reel to pull in anything that chose to nibble on her bait. I don't think anyone expected her to catch anything, but she was trying to be a good sport and join in. My father was roaming back and forth behind us, supervising us all and helping if needed, but not fishing himself. Suddenly Mother got a strike, and in her excitement, instinctively swung her long pole swiftly up and around. At the end of her line was a sucker at least fifteen inches long, hardly a delicacy

---

[52]Jenness to Barbeau, letter dated August 17, 1920, Barbeau Collection, Box 206, Folder 27, Archives, CMC.

[53]The letters referred to here are in the Jenness Correspondence and the Barbeau Collection, Archives, CMC.

by anyone's standards, yet the biggest fish ever caught by anyone in the family. Unfortunately her wiggling projectile followed the arc taken by her pole and struck the side of my father's head with a resounding smack, nearly knocking him to the ground. That was the last straw, as far as he was concerned, and he announced that there would be no more fishing on his property. All fishing ceased therewith until my brother Pete's young sons appeared on the scene many years later with their own fishing rods. By then, however, Father was living at the little bungalow a mile upriver and remained oblivious to the revival of the activity.[54]

Mother enjoyed skiing in her youth and sought to interest my father in participating in that activity. In the early years of their marriage, they skied on some weekends on a hill at Ironsides, a village just north of the city of Hull (or Gatineau, as it is now called), but I don't believe he ever became adept at it or particularly enthusiastic about skiing as an enjoyable activity, and they both stopped skiing sometime in the 1930s.

My father learned how to handle a gun at an early age, for, as a youth in New Zealand, he frequently hunted rabbits and wild pigs in the hills inland from his home. While at Oxford University, he joined the rifle club and for a time had weekly target practice, in due course winning at least two silver spoons for his marksmanship, which were still in my possession in 2006. He later proved his shooting ability by the number of caribou he brought down while living with his "adopted" Eskimo parents on Victoria Island in 1915. His war experiences seem to have ended his interest in guns, however, for he never owned one thereafter.

While he was at Oxford, my father took up rowing and punting for a time when he could no longer afford going to the target range. He did not perform competitively. We always had a rowboat at the cottage, which he certainly knew how to handle well, but by then he was no longer interested in rowing for fitness.

The Cascades House

Little has been said to this point about the Cascades property and house, where my father spent the last years and days of his life. Located about a mile upriver from the Ramsay's Crossing cottage (hence about twenty one miles north of Ottawa), the winterized house sat on a small, level area of post-glacial clay, the front edge of which sloped down to a narrow inlet of the Gatineau River about ninety feet below. Railway tracks separated both this inlet and the lower part of the property from a narrow strip of land along the river. The view down the river had convinced my mother to purchase the lot in 1957. She then arranged for the building of a road from the highway and for the construction of a small, two-bedroom bungalow with basement and furnace. My parents moved in shortly before Christmas 1957.

All of the rooms in the finished house were small, but there was a large picture window in the living room, flanked by two narrow windows, which afforded a splendid view down the river from indoors, as Mother had wished. The house was isolated—five miles from the nearest town, shops, and medical help, and several hundred feet from the highway and their nearest neighbour at the time. Mother loved the little house, largely because of its isolation and quiet,

---

[54]The veracity of this seemingly fictitious story is confirmed in part in a letter from my father to H.B. Collins, dated September 9, 1939, Jenness Correspondence, Box 642, Folder 17, Archives, CMC.

Figure 46 The Jenness bungalow at Cascades, Quebec, about 1960. Diamond Jenness at his front door with his grandson Bill, grandson David playing in the sand. Left of Diamond is the living-room bay window; to his right is the window of the bedroom in which he died in 1969.

Photo by J.L. Pete Jenness

Figure 47 Diamond Jenness, about 1962, immersed in thought in his living room chair at his Cascades home, where he could read and converse with family or visitors.

and partly because she had helped design it and oversaw its construction. It may have been her dream home.

I do not think that my father was ever content there, however, feeling the closeness of the quarters, deprived of a study where he could do his writing, and being so dependent on the weather and the reliability of his automobile. As a result, he escaped the confinement of the house by driving to town as often as he could. He had good reason to feel as he did, for this tiny 720 sq. ft bungalow was smaller than the ground floor of his Broadway Avenue house. And the problem of having to shovel a path in the snow to the highway (where my parents had to leave their automobile for the first few winters), proved extremely challenging. During the last few years of my father's life, when he was not allowed to shovel because of the condition of his heart, he was fortunately able to get a local man to plow the road to the house in the winter time.

After Father's death in 1969, Mother remained in the house year-round for several more years, until increasing blindness forced her to return to Ottawa where we sons could attend to her needs more readily. The house was finally sold after her death in 1993.

Figure 48 View down the Gatineau River from the Jenness house at Cascades in early spring, 1969.
Photo by J.L. Pete Jenness

Honours

My father received several honours over the years, most of them reflecting the high regard in which he was held for his contributions to his profession. They were of four types: honorary degrees from universities; nominations for high offices in prestigious organizations; national awards; and special publications to honour him. A few other honours of varying kind and merit were also bestowed upon him, as I note at the end of this section.

My father received the following five honorary degrees in his later years:

University of New Zealand, Hon. Litt.D., 1935;
Waterloo Lutheran University, Hon. LL.D., 1962;
McGill University, Hon. D.Sc., 1963;
University of Saskatchewan, Hon. LL. D., 1965; and
Carleton University, Hon. LL.D., 1968.

He was greatly touched to be awarded these honours, and personally attended the awards ceremonies of all but the one from the University of New Zealand.[55]

He was elected President of the Society for American Archaeology in 1937, President of the American Anthropological Association in 1939, and Vice-President (Section H) of the American Association for the Advancement of Science in 1939. In addition to these professional honours, he was made an Honorary Fellow of the Royal Danish Geographical Society, an Honorary Member of the Royal Society of New Zealand, an Honorary Member of the Washington Academy of Sciences, and an Honorary Member of the Italian Geographical Society. He was a Fellow of the Royal Society of Canada, the Arctic Institute of North America, the American Ethnological Society, and the Guggenheim Foundation.

In 1954, he was awarded a John Simon Guggenheim Fellowship, the funds from which enabled him to spend the winter in Cyprus researching that island's unusual history. His studies led to the publication of his book, *The Economics of Cyprus: A Survey to 1914*. The book summarizes the historical and geographical development of the island until its annexation from Turkey by Great Britain in 1914.

In the fall of 1941, my father was awarded the first of several medals he received for his achievements in anthropological research: the Rivers Memorial Medal, awarded by the Royal Anthropological Institute of Great Britain and Ireland in recognition of his work in Arctic America.

In May 1962, he was awarded the Massey Medal by the Royal Canadian Geographical Society, for his outstanding contributions to our knowledge of Indians and Eskimos.[56] He was

---

[55]He told me one day, with a mischievous smile, that the only honorary degree he still lacked was an honorary doctor of divinity. When he got back to Ottawa after receiving his honorary degree from the University of Saskatchewan in 1965, he said little about the awards ceremony but told me instead about the undignified manner in which he was taken on board the aircraft for his return trip. With his heart problems, being confronted by a steep set of steps from the tarmac up to the entrance door of the aircraft proved a bit formidable so he asked if there was some way he could be lifted up to the door. After some discussion, the airline personnel produced a large net into which he was placed and then hoisted up most unceremoniously by a crane.

[56]Anonymous, 1962.

Figure 49 Diamond Jenness with his Massey Medal and three sons, Rockliffe Park, Ottawa, June 1962. L. to r.: Bob, Stuart, Diamond, and John (Pete).

Photo by S.E. Jenness

only the fourth person to receive this prestigious award since its inception. It was presented to him by Governor-General George Vanier in a private ceremony at Government House, with his three sons in attendance.

In December 1968, he was appointed a Companion of the Order of Canada, Canada's highest honour, for his services in the field of anthropology. Unfortunately, he was not well enough to attend the scheduled presentation at Government House in April 1969, nor to receive Governor General Roland Mitchener for a proposed later private presentation to him during the summer at his bungalow in the Gatineau Valley. Thus, he never saw his medal. Governor General Mitchener ultimately presented the medal to my mother in a private ceremony at Government House on March 25, 1970, with her oldest son, John (Pete), in attendance.

My father also received some other honours, most of them after his death. In a class by themselves were the two groups of scholarly publications issued in his honour. The first of these was a collection of anthropological papers, which his friends, Jim and Pat Lotz, coordinated and edited into a special "Festschrift" issue of *Anthropologica* in 1971, aptly entitled "Pilot not Commander—Essays in Memory of Diamond Jenness."[57] The list of the sixteen contributors reads almost like a *Who's Who in Anthropology* of the day. The second group, initiated in 1976

---

[57] *Anthropologica*, N.S., vol. XIII, nos. 1 & 2, 1971, 323 pp.

Figure 50 Eilleen Jenness and her three sons in the office of William Taylor, Jr., Director of the Museum of Man, Ottawa, April 5, 1972, with the Presentation Copy of the topographic map showing the newly named Diamond Jenness Peninsula on Victoria Island. L. to r.: J.L. (Pete), Stuart, Bob, and Eilleen.

by William E. Taylor, Jr., the Director of the Museum of Man in Ottawa, consisted of the designation of a select group of publications in the museum's Mercury Series of anthropological reports by a specially patterned black band affixed across their covers, together with the wording "A DIAMOND JENNESS MEMORIAL VOLUME." Inside each of these special volumes is a page dedicating the volume to my father and carrying a photograph of him. Over the next ten years, until the museum became the Canadian Museum of Civilization (in 1986), sixty-five of its reports were designated in memory of my father. Somehow, I think that these special tributes to "the founding Father of Canadian anthropology," as George F. MacDonald (the first director of the new Canadian Museum of Civilization) described my father, might have been the honours that most pleased him.

Still other honours involved the use of his name for varying objects, some significant and just cause for family pride, others less so. They were: (1) a large peninsula on Victoria Island (Diamond Jenness Peninsula); (2) an Arctic river (Jenness River); (3) a very small Arctic island (Jenness Island); (4) a high school at Hay River, Northwest Territories (Diamond Jenness High School)[58]; (5) a house on the campus of my father's alma mater, Victoria University College

---

[58]Opened in September 1973, the Diamond Jenness High School proclaims as its mission a goal my father would surely have approved—"to provide a safe, caring and vibrant learning environment that inspires all students to achieve excellence in the pursuit of life-long learning." A decade later, the school's architect, Douglas J. Cardinal, designed the buildings my father had hoped one day might house (and display) the vast collection of native Canadian artifacts that he had helped accumulate, the Canadian Museum of Civilization.

(Jenness House);[59] (6) a two-winged fly he had collected on Victoria Island in 1915, named *Diamesa arctica*; (7) "Chemin Jenness," the gravel road from the highway to the house that was the Jenness bungalow at Cascades; (8) a farm horse named "Diamond," which belonged to the Ramsay family near the Jenness' cottage in the 1940s; (9) an entry in a crossword puzzle in the *National Post* newspaper in 2003 that required his full name to be listed; and (10) most recently (August 2004) a small, strange rock in a crater on the planet Mars, which has been given the name "Diamond Jenness"![60] Of these various honours, all but the following were announced after his death: the high school, the fly, the island, and the horse.

My father's outstanding scientific contribution to Canada was also recognized in 1998 when *Maclean's* magazine listed him as one of the 100 most important Canadians in history, as well as third among the ten foremost Canadian scientists.[61]

Figure 51 Diamond Jenness with volume 1 of his Arctic diary, about 1958.

Photo by Newton Associates, *Ottawa Citizen*

Miscellaneous Recollections

Father and Writing

Father did a lot of writing both at his office and in his study in the evenings during the 1920s and 1930s, much of it by hand. His handwriting was small and neatly legible. It frequently slanted upwards on the page, however, about which he once wrote with tongue in cheek to his friend Bill Newcombe, "Is it a sign of senility to write askew? I never do write straight across the page."[62] At some stage early in his life he had learned to typewrite properly. For years, he had a desk in his study into which a heavy Royal manual typewriter folded. The desk thus served the useful dual purpose of providing either a writing or drawing surface, or a typing facility, according to his needs.

---

[59] The college is now Victoria University of Wellington. The Anthropology Department occupied Jenness House commencing in the mid-1980s, but it was demolished a few years later after the department moved to new quarters, wherein the Anthropology Library is now known as the "Diamond Jenness Room."

[60] R. Boswell, 2004.

[61] J. Granatstein, 1998, p. 39.

[62] Jenness to W.A. Newcombe, letter dated May 8, 1933, Newcombe Collection, GR 111, Box 7, File 4, Archives of British Columbia, Victoria, B.C.

Figure 52 Diamond Jenness at work on his memoirs at his cottage, 1968.
Photo by J.L. Pete Jenness

When our house on Broadway Avenue was renovated in 1946, Father lost the use of both the study and the typewriter desk, and was forced to revert to writing with pen and ink for a year or two until he purchased a portable typewriter. On this lightweight machine, thereafter, he wrote his subsequent articles, reports, books (including the chapters in this book), and letters, sometimes outdoors at the cottage or upriver at the bungalow at Cascades. He took this typewriter with him when he travelled to Italy, Cyprus, Mexico, Florida, or the Caribbean.

When Mother and Father were on their travels, she faithfully wrote her three sons weekly about their activities, letters which for the most part, alas, we did not save.[63] As she enjoyed the role of family correspondent, Father seldom wrote, which left him more time to carry out his research work. During the two winters when he was away alone, however, he wrote detailed accounts of his activities to Mother almost weekly, always including an affectionate salutation and ending. She retained his letters from Italy in 1949–1950, but not, unfortunately, those from France a decade later. He did not retain hers. He also wrote his sons from time to time when he was in Europe alone. A few of these letters have survived.

When he wrote professional material, Father would hand-write or type his first draft, then meticulously edit it several times, polishing up what he had written in a real labour of love. The result was often excellent prose, but it did not come without considerable effort. Mother

---

[63]Perhaps if Father had been less modest and his sons had been more aware of his importance in his profession, we might have recognized the historical value of the letters and saved them.

acted as his editor and critic most of the time, which usually led to somewhat agitated scenes, for she was frequently blunt in her criticism. For example, she wrote along the margin of the middle section of Chapter 1, which described his voyage to England, "Article on D's first ocean trip to college at Oxford is *very bad*," and at the start of Chapter 14, "This article interesting, but not very important." He removed both sections as a result, but I have re-instated them because of the valuable information they include. She always wanted his work to be of the highest standard, but her concept of what that required did not always match his own.

My father wrote much of his book, *Dawn in Arctic Alaska*, while he and Mother wintered on the Italian Riviera between 1953 and 1955. From Alassio, Mother wrote to me, "Dad is getting on really well with his Arctic book, & is really enjoying being able to do it leisurely.... He still doesn't take too well to criticism tho'! ... Fortunately, his work lately hasn't needed anything more than a word here & a word there."[64] A nearly destitute local artist my parents befriended in 1955 in Albisola, Señor Giacomo Raimondi, charmingly illustrated Father's Arctic book, and I drafted its maps and a piece of music. Mother also commissioned Señor Raimondi to do a pastel portrait of my father, which proved to be quite a good likeness.

My father's writing was so admirably and clearly expressed that when I edited his lengthy Arctic diary, which he had written virtually without corrections under the most difficult conditions of temperature, weather, and location, I found nothing to correct more significant than an abbreviation here and there, an occasional punctuation mark, and a few spelling inconsistencies of Eskimo names.

Christmas Activities When We Were Young

When we three boys were young, we helped Mother or Father set up and decorate our Christmas tree in Father's study and hung our Christmas stockings on hooks in the mantelpiece over the fireplace. A few days before Christmas, we were each instructed to write a note to Santa Claus listing our Christmas wants, then Father would help us individually set our notes alight in the fireplace, in that manner "sending our requests to Santa Claus." In the process, of course, he had the opportunity to read what we wanted for Christmas. On Christmas Eve, Father (or Mother) would place a glass of milk and a cookie on a plate in his study as a thank-you for Santa Claus, and I recall being excited at finding the glass empty and the cookie gone in the morning, with a note of thanks from Santa. It did not occur to me until years later that the handwriting on the note looked suspiciously like Father's or Mother's (their handwriting was somewhat similar).

On Christmas morning, the dark curtain was drawn across the entrance to the study to conceal the contents that lay within, and we were not permitted to see those contents until after breakfast. Mother insisted we all eat a hearty breakfast before we could look at our presents. Afterwards, Father lit a fire in the study fireplace to warm up the room, then lined us up in

---

[64]E. Jenness to S.E. Jenness, letter dated February 23, 1954, in possession of S.E. Jenness in 2006. Fifty years later, when I mentioned mother's comment to Mrs. Diana Rowley, who edited the five volumes of my father's Eskimo Administration series for the Arctic Institute of North America in the 1960s, she remembered that mother was inclined to be far too negative in her criticism of his writing. His writing, she volunteered, was much too good to improve upon.

the hall, youngest son (Bob) first, then me, and then Pete, before the curtain was drawn aside and we were allowed to enter. Our gifts in those days generally included socks, mittens, a book, and one or two toys or sporting items, hockey sticks being provided most years. The stockings hanging on the mantelpiece were invariably filled with an orange, an apple, some nuts, a small gift-wrapped toy, and one or two other items, sometimes as a fatherly prank including a lump of coal or a potato from the cellar.

We always had a large turkey for Christmas dinner, which Mother roasted to perfection. Father carved excellently, some years with the "special-occasions" cutlery, other years with an old, bone-handled carving knife, the long blade of which was well worn down from his frequent sharpening. While he carved, we snapped the traditional Christmas crackers and retrieved the coloured paper hats within, placing them on our heads to liven up the occasion. To accompany the turkey, Mother generally offered mashed sweet potatoes, mashed turnips or parsnips, tinned beans or peas, cranberry jelly, and gravy. This first course was followed by a large round plum pudding, which Mother had prepared and steam-cooked in November, then hung in cheesecloth from a ceiling fixture in the pantry for weeks to mature. She used an old English recipe. The pudding was served hot with a hot, creamy, unsweetened white sauce, providing a treat I can still savour today. Tea or milk comprised the beverages we consumed, never coffee, wines, or liquors. Our Christmas dinner was always a special event and greatly enjoyed.

Birthdays

Children's birthdays were low-keyed in our home when my brothers and I were growing up. Neighbour's children were not invited, and there were no decorations. Mother generally made a white or yellow cake for the occasion, with chocolate icing on top and in the middle, and would place small-valued coins (one-, five-, and ten-cent pieces) here and there around the outer edge of the top of the middle layer of the cake. Finding a ten-cent piece in those depression days of the 1930s seemed a fortune.[65] Our parents gave us a toy, a book, or an item of apparel as our birthday present. They made no equivalent fuss for their own birthdays, foregoing even the presentation of cards or gifts, if memory serves me rightly. In later years, we three sons tried to remember our parents' birthdays with greeting cards or cheerful phone calls.

Thus it was perfectly natural that our family made no plans for Father's eightieth birthday on February 10, 1966. We were only following his wishes, for he had said that he did not want a fancy celebration. However, he had not reckoned on some of his friends and acquaintances. A considerable number of good wishes reached him at the time, including telegrams from Helge Larsen in Copenhagen, Henry B. Collins in Washington, Canada's Governor-General George P. Vanier, the Arctic Institute, and the National Museum of Canada. Additional greetings came by mail from Prime Minister Lester Pearson, the Honourable Arthur Laing (then Minister of Northern Affairs and Natural Resources), and the Geological Survey of Canada. And on the day of his special birthday, several of his museum friends, led by W.E. Taylor, Jr., descended upon my father's house at Cascades and warmly congratulated him, then informed him that they had commissioned well-known Ottawa portrait artist Robert Hyndman to paint my father's portrait. Some sixty of his friends, both local and far afield, had contributed

---

[65]Unlike today's children, we did not receive allowances.

Figure 53 Diamond Jenness alongside his portrait painted by R. Hyndman, in his living room at Cascades, 1968.

to its cost.[66] Hyndman visited my father at Cascades on several occasions thereafter to work on this painting.[67]

In due course, Taylor returned to present the finished painting to my father. He was accompanied on that occasion by Mrs. Diana Rowley, Dr. Erling Porsild, and Captain Joe Bernard. Mrs. Rowley had edited my father's five Eskimo Administration reports. Porsild was the chief botanist at the National Museum of Canada and Father's friend since their meeting on Little Diomede Island in 1926. Bernard was the first white trader in Coronation Gulf, whom my father had met on several occasions since the summer of 1916. The framed painting rested on the mantelpiece at Cascades for the next decade or so, then was presented with the family's approval to the National Museum of Man (now the Canadian Museum of Civilization), where it currently resides.

A little-known curiosity about our family is the cluster of birthdays in February. Father's birthday was February 10. Mother's birthday and my brother Pete's birthday were on the preceding day, February 9. And the birthday of one of Mother's younger brothers, Hal, was

---

[66]Many of the contributors were friends from his days at the museum, including, interestingly enough, Marius Barbeau (see Appendix 1).

[67]Hyndman evidently had an interesting career (Gessell, 2003). I understand that he deliberately enlarged my father's hands in his portrait to reflect my father's literary talents. I have always suspected that the stern look of my father in this portrait reflected his disapproval either of having to sit for the painting or of the artist himself.

February 8. Persons born in February come under the sign Aquarius, and horoscope believers might be able to offer some creative speculations about what, if anything, this clustering of family birth dates might mean.

Automobiles and Transportation

To Father, an automobile was a convenient mode of transportation. He was not concerned about the kind of automobile he owned, nor its size, nor how old it was, just so long as it started and ran reliably, with a minimum of mechanical or electrical trouble. He purchased all of his automobiles new, except for the one he bought in 1936, and always paid outright for them. He purchased his first car in 1929, a new two-door Chevrolet, and replaced that in 1936 with a 1934 Chrysler four-door sedan. From 1939, his third car, a new four-door Dodge, served him well for fifteen years, then he gave it to me and bought a new Volkswagen "Beetle," the first of several he owned until his death.

He patiently taught his wife and three sons the basics of driving, and kindly let us borrow his automobile from time to time after we obtained our licences. I recall how, in 1951, he let me borrow his automobile to drive to Pennsylvania so that I could move my wife and infant son to New Haven, Connecticut, then came uncomplainingly by train and retrieved it when I was immediately involved with graduate-school studies and could not spare the time to drive it back to Ottawa.

While he lived at 108 Broadway, he stored his automobile in our garage every winter, supported on wooden blocks, the battery removed and brought into our house to prevent freezing. At the cottage, he parked his automobile under the trees, unprotected from rain, insects, tree gum, and bird droppings. On wet or damp days, it sometimes failed to start. On such occasions he would usually clean and dry the spark plugs with his old but trusty pocket knife, and then try to start the automobile again. That was about the limit of his knowledge of auto mechanics. His efforts generally proved successful, however, and he was able to proceed to town, but when they failed, he took the train to town and went to his office, or stayed at the cottage.

A Near-fatal Car Accident

One afternoon shortly before Christmas in 1957, my father headed back from Ottawa to his newly completed bungalow at Cascades. His almost-new Volkswagen "Beetle" was loaded with groceries plus some gifts he had purchased for Mother. The weather had taken a warm turn and a dense ground fog coming off the Gatineau River shrouded the highway in several places. He drove extra carefully in the foggy, late-afternoon darkness, relying upon his headlights to illuminate the white dividing line in the middle of the two-lane highway to keep him safely on the road. Fortunately, there was almost no traffic. In places, he could see only a few yards of road in front of him through the fog. When he was about half way between the communities of Old Chelsea and Tenaga, his car suddenly lurched, bumped heavily, then plunged forty feet down the steep slope of an abandoned sand quarry. It bounced once near the bottom of the sandpit, flipped upside down, and landed in a pool of water several feet deep at the bottom. The car was flattened, a total write-off.

I examined the scene of the accident the next day and saw that at the place where he had driven off the highway, the road curved to the left and a gravel road from the sandpit joined the highway on the right. At that precise locality, the mid-road white line ceased for several yards, reappearing around the curve. Without the white line as a guide and unable to see the curve in the fog, my father had obviously driven straight ahead, right into the deep sand quarry.

Fortunately, he was not wearing his seatbelt at the time, despite a newly introduced law requiring its use, for the novelty of the new safety device in his car had not yet instilled in him an instinctual reaction to buckle it whenever he got into the car. That oversight actually saved his life, for when the car bounced on its nose and flipped over, the door alongside him sprung open, and he was thrown out onto the slope of the sandpit. He had no idea how long he lay there, but he finally crawled up the steep bank and walked unsteadily down the road to a small restaurant a few tens of yards away. There, his face badly scraped and bloody, he was given immediate assistance, and at his suggestion, the restaurant owner telephoned Mother's brother, Hal, who lived at the Larrimac golf course about seven miles farther up the highway. Hal arrived within a few minutes and promptly drove my father to the hospital at Wakefield, several miles beyond his house at Cascades, for treatment. Father spent the next few days resting and under observation in the hospital, recovering from what thankfully proved to be largely superficial injuries.

At some time during that hospital stay of about ten days, which included Christmas, the founder of and senior doctor at the hospital, Dr. Harold J. Geggie, a quiet, sage gentleman whom my father knew fairly well, informed him that he was a very lucky man to be alive. "A thick skull with nothing under it is what saved you," the doctor jokingly said to him at the time.[68] My father enjoyed recounting that comment to his friends for many years afterwards.

He was 71 years old at the time of the accident. While he was hospitalized, I arranged for the removal of his vehicle from the sandpit and the purchase of a replacement Volkswagen for him. I am glad that neither he nor Mother ever saw the flattened accident vehicle, for it might have given them nightmares on many a night afterwards.

The Jenness Plaque

Early in the 1970s, Dr. William E. Taylor Jr., Director of the National Museum of Man, and a great friend and admirer of my father, urged the National Historic Sites and Monuments Board to commemorate my father's significant contribution to Canada's knowledge and understanding of its Native people by putting a plaque in his memory at the front of the Victoria Memorial Museum Building. Months passed before any action was taken.[69] Finally, on June 26, 1976, my mother, flanked by her three proud sons, a few invited guests and Dr. Taylor, formally unveiled a handsome gold and maroon plaque at the front door of the building in which my father had worked for nearly thirty years. The dedication speech was given by "Confucius," Father's wartime friend, Reverend Gordon Taylor.[70] The plaque was mounted prominently

---

[68]Jenness to Professor Harry Hawthorn, letter dated June 4, 1958; Harry Hawthorn Collection, Special Collections and University Archives, Library, UBC.

[69]Dr. Taylor notified my mother in November 1973 that the National Historic Sites and Monuments Board had recommended that my father was of national historic significance and should be commemorated. Mother evidently responded to Dr. Taylor by expressing our family's appreciation, then adding my comment upon reading his letter, "I had always thought so many wonderful things about my father, but I never dreamed that Canada would finally proclaim him a "National Historic Site."

[70]Gordon R. Taylor was not related to Dr. William E. Taylor, Jr.

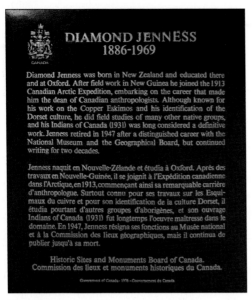

DIAMOND JENNESS
1886-1969

CANADA

Diamond Jenness was born in New Zealand and educated there and at Oxford. After field work in New Guinea he joined the 1913 Canadian Arctic Expedition, embarking on the career that made him the dean of Canadian anthropologists. Although known for his work on the Copper Eskimos and his identification of the Dorset culture, he did field studies of many other native groups, and his Indians of Canada (1931) was long considered a definitive work. Jenness retired in 1947 after a distinguished career with the National Museum and the Geographical Board, but continued writing for two decades.

Jenness naquit en Nouvelle-Zélande et étudia à Oxford. Après des travaux en Nouvelle-Guinée, il se joignit à l'Expédition canadienne dans l'Arctique, en 1913, commençant ainsi sa remarquable carrière d'anthropologue. Surtout connu pour ses travaux sur les Esquimaux du cuivre et pour son identification de la culture Dorset, il étudia pourtant d'autres groupes d'aborigènes, et son ouvrage Indians of Canada (1931) fut longtemps l'oeuvre maîtresse dans le domaine. En 1947, Jenness résigna ses fonctions au Musée national et à la Commission des lieux géographiques, mais il continua de publier jusqu'à sa mort.

Historic Sites and Monuments Board of Canada.
Commission des lieux et monuments historiques du Canada.

Government of Canada - 1976 - Gouvernement du Canada

Figure 54 The Diamond Jenness plaque.

on one of the supporting stone pillars at the top of the steps leading to the huge front doors of the building.

One winter evening about two years later, I went to the museum to attend a lecture by the well-known African archaeologist, Richard Leakey. A considerable crowd gathered long before the lecture, and the waiting line of people stretched from the front entrance out into the snow-covered roadway in front of the museum. Finally the big doors swung open, and the attendants began admitting people, but they did so very slowly, for the museum's auditorium held only about four hundred and fifty persons and they did not want to let too many people enter. I finally reached the foot of the wide stairs leading to the big entrance doors, alongside which was the pillar that held the plaque honouring my father. A young boy of perhaps twelve, who was with his parents immediately ahead of me, grew restless at the slowness of the admission process and wandered up the stairs, stopping briefly to look at the plaque. Then he returned and said to his father, "Dad, who was this guy Jenness whose name is on that sign?" The father, no more than three feet in front of me, shook his head and replied, "I don't know. Probably some old bugger who worked here!" I believe that my father would have been just as amused as I was at that unflattering description.[71]

The Day I Conned My Father

During the summer of 1962, while he was writing the second of his five Eskimo administration reports in an office downtown, my father sometimes joined me for lunch in my office at the Geological Survey of Canada. Each of us had a bag with sandwiches and fruit prepared for us by our wives. Those were quiet times we shared, talking of family and other matters, the memory of which I treasure to this day.

At some point, I realized I did not have a single good photograph of my father and decided to remedy the matter. I knew that my father had known Ernie Elliott, the head of the Photographic Section at the Geological Survey, for many years and liked him, so I told Ernie

---

[71]In 2003, the Canadian Museum of Civilization sought to have the plaque moved to its new building in Gatineau, Quebec, where the anthropologists in the federal government now work. I was asked if the Jenness family had views about the planned move and replied that we had no serious objection provided it was given a prominence in its new location comparable to that it had enjoyed in the Victoria Memorial Museum Building. I subsequently heard that the current director of this museum (now the Canadian Museum of Nature) did not want it to be removed, so that it remains near the entrance where it was originally placed. I now think that was the correct decision, for my father knew nothing of the new building.

about my desire to obtain a good portrait photograph of my father and asked his help. He willingly agreed, and we arranged for me to alert him (Ernie) the next time my father came for lunch and then bring him up to Ernie's laboratory for a photo session. All went as planned, but I deliberately avoided telling my father the real purpose of the visit, merely saying his old friend Ernie would like to see him again. Father willingly came along with me, and I ushered him in to Ernie's lab. There he was greeted warmly by Ernie and one of his assistants, and was shown to a stool, which had been strategically placed for the photographing. The assistant was ready for action, and snapped the camera shutter just as my father realized he had been conned. He captured beautifully my father's slightly amused expression, as can be seen in Figure 55. Fortunately, Father was not the least bit angry, and the family obtained what I regard as the best photograph we own of him.[72] This later became Mother's favourite picture of him as well.[73]

Figure 55 Diamond Jenness, 1962.

A Prophet is Without Honour

Some years ago an American comedian, Roger Dangerfield, built a career around the expression "I get no respect!" My father had no knowledge of this comedian, nor I expect would he have found him especially amusing. He would, however, have had some understanding of the basis for the comedian's act.

---

[72]The famous photographer Yousuf Karsh photographed my father on August 21, 1944, soon after he (Karsh) had established his reputation as a photographer of famous people. Mother did not like the results, so no prints were ordered until sometime in the 1980s, when I decided that the family ought to own one copy. It carries his photo no. 9272. Karsh soon afterwards presented all his photographs to the National Archives of Canada, where they are identified as Karsh Collection, Accession No. 1987-054.

[73]"At long last *this* is the one picture of Diamond that I like the best, as its expression shows his really sympathetic nature." E. Jenness to H. Hawthorn, letter dated February 2, 1971. Anthropology Professor Frederica de Laguna of Bryn Mawr wrote: "I wish that I'd had a copy of the photograph you used for the AA [an obituary of Diamond Jenness in *American Antiquity* (De Laguna, 1971)], for it is admirable—just as I remember him: kind, thoughtful, and about to give friendly counsel with a warm smile;" de Laguna to H. Hawthorn, August 3, 1971, Harry Hawthorn Collection, Special Collections and University Archives, Library, UBC.

Figure 56 Last known photograph of Diamond Jenness, with his pith helmet, Cascades, Quebec, 1969.

Photo by permission of Manuel Maples, Ottawa

My father was Chief of the Anthropology Division during a very trying period. He succeeded Dr. Edward Sapir, a man whose abilities my father greatly admired and whose vision he sought to follow, but in this, my father's timing, which had favoured him so often in the Arctic, in British Columbia, and in Newfoundland, largely abandoned him. In contrast to the fast start made by Dr. Sapir in developing the division in 1911, much aided by the strong support of Dr. Brock, who was then the Director of the Geological Survey, my father promptly encountered the chilly disinterest of different Survey administrators, the almost immediate opposition and unfriendliness of Marius Barbeau (the one person he thought he could depend upon), and, within a few years, the prolonged depression of the 1930s and the world war that followed. Between 1925 and 1940, he received recognition for his anthropological work from individuals and institutions abroad, but almost constantly battled for every inch of progress, and every penny or pencil for the people in his division. And when he finally went home each evening to seek a little peace and quiet, he was regularly beset by the thoughtless demands and behaviour of three growing sons for whom he was not Canada's foremost anthropologist, just simply "Dad" or worse, "Pop." It is little wonder, then, that one of my father's favourite quotations, which I heard him recite on several occasions, was the well-known biblical passage, "A prophet is not without honour, save in his own country, and in his own house."[74] Fortunately, with the passing of time and the accumulation of at least some wisdom, this seeming lack of respect by his fellow countrymen and family has been replaced by a growing appreciation and admiration for what my father managed to accomplish under highly unfavourable conditions. Unfortunately, none of this was of any benefit or comfort to him while he was alive, and he was forced to settle with the belief that he had done his best, in spite of adversity.

And in the End

My father's health failed noticeably during his last six months. On April 29, 1969, his fiftieth wedding anniversary, he was bedridden and on oxygen in the Wakefield Hospital (a few miles north of his home) with a weakened heart, forced to remain there for several days. He then spent a quiet summer at his Cascades home, doing what writing he could, reading, and listening to classical music.

---

[74]The Gospel According to St. Matthew, Ch. 13:57.

(a) (b) (c)

Figure 57 Three portraits of Diamond Jenness. (a) by Jean Jenness, oil, 1986; (b) by Giacomo Raimondi, pastels, 1955; and (c) by Robert Hyndman, oil, 1966.
Photos by S.E. Jenness

Shortly before 1 p.m. Saturday, November 29, 1969, after a night spent combating waves of nausea, he was resting in bed quietly reading a book and listening to classical music on his radio when he suddenly suffered a fatal heart attack and died. Mother was preparing his lunch when the end came. In response to a note of condolence from Father's friend, Professor Harry Hawthorn, Mother wrote:

> In a world so irrational and confused, Diamond did seem to keep intact his courage and sanity of outlook, softened always by compassion. I know, also that he appreciated your own efforts, and he counted on you to continue that fine work on behalf of all the Indians and Eskimos and Metis.
> I think you will be glad to know that his last morning on earth was one of complete serenity and contentment, at home, in our beautiful surroundings. Suddenly, Death came— merely as an utterly peaceful, mystic transition. I am consoled for the rest of my life. I could ask no more."[75]

Father's funeral was held several days later. The peaceful service included the 21st Psalm, one he particularly liked. In the crowded small chapel at the funeral home, sitting quietly near the back, were a number of Eskimo men and women who had come to pay their last respects. My mother later told me she had noticed several of them with tears streaming down their faces during the service and was highly moved by their show of affection towards Diamond, the government man who had always tried to help and protect their people.

---

[75]E. Jenness to H. Hawthorn, letter dated December 10, 1969, University of British Columbia Library, University Archives, Harry Hawthorn Collection, Box 7, File 2.

Later that cold and dreary early December day, his coffin was slowly lowered into its resting place under the trees at Beechwood Cemetery, Ottawa, as his family and a few friends stood silently alongside. In his classical fashion, he had entered the dugout of Pluto's boatman, Charon, and started his final journey across the River Styx.[76]

---

[76]On a small piece of paper glued to the title page of my copy of Vol. 5 "Analysis and Reflections", my father wrote in ink "This copy of *Vol. 5 Eskimo Administration* carries a special preface acknowledging the author's indebtedness to Graham and Diana Rowley. It is one of the only eight copies printed; all others contain a more commonplace preface." It is dated August 1968 and signed by my father

In this special preface, my father explains that the surly Charon had refused to ferry him across the murky river Styx [to the underworld] until he composed a brief summary of the first four volumes "which would release tired administrators, and historians curious about mankind's past frailties, from any obligation to read them." "What follows is the required summary," he wrote, but he was not yet finished. Having acknowledged that Graham's departmental organization in the federal government had subsidized the series, he added: "Yet I fear that Charon may demand a further toll. Accordingly, to ensure for myself safe passage on his boat, I would urge those tired administrators whose heads throb over the summary's first pages to turn as quickly as they can to its Appendix, where a staccato list of recommendations will provoke a violent but, I trust, transitory migraine; and I would counsel those curious historians who are deeply distressed by human frailties to cast only a fleeting glance at the essay's dusty ears of factual wheat, but to weigh most carefully the meditative tares which have maliciously invaded the grain-field. Then, stopping my ears against the siren voices of other readers, I will make my way once more to Charon's leaky dug-out, singing the praises of my editor, Diana Rowley, and vowing never again to inflict on her, my publishers, or the long-suffering Mr. Everyman, another line of manuscript, typescript, or printer's ink."

TABLE 1 **363**

Table 1 Native peoples investigated in the field by Diamond Jenness, 1911–1936

Name	Dates	Locations (References)
Bwaidogan	Dec. 1911 – Dec. 1912	Goodenough I., eastern Papua (Jenness and Ballantyne, 1920)
N. Alaskan Eskimos	Oct. 1913 – July 1914	Northern Alaskan coast (Jenness, 1957, 1985, 1991)
Copper Eskimos	Aug. 1914 – July 1916	Bernard Harbour; Coronation Gulf Victoria Island (Jenness, 1922, 1923b,c, 1928a, 1959, 1991)
Sarcee Indians	July – Aug. 1921	Reserve near Calgary, Alberta (Jenness, 1938)
Carrier Indians	Oct. 1923 – June 1924	Hazelton, Fraser Lake area, and Stony Creek reserve, northern B.C. (Jenness, 1934a, 1943)
Sekani Indians	June 1924	Ft. McLeod, Ft. Grahame, northern B.C. (Jenness, 1937b)
Beaver Indians	July 1924	Peace River, Alberta (Jenness, 1932)
Beothuk Indians (extinct)	June – Aug. 1927	North–central coast of Newfoundland (Jenness, 1927a, 1934b)
Ojibwa Indians	July – Aug. 1929	Parry Sound region, Lake Huron, Ont. (Jenness, 1935)
Coast Salish Indians	Sep. 1935 – Mar. 1936	Near Sydney and Duncan, Vancouver Island; and Fraser Valley, southwestern B.C. (Jenness, 1955)

Table 2 Diamond Jenness' travels, 1947–1969

Year	Season	Duration	Country	Comments
1947–1948	Winter	3 months	New Zealand	Alone; first trip there since 1919
1948–1949	Winter	3–4 months	Italy	With wife; Bergeggi, Rome
1949–1950	Winter	5 months	Italy	Alone; by car around Italy and Sicily
1950–1951	Winter	3–4 months	Mexico	With wife; by car to Orleans; Yucatan, Mexico City
1951	Fall	4 months	British Columbia	Alone; visiting professor at UBC
1951–1952	Winter	4–5 months	Spain and France	With wife; by car to Málaga and Brittany
1952–1953	Winter	3–4 months	Mexico	With wife; by car to Guadalajara
1953–1954	Winter	6 months	Italy	With wife; by car to Alassio
1954–1955	Winter	~6 months	Italy	With wife; by car to Albisola
1955–1956	Winter	6 months	Cyprus	With wife; by car to Kyrenia
1957	Winter	3 months	Florida	With wife; by car to Daytona Beach
1958	Winter	3 months	Portugal	Christmas at Cascades; with wife to Almogarve
1959	Winter	2 months	Martinique	Christmas at Cascades; with wife to Fort-de-France
1959–1960	Winter	6 months	France	Alone; by car, studying mediaeval church architecture
1960–1961	Winter	6 months	Mexico	With wife; by car to Manzanillo
1961–1962	Winter	6 months	Spain	With wife; by car to Gandia Playa
1962–1963	Winter	4 months	Florida	With wife; by car to New Smyrna Beach
1963	Summer	1 month	Labrador	Alone, by coastal ship to Ft. Chimo
1963–1964	Winter	6 months	Ottawa	With wife; Lexington Apts.
1964	Summer	~6 weeks	Greenland	Alone; Denmark and Greenland
1964–1965	Winter	5 months	Portugal	With wife; Albufeira
1965–1966	Winter	4 months	Florida.	With wife; Daytona Beach
1966–1967	Winter	3 months	Ottawa	With wife; 890 Echo Drive
1967–1968	Winter		Ottawa	With wife; Parkdale Towers Apts.
1968–1969	Winter		Cascades (Quebec)	With wife

APPENDIX 1

List of Donors for Portrait of Diamond Jenness

Painted by Robert Hyndman

On the Occasion of his 80th Birthday, February 10, 1966
as a token of their affection and admiration

Charlotte Abbott
F.J. Alcock
A.W.F. Banfield
Marius Barbeau
Selma Barkham
Junius and Margaret Bird
Kaj Birket-Smith
Hugh S. Bostock
Kathleen Bowlby
Douglas S. Byers
N.O. Christensen
C.H.D. Clarke
Henry Collins
Nan Cooke
Jack and Corolyn Cox
Audrey Dawe
Frederica de Laguna
M.J. Dunbar
C.R. Dunlop
E.C. Elliott
Richard Finnie
James A. and Ethel C. Ford
Nansi Swayze Glick
R.G. Glover
A.D.P. Heeney
William N. Irving
Frederick Johnson
H.L. Keenleyside
Helen Kummermann

Helge Larsen
W.S. Loughlin
Trevor Lloyd
Richard S. MacNeish
Tom Manning
Catharine McClellan
Evelyn Stefansson Nef
Cornelius Osgood
Ralph Parkin
A.J. Pick
A.E. and Margrit Porsild
R.T. and Elly Porsild
George I. Quimby
Hugh and Lucy Raup
Graham and Diana Rowley
Richard Slobodin
C.M. Sternberg
Winnifred Strong
Martha Taverner
Wm. E. and Joan Taylor
Frank Vallee
Geert van den Steenhoven
Maja van Steensel
Linc and Tahoe Washburn
C.P. Wilson
R.F. Wodehouse
Nora Woods
J.V. Wright

APPENDIX 2

The Publications of Diamond Jenness

Stuart E. Jenness

Diamond Jenness authored (or co-authored) at least 138 publications, as follows: scholarly books (21); popular books (5, including this one); articles in scholarly publications (52); articles in popular magazines (19); chapters, prefaces, or forewords in books by others (12); articles in the *Encyclopaedia Britannica* (3); book reviews (11); obituaries (3); and other publications (12). One of his book reviews, published in 1922, covered five different books, but I have listed it as a single review rather than five. One hundred and three of his publications dealt with either the Eskimos (69) or the Indians (34). He co-authored four books and one article; two of his co-authored books were with his missionary brother-in-law, Reverend Andrew Ballantyne, very early in Jenness' career. Being the sole author of all but five of his publications was a reflection of both the times and his working habits.

The best-known list of Jenness' publications heretofore has been that of Collins and Taylor, Jr. (1970), which appeared in an obituary of Jenness published in *Arctic* the year after his death. Their list contains 98 entries, which they stated was a combination of lists compiled to 1956 by Asen Balikci (1957) and covering 1957 to 1971 prepared by Jenness himself. One article on the Collins-and-Taylor list does not appear to exist. This is "The land of the midnight sun," identified as being in the December 1928 issue of the magazine, *The Country Gentleman*. The article is not in that issue or in any issues of that American magazine during that year, the year earlier, or the year later. It may have been published elsewhere, but until it is located, I have deleted it.

In 1990, Anne McDougall produced a valuable annotated bibliography of Jenness' publications in the French Arctic journal, *Inter-Nord*, which included seven items not on the Collins-Taylor list or among the thirty additional publications I have added. I have included those seven publications in the following listing.

Jenness' first-known publication was a short Fijian folktale, which he sent in manuscript form to his teacher, R.R. Marett, at Oxford, who in turn arranged for its publication in 1913. My father may have gathered the story during a brief ship stop at Fiji, in April of 1913, while en route from Auckland to Victoria, British Columbia, then mailed it from Victoria while he was waiting there to go north with the Canadian Arctic Expedition. His last-known publication (prior to the present one) was an essay on the Eskimos, probably written sometime in 1969 and published in the *Encyclopaedia Britannica* in 1971, two years after his death.

Jenness' entire professional career was spent as an employee of the Canadian government, all but the final seven years of it at the National Museum of Canada. As he worked from 1913 onwards for the museum (except for the two years between 1917 and 1919 when he was with the Canadian Expeditionary Force overseas), first as a scientist and later as a scientist-administrator, it is understandable that eleven of his publications were issued by that organization, commencing in 1927. From its inception in 1910, the Anthropology Division within the National Museum of Canada had been a small scientific organization within the long-established Geological Survey of Canada. Jenness was still a member of the museum's staff when he retired late in 1948, but carried out important intelligence work from 1940 to 1946 with the Royal Canadian Air Force and the Department of National Defence, then for two years helped organize and develop the Geographic Bureau within the Department of Mines and Resources.

In perusing the following list of publications, I found it interesting that for one trained in the Classics and Anthropology, Jenness published so many articles (18) in two geographical journals: the *Geographical Review* (9), and the *Canadian Geographical Journal* (9). Furthermore, all but two of those articles were published before 1940. It is also noteworthy that as early as 1932, he published on Canada's population possibilities, followed almost twenty years later with a paper concerned with Italy's population. And in 1933 he published some views about Canada's fisheries. Perhaps his studies in geography while at Oxford years before had somehow sparked his interest in these non-anthropological directions.

The current list of Jenness' publications appears below. Each of the forty items not included in Collins and Taylor (1970) is identified by an asterisk (★) after the date.

List of Diamond Jenness' Publications

Jenness, D. 1913.★ The magic maker: a Fijian folk-tale. *Folk-Lore* (Folklore Society of the Royal Anthropological Institute), vol. 24, no. 1, pp. 233–234.

———— 1916a. The ethnological results of the Canadian Arctic Expedition, 1913–1916. *American Anthropologist*, vol. 18, no. 4, pp. 612–615. Also in *Summary Report 1916*, Geological Survey of Canada, pp. 392–394.

———— 1916b.★ Return from Canadian Arctic Expedition. *Geographical Review*, vol. 2, pp. 232–233.

———— 1917a. The Copper Eskimos. *Geographical Review*, vol. 4, no. 2, pp. 81–91.

———— 1917b.★ Ethnological results of the Canadian Arctic Expedition. In *Summary Report of the Geological Survey for Calendar Year 1916*, Printer of the King's Most Excellent Majesty, Ottawa, pp. 392–394.

———— 1917c.★ Work on Canadian Arctic Expedition. *Geographical Review*, vol. 4, pp. 241, 246.

———— 1918. The Eskimos of northern Alaska: a study in the effect of civilization. *Geographical Review*, vol. 5, no. 2, pp. 89–101.

———— 1919.★ Along old cannibal trails. *Travel*, vol. 33, no. 3 (July), pp. 34–37, 41.

———— and A. Ballantyne, 1920. *The Northern D'Entrecasteaux*. Preface by R.R. Marett. Clarendon Press, Oxford, 219 pp.

———— 1920a. Papuan cat's cradles. *Journal of the Royal Anthropological Institute*, vol. 50, pp. 299–326.

———— 1920b. Proposals for ethnological research in New Zealand. *New Zealand Journal of Science and Technology*, vol. 3, no. 4, pp. 213–216.

———— 1920c.★ Heroes of the frozen North. *Travel*, vol. 34, no. 4 (February), pp. 10–13, 54.

———— 1920d.★ A note on "Eskimo Stone Rows in Greenland. *Geographical Review*, vol. 10, p.47.

———— 1920e.★ Note on Cadzow's "Native copper objects of the Copper Eskimo", in "Discussion and Correspondence, *American Anthropologist*, vol. 23, p. 235.

———— 1921a. The 'blond' Eskimos. *American Anthropologist*, vol. 23, no. 3, pp. 257–267.

———— 1921b. The cultural transformation of the Copper Eskimo. *Geographical Review*, vol. 11, pp. 541–550.

———— 1922a. Eskimo art. *Geographical Review*, vol. 12, pp. 161–174. Also in *Readings in the Geography of North America*. American Geographical Society, 1952, pp. 23–36.

———— 1922b. Eskimo music in northern Alaska. *The Musical Quarterly*, vol. 8, no. 3, pp. 377–383.

———— 1922c.★ Hunting caribou with the Copper Eskimo. *Travel*, vol. 39, no. 3 (July), pp. 21–25, 42.

———— 1922d.★ "The friendly Arctic." Comments on a review of V. Stefansson's book by Professor Richard Pearl in *Science*, vol. 56, no. 1436, July 7, 1922, pp. 8–12.

———— 1922e. "The Copper Eskimos, Part A: The Life of the Copper Eskimos." *Report of the Canadian Arctic Expedition, 1913–1918*, vol. 12, 277 pp.

———— 1922f.★ Review of five works on oceanic cultures: *Migrations of cultures in British New Guinea*, by A.C. Haddon; *Racial and cultural distributions in New Guinea*, by A.C. Haddon; *A new theory of Polynesian origins*, by R.B. Dixon; "Review of *A new theory of Polynesian origins*," and "*The Islanders of the Pacific, or the children of the Sun*," by T.R. St.-Johnston. *Geographical Review*, vol. 12, pp. 503–506.

———— 1922g.★ Copper objects of the Copper Eskimo — a reply to Mr. Cadzow. *The American Anthropologist*, n.s., vol. xxiv, pp. 89–92.

———— 1923a. Eskimo string figures. *Journal of American Folk-Lore*, vol. 36, pp. 281–294.

———— 1923b. The Copper Eskimos, Part B. Physical characteristics of the Copper Eskimos. *Report of the Canadian Arctic Expedition, 1913–1918*, vol. 12, 89 pp.

———— 1923c. The Copper Eskimos, Part C. Introduction (3c–5c). In Cameron, J. *Osteology of the Western and Central Eskimos* (6c–58c), and Ritchie, S.G. *Dentition of the Western and Central Eskimos* (59c–67c). *Report of the Canadian Arctic Expedition, 1913–1918*, vol. 12, 79 pp.

———— 1923d. Origin of the Copper Eskimos and their copper culture. *Geographical Review*, vol. 13, pp. 540–541.

———— 1923e.★ The play hour in New Guinea. *The Christian Herald*, January 27, 1923, pp. 68, 178.

———— 1923f.★ Two monuments in Arctic Canada. *Canadian Historical Association, Annual Report 1923*, pp. 72–75.

———— 1923g.★ Review of *Among unknown Eskimo: An account of twelve years intimate relations with the primitive Eskimo of ice-bound Baffin Island, with a description of their ways of living, hunting customs & beliefs*, by J.W. Bilby. *Geographical Review*, vol. 13, p. 642.

———— 1923h.★ Review *A summer in Greenland*, by A.C. Seward. *Geographical Review*, vol. 13, pp. 642–643.

———— 1923i.★ Indian religion. *The Canadian Magazine*, vol. 61, pp. 66–70.

———— 1924a. Eskimo folk-lore. Part A: Myths and traditions from Northern Alaska, the Mackenzie Delta and Coronation Gulf. *Report of the Canadian Arctic Expedition, 1913–1918*, vol. 13; Southern Party, 1913–1916, 90 pp.

———— 1924b. Eskimo folk-lore. Part B: Eskimo string figures. *Report of the Canadian Arctic Expedition, 1913–1918*, vol. 13, 90 pp.

———— 1924c.★ The singing people of the South Seas. In *The Outline of Knowledge*, vol. XV (Travel), edited by J.A. Richards, J.A. Richards Inc., New York, pp. 192–202.

———— 1924d.★ Wolf! Wolf! *Victoria University College Review ("The Spike")*, Silver Jubilee Number, Easter 1924, pp. 29–31.

———— 1925a. A new Eskimo culture in Hudson Bay. *Geographical Review*, vol. 15, no. 3, pp. 428–437.

———— 1925b.★ The shudd'ring tenant of the frigid zone. *Travel*, vol. 45, no. 4 (August), pp. 21–22.

———— and Helen H. Roberts, 1925. Songs of the Copper Eskimos. *Report of the Canadian Arctic Expedition, 1913–1918*, vol. 14, 506 pp.

———— 1926.★ Review of *Primitive Labour* by L.H. Dudley Buxton. *Geographical Review*, vol. 16, pp. 347–348.

————— 1927a. Notes on the Beothuk Indians of Newfoundland. *National Museum of Canada, Bulletin no. 56*, pp. 36–38.

————— 1927b. Notes on the phonology of the Eskimo dialect of Cape Prince of Wales. *International Journal of American Linguistics*, vol. 4, nos. 2–4, pp. 168–180.

————— 1927c.★ Review of *Early Migrations of the Eskimo Between Asia and America*, by Waldemar Bogoras. *Geographical Review*, vol. 17, pp. 342–344.

————— 1928a. Archaeological investigations in Bering Strait, 1926. *National Museum of Canada, Bulletin no. 50*, pp. 71–80.

————— 1928b. Eskimo language and technology. Part A. Comparative vocabulary of the Western Eskimo dialects. *Report of the Canadian Arctic Expedition, 1913–1918*, vol. 15: Southern Party, 1913–1916, 134 pp.

————— 1928c. Ethnological problems of arctic America. pp. 167–175 in Problems of Polar Research. *American Geographical Society, Special Publication no. 7.*

————— 1928d. *The People of the Twilight*. The Macmillan Co., New York, 247 pp. Published in a softcover edition in 1959 with an epilogue, The University of Chicago Press, Chicago, 251 pp.

————— 1928e. The National Museum of Canada. In *Anthropological Notes and News*, *American Anthropologist*, vol. 30, no. 1, pp. 178–180.

————— 1928f.★ Review of *Archaeology of the Central Eskimos: I. Descriptive Part. II. The Thule Culture and its Position within the Eskimo Culture. Geographical Review*, vol.18, pp. 696–698.

————— and A. Ballantyne, 1928. *Language, mythology, and songs of Bwaidoga, Goodenough Island, S.E. Papua.* Polynesian Society, Memoir no. 8, 270 pp. Also in *Journal of the Polynesian Society*, 1926–1929. Bwaidogan grammar. vol. 35, no. 4, pp. 290–314 (1926); Folk-lore and translations. vol. 36, no. 1, pp. 48–71; vol. 36, no. 2, pp. 145; vol. 36, no. 3, pp. 207–238; vol., no. 4, pp. 303–329 (1927); Incantations. vol. 37, no. 1, pp. 30–56; vol. 37, no. 2, pp. 139–164; War chants. vol 37, no. 3, pp. 271–299; Bwaidogan vocabulary. vol. 37, no. 4, pp. 377–402 (1928); and Bwaidogan vocabulary (cont'd.). vol. 38, no. 1, pp. 29–47 (1929

————— 1929a. The ancient education of a Carrier Indian. *National Museum of Canada, Bulletin no. 62*, pp. 22–27.

————— 1929b. Ivory carving of North America. *Encyclopaedia Britannica*, 14th ed., vol. 12, pp. 843–844.

————— 1929c. Little Diomede Island, Bering Strait. *Geographical Review*, vol.19, pp. 78–86.

————— 1929d.★ Review of *The Silent Force: Scenes from the Life of the Mounted Police of Canada. Geographical Review*, vol.19, pp. 523–524.

————— 1929e.★ Review of *The Cruise of the Northern Light. Geographical Review*, vol.19, pp. 350–351.

————— 1929f.★ A demographic inquiry into the Eskimo population. *Geographical Review*, vol. 19, pp. 336–337.

————— 1929g.★ Review of *Alcuni data demografici sugli Esquimesi* by Giorgio Carega. *Geographical Review*, vol. 19, pp. 336–337.

————— 1930a. The Indian's interpretation of man and nature. *Transactions of the Royal Society of Canada*, vol. 24, section II, pp. 57–62.

————— 1930b. The Yukon telegraph line. *Canadian Geographical Journal*, vol. 1, no. 8, pp. 695–714.

————— 1930c. The Indians of Canada. In *The Cambridge History of the British Empire*, vol. 6, *Canada and Newfoundland*, Cambridge, pp. 79–91.

————— 1930d.★ The trials of a polygamist. *Toronto Star Weekly*, January 11, 1930, p. 5.

————— 1931a. Wild rice. *Canadian Geographical Journal*, vol. 2, no. 6, pp. 477–482.

————— 1931b. Indian prehistory as revealed by archaeology. *The University of Toronto Quarterly*, vol. 1, no. 2, pp. 164–182.

————— 1931c. Biographical Foreword to Wilkins, G.H., 1931, In polar lands. *Canadian Geographical Journal*, vol. 2, no. 6, p 425.

————— 1931d.★ Who are the Eskimos? *The Beaver.* Outfit 262, pp. 267–270.

————— 1932a. Fifty years of archaeology in Canada. *Royal Society of Canada Anniversary Volume, 1882–1932*, Ottawa; Royal Society of Canada, pp. 71–76.

————— 1932b. The population possibilities of Canada. *University of Toronto Quarterly*, vol. 1, no. 4, pp. 387–423.

————— 1932c. Three Iroquois wampum records. *National Museum of Canada, Annual Report for 1931*, pp. 25–28.

————— 1932d.★ Java, land of mystery. *Canadian Geographical Journal*, vol. 5, no. 2 (August), pp. 112–127.

————— 1932e. *The Indians of Canada. National Museum of Canada, Bulletin no. 65, Anthropological Series no. 15*, 445 pp.; Second edition, 1934; Third edition, enlarged, 452 pp., 1955; Fourth edition, 1958; Fifth edition, 1960; Sixth edition, 1963; Seventh edition, University of Toronto Press, with a new Foreword by William E. Taylor, Jr., 432 pp., 1970.

————— 1933a. Canada's fisheries and fishery population. *Proceedings and Transactions of the Royal Society of Canada*, vol. 27, section 2, pp. 41–46.

————— 1933b. *The American aborigines, their origin and antiquity.* A collection of papers by ten authors published for presentation at the Fifth Pacific Science Congress, Canada, 1933, edited with preface by Diamond Jenness. University of Toronto Press, 396 pp.

————— 1933c. The problem of the Eskimo. In *The American aborigines, their origin and antiquity.* Edited by D. Jenness. University of Toronto Press, pp. 373–396.

————— 1933d. An Indian method of treating hysteria. *Primitive Man*, vol. 6, pp. 13–20. Also in *Anthropological Quarterly*, vol. 4, no. 1, pp. 13–20.

————— 1934a. The vanished Red Indians of Newfoundland. *Canadian Geographical Journal*, vol. 8, no. 1, pp. 27–32.

————— 1934b. Fading scenes on Quatsino Inlet. *Canadian Geographical Journal*, vol. 8, no. 2, pp. 89–97.

————— 1934c. Indian-Vikings of the northwest coast. *Canadian Geographical Journal*, vol. 8, no. 5, pp. 235–246.

————— 1934d. Myths of the Carrier Indians of British Columbia. *Journal of American Folk-lore*, vol. 47, nos. 184–185, pp. 98–257.

————— 1935a. The Ojibwa Indians of Parry Island, their social and religious life. *National Museum of Canada Bulletin no. 78, Anthropological Series No. 17*, 115 pp.

————— 1935b. Review of A.L. Kroeber's *Native American Population. Geographical Review*, vol. 25, pp. 514–516. (Listed in Collins and Taylor Jr. 1970, as "The Population of Aboriginal America, North of Mexico," Review of A.L. Kroeber's "Native American population.")

————— 1936a. Foreword in *The Eskimos* by Kaj Birket-Smith, Methuen, London, 250 pp.

————— 1936b. The prehistory of the Canadian Indians; pp. 63–84 in *Custom is King, Essays presented to R.R. Marett*, edited by L.H.D. Buxton. Hutchinson's Scientific and Technical Publications, London.

————— 1936c. The village of the crossroads, Pond Inlet, the Dominion's most northerly habitation. *Illustrated Canadian Forest and Outdoors*, January 1936, pp. 14, 20.

————— 1936d. The Canadian field. *American Antiquity*, vol. 1, no. 4, pp. 253–255.

————— 1937a. Arrow-straighteners, thong-smoothers, and batons-de-commandement." *Man*, vol. 37, pp. 73–74.

————— 1937b. The Hare Indian dog. *The Canadian Field-Naturalist*, vol. 51, no. 4, 47–50.

———— 1937c. The Indian background of Canadian history. *National Museum of Canada, Bulletin no. 86, Anthropological Series no. 21*, 46 pp.

———— 1937d. The Sekani Indians of British Columbia. *National Museum of Canada, Bulletin no. 84, Anthropological Series no. 20*, 82 pp.

———— 1938a. Review of *Archaeology of St. Lawrence Island*, by Henry B. Collins. *American Antiquity*, vol. 4, no. 2, pp. 173–176.

———— 1938b. Guide leaflets to the Indians of Canada. *National Museum of Canada*, Ottawa.

———— 1938c. Report of the American Association for the Advancement of Science, 101st session, Section H, Anthropology, Ottawa, 1938. In *Science*, N.S., vol. 88, no. 2, pp. 96–97.

———— 1938d. The Sarcee Indians of Alberta. *National Museum of Canada Bulletin no. 90, Anthropological Series no. 23*, 98 pp.

———— 1939a. Canada's debt to the Indians. *Canadian Geographical Journal*, vol. 18, no. 5, pp. 269–275. Republished in *Canadian Geographical Journal*, 1962, vol. 65, no. 4, pp. 112–117.

———— 1939b. The Snare Indians. *Proceedings and Transactions of the Royal Society of Canada*, series 3, vol. 33, section 2, pp. 103–105.

———— 1939c.★ Edward Sapir (1884–1939). Obituary. *Proceedings and Transactions of the Royal Society of Canada*, 3rd Series, vol. 33, pp. 151–153.

———— 1940a. Prehistoric culture waves from Asia to America. *Journal of the Washington Academy of Science*, vol. 30, no. 1, pp. 1–15. Also in *Smithsonian Institution Annual Report 1940*, pp. 383–396.

———— 1940b.★ Introduction; pp. xv–xvi in *Lure of the North* by Richard Finnie. David McKay Company, Philadelphia, 227 pp.

———— 1941a. An archaeological collection from the Belcher Islands in Hudson Bay. *Annals of the Carnegie Museum*, vol. 28, pp. 189–206.

———— 1941b. William John Wintemberg. *American Antiquity*, vol. 7, pp. 64–66. Also in *Proceedings and Transactions of the Royal Society of Canada*, third series, vol. 35, pp.

———— and Robert Bentham, 1941. Eskimo remains in S.E. Ellesmere Islands. *Proceedings and Transactions of the Royal Society of Canada*, third series, section H, vol. 35, pp. 41–55.

———— 1942. Canada's Indian problems. *America Indigena*, vol. 2, no. 1, pp. 29–30. Reprinted in *Annual Report of the Smithsonian Institution for 1942*, pp. 367–380 (1943).

———— 1943. The Carrier Indians of the Bulkley River, their social and religious life. *Bureau of American Ethnology Bulletin no. 133, Anthropological Papers no. 25*, pp. 469–586.

———— 1944a. Eskimo language. Part B: Grammatical notes on some Western Eskimo dialects. *Report of the Canadian Arctic Expedition, 1913–1918*, vol. 15, 34 pp.

———— 1944b. The Eskimos: Their past and future. *Queen's Quarterly*, vol. LI, no. 2, summer, pp. 132–148. (The author's first name is misspelled "Desmond" under the title of this article.)

———— 1946a. Material culture of the Copper Eskimo. *Report of the Canadian Arctic Expedition, 1913–1918*, vol. 16, Southern Party, 1913–1916, 148 pp.

———— 1946b.★ Ethnology and Archaeology; pp. 57–59 in *A Program of Desirable Scientific Investigations in Arctic North America*, compiled by R.F. Flint. *Arctic Institute of North America Bulletin no. 1*.

———— 1949.★ Some impressions of post-war Italy. *International Journal* (Quarterly of the Canadian Institute of International Affairs), vol. 4, no. 4 (autumn), pp. 342–350.

———— 1950a. The recovery program in Sicily. *Geographical Review*, vol. 40, no. 3, pp. 355–363.

———— 1950b.★ Italy's demographic crisis. *Queen's Quarterly*, vol. LVII, no. 3, pp. 269–280.

———— 1950c.★ Bergeggi-on-the-Riviera. *Canadian Geographical Journal*, vol. 41, no. 6, pp. 270–275.

———— 1950d. Discussion of *The Ipiutak Culture, its Origin and Relationships*, by Helge Larson; pp. 30–34 in *Indian tribes of Aboriginal America: selected papers of the 29th International Congress of Americanists*, Sol Tax, editor, vol. 3. University of Chicago Press.

————— 1952. Preservation of archaeological remains in Canada; pp. 60–65 in *Alaskan Science Conference of the National Academy of Sciences, National Research Council, Washington, D.C. November 9–11, 1950: Selected papers edited by Henry B. Collins.* Washington, D.C.

————— 1953a. Did the Yahgan Indians of Tierra del Fuego speak an Eskimo tongue? *International Journal of American Linguistics,* vol. 19, no. 2, pp. 128–131.

————— 1953b. Stray notes on the Eskimo of Arctic Alaska. *Anthropological Papers of the University of Alaska,* vol. 1, no. 2, pp. 5–13.

————— 1954a. Among the Eskimos. *The Beaver.* Outfit 285, Winter 1954–55, pp. 24–30.

————— 1954b. Canada's Indians Yesterday. What of Today? *Canadian Journal of Economics and Political Science,* vol. 20, no. 1, pp. 95–100.

————— 1955a. Canadian Indian religion. *Anthropologica,* no. 1, pp. 1–17. Reprinted as pp. 71–78 in *Religion in Canadian Society,* edited by Stewart Crysdale and Les Wheatcraft. Macmillan of Canada, Toronto, 466 pp., 1976.

————— 1955b. The faith of a Coast Salish Indian. *British Columbia Provincial Museum Memoirs,* no. 3, 92 pp.

————— 1956a. The Chipewyan Indians: an account by an early explorer. Edited by Diamond Jenness. *Anthropologica,* no. 3, pp. 15–33.

————— 1956b. The Corn Goddess and other tales from Indian Canada. *National Museum of Canada, Bulletin no. 141,* 111 pp.

————— 1957. *Dawn in Arctic Alaska.* University of Minnesota Press, Minneapolis, 222 pp. Republished in a softcover edition by the University of Chicago Press, 1985.

————— 1958.★ Eskimo. *Encyclopaedia Britannica,* vol. 8, pp. 708–710.

————— 1961.★ Obituary — R.M. Anderson. *Arctic,* vol. 14, no. 4, p. 268.

————— 1962a. *The Economics of Cyprus: A Survey to 1914.* McGill University Press, Montreal, 219 pp.

————— 1962b. Eskimo administration, vol. I: Alaska. *Arctic Institute of North America, Technical Paper no. 10,* 64 pp.

————— 1963.★ Appendix B, pp. 165–166 in *The Search for a Country: the Autobiography of G.W. von Zedlitz.* Latimer, Trend & Co., Plymouth, Great Britain, 166 pp.

————— 1964a. Eskimo administration, vol. II: Canada. *Arctic Institute of North America, Technical Paper no. 14,* 186 pp.

————— 1964b. The Canadian Eskimo. In *The Unbelievable Land,* edited by I. Norman Smith. Queen's Printer, Ottawa, pp. 6–10.

————— 1965. Eskimo administration, vol. III: Labrador. *Arctic Institute of North America, Technical Paper no. 16,* 94 pp.

————— 1966. The administration of northern peoples: America's Eskimos — pawns of history. In *The Arctic Frontier,* edited by R. St. J. MacDonald. University of Toronto Press, Toronto, pp. 120–129.

————— 1967a. Ascent of Mount Madawana, Goodenough Island (New Guinea). *Canadian Geographical Journal,* vol. 74, pp. 100–108.

————— 1967b. Eskimo administration, vol. IV: Greenland. *Arctic Institute of North America, Technical Paper no. 19,* 176 pp.

————— 1967c.★ The Indians. In *Canada,* edited by Earle Toppings. Ryerson Press, Toronto, pp. 15–16.

————— 1968a. Eskimo administration, vol. V: Analysis and Reflection. *Arctic Institute of North America, Technical Paper no. 21,* 72 pp.

————— 1968b. America's Eskimos, can they survive? pp. 137–143 in *Readings in Canadian Geography,* Holt, Rinehart Winston Co., Toronto. (Given as a graduation address, 1962, Convocation, Waterloo Lutheran University, Waterloo, 15 pp.)

——— 1970. Preface to "Banksland Story" by Father Lemer, Sachs Harbour School Year Book 1968–1969 (typescript produced in February 1970).

——— 1971. Eskimo. *Encyclopaedia Britannica*, London, vol. 8, pp.702–705.

——— and Stuart E. Jenness, 2008.★ *Through Darkening Spectacles—Memoirs of Diamond Jenness*. Canadian Museum of Civilization, Mercury Series History Paper 55, 436 pp.

Collins and Taylor Jr. (1970, p. 81) listed one additional item as "in press", which I have not included on the foregoing list. It was entitled "The Canadian Eskimo," an article evidently prepared by my father, a few months prior to his death in November 1969, for publication in a book called *The United States and Canada Handbook, Book II*, which was to be published by Anthony Blond Ltd., London. I corrected the galley proofs for that article and returned the master copy to the publisher early in March 1971. I heard nothing further about it. Today the publishing company is no longer in business, and I suspect that it went out of business before it was able to produce the book containing my father's article.

In her bibliography of Jenness' publications McDougall (1990, p. 190) annotated a review by Jenness of William Thalbitzer's 1912 book, *The Ammassalik Eskimos*, and indicated it was in the *Geographical Review*, vol. 26, no. 4, 1924. The volume for 1924, however, is 14, not 26, and my search of all volumes between 1916 and 1940 failed to reveal the review McDougall cited. I suspect that it appeared in some other publication.

APPENDIX 3
Publications about Diamond Jenness

Prepared by Stuart E. Jenness, with contributions by Sylvia Mauro, Reference Librarian, Canadian Museum of Civilization

Anonymous, 1928. Review of *People of the Twilight* by Diamond Jenness. *Geographical Review*, vol. 18, p. 638.

———— 1962. Dr. Diamond Jenness: Massey Medal, 1962. *Canadian Geographical Journal*, vol. LXIV, no. 6, pp. 186–187.

———— 1969. Diamond Jenness is awarded the Order of Canada. *Arctic*, vol. 22, no. 1, p. 77.

Balikci, Asen, 1957. Bio-bibliography of Diamond Jenness. *Anthropologica*, no. 4, pp. 37–46.

Barton, F.R., 1921a. Review of *The Northern D'Entrecasteaux* by Diamond Jenness and the Late Rev. A. Ballantyne. *Man*, vol. 27 (111), pp. 187–189.

———— 1921b. Review of *The Northern D'Entrecasteaux* by Diamond Jenness and the Late Rev. A. Ballantyne. *American Anthropologist* (23), pp. 226–227.

Collins, Henry B., 1967. Diamond Jenness and Arctic Archaeology. *The Beaver*, vol. 78, Autumn, 1967, pp. 78–79.

———— 1971. Diamond Jenness: An Appreciation. *Anthropologica*, vol. 13 (1/2), pp. 9–12.

Collins, Henry B. and William E. Taylor, Jr., 1970. Diamond Jenness (1886–1969). *Arctic*, vol. 23, no. 2, pp. 71–81.

Cox, Corolyn, 1944. New Zealand birthplace of the chief authority on Eskimos. *Saturday Night*, 9 Sept. 1944.

Cummins, Bryan D. and John L. Steckley, 2005. *The Ethnographic Experience*. Pearson Education Canada, Toronto, 27 pp.

Edwards, Elizabeth, 1992. Wamo: D'Entrecasteaux Islands, New Guinea, 1911–1912: Photographs by Diamond Jenness. *Pacific Arts*, vol. 5, pp. 53–56.

———— 1994. Visualizing history—Diamond Jenness's photographs of D'Entrecasteaux Islands, Massim, 1911–1912—a case study in re–arrangement. *Canberra Anthropology*, vol. 17, no. 2, pp. 1–25.

———— 2001. Visualizing History: Diamond Jenness's Photographs of the D'entrecasteaux Islands, Massim, 1911–1912. Chapter 4 in *Raw Histories — Photographs, Anthropology and Museums*. Berg Publishing Co., Oxford and New York, pp. 83–105.

Fowke, E., 1970. Diamond Jenness, 1886–1969. *Journal of American Folklore*, vol. 83, (329), p. 350.

Hancock, Robert L.A., 2002. The potential for a Canadian Anthropology: Diamond Jenness's Arctic Ethnography. Master of Arts thesis, Department of History, University of Victoria.

Hawthorn, Harry, 1970a. Diamond Jenness 1886–1969. *Proceedings of the Royal Society of Canada*, Ser. IV, vol. VIII, pp. 92–95.

———— 1970b. Diamond Jenness (1886–1969). *Canadian Review of Sociology and Anthropology*, vol. 7 (Feb.), pp. 83–84.

Helmer, James, 1983. Arctic profile — Diamond Jenness (1886–1969). *Arctic*, vol. 36, no. 1, pp. 108–109.

Jenness, Diamond and Stuart E. Jenness, 2008. *Through Darkening Spectacles—Memoirs of Diamond Jenness*. Canadian Museum of Civilization, Mercury Series History Paper 55, 436 pp.

Jenness, Stuart E. (ed.), 1991. *Arctic Odyssey — The Diary of Diamond Jenness 1913–1916*. Canadian Museum of Civilization, Hull [now Gatineau], Quebec, 859 pp.

Jenness, Stuart E., 1985. Arctic wolf attacks scientist — A unique Canadian incident. *Arctic*, vol. 38, no. 2, pp. 129–132.

————— 1989. Letter to the Editor. *Arctic*, vol. 42, no. 3, pp. 297.

————— 1990. Diamond Jenness's archaeological investigations on Barter Island, Alaska. *Polar Record*, vol. 26, no. 157, pp. 91–102.

Kulchyski, Peter, 1993. Anthropology in the service of the state: Diamond Jenness and Canadian Indian Policy. *Journal of Canadian Studies*, vol. 28, no. 2, pp. 21–50.

Laguna, Frederica de, 1971. Obituary — Diamond Jenness, C.C. *American Anthropologist*, vol. 73, 1971, pp. 248–253.

Lehmer, Derrick Norman, 1927. Review of *Songs of the Copper Eskimos* by Helen Roberts and D. Jenness. *American Anthropologist*, (XXIX), pp. 712–714.

Lotz, P., and J. Lotz, 1971. Pilot Not Commander: Essays in Memory of Diamond Jenness. *Anthropologica*, vol. 13 (1/2), pp. 15–22.

MacDonald, George F., 1969. Diamond Jenness (1886–1969). *Canadian Archaeological Association Bulletin*, vol. 1, pp. 43–45.

Maxwell, Moreau S., 1972. Diamond Jenness, 1886–1969. *American Antiquity*, vol. 37 (1), pp. 86–88.

Marshall, Duncan, 2004. A gem in the Gatineau. *Up the Gatineau*, vol. 30, pp. 17–23.

McDougall, Anne, 1981. Diamond Jenness and his Contribution to the Study of Eskimo Art History. Master of Arts Thesis, Carleton University, Ottawa

————— 1992. Jenness on Inuit art — Documentation with sympathy and no pretension. *Inuit Art Quarterly*, vol. 7, no. 1, pp. 22–29.

McDougall, Anne, Jean Malaurie, Graham Rowley, 1990. Homage to Dr. Diamond Jenness (1886–1969). *Inter–Nord* (International Journal of Arctic Studies, Paris), no. 19, pp. 185–200. (a) A French homage to Dr. Diamond Jenness, by Jean Malaurie, pp. 185–187; (b) Diamond Jenness: Canada's renowned pioneer anthropologist who wrote up his notes, by Anne McDougall, pp. 187–199; (c) Diamond Jenness, by Graham Rowley, p. 200.

Morrison, David, 1991. *The Diamond Jenness Collections from Bering Strait*. Mercury Series; Archaeological Survey of Canada, no. 144, Canadian Museum of Civilization, Hull, Quebec, 171 pp.

————— 1992. *Arctic Hunters: The Inuit and Diamond Jenness*. Canadian Museum of Civilization, Hull, Quebec, 66 pp.

————— 2002. Diamond Jenness; the first Canadian Arctic archaeologist. In W. Fitzhugh, S. Loring and D. Odess (eds.), *Honoring our Elders: A History of Eastern Arctic Archaeology*. Contributions to Circumpolar Anthropology, vol. 2, National Museum of Natural History, Smithsonian Institution, pp. 61–68.

Noice, Harold H., 1922. Further discussion of the 'Blond' Eskimo. *American Anthropologist*, vol. XXIV, pp. 228–232.

O'Reilly, Kathleen Marie, 2003. Two Arctic Adventures: A comparison of the Arctic collections of Diamond Jenness and Joseph Bernard. Master of Arts thesis, Carleton University, 90 pp.

Osler, Morris, 1959. Review of *The People of the Twilight* by Diamond Jenness. *Midwest Folklore*, vol. IX, no. 4, pp. 238–240.

Richling, Barnet, 1989. An anthropologist's apprenticeship: Diamond Jenness' Papuan and Arctic Fieldwork. *Culture*, vol. 9, pp.71–85.

————— 1990. Diamond Jenness and the National Museum of Canada. *Curator*, vol. 33, pp. 245–260.

————— 1991a. Diamond Jenness. In C. Winters (ed.), *International Dictionary of Anthropologists*, University of Chicago Library-Anthropology Resource Group, New York; Garland Publishing, pp. 324–325.

————— 1991b. Diamond Jenness and 'Useful Anthropology' in Canada, 1930–1950. *Stout Centre Review*, vol. 2, pp. 5–8.

————— 1995a. Applied anthropology and Aboriginal peoples in Canada, 1910–1939. *Australian Canadian Studies*, vol. 13, pp. 49–62.

————— 1995b. Politics, bureaucracy, and Arctic archaeology in Canada, 1910–1939. *Arctic*, vol. 48, pp. 109–117.

————— 2004a. Diamond Jenness. In Hallowell, Gerald (ed.), *The Oxford Companion to Canadian History*. Oxford University Press, Don Mills, p. 330.

————— 2004b. Diamond Jenness. In Nuttall, Mark (ed.), *Encyclopedia of the Arctic*. Routledge, New York, pp. 1043–1044.

————— 2005. Scaenae ex matrimonio infelici (Scenes from an unhappy marriage). *Museum Anthropology*, vol. 28, pp. 57–65.

Rowley, Graham W., 1970. Obituary: Diamond Jenness (1886–1969). *Polar Record*, vol. 15, no. 96, pp. 361–362.

Schuhmacher, W.W., 1989. Diamond Jenness' Eskimo–Fuegian Hypothesis revisited (Comments on "Did the Yahgan Indians of Tierra del Fuego speak an Eskimo tongue?" by Jenness in *International Journal of American Linguistics*, vol. 19, pp. 128–131). *Anthropos*, vol. 84, (4/6), pp. 547–549.

Steckley, John, *in press. White lies about the Inuit*. Broadview Press, Peterborough, Ontario.

Steckley, John, and Bryan Cummins, 2005. Pegahmagabow of Parry Island: from Jenness informant to individual. *The Canadian Journal of Native Studies*, vol. xxv, no. 1, pp. 35–50.

Steckley, John, and Guy Kirby Letts, 2006. Diamond Jenness Learns Exceptions to a 'Rule' of Inuit Family Socialization; pp. 107–108 in *Elements of Sociology: A critical Canadian Introduction* by John Steckley and Guy K. Letts. Oxford University Press, Toronto, 350 p.

Sullivan, Louis Robert, 1922. The 'Blond' Eskimo — A question of method. *American Anthropologist*, vol. XXIV, pp. 225–228.

Swayze, Nansi, 1960. *The man hunters: Diamond Jenness, Marius Barbeau, William J. Wintemberg*. The Canadian Portraits Series — Clarke, Irwin & Company Limited, Toronto, 180 pp.

Taylor, William E. Jr., 1985. "Diamond Jenness." *Canadian Encyclopedia*, Hurtig Publishers Ltd., Edmonton, Alberta, vol. II, pp. 915–916.

————— 1991. Foreword. Pp. xv–xvii in *Arctic Odyssey: The Diary of Diamond Jenness, 1913–1916*, edited by Stuart E. Jenness. Canadian Museum of Civilization, Hull, Quebec.

Tepper, Leslie H., 1983. The Expedition Diaries of Diamond Jenness, 1913–1916. *The Beaver*, Outfit 314:1, Summer, 1983, pp. 4–13.

Wissler, Clark, 1928. Review of *The Life of the Copper Eskimo* by Diamond Jenness. *Geographical Review*, vol. 12, no. 3, pp. 506–507.

————— 1933. Review of *The Indians of Canada* by Diamond Jenness. *Geographical Review*, vol. 23, pp. 345–346.

Wright, Terence, 1991. Fieldwork photographs of Jenness and Malinowski and the beginnings of modern anthropology. *Journal, Anthropological Society of Oxford*, vol. 22, no. 1, pp. 41–58.

Also:

1. Diamond Jenness is listed in *The Canadian Who's Who*, editions from 1936 to 1969.
2. Diamond Jenness is discussed in *The Canadian Encyclopedia Online* under a dozen topical headings at www.thecanadianencyclopedia.com.

REFERENCES

Prepared by Stuart E. Jenness

Archival Sources

More than one hundred unpublished letters to or from D. Jenness (and others) are cited in Footnotes throughout this book, complete with dates and archival sources. Only a select few are repeated here.

Anderson, R.M., 1921. Letter dated March 26, 1921, to J. Eugene Law, Museum of Vertebrate Zoology, University of California at Berkeley, California; Dr. R.M. Anderson Papers, Canadian Arctic Expedition files, Correspondence Folder B–M, Library Archives, Canadian Museum of Nature, Gatineau, Quebec.

———— 1923. Letter dated April 24, 1923, to Dr. Charles Camsell, Deputy Minister, Department of Mines; Ac.1-1996-077, Series A — R.M. Anderson, Box 53, File No. 22, Library Archives, Canadian Museum of Nature, Gatineau, Quebec.

Barbeau, C. Marius, 1957–58. Unpublished memoirs, Carmen Roy Collection, Box 622, Archives, Canadian Museum of Civilization, Gatineau, Quebec.

———— 1965. *The Barbeau Reminiscences*, English transcript of interviews with Marius Barbeau summarizing his life, taped for the Canadian Broadcasting Corporation in February 1965 by Lawrence Nowry, Box I-122, Archives, Canadian Museum of Civilization, Gatineau, Quebec.

Camsell, C. 1926. Letter dated November 24, 1926, to the Secretary of the Interior, Washington, D.C. RG 45, vol. 49, File 3109A, Library and Archives Canada., Ottawa, Ontario

Caulkin, Inspector T.B., 1926. Letter dated Oct. 27, 1926, to RCMP Superintendent J. Ritchie, Edmonton, RG 18, vol. 3303, File HQ 681-G-2, National Archives of Canada, Ottawa.

Chipman, K.G., 1913–1916. Arctic diary. 3 volumes. Chipman papers, MG30 B66. Library and Archives Canada, Ottawa.

Jenness, Diamond, 1913–1916. Diary, 3 volumes, Canadian Arctic Expedition 1913–1916. Jenness papers, MG 30 B 89. Library and Archives Canada, Ottawa.

Wilkins, George Hubert, 1913–1916. Diary, Stefansson Special Collection, Wilkins Papers, Box 1, Folder 2.12, Rauner Library, Dartmouth College, Hanover, New Hampshire.

Published Sources

Ami, Henri, 1927. The Canadian "School of Prehistory" in France. Memoirs of the *Royal Society of Canada*, pp. LXII–LXIII.

Anonymous, 1962. Dr. Diamond Jenness: Massey Medal, 1962. *Canadian Geographical Journal*, vol. 64, no. 6, pp. 186–187.

———— 2003. Island monastery to be freed from decades-old sludge. *National Post*, February 13, 2003, p. A 18.

Balikci, Asen, 1957. Bio-biography of Diamond Jenness. *Anthropologica*, vol. 4, pp. 37–44.

Barker, John, 1992. Introduction in McIlwraith, T.F., *The Bella Coola Indians*. The University of Toronto Press, Toronto, vol. 1, 768 pp.

Bartlett, Robert A. and R.T. Hale, 1916. *The last voyage of the* Karluk, *flagship of Vilhjalmur Stefansson's Canadian Arctic Expedition of 1913–1916*. McClelland, Goodrich & Stewart, Publishers, Toronto, 329 pp.

Beaglehole, J.C., 1949. *Victoria University College — An essay towards a history*. New Zealand University Press, Wellington, N.Z., 319 pp.

Beuchat, Henri, 1906. Essai sur les variations saisonnières des sociétés eskimos. *L'Année Sociologique*, vol. 9, pp. 39–130.

——— 1912. Manuel d'archéologie américaine, Amérique préhistorique, civilisations disparues. A. Picard, Paris, 352 pp.

Birket-Smith, Kaj, 1971. *Eskimos*. Crown Publishers Inc., New York, 278 pp.

Bleakney, F. Eileen, 1918. Folk-lore from Ottawa and vicinity. *Journal of American Folk-Lore*, vol. 31, no. 119–120, pp. 158–169.

Bloomfield, Leonard, 1930. *Sacred stories of the Sweet Grass Cree*. National Museum of Canada Bulletin 60, Anthropological Series No. 11, 346 pp.

Bockstoce, John R., 1986. *Whales, ice, & men — the history of whaling in the Western Arctic*. University of Washington Press, Seattle, 400 pp.

Boswell, Randy, 2004. Ottawa man "astounded" to learn NASA named Mars rock after father. *Ottawa Citizen*, September 22, 2004, pp. A1, A11.

Collins, H.B., 1931. Ancient culture of St. Lawrence Island. Explorations and field-work of the Smithsonian Institution for 1930, Washington, pp. 135–144.

——— 1967. Diamond Jenness. *The Beaver*, Autumn issue, pp. 78–79.

——— 1971. Diamond Jenness — An appreciation; pp. 9–12 in Lotz, Pat and Jim (Eds.), Pilot not commander — Essays in memory of Diamond Jenness, *Anthropologica*, N.S., vol. XIII, nos. 1 & 2 (special issue), St. Paul University, Ottawa, 323 pp.

Collins, Henry B., and William E. Taylor Jr., 1970. Diamond Jenness (1866–1969). *Arctic*, vol. 23, no. 2, pp. 71–81.

Cowan, William, Michael Foster, and E.F.K. Koerner (Editors), 1986. New perspectives in language, culture, and personality. Proceedings of the Edward Sapir Centenary Conference, Ottawa (1–3 October, 1984). John Benjamins, Amsterdam, Netherlands, 627 pp.

Chrisman, Donald, Richard S. MacNeish, Jamshed Mavalwala, and Howard Savage, 1996. Late Pleistocene human friction skin prints from Pendejo Cave, New Mexico. *American Antiquity*, vol. 61, no. 2, pp. 357–376.

Dall, William, 1877. On succession in the shell-heaps of the Aleutian Islands; pp. 41–91 in *Tribes of the Extreme Northwest*, Contributions to North American Ethnology no. 1, Washington.

Dyck, I., 2001. Founding the Anthropology Division at the National Museum of Canada: An intertwining of science, religion, and politics; pp. 3–41 in *Revelations: Bi-Millenial papers from the Canadian Museum of Civilization*, by B. Klymasz and John Willis, Mercury Series Paper 75, Canadian Museum of Civilization.

Edwards, Elizabeth, 1994. Visualizing history — Diamond Jenness's photographs of D'Entrecasteaux Islands, Massim, 1911–1912 — a case study in re-arrangement. *Canberra Anthropology*, vol. 17, no. 2, pp. 1–25.

——— 2001. Visualizing history: Diamond Jenness's Photographs of the D'Entrecasteaux Islands, Massim, 1911–1912; Chapter 4, pp. 83–105 in *Raw histories — Photographs, anthropology and museums*. Berg Publishing Co., Oxford and New York, 270 pp.

Encyclopaedia Britannica (1956 Edn.), 1956a. John Loudon McAdam (1756–1836), vol. 14, p. 543.

——— 1956b. Thomas Telford (1754–1836), vol. 21, p. 914.

Finnie, Richard S., 1940. *Lure of the North*. David McKay Company, Philadelphia, 227 p.

——— 1945. *Canol — The sub-Arctic pipeline and refining project constructed by Bechtel-Price-Callahan for the Corps of Engineers, United States Army 1942–1944*. Ryder & Ingram, Publishers, San Francisco, CA, 210 pp.

Gessell, Paul, 2003. A career exhibited in landscapes and nudes. *Ottawa Citizen*, April 29, 2003, pp. D1, D2.

Granatstein, Jack., 1998. Sir William Logan. *Maclean's magazine*, vol. 111, no. 26 (July 1), pp. 38–40.

Grottke, Hans, 1961. "Integrate Eskimos in Canada" expert tells Resources meet. *Montreal Gazette*, October 27, 1961.

Hall, E.S., Jr., 1971. Kangiguksuk: a cultural reconstruction of a sixteenth-century Eskimo site in northern Alaska. *Arctic Anthropology*, vol. 8, no. 1, pp. 1–101.

——— 1987. *A land full of people, a long time ago: an analysis of three archaeological sites in the vicinity of Kaktovik, northern Alaska.* Technical Memorandum No. 24, private report, Edwin Hall and Associates Brockport, New York, 360 pp.

Hawthorn, H.B., 1970. Diamond Jenness, 1886–1969. *Proceedings of the Royal Society of Canada*, Series IV, vol. VIII, pp. 93–95.

Hurlbut, C.S. Jr., 1952. *Dana's Manual of Mineralogy*. John Wiley & Sons, New York, N.Y., 530 pp.

Jenkins, McKay, 2005. *Bloody Falls of the Coppermine: Madness, murder, and the collision of cultures in the Arctic, 1913.* Random House, New York, 278 pp.

Jenness, Diamond, 1918. The Eskimos of northern Alaska: a study in the effect of civilization. *Geographical Review*, vol. 5, no. 2, pp. 89–101.

——— 1919. Along old cannibal trails. *Travel*, vol. 33, no. 3 (July), pp. 34–37, 41.

——— 1922. The Copper Eskimos, Part A: The life of the Copper Eskimos. *Report of the Canadian Arctic Expedition 1913–1918*, vol. 12, 227 pp.

——— 1923a. The play hour in New Guinea. *The Christian Herald*, January 27, 1923, pp. 68, 78.

——— 1923b. The Copper Eskimos, Part B: Physical characteristics of the Copper Eskimos. *Report of the Canadian Arctic Expedition, 1913–1918*, vol. 12, 89 pp.

——— 1923c. *The Copper Eskimos*. Introduction to Part C: *Osteology and dentition of the western and central Eskimos*; pp. 3c–5c in Report of the Canadian Arctic Expedition, 1913–1918, vol. 12, 67 pp.

——— 1924a. The singing people of the South Seas. In *The Outline of Knowledge*, vol. XV (Travel), edited by J.A. Richards, J.A. Richards Inc., New York, pp. 192–202.

——— 1924b. Eskimo folk-lore, Part A: Myths and traditions from Northern Alaska, the Mackenzie Delta and Coronation Gulf. *Report of the Canadian Arctic Expedition, 1913–1918*, vol. 13: Southern Party, 1913–1916, 90 pp.

——— 1924c. Eskimo folk-lore, Part B: Eskimo string figures. Report of the Canadian Arctic Expedition, 1913–1918, vol. 13: Southern Party, 1913–1916, 90 pp.

——— 1924c. Wolf! Wolf! "The Spike" (Victoria University College Review), Silver Jubilee Number, Easter 1924, p. 29–31.

——— 1925. A new Eskimo culture in Hudson Bay. *Geographical Review*, vol. 15, no. 3, pp. 428–437.

——— 1926. Bwaidogan grammar. *Journal of the Polynesian Society*, vol. 35, no. 4, pp. 290–314.

——— 1927a. Notes on the Beothuk Indians of Newfoundland. National Museum of Canada, Bulletin no. 56, pp. 36–38.

——— 1927b. Notes on the phonology of the Eskimo dialect of Cape Prince of Wales. *International Journal of American Linguistics*, vol. 4, nos. 2–4, pp. 168–180.

——— 1928a. *People of the Twilight*. The MacMillan Co., New York, 247 pp.

——— 1928b. Archaeological investigations in Bering Strait, 1926. *National Museum of Canada, Bulletin no. 50*, pp. 71–80.

——— 1928c. *Eskimo language and technology, Part A: Comparative vocabulary of the Western Eskimo dialects.* Report of the Canadian Arctic Expedition, 1913–1918, vol. 15: Southern Party, 1913–1916, 134 pp.

——— 1929. Little Diomede Island, Bering Strait. *Geographical Review*, vol. 19, no. 1, pp. 695–714.

——— 1930a. The Yukon telegraph line. *Canadian Geographical Journal*, vol. 1, no. 8, pp. 695–705.

———— 1930b. The trials of a polygamist. *Toronto Star Weekly*, Saturday January 11, 1930, p. 5.

———— 1931. Foreword in Wilkins, G.H., In polar lands, *Canadian Geographical Journal*, vol. 2, no. 6, p. 425.

———— 1932. The Indians of Canada. *National Museum of Canada, Bulletin No. 65*, Anthropological Series No. 15, 446 pp. Second edition 1934; Third edition, enlarged, 1955; Fourth edition 1958; Fifth edition 1960; Sixth edition 1963; Seventh edition 1977.

———— 1933a. An Indian method of treating hysteria. *Primitive Man*, vol. 6, pp. 13–20.

———— 1933b. *The American aborigines — Their origin and antiquity*. University of Toronto Press, Toronto, 396 pp.

———— 1934a. Myths of the Carrier Indians of British Columbia. *Journal of American Folk-lore*, vol. 47, no. 184–185, pp. 98–257.

———— 1934b. The vanished Red Indians of Newfoundland. *Canadian Geographical Journal*, vol. 8, pp. 27–32.

———— 1935. The Ojibwa Indians of Parry Island, their social and religious life. National Museum of Canada Bulletin No. 78, Anthropological Series No. 17, 115 pp.

———— 1936. The prehistory of the Canadian Indians; pp. 63–84 in *Custom is King. Essays presented to R.R. Marett*, edited by L.H.D. Buxton. Hutchinson's Scientific and Technical Publications, London.

———— 1937a. The Indian background of Canadian history. National Museum of Canada, Bulletin no. 84, Anthropological Series no. 21, 46 pp.

———— 1937b. The Sekani Indians of British Columbia. *National Museum of Canada, Bulletin No. 86*, Anthropological Series No. 20, 82 pp.

———— 1938. The Sarcee Indians of Alberta. *National Museum of Canada, Bulletin No. 90*, Anthropological Series No. 23, 98 pp.

———— 1939. Edward Sapir (1884–1939), An obituary. *Proceedings and Transactions of the Royal Society of Canada*, 3rd Series, vol. 33, pp. 151–153.

———— 1940a. Prehistoric culture waves from Asia to America. *Journal of the Washington Academy of Science*, vol. 30, no. 1, pp. 1–15.

———— 1940b. Introduction, pp. xv–xvi in *Lure of the North* by Richard S. Finnie, David Mackay Company, Philadelphia, 227 pp.

———— 1943. The Carrier Indians of the Bulkley River, their social and religious life. *Bureau of American Ethnology, Bulletin No. 133*, Anthropological Papers No. 25, pp. 469–586.

———— 1944a. Eskimo language, Part B: Grammatical notes on some Western Eskimo dialects. *Report of the Canadian Arctic Expedition 1913–1918*, vol. 15, 34 pp.

———— 1944b. The Eskimos: Their past and future. *Queen's Quarterly*, vol LI, no. 2, summer, pp. 132–148.

———— 1946. Material culture of the Copper Eskimo. *Report of the Canadian Arctic Expedition, 1913–1918*, vol. 16: Southern Party, 1913–1916, 148 pp.

———— 1947. *Schneehütten Völkchen: Ein Reise bericht aus der Arctik*. German translation by Dr. Herta Hartmanshenn of D. Jenness' "The People of the Twilight." Verlag Herta Hartmanshenn, Wiesbaden, Germany, 139 pp.

———— 1950a. The recovery program in Sicily. *Geographical Review*, vol. 40, no. 3, pp. 355–363.

———— 1950b. Italy's demographic crisis. *Queen's Quarterly*, vol. LVII, no. 3, pp. 269–280.

———— 1950c. Bergeggi-on-the-Riviera. *Canadian Geographical Journal*, vol. 41, no. 6, pp. 270–275.

———— 1955. *The faith of a Coast Salish Indian*. British Columbia Provincial Museum Memoirs, No. 3, 92 pp.

———— 1957. *Dawn in Arctic Alaska*. University of Minnesota Press, Minneapolis, 222 pp.

————— 1959. *The people of the twilight* (with author's 1958 Epilogue). University of Chicago Press, Chicago, softcover edition, 251 pp.

————— 1962a. *The economics of Cyprus — A survey to 1914.* McGill University Press, Montreal, 219 pp.

————— 1962b. *Eskimo administration,* I: *Alaska.* Arctic Institute of North America, Technical Paper No. 10, 4 pp.

————— 1963. Appendix B, pp. 165–166 in *The search for a country: the autobiography of G.W. von Zedlitz.* Latimer, Trend & Co., Plymouth, Great Britain, 166 pp.

————— 1964. *Eskimo administration,* II: *Canada.* Arctic Institute of North America, Technical Paper No. 14, 186 pp.

————— 1965. *Eskimo administration,* III: *Labrador.* Arctic Institute of North America, Technical Paper No. 16, 94 pp.

————— 1967a. *Eskimo administration,* IV: *Greenland.* Arctic Institute of North America, Technical Paper No. 19, 176 pp.

————— 1967b. The ascent of Mount Madawana, Goodenough Island (New Guinea), *Canadian Geographical Journal,* vol. 74, pp. 100–108.

————— 1968a. *Eskimo administration,* V: *Analysis and Reflections.* Arctic Institute of North America, Technical Paper No. 21, 72 pp.

————— 1968b. The economic situation of the Eskimos; pp. 127–148 in *Eskimo of the Canadian Arctic,* edited by Victor F. Valentine and Frank G. Vallee, Carleton Library No. 41, McClelland & Stewart Limited, Toronto. Reprinted from Chapters 11 and 12 in *Eskimo Administration, II: Canada* by Diamond Jenness, pp. 99–119.

————— 1985. *Dawn in Arctic Alaska.* University of Chicago Press, Chicago, softcover edition, 220 pp.

Jenness, Diamond, and Andrew Ballantyne, 1920. *The northern D'Entrecasteaux.* Clarendon Press, Oxford, 219 pp.

————— 1928. *Language, mythology, and songs of Bwaidoga, Goodenough Island, S.E. Papua.* Polynesian Society, Memoirs, 8, 270 p. Also in the *Polynesian Society Journal,* 1926–1929, vol. 35, pp. 290–331; vol. 36, pp. 48–71, 145–179, 207–238, 303, 329; vol. 37, pp. 30–56, 139- 164, 271–299, 377–402; vol. 38, pp. 29–47.

Jenness, Diamond, and Helen H. Roberts, 1925. Songs of the Copper Eskimos. *Report of the Canadian Arctic Expedition, 1913–1918,* vol. 14, 506 pp.

Jenness, Eileen, 1933a. Little Diomede — An Arctic "Bonaventure Island." *Canadian Geographical Journal,* vol. 7, no. 2, pp. 87–92.

————— 1933b. *The Indian tribes of Canada.* The Ryerson Press, Toronto, 123 pp.

————— 1953. Málaga: Spain's port of sunshine and tragedy. *Canadian Geographical Journal,* vol. 47, no. 4, pp. 166–172.

Jenness, John L. (Pete) and Mary A. Jenness, 1998. An ancestral history of Jenness and Ottman Families; Book 1 — Jenness and Bleakney Families, 173 pp; Book 2 — Ottman and Grover Families, 127 pp., privately published, Greely, Ontario.

Jenness, Stuart E., 1985. Arctic wolf attacks scientist — a unique Canadian incident. *Arctic,* vol. 38, pp. 129–132.

————— 1989. Letter to the Editor. *Arctic,* vol. 42, p. 297.

————— 1990. Diamond Jenness's archaeological investigations on Barter Island, Alaska. *Polar Record,* vol. 26, no. 157, pp. 91–102.

————— (Ed.), 1991. *Arctic Odyssey — The diary of Diamond Jenness 1913–1916.* Canadian Museum of Civilization, Hull, Quebec, 859 pp.

————— 1992. Letter to the Editor. *Arctic,* vol. 45, no. 2, pp. 208–209.

————— 1996. Conflict and adversities — The Southern Party of the Canadian Arctic Expedition 1913–1916. *The Beaver.* Vol. 76, pp. 34–41.

————— 2004. *The making of an explorer — George Hubert Wilkins and the Canadian Arctic Expedition 1913–1916.* McGill–Queen's University Press, Montreal, 432 pp.

Jenness, Stuart E., and Jean M. Spencer Jenness, 2003. Solving a Military Puzzle. In Geotales: A Collection of Stories about Earth Scientists, *Northeastern Geology and Environmental Sciences,* vol. 25, no. 2, pp. 148–149.

Keim, Charles J., 1969. *Aghvook, white Eskimo.* The University of Alaska Press, College, Alaska, 318 pp.

Kulchyski, Peter, 1993. Anthropology in the service of the state: Diamond Jenness and the Canadian Indian Policy. *Journal of Canadian Studies,* vol. 28, no. 2, pp. 21–50.

Laguna, Frederica de, 1971. Obituary — Diamond Jenness, 1886–1969. *American Anthropologist,* vol. 73, 1971, pp. 248–254.

Lotz, Pat, and Lotz, Jim (Eds.), 1971. Pilot not commander — Essays in memory of Diamond Jenness. *Anthropologica,* N.S., vol. XIII, nos. 1 & 2 (special issue), St. Paul University, Ottawa, 323 pp.

Lytton, Bulwer,1864. *The last days of Pompeii.* Routledge, Warne, and Routledge, London, 304 pp.

Marett, R.R., 1920. Preface in Jenness, D. and Andrew Ballantyne, 1920, The Northern D'Entrecasteaux, Clarendon Press, Oxford, pp. 5–9.

Mathiassen, T. 1927. *Archaeology of the Central Eskimos,* parts 1 & 2, Report of the Fifth Thule Expedition, 1921–1924, vol. 4, Copenhagen.

MacInnes, Tom (Ed.), 1932. Klengenberg of the Arctic, an autobiography. Jonathan Cape, London, 360 pp.

McIlwraith, Thomas F., 1948. *The Bella Coola Indians.* The University of Toronto Press, Toronto, vol. 1, 768 pp., vol. 2, 672 pp. Reprinted 1992.

McKinlay, W.L., 1975. *Karluk — The Great Untold Story of Arctic Exploration.* Weidenfeld and Nicolson,London, England, 170 pp.

Mech, L.D., 1981. *The Wolf: The Ecology and Behavior of an Endangered Species.* University of Minnesota Press, Minneapolis, Minnesota, 385 pp.

Morrison, David, 1991. *The Diamond Jenness collections from Bering Strait.* Canadian Museum of Civilization, Archeological Survey of Canada, Mercury Series Paper 144, 171 pp.

Moyles, R.G., 1979. *British law and Arctic men.* Western Producer Prairie Books, Saskatoon, Saskatchewan, 93 pp.

National Post, 2003. Island monastery to be freed from decades-old sludge. February 13, 2003, p. A 18.

Nelson, Ray, 1992. Dig uncovers proof of America's oldest man. *New Mexico Magazine,* vol. 70, no. 2, (February), pp. 58–63.

"Nemo," 1918. Notes on past students — Dr. D. Jenness. "The Spike" (The Victoria University College Review), no. 34, pp. 36–37.

Niven, Jennifer, 2000. *The ice master — the doomed 1913 voyage of the* Karluk. Hyperion, New York, 402 pp.

————— 2003. *Ada Blackjack* — The true story of survival in the Arctic. Hyperion, New York, 431 pp.

Nowry, Laurence, 1995. *Man of Mana — Marius Barbeau — a biography.* NCPress Limited, Toronto, 445 pp.

Rasmussen, Knud, 1924. *Across Arctic America — Narrative of the Fifth Thule Expedition.* G.P. Putnam's Sons, N.Y., 388 pp.

Richling, Barnet, 1989. An anthropologist's apprenticeship: Diamond Jenness' Papuan and Arctic fieldwork. *Culture,* vol. 9, pp. 71–85.

————— 1990. Diamond Jenness and the National Museum of Canada. *Curator,* vol. 33, pp. 245–260.

————— 1991a. Diamond Jenness. In Winter's (ed.), *International Dictionary of Anthropologists,* University of Chicago Library — Anthropology Resource Group, New York; Garland Publishing, pp. 324–325.

——— 1991b. Diamond Jenness and "Useful Anthropology" in Canada, 1930–1950. *Stout Centre Review*, vol. 2, pp. 5–8.

——— 1995a. Applied anthropology and Aboriginal peoples in Canada, 1910–1939. *Australian Canadian Studies*, vol. 13, pp. 49–62.

——— 1995b. Politics, bureaucracy, and Arctic archaeology in Canada, 1910–1939. *Arctic*, vol. 48, pp. 109–117.

——— 2004a. Diamond Jenness. In Hallowell, Gerald (ed.), *The Oxford Companion of Canadian History*. Oxford University Press, Don Mills, Ontario, p. 330.

——— 2004b. Diamond Jenness. In Nuttall, Mark (ed.), *Encyclopedia of the Arctic*. Routledge, New York, pp. 1043–1044.

——— 2005. Scaenae ex matrimonio infelici (Scenes from an unhappy marriage). *Museum Anthropology*, vol. 28, pp. 57–65.

Robertson, Alan, 1984. *Blue Guide France 1990*. W.W. Norton & Company Inc., New York, 923 pp.

Royal Canadian Mounted Police (RCMP), 1926. *Shooting of Uluksak*; pp. 47–48 in Report of the Royal Canadian Mounted Police for the year ended September 30, 1925.

——— 1927. *The Western Arctic*; p. 27 in Report of the Royal Canadian Mounted Police for the year ended September 30, 1926.

Steinberg, Neil, 2004. *Hatless Jack: The President, the Fedora, and the History of an American Style*. Plume, N.Y., 342 pp.

Stefansson, Vilhjalmur, 1922. *The friendly Arctic*. The MacMillan Co., New York, 784 pp.

———, 1925. *The adventure of Wrangel Island*. The MacMillan Co., New York, 424 pp.

Stewart, R.E.A., 1990. Letter to the Editor, *Arctic*, vol. 43, no. 1, p. 97.

Streisinger, Erwin, 1991. Letter to the Editor, *Arctic*, vol. 44, no. 2, pp. 172–173.

Swayze, Nansi, 1960. *Canadian portraits: Jenness, Barbeau, Wintemberg — The man hunters*. Clarke, Irwin & Company Limited, Toronto, 180 pp.

Taylor, W.E., Jr., 1990. Foreword, pp. xvi–xviii in *Arctic Odyssey — The Diary of Diamond Jenness 1913–1916*, edited by Stuart E. Jenness. Canadian Museum of Civilization, Hull [now Gatineau], Quebec, 859 pp.

Tepper, Michael, 1978. *Passengers to America*. Genealogical Publishing Company, Baltimore, Md., 554 pp.

Tucker, Alan (Gen. Ed.), 1990. *The Penguin Guide to France*. Penguin Books U.S.A. Inc., New York, 611 pp.

Vodden, Christy, and Ian Dyck, 2006. *A World Inside — A 150-Year History of the Canadian Museum of Civilization*. Canadian Museum of Civilization Corporation, 104 pp.

Wallis, Wilson, 1957. Anthropology in England in the present century. *American Anthropologist*, vol. 59, no. 5, pp. 781–790.

Wilkins, Sir Hubert, 1931. In polar lands (with a biographical foreword by Diamond Jenness). *Canadian Geographical Journal*, vol. 3, no. 6 (June), pp. 424–438.

Zaslow, Morris, 1975. *Reading the Rocks — The Story of the Geological Survey of Canada 1842–1972*. Macmillan Company of Canada, Toronto, 599 pp.

INDEX

(n indicates that the item is in a footnote)